The Rise and Fall of the Communist Party of Iraq

This is the first comprehensive work to examine the complex transformation of the Iraqi Communist Party from vanguard actor under Iraq's conservative monarchy to rearguard lackey under US occupation. Born in the interlude between two world wars, the Communist Party of Iraq was fostered by Iraq's embryonic intelligentsia as an approach to national liberation during the period of British domination. Driven underground or into exile by successive waves of Baᶜathist repression beginning in 1963, the Party's leadership became progressively dependent on and subservient to the Soviet Union. The efforts of reformers dissatisfied with the Party's irrelevance to Iraq's socio-political dynamics were thwarted by the old-guard leadership, and in the mid-1970s the Party fragmented. With the fall of the Hussein regime and the US occupation of Iraq in 2003, the remnants of the Party's old guard connected with the US-installed government and became part of the US project in Iraq.

Tareq Y. Ismael is Professor of Political Science at the University of Calgary, Canada. He also serves as President of the International Centre for Contemporary Middle Eastern Studies and as the co-editor of the *International Journal of Contemporary Iraqi Studies*. Additionally, he is author or editor of numerous books on Iraq and the Middle East, including *Middle East Politics Today: Government and Civil Society* (2001); *Iraq: The Human Cost of History*, with William H. Haddad (2003); *The Iraqi Predicament: People in the Quagmire of Power Politics*, with Jacqueline S. Ismael (2004); and *The Communist Movement in the Arab World* (2005).

The Rise and Fall of the Communist Party of Iraq

TAREQ Y. ISMAEL
University of Calgary

CAMBRIDGE
UNIVERSITY PRESS

CAMBRIDGE UNIVERSITY PRESS
Cambridge, New York, Melbourne, Madrid, Cape Town, Singapore, São Paulo, Delhi

Cambridge University Press
32 Avenue of the Americas, New York, NY 10013-2473, USA

www.cambridge.org
Information on this title: www.cambridge.org/9780521873949

First published 2008

Printed in the United States of America

A catalog record for this publication is available from the British Library.

Library of Congress Cataloging in Publication Data

Ismael, Tareq Y.
The rise and fall of the Communist Party of Iraq / Tareq Y. Ismael.
p. cm.
Includes bibliographical references and index.
ISBN 978-0-521-87394-9 (hardback)
1. Hizb al-Shuyu'i al-'Iraqi – History. I. Title.
JQ1849.A98S4937 2008
324.2567'075 – dc22 2006103456

ISBN 978-0-521-87394-9 hardback

To my brother Khalid and to my wife, Jacqueline

Contents

Preface — *page* ix

1 The Communist Party of Iraq: Origins and Foundations — 1
Iraq Before the First World War — 1
Foreign Influences — 4
British Ascendancy — 7
Al-Raḫḫâl and the First Challenge — 17
Early Communist Organization — 20
The Importance of al-Ahâlî — 24
The Party in the 1940s — 25
The Party in the 1950s — 40
Nasser's Pan-Arabist Challenge — 58
Rebuilding the Party — 59

2 Ascent of the ICP in Iraqi Politics — 71
Politicization of the Army and the Qâsim Coup — 74
The Communists After the 14 July 1958 Revolution — 79
The Fall of the Clique of Four — 102
The Fall of Qâsim — 106
The Rashid Putsch and the Death Train — 109

3 Party Rift: The Emergence of the Central Leadership — 114
Grassroots Reaction to the August Line — 125
Party Leadership Responds to Internal Tensions — 137
The Formation of the ICP-CL — 154
The Factions Face the Baʿth — 159

4 Alliance with the Baʿth — 166
The Third National Congress — 177
The Baʿth Turn on the ICP-CC — 181
The Public Dimension – Issues and Pronouncements — 188

5 The Rebirth of the Central Leadership in the 1970s 204
The Basic Ideology of the ICP-CL 207
Maḥmûd's Grounding of ICP-CL Thought 212
The Plenary Session of the Central Committee (July 1959) 214
The Moscow Meeting (November 1960) 217
The Failures of the National Democratic Movement 219
Portrait of a Torture Victim from the ICP-CL 225
The Third Party Conference (January 1974) 226
Wiḥdat al-Qâʿidah *and the Splintering of the ICP-CL* 236
The Theory of al-Mushtarak 241
The Interpretations of al-Muqâydah 247
The Iraqi Progressive Opposition After the First Gulf War 258
The ICP-CL Responds to the American Empire (1990–Present) 261

6 Crisis: Disintegration or Renewal? 264
The Iraqi Communist Party and Kurdistan 268
The Iraqi Communist Party and Perestroika 269
Preparations for the Fifth Congress 272
The International Situation 279
The Arab Front 280
The Local Level 281
An Examination of the By-laws and Their Relationship to the Party Programme 283
The Concept of Democratic Centralism 285
The Fifth National Congress 286
The Kurdish Connection 289
The Sixth Congress 291
The ICP and the US Occupation 296
The ICP Before Occupation 297
The Governing Council 301
Whither Socialism? 303
The Iraqi Communist Party Cadre 304

7 Conclusion: From Vanguard Activism to Rearguard Opportunism 311
Vanguard Activism 311
Rearguard Opportunism 316
Journey's End? 318

Index 323

Preface

This book has a story for me. As a young boy in February 1949, in my first year of grammar school, on a sunny morning in Baghdad, I passed by some bodies of communists who had been hanged. Later, my father and I had the following conversation:

> "Hanged. They must be criminals."
> "Not quite."
> "They were hanged; they must have done something."
> "Well, they really didn't act, but they were contemplating."
> "They did something, then."
> "No, no, no, they didn't. They were thinking of, hoping for, an action."
> "But you told me the law does not punish you until you do something."
> "When you grow up, you will understand."

I went home and clipped the newspapers that day, and have done so every day since. And since that day, I have been trying to understand.

Though I have never joined any political party, nor been actively involved in one, from my undergraduate years on I have felt driven to understand, and eventually as an academician to explain, but never as an apologist, the communist movement in Iraq. I wanted to write my first book on this topic but had to wait a quarter of a century to see the conclusion of the Cold War. I felt that to understand a movement, one had to have the writings of the participants and their official literature and be able to study their experiences from their own perspectives. Thus, placing the literature and personal experiences of Iraqi communists within a historical, political, social, and international context became the basis for my often critical analysis, rather than any preconceived notions I may have had. This approach differs from that in Hanna Batatu's monumental work *The Old Social Classes and the Revolutionary Movements of Iraq*, which thirty years ago could not access this personal information, let alone document the last three decades of the story.

Acquiring the Iraqi communist movement's documents has been a difficult and time-consuming process. Keeping them has been a legal venture of some scale, and transporting them to safe places has been a risk with consequences of a decidedly physical nature.

The present time of conflict is an important period in history – Iraqi, Arab, and global – and if history is always written by the victors, then if it is not documented, it could be lost entirely. The importance of the Iraqi communists is not in any proportion to the power they attained for themselves. It lies, instead, in the agenda they set for others to follow, for they were frequently the only voice that spoke for the masses, the majority of the people. Because of the communists' energy and commitment, their one-sided solutions to the problems only they cared about were vigorously propagated. This forced those opposed to them to respond to the issues they raised, and to copy their party structures, programs, and activities. Because the communists formed the earliest political organizations in the Arab world (in Egypt in 1919 and in Syria in 1924), they left an indelible mark on its political structure, despite never actually ruling an Arab state.

This book is the second to last in my projected quintuple series on the communist movement in the Arab world, and it concludes the journey I began on that sunny Baghdad morning in February 1949. Previous books in this series are *The Communist Movement in Egypt* (Syracuse University Press, 1990), *The Communist Movement in Syria and Lebanon* (University Press of Florida, 1998), and *The Communist Movement in the Arab World* (Routledge Curzon Publishers, 2005).

The system of transliteration adopted in this study generally follows the format used by the *International Journal of Middle Eastern Studies*.

I would be remiss if I did not acknowledge that this endeavour would not even have been possible without direct and indirect input from many others: those who made documents available or arranged for contacts with principal participants in the movement, as well as those who offered formal and informal suggestions and joined in discussions over the last thirty-five years. In addition, a number of my students and friends contributed in many different ways, helping to gather information and locate important documents all over the world. I dare not attempt to name them all for fear that I would miss some.

However, my special thanks go to my research assistants: Mark Bizek, who chased down all of the available English documents related to the updating of the last part of Chapter 6; Gamal Selim, who laboured over the transliterations; Christopher Langille and Candice M. Juby, who worked hard to finalise the manuscript and coordinate all of the numerous changes and revisions. I must also express my gratitude to Lindy Ayubi, who aided in style adaptation for Cambridge University Press. Finally, I would be remiss if I did not thank Lewis Bateman, the senior editor for political science and history at Cambridge University Press, New York, who shepherded the writing of this book with patience and understanding.

I would also like to gratefully acknowledge the support given to me by the Social Sciences and Humanities Research Council of Canada; the University of Calgary Grants Committee; and the Killam Resident Fellowships Committee, which awarded me a fellowship to prepare this book for press.

As always, all research was done under my direct supervision, and I take full responsibility for all of the analysis and views expressed herein, as well as for any errors. All translations from Arabic are my own.

July 2007
Calgary, Alberta, Canada

1

The Communist Party of Iraq

Origins and Foundations

The introduction of Marxist thought in Iraq must be accredited to Ḥusain al-Raḥḥâl (1901–1981), who, though he never became a communist himself, was the first to introduce Marxist thought into intellectual circles in Baghdad. Al-Raḥḥâl was a high school student in Berlin in 1919 when the Spartacist uprising, an attempt by the Communist Party of Germany (KPD) to seize control of Berlin, took place; this event left a deep impression on him, and kindled his interest in socialism and Marxism.[1] Returning to Iraq a year later, and profoundly affected by the unstable conditions of the country, under British occupation, he gradually started to teach Marxist and socialist thought. However, in his last days he expressed deep disappointment:

> With the seeds I have sown and worked so hard to intellectually nurture... I wanted to create an intellectual environment where scientific socialism would be the base of inquiry to understand our backward conditions, but we ended up somewhere else.... The impoverishment of Marxist thought today [1973] is much more alarming because it is much more regressive than it was fifty years earlier.[2]

Iraq Before the First World War

The history of modern Iraq can be traced back to 1749 when the Ottoman Sultan appointed Sulimân Aghâ Abû-lailah, a Georgian Mamluk officer who was the governor of Basra (1749–1761), to the position of Wâlî (governor) of Baghdad. This appointment initiated the establishment of a semi-autonomous state in Iraq under Mamluk suzerainty. Although formally appointed by the Ottoman Sultan, a succession of Mamluks formed a dynasty that in effect ruled Iraq for the next eight decades. Even so, Mamluk control over Iraq was always incomplete because of overlapping jurisdictional rights in the

1 For an overview of al-Raḥḥâl's life, see Hanna Batatu, *The Old Social Classes and Revolutionary Movements of Iraq* (Princeton, NJ: Princeton University Press, 1978), pp. 389–404.

2 Interview by author with Ḥusain al-Raḥḥâl, Baghdad (19 October 1973).

empire.[3] An Ottoman focus on potential Persian incursions into the territory forced Mamluk officials and the Sublime Porte[4] into grudging cooperation, so that despite their efforts, Mamluk rule over Iraq was "restricted to fluctuating success over an 80 year period ... and the downfall of the Mamluk regime in 1831 meant the unwelcome restoration of alien rule in [the city of] Baghdad."[5] The city's population had grown from twenty thousand inhabitants in the seventeenth century to one hundred thousand by 1800, and had reached some hundred fifty thousand in 1831,[6] at the time Mamluk rule ended.

Dâûd Pasha, the last of the Mamluk rulers (1817–1831), instituted political and economic policies that successfully united what was to constitute modern Iraq. By steering the country even further away from Istanbul's control, he was also able to reduce the influence of C. J. Rich, the British resident in Baghdad, and of representatives of the British East India Company. In a move that gained him popular support, particularly among Iraq's merchants, Dâûd Pasha also forced the British to pay duties on all imported goods, taxes from which they had previously been exempt.

Dâûd Pasha modelled his rule on that of Muḥammad ʿAlî in Egypt. Like Muḥammad ʿAlî, he strove to create a modern centralized governmental infrastructure. He initiated governmental reforms, restored law and order, and created judicial and educational institutions. He also modernized the army, enlarging it to approximately one hundred thousand men; built factories; established a newspaper; and organized irrigation works.[7] As noted by the scholar Tom Nieuwenhuis, "The previous [Mamluk] period of local rule becomes significant, marking an era ... for local progress ... [in which] schools, baths, mosques, khans [inns] ... and *suqs* (markets) [were built or expanded]."[8] One distinguished Iraqi economist, Muḥammad Salmân Ḥasan, considers Dâûd and his reign to be a first attempt at independent economic development – however embryonic – in the modern history of Iraq. In 1831, at the instigation of the British, the Ottoman army marched into Baghdad and arrested Dâûd Pasha. Dâûd was imprisoned for the rest of his life and the Mamluk elite was removed from power, thus ending Iraq's first experiment in autonomy.[9]

3 Hala Fattah, *The Politics of Regional Trade in Iraq, Arabia and the Gulf: 1745–1900* (Albany: State University of New York Press, 1997); Thabit Abdullah, *A Short History of Iraq* (New York: Seven Stories Press, 2003); and Thabit Abdullah, *Merchants, Mamluks and Murder: The Political Economy of Commerce in Eighteenth Century Basra* (Albany: State University of New York Press, 2000).

4 An administrative department directly related to Istanbul and not under the Mamluk Pasha.

5 Tom Nieuwenhuis, *Politics and Society in Early Modern Iraq: Mamluk Pashas, Tribal Shayks and Local Rule Between 1802 and 1831* (Hague: Martinus Nijhoff, 1982), p. 171.

6 ʿAbd al-Aziz al-Duri, "Baghdad," *Encyclopedia of Islam* (Leiden, Netherlands: E.J. Brill, 1960), p. 925.

7 ʿU<u>th</u>mân Ibn Suʿûd al-Baṣrî al-Wâilî, *<u>Kh</u>amsah wa <u>Kh</u>amsûn ʿÂm min Târî<u>kh</u> al-ʿIrâq 1188–1242-Wa Mu<u>kh</u>taṣar Maṭâliʿ al-Suʿûd Biṭayyibî A<u>kh</u>bâr al-Wâlî Dâûd* (Cairo 1371H), p. 2; Zaki Saleh, *Mesopotamia (Iraq), 1600–1914* (Baghdad: al-Rabitah Press, 1957), p. 133; Sulaimân Fâʾiq, *Târî<u>kh</u> Bag<u>h</u>dad*, trans. Mûsâ Kâ<u>dh</u>im Nûras (Baghdad: al-Maʿârif Press, 1962), p. 61.

8 Nieuwenhuis, *Politics and Society*, p. 173.

9 Muḥammad Salmân Ḥasan, *Al-Taṭawwur al-Iqtiṣâdî fî al-ʿIrâq* (Beirut: al-Maktabah al-ʿAṣriyyah, 1965), pp. 30–33. See also Ḥalîm Aḥmad, *Mûjaz Târî<u>kh</u> al-ʿIrâq al-Ḥadî<u>th</u>* (Beirut:

The restoration of direct rule from Istanbul coincided with the "emergence of British influence in Iraq"; according to Nieuwenhuis, both the Turks and the British were largely responsible for the "retarded" development of Iraq.[10] Nevertheless, with its return to Ottoman control Iraq began to be feel the affects of the politics and enlightened reforms then taking place in Istanbul and which, in 1839, initiated the "Age of Tanzimat." In this environment, law, diplomacy, government administration, and education were all modernized, and secular ideas and democratic principles were introduced.

In 1868, Midḥat Pasha, a leading advocate of reform, became the first president of Council of State in Istanbul, one of the two most important institutions of the Tanzimat. The following year he was appointed Wâlî of Baghdad (1869–1872) and from this position put his reform ideas into practice. He centralized government rule, established law and order, surveyed the land, instituted land reforms that gave peasants some protection and reduced feudal control, reestablished modern education, and built factories, in essence reinstating the programme of Dâûd Pasha's government. He also established a newspaper, *Al-Zawrâ͗*, importing a special press for the purpose; the paper survived him by half a century. Most government revenue was spent on public projects, and little was sent to the treasury in Istanbul. Partly as a result of his success in Iraq, court jealousies and intrigue led to Midḥat Pasha's recall three years later, though he soon took over the prime ministership of the empire. According to one Iraqi educator and literary figure, writing in 1930:

> As soon as Midḥat Pasha entered Baghdad ... he began studying Iraqi conditions and its finances from the perspectives of security, administration, order, education, industry, agriculture, economics, and health, and [the creation of] a modern infrastructure.... he announced his intention of implementing his program, and soon worked to put this into action. Although he was gentle and respectful, he was serious about its implementation. In a few days, the signs of reform and prosperity began to appear [in the country] and the social conditions were on the verge of a dramatic transformation. People were happy, justice prevailed and rights were respected. Three years later, in 1873, in Government House, with a grim face, he declared, "This is what I promised you and God the day I met you in this place, and I would have fulfilled this but for the misfortune [of having to leave]. I bid you farewell, my dear Iraqi friends.... " With tearful eyes [his audience] responded.[11]

In 1876, Iraq entered a renewed constitutional experiment under the Ottoman Sultan ͨAbd-ul-Ḥamîd II, who was brought to power by the reformist Midḥat Pasha, now the Grand Vizier, and his liberal compatriots in Istanbul. The newly enthroned ͨAbd-ul-Ḥamîd II promulgated this constitutional experiment on 23 December 1876. However, it came to an abrupt end when ͨAbd-ul-Ḥamîd II reversed his views, sending Midḥat Pasha into exile in Mecca and

Dâr Ibn Khaldûn, n.d.), pp. 31–33. For an excellent history of the Mamluk period in Iraq, see ͨAbbâs al-ͨAzzâwî, *Târîkh al-ͨIrâq Baina Iḥtilâlain*, vol. 6 (Baghdad: Sharikat al-Tijârah wa al-Ṭibâͨah, 1954).

[10] Nieuwenhuis, *Politics and Society*, p. 171.

[11] Fahmî al-Mudarris, *Alͨ Âlam al-ͨArabî*, no. 1965 (Baghdad, 9 August 1930).

initiating a period of despotic rule and corruption that ended with the revolution of the Young Turks in 1908. This powerful military Pan-Turkish nationalist clique, which led Turkey into World War I, practised a policy of Turkification that roused and angered many Ottoman Arabs, including the Iraqis, especially those making up the embryonic intelligentsia.

In their opposition to Turkification, Ottoman Arabs used secret societies and clandestine Arabic newspapers to advance the nationalist cause; as non-Turkish separatist movements in the empire (e.g., in Bosnia, Bulgaria, and Crete) became more vocal, they inspired Arab nationalists in Iraq and Syria. Arab officers in Istanbul, the most influential group in society to benefit from these developments and exposure to technical (often Western) training, assumed important roles within the growing underground movement. Iraqi officers, who were often the most prominent members of secret societies like *al-ᶜAhd* that were formed among the Arab components of the Ottoman army, committed themselves to working for Arab independence. Similar in purpose to *al-ᶜAhd* in Iraq, a branch of the Ottoman Decentralization Party – *al-ᶜUṣbah al-Ḥamra* – was founded in Cairo for the purpose of winning equality and autonomy for the Arab provinces within the framework of the Ottoman Empire. Even though such efforts weakened the Ottoman Empire in the face of European encroachment, many Arabs regarded their demands for decentralization as necessary to protect their cultural and linguistic identity in the face of the reforms emanating from Istanbul. With the return of the constitution in 1908, and with branches of Arab nationalist societies beginning to appear, predominantly in Basra and Baghdad but also in Mosul and other Iraqi cities, the seeds of political and social awakening grew rapidly.

In addition, Arab newspapers and journals proliferated, with the number of dailies in Iraq rising from a single one between 1894 and 1904 to sixty-one between 1904 and 1914. Even though many existed only for a short period before Ottoman efforts to closed them, the flowering of a new intellectual expression took hold of the Arab population. Following the introduction of the modern printing press, Egyptian journals and newspapers became readily available to other Arabs and facilitated greater contact between the rising young intellectual class in Iraq and the rest of the Arab world. The increased availability of Arabic journals through the foreign postal services – bypassing Ottoman censorship – acted as a catalyst in the rapid development of socialist consciousness throughout Iraq. Journals such as *Al-Muqtaṭaf, Al-Hilâl, Al-Siyâsah*, and *Al-Muqaṭṭam* soon became part of the regular diet of discerning members of Iraq's emerging educated classes.[12]

Foreign Influences

In addition to Arabic journals, the publications of the Communist Party of Britain also began to circulate among a limited number of intellectuals in Iraq,

[12] For more detail, see Philip Willard Ireland, *Iraq: A Study in Political Development* (London: Jonathan Cope, 1937), pp. 222–236.

including al-Raḥḥâl, who translated them into Arabic and held discussions about them with his friends in Baghdad. At the same time, the French Communist Party newspaper, *L'Humanité*, available to those Iraqis who spoke French, was also translated into Arabic and made available to Raḥḥâl's circle. The development of socialist thought among Iraqis was further influenced by the progressive foreign socialists who worked with the British in Iraq. Among these was a Scotsman, Donald M. McKenzie, who opened McKenzie's Bookshop in Baghdad in 1925 and operated it until his death in 1946. McKenzie made a number of foreign books, especially those examining socialist ideas, available at cost to young Iraqi socialists, while selling them at a profit to the British and to wealthy Iraqis.[13] His wife also played an important role in spreading socialist ideas among women's groups and was credited with connecting these groups through the first Eastern Women's Congress, held in Damascus in July 1930.[14] In addition, between 1919 and 1926 an Australian named Riley, who worked as a teacher in the British Department of Education in Mosul before becoming the director of education, gave lectures on social conditions, informed by socialist notions, to students and the Iraqi elite. Returning to Australia in 1926, he took up journalism and ended up in China, where he was killed. Finally, McKenzie's wife and an American woman by the name of Miss Kerr lectured in girls' clubs and schools in Baghdad, where socialist notions were also advanced.[15]

Russians and Iraqis had limited contact until World War I, when, as part of the Ottoman armies, Iraqi soldiers and officers met their Russian adversaries on the Russian front. Interaction between civilian Iraqis and Russians following Russia's October 1917 revolution was also limited, but the opinion of Iraqis who did encounter the revolutionaries was favourable to the Bolsheviks. When the Ottoman armies were retreating in early 1917, the Russian forces occupying the northern and western parts of Ottoman Iraq treated the population humanely, and in this environment, some of the Russian soldiers who were politically inclined towards Bolshevist notions spread the seeds of those ideas, which the Iraqis began to propagate.

In addition, because Kurds and Arabs who became Russian prisoners of war (POWs) after the Russian revolution were treated well, they began to spread vague revolutionary notions on their return to Iraq. Some become known in Iraq as Bolsheviks. One such Baghdadi, known as Bolshevik Ṣâliḥ (1892–1973), adopted his nom de guerre and used it for the rest of his life. In a 1968 interview he remarked:

> My contact with the Bolsheviks was a humane one, and even when I was in captivity during the Tsarist period I could tell from the way our guards treated us who was a Bolshevik and who was not. As soon as the revolution took place I was freed, and

[13] See Muḥsin Dizaya, *ʾAḥdâṯẖ ʿÂṣartuhâ* (Erbil, Kurdistan: Aras, 2001), p. 164.
[14] Ibid.
[15] Interviews by author with Ḥusain al-Raḥḥâl and Zakî K͟hairî, Baghdad (18 January 1976).

became part of the comradeship, which is how I acquired my name – and I am proud of it. Although I have never been a communist, I thought the Bolsheviks were very caring, and thus, their ideology must also be of that nature.[16]

In Iraqi Kurdistan, returning Kurds were also dubbed Bolsheviks,[17] and in the religious centres of Shiᶜism in Najaf and Karbala, the same appellation was applied simultaneously to many returnees. Some Shiᶜi ᶜUlama believed that the Bolsheviks were favourably inclined towards Islam, and soon after World War I, the Mosul branch of *al-ᶜAhd* society, in a letter sent to the headquarters in Damascus, called for the formation of an Islamic-German and Bolshevik alliance to challenge the colonialist occupiers.[18]

When al-Raḥḥâl left Iraq around 1914, the country was one of the most remote and least developed provinces of the Ottoman Empire. According to Hanna Batatu, prior to the British military campaign during World War I "private property, in the sense of private appropriation of the means of production, was non-existent outside Iraq's towns and their immediate hinterland, and even in the towns had a precarious basis . . . exposed to recurring confiscation."[19] Some incipient economic classes existed in the towns, but only in a "rudimentary form and in parallel structures within the recognized religious communities," and nationwide social classes had yet to emerge.[20] Iraqi "society" still remained deeply divided along ethnic and sectarian lines, with Sunni Muslims in privileged positions and with very little interaction and few common interests among the various other segments of the population.

Around 75 per cent of Iraq's population was Arab, with Kurds, Persians, Turkomans, Armenians, and some smaller groups making up the remaining 25 per cent. The vast majority of the population were Muslim, divided between Shiᶜi and Sunni. However, there were also some small Christian, Jewish, and Sabean minorities. Out of a total population of 2.25 million at the turn of the twentieth century, 59 per cent were rural peasants, 17 per cent were nomadic and seminomadic herders, and only 24 per cent were urban dwellers;[21] in total, only one per cent of the population was literate.[22]

Internal social stratification was based on a hierarchy of status that gave special privileges to the holders of religiously based positions, such as *sadah*, or descent from the Prophet, and to the leaders of the Ṣûfî orders, as well as to Sunni and Shiᶜi *ᶜUlama* (religious leaders) and to the *chalabis* (rich merchants) who were concentrated mainly in Baghdad, in addition to the small group of high Ottoman officials (mainly of non-Iraqi origin) who ruled the

[16] Interview by author with Bolshevik Ṣâliḥ, Baghdad (18 March, 1968).

[17] Jalâl al-Ṭâlabânî, *Kurdistân wa al-Ḥarakah al-Kurdiyyah* (Beirut: Dâr al-Ṭalîᶜah, 1969), p. 58.

[18] ᶜÂmir Ḥasan Faiyyâḍ, "Judhûr al-Fikr al-ᵓIshtirâkî fî al-ᶜIrâq, 1920–1934" (MA thesis, College of Law and Politics, Baghdad, December 1978), pp. 233–240.

[19] Batatu, *Old Social Classes*, p. 8.

[20] Ibid.

[21] Ḥasan, *Al-Taṭawwur al-Iqtiṣâdî fî al-ᶜIrâq*, p. 52.

[22] Hâshim Jawâd, *Muqaddimah fi Kiyân al-ᶜIrâq al-Ijtimâᶜî* (Baghdad: al-Maᶜârif Press, 1946), p. 104.

country. The privileged strata together constituted a very small proportion of the population. A small middle class made up of professionals, artisans, and domestic merchants occupied another level, while the vast majority of the urban population consisted of poor service workers. An industrial working class was virtually non-existent until the late 1920s,[23] and in the countryside the tribal system, which had existed for centuries, was still largely intact. The *Shaikh al-Mashâyikh* (chief of tribal confederations), the *shaikhs* (leaders) of the tribes among the Arabs, and the tribal *begs* (community sub-leaders) or *aghas* (tribal chiefs) among the Kurds remained in firm control of the affairs of their tribal communities. All in all, Iraq was a mosaic of social groups, stratified along tribal, religious, class, and ethnic lines. Each community lived in accordance with its inherited traditional patterns, into which it assimilated foreign influences and modern practices. In other words, historic and inherited cultural norms were more complex in nature, and had been passed down from the time of the Sumerians, and more recently, from the Abbassid period in the eighth century. These values allowed communities to adapt to change and to adopt new ideas and ways of living, initially difficult for Westerners to comprehend.

British Ascendancy

Britain's penetration of the Persian Gulf in the seventeenth century, as a direct result of the merging of British government and British East India Company interests, led to its eventual control of the Iraqi Tigris and Euphrates valleys during the First World War. The British East India Company initiated commercial activity in Basra in 1635, and established its first factory there eight years later, making Basra an important outpost for the company in the region. Later, in 1764, Britain opened an official consulate in Basra to consolidate British political and economic influence and to replace the British East India Company representative. The British presence was expanded further in 1798, when a permanent residency opened in Baghdad. Eventually, Baghdad became the centre of British activities in Arabia, replacing Basra as a response to heightened French interest in Iraq, which was masked by Napoleon's challenge to British control of India at the end of the eighteenth century.[24] By 1834, the introduction of gunboats on the Tigris had created a safe environment for transport on the river, thus increasing British economic penetration. Thus during the mid-nineteenth century, Iraq became incorporated into the British imperial market system, and Ottoman Iraq was transformed into an area of vital British influence and interest. According to one student of British foreign policy in Iraq, the British viewed Iraq as the cornerstone of the survival of the British Indian Empire: "This conception, originating with the British about the year 1830, and developing during the ensuing four decades, was firmly established by

[23] Batatu, *Old Social Classes*, p. 11.

[24] ʿAbd-ul-Raḥmân al-Bazzâz, *Al-ʿIrâq min al-Iḥtilâl Ḥattâ al-Istiqlâl*, 3rd ed. (Baghdad: al-ʿÂnî Press, 1967), p. 46, and Aḥmad, *Mûjaz Târîkh al-ʿIrâq al-Ḥadîth*, p. 43.

the year 1878.... Mesopotamia was virtually turned into a British sphere of influence."[25]

By the second half of the nineteenth century, however, some changes started to become noticeable. The opening of the Suez Canal in 1869, and the development of powered transportation on the Tigris and the Euphrates rivers, made Iraq more accessible to penetration by products and ideas from the outside world, particularly those of British origin.[26] This caused a decline in indigenous commerce and production, reducing Iraq to the status of a dependent market for British goods and a source of cheap raw materials for British industry, and increasingly connecting Iraq to the international, imperial market. In contrast to the trend up to the late eighteenth century, when Iraqi trade had been predominantly with other Middle Eastern countries, Iraqi commerce now was mainly with industrial Europe in general, and with Britain in particular.[27] Indeed, the value of European imports coming into Iraq through Basra increased from £51,000 in 1868–1870 to £3,066,000 by 1907–1909.[28] A large part of these imports consisted of inexpensive British-made textiles, whose growing influx caused the gradual ruin of the domestic handloom industry in Iraq, as had previously occurred in both Lebanon and Syria. At the same time, however, Iraq's agricultural production rose rapidly. From the 1860s to the 1920s, grain production increased by around one per cent per annum, and the yield of dates increased by even greater margins. In addition, the area under cultivation expanded, from perhaps less than 100,000 *dunums* in the 1860s to about 1,613,000 *dunums* by 1913.[29] The character of crop production also underwent a transformation, from the peasant subsistence economy that had previously prevailed to an economy based on cash crops, mainly cereal grains, the export of which increased about twenty times over the periods 1867–1871 and 1912–1913.[30]

On the eve of the First World War, Great Britain's standing as the dominant power in the Persian Gulf was about to enter a new phase. Three centuries of Britain's efforts to expand and protect its trade, as well as to increase its diplomatic and strategic influence and to protect the land route to India from domination by other powers, were settled through negotiated agreements. Over

[25] Zaki Saleh, *Mesopotamia (Iraq), 1600–1914: A Study in British Foreign Affairs* (Baghdad: al-Maaref Press, 1957), p. 170. For details on the Gulf region and Iraq, see Jacqueline S. Ismael, *Kuwait: Social Change in Historical Perspective* (Syracuse, NY: Syracuse University Press, 1982), pp. 37–53.

[26] Ibid., p. 239. On the eve of World War I, Britain's share of the trade in Iraq and the Gulf area amounted to £9,600,000, about three-quarters of the total; Marion Farouk-Sluglett and Peter Sluglett, *Iraq Since 1958: From Revolution to Dictatorship* (London: KPI, 1987), p. 7.

[27] Ḥasan, *Al-Taṭawwur al-Iqtiṣâdî fî al-ʿIrâq*, p. 87.

[28] Batatu, *Old Social Classes*, pp. 239–240.

[29] Ḥasan, "The Role of Foreign Trade in Economic Development in Iraq, 1864–1964: A Study in the Growth of a Dependent Economy," in M. A. Cook (ed.), *Studies in the Economic History of the Middle East from the Rise of Islam to the Present Day* (London: Oxford University Press, 1970), p. 350. See note 50 for the dimensions of the *dunum*.

[30] Farouk-Sluglett and Sluglett, *Iraq Since 1958*, p. 3.

a series of meetings and exchanges dating from 1909 to 1913, Great Britain achieved recognition of its position from Germany, from France, and from the government of the Ottoman Empire. Under the terms of the Anglo-Turkish Agreement, signed on 29 July 1913, Britain completed its de facto annexation of the Persian Gulf and cemented its dominant position within the Mesopotamian *vilayets* (provinces) of the Ottoman Empire. Further, it secured recognition of its "special position" in the Persian Gulf and of the validity of its existing treaties with the sheikdoms of Kuwait and Bahrain; limited the terminus of the Baghdad railway to Basra (beyond which the rail line could not be extended without British consent); gained sole control over the development of the port of Basra and the city of Baghdad (thereby denying port facilities in the Gulf to Germany or any other power); and achieved Ottoman recognition of its right to buoy, to light, and to police the Shaṭ al-ʿArab and the Persian Gulf. These measures were seen as insurance for British claims on Mesopotamia in the event of the break-up of the Ottoman Empire.[31]

In attempting to extend its influence in the region further, Britain used the agreement to control access to water. In this way British authorities could promote economic growth through agriculture and control revenue assessment and collection despite the shared role it was to have with Germany in developing irrigation for the Cilician Plain in Asia Minor. Finally, the Ottoman oilfields were transferred to British control, and Germany was forced to recognize further oil exploration in southern Mesopotamia and in southern Persia as the exclusive domain of the Anglo-Persian Oil Company. However, because of diplomatic concerns requiring Britain and Germany to heed deliberations by the French, Italian, and Russian representatives, the Anglo-German Agreement was not signed until 15 July 1914, and ratification was further delayed until separate Turko-German negotiations were concluded.

With the outbreak of World War I on 28 July 1914, the Anglo-German treaty and its considerations were, in effect, nullified, and in the ensuing conflict British arms were required to confirm what British commerce and diplomacy had established before the war. With Britain's occupation of Basra in 1914, then of Baghdad in 1917, and finally, of Mosul in 1918, as well as with treaty arrangements farther south in the Gulf proper, British hegemony became incontestable, and suzerainty passed – without the consent or involvement of the region's Arab population – from the Ottomans to the British Empire. The cost to Britain was immense, involving over two hundred million pounds and some hundred thousand casualties in the Mesopotamia campaign.

Commensurate with those developments was the population's growing tendency towards sedentarization, and the increase in the number of peasants who cultivated the land. Indeed, the percentage of nomads among the region's rural

[31] For a discussion of British diplomacy in the treaty, see Jill Crystal (ed.), *Oil and Politics in the Gulf: Rulers and Merchants in Kuwait and Qatar* (Cambridge: Cambridge University Press, 1994); see also Richard Schofield (ed.), *The Iran-Iraq Border: 1840–1958*, 11 vol. (Buckingham, UK: Archive Editions, 1989), for a copy of the 1929 Anglo-Turkish Agreement.

population fell from 35 per cent to 17 per cent between 1867 and 1905, while the percentage of cultivators increased from 41 per cent to 59 per cent. By using the Ottoman Land Code of 1858, tribal *shaikhs*, former tax farmers,[32] and rich city merchants began to acquire title deeds (*tapu sanads*) to previously state-owned or communally held properties.[33] On the eve of the war this process had not progressed all that far, and the Ottoman authorities attempted to repossess land that had already been registered as private property.[34] But with the collapse of the Ottoman Empire and the British occupation of Iraq, the pace of change accelerated rapidly, exaggerating social tensions, economic disparities, and political discord.[35] In the political settlements following the First World War, Britain and France carved the Middle East into spheres of influence, prearranged by the 1915 Sykes-Picot Agreement and implemented at the San Remo conference in April 1920.[36] Britain received mandates over both Iraq and Palestine. This was a transparent attempt to legalize the British occupation of Iraq, and Iraqi nationalists viewed it as "imperialism in a new guise and as colonization under a new name."[37]

Spearheaded by tribal *shaikhs* in the Middle Euphrates and by the Shiʿi leadership of Najaf, Iraqi agitation against the British mandate was initiated in the summer of 1920, just six weeks after the formal announcement of the arrangement. This agitation soon grew into a popular insurrection, and on 4 July 1920, British garrisons and offices came under attack throughout Iraq in what one historian considers the first national 'war of liberation' against British imperialism, with "a chief feature of the movement being the unprecedented cooperation between the Sunni and the Shiʿi communities."[38] Significantly, the 1920 revolution was "the first manifestation of a form of Iraqi national identity."[39] Although the British were able to suppress the insurrection, the repression encountered heavy criticism at home for its human and financial costs, utilization of chemical weapons against the rebels, and overall heavy handedness.

Subsequently, the British Colonial Office set up a sub-department for the newly acquired Middle Eastern territories, and at a conference in Cairo in March 1921, chaired by Colonial Secretary Winston Churchill, new structures

[32] In "tax farming" the central authority contracted with local businessmen or headmen to collect a specific sum as tax from an area by whatever means they saw fit; tax farmers would generally collect a much larger amount than required and keep the difference for themselves.

[33] Roger Owen, *The Middle East in the World Economy, 1800–1914* (London: Methuen, 1981), p. 186.

[34] Interviews by author with Ḥusain al-Raḥḥâl; Zakî Khairî, Baghdad (18 January 1976).

[35] Farouk-Sluglett and Sluglett, *Iraq Since 1958*, p. 4. During the whole period, the increase in privately registered land was still rather modest. The *miri* (state land) fell from about four-fifths in the 1860s to about 60 per cent in the 1933–1958 period, and the *topu* land rose from about 20 per cent in the 1860s to about 30 per cent on the eve of the 1958 Revolution. See Ḥasan, "The Role of Foreign Trade in Economic Development in Iraq, 1864–1964," p. 350.

[36] David Fromkin, *A Peace to End All Peace: The Fall of the Ottoman Empire and the Creation of the Modern Middle East*, 2nd ed. (London: Henry Holt, 2001).

[37] Philip W. Ireland, *Iraq: A Study in Political Development* (London: Jonathan Cape, 1937), p. 262.

[38] Phebe Marr, *The Modern History of Iraq* (Boulder, CO: Westview Press, 1985), p. 33.

[39] Farouk-Sluglett and Sluglett, *Iraq Since 1958*, pp. 10–11.

were established for these territories. Iraq was to be ruled indirectly, nominally through a national cabinet and civil service headed by an Arab. Power would, however, continue to be held by British advisers, and Britain would have veto power over financial and military matters. In addition, Britain would administer Iraq's foreign relations.

Amîr Faiṣal, the son of Sharîf Ḥusain, leader of the Arab Revolt of 1916, was the British choice to rule Iraq as he had just been expelled by the French from his short tenure upon the throne as King of Syria and thus had only limited support among the local elites. He did, however, have some support in Iraq, especially among Iraqi officers who had served with him in the Arab Revolt of 1916 against the Ottomans and many of whom had been part of his short-lived administration in Syria. Other candidates, some of whom had been active in the 1920 revolution, were more popular, but they were either not trusted by or were seen as antagonistic to the British. Because of his limited local acceptance, Faiṣal was viewed by the British as dependent upon them, and therefore as amenable to British pressure. At the same time, he would further divide the leaders of the anti-British national movement since as a descendant of the prophet Muḥammad he commanded the loyalty of many Muslims. This accorded him some popular support and allowed him to transcend sectarian divisions, making an open challenge to his nomination virtually unthinkable. In the spring of 1921, the British stage-managed the election of Faiṣal as a constitutional monarch, crowning him Faiṣal I.

Under Faiṣal, the Anglo-Iraqi Treaty of October 1922 replaced the mandate and formalized British control for a twenty-year period. It gave Britain the right to oversee Iraq's financial and international affairs and to station armed forces on Iraqi soil; it also stipulated that "the king would heed Britain's advice on all matters affecting British interests."[40] In return, Britain agreed to provide military and civilian aid to Iraq and to support its application for membership in the League of Nations. Within two months of the public announcement of the Anglo-Iraqi Treaty, two major political parties – *Ḥizb al-Nahḍah al-ʿIrâqiyyah* (the Iraqi Renaissance Party), headed by Muḥammad al-Ṣadr, and *al-Ḥizb al-Waṭanî* (the National Party), headed by Ja'far Abu-l-Timmân (both men were prominent Shiʿi leaders) – were formed, largely in protest against the treaty. A pro-British party – *al-Ḥizb al-Ḥurr al-ʿIrâqî* (the Liberal Party of Iraq), headed by Maḥmûd al-Naqîb – was also formed.

On 23 August 1922, spontaneous mass demonstrations protesting the treaty broke out. Because of the strong opposition, King Faiṣal and his government refused to ratify the agreement, and, on 29 August, the government resigned. In response, the British High Commission banned political parties, dissolved the parliament, and ruled directly. Through the Anglo-Iraq Treaty, which was finally ratified in January 1926, and the constitution, which had been passed by a constituent assembly in 1924, the mandate was replaced with indirect British rule. The constitution vested considerable power in the monarch (whom the British nevertheless controlled) and provided only a facade of democratic

[40] Marr, *Modern History of Iraq*, p. 38.

TABLE 1.1. *The Population of Iraq (in thousands)*

Type	1905	% of Total	1930	% of Total	1947	% of Total
Bedouin	393	17	234	7	250	5
Rural	1,324	59	2,346	68	2,703	57
Urban	533	34	808	35	1,864	38
Total	2,350		3,388		4,817	

Source: Muḥammad Salmân Ḥasan, *Al-Taṭawwur al-Iqtiṣâdî fî al-ʿIrâq* (Beirut: al-Mattabah al-ʿAṣriyyah, 1965), p. 53.

representation in parliament.[41] In response to the Anglo-Iraqi Treaty of 1930, Nûrî al-Saʿîd formed the *al-ʿAhd* (Allegiance Party) to offset agitation by anti-British parties, particularly from the new *al-Ikhâʾ al-Waṭanî* (National Fraternity), which was created by Yâsîn al-Hâshimî to challenge British rule and the treaty that entrenched it. Two of *al-Ikhâʾ al-Waṭanî*'s active personalities, who later became major figures in Iraqi political life, were Rashîd ʿAlî al-Gailânî and Ḥikmat Sulaimân.

Under the rule of the British authorities and the Iraqi constitutional monarchy created by the British in 1921, Iraq was recognized as an independent state in 1932. The country then began a process of rapid social transformation, the scope of which was reflected in its changing demographic composition. Between 1930 and 1947 Iraq experienced rapid population growth, primarily as a result of lower infant mortality rates (Table 1.1). The trend towards settlement of the Bedouin population, which had contributed to the substantial increase in rural population between 1905 and 1930, continued because of the rapid expansion of arable land. Between 1918 and 1943, the total cultivated area in the irrigation zone increased from 936,500 acres to 4,241,718 acres.[42]

Iraq's urban population also increased dramatically between 1930 and 1947, reflecting the economic changes that were occurring in the country. These included the development of oil production, the beginnings of industrialization, and the organization of the modern centralized bureaucratic state. Regarding the condition of labour in Iraq in the mid-1920s, a British Colonial Office report to the Council of the League of Nations observed:

> In Iraq there are hardly any organized industries worth mentioning. Local industries are mostly of the cottage variety, namely tanning, weaving, copper and iron smithing, and a few others of less importance. Families in their homes carry on these industries. There are no factories in the ordinary sense of the word and the problems associated with factory conditions do not exist.[43]

41 Ibid., pp. 38–39.

42 Doreen Warriner, *Land and Poverty in the Middle East* (London: Royal Institute of International Affairs, 1948), p. 99.

43 His Britannic Majesty's Government, *Report on the Administration of Iraq for the Year 1926* (London: HMSO, 1927), p. 28.

The British observations herein accurately captured the primitive nature of Iraq's labour conditions.

The British, having little legitimacy in the eyes of the local population and, at the same time, trying to limit their expenditures, attempted to establish an internal social basis for their continued rule by creating a bureaucratic bourgeoisie, composed mainly of high officials and military officers to whom they gave large salaries and many privileges. The British also supported the class of intermediary middlemen whose interests were closely interwoven with those of foreign companies, by either marketing their products or providing them with cheap raw material and labour.

In addition to those classes, the British strengthened the semi-feudal authorities in rural areas.[44] The Tribal Criminal and Civil Disputes Regulation, enacted in 1916 and formally incorporated into the Iraqi Constitution in 1925, secured substantial judicial and tax-levying powers for the monarchy.[45] More important, perhaps, those *shaikhs* in the south and *aghas* in the north who were loyal to the British mandatory power, were generously rewarded with huge tracts of land that had previously been state property and that historically had been enjoyed by all tribal members, a practice known as Lazmah. Until 1927, *shaikhs* and *aghas* had had total immunity from property taxes,[46] and even later, their tax burden remained relatively light. The Lazmah custom (land tenure law), and the Settlement of Land Rights Law of 1932, provided justification for land-grabbing by tribal chiefs and other members of the emerging landowner class, such as high government officials and rich town merchants, as well as giving them legal title to the land they seized. These laws allowed the new landowners to deprive the peasants of their communal land rights and, concurrently, their means of living.

As a result, enormous private estates were created, and land ownership became concentrated in a few hands. By 1952 over half a million acres of former state land in the province of Kut were owned by only two families, and in the province of ᶜAmara, eight families held 53 per cent of all the land.[47] Iraq resembled a patchwork quilt, as forty-nine families held some 1,145,000 acres.[48] In 1958, in the country as a whole, 2,480 landowners, or one per cent of the population, held 55 per cent of all agricultural lands, whereas about six hundred thousand peasant families were completely landless, and 64 per cent of the rural population owned only 3.6 per cent of all cultivated land.[49] Although this period witnessed extensive growth in agricultural production, increasing numbers of peasants were now forced by poverty to leave their villages and

44 Zakî Khairî and Suᶜâd Khairî, *Dirâsât fî Târîkh al-Ḥizb a- Shiyûᶜî al-ᶜIrâqî*, vol. 1 (n.p., 1984), pp. 18–19.

45 Farouk-Sluglett and Sluglett, *Iraq Since 1958*, p. 30.

46 Batatu, *Old Social Classes*, p. 98.

47 Farouk-Sluglett and Sluglett, *Iraq Since 1958*, p. 32.

48 Ibid., p. 56.

49 Yousif Sayigh, *The Economies of the Arab World: Development Since 1945* (London: Croom Helm, 1978), p. 28.

migrate to overcrowded *Ṣarîfas* (shanty towns) on the outskirts of Iraq's major cities, particularly Baghdad and Basra. By 1958, "no fewer than 32 million *dunums* of land were in private hands,[50] and . . . of the area ploughed in that year less than one-fourth was in cultivation before the First World War, and a far smaller proportion privately owned."[51]

Nevertheless, productivity declined from 225 kilos per *dunum* during the 1920s to 187 kilos in the 1930s, and even further, to 143 kilos, prior to 1958. The standard of living for the majority of the population declined dramatically. In addition to the appalling conditions in which the peasants now lived as a result of their mass migration to the towns and the worldwide economic crisis of the early 1930s,[52] the situation of the majority of the urban population also deteriorated sharply.[53] Despite the inflation of the 1930s, the daily wage of unskilled labour declined steeply, from 75 fils in 1926 to 56 fils in 1930,[54] and to 50 fils annually from 1935 to 1937.[55] This trend continued through the 1940s and into the 1950s; in 1953 a report prepared by the International Labour Office expressed the opinion that "taking into account the cost of living, numbers of wage earners must be living at or near subsistence if not below."[56] In the meantime, the size of the national bourgeoisie was slowly growing. Iraq's industry was likewise in an embryonic state; the first law to protect national industry was enacted in 1929, it provided tax exemption only to mechanized industry using Iraqi raw materials and whose products were needed by the country.[57]

Although some merchants and financiers made large fortunes [at that time,] the salaried but small middle class made up of civil servants, teachers, clerks in commercial houses, and writers and journalists was excluded from political power and its members found themselves in a very precarious and unstable economic situation.[58] Although their numbers grew with the development of the public school system and availability of government scholarships,[59] their economic distress made them increasingly attracted to anti-establishment ideologies in the period between the two world wars.

The end of the 1930s and the outbreak of the Second World War opened a new chapter in the history of pre-revolutionary Iraqi society. Several different and yet interrelated factors contributed to the socio-economic transformation

[50] One *dunum* is roughly equal to 0.25 acres.

[51] Batatu, *Old Social Classes*, p. 110.

[52] Ibid., pp. 139–147.

[53] Ibid., pp. 136–139.

[54] One *fils* equals three-tenths of a cent U.S.

[55] Batau, *Old Social Classes*, p. 137.

[56] Ibid., pp. 137–138.

[57] Khaîrî and Khaîrî, *Dirâsât fî Târîkh al-Ḥizb a-Shiyû ʿî al-ʿIrâqî*, p. 19.

[58] Batatu, *Old Social Classes*, p. 473.

[59] For relevant data on the development of schools and intelligentsia in Iraq during that period, see *Muʿjam-al-ʿIrâq*, vol. 1 (Baghdad: al Najâḥ Press, 1953), pp. 166, 267; See also Batatu, *Old Social Classes*, pp. 34–35.

and had a major impact on the development of the Iraqi political environment. First, and probably most decisively, was the war itself, which returned allied armies of occupation and a great number of foreigners to Iraq. The British war effort stimulated both local industry and oil extraction. Under wartime conditions, and with the need for import substitution, local firms found an obvious incentive to expand production or to initiate new ventures. The boom continued in the early post-war period, and by 1957, fixed investment in industrial capital had already eclipsed commercial capital (ID 27.25 millon versus ID 20.80 million).[60] As a result of the accelerated rate of capital accumulation from economic growth in the 1940s and 1950s, by 1958, of the seventeen Baghdad families listed for that year as worth one million or more dinars, only one, the Lâwî family, "had two decades earlier ranked as 'first class' members whose 'financial consideration' (in the Chamber of Commerce) ranged between 22,500 and 75,000 *dinars*."[61] The urban working class – those Iraqis employed in industry, transport, communications, and services – also increased and by 1958 numbered 442,000 persons, which represented about 20 per cent of the country's 2.6 million urban residents.[62] Because of this economic development, Iraqi society was divided between a rich and powerful petite bourgeoisie, in which "23 families held, on a conservative estimate, 30 to 35 million dinars in assets of all sorts . . . an amount equalling, in rough terms, 56 to 65 per cent of the entire private corporate, commercial and industrial capital [of the country],"[63] and a large and still growing mass of dispossessed labourers, who had no access to political power and were barely able to eke out an existence. Nevertheless, such socio-economic cleavages had not yet created a marked popular polarization.

According to Hanna Batatu, "Common pauperism had not, by 1958, created any enduring common feeling between the *Ṣarîfa* dwellers and the city workers."[64] However, the poverty and new social challenges could not remain without any reaction. Workers' unions, strikes, and other forms of political mobilization emerged and started to have an impact on the political situation in the country. As early as July 1931 the first labour union in Iraq, *Jamᶜiyyat Aṣḥâb al-Ṣanâiᶜ* (the Artisans' Association), led by Muḥammad Ṣâliḥ al-Qazzâz, organized a massive strike in Baghdad, which soon spread to the provincial towns and took on a political dimension.[65] Despite the authorities' subsequent closure of this union, similar outbreaks of popular discontent were repeated in the 1930s and early 1940s, and at the end of the Second World War, at the

60 Farouk-Sluglett and Sluglett, *Iraq Since 1958*, p. 35.

61 Batatu, *Old Social Classes*, p. 274.

62 Ḥasan, "The Role of Foreign Trade in Economic Development in Iraq, 1864–1964," pp. 363–364.

63 Batatu, *Old Social Classes*, p. 274.

64 Ibid., p. 136.

65 Marion Farouk-Sluglett and Peter Sluglett, "Labour and National Liberation: The Trade Union Movement in Iraq, 1920–1958," *Arab Studies Quarterly*, vol. 5, no. 2 (Spring 1983), pp. 148–149.

time of the British and American alliance with the Soviet Union, when domestic repression was consequently more relaxed, Iraqi authorities granted permission for the establishment of sixteen new labour unions. Members of the Iraqi Communist Party (ICP) quickly took over, the leadership of twelve of these unions, and all of them came to play an important role in the social and political events of the late 1940s and early 1950s.[66] As was typical for Iraq, the largely class-determined socio-economic struggle and the national political struggle were frequently interwoven. Thus during the great upheaval of *al-Wathbah* (the Leap) of 1948, the masses protested against both increased food prices and the abortive Portsmouth Agreement with Britain, which was perceived to be similar to the hated Anglo-Iraqi Treaty of 1930.[67] In this protest the population was also turning against the government and the state apparatus that it controlled, which were ready to accept and enforce both the economic conditions that the majority found unacceptable and the humiliating treaty.

From its inception in 1921 until the 1958 revolution, the Iraqi state apparatus remained largely, if not completely, alienated from its own population, and there was often no close correlation even between the new upper classes and the nation's rulers. As Batatu notes, "The crucial political decisions were made by non-Iraqis, or outside the country's frontiers . . . and there was often no close correspondence between the local distribution of wealth and local distribution of power."[68] In addition, as a result of the influx of revenue from the oil companies "the state became, in large measure, economically autonomous from society,"[69] and this dislocation heightened its potential for despotism. At the same time, however, the state became even more connected to, and dependent on, external financial and political powers, and was increasingly ready to serve their interests.[70] As economic growth was not associated with any meaningful social or democratic progress, legal channels for the expression of discontent and calls for social reforms were barred. There was a huge political void beneath the Iraqi state structures and, below this, a vast undercurrent of popular dissatisfaction with, and a questioning of, a socio-economic and political system that was failing to meet the needs of the majority of the population. No formulated ideology or organization, however, yet existed through which this dissatisfaction could be expressed. Nevertheless, the potential for a truly revolutionary situation existed and provided many opportunities for radical movements.This inchoate situation ultimately, and perhaps inevitably, culminated in the dramatic violence of a military coup in July 1958.

66 Farouk Sluglett and Sluglett, *Iraq Since 1958*, pp. 38–39.

67 Farouk-Sluglett and Sluglett, "Labour and National Liberation," pp. 153–154.

68 Batatu, *Old Social Classes*, pp. 274–275.

69 Ibid, pp. 283 and 353. See also Farouk-Sluglett and Sluglett, *Iraq Since 1958*, p. 35.

70 According to Suᶜâd Khairî, brutal repression of the Kirkuk oilfield workers in 1946 proved to many Iraqis that the government was perfectly prepared to oppress them in defence of British economic interests. *Min Târîkh al-Ḥarakah al-Thawriyyah al-Muᶜâṣirah fî al-ᶜIrâq, 1920–1958*, vol 1.1 (Baghdad: Maṭbaᶜit al-Adîb al-ᶜArabî, 1974), pp. 150–152.

Radical movements had a significant impact on Iraqi socity even before the coup. One direct result of the activities of al-Raḥḥâl and his associates was the creation, in mid-1926, of the *Nâdî al-Taḍâmun* (Solidarity Club); its basic declared aims were the unity of youth, the propagation of knowledge, the progress of national industry, and the fulfillment of all "principles leading to the improvement of the life of the society."[71] Many young people who joined the club, such as ᶜAzîz S͟harîf, ᶜÂṣim Flayyiḥ, Ḥusain Jamîl, Zakî K͟hairî and Jamîl Tûmâ, later became leading leftists and communists.[72] In April 1926, to counteract this tendency, the Iraqi government joined in a regional agreement, sponsored by Britain, to combat communism,[73] and as a result, political activism became more difficult. Nevertheless, the *Nâdî al-Taḍâmun* expanded its activities, and on 1 January 1927 it organized its first public demonstration, calling for freedom of the press. In response, the government closed the main high school in Baghdad for ten days, and a number of students and teachers were arrested or expelled, later to be released and reinstated as a result of pressure from a number of public protests. On 8 February 1928, the club again organized a mass demonstration, this time to protest against the visit to Baghdad of the well-known British Zionist Sir Alfred Mond; the demonstration, in which over twenty thousand people took part, ended in a violent scuffle with the police.[74]

The significance of these demonstrations transcended the specific events; in effect, they signalled the birth of mass politics and mass political mobilization in Iraq. Furthermore, they heralded the issues (British imperialism and Zionism) and the processes (oppression and human rights abuses) that would come to dominate modern Iraqi politics. Until this point, politics and government had been the monopoly of the elite, and the masses had had little input and, perhaps more significantly, did not expect to have any input. Though both *Ḥizb al-Nahḍah al-ᶜIrâqiyyah* and *al-Ḥizb al-Waṭanî* had spearheaded the 1922 demonstrations, they had not organized them, and despite the wide popular support they enjoyed, their legitimacy derived from the institutional underpinnings of elite politics rather than from the democratic foundations of mass politics. Indeed, the political process they engaged in was unabashedly elitist, and not participatory.

Al-Raḥḥâl and the First Challenge

In the context of this volatile political environment, Ḥusain al-Raḥḥâl began translating and disseminating the works of European socialists for a circle of young Iraqi intellectuals, gathering around himself a number of young

71 K͟hairî and K͟hairî, *Dirâsât fî Târîk͟h al-Ḥizb a-S͟hiyû ᶜî al-ᶜIrâqî*, p. 29.

72 Ibid.

73 ᶜAbd-ul Razzâq al-Ḥasanî, *Târîk͟h al-Wizârât al-ᶜIrâqiyyah*, vol. 2, 7th ed. (Baghdad: Afâq ᶜArabiyyah, 1988), p. 59.

74 K͟hairî and K͟hairî, *Dirâsât fî Târîk͟h al-Ḥizb a-S͟hiyû ᶜî al-ᶜIrâqî*, p. 30; see also, K͟hairî al-ᶜUmarî, *Ḥikâyât Siyâsiyyah min Târîk͟h al-ᶜIrâq al-Ḥadît͟h* (Cairo: Dâr al-Hilâl, 1969), pp. 173–194.

nationalists and socially concerned students such as Muḥammad Salîm Fattâḥ, Muṣṭafâ ᶜAlî, ᶜAbd-ul-lah Jaddûᶜ, ᶜAwnî Bakr Ṣidqî, and Maḥmûd Aḥmad al-Saiyyid. Saiyyid (1903–1937), the most prominent among these intellectuals, was pioneer Iraqi realist short story writer. In a 1923 letter to the well-known Egyptian socialist Nicola Ḥaddâd, al-Saiyyid described a major obstacle to the dissemination of socialist thought among the young Iraqi intelligentsia:

In our isolation from the intellectual heritage of the civilized world, our only contact is "Reuters" news wires.... The extent of our understanding of socialism does not go beyond your book.... The socialists in France sent us only French publications, which only Iraqis with a knowledge of French can read. [The Iraqi majority] is still thirsty for reading more about socialism in our own language. Did you ever think of writing or translating to Arabic books on contemporary socialism that deal with socialist systems, administration, governance, and historical background?[75]

In 1929, al-Raḥḥâl, with al-Saiyyid's cooperation, established the bi-monthly *Al-Ṣaḥîfah* (The Journal), which became the realization of al-Raḥḥâl's efforts to introduce scientific socialist thought into the intellectual circles of Iraq. As al-Raḥḥâl later stated:

After the initial five years of thinking out loud in Baghdad's coffee shops, discussing and learning through the translation of foreign socialist journals and magazines – as I spoke English, French, German, and Turkish and thus had more access to socialist thought – I gathered around me a number of eager, thirsty young critical minds looking for answers to their country's problems. I felt like Aristotle, and these were my disciples. Our circles became wider, so we decided on 28 December 1924 to start the journal in order to publish mature analyses of a scientific socialist approach.[76]

As described by al-Saiyyid, the journal's aim was to "disseminat[e] the ideas of revolution and Marxism."[77] Al-Saiyyid was in touch with many Arab socialists, such as Yûsuf Ibrâhîm Yazbak in Lebanon and Shiblî Shumaiyyil and Nicola Ḥaddâd in Egypt, and he soon developed a strong following through his own writings. In a personal letter to Yazbak, dated 19 April 1929, al-Saiyyid, who served as director of correspondence for the Baghdad municipality, described the journal as

dedicated... to the spread of revolutionary thought and Marxism.... In Baghdad these days there is a labour movement [1929] as workers have petitioned the Ministry of the Interior, to form a union in the footsteps of the Barbers' Union and other [nascent] labour organizations.... There is no foundation to the recent scurrilous article in the *Shûrâ* newspaper attributed to their correspondents in Baghdad, the gist of which suggested that these movements have the smell of Bolshevism. I believe these people want nothing more than to discourage our workers. I also enclose, herewith, the appeal I issued to

75 Quoted in ᶜAzîz Sibâhî, *'Uqûd min Târîkh al-Ḥizb al-Shiyûᶜî al-ᶜIrâqî*, vol. 1 (Damascus: Thaqâfah al-Jadîdah Publications, 2002), p. 19.
76 Interview by author with Ḥusain al-Raḥḥâl, Baghdad (18 October 1973).
77 Personal letter from al-Saiyyid to Yûsuf Ibrâhîm Yazbak (19 April 1929). Copy of letter supplied to author by Professor Majid Khadduri.

workers in the capital [Baghdad]. The tone of this call is the most you can aspire to in the world of journalism here.[78]

Al-Raḥḥâl continued:

In 1922, we tried to form the first socialist circle. It had no name and our group was basically for intellectual debate. We held Marxist meetings in a mosque maintained by al-Saiyyid's father. We were basically personal friends, and we produced one serious report on the social, political, and economic conditions of Iraq in 1923. To impress Lenin we translated it into Russian and had it delivered to the Russian Embassy in Tehran to send to him. The embassy later advised us to join the Iraqi Nationalist Party, though we did not do this. Thus, when we established *al-Ṣaḥîfah* with its title in red, we hoped it would become the intellectual socialist articulator of all revolutionaries [in Iraq].[79]

The articles in *Al-Ṣaḥîfah* were very radical and focused on three main issues. First, they openly approached sensitive social subjects related to social justice and human rights against state and class-based oppression. Within this context, they emphasized women's rights, describing the current situation as

the remnants of the feudal ages; the *Ḥarîm* and the *Ḥijâb* [veil] continue the features of the feudal system. The aristocracy of that period was able, through the exploitation of the work of the *fallâḥ* [peasants], to build the *Ḥarîm* system to keep women captive. The *Ḥarîm* and *Ḥijâb* were up to that time unknown [in Iraq] and will wither away once again when the people's classes establish their state.[80]

This call for women's rights produced a public outcry from Iraq's conservative elements and religious leadership. Second, *Al-Ṣaḥîfah* called for the creation of a regime that championed social justice and defended the underprivileged classes. It propagated the theoretical principles of socialism and Marxism, which made the paper an intellectual centre for progressive elements of the society and channelled them toward socialism. Third, the journal called for more public participation in politics and took a staunchly anti-British attitude. Largely because of government reaction to this third focus, *Al-Ṣaḥîfah* was able to publish only six issues before it was suspended by the authorities.[81]

In 1925, al-Raḥḥâl established another journal, *Sînamâ al-Ḥayât* (Theatre of Life), which published its first weekly issue on 17 December 1926. An editorial in this issue described the journal as a forum for "popular socialism from the people to the people."[82] In 1928 publication of this journal also ended, not because of government pressure, but as the result of a split that occurred between al-Raḥḥâl and al-Saiyyid. Both men subsequently entered the Iraqi civil service and, in effect, ceased their activist efforts. However, leftist groups of the 1930s, particularly the *Ahâlî* group, organized in 1932, and the communist

78 Ibid.

79 Interview by author with Ḥusain al-Raḥḥâl, Baghdad (18 October 1973).

80 Khairî and Khairî, *Dirâsât fî Târîkh al-Ḥizb a-Shiyû ʿî al-ʿIrâqî*, p. 29.

81 Ibid.

82 Râfaʿîl Buṭṭî, *Al-Ṣaḥâfah fî al-ʿIrâq* (Cairo: Institute of Higher Arab Studies, 1955), p. 124.

group *Lajnat Mukâfahat al-Isti^cmâr wa al-Istithmâr*, organized in 1934, emerged from among al-Raḥḥâl's disciples. These followers included Yûsuf and ʿAbd-ul-Qâdir Ismâʿîl al-Bustânî (al-Saiyyid's cousins), Zakî Khairî, ʿÂṣim Flayyiḥ, ʿAbd-ul-lah Jaddûʿ, Faḍîl Muḥammad, Muṣṭafâ ʿAlî, ʿAwnî Bakr Ṣidqî (al-Raḥḥâl's brother-in-law), Salîm Fattâḥ, Muḥammad Ṣâliḥ al-Qazzâz, Ḥusain Jamîl, and Rashîd Muṭlaq, all of whom subsequently became prominent members of the communist movement.

Early Communist Organization

Whereas al-Raḥḥâl's efforts to introduce Marxist thought into Iraq in the early 1920s were successful, the origins of Iraq's communist organizations are less clear. As early as January 1925, a pro-British newspaper warned that communism was spreading in Iraq and warned the government and religious leadership to be wary of it.[83] There are several versions of how communism developed, reflecting both the diversity and the interconnectedness of influences operating on leftist political mobilization in this period. Some historians contend that in 1929 the chairman of the Palestine Communist Party, Haim Auerbach (alias ʿAbbûd), corresponded with a young Iraqi political activist, Yûsuf Salmân Yûsuf (alias Fahd) (1901–1949), leading to the creation of the *al-Nasiriyah* Marxist circle.[84] Shortly thereafter, Yûsuf Salmân Yûsuf, Ḥamîd Majîd (from Nasiriyah), Sâmî Nâdir, and Dhâfir Ṣâliḥ (from Basra) formed the short-lived *Jamʿiyyat al-Aḥrâr al-lâ-Dîniyyah* (Secular Liberal Society) according to Marxist principles. The group kept in touch with ʿAbbûd, who sent them the Beirut periodical *Al-Shams*.

Another version suggests that the Comintern agent Buṭrus Abu Nâṣir (also known as Pyotr Vasili, or Petros), posing as a tailor, arrived in Nasiriyah in 1929 and converted Yûsuf Salmân Yûsuf to Marxism.[85] He enabled Yûsuf to travel to Moscow in 1935 to study Marxism-Leninism-Stalinism in the Communist University of the Toilers of the East (KUTV). Returning home in 1938 to lead the Iraqi Communist Party, Yûsuf adopted the pseudonym "Fahd," and Petros, his mission accomplished, returned to Moscow. Yet another version of the story asserts that Iraqi Marxists tried to establish a communist organization in the 1920s, even before the creation of trade unions. The pioneers were Ḥusain al-Raḥḥâl, ʿAwnî Bakr Ṣidqî, Maḥmûd Aḥmad al-Saiyyid, ʿAbd-ul-lah Jaddûʿ, Muṣṭafâ ʿAlî, and Fâḍil Muḥammad. This account also acknowledges Fahd's adoption of Marxism in Nasiriyah in 1929.[86] In a further version, an

83 *Al-ʿÂlam al-ʿArabî*, no. 243 (Baghdad, 7 January 1925).

84 ʿAbd-ul-lah Amîn, *Al-Shiyûʿiyyah ʿAlâ al-Ṣufûd* (Baghdad: Shafîq Press, 1974), p. 81; and ʿAbd-ul-Jabbâr al-Jubûrî, *Al-Aḥzâb wa al-jam ʿiyyât al-Siyâsiyyah fî al-Quṭr al-ʿIrâqî, 1908–1958* (Baghdad: Dâr al-Ḥuriyyah, 1977), pp. 108–109.

85 Qadrî Qalʿajî, *Tajrubat ʿArabî fî al-Ḥizb al-shiyû ʿî* (Beirut: Dar al-Kâtib al-ʿArabî, 1959), p. 23.

86 Suʿâd Khairî, *Min Târîkh al-Ḥarakah al-Thawriyyah al-Muʿâṣirah fî al-ʿIrâq*, p. 55.

active communist circle, led by Mullah S̲h̲arîf ᶜUt̲h̲mân, known locally as the "Red Mullah," was established in Irbil in the early 1930s, and this group amalgamated with Fahd's to form the Communist Party of Iraq.[87] An even more detailed version credits Fahd with spreading Marxism-Leninism in 1932, and even with propagating those ideas under the name of the Communist Party of Iraq, issuing pronouncements titled "Workers and Peasants of the Arab World Unite."[88] Fahd was arrested in 1933; during his trial, he admitted that he was a communist, making him the first person to accept the communist label and defend communism in such a public forum.[89]

Whatever the truth of the origins of communism in Iraq, a meeting of Iraqi communists held on 31 March 1934 was of primary significance in the development of the country's Communist Party. Those present agreed to organize *Lajnat Mukâfaḥat al-Istiᶜmâr wa al-Istit̲h̲mâr* (the Committee for Combating Imperialism and Exploitation), to be led by ᶜÂṣim Flayyiḥ. Other notable participants were ᶜAbd-ul-Qâdir Ismâᶜîl al-Bustânî, Yûnân Frankûl, Zakî K̲h̲airî, ᶜAbd-ul-Wahâb Maḥmûd, Mûsâ Ḥabîb, Mahdî Hâs̲h̲im, Wadîᶜ Ṭalyah, Yûsuf Mattî, Nûrî Rufâᶜîl (Baghdad), Fahd and Ḥamîd Majîd (Nasiriyah), and Sâmî Nâdir and D̲h̲âfir Ṣâliḥ (Basra). The committee called for the annulment of all debts and mortgages; national control of oil plants, railways, and banks; the protection of motherhood; and the dictatorship of workers and peasants. According to ᶜÂṣim Flayyiḥ:

This committee was the first formal organization of any communist group in Iraq. Previous groups were basically pseudo-intellectual exercises that did not include in their ranks any workers or peasants. We created a formal national organization that included workers (although there were no peasants). My selection as the secretary was based solely on the fact that I was an artisan, the closest of the group to being a worker. The intention in organizing the committee was to begin serious communist action in the country. We selected as members, action-oriented people. Thus, I was the first general secretary of the Communist Party of Iraq and our committee was the first Central Committee.[90]

At the end of 1935 the committee decided to adopt as its name the Iraqi Communist Party (ICP), and to collaborate with the *al-Ahâlî* group, progressive liberal intellectuals who agitated for social reform, cultural emancipation, and national liberation. The group was also committed to reform through raising public awareness, and as its primary activity published a daily paper in Baghdad, *Al-Ahâlî*; the first issue appeared on 2 January 1932. Most of Iraq's progressive activists started with the *al-Ahâlî* group, which remained a public

[87] Sâmî S̲h̲ûrsh, "Ṣafaḥât min Târîk̲h̲ al-Yasâr al-Kurdî (al-ᶜIrâqî)," *Abwâb*, no. 8 (London, 1996), p. 73.
[88] ᶜAbd-ul-Karîm Ḥasan al-Jârâllah, *Taṣadduᶜ al-Bas̲h̲ariyyah min K̲h̲ilâl Wailât al-Istibdâd wa al-ᶜUbûdiyyah* (Saidon, Lebanon: al-Maktabah al-ᶜAṣriyyah, 1969), pp. 77–80.
[89] Suᶜâd K̲h̲airî, "Short Study of the Iraqi Revolutionary Movement, Pt. 2," *Al-T̲h̲aqâfa al-Jadîdah* (October 1972), p. 32.
[90] Interview by author with ᶜÂṣim Flayyiḥ, Baghdad (18 February 1959).

social conscience for several decades.[91] Notable affiliates and alumni of *al-Ahâlî* include ʿAbd-ul-Fattâḥ Ibrâhîm, Kâmil al-Châdirchî, Ḥusain Jamîl, ʿAbd-ul-Qâdir Ismâʿîl al-Bustânî, Yûsuf Ismâʿîl al-Bustânî, and Muḥammad Ḥadîd.

Al-Ahâlî's ideas were initially rather vague and incoherent. In an editorial in its paper's first issue, under the title "Interests of the People Above All Other Interests," the group declared that it aimed to work for the benefit of the majority of the country's inhabitants by raising their standard of living. It wanted to create "a sound political and economic order and make the best use of the country's intellectual talents and material resources." As its ideology became more explicit, the group identified itself with a reformist and liberal democratic version of socialism called *al-Shaʿbiyyah* (populism), whose meaning was explained best in one of the group's leaflets, *Muṭâlaʿât fî al-Shaʿbiyyah* (Studies in Populism).[92] The group understood the word "people" to mean the majority of people – not one special class among them[93] – and it called for a government that would be able to combine its authority with the preservation of the rights of the population.[94] Consequently, the rights of individuals had to be protected by an independent judicial system,[95] and the government's primary duties would be to serve the majority, to ensure security, to supervise certain economic matters,[96] and to see to the abolition of economic disparities and inequalities.[97]

The *Ahâlî* group insisted, however, that they differed from the communists since (1) they did not believe in the decisive role of class conflict and the special leading role of the working class; (2) they were not against family and religion;[98] (3) they emphasized anti-imperialism but did not subscribe to the communist concept of social and political revolution;[99] (4) they cautioned against nationalist chauvinism while espousing patriotism;[100] and (5) they perceived a need for cooperation to create a progressive Arab society based on the principles of *al-Shaʿbiyyah*. Reflecting the group's reformist tone, they began discussions in the summer of 1935 about transforming *al-Shaʿbiyyah* into a formal party; ʿAbd-ul-Fattâḥ Ibrâhîm rejected this direction, preferring the movement to remain underground.[101]

A rift emerged between the two groups, with the communists characterizing *al-Ahâlî*'s ideas as naïve and not much more radical than various official

[91] For a history of *al-Ahâlî* group, see Fûʾâd Ḥusain al-Wakîl, *Jamâʿât al-Ahâlî fî al-ʿIrâq* (Baghdad: Ministry of Culture, Rashid Publishing House, 1979).
[92] *Muṭâlaʿât fî al-Shaʿbiyyah* [Studies in Populism] (Baghdad: Ahali Press, 1935).
[93] Ibid., p. 7
[94] Ibid., p. 10.
[95] Ibid., p. 12.
[96] Ibid., p. 13.
[97] Ibid., p. 23.
[98] Ibid., p. 35.
[99] Ibid., pp. 35–36.
[100] Ibid., p. 45.
[101] Muḥammad Ḥadîd, *Mudhakkarâtî: Al-Ṣirâʿ min ajl al-Dîmûqrâtiyyah fî al-ʿIrâq* (London: Dar al-Saqi, 2000), pp. 144–149.

governmental reform programmes. In particular, they attacked its understanding of the concept of socialism, and one communist, Qâsim Ḥasan, dedicated thirty-one pages of his seventy-nine-page pamphlet, *Fî al-Maizân: Ḥawla Risâlat al-Ahâlî; Muṭâlaᶜât fî al-Shaᶜbiyyah* (On the balance: On the message of *al-Ahâlî*; studies on *al-Shaᶜbiyyah*) *al-Shaᶜbiyyah* to this single issue. On the other hand, a number of leading communists cooperated with and penetrated the *Ahâlî* group, including ᶜAbd-ul-Qâdir Ismâᶜîl al-Bustânî, who served as the editor in chief of the *Ahâlî* newspaper; Yûsuf Ismâᶜîl al-Bustânî, his brother, also one of the *Ahâlî* editors; ᶜAbd-ul-lah Jaddûᶜ; Yûsuf Mattî; ᶜAwnî Bakr Ṣidqî; and even the future leader of the party, Fahd himself, who was the correspondent for the *Ahâlî* paper in Nasiriyah city.[102]

On 19 July 1935, the ICP started to publish the first clandestine Iraqi paper, *Kifâḥ al-Shaᶜb* (The Struggle of the People), which carried the Marxist slogan "Workers of the World Unite," as well as the communist insignia of the hammer and sickle, on its masthead. The paper was dedicated to a rather simplistic dissemination of Marxist-Leninist ideology. For example, in its second issue, in August 1935, it expressed faith in the leadership of the Comintern, stating that the Comintern's forthcoming Seventh Congress would "set for us rules and plans to guide us in challenging our enemies." It also warned its sympathizers to avoid unnecessary conflict and polemics on side issues such as Islamic beliefs, social customs regarding women, and other sensitive subjects. As it argued:

> There is a mistake committed by some of our comrades in the propagation of their ideas which results in arguments and conflicts.... they focused on the issues of religion, the situation of women, and the Islamic family or the family in general. Comrades, although we believe that all those issues are very important and we appreciate their impact on the march of the socialist revolution,... we nevertheless have a programme which we have to follow and we must remember which goals are of primary importance.

Partly because of the lack of any other progressive media, *Kifâḥ al-Shaᶜb* achieved some popularity and had a circulation of over five hundred copies. However, it stopped publication after the fifth issue, in November 1935, since the Party was dismantled following a police crackdown,[103] and most of its active members abandoned their political activities. The Party's secretary-general, ᶜÂṣim Flayyiḥ, gave the authorities a written guarantee that he would stop his political activity, and he then devoted all his time to improving his tailoring business. ᶜAbd-ul-Qâdir Ismâᶜîl al-Bustânî and his brother Yûsuf departed to Syria, where ᶜAbd-ul-Qâdir joined the Syrian Communist Party. Yûsuf continued on from Syria to France, where he joined the French Communist Party. Mûsâ Ḥabîb became a contractor; during the 1950s he was editorial secretary of the Baghdad-based newspaper *Al-Bilâd* (The Country). Yûnân Frankûl also became a successful contractor.

102 Al-Wakîl, *Jamâᶜât al-Ahâlî fî al-ᶜIrâq*, pp. 186–187.

103 Khairî and Khairî, *Dirâsât fî Târîkh al-Ḥizb a-Shiyûᶜî al-ᶜIrâqî*, pp. 38–39.

The Party had apparently disintegrated, but its renewal and revitalization were imminent. Some communist cells had broken away earlier from the main body of the Party and survived the crackdown. Others quickly reestablished themselves, especially after the Arab world's first military coup, on 29 October 1936, which was led by the Iraqi military's chief of staff, General Bakr Ṣidqî, a former member of *al-Sha^c^biyyah*.[104] Some leading communists, such as Mahdî Hâshim and Zakî Khairî, were released from prison, at least temporarily. In addition, many communists, acting as individuals, had never stopped their political activities and took an active part in the preparation for and execution of the coup. For that purpose, they cooperated closely with the *al-Ahâlî* group, whose members held half the portfolios of the post-coup government of Ḥikmat Sulaimân. As Muḥammad Ḥadîd's memoirs reveal, the *Ahâlî* group was a crucial actor in the Ṣidqî coup. More than mere sympathizers, *al-Ahâlî*, having written the cadre's basic programme and chosen the regime's cabinet, acted as a brain trust for the coup leaders.[105]

The Importance of *al-Ahâlî*

On 1 November 1936, Iraq's leftist groups, including the communists, and their sympathizers issued a statement calling for a public demonstration in support of seven demands: (1) eradicating the tyranny of the past; (2) strengthening the army; (3) offering an amnesty for all political prisoners; (4) allowing trade unions and newspapers to resume their activities; (5) reducing poverty and unemployment, and encouraging national industry; (6) fostering equality among the Iraqi people and spreading education throughout the country; and (7) furthering efforts towards the unity of all Arab progressive forces. On 3 November, the communists led the public demonstrations, and over fifty thousand people gathered in Baghdad to support the post-coup government.[106] The same month, the communists gave wholehearted support to an *al-Ahâlî* initiative when the *Jam^c^iyyat al-Iṣlâḥ al-Sha^c^bî* (Association of the People's Reform) called for "democratic freedoms," the encouragement of workers' organizations, a minimum wage, an eight-hour working day, and progressive taxation.[107] Iraqi conservatives soon branded the members of the *al-Ahâlî* group as "communists," a charge from which the ICP benefited immensely, since politically unsophisticated Iraqis soon equated the ICP with the only other group in Iraq actively seeking to bring about social and political change.

In the following month, the rift between the relatively progressive civilian ministers and the country's military leadership widened, resulting in a

[104] Ḥadîd, *Mudhakkarâtî*, p. 143.
[105] Ibid., pp. 151–165.
[106] Al-Ḥasanî, *Târîkh al-Wizârât al-^c^Irâqiyyah*, p. 238; and Khairî and Khairî, *Dirâsât fî TârîKh al-Ḥizb a-Shiyû ^c^î al-^c^Irâqî*, pp. 44–45.
[107] Khairî and Khairî, *Dirâsât fî Târîkh al-Ḥizb a-Shiyû ^c^î al-^c^Irâqî*, p. 48.

crackdown by the new regime on all leftist groups and organizations, including *al-Ahâlî* and the communists.[108] General Ṣidqî, although having no formal role within the government, worked to control the regime from the outside; consequently, the differences between the military regime and its civilian supporters became irreconcilable.[109]

The *Ahâlî* members had to resign from their ministerial posts on 6 June 1937, and the Association of the People's Reform was banned in July, because, as the Interior Ministry claimed, "it was proven to be detrimental to the existence of the Kingdom and the security of the people, and because of its propagation of the poisonous communist thought."[110] With the assassination of Bakr Ṣidqî, a conservative civilian rule returned to power on 17 August 1937 bringing with it the old guard, including Jamîl al-Madfaᶜî, the pro-British former prime minister. The old guard and Madfaᶜî, who considered the communists to be responsible for the 1936 coup and its aftermath, arrested the leaders of the ICP, sentencing them to jail and exile, and even revoking the citizenship of some of them.[111]

The first communist cells in the Iraqi army were organized in Kirkuk and Baghdad in 1935. Two years later, sixty-five non-commissioned officers were arrested, three of whom were condemned to death before having their sentences stayed, while heavy prison sentences were imposed on the rest. Zakî Khairî, the Party liaison with the army, was given two years in jail and two years of probation. Despite this crackdown, one hundred officers maintained their membership in the Iraqi Communist Party, prompting the government to adjust the Iraqi penal code by adding Article 89a, imposing the death sentence on anyone propagating communist ideas within the army.[112]

The Party in the 1940s

The years between 1939 and 1941, during which Iraqi nationalists and pro-British elites constantly clashed, represented one of the most complicated periods in Iraqi history. The Bakr Ṣidqî coup of 1936 initiated military involvement in Iraq's politics and could be considered a historic victory for the forces of nationalism, despite the fact that the Ṣidqî regime lasted for less than a year. After its collapse, there was a gradual return to the conservative pro-British elements, culminating in March 1939 in Nûrî al-Saᶜîd's formation of a government with the proclaimed goal of restoring "order." Within days of the formation of this government, the young nationalist King Ghâzî I died in a car accident,

[108] Suᶜâd Khairî, *Min Târîkh al-Ḥarakah al-Thawriyyah al-Muᶜâṣirah fî al-ᶜIrâq*, pp. 150–152.
[109] Ḥadîd, *Mudhakkarâtî*, pp. 166–170.
[110] Al-Ḥasanî, *Târîkh al-Wizârât al-ᶜIrâqiyyah*, see also Suᶜâd Khairî, *Min Târîkh al-Ḥarakah al-Thawriyyah al-Muᶜâṣirah fî al-ᶜIrâq*, p. 70.
[111] ᶜAbd-ul Razzâq al-Ḥasanî, *Târîkh al-ᶜIrâq al-Siyâsî*, vol. 3 (Saidon, Lebanon: al-Maktabah al-ᶜAṣriyyah, 1958), p. 178.
[112] Khairî and Khairî, *Dirâsât fî Târîkh al-Ḥizb a-Shiyû ᶜî al-ᶜIrâqî*, pp. 39, 40.

and with the outbreak of the Second World War, tension between nationalist and pro-British forces erupted again, as the Nûrî al-Saᶜîd government – per its treaty obligations – declared war on Germany. In the meantime, the increasing politicization of the army produced a number of movements among nationalistic young officers. This forced the pro-British Regent to appoint an anti-British prime minister, Rashîd ᶜAlî al-Gailânî, whose "National Defence Government" moved closer to the Axis and declared Iraq to be neutral. Within days, conflict broke out between Gailânî and the Regent, who fled with the pro-British leadership to the British garrison in Basra. Within a month, however, British forces had removed al-Gailânî and once again occupied Iraq, placing it under direct military control and thereby turning the country into a British colony in all but name, regardless of its legal sovereignty.

The influence of the ICP during the 1930s and 1940s was limited by the local context, namely, the lack of a substantial and organized working class. Trade unionism began in 1928 but only in a few occupations, and because of the movement's political ramifications unions were prohibited by the government between 1931 and 1944. By 1938 the propagation of communist ideas had also been made a crime,[113] though the Communist Party of Iraq did enjoy some successes. Following the downfall in May 1941 of the short-lived nationalist regime of Rashîd ᶜAlî al-Gailânî (which the Communist Party of Iraq had initially backed, following the Soviet line), and the entry of the Soviet Union into the war, the Iraqi communists supported the Allied war effort against fascism. In exchange for this support, the suppression of communist activities in Iraq was relaxed. With the removal of heavy-handed government tactics, the nascent Iraqi trade union movement stepped up its organizational efforts in the mid-1940s, and the communists became influential among dock workers at the Basra port, tobacco workers in Baghdad, oil field workers in Kirkuk, and railway employees across the country. Even so, the "working class" was still numerically small and was concentrated primarily within British-controlled industries and transportation. In addition, the ICP was unable to rouse the peasantry, who failed to understand either the Party's ideology or its approach to land reform.[114]

On 30 January 1938, Fahd returned from Moscow, where he had been undergoing further education and training. He opened a private commercial translating business as a front and started to organize the Party again from scratch. He contacted Marxist and leftist sympathizers but avoided the old communist groups that had been deeply penetrated by the police or were known to the government's security agencies. Initially, he constructed the Party out of unreliable and volatile material – mostly students, teachers, and government employees, predominantly from well-to-do families. The same types were also

[113] Article 89a of the Penal Code. See M. S. Agwani, *Communism in the Arab East* (Bombay, India: Asia Publishing House, 1969), p. 34.

[114] For a detailed breakdown of known ICP membership in the 1940s by occupation, ethnicity, gender, and age, see Batatu, *Old Social Classes*.

drawn to fascist groups, and their Party loyalty was shallow. Therefore it is not surprising that the Party exhibited ideological confusion and a tendency towards fragmentation; a number of splits soon occurred.

In December 1940, the Party began to publishing its new organ, *Al-Sharârah* (The Spark), which was modelled on Lenin's publication of the same name. Its initial circulation was only ninety copies, but in 1942, after the Party acquired its own printing press, circulation increased to two thousand copies.[115] Initially, the communists supported the Gailânî revolt of April–May 1941 because it was the first popular uprising since 1920 of the Iraqi people against British imperialism, because it was a protest against British manipulation and misinterpretation of the 1930 treaty, and because the Soviet Union recognized the Gailânî regime in May 1941.[116] However, the Party started to revise its stand on the Rashîd ᶜAlî al-Gailânî movement following the defeat of the Gailânî nationalists at the end of May and the reoccupation of Iraq by the British, and, especially, after the German invasion of the Soviet Union on 22 June 1941. The Party now considered the Gailânî revolt to be nothing more than an army coup; it criticized the revolt as badly timed and condemned it for "withholding from the people their constitutional right to organize themselves into parties and trade unions."[117]

In retrospect, the Party interpreted the army's involvement in politics as resulting from the absence of democracy and democratic institutions such as trade unions and poltical parties.[118] Eventually, the leaders of the 1941 nationalist al-Gailânî movement were described in *Al-Sharârah* as "fascist and reactionary sympathizers."[119] In June 1943, the communists even admitted that "our support of the Rashîd ᶜAlî al-Gailânî movement, though not unqualified, was a political mistake."[120]

As Fahd became established as the main organizer of the ICP, challenges to his leadership crystallized. The first such challenge to emerge occurred in August 1942, when Thunûn Aiyyûb (Qâdir), a member of the Central Committee, and Yaᶜqûb Cohen (Fâḍil), along with their followers, were expelled from the Party and started to publish their own organ, *Ila al-Amâm* (Forward). In an interview with the author, Aiyyûb explained that he was expelled because he had refused to obey Fahd, whom he found "naive and ignorant." He added, "Cohen followed me as my protégé."[121] In Aiyyûb's view, Fahd was not acceptable on account of his ethnic and religious background, "as his family originally came from Turkey."[122] He also accused Fahd of getting drunk during one social event and flirting with Ayyûb's wife.

115 Khairî and Khairî, *Dirâsât fî Târîkh al-Ḥizb a-Shiyû ᶜî al-ᶜIrâqî*, p. 52.
116 Suᶜâd Khairî, *Min Târîkh al-Ḥarakah al-Thawriyyah al-Muᶜâṣirah fî al-ᶜIrâq*, pp. 80–81.
117 *Al-Sharârah*, nos. 6–7 (May–June 1941).
118 Ibid., no. 8 (July 1941).
119 Ibid., no. 11 (November 1941).
120 *Al-Qâᶜidah*, no. 5 (June 1943), p. 5.
121 Interview by author with Thunûn Aiyyûb, Baghdad (18 November 1988).
122 Ibid.

A more serious split took place a few months later, in November 1942, while Fahd was away in Moscow. During his absence he had entrusted the Party to one of his closest associates and the most prominent member of his Central Committee, ᶜAbd-ul-lah Masᶜûd Qurainî (Riyâḍ). But Qurainî, along with three other committee members, summoned a Party congress and took over the Party's organization, including *Al-Sharârah*. The three remaining Fahd supporters on the Central Committee, Dâûd Ṣâyegh, Ḥusain Muḥammad al-Shabîbî (Ṣârim), and Zakî Muḥammad Bâsim (Ḥâzim), thereupon established their own paper, *Al-Qâᶜidah* (Base), to replace *Al-Sharârah* as the official Party organ; publication began in January 1943.[123] Thereafter, although both groups claimed to represent the ICP, each was known by its publication. Despite mutual bitterness and recriminations, the *Sharârah* group suggested to the *Qâᶜidah* group that its followers would return to the mainstream *al-Qâᶜidah* group if they were given the right to express their views freely; they even declared, on 6 June 1943, that they were willing to close *Al-Sharârah*. As *al-Sharârah*'s people asserted: "Neither we nor you are, in fact, a Party in the real sense of the word, and the leadership of the Party, regardless of its [formal] titles . . . has already committed many mistakes. Some of them were so detrimental that they may be classified as criminal."[124]

At about the same time, in early 1943, the dissolution of the Comintern took place, an event that Fahd saw as advantageous to the international communist movement in general and to the ICP in particular. The end of the Comintern released the Party from nominal control of the Communist Party of the Soviet Union (CPSU), which had overtaken the international communist movement, giving the Party more room to manoeuvre within Iraq's national and regional contexts and allowing Fahd to set the foundation for a new theoretical and organizational direction for the ICP. This new vision was articulated less than a year later, at the ICP's First Party Conference. In a March 1943 article on the impact of the dissolution, Fahd delineated its importance to the Party and the Iraqi situation, declaring:

> Before the [Second World] War when internal and external conditions in different countries were becoming complex, solving the issues of the workers' movements in each country if it had a [controlling] international centre, could face obstacles [locally] that could not be overcome as the profound differences in the historic process of development in each country would at times result in a conflict [between International Centre] positions and those of other countries. The variations in the level of process of the social and political development, [in each country,] in addition to the divergences among the workers' [socio-political] consciousness and organization, all these would result in placing varying responsibilities on the working class [Party] in each country.[125]

[123] Interview by author with Dâûd Ṣâyegh, Baghdad (18 June 1967).

[124] *Al-Sharârah*, no. 7 (August 1943).

[125] *Kitâbât al-Rafîq Fahd* [The Works of Comrade Fahd] (Beirut: Dâr al-Fârâbî, 1976), pp. 358–359.

He explained that the freedom given the ICP by its release from the Comintern increased the Party's responsibilities since it allowed the Iraqi communists to work with "democratic and popular" forces. This now became the approach followed by the Party under Fahd's leadership.[126]

In February 1944, Dâûd Ṣâyegh, who had supported Fahd in the 1942 split, broke with him and established his own organization, *Râbiṭat al-Shiyûᶜiyyîn al-ᶜIrâqiyyîn* (the League of Iraqi Communists), including its own publication *Al-ᶜAmal* (Action). In its first editorial, in November 1944, *Al-ᶜAmal* attacked Fahd, accusing him of having followed "an adventurist policy despite strong objections and criticism . . . which led to a number of splits and Party revolts." It also published the new group's by-laws and raised the slogan, "Gather around *Al-ᶜAmal* to form a unified and strong Iraqi Communist Party." Later, Ṣâyegh articulated his reasons for breaking away: "We wanted to have a clear programme and publish internal by-laws for the Party. Also, we wanted to have more democracy and less control by the secretary-general. . . . Fahd was an overwhelming personality, but he was also not flexible and sometimes, very dictatorial."[127] He also suggested that Fahd's social background and inellectual limitations made it difficult for Fahd to lead the well-educated intelligentsia of the country.

Other splinter groups, however, began to think seriously of reuniting with the "mother" party, or at least of finding some accommodation with it. Consequently, the *Sharârah* group formally suggested to Fahd that they seek unity, since the police crackdown on every communist splinter group was indiscriminate and the divisions made the crackdown more successful. The *Sharârah* group proposed an immediate merger under a unified temporary central committee that would represent both groups equally and undertake to hold a joint congress within six months. In addition, one Party organ would be published, with an editorial committee representing both groups. At the same time, the two groups would have unified by-laws and programmes on the organizational structure, and the status of members would remain fixed until the congress.[128] Fahd, however, rejected this offer; although he thought the principle of unity was acceptable, the conditions were not. As he explained in an internal Party memo,[129] "The proposed unity of the Central Committee would be artificial and impractical, and in practice would amount to appointing two different Central Committees leading to two different organizations, leaderships, and policies in one Party."[130] Failing to get a favourable response from Fahd, the *Sharârah* group turned its attention to other splinter groups.

126 Ibid., p. 369.

127 Interview by author with Dâûd Ṣâyegh, Baghdad (18 June 1967).

128 Typewritten memorandum from the Shararah Central Committee to the Qâᶜidah Central Committee (n.d.). *Al-Sharârah*, nos. 6–7 (May–June 1941), and *Al-Qâᶜidah*, no. 5 (June 1943).

129 *Al-Qâᶜidah*, Vol. 2, no. 6 (April 1944).

130 An internal memo to all Party members, from the 6th Central Committee (n.d. but probably June 1944).

In September 1944, recovering from severe political repression and in an effort towards reconciliation, the remnants of the *Ila al-Amâm* (Forward) group united with what was left of the *Sharârah* group to create a new organization, *Waḥdat al-Niḍâl* (Unity of the Struggle), with a publication of the same name printed in both Kurdish and Arabic.[131] Further efforts to achieve a more comprehensive reconciliation continued, but Fahd remained strongly critical of his opponents. He rebuffed the splinter groups as opportunists who were out to destroy the Party and compared them to "Mensheviks and traitors."[132] According to Fahd, the splits occurred largely because the Iraqi proletariat was of very recent origin and most of its members had either peasant or artisan backgrounds. This explained why it had not cast off its petit-bourgeois mentality. In addition, the splinter groups had neither experience with opportunistic methods nor sound knowledge of revolutionary theory or practice. Furthermore, a lack of democracy in the country and the ideological confusion caused many people to join the Iraqi Communist Party without themselves being communists, and their presence in the Party's rank and file created more tension and many contradictions.

Fahd dismissed the opposition groups' repeated demands that he call a Party congress to elect a legitimate central committee and establish the Party according to democratic principles. As he put it, the only result would be to expose active Party members to the security forces and send them back to prison, thus allowing traitors and spies to lead the movement in accordance with the interests and wishes of the imperialists.[133] Fahd insisted that all the groups dissolve their memberships and, after they had formally disbanded and delivered their printing equipment and literature to the ICP, return unconditionally, as individual applicants for membership, to the Party. As a result, the Party admitted the Arab section members of the Unity of Struggle group as individuals, not as a group, to avoid "the treachery of local reactionaries, imperialists, and the intrigue of opportunists and terrorists."[134]

Kurdish section members, however, refused to disband, and they continued to "work as a Kurdish Communist Party," known as the *Shursh* group,[135] issuing a paper in Kurdish under the name *Shursh* (Revolution). In 1946 they played an important role in the establishment of the Rizgari Kurd Party (Kurdish Freedom Party), the first popular democratic Kurdish party. The Kurdish Democratic Party, established in August of the same year, later incorporated the majority of Rizgari and a segment of *Shursh*, as well as others; the rest of *Shursh*'s membership either disbanded or rejoined Fahd's party. Among those who rejoined

131 Iraqi Directorate of Criminal Investigation, *Mawsûʿah Sirriyyah Khâṣṣah bi al-Ḥizb al- Shiyûʿî al-ʿIrâqî al-Sirrî*, vol. 3 (Baghdad Government Press, 1949), p. 616.

132 *Kitâbât al-Rafîq Fahd*, p. 75.

133 Ibid., p. 56.

134 *Al-Qâʿidah*, vol. 3, no. 6 (April 1945).

135 ʿAzîz al-Ḥâjj, *Dhâkirat al-Nakhîl* (Beirut: al-Muʾassasah al-ʿArabiyyah lil Dirâsât wa al-Nashr, 1993), p. 147.

were Ṣalâḥ al-Ḥaidarî, his brother Jamâl al-Ḥaidarî, Ḥamîd ᶜU<u>th</u>mân, and Nafiᶜ Yûnus.[136]

The period 1940–1944 witnessed Fahd's unification of the Party, his increasing public exposure, and a newfound public presence for the ICP. Opposition to Fahd was dismissed as jealousy or personal ambition, and as showing little sophistication in Marxist theory or general political understanding. Fahd's leadership qualities, charisma, and political commitment were increasingly unassailable. For example, Ṣalâḥ al-Ḥaidarî, a close Fahd associate, described Fahd as an "exemplary popular leader in his daily conduct as well as in his relationships with other comrades, in addition to his discernment of the issue of his people, and his acumen of Marxism. However, he was vainglorious."[137] In February 1944, confident of his grip on the leadership, Fahd held the First Party Conference, dubbed the National Charter Conference, in Baghdad. Now in firm control of the Party apparatus, he did not expect any major challenges from the members. Additionally, because of wartime conditions and the British alliance with the Soviet Union, the persecution of the communists in the country had been somewhat relaxed, thus reducing the potential risks involved in organizing the conference. Fahd was also motivated by the example of the Communist Party of Syria and Lebanon, which had just held its own first congress in Beirut from 31 December 1943 to 2 January 1944. Fahd wanted to integrate Marxist-Leninist principles into the specific conditions found in Iraq.[138]

In his report to the conference as secretary-general, Fahd addressed the domestic and international situations. He focused especially on the struggle of the Soviet and Allied nations to speed up the conclusion of the war in order to return to the peaceful world that had been disrupted by the aggression of "Hitler's gang."[139] He stressed that Iraq was still under foreign control, both politically and militarily, and that its foreign policy regarding its Arab and non-Arab neighbours was a tool of British interests.[140] Further, its domestic policy was also influenced by imperialist requirements. Fahd described how Iraq's traditional cottage industries had been destroyed, and how the proletariat was being exploited and forced to live in miserable social and cultural conditions. According to him, the three main causes for this were (1) the theft of Iraqi national wealth by foreign companies; (2) the feudal conditions imposed on peasants (the taxes they paid to *<u>sh</u>ai<u>kh</u>s* and middlemen amounted to more than half the peasant's income); and (3) the confiscation of public land (*miri*) from the peasants and its transfer to feudal landlords, rich speculators, and government bureaucrats.[141]

[136] Ibid., pp. 147–148.
[137] As quoted by ᶜAzîz Sibâhî, *ᶜUqûd min Târî<u>kh</u> al-Ḥizb al-<u>Sh</u>iyû ᶜî al-ᶜIrâqî*, p. 219.
[138] For more details, see Tareq Y. Ismael and Jacqueline Ismael, *The Communist Movement in Syria and Lebanon* (Gainesville, FL: University Press of Florida), pp. 33–38.
[139] *Kitâbât al-Rafîq Fahd*, p. 103.
[140] Ibid., p. 106.
[141] Ibid., pp. 107–108.

The main item on the conference agenda was a discussion of the draft of the Party programme, or National Charter. The draft, which Fahd proposed and was later unanimously accepted by the conference, focused on national and broadly democratic goals, with only a few specifically communist demands and ideological concepts included. The Charter called for:

1. National sovereignty to make Iraq a truly independent country (Article 1).
2. Reinstatement of the constitution and implementation of its suspended articles related to the people's democratic rights, including the right to have an elected and truly representative parliament and municipal council (Article 2).
3. Control of speculation and profiteering; provision of basic necessities to the people at reasonable prices (Article 3).
4. Development of the national economy (Article 4).
5. An end to domination by foreign companies over Iraqi agriculture; creation of free markets (Article 4b).
6. A halt to the usurpation of public lands (*miri*) by those in power, and redistribution of those lands in small plots, without charge, to Iraqi peasants (Article 5).
7. Implementation and expansion of Labour Law No. 72 of 1936, and protection of workers and of their right to organize (Article 6).
8. The lifting of the tax burden from people with low incomes, exemption of craftsmen and shopkeepers from municipal fees, and reduction of all indirect taxes (Article 7).
9. Expansion of education among the people without regard to gender or ethnic or social distinctions (Article 8).
10. Recognition of Iraqi women as full citizens with the same social, economic, and political status as Iraqi men (Article 9).
11. The granting of equal rights to Kurd and other minorities in the country (Article 10).
12. Improvement of the lot of Iraqi conscripts, including training them humanely, without flogging or other cruel methods (Article 11).
13. Friendship and cooperation in political, economic, and cultural terms with all democratic peoples; establishment of diplomatic relations with the USSR.
14. Political cooperation among all Arabs and their political groups and parties.
15. National liberation and sovereignty for Palestine and for other colonized Arab countries, and full independence for Iraq, Egypt, Syria, and Lebanon.
16. Cooperation among organizations of workers, students, and intellectuals to raise their national consciousness and exercise their national freedom.

17. Economic cooperation among the Arab countries to protect their national wealth and raise the standard of living of their peoples; erasing of customs barriers and improvement of communications and commercial exchange.
18. Struggle against political and economic Zionist aggression.[142]

The draft of the National Charter was addressed to the various segments of Iraqi society at the "present stage of national liberation in their struggle for democratic rights,"[143] and its spirit was expressed in the final slogan accepted by the conference: "A Free Homeland and a Happy People." A resolution was then passed to hold the Party's first congress one calendar year later.

Events at the time seemed to promise further communist expansion. On 25 August 1944, Iraq officially recognized the USSR and established full diplomatic relations with Moscow. Two weeks later, on 7 September 1944, the Iraqi government permitted railway workers to organize their own trade union; its inaugural conference was held in November. The conference was attended by over ten thousand railway workers, and the well-known communist and Central Committee member ᶜAlî Shukr was elected president of the union. Meanwhile, the communists were also active in union building among Iraq's other labour groupings.[144] Momentum seemed to be in the Party's favour, and on 19 April 1945, the First Party Congress, known as the "Organization Congress," attended by representatives from all Party districts, gathered in Baghdad under the banner "Strengthen Your Party Structure and Strengthen the National Movement's Organization."[145] The highlights of the congress's agenda included the political report of the Central Committee, adoption of the draft of the internal by-laws of the Party, and the election of officers. In his political report, Fahd emphasized the need to work diligently to disseminate communist ideas and condemned British imperialism for its violation of Iraq's sovereignty and interference in Iraqi affairs. He also warned about the British and American rivalry over control of Iraq, and he appealed to the Iraqi people for national unity in their struggle against their common enemies.

Fahd also noted that "the Kurdish issue is a part of the Iraqi liberation package, and the Party is calling for Arab-Kurdish friendship, and a united struggle by both peoples for the solution of their problems."[146] The Party's by-laws recognized its character as being that of a "secret, fighting Party, welded together by iron discipline . . . and committed to the practice of self-criticism" (Article 3). This article was grounded in Iraqi domestic conditions, in which the Party confronted "organized and powerful enemies" and lived under the

142 Ibid., pp. 133–135, 136–137.
143 *Al-Qâᶜidah*, vol. 2, no. 2 (March 1944).
144 Khairî and Khairî, *Dirâsât fî Târîkh al-Ḥizb a-Shiyû ᶜî al-ᶜIrâqî*, p. 91.
145 Iraqi Directorate of Criminal Investigation, *Mawsûᶜah Sirriyyah Khâṣṣah bi al-Ḥizb al- Shiyûᶜî al-ᶜIrâqî al-Sirrî*, p. 771.
146 *Kitâbât al-Rafîq Fahd*, p. 144.

rule of "arbitrary and 'Nazi' laws" (Article 21). Moreover, the influence of the then-dominant Stalinist political ideas and patterns within the Party (reflected in Articles 20, 22, 23, and 25 of the by-laws), secured the secretary-general's complete hegemony over the Party apparatus, so that the Central Committee, which he dominated, was empowered to "annul or suspend the resolutions of the Party congresses... should the grounds that led to their adoption lapse, or if, in the wake of a change of conditions, their continued enforcement would bring harm to the Party" (Article 13b).

The development of the ICP in the 1930s and 1940s coincided with the rise of Stalinism in the Soviet Union. Fahd's leadership was modelled on Stalinism. According to the semi-official Party historian ᶜAzîz Sibâhî, Fahd returned from the Soviet Union influenced by Stalinist dogma; he quoted Fahd as saying, "Whatever Stalin uttered or commanded became a sacred duty to be obeyed, not only by the Soviet party members, the class of the Soviet proletariat, and the Soviet people but also by the international proletariat."[147]

Although Fahd became the undisputed leader of the Party, the character of his leadership and the main focus of his attention both changed after the 1944 conference. Before the conference, he was primarily an organizer, laying the foundation for the ICP in accordance with the Comintern's basic guidelines. After that date, he concentrated more on ideological issues, both to make the Party's orientation more Marxist and to adapt the Party to the unique conditions of Iraq. Soon after the conference, in the autumn of 1945, the ICP publicly advocated the creation of a national front that would unify all national and progressive forces so as:

1. To promote the independence of Iraq and strengthen its national sovereignty by the removal of imperial influence in the country; amend the Iraqi-British Treaty [of 1930]; abolish all articles of the 1930 treaty, that restricted national sovereignty and independence, such as the acceptance of foreign bases and armies; and remove foreign advisors and missions.
2. To introduce a democratic system that would secure and promote public freedom by allowing political parties to form, as well as by ending press censorship and lifting extraordinary and martial laws.[148]

The Party considered this front to be its only safeguard against national and international reactionary groups.[149] During 1945–1946, under Fahd's leadership, the Party further elaborated its strategy and tactics, and became very active in the domestic life of the country.

In the euphoria that followed the end of the Second World War, the Regent and Crown Prince, ᶜAbd-ul-ilâh, issued a declaration on 27 December 1945 in which he promised a more democratic Iraq. He blamed all past disturbances on the absence of democracy and called for a new approach to the management

147 Ibid., p. 217.
148 *Al-Qâᶜidah*, vol. 3, no. 17 (September 1945).
149 Ibid.

of Iraqi politics. A short-lived democratic experiment was thus initiated. The public demanded political reforms, and it was especially mobilized against continued British control as articulated in the 1930 treaty. The treaty's abolition became a popular demand articulated in editorials in most newspapers of the time, newspapers that were now free to express all shades of opinion under the new liberalization experiment. To implement the reforms, the semi-liberal government of Tawfîq al-Suwaidî (a liberal, although from the "old guard") was formed in February 1946. The new government, in which al-Suwaidî kept the Ministry of Foreign Affairs portfolio for himself, included in its platform the renegotiation of the 1930 treaty on the basis that conditions had changed since its signing sixteen years earlier. As al-Suwaidî noted, "It became imperative to amend the Treaty as Iraq had progressed . . . towards independence, and to align with international development and the spirit of the newly formed United Nations."[150]

The Interior Ministry was entrusted to a respected reformist, Saᶜd Ṣâliḥ, who, with Suwaidî's encouragement, promoted a democratic environment, relaxed government controls, and allowed freedom of the press. Ṣâliḥ also had the support of the palace and the Crown Prince. Five political parties were officially licensed, with the prime minister heading the Liberal Party (*al-Aḥrâr*), and the Independence Party (*al-Istiqlâl*), having mainly a traditional Arab nationalist orientation, headed by Muḥammad Mahdî Kubbah, a respected political figure. On the moderate left, the National Democratic Party (*al-Waṭanî al-Dîmuqrâṭî*) was headed by Kâmil al-Châdirchî, a well-known intellectual politician with Fabian tendencies, whose 1930 roots extended to the *al-Ahâlî* group discussed earlier. The National Unity Party (*al-Ittiḥâd al-Waṭanî*) was headed by a well-known anti-imperialist and leftist (though not Marxist) intellectual, ᶜAbd-ul-Fattâḥ Ibrâhîm, and finally, the People's Party (*al-Shaᶜb*) was headed by the Marxist, though then not communist, ᶜAzîz Sharîf. The government allowed each party to publish its own official newspaper.

However, Suwaidî's government lasted no longer than three months, since it aroused the opposition of the traditionaly pro-British, antiliberal, staunchly reactionary establishment, who viewed any relaxation of political control as a surrender to the communist-led left and as a return to the chaos of the 1936–1941 period. The old guard viewed the changes in the political environment unleashed by the liberalization measures of the Suwaidî government as endangering to the stability of the country and harmful to their particular interests. This conservative group was led by the famous pro-British personality Nûrî al-Saᶜîd, who was in disfavour in palace circles because of his lack of popular support, and by his protégé, Arshad al-ᶜUmarî, who replaced al-Suwaidî as prime minister on 1 June 1946.[151]

150 Iraqi Parliament Minutes – Ordinary Meetings, 1945–1945 (Baghdad Government Press), p. 205.

151 Tawfîq al-Suwaidî, *Mudhakkarâtî: Niṣf Qarn min Târîkh al-ᶜIrâq wa al-Qaḍiyyah al-ᶜArabiyyah* (Beirut: Dâr al-Kâtib al-ᶜArabî, 1969), p. 45.

For the first time, and to destabilize the political environment, seventeen members of the Senate absented themselves from meetings, making it impossible to form a quorum. This convinced the Crown Prince of the dangers of those liberalization measures to the monarchy.[152] Although Nûrî al-Saᶜîd was not a member of the new government, a number of his protégés held important cabinet posts. Despite his claim that his government was to be a transitional one aimed at promoting justice and neutrality, Al-ᶜUmarî, a hardliner, was known even in conservative circles (including Nûrî al-Saᶜîd's closest allies) as "the least democratic and [most] non-supportive of [the formation of] political parties, and [totally unable to accept] criticism and [political] opposition."[153] Al-ᶜUmarî declared that his government would not be addressing the Anglo-Iraqi Treaty.[154]

Since al-ᶜUmarî was known to be staunchly pro-British and conservative and against liberalization, the public's reaction to his government, especially among the progressive forces, was swift. In an initial editorial response ("The People's Primary Demands and the New Cabinet") in its official newspaper the head of the *Shaᶜb* party echoed public sentiment by denouncing the old guard's tactics in forcing the resignation of the Suwaidî government. The editorial outlined the party's demands as "the achieving of independence, national sovereignty, and the freeing of the people from the political, military and economic shackles of colonial control."[155] A series of three editorials ("To the New Government," "The People's Imperative," and "Urgent Demands") summarized these demands as the solution to unemployment and inflation, the exercise of free democratic rights, and a solution to the Palestine issue.[156] Responding to the programme of the new cabinet, the editorials concluded that Iraqi sovereignty was being compromised, and that British penetration of Iraqi affairs had increased. *Shaᶜb*'s message was also sceptical about the government's pending elections, and it condemned all government measures to de-license various newspapers and journals.[157] In another editorial ("Imperialism and Its Allies, An Account of the ᶜUmarî Cabinet Actions and the Events That Have Occurred Under It"), the newspaper complained that al-ᶜUmarî's government had unfairly accused the national movement of falsehood and was opposing the movement under the guise of combating communism. It also condemned the government as undemocratic, particularly in its arrests of citizens, workers, students, and Party members.[158] This editorial was immediately followed by another, which asked, "In Whose Interests Are Events Occurring?" openly asserting in reply that these events were occurring solely in the interests of the British.[159]

152 Minutes of the Iraqi Senate – Regular Meetings, 1945–1946 (Baghdad Government Press), p. 107.
153 Khalîl Kannah, *Al-ᶜIrâq: Amsuhu wa Ghaduhu* (Beirut: al-Maktabah al-ᶜAṣriyyah, 1966), p. 77.
154 *Al-ᶜIraq*, no. 7135 (Baghdad, 6 June 1946).
155 *Al-Waṭan*, no. 146 (Baghdad, 7 June 1946).
156 Ibid., nos. 148–150 (4–6 June 1946).
157 Ibid., nos. 151, 161, and 164 (7, 19, 23 June 1946).
158 Ibid., no. 217 (27 August 1946).
159 Ibid., no. 218 (16 August 1946).

Eventually, the newspaper asserted that the only alternative left to the national movement for opposing the ᶜUmarî oppression was for the Iraqi people to continue "the struggle for liberty and independence."[160] With this in mind, the People's Party (*al-Shaᶜb*) moved to forge a unified position with both the National Democratic Party and the National Unity Party (NUP), and on 30 August 1946 the three parties held a public meeting in the NUP's headquarters. ᶜAzîz Sharîf led the criticism of the government, reiterating the same charges that had already been published. Subsequently, the parties issued a joint communiqué calling on the government to resign,[161] and the newspaper *Al-Waṭan* declared, "The policy of the current government has failed and [the government] has to resign."[162]

Azîz Sharîf was arrested and tried, and his paper was suspended for twenty days. However, his own and his party's popularity simply increased, and fifty-five lawyers came forward to defend him in court.[163] *Al-Waṭan*, accepted as the official newspaper of the opposition parties, rapidly became more vocal, more visible, and more popular. When Nûrî al-Saᶜîd's ninth government was formed, on 21 October 1946, Sharîf declared in an editorial in *Al-Waṭan* that this was just a continuation of the previous ᶜUmarî government. "The ᶜUmarî government simply prepared the ground for al-Saᶜîd's return to power."[164]

In March 1946, Ḥusain Muḥammad al-Shabîbî (Ṣârim), a member of the Central Committee of the Iraqi Communist Party, applied to the authorities for permission to establish a legal political party under the name *Ḥizb al-Taḥarrur al-Waṭanî* (the Party of National Liberation). While the application was being considered (it was ultimately rejected), the founding committee operated as if the Party were legal and able to conduct activities and propagate its views. One of the cornerstones of *al-Taḥarrur al-Waṭanî*'s strategic position was the creation of a national front through cooperation with all anti-imperialist and progressive forces who agreed with the party's proposed goals (they were almost identical to its policies six months earlier). Shabîbî's pamphlet, *Al-Jabhah al-Waṭaniyyah al-Muttaḥidah: Ṭarîqunâ wa Wâjibuna al-Târîkhî* (The United National Front Is Our Path and National Duty), outlined these goals:

1. Achieve complete political independence and strengthen national sovereignty; resist foreign intervention in Iraq's internal affairs; and abolish special military concessions and privileges for foreign armed forces; abrogate the Anglo-Iraqi Treaty of 1930.
2. Closely cooperate with the Arab peoples and governments striving to free themselves from special foreign privileges and domination; help Arab peoples still under colonial rule to achieve their freedom and exercise their rights to self-determination by forming a national government.

160 Ibid., no. 220 (28 August 1946).
161 Ibid., no. 221 (1 September 1946).
162 Ibid., no. 225 (5 September 1946).
163 Muḥâkamat al-ʾUstâdh *ᶜAzîz Sharîf Raʾîs Ḥizb al-Shaᶜb* (Baghdad: Dâr al-Amal, 1946).
164 *Al-Waṭan*, no. 246 (Baghdad, 30 November 1946).

3. Strengthen the democratic system in Iraq through the abolition of all laws and policies that deny or stand against the right of citizens to exercise their democratic freedoms, and enact new laws to implement their freedom.
4. Purge the administrative apparatus of corrupt elements and practices and make it an efficient agency dedicated to serving the interests of the people.
5. Enforce comprehensive reforms in the social and economic life of the country, including agriculture and industry; expand education to the masses; and provide welfare to the poor.[165]

National unity was stressed by Fahd as well:

Our aim is to eliminate the conditions of suffering of the Iraqi people by working within a framework of a true and conscious national movement whose aim is to struggle to achieve our democratic freedoms and economic and political rights. The National Front unifies activities for the sake of achieving the aims which all participants are striving for, such as: (1) the right to both political and non-political organizations; (2) freedom of the press and of association; (3) repeal of all emergency regulations; (4) protection of the country's independence and its national sovereignty; and (5) combating fascism.[166]

Although in 1946 Tawfîq al- Suwaidî's government permitted the formation of political parties and restrained government oppression, it did not extend the right to organize to the Iraqi Communist Party. As a result, the communists sought to penetrate legal left-wing parties, particularly the People's Party (*al-Sh̲aᶜb*), the National Unity Party (outlawed one year after its establishment), and the rival National Democratic Party (which also was eventually outlawed in 1954). During this period, the ICP succeeded in broadening its support among students and women's and trade union organizations, and in leading a wave of labour unrest in 1946–1947. On 21 December 1946, al-Sh̲abîbî sent a letter from his prison cell on behalf of the founding executive of the National Liberation Party to the minister of the interior denouncing Nûrî al-Saᶜîd's government for its anti-democratic and non-nationalist approach, and describing it as an extension of the reactionaries' designs to "resist the people's national movement and deny their democratic freedoms."[167]

Al-Saᶜîd's government responded four weeks later, on 18 January 1947, when it arrested the top sixteen members of the Party leadership, including Fahd, on charges of advocating communism. According to Article 89a of the Iraqi Penal Code, communism was designed to subvert constitutional order and incite armed insurrection through infiltration of the armed forces, with the financial assistance of, and contact with, a foreign state (the Soviet Union), a charge rejected by all the accused. Fahd, who never denied that he was the secretary-general of the Party, attempted to rebut the charges in court. On 24 June 1947, he was found guilty and sentenced to death, as were his second in command,

[165] *Kitâbât al-Rafîq Ḥusain Muḥammad al-Sh̲abîbî* [The Works of Comrade Hussein] (Baghdad: Adib Press, 1974), p. 7.
[166] *Kitâbât al-Rafîq Fahd*, p. 57.
[167] Letter from Ḥusain Muḥammad al-Sh̲abîbî, published 21 January 1947.

Zakî Bâsim, and Ibrâhîm Nâjî Shumaiyyil; the others arrested were sentenced to various terms of hard labour. The death sentences were commuted on 13 July; Fahd was sentenced to life imprisonment and Shumaiyyil and Bâsim were each given fifteen years. The sentences of the remaining ICP leaders were similarly reduced. According to the Party newspaper, the crackdown took place because the government "fears the Communist Party will hinder the colonial projects."[168]

Although the ICP members' trial before the Iraqi high court dragged on for almost two years, this did not prevent Fahd and the ICP from playing a leading role in the *al-Wathbah* riots that compelled Prime Minister Ṣâliḥ Jabr to resign on 27 January 1948. Even though Fahd was in prison in October 1947, in a strategically bold move he directed the caretaker leadership of the Party to call for the creation of the *Lajnat al-Taᶜâwun al-Waṭanî* (Committee for National Cooperation). This committee was to include all leftist parties, including *al-Shaᶜb*, the National Unity Party, the progressive members of the National Democratic Party, and the underground Kurdish Democratic Party of Iraq. A leftist non-communist, Kâmil Qazanchî, was chosen to chair the committee, which took on a powerful role three months later in organizing and directing the activities of the *Wathbah* (uprising).

According to police records, on 23 January 1948 Qazanchî inflamed the demonstrators in a speech that he gave during the huge demonstrations in Baghdad. He proclaimed: "Let us declare it a great people's revolution, and struggle to reform [this execrable] situation until the formation of a people's government, including all classes."[169] The *al-Wathbah* swept Baghdad and other large cities following the government's provisional signing of the Portsmouth Treaty with Britain on 15 January 1948. The 1930 treaty, which was due to expire in 1958, tied Iraq strategically to Britain through Britain's establishment and control of military bases across Iraq, and its abrogation was the principal demand of the Iraqi opposition. An ICP pamphlet entitled *The Treaty Is Null and We Must Declare Its Abrogation,* expressed official ICP policy; it maintained that the 1930 treaty was illegal since it had been concluded under duress. In addition, treaty articles that required Iraq to consult with Britain restricted Iraq's foreign policy and tied it to a colonial foreign policy that negated Iraq's sovereignty, which was implicit in the country's membership in the United Nations.[170] The pamphlet also asserted that the treaty changed "the temporary mandate into a permanent occupation."[171]

By the end of December 1947, an agreement had been reached between Britain and the pro-British government of Ṣâliḥ Jabr, the first Shiᶜi prime minister in Iraq's modern history. The opposition, however, interpreted this

168 *Al-Qâᶜidah*, vol. 5, no. 3 (June 1947).

169 Police Records of the Criminal Investigation, Confidential Letter no. 266, 24 January 1948, in a file entitled, "Demonstrations and Strike."

170 ᶜAbd-ul-Raḥîm Sharîf, *Muᶜâhadat 1930 Bâṭilah: Yajibu Ilghâ'uha* (Baghdad: al-Shaᶜb Party, 1948), pp. 6–11.

171 Ibid., p. 7.

agreement as a capitulation to the British since the proposed treaty prolonged Britain's control of the Iraqi military for a further twenty-five years by institutionalizing Iraqi dependence upon British supplies and military training and by surrendering Iraqi bases to Britain in times of war. The agreement was clearly designed to integrate Iraq into regional military pacts that would serve British interests. Following Jabr's resignation, the caretaker government of Muḥammad al-Ṣadr, though respected by most of the nationalist forces, who had urged him to accept the position, dissolved parliament and declared martial law on 22 February 1948. But al-Ṣadr acquiesced to popular Iraqi opinion by promising not to ratify the Portsmouth Treaty. The proposed revision of the treaty had been pushed by the Regent to win favour with the nationalists, though ultimately his plan backfired because they continued to portray him as a British stooge. Britain's role and actions in Palestine, which were increasingly regarded by all Arab nationalists, including the Iraqi opposition, as yet another betrayal of the Arabs by the British, reinforced the negative view of the Regent.

In early 1948, the ICP reached the pinnacle of its influence, recruiting Iraqi students studying across the Arab world and as far away as Europe. The Party even briefly issued a daily paper called *Al-Asâs* (The Foundation), edited by Sharîf al-Shaikh, an active communist and well-known lawyer, but it was soon banned by the authorities.[172] In addition, starting in October 1948 the Iraqi police once again made a concerted effort to spy on and suppress the ICP. Guided by information provided them by Mâlik Saif, the interim secretary-general who turned informer,[173] the authorities arrested hundreds of communists, including many of the Party's top leaders and organizers. Fahd and the rest of the leadership were again forced to stand trial, which this time resulted in their execution in Baghdad on 14 February 1949. Reeling from the decapitation of its leadership and the persecution of its cadres, the Party went through a period of fragmentation between November 1948 and June 1949. During this time, five splinter groups emerged, each describing itself as the "true" Iraqi Communist Party, each maintaining individual politburos and central committees, and each producing its own newspaper. According to Hanna Batatu, "The Communists split into five mutually hostile groups – *al-Ḥaqiqah* (The Truth), *al-Najmah* (The Star), *al-Ṣawâb* (The Right), *al-Ittiḥâd* (The Union), and the old *Qâʿidah* (the Grassroots) group."[174]

The Party in the 1950s

Hitherto insulated from developments abroad, the ICP during the 1950s must be understood within its local, regional, and international contexts. Iraq suffered a number of political upheavals during this period, and in the span of three years,

[172] Interviews by the author with Zakî Khairî, Damascus (18 March 1987), and ʿAbd-ul-Khâliq al-Bayâtî, Baghdad (27 September 1960).
[173] Batatu, *Old Social Classes*, pp. 567–568.
[174] Ibid., p. 571.

1948 to 1952, five governments passed in rapid succession. During Nûrî al-Saᶜîd's eleventh government, lasting from 16 September 1950 to 12 July 1952, oppression of leftist activities again became a focus of the Iraqi government. In September 1951, so that opposition forces could confront Nûrî al-Saᶜîd's government, the ICP proposed a programme of cooperation in the form of a national front. The National Front put forward a number of bold proposals including nationalization of the oil industry, radical land reform, freedom of expression, freedom of assembly, the right to form political parties and unions, and recognition by Iraq of the People's Republic of China. Although this agenda did not produce immediate results, the steps set in motion by the formation of a national front led six years later to the 1958 Qasim coup.[175] In 1952, al-Saᶜîd's government refused to accede to the demands for more democratic reforms that emanated from legal opposition parties such as *al-Istiqlâl* (the Independence Party) and the the National Democratic Party, from prominent individuals, and from the clandestine Peace Partisans of the ICP. All, and particularly the nationalist and leftist organizations, called for an easing of Nûrî al-Saᶜîd's ban on radical opposition parties and a reduction in Iraq's dependence on Western-sponsored military alliances. These democratic and nationalist forces further demanded the complete rejection of Iraq's integration into the US-sponsored Baghdad Pact, to which Nûrî al-Saᶜîd was preparing to tie Iraq.

The crisis came to a head with the opposition's demand that the government curtail foreign control of Iraq's petroleum sector. Britain's control of Iraq's oil had become the most pronounced symbol of British domination of the country and demands that Iraq emulate Iran's nationalization of the petroleum sector gave opposition political forces an issue around which to rally the public.[176] The government settled for a less confrontational policy by renegotiating its revenue agreements with the Iraqi Petroleum Company.[177] On 12 July 1952, after less than two years in office, Nûrî al-Saᶜîd was again forced to resign as prime minister, but this did not satisfy opposition groups, and unrest continued as the opposition parties successfully mobilized the population against the conservative pro-British government that followed him. This mobilization was fuelled by the 26 May 1951 licensing of a new political party, *Al-Jabhah al-S͟haᶜbiyyah al-Muttaḥidah* (Popular Unified Front Party), which immediately and successfully moved to coordinate its activities with other opposition groupings, particularly the National Democratic Party.

At the same time, other opposition groups, including communist-sponsored leftist organizations such as the Union of Democratic Youth, the League of Women's Rights, the General Union of Iraqi Students, and a number of Peasant Associations, as well as the Arab Baᶜt͟h Socialist Party and the Arab Nationalist

175 *Al-Qâᶜidah*, vol. 9, no. 16 (end of September 1951).

176 *Al-Qâᶜidah*, vol. 8, no. 3 (April 1950), and *Al-Qâᶜidah*, vol. 9, no. 13 (early April 1952).

177 *Liwâ᾽ al-Istiqlâl* (Baghdad, 19 May 1954); *Ṣawt al-Ahâlî* (Baghdad, 16 May 1954); also see Fâḍil Ḥusain, *Târîk͟h al-Ḥizb al-Waṭanî al-Dîmuqrâṭi, 1946–1958* (Baghdad: al-S͟haᶜb Press, 1963), p. 352.

Movement (ANM), all emerged to oppose the government through increasingly sophisticated organizational and ideological support for the vocal opposition. Later, in 1951, student unrest sparked massive anti-government riots in Baghdad, forcing the resignation of Muṣṭafâ al-ʿUmarî (Nûrî al-Saʿîd's successor) on 22 November 1952. The increasing disorder forced the Crown Prince to appoint yet another interim government, headed this time by General Nûrî al-Dîn Maḥmûd, the army chief of staff, which lasted from 23 November 1952 to 29 January 1953. In response, the ICP censured the military government, accusing Maḥmûd, the new prime minister, of "[wanting] to establish a military dictatorship through the imposition of martial law and the unleashing of the 'spies of the Gestapo' against the people." Indeed, Maḥmûd arrested thousands of Peace Partisans, communists, and democrats for the sole purpose of suppressing the popular movement and reinforcing the dictatorial and feudal colonial system.[178] He also declared martial law and banned all political parties.

Elections held on 17 January 1953 saw Nûrî al-Saʿîd's party win 77 of the 138 parliamentary seats through acclamation. Only 11 seats were won by the Popular Unified Front, which, although banned, was supported by the opposition.[179] On 5 October 1953, soon after martial law ended and the order to ban opposition parties was lifted, normal political activities resumed. A succession of cabinets followed, none of which lasted longer than nine months. Nûrî al-Saʿîd became prime minister once again in August 1954 and almost immediately began to suppress all political opposition. He also opened negotiations with Turkey, Britain, Iran, and Pakistan over a pro-Western "Northern Tier" defence system. As a result of these discussions Iraq joined the Central Treaty Organization (CENTO), which thereupon changed its name to the Baghdad Pact. The organization's first meeting was held in Baghdad in November 1955.

By the mid-1950s, events in other Arab countries had begun to affect the political climate in Iraq. The 23 July 1952 revolution in Egypt soon gained regional prominence through promoting a policy of positive neutralism, including cordial relations and arms deals with the socialist bloc, all in an effort to promote Arab liberation from colonialism and Zionism.[180] The downfall of the military regime of Adîb al-Shishaklî in Syria in February 1954, and the resurgence of Syrian national political life, drew Egypt and Syria closer together. In autumn 1956, parliamentary elections in Jordan saw the job of prime minister go to Sulaimân al-Nâbulsî, the head of a leftist-nationalist coalition that was sympathetic to Nasser's Egypt and was in favour of Arab unity in general and of unity with Syria in particular. The last vestiges of colonialism in the Arab world

178 *Al-Qâʿidah*, vol. 10, no. 26 (end of November 1952).

179 *Al-Zamân* (Baghdad, 18 January 1953 and 19 January 1953).

180 The impact of the Egyptian revolution should not be underestimated, and the feeling at that time in much of the Arab world, and especially in Egypt, was almost as if Nasser were a figure whose significance could rival that of Muḥammad ʿAlî or of Ṣalâḥu-d-Dîn.

seemed to be disappearing. The Algerian revolt began in 1954, and Morocco, Tunisia, and Sudan all won formal independence by 1955. Moreover, Egypt's political victory in the 1956 Suez War served to heighten anti-imperialist sentiment throughout the region, giving Nasser's Egypt a pre-eminent position in Arab politics, and crystallizing Nasserist Pan-Arabism as an almost irresistible political force.

This period also saw two significant developments within the international communist movement. The first of these was the foundation of the People's Republic of China in 1949, which provided Arab Marxists with an alternative, and in many ways (since China was a Third World country) a more attractive, model of social revolution than the Soviet prototype. The second was the death of Stalin in 1953 and the subsequent landmark Twentieth Congress of the Communist Party of the Soviet Union in Moscow in January 1956: this ushered in sweeping changes in Soviet policy towards non-aligned bourgeois states such as Egypt, Syria, Iraq, India, and Indonesia and towards bourgeois nationalist movements in the Third World. The Soviet leadership endorsed the five principles of nonalignment enunciated at the Bandung Conference in April 1955 and also adopted a more favourable position towards Arab liberation movements.

During this period, the Iraqi Communist Party was attempting to recover organizationally from the execution of its leadership in 1949 and to bounce back from being rebuffed by the nationalists following its support of the Soviet recognition of Israel in 1948; at the same time, it was trying to get over the ideological and organizational confusion that had arisen inside the Party itself. Since power remained concentrated in the hands of the secretary-general of the Party, those now at the Party's helm, who though not strictly secretaries-general nevertheless exercised all the functions and authority of the position, sought to emulate Fahd. Accordingly, they attempted to leave their mark by changing the Party's by-laws, procedures, and internal workings. Yet they often found themselves making decisions that were beyond their abilities and intellects, decisions that proved detrimental to the Party. On the organizational level, in June 1949, Party leadership was taken up by a young, inexperienced Kurd who used the pseudonym Bahâʾu-d-Dîn Nûrî (Bâsim). A twenty-two-year-old high school dropout, Nûrî came from Takiyah, a small village just outside Sulaymaniyah which had been a centre for Kurdish nationalism in the 1940s. Nûrî rose to the pinnacle of Party leadership in fewer than four years after he joined it. He quickly initiated a major reorganization and restructuring at all levels.[181]

Nearly five decades later, Nûrî admitted that he did not have "the intellectual or practical experience that qualified me for the central leadership . . . in such a highly complex and sensitive [period] as a result of the Party's setback. However, between November 1948 and June 1949 I had to establish another leadership

[181] Bahâʾu-d-Dîn Nûrî, *Mudhakkarât Bahâʾu-d-Dîn Nûrî* (Sulaimaniyyah, Kurdistân: n.p. 1992), p. 36.

centre."[182] According to Bahâ'u-d-Dîn Nûrî, he reconstructed a new Central Committee to replace the executed Party leadership,

which included seven members I chose personally from the cadre. It did not occur to me, or [to] anyone else in those days, that they should be elected in any way. The group included, in addition to myself, a port worker from Basra, Nâṣir ʿAbbûd, a textile worker from Baghdad, Ṣâdiq al-Falâḥî, a dismissed primary school teacher from a strong peasant background by the name of Karîm Aḥmad, the expelled Baghdadi student Muḥammed Râḍî Shubbar, and an expelled government worker from a middle-class background named Sâlim al-Chalabî, and finally, the expelled student from Sulaimaniyah who came from a poor peasant background named Kakah Falâḥ. This step [forming the Central Committee] did not put an end to the practice of the personality cult and the bureaucratic inflexibility which was prevalent in the ICP, as well as in the communist parties in a number of other, particularly underdeveloped, countries. I was raised in this mental setting and practice. We used to idolize Fahd as if he was a god or a prophet.... this glorification of a single person used continuously to strengthen the personality cult in the Party.... we considered Fahd to be a local god, in addition to the greater gods in the world of the communist movement.... I stayed on the top of the [pyramid] of the Central Committee, as was every other secretary within the apparatus of the Party. There was no regularity in the meetings of our Central Committee. Its members were not of a [high] intellectual or political calibre that would have allowed it to exercise any collective leadership. Events proved that I was the most qualified among the members of the Central Committee, despite my low level of qualifications.[183]

Nonetheless, confident of his control, Nûrî embarked at the end of 1951 on an ideological reshaping of the Party.[184] He solidified his leadership in a Party conference in the spring of 1952, at which he imposed a new and radical Party programme without having held any Party congress or conference to discuss or approve the changes. In the 1952 conference, he replaced the earlier, more moderate platform approved by the First Party Congress under Fahd, and for the first time in the ICP's history, there was a call for the establishment of a popular republican regime in Iraq through revolution. Such a regime would eradicate British influence, nationalize the oil industry, and broaden public freedom by unifying all opposition groupings into a popular front spearheaded by the communists. This new programme caused an ideological split within the Party over the tactics to be employed in selecting the groups for the proposed popular front.

ʿAzîz Muḥammad, Jamâl al-Ḥaidarî, and ʿAbd-ul-Salâm al-Nâṣirî, who were all then in prison, disagreed with the Party's new programme, declaring it to be illegal. In addition, Zakî Khairî, who was also in prison, led a strong protest against the new Party platform; this resulted in the immediate expulsion of the dissidents from the ICP, along with all those who supported them, including ʿAbd-ul-Razzâq al-Ṣâfî. Bâsim further denounced the group at the end of February 1953, identifying them by name in *Al-Qâʿidah*, the Party organ, as

[182] Ibid., p. 52.
[183] Ibid., pp. 96–97.
[184] Ibid., p. 103

"opportunist and subversive," and thereby also revealing their identities to the police. Those who were expelled respondend by announcing the formation of their own organization, and Jamâl al-Ḥaidarî emerged as its spokesman. They issued a publication, *Râyat al-Shaghîlah* (The Worker's Banner), which then became the popular name of the group. Al-Ḥaidarî devoted himself and his group to challenging Bâsim and his supporters, and even attempted to win recognition from the international communist movement as the official Iraqi Communist Party by affirming the group's loyalty to the Soviet Union. In the sixth issue of *Râyat al-Shaghîlah*,[185] al-Ḥaidarî's group described the Soviet Union as "our first country in loyalty and love." The group also participated in the International Youth Festival held in Warsaw in 1955. However, the CPSU did not recognize the group and continued to view it as a splinter group.

Even after Bâsim's arrest in April 1953, his group continued its assault on ICP dessidents by repeatedly publishing the names of dissident group members over the 1953–1954 period, calling them agents of the security forces and "royalists, deviationists and destructive" people. The ICP's official leadership continued to expound Bâsim's Party line in the pages of *Al-Qâᶜidah*, and in this environment, another underground Marxist group emerged in late 1950 under the leadership of ᶜAzîz Sharîf. Initially named *Lajnat al-Waᶜi al-Mârkisî* (the Committee for a Marxist Understanding), it eventually transformed itself into *Waḥdat al-Shiyûᶜiyyîn fî al-ᶜIrâq* (the Unity of Communists in Iraq), with roots in *Ḥizb al-Shaᶜb*, the Marxist party mentioned earlier. The licence of *Ḥizb al-Shaᶜb* had been revoked in September 1947, and its paper, *Al-Waṭan* (The Homeland), had been closed down in 1948. It had been distinguished by its passionate attacks on both the Soviet position on the partition of Palestine and the ICP tolerance of this Soviet policy. The basic aim of the new *Lajnat al-Waᶜi al-Mârkisî* was

> to correct both the non-Marxist deviationist approach of the CPSU, and the mindless followers of what was left of the ICP . . . in addition to a renewed study of Marxism, not as exported by Soviet theoreticians, but as read and interpreted by genuine free Arab Marxists. Marx gave only guidelines and principle, and it is the Marxists who should apply these principles and interpret events as these relate to their environment. . . . Marxist analysis could be applied to the Arab national liberation and the Palestine issue in complete independence from the Soviet government line. This would inevitably lead to a different interpretation, and either Marxism would become irrelevant for us, or we would become an arm of the Soviet state.[186]

On these principles, ᶜAzîz Sharîf attempted to build a new communist movement, contending that

> the ICP is no longer a viable progressive Marxist Iraqi organization and its fragmentation is the evidence of its demise. However, there are so many communists who have left it, mainly because of its non-Marxist, non-communist interpretations of Arab and Iraqi

[185] Al-Ḥâjj, *Dhâkiarat al-Nakhîl*, pp. 158–159.
[186] Interview by author with ᶜAzîz Sharîf, Baghdad (18 October 1973).

issues. Thus, we need a new, genuine communist movement, and for that reason we established the *Waḥdat al-Shiyûᶜiyyîn fî al-ᶜIrâq* (Party of the Unity of Communists in Iraq) which will reunite all these splinter groups, along with all the individuals who have deserted the Party, within a truly genuine democratic Marxist, Iraqi Communist Party.[187]

Al-Qâᶜidah exposed the members of the ᶜAzîz Sharîf group by publishing their full names in issue 9 in October 1950. Nevertheless, ᶜAzîz Sharîf's group called for and held a party conference, which was attended by representatives of most of the splinter groups as well as by independent communists. The participants elected a new Politburo and Central Committee and published *Al-Niḍâl* (The Struggle) as its official newspaper. The *Al-Qâᶜidah* group considered this conference to be "opportunist and destructivist against the communist Party."[188] Then, with the arrest of Bâsim, and the further fragmentation of the Party, a new leadership began to emerge within the ICP.

Despite its internal disarray, the worsening political conditions, and increased government oppression, the ICP still managed to devote its energies to the Iraqi political arena. Focusing on the integration of its activities with the democratic and nationalist opposition, the ICP gradually emerged more clearly as a politically moderate and unified party, largely through the efforts of Ḥusain Aḥmad al-Râḍî (Salâm ᶜÂdil). Salâm ᶜÂdil (1922–1963), a Shiᶜi from Najaf, graduated from the Teacher's Preparatory School in 1943 and a year later was appointed a government grammar school teacher in the southern city of Diwaniyah. There he joined the ICP in 1944 and was soon promoted to the city's Party committee. Two years later, he was fired from his teaching job because of his political activities.

ᶜÂdil left Diwaniyah for Baghdad, where he worked as a food vendor and a bus inspector. He soon began organizing the bus conductors and workers to demand better conditions and wages. This resulted in his being fired again, although shortly thereafter he secured a low-paying job as a teacher in a private Kurdish school, with the help of his future father-in-law, the former director of the Diwaniyah Education District and now the principal of a Baghdad preparatory school for rural teachers. Later, after ᶜÂdil's re-instatement to his government teaching position, again with the help of his patron, ᶜÂdil was reassigned to the teachers' preparatory school. He was fired again, at the end of 1948, after which he left teaching and opened a shop that became a pick-up location for the Party. During the public unrest and demonstrations in 1949, he was arrested for organizing and leading demonstrations. He was tried by a military court and sentenced to three years in prison, with an additional two years' probation to be served outside of Baghdad. While he was incarcerated in the notorious desert prison of Nuqrat al-Salmân, his sentence was increased to five years for his continued political activities. After his release in June 1953, he ignored the probationary conditions and managed to go underground,

[187] Ibid.
[188] *Al-Qâᶜidah*, no. 15 (1951).

rejoining the embattled Party at a time when its organization and morale were low.

As already mentioned, following the execution of Fahd, and as a result of widespread surveillance and an intense police crackdown, leadership of the ICP fell into the hands of a succession of young, inexperienced but committed and energetic caretakers, none of whom was selected through proper Party procedures. Many came from the Party's Kurdish section, which, because the surveillance was focused on Baghdad and in the south of Iraq, had been spared the crackdown.

Two months before ᶜÂdil's release, Bâsim, the last of the powerful temporary Party leaders, was himself arrested on 13 April 1953, and with this, the Party structure collapsed once again. Party control then passed to yet another inexperienced leader, Karîm Aḥmad Dâûd, also from the Kurdish section, who attempted to rebuild the repeatedly decimated Party. Although Dâûd was committed to communism, "his intellectual capabilities and organizational skills left much to be desired. As a matter of fact, his ascent to the first position in the Party had been engineered by a fellow Kurd, Ḥamîd ᶜUthmân, who had always influenced him strongly when both served on the Central Committee."[189] Dâûd asked ᶜÂdil to take charge of the organizational section of the southern Party, where he distinguished himself. ᶜÂdil's star continued to rise. A year later, as a result of his successful organizational efforts, ᶜÂdil was elevated to the Central Committee.

On 1 January 1954, in ᶜÂdil's first meeting as a member of Central Committee, the committee discussed the final draft of a political report ("The National Front Struggle Against War and Imperialism") that he had played a prominent role in formulating. He later acknowledged that the report articulated "his vision, and the first theoretical articulation of his ideas" and that it became the foundation on which he built his Party politics.[190] The report stressed that revolutionary conditions in Iraq required the Party to have a clear strategy, since the progressive forces in the country "will view our Party as a political force, only if our policy is realistic . . . [and can] achieve the goals of our people in peace, national independence and democratic freedom. Thus, we must have an [explicit] strategy before we engage in any battle."[191] The report then proposed a framework for action through a broad national front that would

> include all the anti-war and anti-Imperialist forces . . . [and] with these national groups, we must together enter the battle. First, however, there has to be an identification of the forces that make up this front which would be composed of workers, peasants, intellectuals, small business people, professionals, and the [enlightened] bourgeoisie from among the merchants, factory owners, and national capitalists – in the meantime, we must recognize the historic role of the working class in that front.[192]

189 Interview by author with Zakî Khairî, Damascus (18 March 1987).

190 Interview by author with Salâm ᶜÂdil, Baghdad (8 December 1959).

191 Iraqi Communist Party, *Jabhat al-Kifâḥ al-Waṭanî ḍid al-Istiᶜmâr wa al-Ḥarb* (Baghdad: ICP, 1954), pp. 1–4.

192 Ibid., p. 11

In addition, the report outlined the basic goal of the proposed national front as being "the creation of a national democratic government . . . that will march towards building a better society devoid of imperialism, oppression and feudalism."[193] It also explained that such a government would abrogate the 1930 treaty with Britain, expel British forces from Iraq, and refuse to align Iraq through treaties with any imperialist forces. Further, it would nationalize the oil companies, confiscate their property, and liberate the Iraqi national economy from their control.[194] The proposed government would allow democratic freedoms, amend the existing constitution to make government more participatory, abolish reactionary laws, free all political prisoners, dismantle the feudal system by distributing land to the peasants and reducing taxes on them, impose a graduated income tax system, improve the conditions of workers, and, finally, grant the Kurdish people and other minorities political, cultural, and administrative rights.[195] The ideal government advocated by the ICP would be one constructed by "the national front composed of the union of all parties, organizations, and democratic personalities, including the Iraqi Communist Party."[196] It should be noted, however, that these principles and aims were not unique to the ICP and that they in fact reflected the general bearing of almost all the major opposition parties at the time. The party programme signalled a change towards increased cooperation and coordination between the ICP and other opposition groups, as opposed to the previous practice of mutual suspicions.

This bilateral approach of reconciliation and pragmatism allowed ᶜÂdil more space to manoeuvre the Party closer to the democratic and nationalist opposition. As ᶜÂdil argued more than once:

> If we are to succeed as a Party, we must have a political presence; and to have a political presence, we must become politically acceptable and work with the majority of the progressive political forces in the country. On paper, our rhetoric, is very extreme but our political impact is minimal on the ground. . . . Thus, I feel, and argue very strongly in the Central Committee, that at this stage our priority must first be to unite all nationalist and progressive groups into a national front – to be one of them and influence their political actions as they influence ours. . . . Through that, we can serve the people and gain credibility for the Party.[197]

An ICP circular on 2 September 1953 seemed to reflect this new direction, and when it was declared that the ICP's aim was to establish a "national democratic government," ᶜÂdil's influence grew within the Party. His personal qualities also helped him gain the confidence of his Central Committee comrades, to whom he appeared forceful, competent, and self-confident. He was a sportsman, an artist, a skilled calligrapher, an avid reader, and a good speaker, and his colleagues found him pleasant to be with. According to Mahdî ᶜAbd-ul-Karîm, a student

193 Ibid., p. 28.
194 Ibid., p. 31.
195 Ibid., p. 32.
196 Ibid., p. 33.
197 Interview by author with Salâm ᶜÂdil, Baghdad (8 December 1959).

who later became one of ʿÂdil's closest friends, and who knew him for over two decades, ʿÂdil's personality and talents were impressive:

> He had the very unusual talent of making you feel valued, and soon after talking to him you realized he was a man of integrity who liked people but was angry at how people were treated. Yet the manner in which this was expressed was calm and reasoned, and whatever he did, he aroused a trust in himself and in those around him. His ideas took fire and though he was humble, he enforced strict Party discipline.[198]

At about this time, the Iraqi Central Committee was invited by the British Communist Party to attend the Second London Conference of the Communist Parties within the Sphere of British Imperialism, to be held from 21 to 24 April 1954. The ICP chose ʿÂdil to represent the Party. Raḥîm ʿAjînah, then a medical student active in the ICP chapter in Britain, acted as ʿÂdil's translator and host while he was at the conference and even presented the ICP's speech because of ʿÂdil's poor English. Four decades later, ʿAjînah described his experience with ʿÂdil in those early days:

> I was impressed with the man's intellect and his sophisticated understanding of Marxist concepts. While dictating the speech in Arabic, he struggled with every word of its translation, and made me check the meaning so many times in the Oxford dictionary. His theoretical interpretations of the conditions of Iraq and the world were his main preoccupation and were novel but, at first glance, looked far-fetched. ʿÂdil insisted, "Theory is great, but it's an Iraqi party, and theory is to serve and explain, not dictate solutions." When he explained their relevance and the application of the theory, the interpretations sounded refreshing. They were not the usual, rigid Marxist-Leninist approach; rather, they were dynamic, fitted our situation, but were certainly not the orthodox Soviet line.... He kept us all going, was diligent and did not waste a minute while he was in London, meeting all the delegates, and re-establishing the ICP's international contacts, including those with the CPSU and Eastern European countries. Thus he set the foundation for the Party's return to the international communist movement, which had been interrupted with the arrest and eventual execution of Fahd.[199]

According to ʿAbd-ul-Khâliq al-Bayâtî, at the time an Iraqi engineering student active in the London branch of the ICP, as well as president of the Iraqi Student Society in the United Kingdom, ʿÂdil's role was crucial in rejuvenating the Party abroad:

> The group was active but had little contact with the home Party. As soon as ʿÂdil came to London, he held a number of meetings and visited groups and students, even those who had lost contact with us. With his personality, knowledge, and enthusiasm he brought a lot of us back, so much so that we felt reborn, and at the time I was so taken by it that my fiancée and I donated all our wedding savings to the Party, and everybody acted in a similar way. He kept us working as translators and guides for him in London, where he managed to secure appointments with numerous leftist and progressive British

198 Interview by author with Mahdî ʿAbd-ul-Karîm, Arbil, Kurdistan (18 June 1981).
199 Interview by author with Raḥîm ʿAjînah, London (19 April 1994).

political activists. He was meticulous in his preparation and used to grill us on issues, personalities, and our knowledge of ideologies. He was sociable, pleasant, and always on the go.[200]

Similarly, Anîs ᶜAjînah, who was then in charge of the London branch of the ICP, and the most active member of the Iraqi Students' Society in the United Kingdom, saw ᶜÂdil's visit as revitalizing the movement. "With his [ᶜÂdil's] visit, we began regularizing our contributions to the Party on a monthly basis and we delivered more than £3,000 to him, which was a lot of money in those days, in a way giving the Party, in this critical stage, a financial shot in the arm, and also [giving] ᶜÂdil more clout within the financially pressed Central Committee."[201] This support also accorded the London group special standing within the Party, especially when these students returned to Iraq in the mid-1950s, enriching the intellectual foundations of the Party and permeating the professional associations they would belong to. Thus, they made the Party more visible in Iraq, especially as they gradually rose in Iraqi society, in some cases assuming influential positions in their respective professional associations. As time passed, the impact of this influnce became evident, particularly in Baghdad, the political nerve centre of the country.

Returning to Baghdad, ᶜÂdil conneted with the Syrian-Lebanese Communist Party, making it the primary point of contact for the ICP internationally. He also informed the Central Committee of the determination of the international communist movement "to support our Party based on their faithful commitment to the international proletariat."[202] His performance at the conference had enhanced his stature in the Central Committee as an effective international figure. Because of the success of his participation in the April conference in London and the restoration of the ICP's contact, lost in 1949, with the international communist movement, the Central Committee gave ᶜÂdil charge of the Baghdad section. This position gave him the most prominent role in the Party's national scene, placing him in the forefront of Iraqi political opposition and putting him in touch with all the other opposition groups. It allowed him to be directly involved in the national political process, as did his other assignment as liaison officer for national relations between the ICP and the nationalist and opposition forces. These posts gave ᶜÂdil the chance to implement both his personal ideas and the ideas contained in the Central Committee's report "The National Front Struggle Against War and Imperialism." As already noted, this report both reflected his personal views and had convinced the Central Committee to abandon its past extremist positions. Thus was initiated what might be dubbed a "post-Fahd" period, in which a more practical stance brought the ICP closer to other opposition parties and eventually allowed the Party to work with those parties in a national front. Further, it opened up a direction in the ICP's development that has influenced the Party up to the present.

200 Interview by author with ᶜAbd-ul-Khâliq al-Bayâtî, Baghdad (27 September 1960).
201 Interview by author with Anîs ᶜAjînah, Baghdad (17 March 1974).
202 *Al-Qâᶜidah*, no. 5 (June, 1954).

At this crucial point in Iraqi politics, ᶜÂdil had emerged as the most important person in the Party. On 11 May 1954, the ICP made contact with the main opposition parties, *al-Istiqlâl*, the National Democratic Party, and other opposition groups and professional associations, in an effort to create a "national front" that would participate in the parliamentary elections scheduled for the following month.

ᶜÂdil's wife notes that upon his becoming responsible for the Baghdad section of the Party, one of her husband's first actions was to organize within the army:

> The issue of the Party taking over the reins of power of the government was a central focus of his thoughts and concerns . . . and the main issue [was] the organization of the Party in the army. . . . In the past, the activities of the Party in Baghdad centered around students and youth. . . . [ᶜÂdil] strengthened the Party activities in the armed forces, particularly among officers and the lower ranks, and directed . . . that we establish connections with the Army in Baghdad and around Baghdad.[203]

The Iraqi political scene accorded ᶜÂdil the environment needed to revive the Party as a viable political force and halt its organizational disintegration. In addition, the rise in Soviet popularity in the aftermath of the Arab-Israeli conflict of 1948, and strong domestic anti-Western feelings, helped to further strengthen the ICP's role as a credible opposition group. At the same time, successive pro-British Iraqi governments attempted to integrate the country into the Western defence system, in order to secure Western oil supplies and utilize Iraq's geopolitical position in the emerging Cold War. Thus, the West's strategic aim in Iraq became the creation of a Middle East defence system that integrated Iraq into the containment of the Soviet Union. Moving towards that goal, Britain attempted to replace the unequal Anglo-Iraqi and Anglo-Egyptian Treaties of 1930 and 1936, respectively, with a military pact in which the United States would be a partner. In this the British failed, although other arrangements were subsequently advanced for the same purpose of containment. On 21 April 1954, Iraq became a signatory to an Understanding of Military Assistance with the United States, thereby preparing the ground for the Baghdad Pact a year later. This was considered by most of the country's national and progressive forces to be a first step in tying Iraq to the American-sponsored security alliance signed three weeks earlier (2 April 1954) between Turkey and Pakistan. Thus, the ICP, in a circular dated May 1954 entitled "Down with the Pakistan-Turkey Treaty," proclaimed:

> We have no choice except the unity in our national front . . . and to stand up as one people to challenge this treaty, and work for the abolition of the 1930 Treaty, along with the departure of the English occupying armies, the nationalizing of oil companies, the redistribution of land and its irrigation, . . . the increase of the farmer's share [in the tenure system], the abolition of forced labour, the non-involvement of Iraq in any aggressive military project . . . and the establishment of a national government that serves peace and rejects all treaties and imperial military designs.

203 Thamînah Nâjî Yûsuf and Nazâr Khâlid, *Salâm ᶜÂdil: Sirat Munâḍil*, vol. 1 (Cyprus: al-Mada Publishing Company, 2001), p. 80.

With the signing of the Turkish-Iraqi Mutual Cooperation Pact of 24 February 1955, and the special Iraqi-British agreement of 4 April 1955 that would lead to the Baghdad Pact, the integration of Iraq into the Western alliance became complete, achieving Nûrî al-Saᶜîd's goal. The two major nationalist and progressive parties, *al-Istiqlâl* and the National Democratic Party (NDP), reacted to these events by issuing a joint declaration on 30 April 1954 condemning the government and its actions, and they began negotiations with the ICP to discuss the communists' proposed national front. Two weeks later, on 12 May 1954, a temporary national front was formed to coordinate activities for the duration of the forthcoming parliamentary election, thus concretely implementing ᶜÂdil's new direction for the ICP. The front agreement was signed by representatives of the NDP and the *Istiqlâl*, and by representatives of youth, lawyer, doctor, student, labour, and peasant organizations, all of which were either controlled or influenced by the communists. However, although the ICP was the principal architect of the National Front, it could not be a co-signatory to its formation, nor could it appear as a partner at the formal announcement of the front, since the Party was an illegal organization and the nationalists were reluctant to be publicly associated with it. The main pillars of the front's pact were

1. A call for democratic freedoms such as the freedom of the press, expression, and assembly, as well as the for right to form political, labour, and professional associations, including political parties.
2. A call for free elections.
3. Abolition of the 1930 treaty; closure of military bases and the departure of foreign armies; and the rejection of imperialist military alliances, including the Turkish-Pakistani Pact.
4. Rejection of military aid programs whose aims are to restrict Iraqi sovereignty and to tie Iraq to imperialist military pacts.
5. Action to abolish foreign monopolies; achieve social justice; abolish feudalism; solve the existing economic crisis, including the problems of unemployment and inflation; raise the standard of living in general; and encourage national industries.[204]

At the end of May 1954, *Al-Qâᶜidah*, the primary ICP newspaper, hailed the formation of the front in an editorial, and saluted the victory achieved by the democratic forces. While it expressed chagrin at not being given public acknowledgement for its efforts in building the front, *Al-Qâᶜidah* declared that the national front was the only umbrella "that can unify all national and democratic groups against the imperialist forces and the local ruling reactionaries which tie their destiny to that of imperialist control of our country, selling our people's freedom and independence to the British and the Americans." However, it criticized the front for not developing clear positions on anti-imperialism or Arab liberation movements and for limiting "the imperialist forces" to the Americans. In dealing with the eradication of feudalism, the paper also tactfully criticized the front for not specifying the exact form of government it

[204] *Ṣawt al-Ahâlî* and *Liwâʾal-Istiqlâl* (Baghdad, 13 May 1954).

sought and for ignoring issuses pertaining to Kurds, women, and political prisoners. It called "for the members of the Front to become more mature, and worthy [of the public's trust] by more clearly articulating national and popular goals, in order to enable the Front to rally all popular forces to the struggle against imperialism, and towards the achievement of independence." Ten days later, perhaps in reaction to the communists' criticisms, as well as to internal debates, the front added two more articles to its pact: "support for all Arab people, in order to achieve the independence of [all] Arab countries, and the liberation of Palestine," and "striving to free Iraq and other Arab countries from the evils of war."[205]

At about the same time, a radical change in the ICP leadership began to take shape when Ḥamîd ᶜUth̲mân took charge of the Party and reorganized the Central Committee, reducing the influence of ᶜÂdil and signalling a more orthodox Marxist orientation. The ICP Central Committee at the time was made up of Ḥamîd ᶜUth̲mân, Karîm Aḥmad, Salâm ᶜÂdil, Sâlim al-Chalabî, Hâdî Hâs̲h̲im, Farmân Ṭuᶜmâ, ᶜAbd-ul-lah ᶜUmar Muḥyî-d-Dîn, Nâṣir ᶜAbbûd, and ᶜAṭs̲h̲an Ḍaiyyûl. Karîm Aḥmad, ᶜUth̲mân's protégé, replaced ᶜÂdil and was put in charge of the Baghdad section, and Muḥyî-d-Dîn was put in charge of the Kurdish section. ᶜÂdil was moved to the Middle Euphrates region, and Ṭuᶜmâ was put in charge of the south. The acting secretary-general, ᶜUth̲mân, gradually took complete charge of all Party activities and reduced the input of the Central Committee, particularly that of ᶜÂdil, giving the Party a new, radical direction through an emphasis on armed struggle.[206]

When the election was held on 9 June 1954, ten National Front candidates were elected – two from the *Istiqlâl* party, six from the NDP, and two former communists. After convening only for the day of its opening, Parliament recessed on 27 July, and Nûrî al-Saᶜîd, whose party had won 56 out of the 135 total seats, was called upon to form the government. On 4 August, al-Saᶜîd's new government was announced and immediately moved to dissolve Parliament. He also announced the dissolution of his political party, the Constitutional Union, issued an announcement attacking all opposition groups, and called upon the Iraqi people to rally around his government to defend the country from these forces.[207] Immediately thereafter, he revoked the licences of eighteen political newspapers. To further tighten his grip on the country, he issued a number of decrees. On 22 August, in Decree 16, he amended Article 51 of the 1938 Iraqi penal code which mandated seven years imprisonment for anyone who propagated socialist ideas (Bolshevism), communism, or anarchism, or who simply advocated reforming the political system. Nûrî al-Saᶜîd's amendment added to that list any organization, such as democratic youth groups, whose aims he believed coincided with those of the communists. On the same day, he also issued Decrees 17 and 18, authorizing the cabinet, upon the recommendation of the minister of the interior, to revoke the citizenship of those

205 Ibid. (23 May 1954).
206 Yûsuf and K̲h̲âlid, *Salâm ᶜÂdil*, pp. 87–98.
207 *Al-Zamân* (Baghdad, 4 August 1954).

convicted under Article 51. Decree 17 entrusted the minister of the interior with the arrest and deportation of those convicted, and Article 18 closed all labour unions.[208]

Decree 19 followed on 22 September. It authorized the minister of the interior to withdraw the licences of many associations, clubs and theatres, resulting in the closure of some 465 such premises.[209] Two weeks later, on 10 October, Decree 24 authorized the minister of the interior to ban any newspaper or journal.[210] Nûrî al-Saᶜîd also gave the minister of the interior, or his designee, the power to disperse any gathering if law and order were threatened.[211] The NDP vehemently attacked Decrees 16, 17, and 18 and demanded their withdrawal declaring:

> We consider these reactionary Decrees issued by this government the worst of any government's action, not only in Iraq but in the world as a whole.... Not because it is contrary to the basic principles of democracy and violates the constitution, but because it violated one of the natural human rights of citizens which is the right of citizenship and because it included [and limited] our expression of opinion and political freedoms with vague definitions which allow [the government] free interpretation to oppress any and all political activities.... All events prove that oppression, tyranny, suppression of freedoms and the expansion of reactionary decrees will not cure the terrible conditions that create public dissatisfaction and complaints.... This, at the end, will awaken the people's consciousness and they will work to eradicate them.[212]

The *Istiqlâl* party issued similar, though less vehement, condemnations.[213]

Immediately after the NDP attacked the decrees its licence was revoked and its paper ceased to publish. The *Istiqlâl* party reacted strongly to the closure, and its editorial entitled "Grave Responsibilities" described the revocation of the NDP's licence as

> expressing the [depths of] despair reached by the ruling group that is trying, without success, to hold onto its privileges in a time when popular mobilization is taking place and people are looking forward to a rapid and fundamental reform. At the same time these groups and their structures are unable to respond to the demanded reforms. They should have tried to reform the corruption under which people are suffering, instead of oppressing the people further. The *Istiqlâl* party knows well the reasons that caused the delicensing of the NDP, and the motives behind this irregular action.... the party will shoulder its responsibility fully.[214]

In this environment, the Popular Front Party, in despair, dissolved itself, leaving only the *Istiqlâl* in the public political arena. When the election took place

208 *Al-Waqâʾiᶜ al-ᶜIrâqiyyah*, no. 3455 (Baghdad, 14 September 1954).
209 Al-Ḥasanî, *Târîkh al-Wizârât al-ᶜIrâqiyyah*, vol. 9, p. 150; and *Al-Waqâʾiᶜ al-ᶜIrâqiyyah*, no. 3455 (Baghdad, 14 September 1954).
210 Ibid., no. 3479 (10 October 1954).
211 Ibid., no. 3480 (12 October 1954).
212 *Ṣawt al-Ahâlî* (Baghdad, 2 September 1954).
213 *Liwâʾal-Istiqlâl* (Baghdad, 2 September 1954).
214 Fâʾiq al-Sâmarrâʾî, *Liwâʾ al-Istiqlâl* (Baghdad, 5 September 1954).

on 12 September 1954, and with other opposition parties also boycotting the election, *Istiqlâl* participated under the same slogans as in the previous election. Nevertheless, as a result of election "irregularities," only two of its members were elected, while Nûrî al-Saᶜîd's group won a landslide victory, taking all the remaining seats. One hundred and twenty-one seats were won by acclamation, and the other twelve were only weakly contested.[215]

In response to these results, the *Istiqlâl* party decided to withdraw from the parliament, though one member chose to stay on as an independent after resigning from the party. On 22 September 1954, and in accordance with Decree 19, the party was also de-licensed.[216] Confronted by Nûrî al-Saᶜîd's oppression and indiscriminate attack on public freedoms, the Communist Party repeated its call for continuation of the national front, using the success of the 9 June 1954 election and the election of ten members to Parliament as evidence that "it was a successful experiment for any national grouping... and a practical justification for forming a united national front later on."[217]

Nûrî al-Saᶜîd's repression of the political opposition backfired in that the ICP emerged with greatly increased popularity. A cardinal principle of the ICP's strategy at this time seemed to centre on collective political action through a national front to stop Nûrî al-Saᶜîd from steering Iraq towards joining in the Turkish-Pakistani Pact for Friendship and Co-operation for Security. To prepare for this move, Nûrî al-Saᶜîd broke off diplomatic relations with the Soviet Union in January 1955. The Central Committee of the ICP responded with a memorandum, addressed to all national parties and forces, in which it explained the break with the Soviet Union as a realignment of Iraq in preparation for the security pact. The ICP declared:

> The resumption of diplomatic relations with the USSR is of utmost national necessity, dictated by the [defence] of the country's reputation and the nation's honour.... the break with the Soviet Union means Iraq became one of America's client states.... the Central Committee calls upon all brothers in the other political parties, and all those opposition personalities, to show their solidarity. Our Party believes that one simple common action uniting us all together will shake up the government.... we must make a collective response.[218]

Al-Qâᶜidah continued its call for a national front as the only alternative framework for opposition to Nûrî al-Saᶜîd and again pointed out that the temporary national front of May 1954 should have been developed further and become permanent. If "the parliamentary bloc had been able to transform itself into a supreme body for the National Front," argued *Al-Qâᶜidah*, "it would not have been so easy for Nûrî al-Saᶜîd to dissolve the parliament. And even if he had dissolved parliament and the bloc, if the Front had been transformed, it would have had the solid legitimacy of a national organization." As, the Party

215 Al-Ḥasanî, *Târîkh al-Wizârât al-ᶜIrâqiyyah*, vol. 9, p. 181.
216 *Al-Waqâʾiᶜ al-ᶜIrâqiyyah*, no. 2473 (29 September, 1954).
217 *Al-Qâᶜidah* (10 June 1954).
218 Ibid. (mid-January 1955).

asserted in an editorial: "Had it not been for these mistakes, the reactionary forces would not have been able to dismantle the Front, and the step of 12 May 1954 [formation of the National Front] would have become the nucleus of a broad democratic front, which would have been able to steer the direction of politics towards a nationalist and independent policy."[219]

As expected, on 24 February 1955 Iraq joined the Turkish-Pakistani Pact; this move was immediately ratified by the parliament led by Nûrî al-Saʿîd. *Al-Qâʿidah* reacted by declaring:

> Division among the Arabs will be the first fruit of this pact. The Iraqi-Turkish pact is directed clearly against the peace-loving Afro-Asian nations, and against the unity of the Arab people struggling for independence, peace, and progress. At the same time it is also directed against the Kurdish people, who arose courageously to challenge imperial and feudal serfdom . . . in Turkey, Iraq, and Iran.[220]

The next day, the ICP, along with the nationalist forces, played a leading role in mobilizing public demonstrations against the pact in the major cities of Iraq. Scores of citizens were arrested, and a number were killed. A week later, on 3 April, Iraq and Britain signed a special agreement to replace the 1930 Anglo-Iraqi Treaty, and on 5 April Britain joined the Iraqi-Turkish-Pakistani Pact.

In response to there being no formal structure uniting progressive and nationalist forces, ʿUthmân sternly criticized opposition groups and parties, chastising them for not supporting the Party's call for a "common action" against the government. He claimed that the ICP had "asked the interested parties to organize a general political strike to destabilize the Cabinet [of Nûrî al-Saʿîd]; however, we have not received any response from our brethren."[221] ʿUthmân issued this call without consulting anyone else in the Party.

Soon after, again on his own, and without any discussion in the Central Committee or the Politburo, or with any of the Party's partners in the National Front, though nominally under the signatures of the Central Committee, ʿUthmân published an exceptionally radical action programme in *Al-Qâʿidah*. In doing so, he committed the ICP to a strategy and programme that would have significant ramifications for both the Party and the country. He unilaterally stated that as "our Party does not know retreat in the face of challenge, we now offer the required national programme which expresses the interest of the overwhelming majority of the people, based on the internal, national situation, and in the pressing national interests of [the people]." He challenged the opposition forces to act by declaring, "We extend the hand of real struggle to every Iraqi who will stand to implement [the total] programme, or any part of it, even any of its sections or articles."[222] ʿUthmân proposed in this programme, which came to be known as "The Cry of May," that all nationalist forces unite around the following objectives: (1) the withdrawal of Iraq from the Turkish-Pakistani

[219] Ibid. (mid-February 1955).
[220] Ibid. (early March 1955).
[221] Ibid. (mid-January 1955).
[222] Ibid. (May 1955).

Pact; (2) the repudiation of the April Anglo-Iraqi Treaty; (3) the rejection of all American assistance programmes, military or otherwise; (4) the cancellation of all foreign monopolies, including oil concessions; and (5) the overthrow of Nûrî al-Saᶜîd's government and the installation of a national coalition government dedicated to the creation of a democratic environment, the freeing of all political prisoners, the dissolution of the present parliament, and the free election of a new parliament in which women and minorities would have better representation. In addition, the proposed government would improve the health and the cultural and living conditions of the people. The final objective of ᶜUthmân's programme was (6) the reform of the state structure, especially the police, the judiciary, and the army.[223]

At this time, the ICP's popularity increased, and the Party was emboldened to become active in new areas. It moved to organize within the Iraqi armed forces, creating the National Committee for the Union of Officers and Soldiers, with its own newspaper, *Ḥurriyyat al-Waṭan* (The Liberation of the Motherland). The paper's first issue, published in January 1955, declared:

> The Iraqi soldiers should not be treated as slaves, driven to war without a choice, and exploited as servants in officers' homes – we must have a unity of aim and organization – our immediate duty is to work in order to spread national consciousness, to strengthen the spirit of patriotic devotion and the hatred of imperialism.... we must struggle against mistreatment of soldiers, work to prohibit... inhumane treatment of them, and strive towards the improvement of the soldiers' standard of living and education. We must also endeavour to provide schools to raise the technical level of the soldiers... and the unlimited privileges of officers should be terminated.

According to the second issue, in February 1955, "Soldiers are human beings like other Iraqi people and should have rights and opinions.... we are not serfs.... the national committee calls upon you [soldiers] to join the people in their demonstrations, wearing your military uniforms so that the enemies of the people will know that the nation's workers and soldiers are united." Around this time also, the Committee of the Workers' Organization became more vocal and active; it regularly published *Ittiḥâd al-ᶜUmmâl* (The Unity of Workers), its official organ, in which it called for the right of workers to organize into labour unions, carried news of workers' activities in general, and highlighted workers' strikes and grievances. Subsequently, the Party newspaper, *Al-Qâᶜidah*, intensified its coverage of the peasant movement, stressing the need to form peasant organizations.

Incensed by the radicalization of the Party and the personal conduct of the secretary-general, ᶜÂdil refused to abide by "The Cry of May" policy or to distribute *Al-Qâᶜidah* that contained it. He also wrote to ask that the Central Committee convene to debate this "Party" policy.[224] Other members of the Central Committee, likewise alarmed by Ḥamîd ᶜUthmân's extremism, isolation from other national progressive forces, and dictatorial style, also called for

[223] Ibid. (May 1955).
[224] Yûsuf and Khâlid, *Salâm ᶜÂdil*, pp. 99–101.

an assessment of ᶜUthmân's leadership. In an extraordinary meeting in June 1955, the Central Committee decided to remove ᶜUthmân from the secretary-generalship and place him under forced detention. He was expelled from his post on 19 July and warned that if he did not submit to the leadership, he would no longer be under the "protection" of the ICP.[225]

Following this action, the ICP experienced yet another change in direction, characterized by greater emphasis on peaceful activities through the formation of popular groups, such as a separate women's party section, intended to satisfy cultural norms rather than ideological positions. The Party also created the Committee of Democratic Activities to foster creation of professional and popular organizations to work within the Iraqi political environment. The Central Committee placed responsibility for the Party's isolation and adventurist policies directly on ᶜUthmân and roundly condemned his dictatorial style, which had ignored Party by-laws, violated the basic principles of democratic centralism, and encouraged the rise of a personality cult. They also censured ᶜUthmân's tactics vis-à-vis other democratic forces. Finally, the Central Committee elected ᶜÂdil secretary-general, and authorized him to put into action a new vision for the Party's future, involving a restructuring of the Party and a broadening of the Party's collaboration with workers' unions and peasant organizations rather than merely seeking to integrate those associations into the Party structure. The Party also opened itself to full cooperation with other political forces in order to "struggle for democratic freedoms that will never bear fruit without the involvement of the popular masses in a struggle for their immediate and vital interests."[226]

Nasser's Pan-Arabist Challenge

Gamal Abdel Nasser's 1952 coup in Egypt opened the floodgates of revolution in the Arab world, and by the mid-1950s the region was awash with change. It was in this context that ᶜÂdil rose to power in the Party leadership, assuming the post of secretary-general in July 1955, just prior to Nasser's ascent to prominence in the Arab nationalist movement, his increasing anti-Western orientation, and his close cooperation with the socialist bloc.

In early 1955, the Western-engineered Baghdad Pact promoted by Nûrî al-Saᶜîd presented a major challenge to Nasser's Pan-Arab policy and was the catalyst for his anti-imperialist stance. To counter the pact, Nasser attempted to form his own defence alliance, and in March 1955, Egypt and Syria formed the "Defence Organization and Mutual Arab Cooperative to establish a permanent common command [structure] to execute defence, and supervise the war industry and economic cooperation."[227] Yemen declared its support,[228]

[225] Ṣalâḥ al-Kharsân, *Ṣafaḥât min Târîkh al-Ḥarakah al-Shîyûᶜiyyah fî al-ᶜIrâq* (Beirut: Dâr al-Furât, 1993), pp. 76, 77; and *Ittiḥâd al-Shaᶜb* (26 January 1960).
[226] Central Committee Party Minutes and Pronouncements, ICP, August 1955.
[227] *Al-Ahram* (Cairo, 7 March 1955).
[228] Ibid. (7 March 1955).

and a day later Saudi Arabia endorsed the agreement.[229] *Al-Ahram* described the purpose, scope, and nature of the alliance:

What Egypt and Syria seek is the complete integration of the Arab world.... Politically the Arab world ignores the Iraqi-Turkish pact or any other non-Arab pact. Militarily the new Arab world should have an organization which takes care of its defence.... Economically...an Arab economic council will be formed to direct the economic policy.[230]

By mid-1955 it was apparent that Nasser had failed to rally sufficient Arab state support for the proposed Arab Mutual Security Pact, which drove a further wedge between him and the governments concerned. Personality conflicts and policy clashes between Nasser and the other Arab leaders, particularly Nûrî al-Saᶜîd, intensified. Furthermore, Nasser's active opposition to the Baghdad Pact paved the way for a breach with the West. With the Bandung Conference in April 1955, this confrontation intensified, pushing Nasser to the forefront of the Arab nationalist movement. When he signed an arms deal with Czechoslovakia on 17 September 1955, it ended the Western monopoly on arms sales to the region, was the start of closer Egyptian cooperation with the Soviet bloc, and deepened the gulfs between Nasser and the Pan-Arab nationalist movement, and Nasser and the West. Nine months later, the Suez Canal crisis, initiated by Egypt's nationalization of the canal on 26 July, led to an Israeli-French-British attack on Egypt on 29 October. Soviet and Chinese support for Egypt cemented Nasser's role as leader of the Pan-Arab nationalist movement and propelled the Egyptian leader to prominence on the international stage. In addition, these events increased Soviet popularity throughout the Arab world, heightened support for all anti-Western forces in the region, and brought about closer communication, if not outright cooperation, between Arab nationalists and the left in the Arab world. Thus, the crisis cemented the front among all anti-imperialist forces against the West, their common enemy.

Rebuilding the Party

It is within this fluid and dynamic environment that ᶜÂdil's rise to power and his success in bringing the fractured Party together and leading it to become a significant actor in Iraqi politics and in the anti-imperialist front against Nûrî al-Saᶜîd must be understood. Immediately after assuming the position of secretary-general of the Party, and in a gesture of goodwill to other opposition groupings, particularly the nationalists, Salâm ᶜÂdil and his Central Committee pledged their support for his long-held position on formation of a national front.[231] ᶜÂdil confided to his wife that "his new platform would be the unification of the Party, the reintegration of all splinter groups and the formation of a national front."[232]

229 Ibid. (8 March 1955).
230 Ibid. (Cairo, 10 March 1955).
231 For more detail on ᶜÂdil's account, see Yûsuf and Khâlid, vol. 1, *Salâm ᶜÂdil*, pp. 99–101.
232 Ibid., p. 102.

In this environment, ᶜÂdil turned his attention to attracting all the splinter groups into the "mother party." He initiated these activities by establishing links with dissident communist groups, suggesting that they reunite since "none of them is strong enough to be viable on its own, and now that the Party has acceptance within the Iraqi political scene we can have our imprint on the political life of the country."[233] One of ᶜÂdil's first tasks was to rebuild the Party by raising the standard of the intellectual and theoretical education of the cadres. To accomplish this, he published a special issue of *Al-Qâᶜidah* (number 8), at the end of 1955, devoted entirely to this purpose.

On 22 July 1955, only two weeks into his new post, the ICP's new secretary-general moved to attract the most popular splinter communist organization, *Râyat al-Shaghîlah*: he presented it with a four-point plan to discuss and to serve as a basis for possible reunification.[234] *Râyat al-Shaghîlah* initially responded with caution, declaring, "unity will no doubt have to be achieved and the slogan of the 'unity of principles' is becoming a reality." Moreover, its attacks on *al-Qâᶜidah* did not cease.[235] In March 1956, *Al-Qâᶜidah* appealed to all splinter groups to unite in one communist party, claiming that "*Râyat al-Shaghîlah* does not have any good reason to continue its opposition" to the *al-Qâᶜidah* group, especially after the Twentieth Congress of the CPSU in February 1956. Immediately after the dissolution of the Cominform on 17 April 1956, the group the Unity of the Communists in Iraq also dissolved itself and amalgamated with the ICP, with one of its leaders, ᶜAbd-ul-Raḥîm Sharîf, being appointed to the Party's Central Committee. This paved the way for *Râyat al-Shaghîlah*'s eventual return after long negotiations between the two groups, mediated by the Syrian Communist Party and its leader, Khâlid Bakdâsh. Thus, in the middle of June 1956, the final issue of *Râyat al-Shaghîlah* declared the group dissolved and even criticized itself as having been divisive to the unity of the communist movement. Following this, in a circular dated 17 June 1956, the ICP's Central Committee criticized the actions taken in 1952 by the Bâsim Central Committee in expelling the *Râyat al-Shaghîlah* group, and described the expulsion as "childish and bureaucratic." It was a time when

> an ignorant leadership achieved control over the affairs of the Party . . . which resulted in repeated grave political and organizational mistakes that led to the Party being deprived of the experience and knowledge of faithful comrades who [had] sincerely criticized the Party, and were consequently and unjustly expelled because of the suppression of criticism by the then party leadership, later forcing these comrades to join *Râyat al-Shaghîlah*.[236]

To show its new direction and good faith, the ICP leadership decided to replace the Party's newspaper, and *Al-Qâᶜidah* declared its 19 June 1956 issue to be its last. Party members and friends were called on to help choose a suitable

233 Interview by author with George Tallû, Baghdad (18 March 1959).
234 *Al-Qâᶜidah*, no. 11 (December 1955).
235 *Râyat al-Shaghîlah* (28 October 1955).
236 For more details, and for the views of ᶜÂdil, see *Ittiḥâd al-Shaᶜb* (Baghdad, 26 January 1960).

name for the new Party newspaper, and *Ittiḥâd al-Sha*ᶜ*b* (Unity of the People) was issued on 22 July 1956, signalling a new era for the reborn ICP. Confident of Party unity and in its increasing presence on the Iraqi political scene, the ICP made preparations for a second Party conference, the first to be held since the execution of its founder Fahd; the conference took place in September 1956, at the height of the Suez crisis. During the Second Party Conference, the advanced Party and local committees were fully represented, and the secretary-general's draft report was closely scrutinized and discussed before it was unanimously approved.

In the report entitled "Our Political Plan for our National and Patriotic Liberation," Salâm ᶜÂdil presented the Party's new direction and policy orientation to the conference. Essentially, it summarised what he had been putting into practice from the time he assumed the Party's top post, and for which he now sought formal sanction from the entire cadre. He laid out his basic platform, to some extent incorporating changes introduced by resolutions of the Twentieth Congress of the CPSU that brought principles of co-existence into international relations. He also inserted his own moderate views, which had evolved over the past two years, into the programme, emphasizing not the Marxist-Leninist principle of a revolutionary transformation to socialism, but "the current imperative [which is] the creation of a national government whose most important obligations ... are to put an end to its isolation from its sister Arab states and to follow an Arab national policy which guarantees Iraq the honour of participating in Arab alliances, and in the noble efforts to achieve the aspired Arab unity." He added:

> What faces our country now is the need to transform the existing policy of cooperation with imperialism, compromise with Zionism, and isolation from the national liberation movement to an Arab nationalist policy. The nature of the approaching battle ... must be peaceful ... based on the mobilization of nationalist forces in a broad front to change the existing policy to an independent, nationalist Arab policy.[237]

He then went on to explain that "the task of the transition to socialism and the transfer of political power to the hands of workers, peasants and their allies, is not the task that faces the Party under current conditions."[238] Further, the report clarified the basic aims of the Party at this particular stage of Iraq's history, and it emphasized that the way to the achievement of this change would be through cooperation with other national forces by peaceful means and through the formation of a national front coalition government, even though the Communist Party might not be represented in that government.[239]

While the Party did not advocate revolution, it did not rule out the possibility of a popular uprising to create a national government that would steer Iraqi

[237] *Ittiḥâd al-Sha*ᶜ*b*, no. 9 (mid-October 1956), and ICP, *Khuṭaṭunâ al-Siyâsiyyah fî Sabîl al-Taḥarrur al-Waṭanî wa al-Qawmî* (Baghdad: ICP, 1956), p. 23.

[238] ICP, *Khuṭaṭunâ al-Siyâsiyyah fî Sabîl al-Taḥarrur al-Waṭanî wa al-Qawmî*, p. 24.

[239] Ibid. p. 34.

politics towards a more "independent nationalist Arab" policy. Thus, while it advocated change through peaceful means and was "anxious to achieve its aim constitutionally, with the lowest cost, and a minimum of human sacrifice,"[240] it did not rule out a possible uprising in the face of government violence. The report described the tasks of the national front government it envisioned as the establishment of an independent foreign policy that would include withdrawal from military agreements with the West, the immediate annulment of the Baghdad Pact, and the encouragement of an Arab cooperation policy that could lead to Arab unity. On the domestic level, it called for democratization through the repeal of all laws limiting basic human freedom implementation of the constitution, an independent economic policy that would protect the national economy and improve the living conditions of the population, and limitation of the powers of foreign oil companies to secure Iraqi interests rather than those of the petroleum companies through renegotiation of profit-sharing arrangements.[241]

Since the national front was to be the cornerstone of the Party's future activities, a significant proportion of the report was devoted to the front's nature, scope, and form.[242] It described the front as a coalition of all political forces having the common denominator of consensus on major issues, including a commitment to replacing the oppressive regime, while allowing

> each member of the front to exercise its own activities ... while working independently to achieve their own aims through their own specific methods and forms [as they see fit], as long as these do not infringe upon the basic general struggle.... To act as if we are alone in the field, and we alone have the right to lead, is erroneous and a clear violation of the fact that all national forces are united in one front, and not in one party. We should not overburden the front with aims, ideologies, or approaches that may be in contradiction to the class nature of the parties.[243]

The report also devoted extensive space to the Arab national movement and the Kurdish question, in which it asserted that Iraq was an Arab country and that its people were part of the "Arab nation." Nevertheless, the report observed that there existed two major nationalities, Kurdish and Arab, both of which were struggling to achieve independence and liberation "from imperialism." Securing the autonomy of Iraqi Kurdistan would allow liberation and Arab unity but, at the same time, would pave the way for genuine Kurdish self-determination and the eventual possibility of an independent Kurdish state.[244] With this part of the report, ʿÂdil brought the Party into line with the burning issues of the Arab national movement and closer in orientation to the nationalist groupings.

Also at the conference a new Central Committee was chosen, the Politburo being composed of Salâm ʿÂdil, first secretary of the Central Committee;

240 Ibid., p. 31.
241 Ibid, pp. 31–36.
242 Ibid, pp. 36–48.
243 Ibid., p. 45.
244 Ibid., pp. 49–60.

ᶜÂmir ᶜAbd-ul-lah; and Jamâl al Ḥaidarî. The rest of the Central Committee was made up of Nâṣir ᶜAbbûd, ᶜAṭshân Khaiyyûn al-Izzarjâwî, Farḥân Ṭuᶜmâ, Muḥammad Ṣâliḥ al-ᶜAblî and ᶜAbd-ul-Raḥîm Sharîf, with ᶜAzîz Aḥmad al-Shaikh and Ṣâliḥ Mahdî Duglah as Central Committee candidates.[245]

However, this re-shuffling did not go down well with a number of Party veterans, who viewed the conference as a deviation from socialism, let alone Marxist-Leninist principles. According to Hesqal Kojaman, a deeply committed communist who was imprisoned from 1949 to 1958 and again from 1959 to 1962, after which he left Iraq to live in London, the conference was the first betrayal of Fahd's Marxist-Leninist principles, and he saw the ICP shifting towards a moderation unworthy of the name communist party.[246] Kojaman concluded that the Party was becoming a mere reformist party rather than a revolutionary Marxist one that had found accommodation with the ruling elites and the royal regime "to achieve socialism in gradual stages; [the first of which is] the establishment of honest national government that allows the people the chance to march gradually and peacefully, under the leadership of the working class, towards socialism."[247]

Some observers have argued that the ICP never really recovered from the loss of its leaders in 1949. Fahd's leadership qualities were difficult to equal, and even his rivals acknowledged his tremendous intellectual strength. In the words of Mâlik Saif, to whom Fahd left control of the Party during his imprisonment, and who later turned most of the organization over to Iraqi security forces:

> I can say that Yûsuf Salmân Yûsuf (Fahd) was the only Iraqi Marxist-Leninist, not only because he studied at the "Toilers of the East" University, but also because he was able to adapt Marxism-Leninism to fit Iraqi social conditions in that period. He made communism attractive to a lot of people, including those within the petit-bourgeoisie, and sons of the upper classes and ministers, while widening the popular base of the Party to the degree that he was able to dispel the image of communism as atheistic. This allowed the Party the opportunity to convert clerics and their sons.[248]

An example of the strength of Fahd's personal influence was the admission into the Party of Mullah Sharîf ᶜUthmân – the "Red Mullah." ᶜUthmân was elected to the Central Committee at the First Congress, and put in charge of the Party's Kurdish branch, which at the time was almost non-existent. By mid-1946, however, the Kurdish branch was flourishing and published a Kurdish-language newspaper called *Azadi* (Freedom). But with Fahd's arrest in 1947, Sharîf ᶜUthmân abandoned all the work he had done and resigned, saying that Fahd had been the source of his loyalty and inspiration.[249]

Hesqal Kojaman made similar claims regarding Fahd's influence. In his eyes, the leaders who succeeded Fahd never reached the intellectual and theoretical

[245] Al-Kharsân, *Ṣafaḥât min Târîkh al-Ḥarakah al-Shîyûᶜiyyah fî al-ᶜIrâq*, p. 81.

[246] Hesqal Kojaman, *Thawrat 14 Tammûz 1958 fî al-ᶜIrâq wa siyâsât al-Ḥizb al-Shiyûᶜî* (London: n.p., 1985), pp. 40–54.

[247] Ibid., pp. 179–80.

[248] *Lil-Târîkh Lisân* (Baghdad: Ḥurriyah Press, 1983), pp. 67–68.

[249] Ibid., pp. 179–80.

levels or the revolutionary sophistication that would enable them to take mature political stands; in addition, the majority of the active members knowledgeable about Marxist theory had been arrested and imprisoned. Thus, according to Kojaman, those leaders left outside prison were the most inexperienced and least equipped to guide the Party; moreover, the leadership in prison failed to improve their understanding of Marxism.

As far as I know, [between 1949 and 1958,] while we were in prison, nobody from the cadre can deny the impoverished understanding of Marxist thought, which was maintained by the prison leadership [after Fahd's execution]. After the three executions (Fahd, Ḥâzim, and Ṣârim), successive weak prison leadership suffered from the same [intellectual stagnation] which was inflicted on the Party outside.... The [inexperienced and theoretically weak] communist leadership that was charged to rebuild the Party, and revitalize its activities outside, became the leadership in prison once they [too] were arrested. [After the new leadership] was imprisoned, they continued to be naïve and uneducated [in a Marxist sense], despite their urging new recruits to educate themselves in Marxist theory.

According to Kojaman, only four members of the Party – himself, ᶜAzîz al-Ḥâjj, Zakî Khairî, and Ibrâhîm Shâʾûl – had the intellectual facility and Marxist understanding necessary to render decisions about the Party from the proper theoretical perspective. Immediately after their release from prison following the 14 July 1958 coup, this divergent group assumed the leadership of the Party, composing the Central Committee and the Party Politburo.[250]

To deal on the organizational level with the Party's new amalgamation with the splinter groups, the Second Party Conference in 1956 paid special attention to the principle of "democratic centralism" and emphasized the need for Party discipline. In assessing the conference, one of the semi-official historians of the ICP, Suᶜâd Khairî notes:

The Conference was a testament to the Party's success in strengthening its unity, ridding itself of all schisms, ... uniting the leadership and cadre, solidifying the party intellectually and politically, freeing itself from its national isolation, and strengthening its ties to the international communist movement ... [as well as] responding to the new needs of our Iraqi people's national liberation movement and meeting the challenge of the rising Arab liberation movement as a whole. The situation demanded that the Party take into account these new objectives. To effectively augment its role in the national Iraqi liberation, it proclaimed slogans that would unify all opposition forces including Iraqi patriotic and national elements, and Kurdish and minority groups in a united national front ... for the purpose of solidifying the struggle to achieve the formation of a national government.[251]

The ICP leadership under ᶜÂdil was anxious to integrate its activities with other nationalist forces. As a result, in its acceptance of non-violent means for achieving its political aims, its approach was highly pragmatic. According

[250] Kojaman, *Thawrat 14 Tammûz 1958 fî al-ᶜIrâq wa siyâsât al-Ḥizb al-Shiyûᶜî*, pp. 96–98.
[251] Suᶜâd Khaîrî, *Min Târîkh al-Ḥarakah al-Thawriyyah al-Muᶜâṣirah fî al-ᶜIrâq*, p. 273.

to some observers, it had clearly abandoned the principle of class struggle and submitted to the nationalist bourgeoisie. This prompted Suᶜâd Khaîrî to criticize the conference resolutions as tantamount to a betrayal of Party principles:

> The Second Conference did not elaborate or delineate its vision [of the nature of the government] after the achievement of the national revolution because it did not envisage the necessity of the Communist Party's participation in this national government. Nor did it define the leading role of the working class in developing the national democratic revolution, which the national bourgeoisie is unable and unfit to fulfil because of its class make-up. This makes the bourgeoisie unable to achieve the complete objective of national liberation, in addition to its opposition to the transformation to the next stage, [which is] socialism.[252]

To implement the conference resolutions, the Party intensified the efforts it had initiated even before the conference to build the national front. In the spring of 1955, the Party had made formal representation to the NDP and progressive leftist groupings regarding the possibility of cooperation in preparation for such a national front.[253] Conditions in 1956 were ripe for the realization of the ICP's Second Conference resolutions on both Arab and national levels. Gradually, a loose committee, without any specific strategy, came into being, whose purpose was simply to discuss possible conditions for some sort of coordination, at least on basic political issues. However, the political situation in the Arab world generally, and in Iraq in particular, deteriorated, with events moving so rapidly that the various groupings, particularly the NDP, were induced to work more closely together. Even the *Istiqlâl* party gradually considered the idea of cooperation among all the leftist political parties, including the ICP, despite its previous reluctance to interact with leftists and communists. The NDP did not fully share such sensitivity. Indeed, relations between *al-Istiqlâl* and the NDP became so close that on 16 June 1956 they jointly applied to the government for a licence to form a new amalgamated party under the name *Ḥizb al-Muʾtamar al-Waṭanî* (the National Congress Party). This application was denied, prompting the Communist Party's official newspaper to vow that "the national and democratic forces will continue the struggle to remedy the political life of the country, and enforce the right of political organization for all political parties as one of the natural rights of any people, despite differences in their approaches and ideologies, [indeed,] as one of the natural rights of any nation."[254]

Strikes and public unrest ensued, culminating with the ICP, the newly emerging Arab Baᶜth Socialist Party, and the leadership of the proposed National Congress Party jointly calling for national strikes in support of Egypt's resistance to Western pressures and threats. The strike was timed to coincide with the holding of the London Conference of 16 August 1956, which was supposed to coordinate the West's response to Nasser's nationalization of the Suez

[252] Ibid., pp. 273, 274.
[253] Ibid., p. 278.
[254] *Ittiḥâd al-Shaᶜb* (22 July 1956).

Canal.[255] The ICP supported the strike, and in a 13 August pronouncement entitled "The ICP Calls the Iraqi People to a General Strike in Solidarity with the Arab People in Support of Egypt," declared:

> Let us respond to the call of the Arab Central Committee, which was formed by all the political parties and forces in Syria, to make 16 August the day of a total and comprehensive strike.... let us unite all parties and national forces for this sacred occasion in a decisive response to the popular will... to force the government to assent to the will of the people, and declare publicly that Iraq is [in solidarity] with Egypt... and with Arabism against imperialism. Let the government take serious political and economic measures against the imperial states that are threatening aggression against Egypt.... let us get our country out of the Baghdad Pact, the cause of the division among Arabs... let us plan an honourable direction for our country... a patriotic Arab independent direction.[256]

Now in good standing with Arab nationalist forces on the Iraqi scene, ᶜÂdil turned his attention to strengthening the ICP's relations with the Kurdish Democratic Party (KDP) and to negotiations to coordinate activities between the Kurdish branch of the ICP and the KDP. However, the KDP rejected anything other than the dissolution of the ICP's Kurdish branch and its complete integration into the KDP. The majority of the ICP's Kurdish branch eventually chose to join the KDP in June 1957. The secretary-general responded in August, in the name of the ICP, by issuing the pamphlet *A Response to Bourgeois Chauvinist Dismantlers*,[257] which asserted that members of the ICP leadership had, without authorization from the Central Committee or approval by the Kurdish branch leadership, negotiated a merger with the KDP that the Central Committee rejected because the plan had

> no ideological, political or social basis.... it is an opportunist unity at the expense of the Iraqi people, including the Kurdish people, and the communist Party.... instead of the leadership of our branch in Kurdistan standing firm and candidly against this bourgeois, chauvinist, dismantler, deviationist group, it submitted to the [group], and approved the majority of opinions and conclusions of this deviating body.[258]

The pamphlet went on to state that the KDP "is not a Marxist-Leninist organization but rather a bourgeois chauvinist [group]."[259] By the autumn of 1956, the Iraqi situation was approaching a boiling point; moreover, public support for the four-year-old Algerian revolution was reaching its peak. Arab issues became paramount for all Iraqi nationalist and progressive forces, including

[255] Kâmil al-Châdirchî, *Mudhakkarât Kâmil al-Châdirchî wa Târîkh al-Ḥizb al-Waṭanî al-Dîmuqrâṭi* (Beirut: Dar al-Ṭalîᶜah, 1970), p. 676; and Laith ᶜAbd-ul-Ḥasan al-Zubaidî, *Thawrat 14 Tammûz 1958 fî al-ᶜIrâq* (Baghdad: Ministry of Culture, Rashîd Publishing House, 1979), p. 100.

[256] ᶜAzîz al-Shaikh, *Jabhat al-Ittiḥâd al-Waṭanî wa al-Mahâm al-Târîkhiyyah al-Mulqât ᶜAlâ ᶜÂtiqihâ fî al-Ẓarf al-Râhin* (Baghdad: al-Nûr Bookshop, 1959), p. 12.

[257] Reproduced in Yûsuf and Khâlid, *Salâm ᶜÂdil*, pp. 339–389.

[258] Ibid., p. 341.

[259] Ibid., p. 345.

the communists, and, as a result, organizational issues like the Party's conflict with the KDP became secondary.

The major cities in Iraq responded fully to the call to strike, and with teachers and students at the forefront, confrontations with the police ensued. *Ittiḥâd al-Shaᶜb* declared in September 1956 that "the success of the strike proved that national unity is the only means to abort imperialists and their agents' plots." With the Israeli, French, and British Tripartite aggression against Egypt in November 1956, there was an upsurge in public activity and protest throughout Iraq, with large masses of people taking to the streets spontaneously and demonstrating in support of Egypt. Unrest spread out from Baghdad in a ripple effect and quickly engulfed the entire country. From the northern cities of Mosul, Irbil, and Sulaimaniyah to the southern cities of Basra and Najaf the demonstrators confronted the government. In al-Hayy, 225 kilometres southeast of Baghdad, a full-blown armed confrontation against the government materialized. The ICP played a leading role in this confrontation, and as a result, the Party leadership in al-Hayy was arrested and eventually executed. At the same time, Baghdad was seething with discontent, and student demonstrators filled the streets. Martial law was declared, schools and universities were closed, and sixty professors and two college deans were removed from their posts and arrested. The head of the Chamber of Commerce was also detained, and numerous personages were imprisoned, including the chairmen of the banned nationalist and leftist political parties and organizations. The most severe prison sentence, three years in jail, was reserved for Kâmil al-Châdirchî, the chairman of the NDP. This situation demanded improved coordination among the leader of the Iraqi opposition political scene. From the first day of the Tripartite aggression, the four nationalist and progressive parties – the Baᶜth, the ICP, the *al-Istiqlâl*, and the NDP, along with independent nationalist personalities – sought to initiate a more coordinated and structured opposition effort, resulting in the formation of an ad hoc frontline leadership group to direct all spontaneous popular activities.[260]

On 1 May 1957, the Party published a special report written by ᶜÂdil on behalf of the Politburo. This report, "The Uprising of 1956 and Our Responsibilities in the Current Conditions,"[261] was basically the result of the deliberations at the Central Committee meeting in February evaluating the Party's involvement in the events of 1956. It lamented the fact that the uprising would have brought more positive results if the national forces had been able to unite more aggressively and better coordinate their activities, and if they had been integrated within a formal national front. As a first step towards that end, the report attempted to bridge the gap between communist and nationalist forces through an unequivocal recognition of the connection between Arab nationalism and Iraqi liberation. Indeed, the ICP's failure to see the relationship between the two had been the basic reason for the rift between the communists and

260 Al-Shaikh, *Jabhat al-Ittiḥad al-Waṭanî wa al-Mahâm al-Târîkhiyyah al-Mulqât ᶜAlâ ᶜÂtiqihâ fî al-Ẓarf al-Râhin*, p. 12.

261 Reproduced in Yûsuf and Khâlid, *Salâm ᶜÂdil*, pp. 391–451.

nationalists over the past decade. Furthermore, the Party accepted the special position of Nasser in the forefront of the Arab struggle against imperialism, acknowledging

> his heroic role in combating colonialism and its allies, and his leadership of the Arab liberation sovereignty [movement]. For the first time in centuries, the Arab liberation movement appeared to have a degree of vitality, power and unity of direction. For the sake of expelling imperialism from the Arab world, and for the sake of defending [it] against imperialist aggression and conspiracies, the united Arab countries resorted to Arab defence alliances, [and] cultural, economic, and political pacts, in addition to holding conferences to unify their political positions and coordinate their efforts . . . to liberate the Arab world and unify the Arab nation."[262]

The report emphasized the "organic" connection between the Iraqi national movement, the "Arab liberation" and "unity" movements the special role of Egypt, and "the personification of Arab liberation aims [in Egypt] where the main material and organic power resides. . . . The main content of the [1956] uprising is the amalgamation of the policy of Arab liberation led by big sister Egypt, as the only historic route to liberate the Iraqi people."[263] The report went on to say that the events of 1956 took place within

> . . . a decisive battle between the Arab nations and their allies and imperialism. The battle took place in local Arab and international circumstances that forced the Iraqi people to confront the need for a fundamental struggle to transform [Iraqi politics] . . . The latest peoples' uprising [1956] carried with it significant and comprehensive objectives for liberation, and clashed with the imperial policy in historic conditions, as any retreat [by the imperialists] in the face of the overwhelming power of the Arab Liberation movement would lead inevitably to deaths, disasters, and ultimately, a debacle for imperialism.[264]

The analysis continued, emphasizing the crucial strategic position of Iraq in the regional and international milieu for both the colonialist and the nationalist camps. The report noted that Iraq was the only country incorporated into the Western alliances, and the only country still associated with colonial power through its membership in the Baghdad Pact. In addition, Iraq was strategically positioned "close to the Soviet Union" and could be "transformed into a base to attack the Soviet Union."[265] Thus, according to the report, the Iraqi national movement was key in the battle against imperialism in the Arab world. But because it was led mainly by students, the intelligentsia, and professionals, the Iraqi national movement did not attract the participation of the majority of

> decisive forces of peasants and workers. In addition, it did not attract the Kurdish masses. If these forces had entered the struggle, the balance would have tipped in favour of the national movement. . . . While the students and the intelligentsia are not the main forces in the country, their comparatively small forces will not be able to resolve the question

[262] Ibid., p. 396.
[263] Ibid., p. 400.
[264] Ibid., pp. 402, 403.
[265] Ibid., p. 404.

of national liberation, no matter how passionate, committed, and courageous they may be. The main forces that can truly prevail and carry that great task are that force made up of millions of peasants and workers.... We know that the uprising did not attract enough peasants and workers to its ranks. Thus, there is no doubt that it would have been impossible for the forces that did participate in the uprising ... to settle the problem of national liberation and direct the country toward the path of Arab liberation.[266]

The report outlined the reasons for this failure to attract the masses of workers and peasants as

neglect by the Party of both the problems of the peasants and workers, as well as the need to actively organize among these masses. As such, we need to enlarge our Party base among the peasants and workers, and create national labour organizations. For that we are in need of larger numbers of [cadre] who will propagate [the Party's ideas] and carry our voice, slogans, and path to the thousands of workers and peasants.

The Party saw this as the most important lesson to be learned from the uprising. On Kurdish non-involvement, the report pointed out that the Arab liberation movement concentrated on Arab issues and paid less attention to the issues pertaining to other national minorities living in the Arab world.[267] The report also admitted that "the uprising of 1956 could have had much more positive results on the Iraqi scene if the national forces, including the communists, had been prepared to lead and unify all the opposition forces, and to mobilize the masses."[268] It reiterated the need for the Party to "reconsider its present policy regarding the national front ... and follow a more positive stance toward the fraternal national forces, as this [front] is the only path that will [lead] us to success in the battle of liberation from imperialism."[269]

In the meantime, the report noted, some important positive consequences did emerge from the uprising, strengthening "[the] feeling of solidarity and unity of destiny among the Iraqi people and the rest of the Arab world." In addition, the demonstrations had preoccupied the Nûrî al-Saᶜîd regime for three months, thus restraining it from further aggression against other Arab countries, and had shown the world that the regime's policies had no popular support. Furthermore, the uprising had a very salutary effect in awakening public understanding of the nature of the Baghdad Pact and of the treaty's potentially calamitous impact on the "national interest and on the Arab liberation movement." The report also pointed out that "one of the most important effects of the uprising was the realization of the need to coordinate all national forces and the masses ... and [to] prepare by being unified for the coming battle."[270] In delineating the current aims of the national movement, the report called for safeguarding the unity of the movement and for improving the movement's level of preparedness. It also asserted the need to incorporate within the movement

[266] Ibid., pp. 407–408.
[267] Ibid., pp. 408–416.
[268] Ibid., pp. 416–418.
[269] Ibid., p. 429.
[270] Ibid., pp. 438–439.

all "Party and non-party forces" by a sustained effort to win over all the independent groups and personalities, including the masses, despite their ideological differences, and to include them in one unified front.[271] Thus, the report put the Party on the path to a national front that would mobilize all opposition forces and called on the Party to direct its energies towards that end, as well as to put into action the resolutions of the Second Party Conference, which were made imperative by the turmoil that occurred during the Suez crisis a few short weeks after the conference ended.

[271] Ibid., pp. 447–448.

2

Ascent of the ICP in Iraqi Politics

The Tripartite aggression of 20 October 1956 against Egypt polarized politics in the entire Middle East region, including Iraq, with national fervor turning into popular political opposition to the West and its Arab allies. Public outrage in Iraq and the demonstrations that followed brought the major opposition parties closer together, and a committee representing the Baᶜth, *Istiqlâl*, NDP, and ICP, and including some independent democratic personalities, was created to coordinate their activities. They formed a special Field Committee to direct the daily demonstrations that were taking place. However, the members of this committee were almost immediately arrested, forcing the Party representatives to take over the tasks themselves. In addition to forming the sub-committee, they established the Supreme Student Committee to direct and mobilize students, who in fact formed the backbone of the protests and who represented the parties. A representative of the KDP was added to this student committee, although the KDP was not officially part of the initial sub-committee.[1]

In response to these developments, Nûrî al-Saᶜîd's defiance of the opposition intensified and his oppression increased, particularly of the communists and their sympathizers. This spurred closer cooperation among many of the opposition groupings, and by early 1957 the opposition's solidarity had become a pre-condition for their survival. With some effort, an alliance structure began to take shape, and in February 1957 an umbrella organization, the United National Front, was born. Recalling these events three years later, Kâmil al-Châdirchî, the leader of the NDP, explained the creation of the Front as resulting from

> the struggle between the national movement on one side, and on the other imperialism and its ruling allies . . . the idea of forming a national united front materialized to unify the efforts and coordinate actions in order to achieve the national aspirations directed

1 ᶜAzîz al-Shaikh, *Jabhat al-Ittiḥâd al-Waṭanî wa al-Mahâm al-Târîkhiyyah al-Mulqât ᶜAlâ ᶜÂtiqihâ fî al-Ẓarf al-Râhin* (Baghdad: al-Nûr Bookshop, 1959), p. 12; and Hânî al-Fakaikî, *Awkâr al-Hazîmah: Tajrubatî fî Ḥizb al-Baᶜth al-ᶜIrâqî* (London: Riad el-Rayyes Book Limited, 1993), p. 75.

at combating imperialism and its aggressive designs, such as the Baghdad Pact and foreign military bases... [The United National Front] called for the unification of all anti-imperialist forces who rejected the Baghdad Pact, supported the policy of non-alignment, and adhered to a progressive Arab policy.[2]

Ibrâhîm Kubbah, an independent Marxist and University of Baghdad professor of economics, who later oversaw the Economics and Agrarian Reform portfolios in the early period of the Qâsim regime following the 1958 coup, drafted the first formal declaration of the Front. The Front leadership approved Kubbah's draft with no changes.[3] Printed on a press provided by the Communist Party,[4] and highlighting the priorities of the nationalist movement, the declaration to the Iraqi people focused on Arab and international issues in the preface and then moved on to pressing Iraqi problems:

The international situation is characterized by an intensification of the conflict between the imperial states on one side and the forces of national struggle on the other. As a result, the national struggle took new forms after the balance of power within the imperial camp shifted [in favour of the nationalist forces] after the failure of the treacherous and insane aggression against sister Egypt, [resulting] in the cracking of the imperialist edifice, the exposure of the reality of imperialist pacts and alliances, and the ignominious role played by the members of the Baghdad Pact, (especially Turkey and Iraq) in that imperialist aggression. It was inevitable that imperialists would attempt to see the growth of Arab nationalism, the emergence of the liberated Arab bloc, and the crystallization of national consciousness among the Arab people as the greatest threat[s] to their interests.[5]

The Front identified its most urgent internal short-range goals to be (1) the dissolution of Nûrî al-Saᶜîd's government and its parliament as a first step towards the inauguration of an independent nationalist policy; (2) Iraq's withdrawal from the Baghdad Pact and the integration of Iraq's policies with those of the liberated Arab states; (3) rejection of imperialist interference in Iraqi affairs and the adoption of an independent Arab policy based on positive neutralism; (4) the granting of democratic and constitutional freedoms; and (5) the abolition of martial law, the freeing of all political prisoners, and the reinstatement of students, workers, and government employees expelled for engaging in political activities.[6]

The Front became increasingly defiant after its initial declaration, and intensified its challenge to the Nûrî al-Saᶜîd government by issuing public pronouncements elaborating on the basic principles of the draft declaration, and addressing Iraqi and Arab issues as they arose. "A Declaration on the Anniversary of the Aggression against Egypt," issued on 29 October 1957, vehemently attacked France, Britain, Israel, and the United States, and their allies in the Arab world,

[2] Al-Châdirchî, *Mudhakkarât Kâmil al-Châdirchî wa Târîkh al-Ḥizb al-Waṭanî al-Dîmuqrâṭî* (Beirut: Dâr al-Ṭalîᶜah, 1970), p. 676.

[3] Ibrâhîm Kubbah, *Hadha Huwa Ṭarîq 14 Tammûz* (Beirut: Dâr al-Ṭalîᶜah, 1969), p. 13.

[4] *Ittiḥâd al-Shaᶜb* (Baghdad, 17 July 1960).

[5] Kubbah, *Hadha Huwa Ṭarîq 14 Tammûz*, pp. 229–230.

[6] Ibid., pp. 231–237.

and saluted the Egyptian people and Nasser's leadership. On 14 November 1957 the Front issued another bold declaration, "Arab Unity: The Greatest Hope of the Arabs," in which it hailed the creation of the United Arab Republic and announced that "the United National Front expresses, in the name of the Iraqi people, its great pleasure in the union between Egypt and Syria as a nucleus of Arab unity. The Front affirms its strong determination to liberate Iraq and join the march of Arabism and liberation."

To increase its grassroots support outside the capital while affirming its presence throughout the country – as it had been unable to do in the past – the Front created a more formal structure, the Supreme National Committee, located in Baghdad. This committee became the political leadership of the Front, with representatives from all member parties, including the ICP. So that they could be binding on all member political parties, it was agreed that the committee's decisions had to be unanimous. The basic task of the Supreme National Committee, which met weekly and also on an ad hoc basis when the need arose, was to plan, coordinate, and act on behalf of all opposition groups. In addition, a Supreme Executive Committee, in which all political parties and independents were represented, was established to take charge of administrative matters and to implement decisions taken by the Supreme National Committee;[7] committee branches were soon established in the major cities of Iraq.

The ICP mobilized all its organizations in support of the Front, especially the communist-sponsored General Union of Students, Union of Democratic Youth, and League for the Defence of Iraqi Women's Rights. The Party newspaper, *Ittiḥâd al-Shaᶜb* considered

> the creation and proliferation of national committees [of the National Front] to all parts of the country to be the main goal that we should focus our efforts on at this particular juncture, for without this, the unity of the national forces would remain [only] in the Supreme Executive Committee, and [the Front] would move only in a limited circle in terms of its activities and impact on current political events.[8]

The paper encouraged Party members to propagate the message of the Front and generate public support. A few weeks later, on 8 August 1957, an internal Party circular advised the cadre that the new government of ᶜAlî Jawdat al-Aiyyûbî, which had replaced Nûrî al-Saᶜîd's government in June, was merely continuing the policies of the previous government. The circular called upon them to mobilize the masses to challenge the government to "retreat," and so to achieve the "demands" of the people. The circular also emphasized that the Baghdad Pact should be rejected, as well as the Eisenhower doctrine, which provided for economic and military aid, or even direct U.S. intervention, to protect any Middle Eastern nation willing to acknowledge the threat posed

[7] Al-Shaikh, *Jabhat al-Ittiḥâd al-Waṭanî wa al-Mahâm al-Târîkhiyyah al-Mulqât ᶜAlâ ᶜÂtiqihâ fî al-Ẓarf al-Râhin*, pp. 25–27; see also Fâḍil Ḥusain, *Târîkh al-Ḥizb al-Waṭanî al-Dîmuqrâṭî, 1946–1958* (Baghdad: al-Shaᶜb Press, 1963), pp. 391–392.

[8] *Ittiḥâd al-Shaᶜb* (beginning of June 1957).

by international communism. The doctrine was also intended to contain Arab nationalism.

About a year later, the worsening state of the conditions of the peasants in the south of the country became a central issue in galvanizing their opposition to the government and moved the clandestine Peasants' Association of the Party to action. In late June 1957, the association led an armed uprising of the peasantry in the Diwaniyah district. They hoped that the uprising would spread to the rest of the Middle Euphrates region and that it would be the catalyst for an urban revolt that would bring the army into the popular movement and would ultimately lead to a mass revolution. The Party informed the Supreme Executive Committee of its intentions and solicited its support, which was given.[9] By the end of June, the Diwaniyah uprising had become a serious issue for the government. The need for military forces in Diwaniyah prevented the army's First Division (which was based in Diwaniyah) from giving aid to the Royal government in Baghdad when it was needed on the first day of the Qâsim coup two weeks later.

Politicization of the Army and the Qâsim Coup

Like other parts of the society, the Iraqi army was affected by events in Iraq, and as early as 19 September 1952, less than two months after the Egyptian army's coup, a small number of Iraqi officer cliques began to form in different army branches; these groups were structured on the "Free Officer" model, but had no communication with one another. With both the turmoil in Iraqi politics and the increase of Nûrî al-Saᶜîd's oppression, however, these cliques became more politicized and their numbers grew. Gradually, the army groups and the opposition political parties began to communicate with each other, and with the Tripartite aggression of 29 October 1956 against Egypt, the military cells began to consolidate their structures. At the end of 1956 they formed the Supreme Officers' Committee, unifying the leadership of all these cells into a well-integrated and structured organization under Brigadier-General ᶜAbd-ul-Karîm Qâsim. The ICP instructed its military organizations to unite with the Qâsim group in early 1958.[10]

Both historians and participants in the army officers' movement attribute the unification of the leadership of the cliques to the earlier formation of the United National Front.[11] Parallel organizational structures came to exist, one clandestinely in the army and the other in the civilian sphere, which, though not legal, operated openly. Because of their mutual fear of government oppression, the two groups moved cautiously in opening communications. Theoretically,

[9] Ibid. (end of June 1958). See also ICP circulars dated 6 June 1958 and 3 July 1958.

[10] Thamînah Nâjî Yûsuf and Nazâr Khâlid, *Salâm ᶜÂdil: Sîrat Munâḍil*, 2 vols. (Cyprus: al-Mada Publishing Company, 2001), vol. 1, pp. 220–221.

[11] For an excellent history and structure of the army officers' group, see Laith ᶜAbd-ul-Ḥasan al-Zubaidî, *Thawrat 14 Tammûz 1958 fî al-ᶜIrâq*, pp. 115–158; and item, *Al-Dhâkirah al-Târîkhiyyah liThawrat 14 Tammûz, 1958* (Baghdad: Âfâq ᶜArabiyyah, 1987).

all communications of the United National Front had to go through the Secretariat of the Supreme Officers' Committee; however, communications between individual members of the officers' committee and opposition political parties continued. Through a childhood friend, Rashîd Muṭlaq, ᶜAbd-ul-Karîm Qâsim maintained minimal contact with both the NDP and the ICP. The ICP, in turn, communicated informally with the USSR, while other nationalist members of the Supreme Officers' Committee kept in touch with *al-Istiqlâl* and, through it, with the Egyptian Free Officers and Nasser.[12]

According to ᶜÂmir ᶜAbd-ul-lah, then a member of the Central Committee, Qâsim's contact Rashîd Muṭlaq, who was also ᶜAbd-ul-lah's friend, confided to him in the summer of 1956 that Qâsim was planning a coup, and wanted "the Communist Party's cooperation only in 'public mobilization and consultation.'" The secretary-general, Salâm ᶜÂdil, gave his approval, and on 10 September 1956, immediately after the conclusion of the Second Conference, the Central Committee was for the first time informed of the Party's involvement with the impending military coup. Qâsim's main fear was focused on the possibility of outside interference. Because Iraq was a member of the Baghdad Pact, Qâsim expected that the United States, Britain, and Turkey would become involved, and therefore he wanted the Soviet Union to pledge its support for the impending coup.[13] In the meantime, *Ittiḥâd al-Shaᶜb* assessed America's future policy in the region, which would be based on the pretence of combating communism and implementing the Eisenhower doctrine but was in essence no different from the goals of the Baghdad Pact.[14]

Thus, ᶜÂmir ᶜAbd-ul-lah became the link between the Party and the conspirators, and as a result, he was sent by the Party's secretary-general as an envoy to the Syrian-Lebanese Communist Party (which had been acting as the ICP's mentor and guardian, and was the only regional party to have close contact with the ICP). In early 1957, ᶜAbd-ul-lah met Syrian party boss Khâlid Bakdâsh, who at that time was the most trusted and senior communist leader in the region. It was hoped that Bakdâsh's close ties to the CPSU could be utilized to secure Moscow's blessing for and help with Qâsim's impending coup.[15] In an interview with the author in Damascus on 10 October 1974, Bakdâsh recalled his first impressions of ᶜAbd-ul-lah: "He was smooth, very pleasant, careful, handsomely dressed, chose his words to please his audience, showed a very sophisticated understanding of Marxism, and had read most of my writings. I have not known too many Iraqis [who were] as committed and articulate communist leaders as he was." Soon after they met, Bakdâsh invited ᶜAbd-ul-lah to attend a Peace Partisans meeting in Colombo, Ceylon. There ᶜAbd-ul-lah met Zhou Enlai, the Chinese premier, who expressed no interest in becoming

[12] al-Zubaidî, *Thawrat 14 Tammûz 1958 fî al-ᶜIrâq*, pp. 69–146; see also Zakî Khairî and Suᶜâd Khairî, *Dirâsât fî Târîkh al-Ḥizb al-Shiyûᶜî al-ᶜIrâqî*, vol. 1 (n.p., 1984), p. 262.

[13] Interview by author with ᶜÂmir ᶜAbd-ul-lah, London (18 January 1998).

[14] *Ittiḥâd al-Shaᶜb* (February 1957).

[15] Yûsuf and Khâlid, *Salâm ᶜÂdil*, vol. 1, p. 210.

involved in the impending coup, explaining, "China is a far off country and cannot do anything for you."[16] With that, the first humble contact between the Iraqi Communist Party and the international communist movement was initiated, with ᶜAbd-ul-lah as the link. This gave him the chance to become the ICP spokesperson, and to liaise with the CPSU leadership, espouse the impending coup, and convince the Soviets that Qâsim was a serious leader whose base in the Iraqi armed forces was not negligible. In October 1956, ᶜÂmir ᶜAbd-ul-lah was invited to Moscow to attend the First Conference of International Communist Parties, where he was introduced by Bakdâsh to Farajallah al-Ḥilw, the charismatic leader of the Lebanese Communist Party; Fûʾâd Naṣṣar, the leader of the Jordanian Communist Party; and ᶜAbd-ul-Khâliq Maḥjûb, the popular leader of the Sudanese Communist Party, thereby cementing his relationships on the regional level.[17]

ᶜÂmir ᶜAbd-ul-lah was unable to obtain any commitment from the Soviets, or from any other communist country, for help with the coup. ᶜÂdil, however, was able to take advantage of his role as chairperson of the ICP's delegation to the Conference of Communist and Workers' Parties in November 1957 (on the occasion of the fortieth anniversary of the Russian revolution) and secure support from Soviet Premier Nikita Khrushchev. Travelling on to Beijing, he won the blessing of the Chinese leader Mao Tse Tung; he then went to East Germany (DDR), where he was given a warm reception. The DDR Communist Party, in a symbolic gesture of its support, presented him with the printing press it had used during its underground resistance to the Hitler regime, since the ICP's own press had just been confiscated by the Iraqi police. Stopping in Syria on his way home, ᶜÂdil had hoped for a meeting with Nasser but instead received moral support for the impending coup from Nasser's deputy, Kamâl Rifᶜat. ᶜÂdil returned to Baghdad in May 1958 and directed ᶜÂmir ᶜAbd-ul-lah to continue his efforts in Czechoslovakia and Bulgaria.[18] In June 1958, seventeen communist parties established the *World Marxist Review* in Prague as the theoretical and intellectual voice of the international communist movement; as a result of his widespread international contacts, ᶜÂmir ᶜAbd-ul-lah was chosen to represent the Iraqi Communist Party.

Events moved rapidly in the Middle East, widening the gulf between the Iraqi government and the opposition forces, and exacerbating the tense situation between them. When the creation of the United Arab Republic (UAR) was formalized on 4 February 1958, the union was seen by the West as a threat to regional stability since it divided the region into two opposing camps, one an anti-Western nationalist bloc led by Egypt's Nasser, and the other, a pro-Western bloc led by Baghdad Pact members, with Iraq being the principal Arab link. Ten days later, in response to the formation of the UAR, Iraq and Jordan formed the Hashemite Union. With the blessing of Britain, an attempt was initiated to

[16] Interview with ᶜÂmir ᶜAbd-ul-lah, *Abwah*, no. 2 (London, Autumn 1994), p. 82.
[17] Ibid., pp. 182–186.
[18] Ibid., pp. 210–216.

include Kuwait in this nascent conservative union, to cement the polarization of the Arab world.

Five months later, in July 1958, the Hashemite Arab Union sent Iraqi troops to nearby Jordan in response to a nationalist uprising in Lebanon and in support of Camille Chamoun's pro-Western government. Nominally, they were positioned there to help quell the uprising if their assistance was formally requested by the Lebanese government, but this manoeuvre was also intended to deter the agitation of Arab nationalists in Lebanon who were seeking a union with Syria in the UAR. The Iraqi army was mobilized, and Qâsim and other "free officers" were put in charge of the mission, which unintentionally provided them with the cover to execute their planned coup. Qâsim informed the United National Front, on 10 July 1958, of his group's imminent action. He also informed the ICP and the NDP – who backed the action despite Châdirchî's reservations – while ᶜÂrif conveyed the information to the Baᶜth Party.[19]

Because of its contact with Qâsim on 12 July 1958, the ICP was able to issue a directive to all Party organizations hinting at an the impending coup, because of "critical political Arab and internal conditions and the possibility of the development of those conditions." It urged members to emphasize the slogans of the United National Front and stressed "the avoidance of extreme slogans that would glorify one leader or one political group, and an adherence to the basic principles of the United National Front."[20]

The exact time of the impending coup was known only to Qâsim and about a dozen other army officers, although the 250 Iraqi "free officers" were under orders from the Supreme Officers' Committee to be ready to act on short notice. Two infantry brigades, the Nineteenth and the Twentieth, moved through Baghdad on their way to Jordan in the early morning of 14 July 1958. Qâsim commanded the Nineteenth Brigade while two of the three regimental commanders, Colonels ᶜAbd-ul-Salâm ᶜÂrif and ᶜAbd-ul-laṭîf al-Darrâjî, who were Qâsim's most trusted co-conspirators, took command of the Twentieth Brigade. This was the advance unit of the troops to be sent to Jordan, while Qâsim's Nineteenth Brigade was to be the supporting unit. ᶜÂrif and Darrâjî, in command of the Twentieth Brigade, invited all those who did not already belong to the Free Officers' Movement to join them. They then moved to occupy all the most important government buildings in the capital, including the Central Military Headquarters, as well as radio and television stations throughout Baghdad. With this accomplished, they surrounded the palace and hunted for Nûrî al-Saᶜîd. At 6:30 AM the coup leaders issued their first Proclamation. Signed by Qâsim – who had taken the title commander-in-chief of the national armed forces – it declared Iraq to be a republic. In fewer than three hours, the army had the country under its control, and many in the royal family had been assassinated. A day later, Nûrî al-Saᶜîd was captured and killed.

[19] Al-Zubaidî, *al-Dhâkirah al-Târîkhiyyah li Thawrat 14 Tammûz, 1958*, pp. 82, 83.

[20] ICP pamphlet entitled *Naḥwa Ṣiyânat Muktasabât Thawratunâ wa Musânadat Jumhûriyyatunâ al-ᶜIrâqiyyah* [Toward Protecting Gains of Our Revolution and the Support of Our Iraqi Republic] Baghdad (April 1959), p. 4.

Besides serving as the commander-in-chief of the armed forces, Qâsim headed a new cabinet as prime minister and also took the portfolio of minister of defence ᶜÂrif became deputy prime minister and minister of the interior. These two officers now held the most powerful positions in the Iraqi government. They then chose the other cabinet personnel. Colonel al-Darrâjî refused to accept any cabinet position but did play a role in the cabinet selection. The United National Front was assigned minor and technical cabinet positions; the NDP held two portfolios, Agriculture and Finance, assigned to Muḥammad Ḥadîd; the *Istiqlâl* held the portfolio of National Guidance; and the Baᶜth was assigned the Ministry of Development; the rest of the portfolios were distributed mainly through personal friendships and political connections.

Despite its central role in building the National Front – and its ability to secure recognition and support from the states of the international communist movement – the ICP was completely excluded from the Qâsim cabinet. Although Ibrâhîm Kubbah was assigned the portfolio of Economics before shifting to that of Agrarian Reform, no ICP members were invited. Indeed, many of their former Front colleagues quickly abandoned them.

A rubber stamp Sovereignty Council, made up of two retired senior army officers, one of whom was a Kurd and the other a Shiᶜite who headed the *Istiqlâl*, was created to approve cabinet decisions. For all practical purposes, the United National Front had come to an end, and the cabinet's only function was to provide advice to the new government. Ministers who were members of political parties were chosen on the basis of their personal capacities and not as party representatives. The fact that the Communist Party was not represented in the cabinet, and that the other members of the Front lodged no protest on the Party's behalf, signalled the ICP's complete ineffectiveness, if not its demise as a political force. According to Hesqal Kojaman:

> The announcement of the formation of the revolutionary government was, in fact, a proclamation of a bourgeois government terminating the role of the Front, and ending the [Front's] alliance with the ICP. . . . And since the ICP had already forfeited the right to participate openly in the revolutionary government, we cannot then blame the bourgeoisie for what it did. On 14 July 1958, the day of the revolution, Muḥammad Ḥadîd [Qâsim's minister of finance, then a member of the NDP], announced to the ICP member of the Front that the Front had already achieved its aims. A few days later, the Baᶜth, in its own way, announced the end of the Front and identified the ICP as the principal enemy of the revolution over and above imperialism, and threatened to "cut[off] any hand" that was extended to the ICP. Shortly after the revolution, other nationalist forces worked to form the League for the Defence of the Unity of the National Forces from the same elements of the United National Front, excluding the communists. . . . All these actions led to the conclusion that, to the bourgeoisie the Front . . . was not any longer a necessity . . . as the main aim of the bourgeoisie in collaboration with the communists was to take over the powers of the state.[21]

[21] Hesqal Kojaman, *Thawrat 14 Tammûz 1958 fî al-ᶜIrâq wa Siyâsat al-Ḥizb al-Shiyûᶜî* (London: n.p., 1985), p. 134.

When the Qâsim coup took place on the morning of 14 July 1958, ʿÂmir ʿAbd-ul-lah was in Damascus, acting as the spokesperson for the revolutionary government and contacting the Soviet ambassador and representatives of other socialist countries. Returning a few days later to Baghdad after the successful coup, he renewed his contact with his old friend and emerged as liaison between the ICP and Qâsim. By the time the rest of the Central Committee members were freed from prison, or had returned from exile, ʿAbd-ul-lah had achieved a special position, both within the Party and in relation to the new government, from which he was able to gain access to Qâsim at any time.[22] He also built a good relationship with Qâsim's chief bodyguard and confidant, Colonel Waṣfî Ṭâhir, whose cousin, Zakî Khairî, now freed from prison, was a member of the Central Committee and was working closely with ʿAbd-ul-lah. Thus, ʿAbd-ul-lah put himself in the spotlight. On the Party level, after years of oppression, Kojaman relates:

> I know for a fact that the Central Committee, in August 1958, received a detailed report [recommending] that the Party take advantage of the transformation which had taken place after the revolution and the release of [Party] political prisoners, and the return of communist cadres in exile, by holding a Second Party Congress which was to have two main goals. First, to study the mistakes that the Party had committed during the period that followed the execution of the three comrades [in 1949] in which the Party was directed by a succession of enthusiastic leaders who, under the circumstances, worked very hard to regroup the Party and raise its standards. However, by necessity this leadership was unfortunately limited in its intellectual capacity and in its practical experience. Second, to study the [nature] of the class alignment that emerged after the revolution and delineate the strategy for the new stage deriving from that.[23]

The Communists After the 14 July 1958 Revolution

Although aware of the impending coup attempt by the Free Officers, the ICP leadership was slow to react when it proved a success. They did not have any clear strategy for dealing with the new political conditions that emerged, and the leadership found itself responding to events as they arose rather than directing them. Their immediate aim came to be the "defence of the Republic," which translated into the defence of the military regime and its bourgeois leadership. Both the Popular Committees for the Defence of the Republic and a Popular Resistance Militia, supported by the ICP, were formed, and the clandestine Iraqi Union of Democratic Youth and League of Iraqi Women (until 7 March 1960 known as the League for the Defence of Iraqi Women's Rights) become openly active, propagating the revolution and devoting their energies to the media and to mobilizing the masses in support of the revolution. Moreover, soon after the coup, a conflict arose between Qâsim and his second-in-command,

[22] Hanna Batatu, *The Old Social Classes and Revolutionary Movements of Iraq* (Princeton, NJ: Princeton University Press, 1978), p. 719.

[23] Ibid.; see also Kojaman, *Thawrat 14 Tammûz 1958 fî al-ʿIrâq wa Siyâsat al-Ḥizb al-Shiyûʿî*, p. 94.

ᶜAbd-ul-Salâm ᶜÂrif, on the issue of Arab unity, that is, over possible unification with the UAR. The United National Front groupings, having already lost cohesion, split between the Arab nationalists supporting ᶜÂrif (who espoused immediate and unconditional unity with the UAR), and the left of the NDP and the communists supporting Qâsim (who favoured a looser unity in the form of a federal connection). The ICP publicly proclaimed its position, declaring on the day of the revolution that

> we, the communists who have the privilege to advocate the [creation] of the republic and had the honour of persevering with the rest of the nationalist forces... towards its achievements, promise the people... that we shall continue to struggle to preserve our Iraqi Republic... for the sake of an honourable, free, democratic life for the Iraqi people and for the sake of Arab unity, peace, and progress.[24]

A memorandum written on behalf of the Politburo by ᶜÂdil on the second day of the revolution offered the following recommendations to Qâsim and the leadership of the new republic in order to safeguard the revolution:

> First, there should be a clear and firm national policy, and this requires that Iraq immediately withdraw from the Baghdad Pact, the abandonment of the Anglo-Iraqi Treaty [of 1930], a declaration of federal unity with the UAR, a re-examination of Iraq's foreign relations on an independent basis, and an establishing of diplomatic relations with the Soviet Union and the socialist bloc.... secondly, the release of all political prisoners, the espousal of popular committees for the defence of the republic, and the immediate creation of an armed popular militia.... Thirdly, the imposition of firm and immediate control of [the foreign] companies, banks, ports, storage [facilities,] and major economic establishments for the purpose of protecting our revolution and our national economy.... Fourthly, the experience of the first day of the revolution showed the need to take rapid steps toward public guidance, especially by the radio stations, so as to guarantee [the republic's] true expression on the aims of the [revolutionary] movement and its national democratic content, and in order to avoid the creation of division within the ranks of the people.[25]

On 15 July, Iraq withdrew from the Hashemite Union and abrogated any obligations associated with it. On 16 July, the USSR recognized the new Iraqi Republic, and on 17 July, Iraq re-established formal relations with the Soviet Union. On 18 July, an Iraqi delegation headed by ᶜAbd-ul-Salâm ᶜÂrif, along with the ministers of finance, foreign affairs, and national guidance, flew to Damascus, where they met Egyptian President Nasser. An agreement of cooperation between the UAR and the new Iraqi Republic was signed, in which the UAR promised military support to Iraq in the event of any foreign aggression against the Republic, as well as economic and cultural assistance. The new government freed all political prisoners, voided the oppressive decrees of Nûrî al-Saᶜîd, declared its intention to withdraw from the Baghdad

[24] ICP pamphlet entitled *Fî Sabîl Ṣiyânat wa al-Ḥifâẓ ᶜAlâ Muktasabât al-Thawrah wa al-Ḥifâẓ ᶜAlâ Muktasabât al-Jumhûriyyah* [For the Sake of Protecting the Gains of the Revolution and Strengthening the Gains of the Republic] (September 1958).

[25] Ibid., See also Yûsuf and Khâlid, *Salâm ᶜÂdil*, vol. 1, pp. 230–233.

Pact – which it did a year later – and disassociated itself from other aspects of the monarchy's foreign policy. On 27 July, a provisional constitution was adopted in which the republican regime was legally constituted. Executive and legislative power rested in the Council of Ministers, though the relationship between the prime minister and his council was left vague. Since the prime minister appointed the cabinet and controlled the army, the roles of the two government organs became even more blurred. From its first day the cabinet was completely subservient to the prime minister, thus setting the direction of the new republic. This was seen to be particularly true when the Sovereignty Council, supposedly Iraq's highest body, was given no veto powers and was confined to a ceremonial role.

ᶜAzîz al-Ḥâjj described the political scene after his release from prison, immediately following the revolution:

> I found Baghdad, upon my release, in the most jumbled condition. Political parties were suddenly allowed to function . . . [and] began to propagate their views [in a chaotic manner]. Each one considered itself to be the vanguard [of the national movement]. The communists with their slogan: Without Fahd there would not have been ᶜAbd-ul-Karîm Qâsim . . . boasted about the amount of their suffering and torture . . . The nationalists, *Istiqlâl* and the Baᶜth parties responded by [uniting] to stop the communists.[26]

Inevitably, the two groups collided fiercely.

On the Party level, the situation was no different. Following his release from prison sometime at the end of July, Bahâʾu-d-Dîn Nûrî described the organizational disunity on his first meeting with the Politburo:

> [It was] a strange makeup for me as it was composed of Salâm ᶜÂdil, Jamâl al-Ḥaidarî, and ᶜÂmir ᶜAbd-ul-lah, who until my arrest five years earlier was no more than a supporter of the Party who was not organized in any Party cell and knew nothing of internal Party affairs. Jamâl al-Ḥaidarî had spearheaded the splinter group, *Râyat al-Shaghîlah*, until 1956.[27]

This confusion was also reflected in the Party leadership. In these tense and unusual conditions, the secretary-general, rather than going through normal Party channels, continued to make decisions as the need arose, without consultation and in the manner he had done over the past three years when he had been rebuilding the Party during the "underground years."

ᶜÂmir ᶜAbd-ul-lah returned to Baghdad four days after the revolution, confident of his own importance since he had been the representative for the revolution and the Party abroad for more than a year, and had also been the Party liaison with Qâsim, the leader of the new regime. He had built close personal relationships with the regional and international communist movement, becoming virtually the only link that the Party had to the outside world, whereas

26 ᶜAzîz al-Ḥâjj, *Dhâkirat al-Nakhîl* (Beirut: al-Muʾassasah al-ᶜArabiyyah lil Dirâsât wa al-Nashr, 1993), p. 169.

27 Bahâʾu-d-Dîn Nûrî, *Mudhakkarât Bahâʾu-d-Dîn Nûrî* (Sulaimaniyah, Kurdistan: n.p., 1992), p. 173.

ᶜÂdil had remained in official control of the Party. In effect, this created a de facto dual leadership. ᶜÂmir ᶜAbd-ul-lah – self-confident, sure of the secretary-general's style, and well aware of his own relationship with Qâsim and the rest of the coup leadership – resented ᶜÂdil's approach and began to question it, though mildly. He began to meet with the rest of the Party leadership, communicating what he presented as the "advice" of regional communist leaders such as Khâlid Bakdâsh, the Syrian Party boss; Fûʾâd Naṣṣar, the secretary-general of the Jordanian Party; and Nicola Shâwî of the Lebanese Communist Party. This advice was to "Soft pedal your ideas, rather than confronting them, as they are military men, and we, as communists, should learn from the Egyptian experience after the 1952 Nasser coup, especially when the ICP has a sympathetic understanding with the coup leadership."[28]

Nevertheless, as early as the second day of the coup, the secretary-general was advocating that the ICP continue to pressure the regime to implement basic democratic reforms, such as freedom of assembly and organization, that ᶜÂdil had advocated in his Party memorandum to Qâsim on 15 July. ᶜÂdil, disappointed that the Party was the only member of the National Front not represented in the government, sought to influence the military regime through popular demands, which he termed "the tactic of pressure from below."

The discontent between the two leaders eventually surfaced when the Central Committee met on 29 July to deal with the issue of influencing the regime. The Central Committee endorsed ᶜÂdil's approach, with the caveat that the grassroots cadre be instructed on the implications and importance of the Party's approach. One of the first attempts to do this was in a conference with the Baghdad section, the most important section of the ICP, in early August 1958. The secretary-general opened the Baghdad Section Conference and outlined the class nature of the regime, which he described as

> a national bourgeois, anti-imperialist regime, representing the interests of the bourgeoisie. . . . The composition of the revolutionary government does not represent all the national forces, and here lies the contradiction between the core revolutionary forces (workers, peasants, petit bourgeoisie, and national bourgeoisie) and groups which took over power after the revolution, representing the interests of the petit bourgeoisie and the middle class only. This is the foundation for the creation and widening of the conflicts within the national movement and its parties.

ᶜÂdil also analyzed the leadership of the regime, calling Qâsim

> progressive, and leftist, and having some understanding and an elementary grasp of democracy, and who can be influenced to sharpen these tendencies. . . . As for ᶜAbd-ul-Salâm ᶜÂrif, he is anti-communist, has no connection with any progressive circles, and is impetuous, rash, and self-centred to an extreme degree. Our information about when he joined the Supreme Committee of the Free Officers is that he was the worst of them.[29]

[28] Interview by author with ᶜÂmir ᶜAbd-ul-lah, London (19 January 1993).
[29] Yûsuf and Khâlid, *Salâm ᶜÂdil*, vol. 1, pp. 246–247.

ʿÂdil also explained that the government bureaucracy was anti-communist, and that the Party was not represented in the government. Consequently, in ʿÂdil's view, the primary responsibility of the Party was to work from below by pressuring the government to introduce democratic reforms, after which the regime could be forced to allow the right of assembly and organization. In this situation, the Party could mobilize the population into further influencing the government. Thus, "the main objective of the Party's internal life is the necessity to comprehend and deepen the understanding of Party policy by the cadre and membership, who should commit themselves fully to its implementation."[30] The secretary-general seems to have regained control over the Party as a result of its adopting this policy, but the power struggle between the two men continued to fester, gradually leading to the formation of two camps within the Party leadership.

At a Party Central Committee meeting on 2 September 1958 to deal with Party policy (particularly the Party's relationship to the new regime), the Central Committee called for a plenary session, which was held four days later, on 6 September. At this meeting a new Politburo, including the secretary-general, was formally elected. This was the largest such session in the Party's history, and the first after the September 1956 plenary session that followed the Second Party Conference. The secretary-general stated:

> This plenary meeting is held in the best internal conditions experienced by our Party . . . as its organizational Party network has extended to all parts of the country, and as such, its political influence has expanded. This meeting has brought back together all of its cadre by settling its schisms, those freed from jail, along with those who have returned from exile, as a consequence of the victorious revolution and the establishment of the heroic Iraqi Republic.[31]

The secretary-general identified the goals of the Party and the national movement at this time as the defence of the Republic and "the strengthening of its democratic anti-imperialist and anti-feudal direction," along with the institution of democratic freedoms (especially "the freedoms of organization and the press,"[32] respect for Kurdish national rights, and implementation of the clauses in the constitution related to cultural and administrative control). The Party also called for protection of the national economy; land reform; a closer watch over multinational companies, including oil and banking interests; and the encouragement of domestic investment and national industries.

In foreign policy, the Party's aim was to strengthen national independence through Iraq's withdrawal from the Baghdad Pact and its abrogation of the Iraqi-British agreements and of its 21 April 1954 military assistance understanding with the United States. It also called for closer cooperation with the "liberated" Arab countries, and a strengthening of the Arab League to "struggle"

30 Ibid., p. 249.
31 Ibid., p. 252.
32 Ibid., p. 257.

against imperialism and in support of Arab solidarity. It recommended that Iraq join the United Arab Republic, that there be closer cooperation with the Afro-Asian bloc, and that political, economic, and cultural relations with the Soviet Union, China, and other socialist camp countries be strengthened.[33] On the internal front, the Politburo stressed that its aim was to combat rightist deviationist views within the Party, and emphasized its impact on the Arab world:

> As the burgeoning influence of bourgeois nationalism has a "positive dimension" in the aspirations of the Arab peoples for Arab liberation from imperialism and towards "national unity" . . . it also has a "negative side" in that it spreads bourgeois thoughts and creates objective conditions conducive to the development of nationalist, rightist, deviationist thoughts that penetrate the working-class movement and will "feed" the rightist currents in that movement.[34]

The secretary-general's report explained why this phenomenon was much more acute in Iraq, as well as why it would result in a negative reaction from the Kurds who would feel threatened and excluded from the majority Arab population, thus feeding Kurdish the separatist movement. It also called for a widening of the Party's grassroots base, particularly among peasants and workers, by recruiting carefully screened, committed cadres from these groups. It reiterated the need for internal Party discipline: "[The] complete adherence to Party policies, aims and principles is the only condition that will secure success in implementing Party strategies and achiev[ing] our people's goals."[35]

The conference discussed and unanimously approved the secretary-general's report. It gave the secretary-general its unconditional support and affirmed his leadership of the Party; at the same time, it silenced the voices of dissent, at least temporarily. Limited though they were, dissident views were represented mainly by ᶜÂmir ᶜAbd-ul-lah, who disagreed with the secretary-general on tactics and personal style, though not on Party policies. Nevertheless, the seeds of disagreement had been sown, and they would develop within a few months into a full-fledged conflict between the two men, splitting the Politburo and Central Committee in an open struggle for control of the Party.

With the public's support and sympathy, the communists began to openly organize themselves, although this activity was mixed with a certain opportunism, as people saw the new revolutionary government as leftist oriented and to some degree communist influenced. This was particularly evident since the communists were the only group to staff the recently licensed newspapers and journals, and government-run radio and television, and to propagate the new revolutionary vision.

In the meantime, labour and peasant organizations began to spring up, and although they were tolerated, they were not yet formally sanctioned. The ICP

[33] Ibid., pp. 257–258.
[34] Ibid., p. 260.
[35] Ibid., p. 262.

had its own already-functioning clandestine organizational structures, which now came to the surface, visibly filling the organizational vacuum. The executive committee for the workers' unions began its activities under the leadership of a well-respected communist leader, ʿAlî Shukr, and the Union of Peasant Associations also began to operate openly under the nominal leadership of a leftist NDP figurehead and petit landowner, ʿArrâk al-Zigam. The majority of the peasant union's membership had in fact been organized in the 1950s by the ICP under the auspices of the "Friends of the Peasant" associations. Meanwhile, the legal professional organizations of teachers, lawyers, journalists, doctors, and engineers were controlled by the left in general, including both the ICP and its unpredictable ally, the NDP. The General Union of Iraqi Students, the Union of Democratic Youth, and the League of Iraqi Women, all communist-front organizations, were now also formally licensed. The Partisans of Peace also functioned openly and freely under the leadership of ʿAzîz Sharîf, as did the communist-sponsored Committee for the Protection of the Revolution, which penetrated government offices.[36]

In these circumstances, and perhaps in response to the ICR's popularity, a rift opened between the members of the United National Front (particularly *al-Istiqlâl* and the Baʿth, as well as a large number of NDP members) and the communists. These groups feared the control the ICP held over the masses as a result of public misconceptions and sympathy. The communists, disappointed by the new leadership, increasingly became aware of the strength of their own popular support. In the Party's first plenary session on 6 September 1958, the members condemned exclusion of the ICP from the government as a desertion of the masses: "[Since] the government, which emerged after the revolution... is one of a national revolutionary bourgeoisie, but does not represent all the national forces, here lies the contradiction between the leading forces of the national movement [and the coup government]."[37] The rift between the communist movement and the other nationalist forces widened, reaching its climax over unity with the UAR. The leftists and communists insisted on a federation, with democratic processes being allowed to determine the road to unity, whereas the nationalists sought an unconditional, complete, and immediate merger. Gradually, this issue evolved into a conflict between Qâsim, who came to personify the Iraqi left, and ʿÂrif, who now represented the Pan-Arab nationalists;

The nationalist movement was now divided into two polarized camps. ʿAbd-ul-Salâm ʿÂrif advocated the slogan of "immediate unity" with the UAR, supported by the national and populist groups, as well as some military officers. In the other camp, Qâsim was supported by the ICP, [some] of the NDP, and the Kurdish movement who were against the immediate merger and feared being further marginalized in a larger Arab Union. Qâsim's main strategy was to play the game of balancing political forces

[36] Ṣalâḥ al-Kharsân, *Ṣafaḥât min Târîkh al-Ḥarakah al-Shiyûʿiyyah fî al-ʿIrâq* (Beirut: Dâr al-Furât, 1993), pp. 87–88.

[37] Khairî and Khairî, *Dirâsât fî Târîkh al-Ḥizb al-Shiyûʿî al-ʿIrâqî*, pp. 270–272.

and neutralizing each of them in order to strengthen his authority and transform the revolution into a military dictatorship with a narrow personal orientation.[38]

According to Zakî Khairî, three weeks after the revolution the ICP, in a direct challenge to ʿÂrif, threw its weight behind Qâsim and organized public demonstrations

> with the tacit backing of General Qâsim, who was in great need of public support in his opposition [to the nationalist] call for an immediate merger, which [he viewed as stripping him] of all his powers.... The Party prepared slogans and utilized government radio and television to call upon the people to join the demonstrations.[39]

Fearing that a split within the national movement would lead to conflict, Kâmil al-Châdirchî, the head of the NDP, flew to Cairo at the end of September 1958 and tried to convince Nasser to limit his advocacy for an immediate union with the UAR. He also called on Nasser to persuade the Iraqi nationalists and ʿÂrif to defuse the crisis between them and Qâsim, which might, if it continued, result in the demise of the concept of Iraqi unity altogether. Nasser refused to become involved in this internal issue, declaring, "Unify your country. Do not get entangled in a civil war, and I, no matter what, will not advise you to unite or confederate."[40] The crisis reached its peak when the pro-unification nationalists resigned en masse from the government on 5–6 February 1959.

The ICP had reached the height of its influence on the Qâsim government. On 25 January 1959, even while the Party was still illegal, *Ittiḥâd al-Shaʿb* was licensed, thereby giving the ICP a public voice. In its very first editorial, the paper declared itself to be "the voice of 'the toiling masses,' and the brave vanguard of the Iraqi people." The July coup had been a deep expression of the people's wish and a logical result of the revolutionary struggle "whose fire was lit by the daring son of the people, Qâsim and his brave fellow officers." The paper described the current situation in Iraq as the "stage of revolutionary, political, and economic struggle for liberation from colonial control and feudalism."[41] *Ittiḥâd al-Shaʿb* became the most widely read Iraqi daily, with its offices becoming, in effect, the headquarters of the Party's Central Committee. Although ʿAbd-ul-Qâdir Ismâʿîl al-Bustânî was the paper's official editor, ʿÂmir ʿAbd-ul-lah was its true political editor, aided by Bahâʾu-d-Dîn Nûrî and, in June, by Zakî Khairî. However, Salâm ʿÂdil remained the real power behind the newspaper, and all of its editorials, which reflected Party policy, "were either written [by him] or [had] their central ideas dictated by him."[42] Commenting on 9 February 1959 on the mass resignations by the pro-unionist government members, *Ittiḥâd al-Shaʿb* stated:

38 Al-Ḥâjj, *Dhâkirat al-Nakhîl*, p. 169.

39 Zakî Khairî, *Ṣadâ al-Sinîn fî Dhâkirat Shiyûʿî ʿIrâqî Mukhadram* (Göttenberg, Sweden: Arabiska Bokstavscentre, 1996), p. 190.

40 *Al-Ahram* (Cairo, 24 July 1959).

41 *Ittiḥâd al- Shaʿb* [Our Arab Stage of Today] (25 January 1959), p. 2.

42 Khairî, *Ṣadâ al-Sinîn fî Dhâkirat Shiyûʿî ʿIrâqî Mukhadram*, p. 215.

> As soon as the revolution took its first steps . . . the signs of regression against its march began to be evident among some of those in charge who had risen to power in the cabinet by the revolutionary [regime]. . . . [This regression] took the form of direct and indirect sympathy for an anti-republican [regime] in both foreign and domestic [spheres]. . . . In our opinion the latest cabinet shuffle is a positive action that will have great importance at this stage.

Qâsim, supported by the ICP, was suspicious of Nasser and his pan-Arab aspirations, and consequently he continued to encourage the ICP as a counterweight to the Baᶜth Party, the *Istiqlâl*, and other pan-Arab and nationalist groups in the country. With such encouragement, the ICP zealously set about confronting those Arab nationalist forces throughout Iraq bent on union with the UAR. Communist front organizations (such as the mass membership "Partisans of Peace") multiplied and prospered, and many existing revolutionary organizations, notably the Popular Resistance Forces (a newly formed civilian militia) and the Committee for the Preservation of the Republic, revealed their communist inclinations. On 8 March 1959, when nationalist army officers led by Colonel ᶜAbd-ul-Wahhâb al-Shawwâf rebelled against Qâsim in Mosul, the communists played a leading role in the brutal crushing of the revolt. Following their defeat of Shawwâf's forces in bitter fighting, ICP cadres and supporters, together with other anti-nationalist forces, engaged in a merciless three-day purge of the city, during which rebel sympathizers and "class enemies" were subject to summary trial and execution.[43]

The ICP emerged from the Mosul revolt flushed with success and began to press Qâsim for a greater role in the government. One of the secretary-general's first steps was to issue an open letter to Qâsim in which he complained that the Party was not formally consulted on public issues and was not even represented in the cabinet, despite its commitment to the revolution. The letter asserted that "events have confirmed the necessity and significance of greater solidarity. We say, with deep regret, that we are still victims of discrimination among the nationalist forces, and the limited opportunity open to our Party is not in conformity with the very interests of the Republic."[44] In an interview in *Ittiḥâd al-Shaᶜb* on 30 March, fewer than three weeks after the Shawwâf revolt, ᶜÂdil described the rebellion as an Anglo-American plan to overthrow the republican regime by utilizing a fifth column to divide the national ranks. ᶜÂdil identified the Baᶜthists as the group behind the plot. They were

> pushing to amalgamate Iraq with the UAR to achieve their objectives. They worked sedulously in that direction . . . and when they were not able to achieve their aims through practical [political] means . . . and unsuccessful in winning the masses to their slogans and views . . . they gradually sank to the path of conspiracy and violence to achieve these goals.

43 Batatu, *Old Social Classes*, pp. 864–889.

44 *Ittiḥâd al-Shaᶜb* (31 March 1959).

At the end of April, in a number of editorials attributed by Zakî Khairî to ʿÂmir ʿAbd-ul-lah and Bahâʾu-d-Dîn Nûrî,[45] *Ittiḥâd al-Shaʿb* daringly demanded participation in the government. On 28 April, the Central Committee again called for communist participation as a national necessity, complaining that "as early as the first day of the revolution the policy of discrimination between patriotic forces played a negative role, and our Party was excluded from the cabinet."[46] The following day another editorial reiterated that "communist participation was an important factor for securing international, Arab and popular support." On the same day, the ICP also expressed its preference for the important portfolio of Ministry of the Interior, in addition to three other cabinet posts.[47] The demands continued, and on 30 April, another editorial stated that "the sensitivity of other groups to ICP participation in the cabinet [and submission to these groups] will encourage the imperialists and their supporters to interfere in our internal affairs and challenge our national independence." The ICP's successes up to this point, their burgeoning confidence, and the tone of the editorials placed the Party on a collision course with Qâsim, who was clearly unwilling to tolerate alternate power centres within the Iraqi political arena. In a speech that he gave on the evening of 30 April 1959 at the ICP's stronghold, the Iraqi General Union of Labour, Qâsim reacted to the repeated communist demands by vehemently attacking all parties and partisanship, describing them as "ugly demon actions" and hinting that the ICP was a destructive force working against the republic.[48]

The next day, while celebrating May Day, participants in the largest public demonstration ever organized and led by the communists repeated the Party's demands for a communist presence in the cabinet. Passing Qâsim's headquarters, the demonstrators, in a show of force and public solidarity with the Party, chanted what later became their infamous slogan, which equated the leadership of Qâsim with communist participation: "Long live our hero, ʿAbd-ul-Karîm Qâsim. Communist participation is a great public demand."[49] Contrary to Qâsim's usual custom of returning their salute on such occasions, he was "decisively clear in his refusal . . . to go out and greet the demonstrators, and immediately initiated a furious campaign of speeches against the Communist Party. As Qâsim had not expected that[the] May Day celebrations would turn partisan, he had tolerated the participation of police and military academies."[50] Qâsim's furious reaction caught the Party leadership totally by surprise, since they were under the impression (from contacts via ʿÂmir ʿAbd-ul-lah and ʿAbd-ul-Qâdir Ismâʿîl al-Bustânî) that Qâsim was close to the left and to the progressive national movement, including the Communist Party. As a result of the contradiction between this understanding and Qâsim's speeches, ʿÂdil, rather

[45] Khairî, *Ṣadâ al-Sinîn fî Dhâkirat Shiyûʿî ʿIrâqî Mukhadram*, p. 209.
[46] *Ittiḥâd al-Shaʿb* (28 April, 1959).
[47] Al-Kharsân, *Ṣafaḥât min Târîkh al-Ḥarakah al-Shiyû ʿiyyah fî al-ʿIrâq*, p. 91.
[48] *Al-Thawrah* (Baghdad, 1 May 1959).
[49] The ICP leadership had long insisted that the slogan was not sanctioned by the Party, but was the result of spontaneous popular identification.
[50] Khairî, *Ṣadâ al-Sinîn fî Dhâkirat Shiyûʿî ʿIrâqî Mukhadram*, p. 210.

than use a "go between, insisted on meeting Qâsim as soon as possible to discover where the Party stood.

In a meeting with Qâsim in early May, ᶜÂdil tried to discuss the dangers of a rupture between the "national forces" and the regime that would weaken them both. To avoid this, he suggested the desirability of reviving the United National Front and permitting democratic freedoms. Qâsim ridiculed the idea and promptly terminated the meeting, angering and dismaying ᶜÂdil, who concluded that ᶜÂmir ᶜAbd-ul-lah had been "dishonest" in conveying the views of each group to the other.[51] Following his meeting with Qâsim, ᶜÂdil became convinced that the regime's change in attitude towards the Party and the "national democratic movement" following the May Day celebrations had been predictable outcome determined by the class nature of the regime and intended to strengthen Qâsim's dictatorial system.[52] Soon after, the Party Politburo met to discuss Qâsim's reaction to the ICP demands and the increasing tension between Qâsim and the Party. Most of the Politburo blamed Salâm ᶜÂdil for the degenerating situation,[53] but the secretary-general disputed this, pointing out that "the Party paper sponsored this slogan and the demonstrators spontaneously took it up. Can the Party question the masses that respond to the call?"[54] and hinting that ᶜÂmir ᶜAbd-ul-lah, Bahâʾu-d-Dîn Nûrî, and Zakî Khairî were the authors of the Party articles. The Politburo initiated a programme to reduce the intensity of the campaign, praising Qâsim's leadership rather than pursuing its demands to have seats in the cabinet. In a meeting between 8 and 9 June, the Politburo attempted to mollify Qâsim's fears. As noted on the first page of the 10 July issue of *Ittiḥâd al-Shaᶜb*:

> our Party was denied the right of representation in government . . . which had negative results. . . . and the best way to identify those who support [the republic] is through [the actions of] national parties and organizations which have [already] proved their commitment. . . . if we did ask to shoulder the responsibility of [being] in government . . . it is because of our feeling of responsibility.

On both 10 and 11 May, lengthy articles by Bahâʾu-d-Dîn Nûrî appeared on the first page of *Ittiḥâd al-Shaᶜb*; they seemed less concerned with placating Qâsim than with attempting to explain the earlier Party demands:

> The ICP's participation in government will strengthen our national democracy. . . . The question of communist participation in government has become a mature, acceptable, and necessary proposition, more pressing then ever, as proved by the popular demonstrations of 1 May. In addition, the level of maturity achieved by our revolution today requires much more than it did in the past. The re-examination of the composition of the cabinet is essential, so as to make it an efficient tool to put into action the new programs of the revolutionary government.

51 Yûsuf and Khâlid, *Salâm ᶜÂdil*, vol. 2, p. 18.
52 Ibid., p. 12.
53 Ibid., p. 211.
54 Ibid.

In the same issue, *Ittiḥâd al-Sha*ʿ*b* apologized indirectly by suggesting that the slogan raised by the demonstrators on May Day was spontaneous:

The masses were not used to Party activities...and thus it was expected that their enthusiasm would not be without error...and because political parties are not licensed...their activities will be hindered [and] their organizational abilities will be limited, and thus, they will not be able to control the masses.

According to Bahâʾu-d-Dîn Nûrî, this change in tone was imposed upon the communists by the CPSU, which viewed the slogans as leftist extremism and called for complete support for Qâsim.[55] Indeed, in a 12 May editorial along the same lines, the paper tried to soften the earlier demands:

When our Party today calls for our participation in government, it bases this on the premise of a coalition government that should include representatives of all national forces. The Party rests its position – not on the basis of monopolizing [power] – but rather on the foundation of brotherly sharing and cooperation in the republic's interest, and the welfare of its people....this is the Party's official policy when it contemplates participation in the responsibility of power in the cabinet.

In its 10 May editorial *Ittiḥâd al-Sha*ʿ*b* had declared that "the communists are the solid buttress for the democratic republic and the leadership of the genuine son of the people, ʿAbd-ul-Karîm Qâsim, [is] to the detriment of the imperialists, the avaricious, their lackeys, and the divisive." Fearing Qâsim's indignation, the Politburo instructed the membership on 23 May to abandon the demand for communist participation in the government.[56] Nevertheless, alarmed at the increased popularity of the ICP, Qâsim took steps to remove communist influence from the army.[57]

Political tensions now spilled over to the ranks of progressive forces, and between February and March the members of the national democratic left, including the NDP and the communists, clashed sporadically. As late as 8 May the NDP arm *Al-Ahâlî* did not appear to pay much attention to this development. Surprisingly, however, when the NDP held its consultative meetings between 11 and 13 May 1959, its leadership, with Qâsim's encouragement, proposed a "freezing" of NDP activities until the transition to democracy was concluded and political parties were allowed to function. Consequently, on 20 May, the NDP announced that it was ceasing its activities. Two days later, a group of NDP leftists who considered this decision to be premature protested that the declaration had been promulgated by the leadership rather than debated by the Party.[58] The next day, the ICP issued a statement declaring that "the activities of the NDP in Iraqi political life are a historical necessity. The NDP should continue to struggle to strengthen the revolution and its gains, and all parties must revitalize their activities."[59]

55 Nûrî, *Mudhakkarât Bahâʾu-d-Dîn Nûrî*, p. 194.
56 *Ittiḥâd al-Sha*ʿ*b* (23 May 1959).
57 Al-Kharsân, *Ṣafaḥât min Târîkh al-Ḥarakah al-Shiyû*ʿ*iyyah fî al-*ʿ*Irâq*, p. 91.
58 *Ittiḥâd al-Sha*ʿ*b* (22 May 1959).
59 Ibid. (23 May 1959).

To recoup its credibility among nationalists, the ICP now busied itself in attempting to reassemble the facade of the United National Front, to be composed of its sympathizers in the Kurdish Democratic Party and the leftist elements of the NDP. Aware of the communists' tactical manoeuvres to tone down their demands by casting them in terms of a renewed national front, Qâsim at a meeting with the secretary-general of the Party in early May, asked sarcastically, "What does the ICP need a Front for, if it has the support of 70 percent of the population?"[60] On 30 June this new Front was declared by the ICP to be "the expression of the people's struggle... [in] its readiness to organize in order to spoil the conspiracies of the enemies of the Republic."[61] The new Front was described as "a decisive blow to the imperialists and their agents." Membership in the Front was open to all other forces,[62] and it was "hailed as being the only means to mobilize the people and unify their ranks."[63]

Communist-run committees were formed in military units and government offices, and among workers and peasants, to guard against the "enemies of the people," and to extend communist influence in those sectors. The *Istiqlâl* Party and the Baᶜthists had already been driven underground. However, the influence and popularity of the Communist Party in the middle of 1959 could be seen in the wide circulation of the Party's paper, which reached around 23,000 readers. All other papers had circulations of only about 10 per cent of this number. Furthermore, the number of Party members and candidates waiting to join the Party exceeded 20,000; Party front organizations such as the League for the Defence of Iraqi Women's Rights reached 40,000 members; the Iraqi Union of Democratic Youth had 84,000 members; the National Congress of Peasant Societies claimed to have 2,000 societies under its umbrella, totalling some 250,000 members; and the General Union of Labour reckoned that it represented fifty-one labour unions with a membership of 275,000.[64] To balance this perceived communist domination, Qâsim released some Arab nationalist detainees in June and July and placed curbs on the operation of pro-Communist popular resistance forces.

From 14 to 16 July 1959, the Mosul purges were replayed, as pro-communist Kurds fought anti-communist Turkomens in the city of Kirkuk. The communists and the Bârzânî Kurdish groups

> initiated a slaughter, and vicious violations [of human rights] were committed as dozens of innocent Turkomens were arrested, killed... and some even buried alive. This bloody wave was a spontaneous expression of Kurdish chauvinism against [Turkomens], and what exacerbated the matter were the misguided actions of the Iraqi Communist Party.[65]

60 Khairî, *Ṣadâ al-Sinîn fî Dhâkirat Shiyûᶜî ᶜIrâqî Mukhadram*, p. 209.
61 *Ittiḥâd al-Shaᶜb* (30 June 1959).
62 Ibid. (1 July 1959).
63 Ibid. (2 July 1959).
64 Yûsuf and Khâlid, *Salâm ᶜÂdil*, vol. 2, pp. 45, 46; and Batatu, *Old Social Classes*, pp. 896–897.
65 ᶜAzîz al-Ḥâjj, *Maᶜa al-Aᶜwâm: Ṣafahât min Târîkh al-Ḥarakah al-Shiyûᶜiyyah fî al-ᶜIrâq Baina 1958–69* (Beirut: al-Mûᶜassasah al-ᶜArabiyyah lil Dirâsât wa al-Nashr, 1981), p. 62.

Ittiḥâd al-Shaᶜb mistakenly hailed the Kurdish action as supporting the revolution, though a decade later ᶜAzîz al-Ḥâjj revealed that the ICP official in charge of Kirkuk at that time had admitted that the clash was essentially a racist provocation against the Turkomens.[66] In a speech on 19 July following the Kirkuk massacre, Qâsim denounced the incident as being motivated by "cruelty and blind fanaticism."[67] At a news conference ten days later, he repeated his attack on those he identified as responsible, and although he did not mention the communists by name, he signalled a campaign against them.[68]

In response to this further deterioration in the political climate, attempts were made to allocate blame, and recriminations began to fly among members of the Politburo; this resulted in the resurfacing of two factions, one consisting of Jamâl al-Ḥaidarî, and ᶜÂdil, and the other of the remainder of the Politburo. This majority group, led by Qâsim supporters, included the ambitious ᶜÂmir ᶜAbd-ul-lah and the unhappy Bahâᵓu-d-Dîn Nûrî, and was supported by Zakî Khairî and Muḥammad Ḥusain Abû-l-ᶜÎss. It later became known as the "Clique of Four." Zakî Khairî and Muḥammad Ḥusain Abû-l-ᶜÎss, while not official members of the Central Committee (having been co-opted by the secretary-general into the Politburo in a consultative capacity), now acted as if they were full members of the Politburo. These aspirants to Party leadership believed themselves more qualified than ᶜÂdil because of seniority and intellectual ability, and they saw this moment as their chance to play a more decisive role in Iraqi politics. They portrayed Qâsim as a genuine national democrat who had some leftist leanings and could be won over by appropriate Party actions, just as Fidel Castro had been won over by the communists in Cuba. The secretary-general, they claimed, had somehow created a dangerous level of animosity with Qâsim, and thus blame for this crisis must rest on him and on his chief assistant, Jamâl al-Ḥaidarî. They based their argument on the fact that between September 1958 and July 1959, the secretary-general, along with a very limited number of his supporters, had run Party affairs with no formal meetings, discussions, or input from either the Politburo or the Central Committee.[69]

For this reason, the Clique of Four called for formal and more regular Central Committee plenary session meetings. In preparation for these full meetings, the Politburo held its own formal meetings in mid-July to evaluate the events to be discussed at the scheduled Central Committee plenary session. The Clique of Four now prepared to carry their fight further and to disseminate a very clear position to the Central Committee and, eventually, to the general cadre, concerning the secretary-general's approach towards overall Party policies. Adding insult to injury, the clique initiated its attack on ᶜÂdil by rejecting his report, which would customarily have been submitted as the Politburo report at the

66 Ibid., p. 62.

67 *Iraqi Times* (20 July 1959).

68 *Al-Zamân* (Baghdad, 30 July 1959).

69 Khairî, *Ṣadâ al-Sinîn fî Dhâkirat Shiyûᶜî ᶜIrâqî Mukhadram*, p. 210, 211; al-Ḥâjj, *Maᶜa al-Aᶜwâm*, p. 63; and Yûsuf and Khâlid, *Salâm ᶜÂdil*, vol. 2, pp. 49–65.

Central Committee meeting. Bahâʾu-d-Dîn Nûrî became the most vehement propounder of the clique's views, his sole aim being to unseat the secretary-general. ʿÂmir ʿAbd-ul-lah and the rest of the clique stayed in the background and confined themselves to formulating policies and ideological positions that indirectly supported and strengthened Bahâʾu-d-Dîn Nûrî's position, approach, which was evolving into a personal vendetta against ʿÂdil. The tension at the Politburo meeting, which lasted all night, reached such a level that the meeting was adjourned by ʿÂdil and al-Ḥaidarî, although the rest of the participants surreptitiously continued to prepare their strategy for the next day's session.

The plenary meeting on the following day was one of the largest in the history of the Party, with thirty-three Central Committee members in attendance. With regard to the tension between Qâsim and the ICP, the clique presented its position as being the result of the secretary-general's intransigence. They pointed in particular to ʿÂdil's drive to secure Party participation in the cabinet, which was to their minds was the main reason for Qâsim's animosity towards the Party. According to the clique's members, ʿÂdil's focus on the cabinet resulted from his "leftist deviationist" failure to follow the principle of collective leadership. Consequently, they maintained, ʿÂdil must bear the complete responsibility for the debacle. Furthermore, he should be removed from office, and a new Central Committee and Politburo elected at a future Party congress. The summary report of the Plenary Session of the Central Committee, hurriedly cobbled together and modified by ʿÂmir ʿAbd-ul-lah to appease Qâsim,[70] explained that

> an attempt was made by the [imperialists]...and their supporters to disseminate rumours and fabrications in order to sow the seeds of division between the national forces, and turn the members against each other, thus creating mistrust and spreading doubts between the government and its people.... Our Party would like to emphasize – in the name of the masses – its clear policy of supporting the revolution and the leader of the republic, ʿAbd-ul-Karîm Qâsim.... The support of our Party for the national government is based on our logical analysis of the necessity and importance of unifying the ranks in order to safeguard and achieve the common great aims of the people. We support and appreciate the leader, ʿAbd-ul-Karîm Qâsim, as the leader of the great liberating revolution... which destroyed the system of imperialism and the old enslaving regime. [He] restored to the people their freedom, rights and dignity, and because he is committed to an anti-imperialist policy to complete the country's independence and secure the people's freedoms and democratic rights... the ICP declares again that it will stand strongly and firmly against all attempts to undermine the security of the republic and threaten the people's gains. It also emphasizes its firm belief that the solidarity of the people and its national forces, with their national government and brave army under the leadership of ʿAbd-ul-Karîm Qâsim, is a strong and assured guarantee to spoil all treacherous attempts of the imperialists and their reactionary supporters, and the enemies of the revolution.[71]

[70] For ʿÂdil's perspective, see Yûsuf and Khâlid, *Salâm ʿÂdil*, vol. 2, pp. 74–97.

[71] *Ittiḥâd al-Shaʿb* (3 August 1959).

The plenary session was tense and mobilized against ᶜÂdil. Nevertheless, he was allowed to give the report earlier rejected by the Politburo, which was now presented as a personal report to the Central Committee. ᶜÂdil's report analyzed the political situation from a classical communist class perspective, asserting that because of its bourgeois class nature the Qâsim regime had, after attaining power, turned its back on its previous allies in the working class. Despite the clique's opposition, ᶜÂdil was re-elected, although the bulk of the meeting's discussion blamed him for the crisis between Qâsim and the Party. While accepting much of the responsibility for this, he called for "organized retreat" so that the Party's change in direction would not turn into a "rout," even though in a way this weakened his position and strengthened that of the clique's, especially after the election of Zakî Khairî and Abû-l-ᶜÎss to the Politburo as full members.

To soften the blow he had suffered, and to challenge the domination of the Party and the Party newspaper by the Clique of Four, Salâm ᶜÂdil published an editorial in *Ṭarîq al-Shaᶜb* on 2 August in which he defended the Party's position and rejected all the insinuations present in the summary of the plenary session. According to this "rebuttal":

> It was said that we believe in violence within the framework of the national movement, and in our relationship with other national forces. . . . this is fallacious and malicious, and their [those who accuse us] aim is no more than to defame us. . . . We condemn absolutely all forms of aggression against innocent people. . . . Our condemnation of these practices is a principled one.

The summary resolutions of the Plenary Session of the Central Committee revealed deep divisions within the rank and file of the Party, despite attempts to contain internal dissatisfaction with its position vis-à-vis the Qâsim regime. The ICP overlooked the regime's attacks against the Party and its cadres, and adopted a severe degree of self-criticism, which was spoken of in the Party as "self-flagellation." A change in the Party's direction was immediately evident in its newspaper editorials, so much so, in fact, that Qâsim frequently used *Ittiḥâd al-Shaᶜb* editorials to justify his attack on the Party.[72] These editorials angered many of the cadre because of their excessively conciliatory tone regarding Qâsim.[73] Four weeks after meeting, the final, detailed report of the plenary session, while still making concessions to Qâsim, attempted to explain the Party's actions:

> The Party organizations became preoccupied with fighting conspiratorial activities, so that they did not have much opportunity for indoctrination. The Party's qualitative development thus fell behind development of its numerical strength. There were other factors which militated against the Party's resolution of the problem of keeping its organizations clandestine however public its political activity was. It was this which made

72 Yûsuf and Khâlid, *Salâm ᶜÂdil*, vol. 2, p. 82.
73 Al-Ḥâjj, *Maᶜa al-Aᶜwâm*, p. 66.

it difficult to ensure the leadership's thorough monitoring of the Party's bases, and led to the committing of mistakes and abuses. The Party failed to stand firmly against such conduct and made mistakes as a result of the euphoria of victory and conceit resulting from its major triumphs. It thus made political miscalculations by overestimating its power and underestimating the role of the other nationalist forces, which caused it to commit leftist political errors that affected its organizational functioning. The secretary-general violated the Leninist principle of collective leadership and encroached upon the rights of the Central Committee. To the extent that collective leadership was compromised and monolithic leadership prevailed, bureaucratic tendencies emerged, and the level of criticism and self-criticism declined especially among some Party cadres who thus discredited the Party.[74]

It also acknowledged the mistake of raising the slogan of participation in government but declared that

contemporary experiences of a number of countries prove that a coalition government is the best model of political administration, and during the transitional period, this issue occupies a special importance when the representation of all national forces in government is an important factor in the struggle against the anti-government [forces].... speaking in general principles, but on the practical side, our demand to participate in the national government was an error because it did not take into consideration the conditions and relations of the national forces in the country, and did not [take into account] the conditions of the revolution, and its connection to the Arab and international environment.... In the political situation that followed the revolution, when the government pursued an anti-imperialist and anti-feudal policy, and with this transitional government whose elements had been chosen by the leader of the revolution [himself], raising such a slogan [of communist participation in government] without [consulting] the leadership of the government was a wrong and divisive [action] that did not consider the realities of the [political situation] or its [impact] on other national forces, and has to have resulted in a fracture of the unity of the national forces and their solidarity in defending the republic.[75]

The resolutions also condemned the May Day episode and held the ICP newspaper responsible for the government's campaign against the Party. The overreaction of the Party to the NDP's announcement that it was dissolving was also condemned, as was the hasty attempt to build a national front, which was considered to have been another mistake: "It did not achieve its expected aims but rather contributed to intensifying the existing differences, and frustrated the efforts to bridge the gap between the government and the other national forces of the country."[76] The Party's open-door policy in "recruiting members

74 A week later, a more detailed communiqué was issued in a supplement to *Ittiḥâd al-Sha*ᶜ*b* (29 August 1959) entitled "For the Sake of Strengthening the Unity of the National Forces in the Defence of the Republic and the Gains of the Revolution," which is the source referred to from now on.

75 Ibid.

76 Ibid.

without 'political maturity'"[77] was also acknowledged, and all these criticisms were laid at the feet of the secretary-general. The resolutions declared that

the principle of collective leadership was violated during the past few months when the secretary-general arrogated the rights of the Central Committee to himself, as he has not convened any Central Committee meetings for the last ten months. This constituted a violation of Politburo decisions and party by-laws.... A number of serious and improper personal decisions were made with the consultation of only a small number of the Politburo. Some of the decisions were taken without reference to the Central Committee, and, in particular, the campaign of Party participation within the government is within the jurisdiction of the Central Committee, and not within the domain of any other organ.... The violation of collective leadership, and its replacement by an autocratic style, resulted in negative outcomes and grave political and organizational shortcomings that could have been avoided if the collective leadership [principle] had been practised, and the Central Committee meetings held. Holding the Central Committee meetings without the written report having been distributed beforehand is wrong, and contrary to the principle of collective leadership.... the violation of the principles of collective leadership was not limited to the activities of the central Party leadership, but extended to other [Party committees] in varying degrees... as some personal decisions were made by some of the chairmen, or a limited number of members of these committees.... in addition there was a scarcity of Party meetings... with no minutes taken... and no agenda prepared etc., and in some cases the meetings were proforma to approve the opinion of the chairman or the [local] bureau, rather than [meetings] to study the issues and conclude sensible decisions.[78]

The final result was that the secretary-general was reprimanded. The Clique of Four, which hoped for a rapprochement with Qâsim, now found themselves in command of the Party. Under the cloak of improving collective leadership, the clique reduced the power of Secretary-General ᶜÂdil and his supporter Jamâl al-Ḥaidarî and constituted themselves as a new Secretariat to "assist" the secretary-general with the administration of the Party. In effect, Bahâʾu-d-Dîn Nûrî, Muḥammad Ḥusain Abû-l-ᶜÎss, and Hâdî Hâshim al-Aᶜẓamî took over the Party, but the real power remained with ᶜÂmir ᶜAbd-ul-lah and his henchman, Bahâʾu-d-Dîn Nûrî.

In the meantime, overtures were made by the Party leadership early in August to implement the decisions of the plenary Central Committee meetings and to patch up matters with Qâsim through an intermediary. Thus Jamâl al-Ḥaidarî, the second man in command of the Party, met with General Ismâᶜîl al-ᶜÂrif, the minister of education and a confidant of Qâsim, who had been given Qâsim's approval to meet with the ICP leadership. According to al-ᶜÂrif, al-Ḥaidarî

initiated his discussion saying "there is a heated reactionary campaign against the Communist Party, fed by elements that are against the 14 July revolution because of the Party's faithful commitment in support of the revolution. At the same time, the security and intelligence agencies have organized a campaign against Party members and imprisoned

77 Ibid.
78 Ibid.

them. Further, since the ICP cannot work against the revolution, and will continue to support its leadership, then the leadership of the revolution needs to be aware that there is a conspiracy organized against the revolution, by isolating its supporters and preparing for a deadly blow against it." Al-Ḥaidarî asked me to intervene in order to convince Qâsim of the good will of the ICP towards the revolution, in order to stop the attacks on it, and to correct this misunderstanding.... [Al-Ḥaidarî] stresses that he speaks in the name of the Politburo and the Central Committee.[79]

Al-ᶜÂrif adds that Qâsim was furious.[80] Qâsim believed that al-Ḥaidarî's statement was a tactic to regain his confidence, since the ICP knew that it would be publicly bankrupt without his "imagined support." Qâsim was wary of the intentions of the secretary-general whom he regarded as arrogant, and was equally aware of the ambitions of ᶜÂmir ᶜAbd-ul-lah. Moreover, he deprecated ᶜAbd-ul-Qâdir Ismâᶜîl al-Bustânî, who was then editor of *Ittiḥâd al-Shaᶜb* and a member of the Central Committee.[81]

In early September, the Secretariat, continuing its efforts to please Qâsim, "surprised" the Politburo by announcing that the Party's armed forces organization would be dissolved. "It was not surprising that Bahâ'u-d-Dîn Nûrî and Hâdî Hâshim al-Aᶜẓamî demanded this action. It was a surprise that the Secretary-General adopted it."[82] According to the Party's most critical members, who emerged eight years later as the Central Leadership faction[83] of the ICP (ICP-CC),[84] the battered Party came out of the July plenary session with the Clique of Four in complete control, and ready to subordinate every other consideration to "the republic's independence," to "democratic rule," and, especially, to "the restoration of solidarity with Qâsim."

In other words, persistence in the rightist approach to clientilism and to the monolithic military government and its pressures and policies which were against the interests of the mass movement.... The possibility of abandoning Qâsim and seeking out other allies among other nationalist forces to rally and defend the masses was ignored. Rather than criticizing Qâsim's authoritarian actions, the resolutions of the plenary session contained justifications for more and more humiliating concessions to the regime. The leadership failed to realize that fighting against the progressive democratic forces thrust to the fore by the July 1958 revolution could not preserve the young republic.[85]

ᶜÂmir ᶜAbd-ul-lah, and the rest of the clique began a public campaign to prove their loyalty to Qâsim by emphasizing his leadership and their complete faith in

79 Ismâᶜîl al-ᶜÂrif, *Asrâr Thawrat 14 Tammûz wa Ta'sîs al-Jumhûriyyah fî al-ᶜIrâq* (London: Lana Publications, 1986), p. 194.

80 Interview by author with Ismâᶜîl al-ᶜÂrif, Washington, DC (1 December, 1965).

81 Ibid. (4 December 1965).

82 Khairî, *Ṣadâ al-Sinîn fî Dhâkirat Shiyûᶜî ᶜIrâqî Mukhadram*, p. 228.

83 See Chapters 4 and 5 for an examination of the emergence and role of the Central Leadership.

84 *Al-Qiyâdah al-Markaziyyah* is translated as "Central leadership." *Al-Qiyâdah* can also be translated as "a command," but this denotes a military dimension and in this context is incorrect.

85 Al-Ḥâjj, *Maᶜa al-Aᶜwâm*, p. 68.

him. In his public lecture on "the political situation in Iraq," ʿÂmir ʿAbd-ul-lah stated:

After a while the situation began to regress because of the attempt to limit the activities of the democratic movement [ICP], and the toleration [by some agencies in the government] of these reactionaries.... the attempt encouraged by those reactionaries in the government against the democratic forces was to sow the seeds of discord among the national forces. In this critical stage of our history, our Central Committee held a plenary session, adjusted the leftist Party policy of the previous few months and emphasized the necessity of national unity and the support of the leadership of the republic for the defence of the republic against all threats.... For these reasons, the plenary session's resolutions of the Central Committee spoiled the [reactionaries'] cheap designs... and finally, the [reactionaries] put into action their despicable but unsuccessful plot to assassinate the leader, ʿAbd-ul-Karîm Qâsim.[86]

The ICP's self-criticism did little to lessen the pressure on the Party, though some respite came in the last months of 1959 when a Baʿthist assassination attempt against Qâsim on 7 October 1959 led to what appeared to be a temporary relaxation of the suppression policy against the communists. However, no amount of concessions from the ICP would bring official recognition or tolerance from the security agencies of the government.[87] The Party complained in *Ittiḥâd al-Shaʿb* that the freedom permitted the moderate and national forces during the latter part of 1959 had allowed these forces to conduct a "fierce campaign whose ultimate intention is a conspiracy against the republic under the veil of combating communism, while repeating the same approach of Nûrî al-Saʿîd... with stronger hysterical overtones, and more deceit and cunning."[88]

To widen the split in the ʿÂdil leadership of the ICP, Qâsim introduced an additional element – the rehabilitation of an old enemy of ʿÂdil, Dâûd Ṣâyegh, who had left the ICP in late 1957. This was widely interpreted as a "shrewd attempt by Qâsim to resurrect an old foe of the secretary-general, who had been a member of the Central Committee until 1957, but in disagreement with ʿÂdil and ʿÂmir ʿAbd-ul-lah had been expelled."[89] The government granted Ṣâyegh permission to publish a newspaper and facilitated its publication by giving him government advertisements and subsidies. Thus, *Al-Mabdaʾ* (The Principle) was born on 21 November 1959; Qâsim further showed his support for the paper by granting it exclusive interviews, one of which appeared in its first issue. On 10 December 1959, an editorial in *Ittiḥâd al-Shaʿb* carefully responded to Qâsim's maneuvering, hinting at its dissatisfaction and stating that:

one of the most important aims... is the respect and guarantee of democratic freedoms to the people without class distinction, as long as [these democratic] forces are anti-imperialist and anti-feudal. These freedoms cannot prevail unless human rights are

86 *Ittiḥâd al-Shaʿb* (14 December, 1959).
87 Al-Kharsân, *Ṣafaḥât min Târîkh al-Ḥarakah al-Shiyûʿiyyah fî al-ʿIrâq*, p. 96.
88 *Ittiḥâd al-Shaʿb* (October 4, 1959).
89 Interview by author with ʿAbd-ul-Raḥîm Sharîf, Baghdad (28 July, 1961).

achieved through securing the [citizen's] humanity and integrity . . . and allowing equal opportunities to all classes to exercise their parliamentary right [to organize political parties].[90]

The Law of Association, which formally permitted the formation of political parties, was implemented on 1 January 1960. In an editorial on 4 January, *Ittiḥâd al-Sha^cb* hailed this law as "the most necessary action to defend the republic, since political parties have a mutual interest in maintaining communications among themselves and [in] proposing solutions to the political issues the [people] face." The Party wanted to assure the regime of its good intentions in cooperating with other political parties in support of the Republic. It declared that creation of a democratic political life through the formation of political parties did not mean the intensification of differences; rather, "the multiparty [environment] gives another chance for differing opinions to converge, and this will emphasize the importance of peaceful coexistence among the national forces. This coexistence requires democratic freedoms."

On 9 January 1960, Zakî Khairî and fifteen others, in compliance with the Law of Association, petitioned the government for formal permission to establish the Iraqi Communist Party.[91] On the same day, Dâûd Ṣâyegh applied for permission to form a party under the same name. Aware of this ploy, *Ittiḥâd al-Shaᶜb* fiercely criticized Ṣâyegh's group, insisting "there is only one Communist Party." In its editorial the following day, 10 January, *Ittiḥâd al-Shaᶜb* called the "licensing of political parties" a great step towards strengthening "the democratic path of our republic." However, Qâsim's plan to weaken the ICP still further was made clear by the government's refusal to grant it legal party status. Instead, the regime gave legal status to Dâûd Ṣâyegh's rival party, on 9 February 1960. The minister of the interior allowed the ICP to reapply on the condition that the Party revise its by-laws. It did so a month later, only to be rejected again, this time on the basis that a license had already been granted to a party that carried the same name.[92] Dâûd Ṣâyegh's *Al-Mabda'* became the licensed ICP organ; its slogan was "to firmly assure and develop our revolution, the fortress of democracy, peace and national liberation."[93] In response to these developments, *Ittiḥâd al-Shaᶜb* attacked Ṣâyegh's party. In an attempt to pressure Qâsim and discredit Ṣâyegh's party, the paper organized a petition drive, which garnered about 185,000 signatures, demanding that its Party be licensed. On 15 March 1960, *Ittiḥâd al-Shaᶜb* published the editorial "Basic Foundations of the Concept of National Unity," in which it asserted that the existence of classes required the formation of political parties and that for the Republic to fulfill its basic aims, it must accept this principle.

On 24 March 1960, *Ittiḥâd al-Shaᶜb* complained that security agencies were continuing to arrest communists without due process. On the following day,

90 *Ittiḥâd al-Shaᶜb* (10 December 1959).
91 Ibid. (10 January 1960).
92 Ibid. (9 February 1960).
93 Khairî and Khairî, *Dirâsât fî Târîkh al-Ḥizb al-Shiyûᶜî ᶜIrâqî*, p. 332.

it attacked those who hid behind slogans of "moderation" and "democracy," asking, "Who would gain from the attack on democratic organizations?" Three days later, an editorial spoke of the harassment of communists by those who use "religious and nationalist fronts." On 30 March, the paper commented on the arrest of hundreds of workers and labour leaders, and on 2 April, it openly accused security agencies and officials of collusion in their organized attack on communists. During the May Day rally organized by the ICP on 1 May 1960, anti-communists and some nationalists charged into the marchers, leaving some fifty communists and ICP sympathizers injured and five dead. The police intervented and arrested a number of ICP members. On 1 June 1960, *Ittiḥâd al-Sha<u>h</u>ᶜb* denounced the arrests as harassment connected to the regime's crackdown on communist activities in the labour movement. Systematic repression and the campaign of arrests and detention continual. Between February and May 1960, the communist leadership of the labour movement was effectively purged through the arrests.[94] In May 1960, all centres run by communist-supported Union of Democratic Youth, including the union's headquarters, were closed down, although the organization was not legally banned until April 1961. From early June 1960, despite Qâsim's assurances of press freedom, distribution of *Ittiḥâd al-Shaᶜb* was severely curtailed across half of the country, including in major cities, by security restrictions and police harassment.[95] On 16 September 1960, the pro-communist Student Federation was banned.[96] In a mid-June editorial, *Ittiḥâd al-Shaᶜb*, in a display of bravado, declared: "There exists today a political conflict in the country between the anti-imperialists and anti-feudal forces and the forces of reaction that want to return the country to the days of imperialism and backwardness; within this struggle the communists have emerged as one of the most prominent forces among the national groupings."

The Party's difficulties continued, and on 14 July 1961 – the third anniversary of the 14 July 1958 revolution – *Ittiḥâd al-Shaᶜb* called for creation of a democratic, "true" parliamentary form of government, with a permanent constitution, and for an end to the transitional conditions.[97] At the same time, the pro-communist Iraqi poet, Muḥammad Mahdî al-Jawâhirî, the head of the Iraqi Press Syndicate, indirectly protested the campaign against *Ittiḥâd al-Shaᶜb* by denouncing government interference in the press.[98] However, government measures against communist organizations continued. Attacks on communists intensified in the major cities, and assassinations of prominent communists took place throughout Iraq. *Ittiḥâd al-Shaᶜb* itself was banned on 30 September 1961, and its editor was referred to a military court, thus initiating an open anti-communist purge. By the end of 1961, the ICP was mortally weakened,

[94] Batatu, *Old Social Classes*, pp. 946–948.
[95] *Ittiḥâd al-Shaᶜb* (23 June 1960).
[96] Ibid. (17 September 1960).
[97] Ibid. (14 July 1961).
[98] Ibid. (29 July 1961).

with its leadership split into a loyalist camp subservient to Qâsim (the Clique of Four) and an independent faction that resisted cooptation into Qâsim's political domain.

Effectively paralyzed as an independent political party, the ICP undertook a second round of public self-criticism in a futile effort to maintain unity and regain Qâsim's favour. In the winter of 1961 the Clique of Four, under the pretext of concern about his personal safety, forced the secretary-general, Salâm ʿÂdil, to go to Moscow for re-education. Zakî Khairî was appointed as co-secretary-general and took direct charge of the Party. Qâsim continued to support Ṣâyegh's bogus communist party, which was in reality a front for the regime to undermine the communist movement in Iraq. After a number of attempts to embarrass Ṣâyegh by penetrating his party, and still interested in winning favour with the Qâsim regime, the new ICP leader recognized that Qâsim had no intention of tolerating their Party. This led them to seriously consider a takeover of the bogus party, since the Ṣâyegh party was essentially a legal entity without any members and the ICP was a membership without a sanctioned structure. The ICP thought that it could control the empty structure,[99] and on the pretext of negotiating a merger, though with the intention of taking it over, Bahâʾu-d-Dîn Nûrî held discussions with the Ṣâyegh party on behalf of his Central Committee during March, April, and May 1960.[100]

Ṣâyegh insisted that he would not negotiate with the ICP without the expulsion of ʿÂmir ʿAbd-ul-lah, Jamâl al-Ḥaidarî, and Secretary-General Salâm ʿÂdil, since he considered them to be responsible for the ICP's personality cults and autocratic control. However, the ICP refused such conditions. Another attempt on behalf of the ICP to reopen the dialogue was made on 5 June 1960 by ʿAzîz al-Shaikh. He conceded to Ṣâyegh's demands but with a face-saving tactic that involved the three men who Ṣâyegh's objected to asking to be relieved of their Party duties on health grounds rather than be expelled, and then Ṣâyegh's using his good offices with the government to get al-Ḥaidarî and ʿÂmir ʿAbd-ul-lah exit visas so they could join the secretary-general, who was already in Moscow.

At this point, however, Bahâʾu-d-Dîn Nûrî went behind Ṣâyegh's back to his rival, Ṣamad, who sat ʿAbd-ul-Ḥamîd on the Ṣâyegh Central Committee, with an offer to unseat Ṣâyegh and to help Ṣamad ʿAbd-ul-Ḥamîd gain control of the party.[101] Sensing these maneuvres, Ṣâyegh broke off discussions with Ṣamad, as he recognized an attempt to "freeze him out" of the party leadership.[102] At the end of June, *Al-Mabdaʾ* appealed to the cadre of the ICP to reunite the Party in the face of its enemies. A few months later, Ṣâyegh's party withered away.[103]

99 Khairî, *Ṣadâ al-Sinîn fî Dhâkirat Shiyûʿî ʿIrâqî Mukhadram*, p. 231.
100 Ibid.
101 Interview by author with Zakî Khairî, Damascus (18 March 1987). Confirmed by ʿÂmir ʿAbd-ul-lah in an interview, London (18 January 1998).
102 Interview by author with Dâûd Ṣâyegh, Beirut (18 July 1969).
103 *Al-Mabdaʾ* (25 June 1960, 28 June 1960, and 3 July 1960).

All of the anti-communist and anti-republican forces in Iraq were now rallied under the rubric of nationalism. In the process, the ICP was weakened and its effective functioning was radically curtailed. These nationalist forces were given full freedom to check the communists and, afterwards, to fill the political vacuum left by the Party's departure from the political stage, particularly as the security forces were preoccupied with their own anti-communist campaign. The security agencies and the police openly attacked communists, even those who supported Qâsim. This prompted a close Qâsim associate to warn the chief of the State Security Agency of the danger of confusing Qâsim supporters with other communists since, as he knew, the security chief had disliked communists ever since he had been an intelligence officer during the monarchy. But the security chief rejected the advice, saying, "They're all communists."[104] According to the Committee for the Defence of Democratic Freedoms and Rights in Iraq, which was closely associated with the communists, by the end of 1960 22,000 communists were in jail, 270 had been assassinated, and 112 communists and their supporters had been sentenced to death.

At the end of 1960 and into early 1961 there were a number of strikes by the workers in the tobacco industry and by taxi drivers. Labour unrest continued, and the government rigged labour elections to make sure that communists would not be represented in the union hierarchy. In 1961, under the pretext of fiscal restraint, the government laid off seven thousand workers, including office workers. This occurred at a time of high inflation, increasingly isolating the regime from the population.[105]

In late March 1960, the police opened fire on demonstrators protesting against tax increases, killing a number of them. The communists were accused of instigating the demonstrations and a campaign of repression followed. Evaluating the three-year regime of Qâsim, the *World Marxist Review* commented that the regime had "wiped out the democratic freedoms won by the people,"[106] adding that "the government's anti-democratic policy is aimed at strengthening the dictatorship of the national bourgeoisie, at solving the social contradictions in favour of the bourgeoisie, and at placating the counter-revolutionary elements with a view to eliminating the danger of conspiracies on their part."[107]

The Fall of the Clique of Four

International events in 1961 saw the Qâsim regime increasingly isolated. Qâsim, who considered the 1899 agreement between Kuwait and Britain to be illegal since it usurped Iraq's historic rights to Kuwait, declared in June 1961 Kuwait to be an integral part of Iraq. By 1 July 1961 Iraq had stationed its armies on the border with Kuwait, and Britain immediately responded by sending in

104 Al-ᶜÂrif, *Asrâr Thawrat 14 Tammûz wa Taʾsîs al-Jumhûriyyah fî al-ᶜIrâq*, pp. 409–410.

105 Khairî and Khairî, *Dirâsât fî Târîkh al-Ḥizb al-Shiyûᶜî ᶜIrâqî*, p. 338.

106 *World Marxist Review*, vol. 4, no. 6 (June 1961), p. 89.

107 Ibid., p. 88.

British forces, along with a symbolic contingent of Saudi Arabians, to defend the Emirate. With Kuwait's admission to the Arab League on 20 July 1961, the Arab League also decided to send in a military force, consisting of soldiers from four Arab countries, to replace the British, and between September and October, twenty-three hundred soldiers from Sudan, Jordan, Saudi Arabia, and the UAR guarded the Emirate. In response, Qâsim broke off diplomatic relations with all countries that recognized the newly independent Kuwait, thereby increasing Iraq's isolation both within the Arab world and internationally.[108]

The weakening of the Qâsim regime was exacerbated by the state's increasing oppression of the Kurds. When Qâsim first came to power in 1958 the new Republic guaranteed the national rights of the Kurds (Article 3 of the Provisional Constitution), removed restrictions against Kurdish political activism, and welcomed Muṣṭafâ Bârzânî, the Kurdish leader, to Baghdad as a hero. However, by 1960 Qâsim had turned against Bârzânî and the Kurdish Democratic Party, and a campaign against Kurdish political leaders was initiated. Bârzânî was forced to flee Baghdad in the spring of 1961 and return to Barzan, his tribal stronghold. Despite Bârzânî's efforts to mend fences with Qâsim, government harassment of Barzan increased. On 9 September 1961, Qâsim's regime authorized aerial bombardment of the Kurdish region in northern Iraq, and a full-scale Kurdish rebellion erupted on 11 September.[109] Reflecting on these events forty years later, the Kurdish leader Masᶜûd Bârzânî (the son of Mullah Muṣṭafâ Bârzânî) pointed out:

> It is not just or fair that we place all the responsibility [for this] on Qâsim. We cannot blame him for all the criminal acts and atrocities committed against the Kurdish people. There were two other parties that share some of the responsibility. I must admit that our dealings with Qâsim and his regime very often were short-sighted and not astute. Our actions were hasty, immature, and narrow-minded, and did not take into account their potential to endanger Qâsim's regime. Sometimes we acted as if we were a state within a state, [in effect] giving him cause to worry about the threat to national unity, and provoking the [Arab] chauvinists surrounding him . . . into creating mistrust between Qâsim and Mullah Muṣṭafâ Bârzânî, the Kurdish Democratic Party, and the Kurdish people.[110]

To deal with the deteriorating situation, the remaining members of the Central Committee of the ICP met in November 1961 to address the conditions in northern Iraq, the crisis over Kuwait, and the ongoing oppression of the ICP. According to final report "the common feature between [the Iraqi government]

[108] For details of the Qâsim actions on Kuwait, see al-ᶜÂrif, *Asrâr Thawrat 14 Tammûz wa Taʾsîs al-Jumhûriyyah fî al-ᶜIrâq*, pp. 305–314.

[109] Ismet Sheriff Vanly, "Kurdistan in Iraq," in Gerard Chaliand (ed.), *A People Without a Country: The Kurds and Kurdistan* (New York: Olive Branch Press, 1993), pp. 150–152. For details for the split between Qâsim and Bârzânî, see Muḥsin Dizaiyyi, *Aḥdâth* ᶜ*Âṣartuhâ*, vol. 1 (Erbil: Dar Aras, 2001), pp. 180–182; al-ᶜÂrif, *Asrâr Thawrat 14 Tammûz wa Taʾsîs al-Jumhûriyyah fî al-ᶜIrâq*, pp. 396–402.

[110] Masᶜûd al-Bârzânî, *Al-Bârzânî wa al-Ḥarakah al-Taḥarruriyyah al-Kurdiyyah*, vol. 3 (Arbil: Iraqi Kurdistan Ministry of Education Press, 2002), p. 8.

and the government of the old regime centres around its animosity towards democracy, communism, the Kurdish people's national [liberation] movement, and all popular forms of public organization along with public freedoms."[111]

Since the Party had been without a newspaper for more than a year, the Central Committee decided to re-issue the clandestine pre-Qâsim *Ṭarîq al-Sha*ᶜ*b*, which had ceased publication once *Ittiḥâd al-Sha*ᶜ*b* was established under the free press laws. However, Zakî Khairî, the de facto secretary-general (who was now in charge of the Party), and his Central Committee and Politburo rejected any decisive action on the domestic level, such as support for the Kurdish rebellion or (as communist officers in the Iraqi Air Force had suggested) the use of force to topple Qâsim. In a letter to the KDP on 6 June 1962 he articulated the reasons for the Party's rejection of the proposed to topple Qâsim:

> Using force against a nationalist anti-imperialist government in the current situation, by a democratic party, will result, in the best of situations, in two possibilities, [one] either the existing regime will throw itself in the lap of imperialism and ally itself with all the reactionary forces in order to fight this [anti-government] movement, or [two], the imperialists and their agents will exploit this chance to overthrow the existing government and establish a reactionary government which will wipe out all the people's gains.[112]

The temporary leadership of the ICP thus proved ineffective. The Party was in disarray and increasingly losing popular support. Its cadres were demoralized, with many in prison, and its enemies, both nationalist and reactionary, were in control of the Iraqi political arena.

In September 1962, after a year and a half of enforced exile, Salâm ᶜÂdil, accompanied by his comrade al-Ḥaidarî, returned from Moscow to Iraq and this environment. ᶜÂdil immediately took charge and attempted to revitalize Iraq's communist movement. He convened a Plenary Session of the Central Committee, at which it was decided that ᶜÂmir ᶜAbd-ul-lah and Bahâʾu-d-Dîn Nûrî would be removed from all leadership positions and their memberships on the Central Committee frozen pending the results of the Party's investigations of their activities during the previous three years. The plenary session also stripped Zakî Khairî of all his Politburo posts and reduced him to the status of an active Party member assigned to the Middle Euphrates section. Muḥammad Ḥusain Abû-l-ᶜÎss was also stripped of his positions on the Central Committee, and Thâbit Ḥabîb al-ᶜÂnî's position as the reserve nominee for the Central Committee was frozen. Explaining the reasons for these actions, the final communiqué of the plenary session noted:

> The role of the Party in the past three years grew strong, side by side with the combating of opportunism. This reached its peak, especially in the struggle against subservience, indecisiveness, surrenderism, and liquidationism ... which had seeped into the Party under different slogans and concepts. ... these currents expressed themselves ... in

[111] As quoted in al-Kharsân, *Ṣafaḥât min Târîkh al-Ḥarakah al-Shiyû*ᶜ*iyyah fî al-*ᶜ*Irâq*, p. 98.
[112] Ibid., p. 99.

a dangerous way inside the Party leadership, and in particular . . . grew in the Politburo in a parallel line to the creation and growth of the anti-Party front. This group formed a firm opposition front inside the leadership, borrowing concepts, criteria, slogans, and means . . . from the outside anti-Party front. To achieve its objectives the opposition groups in the Politburo tried to conceal their [real] intent under the cloak of demanding change in the leadership, and followed the route of violating Party by-laws by combining to obstruct the work of the leadership. The opportunist, opposition clique composed of comrades Muḥammad (ᶜÂmir ᶜAbd-ul-lah), Nihâd (Bahâʾu-d-Dîn Nûrî), Thâmir (Muḥammad Ḥusain Abû-l-ᶜÎss) and Jandal (Zakî Khairî) obstructed the efforts of the leadership to analyze the situation in the country, and further obstructed the leadership from implementing a well-thought-out, and carefully considered, plan of retreat from a policy by the [Clique of Four] which was imposed on the Party, and which bonded the destiny of the Party and its future to that [bourgeois] stage, adapting Party slogans, policies, and the composition of its leadership according to the interests of the ruling bourgeoisie. The opportunistic opposition clique [Clique of Four] worked to exaggerate those mistakes, and exploited them to distort the face of the leadership and Party. . . . it did not stop with that, but stubbornly continued working to belittle the vanguard role of the CPSU in the international movement for the purpose of nationalist bourgeois thinking on this issue. The same thing applies to the Kurdish national question and the issue of Kuwait.[113]

Ironically, Salâm ᶜÂdil used the same charge that the Clique of Four had used to freeze him out of the Party hierarchy when they sent him and al-Ḥaidarî to Moscow. At the conclusion of the meeting, a new Secretariat was chosen, composed of Salâm ᶜÂdil, who served as first secretary and was in charge of the Baghdad and Central Military Organizations; Hâdî Hâshim al-Aᶜẓamî, who emerged as the Party's second in command and was in charge of the labour unions; Jamâl al-Ḥaidarî in charge of the Peasants' Bureau; and George Tallû, in charge of foreign relations and the international communist movement. The Politburo was now composed of Muḥammad Ṣâliḥ al-ᶜAblî, in charge of internal communications; ᶜAzîz Muḥammad, in charge of the Kurdish Branch Committee; and ᶜAbd-ul-Salâm al-Naṣirî, responsible for Baghdad although he was in Moscow at the time.[114] Responding immediately, Bahâʾu-d-Dîn Nûrî complied with the decision by expressing his complete agreement with the Party's decisions. Abû-l-ᶜÎss also wrote a very detailed self-criticism, accepting blame and explaining:

The reason for the vacillation of [our] opposition was to satisfy the Prime Minister ᶜAbd-ul-Karîm Qâsim more than we should, and the apprehension that mass action . . . would become an anti-dictatorship and anti-police condition. . . . I fully concur with the report of the secretary-general, approve of his aims, and support all the measures he has suggested against me, regardless of how harsh they may be, after they are finally decided by Party organs. On this basis, I condemn the opportunist, opposition clique. I condemn all four of them, including myself. I condemn its thoughts, tendencies, and its means, and all their deleterious actions, and I bear a large personal responsibility for

113 Yûsuf and Khâlid, *Salâm ᶜÂdil*, vol. 2, pp. 329–330.

114 Al-Kharasân, *Ṣafaḥât min Târîkh al-Ḥarakah al-Shiyûᶜiyyah fî al-ᶜIrâq*, pp. 100–101.

strengthening the clique by joining it, and working actively with it. I am responsible for their actions collectively and individually, even those actions that I did not participate in. I bear responsibility for the opportunistic, surrenderist and rightist views.... I bear responsibility for the hysteric activities of Bahâᵓu-d-Dîn Nûrî prior to the plenary session of 1959.... I feel my responsibility and the responsibility of comrade Zakî Khairî were extremely grave because of the harmful role our joining the opposition had in encouraging Bahâᵓu-d-Dîn Nûrî and ᶜÂmir ᶜAbd-ul-lah, and in helping them to cloak their surrenderist, liquidationist objectives, and influencing other comrades in the Central Committee and Politburo.[115]

A more sober evaluation from other members of the Central Committee, and from historians of the Party, concludes that the Party leadership was over-occupied with the so-called Clique of Four. This episode could have had a dramatic effect on the "party's policy towards Qasim ... and there were a number of factors (political, social, and so on) that exacerbated the episode; the Iraqi Communist Party would pay dearly in the future."[116]

The Fall of Qâsim

Shortly after these developments, Salâm ᶜÂdil began to prepare the Party for peaceful opposition to Qâsim by encouraging strikes and demonstrations against police oppression, and by condemning the Iraqi army's harshness towards the Kurdish people, who were by then in full rebellion against the government. *Ṭarîq al-Shaᶜb*, echoing these new policies in January 1963, declared:

Conditions in Kurdistan are similar to a country occupied by a foreign invader's forces, in which a policy of vengeance is practised without the restraints of decency, conscience, or honour. Cities and villages were wiped out, citizens in a great number of cases were killed to terrorize the population or with no reason, and thousands of peaceful homes were attacked, their contents looted and their valuables divided among high-ranking officers. In addition, scores of women were violated, and children and the elderly lived in constant fear. In this environment, and because of the Kurdish war, taxes were increased by the government and inflation climbed. Qâsim's progressive measures, especially as they related to agrarian reform, were reduced to appease the landlords and sheikhs ... as their reforms were considered to be a communist measure.

To put the Party's new direction into action the returning leadership took an active role in asserting its independence and increasing its public support and credibility with the masses. Departing from their previous veiled criticisms, the leadership now openly attacked the Qâsim regime. It issued a boldly worded directive to all Party branches initiating steps

to reactivate the mass struggle, especially among workers, poor peasants, and revolutionary democratic forces, ... against military dictatorship, ... [to] educate the comrades and

[115] Complete Report, reproduced in *Aḍwâᶜ ᶜAlâ al-Ḥarakah al-Shiyûᶜiyyah fî al-ᶜIrâq*, vol. 2 (Beirut: Dar al-Mirṣâd, n.d.), pp. 162–171.

[116] ᶜAzîz Sibâhî, *ᶜUqûd min Târîkh al-Ḥizb al-Shiyûᶜî al-ᶜIrâqî* (Damascus: Thaqâfah al-Jadîdah Publication, 2003), vol. 2, pp. 473–474.

organizations on the weakness of the governing military dictatorship . . . and [to] educate the masses to struggle against isolationism and actively work to solve the Kurdish crisis on a democratic basis.[117]

With the Qâsim regime's isolation at both the regional and the international levels, the increasing oppression of the regime's police agencies, and the regime's harsh treatment of the ICP, Qâsim was left without any organized public support and had to depend heavily on his supporters in the army. The race then began among opposition political parties to cultivate the support of disaffected army officers for the numerous opposition groups awaiting the regime's demise; at the same time, many officers were looking around for ideological groups that they thought had some chance of toppling the regime. Thus, the Baᶜth Party sponsored school strikes on 29 December 1962, which escalated into a nationwide movement. The communists, caught between their enemies – the Qâsim regime, on the one hand, and the Baᶜthists and their Arab nationalist allies, who considered the communists responsible for the evils of Qâsim's regime (including Qâsim's actions in Iraqi and Arab politics), on the other – now found themselves fighting both for their lives and for the survival of the very government that was responsible for their oppression.

On 3 January 1963, the ICP warned of an impending coup and called on all its members to be on the alert. A month later, with the help of the US Central Intelligence Agency (CIA), the regime unleashed a witch-hunt in classic Cold War fashion, with a list supplied by the agency of alleged communists that included all progressive forces (communists, leftists, Kassemites). Over ten thousand individuals were detained, and between three thousand and five thousand were executed. In the early morning of 8 February 1963, an army coup led by the Baᶜthists overthrew the Qâsim government. US National Security Council member Robert Komer told President John F. Kennedy, "The coup is a gain for our side."[118] ᶜAbd-ul-Salâm ᶜÂrif, Qâsim's revolutionary comrade turned political foe, who had aligned himself with the Nasserites, was installed as president and leader of a military-style junta. He gave the coup a nationalist stamp, automatically winning the support of the UAR. Salâm ᶜÂdil reacted by issuing a declaration that called for the masses to rally in support of the Republic and Qâsim. On the same day, to show its deep-seated distrust of communism, the new government broadcast Declaration 13, which called upon all Iraqis "to annihilate all communists wherever they exist."

Despite the crackdown, the communists were able to muster a three-day resistance in some quarters of Baghdad and Basra and in some areas of the Middle Euphrates, even after Qâsim's death at the hands of the army on 9 February. With the coup, a wholesale slaughter of communists and their sympathizers began. Thousands were arrested and tortured by "special committees" and by the Baᶜthist militia known as the National Guard. The campaign of terror that

117 Khairî and Khairî, *Dirâsât fî Târîkh al-Ḥizb al-Shiyûᶜî al-ᶜIrâqî*, p. 344.
118 Mark Curtis, *Unpeople: Britain's Secret Human Rights Abuses* (London: Vintage, 2004), p. 83.

ensured mixed personal, sectarian, and tribal hatreds. The new government initiated systematic torture, and, as one eyewitness graphically described it:

> People's legs were chopped off, piece by piece, . . . children's eyes were bound with ropes until their eyelashes were pushed into their eyeballs, women were beaten and sexually violated, and children were tortured in front of their parents. The torturers used tin snips to cut the hands, legs, and face muscles slowly. . . . Scores of victims were crowded into small rooms; [they were] forced to stand on one leg for a number of hours, and water from sewers was thrown on the wounds of the tortured. Others were left without water or food for days and [their] wounds [predictably] became infected. . . . other victims, both men and women, [were] hung upside down on ceiling fans for days, . . . and others were burned with hot metal objects, their bones broken by iron bars or their eyes blinded by cigarette butts or fingers. Nails were pulled off and electrified cattle prods [were] used to inflict pain.[119]

The secretary-general was arrested on 18 February after his second-in-command, Hâdî Hâshim al-Aᶜẓamî had – under torture – informed the coup leaders of his hideout. The Baᶜthists refused Salâm ᶜÂdil's attempts to open a dialogue,[120] and according to eyewitnesses, he was tortured for fifteen days:

> clubbed, hung from his feet to the ceiling, dropped unconscious headfirst, and then his legs were slashed and salt rubbed into the wounds. . . . almost all of his bones were broken; he was then thrown into a dank dungeon . . . naked, handcuffed, and left [in the coldest days of the year]. . . . He was deprived of food and sleep. . . . His eyes were squeezed until blood began to flow. . . . finally, he was crushed under a steam roller.[121]

All but three of the other members of the Central Committee and Politburo were also arrested and met fates similar to ᶜÂdil's; on 7 March 1963 the government declared that they had all been executed. In addition, Jamâl al-Ḥaidarî, Ṣâliḥ al-ᶜAblî, and ᶜAbd-ul-Jabbâr Wahbî, who had eluded capture and assumed the "central Party leadership," were arrested and executed on 20 July 1963.

The atrocities and torture employed by the new Baᶜthist regime, in which its leading members and most of its cabinet participated, were substantiated in the treatment of the ICP leadership after their arrests. Testimonies by Baᶜthist leaders of that period, documented forty years later, tell a gruesome tale. One army officer who was a member of the Baᶜth Military Bureau recounted:

> I visited ᶜAmmâr ᶜAlwash in the Nihâyah Palace where he was supervising the communist interrogations, and found with him ᶜAbd-ul-Karîm al-Shaikhlî [later to become foreign minister under Saddam Hussein before being executed by him] and Khâlid Ṭabrah [later a general director in Saddam Hussein's regime]. I was surprised to find ᶜAbd-ul-Jabbâr Wahbî [a member of the Central Committee and a professor of physics at Baghdad University] lying on the ground and at the point of death, asking for water. Ṭabrah responded "you pimp, you want water" and none was given.

119 "A Terrifying Report on Iraq," *Al-Ghad*, no. 3 (Prague, July 1964), p. 84.

120 Al-Fakaikî, *Awkâr al-Hazîmah*, p. 262, and ᶜAlî Karîm Saᶜîd, *ᶜIrâq 8 Shibât, 1963: Min Ḥiwâr al-Mafâhîm Ilâ Ḥiwâr al-Dam* (Beirut: Dar Al-Kunûz al-Adabiyyah, 1999), pp. 194–198.

121 Khairî and Khairî, *Dirâsât fî Târîkh al-Ḥizb al-Shiyûᶜî al-ᶜIrâqî*, p. 386.

Also forty years later, another detainee, a Kurdish medical doctor, corroborated this story, but with more details:

> I saw ʿAbd-ul-Jabbâr Wahbî having his leg sawn off at the knee, and next to him I saw another person, one of whose arms had been sawn off, and who was hanging from the roof by the other.[122]

In the meantime, the Baʿthists began to reverse Qâsim's progressive internal policies, such as those related to agrarian reform and to foreign control of the oil industry. They reopened the door to Western economic penetration and suspended many agreements for technical and economic cooperation with socialist countries. By bringing Iraq back into the sphere of Western influence and withdrawing from the socialist and non-aligned blocs, they plunged the country more deeply into the Cold War.

On the regional level, at least in the early days of the coup, Iraq was brought closer to Nasser, and on 17 April 1963 the new regime initialled an agreement that joined Iraq, Egypt, and the Baʿthist regime in Syria (which had come to power only a month earlier) in a Tripartite Pact of Unity. However, only a few weeks later the honeymoon between Nasser and the Iraqi Baʿthists was over. The Baʿthists were not interested in surrendering their power over Iraq to a united Arab state under the leadership of Nasser, and ever since Syria's withdrawal from the UAR in September 1961, Nasser did not trust Baʿthist intentions. The tension between Nasser and the Iraqi Baʿthists gradually translated into a conflict between the Baʿthists, on the one hand, and the Nasserites and nationalist army officers, on the other, and culminated in a wholesale purge by the new Baʿthist regime of the nationalists and the Nasserites and their supporters. In November 1963 a split between moderate and extremist Baʿthists over the policies regarding Nasser and Arab unity exacerbated the situation, with the result that President ʿAbd-ul-Salâm ʿÂrif, helped by moderate Baʿthists, nationalists, and Nasserites, purged the extreme Baʿthists, thereby initiating another short-lived honeymoon with the UAR. Although ʿÂrif continued to pay lip service to Nasser's programme for union, he soon began a complete purge of the Baʿth from the government.

The Rashid Putsch and the Death Train

The anti-communist fever that followed the Baʿthist coup in Iraq was criticized, retrospectively, by the more progressive elements within the Baʿth leadership, who quietly blamed this anti-communist revenge on the chauvinism of ʿÂrif and the conservatives, as well as of army officers and civilian officials. In general, however,

> the core leadership did not dissociate itself from the violence, or condemn it officially or publicly. Rather, it attempted to prevaricate, and even [to] hide that fact. Nevertheless,

[122] ʿAlî Karîm Saʿîd, *Al-ʿIrâq: Al-Biriyah al-Musallaḥah: Ḥarakat Ḥasan Sarîʿ wa Qiṭâr al-Mawt.* (Beirut: al-Furât Publishing House, 2002), p. 59.

the death of Salâm ᶜÂdil and others under torture annoyed some members of the leadership because of their fear of an international and local backlash, though some felt that the speed with which ᶜÂdil was eliminated may have been the result of news leaks, suggesting that he was, in fact, in dialogue with [some] of the civilian Baᶜth leadership . . . which some of the military leadership opposed, fearing a positive response.[123]

Though the Baᶜth atrocities and oppression after their 1963 coup decimated the ICP and left it in disarray, some limited and isolated pockets of ICP organization in the army and among workers remained intact. A few weeks after the coup, these groups started to communicate with one another, with military cells contacting workers' cells belonging to the Baghdad "Workers' Committee" of the ICP. Prior to the coup the Baghdad section had the reputation of being militant and had even challenged official ICP policies. Ibrâhîm Muḥammad ᶜAlî was a leader of the Workers' Central Committee, which was connected directly to the Party's Central Committee and controlled over fifty major labour unions. The committee permeated the working class in Baghdad and throughout the rest of the country. ᶜAlî belonged to a smaller Workers' Committee that had not been decimated by the coup,[124] and he was determined that his committee should act as if it were the Party. However, he continued to seek legitimacy, and he searched for the actual Party leadership of al-ᶜAblî, al-Ḥaidarî, and Wahbî until their murders became public.[125]

Ibrâhîm Muḥammad ᶜAlî attempted to gather in what was left of the other civilian cells; he assigned the task of organizing the cells in the army to a coffee shop worker, Muḥammad Ḥabîb (Abû Salâm), who did manage to connect with Corporal Ḥasan Sarîᶜ, the head of one of the army cells. However, Party turncoats eventually delivered ᶜAlî to the Security Services, and he died under torture without revealing any information. His death left control of the civilian cells as well as of the army cells to Ḥabîb, who, with the same vigour as Ḥasan Sarîᶜ had shown, continued to organize the revolutionary committee *al-Lajnah al-Thawriyyah*. The Sarîᶜ group within the army was organizing itself for military action, whereas Ḥabîb "prepared the political and popular grounds" for this action. In this way, "the civilians prepared the ground for the rebellion by mobilizing any who would be able to carry arms, enter the al-Rashid army camp, and help the soldiers execute the plan," which was to mobilize the imprisoned communists and Qâsim supporters and to overthrow the ᶜÂrif regime.[126]

Muḥammad Ḥabîb and Ḥasan Sarîᶜ, two corporals belonging to the ICP, and a tailor named Ḥâfiẓ Laftah, asked the remaining members of the ICP-CC for direction and informed it of their readiness to revolt. The Central Committee rejected their plan, ordered them to abandon the action, and reprimanded them, describing their proposals as "violations of principles, and in contradiction

123 Al-Fakaikî, *Awkâr al-Hazîmah*, p. 264.
124 Saᶜîd, *Al-ᶜIrâq*, p. 41.
125 Ibid., pp. 33–37.
126 Ibid., p. 297.

to Party discipline."[127] However, Muḥammad Ḥabîb did not reveal the Central Committee's response to his group and continued the planning with Sarîᶜ, leading him to believe that they were working in coordination with the Party leadership and with its blessing. The plan focused on the non-commissioned officers, who were to seize the military camps and then hand over command to the detained leftist officers and political leaders. They believed that such a plan was plausible, knowing, first, that those officers thought in similar political and social terms to them, and second, that if they did not move quickly, they would not have another chance.[128]

At dawn on 3 July 1963, the plotters, in conjunction with the remnants of the Baghdad and Middle Euphrates sections of the Party, mobilized two thousand troops, and were able to take over the most important military camp in Baghdad with the aim of liberating around one thousand army officers who were in detention at that time. The plotters planned to hand over power to the freed officers, who would then take over the leadership of the revolt. But although they succeeded in taking over the entire base at al-Rashid, the rebels met unexpected resistance from the prison guards and were unable to free the officers. This delayed the officers' scheduled arrival at pre-arranged units, which would have initiated the second phase of the uprising during which, according to the plan, the revolt would spread to other army camps. With this unexpected setback, the other units did not join in the revolt, even though the rebels had managed to detain the most important group among the political leadership, that is, the minister of the interior and Baᶜth Party secretary-general of the regional command, the minister of foreign affairs, and all the camp's commanding officers, not to mention the entire leadership of the Baᶜth Party's militia, the National Guard. The plan was detailed, carefully thought out, and daring,

> and its chances of success were high. However, some simple mishaps resulted in delaying the freedom of the imprisoned officers which limited the spread of the revolt, thus giving the government the time needed to respond and causing the revolutionaries to lose the element of surprise and initial momentum.[129]

The delay restricted the revolt to the one military camp only, and enabled the government to isolate the rebels.

Four decades later, the most detailed and documented work to assess the revolt and the responsibility for its failure concluded that the "evidence" comes down against Muḥammad Ḥabîb for his deception, arrogance, and animosity towards the leadership of the ICP. As already noted, Ḥabîb convinced Ḥasan Sarîᶜ that he had the complete confidence and support of the Party and that he

[127] Khairî and Khairî, *Dirâsât fî Târîkh al-Ḥizb al-Shiyûᶜî al-ᶜIrâqî*, p. 414. See also Bâqir Ibrâhîm [al-Mûsawî], *Mudhakkarât Bâqir Ibrâhîm* (Beirut: Dâr al-Ṭalîᶜah, 2002), p. 101.

[128] Saᶜîd, *Al-ᶜIrâq*, p. 44. For more details, see pp. 48–206.

[129] Saᶜîd, *ᶜIrâq 8 Shibât 1963: Min Ḥiwâr al-Mafâhîm Ilâ Ḥiwâr al-Dam*, p. 295.

spoke in the name of the Party leadership.[130] Bâqir Ibrâhîm al-Mûsawî, who took charge of the Party soon after the failed revolt, supports this assessment:

> There was a direct connection between the failure of the al-Rashid camp revolt and the renewal of the campaign of terror against the Party, as more than once a delegate from the leadership of the [attempted coup] movement contacted me . . . and spoke on behalf of the Party leadership without revealing the names of the [ICP] leaders so I could trust [the delegate]. I noticed that they were speaking with full confidence of an impending revolution and asked us to prepare for it. We promised them to do so. . . . then we heard from the cadre station [about] the failure of the revolt. We learned later more details on communication between the leader of the revolt, Muḥammad Ḥabîb, with al-ᶜAblî, who tried hard to persuade Ḥabîb to wait and avoid adventurism, . . . however [al-ᶜAblî] failed. . . . With the failure of the revolt, security pressures succeeded, on 7 July, in arresting Ṣabîh Mubârak and ᶜAdnân ᶜAbd-ul-Qâdir, the liaison members between the revolt and the [Party] leadership. These two led security forces to the hideout of the three leaders who were then arrested.[131]

What followed the failure of the coup was a ruthless hunt for and attack against the remnants of the ICP. Moreover, this unleashed the Baᶜth security forces on the detained officers, now believed to be a threat to the Baᶜth regime, since it assumed that had the officers been able to take command, the revolt could well have succeeded. Thus ᶜAbd-ul-Salâm ᶜÂrif insisted that "they must be killed" to eliminate any hope of utilizing them in a future military action against the state.[132] ᶜÂrif was able to convince Aḥmad Ḥasan al-Bakr of this view, and al-Bakr called upon his military colleagues to arrange for the executions to be carried out at the notorious desert prison of Nuqrat al-Salmân outside Baghdad.

Some in the civilian Baᶜth leadership objected to this plan and wanted to limit the executions to around thirty of the officers, given that most of them had had no knowledge of the plot. Nevertheless, several Baᶜthist army officers wanted all of them to be executed, and they were successful in convincing al-Bakr to send them all to the desert prison while their fate was being determined. All were shipped in chains, crowded together in a cattle train (that would later be called "the Death Train") in 120°F heat, for the six-hour journey into the desert. However, when the driver of the train realized that his cargo consisted of people, he more than doubled the speed of his train. Because his action meant that the train arrived at its destination in two hours (instead of in six), people were able to meet it with food and water for the prisoners. And since some of the men on the train were doctors or had medical training, only one of the officers died because of the trip.[133]

The aftermath of the revolt and the government crackdown left the Party leaderless, as all its resources had been concentrated in Baghdad. The Kurdish and Middle Euphrates sections remained intact, and thus the leadership passed

[130] Ibid., pp. 154–156.
[131] Bâqir Ibrâhîm [al-Mûsawî], *Mudhakkarât Bâqir Ibrâhîm*, p. 101.
[132] Saᶜîd, *ᶜIrâq 8 Shibât 1963*, pp. 302–305.
[133] Ibid., p. 303.

primarily to the experienced but unprepared leaders of these two sections, ᶜAzîz Muḥammad and Bâqir Ibrâhîm al-Mûsawî, both of whom were forced to shoulder the rebuilding of the ICP. Even though the revolt was unsuccessful, and its immediate impact on the Party was disastrous, some scholars consider it to have been the beginning of an armed struggle in Iraq in which the Partisan Marshes uprising of May 1968, five years later, was "nothing more than an extension of the new approach created by the al-Rashid uprising."[134]

[134] Saᶜîd, *Al-ᶜIrâq*, p. 208.

3

Party Rift

The Emergence of the Central Leadership

The Iraqi Communist Party remained popular with the Iraqi people despite the elimination of virtually its entire leadership and organization following the failed 1963 revolt. This allowed several attempts to rejuvenate the Party to take place. During the first few weeks after the 1963 Baᶜthist coup, the remnants of the Central Committee and Politburo – Jamâl al-Ḥaidarî, Muḥammad Ṣâliḥ al-ᶜAblî, and ᶜAbd-ul-Jabbâr Wahbî – continued running Party affairs in Baghdad under the name the Bureau of Central Organization. They attempted to re-establish communication with the scattered membership of the embattled Party and began to rebuild the Party's apparatus. But, on 21 July 1963, they too were arrested and summarily executed.

To fill the vacuum that resulted and direct what was left of the Party, a replacement leadership was hastily constituted, led by Bâqir Ibrâhîm al-Mûsawî, the only surviving member of the Politburo in Iraq, who had been the Politburo official in charge of the Party's Middle Euphrates section. This state of confusion, however, did not extend to the Kurdish branch of the ICP, which, being located in the rebellious northern Kurdish areas, was left virtually intact. The branch had established good working relations with other Kurdish groups, particularly with the KDP and its leader Mullah Muṣṭafâ Bârzânî, who had initiated a rebellion against the Qâsim regime in 1961. After the Party's 1962 plenary session, Salâm ᶜÂdil's Central Committee instructed the Kurdish branch to replace the Central Committee in case of an emergency or if for any reason it ceased to function normally. The efforts of al-Mûsawî in Baghdad therefore were advanced by the Party members located in Iraqi Kurdistan. The ongoing rebellion, and the general inability of government forces to control territory in the north, enabled Party members based in the north to begin the painstaking work needed to reconstruct the Party apparatus, to reconnect disparate and fearful Party members isolated in the rest of the country, and to begin the long process of building relations with the international communist movement.

This effort to build a bridge between the emerging Party of the 1960s and the international movement became critical, since clear signs of a Soviet policy shift were evident by the time of the ᶜÂrif-led coup of 18 November 1963. Altering its position towards the developing world in general, and towards the Arab world and the UAR in particular, Moscow demonstrated a pronounced effort to portray the ᶜÂrif regime in a positive light. Ṣâliḥ Mahdî Duglah, a Central Committee member from the Baghdad section of the ICP and a close Iraqi observer of Soviet politics, who was then residing in Moscow, noted:

> An intellectual foundation for a closer relationship between the Arab communist movement and Nasserism resulted. This orientation was sensed by some leaders of the ICP who exaggerated the [potential] of a relationship. . . . For the purpose of propagating this, and strengthening it, the Arab communist parties in Prague held a conference in the summer of 1964.[1]

These Soviet overtures were welcomed by the ᶜÂrif regime, and a month later its foreign minister informed the Soviet ambassador that he expected the "strained relations" between the two countries soon to become a thing of the past.[2] This was despite the draconian anti-communist measures that continued to be taken by the Iraqi regime, and despite the fact that the ICP's temporary leaders and its Kurdish leaders both continued to condemn the ᶜÂrif regime as an anti-progressive extension of the overthrown Baᶜthist regime.

This shift in the Soviet position signalled the beginning of a divorce between the policies of the CPSU and those of the USSR as a state, irrespective of any government's treatment of local communists. Such a disconnection had been evident, for example, in the Soviet policy towards the UAR throughout the three previous years, despite the UAR's oppression of communist parties. It was an abandonment of the notion of socialist fraternity, and as such, it bewildered communist true believers and initiated a critical evaluation of the USSR throughout the Arab world, while further intensifying discussions among the cadre and the leadership of the ICP. This had a profound impact on the ICP as a whole in the years to come, causing the most serious split in the ICP's history and haunting the Party until the end of the century.

At the same time, the leadership of the ᶜÂrif coup tried to project the appearance of a progressive regime, a fantasy made much easier with Soviet recognition. On the internal level, the ᶜÂrif regime dissociated itself from the atrocities of the Baᶜthist-led regime that immediately followed the coup. It attempted to settle the Kurdish rebellion, initiating negotiations through the good offices of President Nasser of Egypt that eventually concluded on 10 February 1964 in a ceasefire with the KDP and its leader, Muṣṭafâ Bârzânî. The USSR continued its flirtation with the ᶜÂrif regime and warmly endorsed the Kurdish ceasefire

[1] Ṣâliḥ Mahdî Duglah, *Min al-Dhâkirah: Sîrat Ḥayât* (Nicosea, Cyprus, Dar al-Mada, 2000), p. 146.

[2] *Pravda* (Moscow, 21 December 1963).

through a congratulatory message sent by Premier Khrushchev to ᶜÂrif.[3] The new regime also took concrete measures to align itself more closely with the UAR, and the Nasserite influence in Iraq increased dramatically. During Nikita Khrushchev's visit to Egypt on 26 May 1964, ᶜÂrif signed an Iraq-UAR agreement with Nasser in Cairo that created a Joint Presidential Council to oversee the coordination of social, economic, political, and military affairs between Egypt and Iraq in preparation for their eventual unification. Six weeks later, on 14 July, in what appeared to be an implementation of the agreement with the UAR, the Iraqi government took two steps in this direction.[4] First, on the economic front, it nationalized all banks and insurance companies, as well as thirty-two large industrial and commercial complexes, and created an Economic Organization for Banks to oversee the nationalized enterprises. These actions were similar to the socialist measures taken by Egypt earlier in 1961, and they aligned Iraq's economic structure largely with that of Egypt. Second, the Arab Socialist Union was created in Iraq and modelled after Egypt's official party organization, the Arab Socialist Union.[5] Another apparent step towards union occurred three months later, on 16 October, when the Joint Presidential Council was replaced by a Unified Political Command intended to oversee the unification process over the following two years.

Iraqi relations with the UAR quickly began to cool, however, and by September 1964 they were strained as a result of an attempted pro-Nasserist coup by ᶜÂrif's prime minister, Air Brigadier General ᶜÂrif ᶜAbd-ul-Razzâq. Razzâq served as the acting president while ᶜÂrif was attending an Arab summit conference in Casablanca on 15 September 1964. After order was restored and the coup leaders exiled to Cairo, a break with Nasser gradually developed. Publicly, the number of Nasserite cabinet members doubled from three to six by 14 November 1964, and they soon held the most important portfolios, giving the lie to ᶜÂrif's disillusionment.[6] The Soviets considered this to be a further sign that ᶜÂrif headed a progressive regime that was attempting "to raise the revolutionary struggle to a higher level," even though anti-communist and anti-Soviet publications were still spreading throughout Iraq, and the implementation of the Kurdish ceasefire remained largely ineffective. Despite events on the ground, the Soviet Union continued to support the ᶜÂrif regime,[7] and it resumed its arms shipments, which had been interrupted during the first Baᶜthist coup eighteen months earlier.

The ICP continued with efforts to rebuild the Party, wavering between condemning the regime for its anti-democratic, anti-communist stance and trying to find an accommodation with the new ᶜÂrif regime. The Soviets continued their public pronouncements in support of the regime, declaring its domestic policies to be progressive and endorsing it as anti-imperialist. Though Soviet approval

[3] *Tass* (Moscow, 15 February 1964).
[4] *Al-Ahram* (Cairo, 27 May 1964).
[5] *Al-Jumhûriyyah* (Baghdad, 27 May 1964, 15 July 1964, and 19 July 1964).
[6] *Ibid.* (Baghdad, 17 July, 1964).
[7] *Pravda* (Moscow, 18 July 1964).

was qualified with the hope that the government would settle the Kurdish issue fully and ease its anti-communist rhetoric and activities, the Russians failed to coerce the ʿÂrif regime into stopping its campaign against the ICP.[8] Against this background of the continued decimation of the Party at home, most of the surviving ICP leaders were now to be found residing in Eastern Europe and the USSR. This shadow ICP consisted mainly of those individuals who had left Iraq either because they had been frozen out of the leadership or expelled from the Party and were in the process of being rehabilitated, or because they were prominent cadre members who had been sent abroad either for their own protection, or to recuperate, or as scholarship recipients. All now found themselves faced with the responsibility for rebuilding the Party from the ground up and doing so without displeasing their hosts.

This difficult task fell on the Party's overseas organizational structure, the *Lajnat Tanẓîm al-Khârij* (the Committee for the Organization of Members Abroad), which at the time was headed by ʿAbd-ul-Salâm al-Nâṣirî (Anwar Muṣṭafâ). Al-Nâṣirî, who had been living in Moscow for the previous three years, was now the highest-ranking ICP leader and Politburo member outside Iraq. Al-Nâṣirî was familiar with, and had personal relationships with, the CPSU leadership by virtue of his position in Moscow. He developed good working relations with both the Soviet state and the Party apparatus, to the extent that he became the most trusted figure for both with regard to Iraq. In the absence of any legitimate formal Party leadership, and by virtue of his special position as a link between the international communist movement (including the CPSU) and what was left of the Party at home (following the execution of the secretary-general and the disappearance of the Politburo), al-Nâṣirî emerged as the de facto leader of the Iraqi Party and played a critical role in shaping and rebuilding the shattered organization. The Committee for the Organization of Members Abroad now included the Central Committee members Ḥusain Sulṭân and Nâṣir ʿAbbûd; candidate for Central Committee membership ʿAzîz al-Ḥâjj; Thâbit Ḥabîb al-ʿÂni; and Arâ Khâjâdûr, as well as two prominent advanced cadre members, Nûrî ʿAbd-ul-Razzâq Ḥusain and ʿAbd-ul-Raḥîm ʿAjînah.[9]

At the end of 1963, ʿAbd-ul-Salâm al-Nâṣirî convened in Prague the first meeting of the Committee for the Organization of Members Abroad, to discuss Party matters and deal with the aftermath of Party's devastation. His evaluation of the ʿÂrif regime and its policies were heavily influenced by the new official Soviet direction towards the UAR and the Arab world. To conform to the Soviet assessment, al-Nâṣirî called for a re-examination of the ICP's position, indicating that this would meet with the approval of international communism because of the shift in Soviet ideological policy regarding the non-capitalist path to development, in which "progressive" Arab regimes such as the UAR, Syria, and Iraq were seen as leading examples. Under these circumstances, the Committee for the Organization of Members Abroad assumed the leadership

[8] *Ibid.* (13 August 1964).

[9] Ṣalâḥ al-Kharsân, *Ṣafaḥât min Târîkh al-Ḥarakah al-Shiyûʿiyyah fî al-ʿIrâq* (Beirut: Dâr al-Furât, 1993), p. 120; and ʿAzîz al-Ḥâjj, *Ḥadatha Baina al-Nahrain* (Paris: n.p., 1997).

of the Party, utilizing resources put at their disposal by the Soviets. The committee assigned ʿAzîz al-Ḥâjj, the flamboyant and experienced Party journalist and theoretician, to oversee the "Voice of the Iraqi People," a radio station in Sofia, Bulgaria. The station became the Party's only public voice and channel of communication to Iraqis, giving the committee a virtual monopoly on the dissemination of information between the leadership and cadre at home and abroad. In essence, the committee's decisions and actions became de facto Party policy. However, the committee's room to manoeuvre was extremely restricted by its dependence on Soviet support and its close proximity to CPSU control.

The manifold tasks that faced the committee involved rebuilding the Party, conforming to the new Soviet line, reactivating the ICP's role on the Iraqi political scene, and regrouping the progressive elements inside and outside Iraq. To achieve these goals, the committee constructed a worldwide network under the rubric of the Movement for the Defence of the Iraqi People, which was overseen by a supreme committee dominated by al-Nâṣirî. The Movement also published *Al-Ghad*, a bi-monthly newspaper. In April 1964, in East Berlin, a new United National Front, patterned on the 1957 and 1959 models, arose from the movement. Its stated aims were to:

> serve the interests of the Iraqi people with all its nationalities and classes, work for complete national liberation, democracy, and social and economic progress, solve the Kurdish issue on the basis of accepting the legitimate national rights of the Kurdish people, genuinely participate in the Arab national liberation movement, follow the policy of positive neutralism, combat imperialism, and safeguard international peace.[10]

To this end, the Front appealed to "all political parties, groups, anti-reactionary and anti-imperialist elements, regardless of their ideologies and orientations, to work together in this United National Front."[11]

One by-product of the discussions of the Committee for the Organization of Members Abroad was a public evaluation of the Party's activities and leadership during the preceding five years. According to ʿAzîz al-Ḥâjj, right from the start of these meetings, a rift opened among the leaders over the nature of the new regime. Al-Ḥâjj, supported by Arâ Kh̲âjâdûr, Nûrî ʿAbd-ul-Razzâq Ḥusain, and ʿAbd-ul-Raḥîm ʿAjînah, contended that the ʿÂrif coup was a continuation of the old 8 February Baʿth̲ regime. In response to the increased vocal opposition of al-Ḥâjj and his group, al-Nâṣirî suspended the committee meetings, removed al-Ḥâjj from his radio station post, and took charge of the station himself. By the time the Kurdish ceasefire occurred in February 1964, al-Nâṣirî had convinced both the Kurdish and the ICP home leaderships to endorse the ceasefire agreement. In addition, during the meeting of Arab communist parties that was held in Moscow in April of that year, he persuaded the delegates to "bless" the ceasefire, and telegraphed ʿÂrif to that effect.[12] Al-Nâṣirî then moved to

10 *Al-Ghad*, no. 2 (Prague, May 1964), p. 1.

11 *Ibid.* [editorial], no. 3 (July 1964), p. 4.

12 ʿAzîz al-Ḥâjj, *Maʿa al-Aʿwâm: Ṣafaḥât min Târîkh̲ al-Ḥarakah al-Sh̲iyûʿiyyah fî al-ʿIrâq Baina, 1958–1969* (Beirut: al-Mûʾassasah al-ʿArabiyyah lil Dirâsât wa al-Nash̲r, 1981), pp. 182–192.

convene *al-Kâdir al-Mutaqaddim fî al-Khârij* (the Advanced Cadre Abroad), and without consultation with the Central Committee, he rehabilitated ʿÂmir ʿAbd-ul-lah, Bahâʾu-d-Dîn Nûrî, and their old comrade Thâbit Ḥabîb al-ʿÂni and gave them a full voice in the meeting.

Al-Nâṣirî continued to act as if he were in charge: he espoused the Soviet line fully, endorsed the ʿÂrif regime, and disregarded the opposition of ʿAzîz al-Ḥâjj and his three prominent comrades. According to ʿAzîz al-Ḥâjj, an announcement was broadcast to Iraq, contrary to Party by-laws, on the Voice of the Iraqi People radio station, as if the Committee for the Organization of Members Abroad had unanimously approved it for members abroad.[13] Indeed, the pronouncement eventually appeared as the Central Committee statement "For Strengthening National Independence, for Genuine Democratic Government, and Toward an End to the Dictatorship and the Abnormal Situation in the Country," which condemned the overthrown Baʿthist regime as

> the willing tool of the imperialists, a sworn enemy of the democratic movement with an insatiable lust for power.... To cover up their actions ... the Baʿthists used the slogan of Arab unity ... and in the course of accomplishing the February coup, the Baʿth leadership went even further and concluded a secret deal with the Anglo-American intelligence services and oil companies.... Despite its ruthless measures it was unable to destroy the Communist Party.[14]

The report claimed that a crisis that had begun to develop was eventually resolved in favour of the national movement by the coup of 18 November 1963, in which Nasserite elements and other nationalists participated, and noted:

> Under the impact of mounting discontent among the people and the armed forces, the November coup was compelled to direct its main blow at the fascist regime. The ultra-reactionary Baʿthist clique, the tool of the imperialists, was removed from the helm of the government. The fascist National Guard was disbanded. These measures conformed to the wishes of the people, and were indeed the result of their struggle and sacrifices. This inevitably led to a slackening of the terror against the people and helped to create more favourable conditions for the national-democratic movements. The Party considers that political independence is indispensable for completing national liberation and securing the economic independence of the country. Our Party, as before, resolutely opposes all views and trends which underestimate the importance of the cause of national independence and subordinate it to other, less important matters.... Imperialism is "Enemy No. 1," not only of national independence, but also of democracy both in Iraq and in all other Arab countries. The imperialists realize full well the importance of democracy for strengthening the national-liberation movement and enhancing the vigilance and militancy of the masses.... Our Party considers that the best way to strengthen national independence would be to establish a national-democratic regime in conformity with the will of the people, and in accordance with a republican democratic constitution guaranteeing the rights of the people.[15]

[13] Ibid., pp. 192–197.

[14] *World Marxist Review*, information bulletin, no. 17 (25 August 1964), pp. 33–35.

[15] Ibid., pp. 39–40.

The Central Committee report called for support for this potentially progressive ʿÂrif regime and expressed the Party's willingness to cooperate with the regime provided that it widen its popular base and relax its control to allow national forces to participate in the creation of the United National Front. In keeping with typical Soviet doctrine of the 1960s, the report stated:

> The key to the solution of the problems facing the national movement is a tried and tested way to a regime representing the will and interests of all the anti-imperialist classes.... today our people need unity more than ever before in order to restore the United National Front, which is a guarantee of the solution of the present crisis in the interests of the people, a barrier to imperialist conspiracies and military gambles of the reactionaries, and a means of effecting the transition to a normal democratic life in the country.
>
> All patriotic parties and strata, communists, democrats and other patriots, nationalists fighting imperialism ... must draw a lesson from past experience, and take an active part in setting up the United National Front as a union of all the political forces opposed to imperialism and reaction.
>
> While working for the alliance of all the anti-imperialist forces without exception, our Party does not rule out bilateral cooperation with any individual organization or patriotic force. The Party sincerely stretches out a hand to all who are prepared to cooperate on the basis of all, or part of, the common aims.
>
> In the Party's opinion, agreement on limited joint actions by patriotic forces in day-to-day struggles could be a preliminary step towards subsequent cooperation at a higher level in building the United National Front.[16]

In effect, this report opened the door for the full implementation of the Soviet line by Iraqis and served notice that the ICP was willing to cooperate with all national forces as well as with the ʿÂrif regime. On 20 June 1964, al-Nâṣirî issued an internal memorandum to members indicating the Party's complete adherence to the Soviet line and its change in policy towards the ʿÂrif regime, which it described as "anti-imperialist" while pointing out its "anti-democratic" leadership:

> Our Party refuses to raise the slogan of overthrowing the existing government in Baghdad, but rather, will follow the tactic of endorsing and strengthening its national content, by supporting every national and progressive measure it undertakes, and will further struggle ... to encourage the rulers to follow a decisive national policy against imperialism and its supporters ... and a democratic policy, respond to the interests of our people and align itself with the governments of Cairo and Algiers.

A month later, in July 1964, ʿÂrif put his nationalization measures into action; this was considered to be further proof of the progressive nature of the regime and was endorsed by the leadership of the ICP. The ICP immediately called for the "masses and decent forces in the country to unite and consolidate their ranks ... in order to safeguard these measures and strengthen them."[17] One

[16] Ibid., pp. 42, 43.

[17] A statement by the ICP on the occasion of the sixth anniversary of the 14 July 1958 revolution (middle July 1964).

month later, in August 1964, and for the first time, a Central Committee plenary session took place outside Iraq, further indicating the changes in the Party's decision-making process and widening the gap between the leadership and the grass roots.

Almost inevitably, frustration with this new decision-making process expressed itself in schisms and continuous tension between the Central Committee and the Politburo, and the Party's grass roots. Splits within and among these groups resulted in the fragmentation of the ICP and ultimately, over the next thirty years, of almost all political influence in Iraq. By the time of the Prague plenary session and the re-establishment of the Party structure through the election of the Central Committee, Politburo, and secretary-general, the Party programme was almost completely a Moscow decision and put in motion for the ICP by the Committee for the Organization of Members Abroad.

In its post-meeting final communiqué, the Party announced the selection of a new secretary-general, ᶜAzîz Muḥammad, whose Kurdish section of the Party was then the most intact of the Party's sections in Iraq. The naturally pleasant and diplomatic ᶜAzîz Muḥammad was also the least controversial of the possible candidates. The plenary session report expressed the Party's willingness to collaborate with the regime, justifying this tactic in theoretical terms:

> The positive position taken by our Communist Party toward the Arab Socialist Union sprang from the progressive thoughts, espoused or called for by the progressive elements in this organization, and based also on the potential future transformations in the composition of its leadership and future programmes.... our Party will not take a negative stand against this organization. On the contrary, it will take all necessary steps to cooperate with it, to strengthen the progressive nature of its policy, and [to] advance its ideology.[18]

A few weeks later, *Pravda* reported on the meeting's resolutions, which declared that Iraq was now "moving towards the non-capitalist path," praised the Arab Socialist Union as an anti-imperialist organization committed to social progress and Arab unity, and declared the ICP's support for the ᶜÂrif regime.[19]

The new Politburo now included Bahâʾu-d-Dîn Nûrî, ᶜÂmir ᶜAbd-ul-lah, Bâqir Ibrâhîm al-Mûsawî, and ᶜAbd-ul-Salâm al-Nâṣirî, in addition to Secretary-General ᶜAzîz Muḥammad. These members, who had rallied around Qâsim, and in 1968, around the Baᶜth regime, now became staunch supporters of what was labelled "the August Line." Although the plenum resolutions of the August meeting were not published, excerpts appeared in the *World Marxist Review* three months later.[20] They describe the Algerian and Egyptian revolutions as having moved beyond the framework of political independence and

[18] *Fî Sabîl Wiḥdat al-Qiwâ al-Waṭaniyyah wa al-Taqaddumiyyah; fî Sabîl Taᶜzîz al-Istiqlâl al-Waṭanî wa al-Taqaddum al-Ijtimâᶜî* [Toward the Unity of the Nationalist and Progressive Forces for the Sake of Strengthening Our National Independence and the Report of the Central Committee of the ICP] (Prague, August 1964), pp. 32, 33.

[19] *Pravda* (Moscow, 4 September 1964).

[20] *World Marxist Review*, vol. 7, no.1 (November 1964), p. 83.

as now influencing the struggle of the Arab and African people. Arab unity, as advocated by the two regimes, now had a "more progressive content." The report praised the November coup as "an action which ended the nightmare of fascist rule and created more favourable conditions for the struggle of the anti-imperialist forces, for the preservation of national independence, [for] changing official policy and returning Iraq to the camp of Arab liberation." The measures taken by the new Iraqi government corresponded to the interests of the people, such as stopping the war against the Kurds, creating a National Oil Company Law, improving relations with the UAR (including signing a coordination agreement with it), stressing the policy of peace and non-alignment, trying to restore and improve relations with the Soviet Union and the other socialist countries, and advancing nationalization laws.[21] The report continued:

The present regime, if it wants to strengthen and deepen the anti-imperialist trend, if it wants to pursue a progressive policy similar to that of the fraternal UAR and Algeria, must follow the example of the leaders in Cairo and Algiers in pursuing a clear and firm policy against imperialism and its agents. In this way it would safeguard the just oil rights of Iraq, implement and deepen agrarian reform, and release the political prisoners and detainees.

The Party will support all the patriotic and progressive measures taken by the present regime. It supports the co-ordination agreement between Iraq and the UAR and the steps towards unity, which will follow from it. It extends the hand of cooperation to all organizations and groups determined to uphold national independence, and will support the government in following a policy similar to that of the UAR and Algerian governments.

Our Party will, as it has always done, continue to fight for the just rights of the people. It determines its position on the basis of the attitude of the regime vis-à-vis imperialism (in its old and new forms), the demands of the workers, peasants and the masses of the people, and the problem of planned economic development, industrialization and social progress.

The Central Committee meeting stresses that imperialism was and remains the chief enemy of our people. Iraq is still at the crossroads. It has not yet achieved economic independence, and will not do so until it wrests its oil wealth from the grip of imperialist monopolies, and until it establishes industries on the basis of modern technology.

The tasks facing our country are the complete liquidation of imperialist positions, namely the economic positions, the realization of radical social and democratic changes, and above all, agrarian reform.

The meeting notes that the new developments in the Arab world, and on the international scene, open before Iraq the possibility of taking the non-capitalist way of development now being followed by the UAR and Algeria.

The meeting sees the problem of Arab unity in the context of the new developments on the Arab scene – the non-capitalist path and social progress, which enrich the progressive content of the Arab unity movement, and make it a movement aiming at both national and social liberation.

The Party is fighting, as it always has done, for the unity of all the anti-imperialist forces without exception, to uphold and consolidate national independence, and for

[21] Ibid., p. 83.

democracy and social progress. Our Party declares its readiness to conclude bilateral and multilateral alliances with all forces concerned with realizing social transformations and opting for the non-capitalist way for Iraq.[22]

The plenum paid lip service to the principle of collective leadership and called on members to:

close their ranks, sharpen their vigilance, consolidate the unity of their glorious party, strengthen discipline, and stand firm in the face of all forms of opportunism. The basic danger against which our Party should concentrate the ideological struggle in the present period is dogmatism and "leftist" [revisionist] sectarianism, which has its tradition in the revolutionary movement in Iraq, and has now suitable objective [existing] conditions on both the local and international levels.[23]

An article by Munîr Aḥmad (Bahâʾu-d-Dîn Nûrî) – once again a member of the Politburo – appeared in the December 1964 issue of *World Marxist Review* and was, in effect, an elaboration of the the August Line in tactics, strategy, and theory.[24] The article echoed the new Soviet line and operationalized the August resolutions. This signalled the ICP's abandonment of the classic communist doctrine that the leadership of the working class is essential; it advanced the idea that the "petit bourgeoisie . . . has to play an active part in the national struggle,"[25] and indicated that the Party was ready to be partners with these forces in leading the country towards the non-capitalist path through peaceful means. With this reasoning, the author dissociated the ʿÂrif regime from the Baʿth and portrayed it as a potentially progressive government:

Under Baʿthist rule there could be no question of non-capitalist development for Iraq. The reactionary policy of the government was a mockery of the socialist ideas it professed. However, the weakness of the regime soon became apparent and shortly after the February putsch it found itself in an embarrassing situation. The democratic forces, having not yet fully recovered from the heavy losses inflicted by the Baʿthist coup, and being not sufficiently united, were unable at this juncture to take the initiative and find a way out of the crisis. In these circumstances a group of army officers, former members of the Baʿthist party, staged another *coup d'état* on 18 November 1963, and overthrew the Baʿthist government, a move that ended the fascist regime and created more favourable conditions for the struggle to consolidate national independence, and enable Iraq to rejoin the mainstream of the Arab national-liberation movement.[26]

Despite its criticism of ʿÂrif's oppressive domestic policy vis-à-vis Kurds and communists, this article clearly rehabilitated the regime, which it judged to have taken definite steps in the interests of "our people." The article emphasized that future cooperation between the ICP and the ʿÂrif regime hinged on the

22 **Ibid., p. 83.**
23 Ibid., pp. 84, 85.
24 "The Situation in Iraq and the Policy of the Communist Party," *World Marxist Review*, vol. 7, no. 12 (December 1964), pp. 37–41.
25 Ibid., p. 39.
26 Ibid., p. 37.

regime's adopting a non-capitalist path of development. It declared that the Iraqi communists were "revising their method of struggle for political alliances in the light of this non-capitalist perspective," thus opening the door to the possibility of co-optation by the new regime. The Party declared:

The present leaders will not be able to steer the country onto the path the UAR and Algeria have taken unless they drastically change their policy, and unite all the progressive forces of the country. However, we believe that the struggle of the people to consolidate national independence and carry out radical socio-economic reforms, combined with progressive steps by the government, under the impact of the international situation, and the changes in the Arab world, can lead to changes in the government's policy in a democratic direction. This can be achieved, provided all the national forces – communists, democrats, nationalists, Arabs, Kurds, and other national minorities – unite in a common program of action. The choice of the non-capitalist path need not necessarily hinge on the removal of the present government. The transition could be effected by gradually changing the social structure of the government through support for those of its measures, which conform to the interests of the people, and by combating all anti-democratic moves.[27]

Bahâʾu-d-Dîn Nûrî further committed the Party when he declared that its main aim was the achievement of the "non-capitalist way," and that "we have changed our views on this question and are willing even to disband the Party and amalgamate with the regime's single organization, the Arab Socialist Union, just as the Egyptian Communist Party was in the process of doing."[28] The Nûrî article concluded:

Our attitude to the present regime is a tactical problem that can be solved, depending on the situation and on the position taken by the government. The possibility of the non-capitalist path for Iraq is an objective process that does not depend on the will or desire of anyone within or without the government. The movement in favour of taking the non-capitalist approach is steadily gaining momentum, representing a social force which, despite the difficulties and obstacles, is capable of imposing its will.

The Communist Party is working to give to the slogan of the non-capitalist path a political impact, powerful enough to influence any government in Iraq, and compel it to adopt this path or step down. We communists are not the only ones who advocate this idea. The communists are revising their methods of struggle for political alliances in the light of this non-capitalist perspective.

The Communist Party is ready to cooperate with the Arab Socialist Alliance in the fight against imperialism, and for democracy, social progress, and solidarity and unity with the UAR and other fraternal Arab countries. At the same time, we say that the Socialist Alliance must abandon its reactionary anti-communism as being incompatible with the interests of our people. We support the desire of all patriotic groups and elements to join in a single progressive political organization, which would occupy a worthy place in the struggle of our people, and all the Arab countries. However, we believe that this organization should not have a monopoly on the right to political action. We are

[27] Ibid., pp. 37–38.
[28] Ibid., pp. 38–40.

confidant that time will expose and isolate any reactionary elements that try to capitalize on nationalist slogans.

In the past, the Communist Party held that the establishment of a popular regime, under the leadership of the working class, was an essential prerequisite for the realization of radical social reforms and for building socialism in Iraq. In the new conditions, with [this] struggle for the non-capitalist path as the general political line of our party, we have changed our views on this question. We believe that at this given stage the best government in Iraq would be a coalition of all the patriotic forces fighting for complete emancipation and social progress.[29]

Grassroots Reaction to the August Line

In January 1965, ICP Secretary-General ᶜAzîz Muḥammad (alias Nâẓim ᶜAlî), moved to Moscow to further his education at the Communist University of the Toilers of the East (KUTV), as he had had very little formal education and wished to strengthen his understanding of Marxism. While there, he praised the positive changes taking place in the Arab liberation movement.[30] Thus, the new Party leadership moved fully into line with the Soviets, creating tension with dissident groups both outside and inside Iraq, who openly expressed their dissatisfaction.

ᶜAzîz al-Ḥâjj continued his subtle opposition to the direction of the Party leadership. As early as April 1964, in his capacity as the ICP representative on the editorial board of the *World Marxist Review*, he utilized the occasion of the thirtieth anniversary of the ICP to write a veiled attack on the ᶜÂrif regime. While still paying lip service to the CPSU, he noted:

The Iraqi communists are fighting to end the present military rule and establish a patriotic government of national coalition which will guarantee democratic rights (freedom for political parties, for trade unions and for the press), release of the victims of the fascist terror, genuinely free elections, to ensure a democratic solution to the Kurdish question, and to take a decisive stand against imperialism and the robbery effected by the foreign oil companies. The Iraqi Communist Party, a unit in the international communist army, has always held aloft the banner of proletarian internationalism. It has educated its members, supporters and the working people to support the great Soviet Union and its Communist party. Fahd said, "The enemy of the October Revolution is the enemy of our national cause."[31]

In addition, ᶜAzîz al-Ḥâjj took his criticism of the August Line to the Movement for the Defence of the Iraqi People and published his complete rejection of the August Line in its newspaper, *Al-Ghad*:

What is needed in Iraq today is not a one-party [organization]. . . . what is needed is a national, unified, broad front that will encompass the major political parties . . . and the elements and groups that are anti-imperialist and anti-reactionary. . . . The Pan-Arabist

[29] Ibid.

[30] *Pravda* (Moscow, 22 January 1965); see also *Al-Wasat*, no. 288 (London, 4 August 1997), p. 31.

[31] "The True Champion of the Working People," *World Marxist Review*, vol. 7, no. 3 (April 1964), p. 42.

groupings that talk about the proposed unified organization ... will do much better if they amalgamate themselves into a Pan-Arabist party.... This is their natural right. However, it is not their right, at all, to impose this party, by force or the usage of state agencies, on the entire nation. It is not their right to try to monopolize political action, and deprive the other political parties of it.[32]

Perhaps because of his non-conformity with the August Line, ʿAzîz al-Ḥâjj was replaced by Zakî Khairî as the ICP representative on the *World Marxist Review*.[33] One of his last official acts before his replacement arrived in Prague occurred in the middle of June 1965, at a public forum, the "Problem of the National Liberation Movement of the Arab People," where he deliberated with other Arab communist theoreticians on the notion of "Arab socialism," in an attempt to reconcile it to the new Soviet evaluation. Along with the sponsor of the August Line, ʿAbd-ul-Salâm al-Nâṣirî (Anwar Muṣṭafâ), al-Ḥâjj represented the Communist Party of Iraq. Al-Ḥâjj continued his low-key agitation against the August Line, opposing the accepted position by questioning the "non-capitalist path," the UAR as a model of non-capitalist development, and Nasserism as a successful socialist experiment. He noted that although in the UAR Nasserism was a progressive ideology and, in the long run, could develop in a revolutionary socialist direction:

Nasser's "Arab socialism" is not scientific. His ideology is a mixture of scientific, utopian, religious and other ideas ... [and] his ideology and practice should be examined in the process of development. From an ideological point of view, the UAR leaders have progressed from frank hostility to scientific socialism to borrowing and utilizing some of its ideas, albeit in distorted form. This general evolution of ideology should be taken into account.... The weakest link in that country, however, is the lagging of the political and ideological superstructure behind the revolutionary nature of the basis, in particular the exclusion of the masses from broad and vigorous participation in the government of the country.[34]

Al-Ḥâjj's agitation extended beyond formal Party leadership meetings and publications to public venues, and in early February 1965, while attending an Iraqi student meeting in Prague, he openly criticized the ʿÂrif regime and called for its overthrow. His final protest before he was replaced on the *World Marxist Review*'s board was published under a pseudonym in March 1965, and entitled "Freedom for the Patriots in Iraq." Since he had been a long-standing editorial board member, the *World Marxist Review* must have either approved or solicited the article. In this article, the author reminds his readers that the Iraqi regime was continuing to fill prisons with thousands of communists, who were mistreated and whose conditions had worsened. This was in spite of the ʿÂrif regime's promise

32 "On the Unified Popular Organisation ... or the Pan-Arabist Unified Organisation," *Al-Ghad*, no. 2 (Prague, May 1964), pp. 15–16.

33 Zakî Khairî, *Ṣadâ al-Sinîn fî Dhâkirat Shiyûʿîʿ Irâqî Mukhadram* (Göttenberg, Sweden: Arabiska Bokstavscentre, 1996), pp. 363–364; *World Marxist Review*, vol. 7, no. 9 (July 1964), pp. 74–82.

34 *World Marxist Review*, vol. 7, no. 9 (Sept. 1964), p. 58.

to restore law and order, and end the barbarous crimes of the Baᶜthist regime. This pledge was honoured only in part. All that the government has done is to correct its own injustice, while doing nothing at all to abolish the acts of lawlessness committed by the previous Baᶜth regime.

Commenting on these developments, the Beirut newspaper *al-Nahâr* stated that the total number of those to be released was not known. There is reason to believe that about 1,000 prisoners have been released. But even if this figure is correct, it means that only a tenth of those arrested at the time of the Baᶜthist coup of February 1963 will be set free.... Meanwhile, still larger protest campaigns, and still greater pressure by public opinion throughout the world, can do much to improve the conditions of the Iraqi political prisoners and wrest them from the dungeons.[35]

As a result of these activities, the ICP leadership accused al-Ḥâjj of having worked from 1965 to divide the Party.[36] In the meantime, the Party leadership attempted to silence the voices of criticism against the ᶜÂrif regime. In February 1965, it sent Nazîhah al-Dulaimî, one of its Central Committee members and a former Qâsim cabinet minister, to London to restrain the zeal of anti-ᶜÂrif Iraqi communist groupings. At that time, these groups were successfully soliciting the support of British human rights organizations that were preparing for a conference on the treatment of political prisoners in Iraq. Khâlid Aḥmad Zakî, an ICP official who was responsible for the student section in England, was the most active Iraqi student leader in Britain at that time and had worked for over six months to secure the sponsorship of these human rights organizations. He explained how:

I was so incensed that the Party leadership was trying to silence us, and ask us formally to reduce our involvement in this prestigious public forum, after we had worked so hard to enlist its support and sponsorship, so much so that I lost my temper in dealing with Dr Dulaimî, and most of those present in that meeting were about to walk out. Hearing and seeing this, Dulaimî had to modify her demands and tone, asking us only to reduce our antagonistic stance, especially when we spoke in the name of the Party. This was an eye-opener for me, as I discovered, to my dismay, there were some delicate negotiations via the UAR to open further dialogue with the ICP that would lead to the relaxation of the oppression, and effect further democratic changes. I began to see the degree of the leadership's corruption and the need for reform.[37]

Conference sponsors were the prestigious Bertrand Russell Peace Foundation, the British Committee for the Defence of Human Rights in Iraq, and the Supreme Committee of the Movement for the Defence of the Iraqi People, in which the ICP itself was an active member. The final communiqué of the London conference condemned the ᶜÂrif regime for its treatment of political prisoners and called for a worldwide campaign for their release. This was reported in *Pravda* as a news item and without commentary.[38] However, the conference

[35] Ibids., vol. 18, no. 3 (March 1965), p. 80.

[36] *Munâḍil al-Ḥizb*, vol. 14, no. 7 (mid-October 1968); see also al-Ḥâjj, *Maᶜa al-Aᶜwâm*, p. 222.

[37] Interview by author with Khâlid Aḥmad Zakî, London (17 March 1965).

[38] *Pravda* (Moscow, 10 February 1965).

produced an immediate response from President ʿÂrif, who, in a speech at the opening session of the Baghdad Industrial Conference on 11 February 1965, vehemently attacked the British human rights groups as agitators trying to interfere in the internal affairs of Iraq.[39]

ʿAzîz al-Ḥâjj's dissenting voice continued and was heard by ever wider audiences. He decided to write a critical evaluation of the Party to be entitled "The August Line." It was to be distributed to the Party cadre. Zakî Khairî, who was then also claiming to share these ideals, supported this initiative and agreed to co-write the work with al-Ḥâjj, but he withdrew his endorsement at the last minute after joining the board of the *World Marxist Review*. This post gave him the chance to be reunited with his wife and child for the first time since his marriage; they had been living in Moscow since the Party had banished him to the Middle Euphrates in the middle of 1962. ʿAzîz al-Ḥâjj continued to take his efforts to the public, however, and wrote an article in English for the British Communist Party newspaper *The Labour Monthly*, which criticized the August Line, attacked the ʿÂrif regime, and called the regime's its overthrow.[40] However, in her February 1965 visit to London, Dr Nazîhah al-Dulaimî succeeded in stopping publication of the article, and al-Ḥâjj was reprimanded by the Central Committee, which regarded his activities as a breach of Party discipline.

At the same time, on the ground in Iraq and Egypt, while the Iraqis were speaking of unity with the UAR, Nasser was being much less forthcoming than the pro-unionist Iraqis wished, almost certainly because of his negative experience with his first attempt at unity; for example, the formation of the UAR with Syria in February 1958, and its subsequent break-up in September 1961. Furthermore, and despite its pretence of social and economic progress, the ʿÂrif regime was suffering from many setbacks at home. Unemployment had soared, so that by autumn 1965 more than twenty thousand workers had been laid off, and the nationalized industries were facing real difficulties.[41] Nasserite ministers were now at odds with the government because, according to General ʿÂrifʿAbd-ul-Razzâq, President ʿÂrif was not interested in any serious socialist initiatives; his only purpose in employing them had been to gain more popularity as an Arab nationalist, on the back of Nasser's reputation and political clout.[42] Out of the combination of Iraq's economic problems and the government's lack of commitment to socialist reforms, a crisis began to develop between ʿÂrif and his Nasserite ministers. On 4 July, the ministers resigned en masse in protest against obstacles to implementing the socialist measures and against the increasing influence of conservative elements on ʿÂrif's thinking. On 6 September, continuing the pretence of supporting Nasserist notions,

39 *Al-Jumhûriyyah* (Baghdad, 12 February 1965).

40 Al-Ḥâjj, *Maʿa al-Aʿwâm*, p. 224; and Khairî, *Ṣadâ al-Sinîn fî Dhâkirat Shiyûʿî ʿIrâqî Mukhadram*, p. 263.

41 Ministry of Finance in Iraq, *Taqrîr ʿAn al-Siyâsah al-Iqtiṣâdiyyah fî al-ʿIrâq* (December 1965), p. 12.

42 Interview by author with ʿÂrif ʿAbd-ul-Razzâq, Cairo (27 December 1971).

ᶜÂrif appointed Air Staff Brigadier General ᶜÂrif ᶜAbd-ul-Razzâq, a well-known Nasserite, as prime minister. But nine days later he exiled al-Razzâq to Egypt, having accused him of plotting to overthrow the regime while ᶜÂrif was in Casablanca at an Arab summit meeting. In returns, General al-Razzâq accused President ᶜÂrif of orchestrating the entire affair, enticing him to stage the coup only to assure its failure, in a political ploy to portray the Nasserites as "bumbling plotters." To show his own commitment to Nasserism, to continue to exploit its public appeal, and to allay Cairo's fears, the president publicly portrayed the coup attempt as a personal initiative of the general and not as a pro-Nasserist plot.[43] The following day, ᶜÂrif appointed in Razzâq's place a conservative Arab nationalist, ᶜAbd-ul-Raḥmân al-Bazzâz, who had served as ᶜAbd-ul-Razzâq's civilian deputy. A respected law professor and conservative nationalist with Nasserite leanings and good UAR contacts, Bazzâz became the first civilian prime minister since the 1958 coup. This manoeuvre secured Nasser's support, which was essential for a vulnerable regime with little popular appeal and facing the possibility of a Baᶜthist counter coup.[44]

In ICP circles, meanwhile, al-Ḥâjj continued his veiled but now more vocal attacks on the August Line. At the end of February 1965, while in Prague, he published a pamphlet examining non-capitalist development in Iraq, in which he criticized the concept as a non-scientific and ambiguous approach, rejected the inevitable leading role of the petit bourgeoisie; attacked the ᶜÂrif regime as non-democratic, called for the ᶜÂrif regime's overthrow,[45] and posed the question, "How can a rightist military rule lead the country to a non-capitalist goal?"[46] Indirectly, he was criticizing Soviet interference in Iraqi communist affairs, and the naiveté of theoreticians,[47] but he reserved his most scathing attack for the ICP leadership, stating that "communists in every country will serve the aim of the international proletariat... to the degree that they adopt a reasonable policy for their country's revolutionary national movement, and to the same degree that they work courageously and firmly to improve this [local] movement."[48]

Al-Ḥâjj did not stop with this critique, and he continued his opposition to the August Line by publishing a limited edition of the revised text of his August 1966 lecture in Brno, Czechoslovakia. The event brought together Iraqi students studying outside the country, and in his lecture, entitled "Observations on Neo-Imperialism and How It Should Be Combated," he attacked the August Line with vigour. While the entire Party leadership was now in either Prague or Moscow, conditions within Iraq were deteriorating further. With virtually no

[43] Interview by author with Colonel Ṣubḥî ᶜAbd-ul-Ḥamîd; Col. Ra<u>sh</u>îd Muḥsin, director of military intelligence under ᶜÂrif, and Col. Hâdî <u>Kh</u>ammâs, Cairo (24–26 December 1971).

[44] *New York Times* (April 15, 1966).

[45] *Ḥawla al-Taṭawwur <u>gh</u>air al-Raʾsimâlî fî al-ᶜIrâq: Mulâḥaẓât <u>Sh</u>a<u>kh</u>ṣiyyah* (Prague, 1965), pp. 1–7.

[46] Ibid., p. 14.

[47] Ibid., pp. 13–14.

[48] Ibid., p. 29.

leadership present in Iraq to direct day-to-day Party operations, its ineffectual response to the crisis in the country marginalized the Party.

While the ICP languished in internal disarray, ʿÂrif gradually consolidated his personal power within the army; he also dissolved the National Council of the Revolutionary Command in early September 1965 and transferred its legislative powers to the cabinet, leaving defence and internal security to a National Defence Council whose membership came predominantly from the military and therefore, was loyal to him personally. Al-Bazzâz introduced a political framework for ʿÂrif's ideology under the rubric of "mature Arab socialism." This became the new orientation of the cabinet, at the same time further reducing the socialist character of the previous Nasserite-oriented programmes. ʿÂrif also continued to conciliate conservative elements through a balance of private- and public-sector economic initiatives; all the while he paid lip service to Nasserism and cooperation with the UAR in order not to lose populist appeal.

Some relaxation of government controls and restrictions, and the need to return to operations on the ground, encouraged the ICP leadership to return to Iraq. The three newest members of the Central Committee, Bahâʾu-d-Dîn Nûrî, ʿÂmir ʿAbd-ul-lah, and ʿAbd-ul-Salâm al-Nâṣirî, slipped back into the country during the winter of 1965.[49] They took charge of the Party and began the process of restructuring it, implementing the August Line through a new administrative structure. These three Central Committee members became the Party's highest policy-making group, supported by the new structure the *Lajnat al-Tanẓîm al-Markazî* (Committee for Central Organization), and in effect they became the entire Central Committee and Politburo for the Party. Bahâʾu-d-Dîn Nûrî, officially described as simply the most senior Party official residing within Iraq, in reality acted as its secretary-general. However, the widespread grassroots rejection of the August Line now threatend to engulf the entire Party and posed a serious obstacle to the new leadership. According to an internal Central Organization Committee circular, fifty per cent of both the student organization and the Baghdad district – the largest, most active, and most ideological groups in the Party at this time – had resigned in protest against the August Line, while the majority of those who remained were also against it. In addition, the Middle Euphrates and Southern sections reported membership losses of 25 per cent.[50]

Rival factions began to emerge across Iraq to challenge the ICP. In early 1965, a previously unknown group of younger Party members accused the Party leadership of a betrayal of Marxist principles and of complete subservience to Moscow; they expressed their disillusionment with the Soviet policy towards the ʿÂrif regime and, in reaction to the August Line, broke away from the Party. Their 8 March 1965 circular accused the Party of becoming a tool of the Soviets, whom they blamed for the split in the international communist movement. The group evidenced pro-Maoist leanings and identified themselves

[49] Khairî, *Ṣadâ al-Sinîn fî Dhâkirat Shiyûʿî ʿIrâqî Mukhadram*, p. 263.
[50] *Munâḍil al-Ḥizb* (10 September 1965).

as *al-Lajnah al-Qiyâdiyyah al-ᶜUlyâ li al-Ḥizb al-Shiyûᶜî al-ᶜIrâqî* (Supreme Leadership Committee for the Iraqi Communist Party).

This group described the ICP leadership as "opportunist" and rigid, and as "having nothing in common with communist ideology but the name." It further maintained that "like a parrot repeating what Radio Moscow announces, they [the ICP] wait for their policies to be drawn from Radio Moscow." The group stated that its new organization was committed "to struggle against opportunism, treason and Khrushchevism" and promised that it would follow its own independent approach to communism. In early February 1966, the group issued a widely circulated detailed ideological statement entitled "Observations on the Chinese-Soviet Dispute." The statement traced the roots of the Sino-Soviet split, laying the blame squarely on the CPSU and Khrushchev, accepting the Chinese version of events, and bringing to the attention of the members a supporting publication by the Foreign Language Publishing House in Peking entitled *A Debate on the General Direction of the International Communist Movement*. The group also called on the new CPSU leadership under Leonid Brezhnev, which had come to power in 1964, to correct the errors of the previous Khrushchev regime. It warned the new Soviet leadership that if they did not relinquish control of the international socialist leadership,

> and [did] not punish the surrenderists, revise comments, and correct the dangerous direction [of Marxism-Leninism] and its violation, then our Party, and all other parties and genuine communists in the world, will struggle forever under the leadership of the brotherly Chinese People's Communist Party to expose and isolate the new leaders [of the Soviet Union under Leonid Brezhnev], and march to spread and safeguard Marxism-Leninism for the sake of protecting socialism and peace.

Although the splinter group had no impact on the Iraqi political scene, it continued to grow in size, which gave it the confidence to style itself the one true Marxist-Leninist party that would represent "our people's glory and our national culture," and later to publish a party newspaper, *Kifâḥ al-Shaᶜb* (The Struggle of the People).

In early 1964, a number of leftist officers from the lower echelons of the army and police, many of whom had been expelled from the armed forces during and after the overthrow of Qâsim, began to hold the ICP leadership responsible for the slaughter that had followed the Baᶜthist coup. Calling themselves *al-Lajnah al-Thawriyyah* (the Revolutionary Committee), they identified as the main cause of the Party's problems its faulty leadership and policies. Moreover, they considered the Party's adherence to the August Line to be an extension of its erroneous direction. They began preparing to challenge the ᶜÂrif government by recruiting dissatisfied Party members, especially among the military. In preparation for an "armed struggle," they concentrated their energies on recruting well-known army officers who had joined the Kurdish rebellion in the north after the overthrow of Qâsim and succeeded in enlisting the most senior communist army officer, the respected Staff Lieutenant Colonel Salîm al-Fakhrî. Al-Fakhrî had been expelled from the army in 1949. Released after spending almost ten years in prison, he had worked as Qâsim's radio and television director between late 1958 and early 1959. Despite his having formally left the Party, he fell out of favour again during the rift between Qâsim and the communists because of his communist convictions. In late October 1964 al-Fakhrî agreed to lead the proposed coup, after receiving the plotters' exaggerated assurance that they had "thousands [of supporters] in the army and had stashed away enough weapons that their members would be able to use." After he joined the plot, he supplied the group with the names of a proposed new government which would be led by a Revolutionary Popular Council. However, a month later, the conspirators were arrested and their organization withered away. Salîm al-Fakhrî and about four hundred suspects were imprisoned, where they remained until the second Baᶜthist coup of July 1968.[51]

In the face of this widespread dissatisfaction and Party fragmentation, the "home" Party leadership, led by Bahâᵓu-d-Dîn Nûrî and his colleagues, had no choice but to reassert control. The trio attempted to appear democratic by reflecting cadre wishes and to exercise responsibility while not antagonizing those who held official and legal Party power – the majority of the Central Committee, the Politburo, and the secretary-general, who were all residing outside Iraq. Nevertheless, because of the difficulties in communicating with the leadership abroad, as well as because of increasing pressure at the grass roots, Party action began to suffer a certain paralysis. This only added to the confusion among the grassroots Party membership, and contributed to the creation of two antagonistic power centres, one within Iraq that was forced to deal with the restive cadre, and a second, residing in Eastern Europe, who formulated ICP policies to be more in line with those of the Soviets, and who were less responsive to the rank-and-file membership. The leadership within Iraq asked for instructions from the secretary-general, who responded in March 1965 by giving the green light to a conference for the advanced cadre and the Central Committee then in Iraq, to be held in mid-April in Baghdad. Accordingly, a draft statement was forwarded to the home leadership and circulated on a very limited scale; its basic purpose was to reduce antagonism to the August Line. In March 1965, in order to legitimize this action and to appear more consultative than his predecessors, the secretary-general convened the Central Committee within Iraq for what he expected would be pro forma approval. Although the draft statement did not negate the basic premise of the August Line, it did try to reformulate some of its ideas in more acceptable terms. However, influenced by ᶜAzîz al-Ḥâjj and Zakî Khairî's opposition to the draft, the Central Committee rejected it on the grounds that it did not address the basic issues of the Kurdish problem and the overthrow of the ᶜÂrif regime.[52] The Central Committee then charged ᶜAzîz al-Ḥâjj and Zakî Khairî with developing a new draft to be circulated to the advanced cadre in Iraq.[53]

[51] Interview by author with Salîm al-Fakhrî, London (27 February 1990).
[52] Al-Ḥâjj, *Maᶜa al-Aᶜwâm*, pp. 224–229.
[53] Interview by author with Zakî Khairî, Damascus (18 March 1987).

Amid mounting pressure, the Central Committee at home followed the instructions from the secretary-general and scheduled a meeting for mid-April to present the original draft statement. Party members in Iraq were unaware of the Central Committee's discussions and revision; the new statement from the secretary-general and the Central Committee did not arrive in time to be considered for the conference. Responding to the general mood of the Party, *Ṭarîq al-Shaᶜb*, in its mid-March 1965 issue, mildly criticized the regime for its nationalization measures, suggesting that these could not be understood in isolation from the nature of the regime and the relations of production in Iraqi society. *Ṭarîq al-Shaᶜb* argued that the measures "did not result in any fundamental change in the makeup of the regime, its policies, or in the semi-feudal and capitalist relations of production. The oil sector is still, in effect, controlled by multi-national corporations."

To implement the new direction of Soviet foreign policy in the Arab world, Arab communist parties began to shift their rhetoric in early 1964; Nasser was lauded as the main advocate of friendship with the USSR, and his experiment in government was called the best example of non-capitalist development. The ICP leadership also seemed to be moving in this direction. The main source of dissatisfaction lay in the need for new leadership, since those in charge were the same individuals who had participated in the debacle that decimated the Party in 1963. For example, Bahâʾu-d-Dîn Nûrî, who had been expelled from the Party at that time, was now in charge of the Party. Thus a serious organizational flaw still needed to be addressed through a Party Congress and the election of new leader. The Party leadership began sending some of its most committed functionaries, who were living in Eastern European countries and in the USSR, to Iraq to prepare the intellectual ground. The aim was to take charge of the key sections of the Party, the main one being the Baghdad district; the leadership chose Khiḍr Salmân (Abu Jaᶜfar), Ḥusain al-Gumar (Walîd) and Peter Yûsuf to return to Iraq.[54]

Activists also arrived in Iraq from Western Europe, especially Britain, and began to join the Baghdad district. Among the returnees, two important personalities, Najim Maḥmûd in 1958 and, a decade later, Khâlid Aḥmad Zakî (Ẓâfir), introduced fresh ideas that helped mobilize the Baghdad section. Prominent among these ideas was an embrace of protracted civil war and a rejection of the the old guard's reliance on the army as the major instrument of revolutionary change (though they acknowledged the role of revolutionary elements within the army). Both Ẓâfir and Najim Maḥmûd had grievances against the leadership and had openly condemned the August Line from its inception.[55] When the conference was held in mid-April 1965, these grievances surfaced and dissatisfaction marked the deliberations. There was agreement on the need to change Party policy towards the regime, however, and a call for the regime's

[54] Numerous personal interviews with Zakî Khairî, Damascus (18 March 1987); Najim Maḥmûd, Paris (18 May 1982): and ᶜÂmir ᶜAbd-ul-lah, London (18 December 1997).

[55] Central Leadership, *Fî Dhikrâ Istishhâd Khâlid Aḥmad Zakî* (Baghdad, 1971), pp. 30–71.

overthrow was endorsed. Two views began to emerge on the tactics of gaining power, both of which rejected the August Line in its entirety and accepted the principle of "decisive action"; they disagreed over whether the decisive action should be a military takeover or a popular armed revolution.

In the end, the conference called for the overthrow of the regime through a military coup d'état led by the Communist Party. ᶜÂmir ᶜAbd-ul-lah championed the view that only after the success of the coup would non-communist opposition forces be invited to assume public leadership roles in the new government, since tight secrecy and a sudden strike against the regime through the army were essential for a successful coup. In contrast, Bahâ᾽u-d-Dîn Nûrî argued for input from opposition forces in the planning and execution of the proposed coup. As a result, separate reports were delivered to the Central Committee members in Europe, presenting each of these positions.

The abridged communiqué from the conference, written by Zakî Khairî, attempted to reflect both views and to acknowledge the Party's grassroots wishes when it declared that "in the future, Party functionaries and rank and file [members] will have a bigger say in determining the attitude of the Party and in formulating its policy."[56] To quell Party unrest, the statement condemned the government and for the first time called for the "overthrow of the dictatorial military regime ... and for a provisional government of a national coalition ... for democratic freedoms, for a democratic settlement of the Kurdish question and for reinvigorating the country."[57] The communiqué criticized the actions of the government, pointing out that the number of executions of leftists and communists in a single year under the ᶜÂrif regime had exceeded that for the entire monarchical period. The regime's oppression of the Kurdish people was also highlighted, and the communiqué pointed out that

> several thousand communists and democrats [continue to] languish in jail. Power is concentrated in the hands of the military junta, which has deprived the patriotic forces of any legitimacy and freedoms. The present rate of the implementation of the land reform laws is such that it will take twenty-five years to implement.[58]

The communiqué also accused the regime of being a tool of the multinational oil companies. The communiqué paid lip service to the UAR government while noting the UAR's support of the dictatorial regime in Iraq.[59] But by the time the final document was approved by the Central Committee, the session was billed as "Documents of the Plenary Session of the ICP," further details were introduced, and the attack on the ᶜÂrif regime was much more explicit:

> The rulers persist in seizing on methods of despotic and dictatorial rule, thereby defying the will of the people and all their patriotic forces. They are using what is called

56 "The Situation in Iraq and the Position of the Communist Party," *World Marxist Review*, vol. 8, no. 6 (June 1965), p. 80.

57 Ibid.

58 Ibid.

59 Ibid., p. 81.

the "transition period" as a pretext to monopolize political power, maintain abnormal conditions and martial administration or a state of emergency, to enact reactionary and freedom-inhibiting laws. They try to camouflage the dictatorial character of the present military rule by means of the so-called "consultative college," and by forming state security courts. The "transition period" was also used as a pretext for vesting legislative, executive, and even judicial functions in the hands of the command of the armed forces, the presidency of the republic, most of the cabinet portfolios, and in a small clique of highly placed military personnel bent on despotism and on invoking military procedure in administration and rule.

The condemnation by the present rulers of the one-man dictatorship does not prevent them from dedicating all the press and official information organs to deify the present President of the republic, and to portray him as a military dictator with unlimited prerogatives.

The masses of the people and all anti-imperialist forces, irrespective of nationality and political views, are therefore called upon to pool efforts: First, to overthrow the ᶜÂrif-Yaḥyâ military dictatorship, and install a government of national unity embracing all patriotic parties, groups and personalities from among the democrats and anti-imperialist nationalists. Second, this government is to start, forthwith, to eradicate the remnants of the terror and emergency law of the previous dictatorships, ensure democratic liberties, evolve a peaceful and democratic settlement of the Kurdish question, and hold free general elections to transfer the country to parliamentary-constitutional life as a prelude to forming a government emanating from the will of the people.

The report of the plenary session connected the Kurdish issue to the question of democracy in Iraq, and it offered specific solutions to the problem:

The settlement of the Kurdish question is organically bound up with that of democracy and the installation of a democratic regime in Iraq. The governments, which denied the legitimate national rights of the Kurds and oppressed them, are the selfsame governments that simultaneously ignored the democratic rights of the Iraqi people, and oppressed citizens of different views and diverse nationalities.

There will never be a just and solid settlement for the Kurdish question short of complete autonomy for the Kurdish people within the framework of the Iraqi Republic. National unity in Iraq cannot be maintained and consolidated unless account is taken of the legitimate rights of the Kurdish people.

The junta usurping the power has, through its outrageous policy, torn national unity asunder, and has not observed its former pledge to observe the ceasefire agreement of February 1964. Therefore, the Kurdish revolutionary movement has the right to doubt their [good faith] and refuse to lay down their arms until their legitimate demands are met, and constitutional and practical guarantees made to secure and respect these.[60]

On the issue of democracy, the statement was much more explicit in its rejection of the August Line:

In the conditions prevailing in Iraq, democracy assumes a place of prime importance, inasmuch as, in the modern history of Iraq, it has been a pivot of protracted struggle between the people and the reactionary rulers.

[60] *Information Bulletin*, no. 52 (2 September 1965), pp. 22–28.

Experience has shown that the path to uniting national ranks is that of free party life and optional collaboration in a national front, not that of decrees and administrative orders imposing one particular form of organization. There can be no other alternative than to allow all anti-imperialist parties and groups, irrespective of nationality and political views, to enjoy equal rights to publication and political activity, and to allow the people to choose the ideas and slogans corroborated by life in the course of application, and to discard what is erroneous and futile. . . .[61]

The Arab Socialist Union has the right to be one of the political parties in the country, but cannot [alone] be a substitute for [democratic] party life under conditions in Iraq, which are distinct from those in other Arab countries.[62]

The report also went into detail about the proposed national coalition, citing the following twelve bases for the front:

1. A solid, democratic settlement of the Kurdish question by responding to legitimate Kurdish national rights, including autonomy within the framework of the Iraqi Republic.
2. An amnesty for all those condemned to death, as well as for political prisoners and detainees; a restoration of the rights of citizenship that had been withdrawn from Iraqis, an end to police persecution and "renunciations"; and an inquiry into the perpetrators of crimes of murder, plunder, and sedition under the fascist regime.
3. The reinstatement of servicemen and civilians dismissed for political reasons.
4. Democratic freedoms, including the freedom to publish and to organize parties and trade unions, for all patriotic forces to the exclusion of none.
5. A purge of imperialist agents from state organs.
6. A resolution of the acute living problems of the people, provision of foodstuffs at reasonable prices, combating of speculation in and manipulation of food prices, and an improvement in peoples sanitary and cultural standards.
7. A resolution of the problems of unemployment, an end to wholesale dismissals, the fixing of a reasonable minimum for wages, and guaranteed social security for workers and their families in cases of disease, old age, and death.
8. Restoration of Iraqi's legitimate right to [its own] petroleum, and putting into effect the proposal to establish a national petroleum company.
9. A lowering of the present ceiling on land ownership, revoking payment for land allocated to the peasants, providing peasants with instructions and material aid, and forming an effective body to carry out the agrarian reform.
10. A plan to develop the national economy on a sound scientific basis and with the active participation of the people, and with a view to industrializing the country and developing the state sector of the economy,

[61] Ibid., p. 28.
[62] Ibid., p. 27.

taking into account the protection of national capital from foreign competition.

11. The consolidation of Arab solidarity; the provision of effective aid to secure Arab rights to Palestine, Aden, and the Arab South; the improvement of Iraqi relations with the UAR and other liberated Arab countries so as to gradually proceed along the path of realizing inter-Arab unity on a solid democratic basis, and with reliance on the will of Arab peoples.
12. The pursuit of a clear policy in the struggle against imperialism, and for peace; the support of national liberation movements; and a consolidation of friendship and cooperation with the Soviet Union and the rest of the socialist world.[63]

The April session pacified some groups but antagonized others, particularly those of the Baghdad district. They felt that the conference had not addressed substantive issues, such as the accountability of the leadership for the August Line, and when to hold the next Party Congress, the last one of which had been twenty years earlier. Also, a good number of the cadre felt that the April plenary session had only been a delaying tactic to forestall action against the Party leadership, especially when the "decisive action" discussed at the conference had ended up being a military coup rather than a popular revolution. More puzzling, the call for a military take-over was being propagated at a time when the Party was infiltrated by the regime's intelligence services. In addition, the same time, the Central Committee and the secretary-general, looking at events from Eastern Europe, were apprehensive about the call to overthrow the regime. The April resolutions committed the Party to a violent path, which was contrary to the peaceful approach the Party had followed since the secretary-general had assumed office. Moreover, such a policy was contrary to CPSU dictates. In Iraq, preparations were made for a Central Committee meeting in July, at which the resolutions of the April session could be operationalized, thus hastening a confrontation with ʿÂrif.

Party Leadership Responds to Internal Tensions

By 5 April, ʿÂrif had broken a ceasefire and resumed his military actions against the Kurds. This initiated a schism between the ʿÂrif regime and the Nasserist bloc and caused the mass resignation of all the Nasserites from the cabinet on 4 July. The July Central Committee meeting took place in this environment. Its resolutions, which were released at the end of August 1965, reversed the August Line, and rejected the Party's official coexistence policy with the ʿÂrif regime. The resolutions also branded the regime the most reactionary, chauvinistic, and despotic wing of the ruling class, stating:

> The despotism, chauvinism and political reactionism of the government have enraged the people, especially after the aggressive war against the Kurdish people. Such attitudes and

[63] Ibid., pp. 26–27.

policies have been accompanied by attempts made by . . . ʿÂrif and his closest supporters to impose a policy that seriously threatens the national interests and, in its essence, is hostile to the Arab liberation movement and the struggle for solidarity and national unity. The attempt to reach a new "agreement of thieves" with the foreign oil monopolies, the failure of the general offensive launched by the forces of the government against the Kurdish revolutionaries, the excessive actions against the interests of the people, the reliance on reactionary elements, and the denial of the supreme national interests have increased the anger and indignation of the people against this government and, at the same time, have increased both the isolation of the regime and the contradictions within it.[64]

In an obvious attempt to discredit the regime, the resolutions declared that the regime had wavered in its course and was no longer in the progressive camp, and thus that it was to be condemned. Cairo was advised to follow suit:

The ʿÂrif bloc with its policy, which is basically against the interests of the national struggle for liberation, can never be the representative of Arab nationalism in Iraq. Add to this the fact that with its policy, which is hostile to the people, it is inflicting harm on Cairo, its progressive policy and leadership, and the ties of solidarity and brotherhood between the two peoples.[65]

The resolutions censured the ʿÂrif regime for being oppressive and non-democratic, and officially signalled the Party's retreat from any further cooperation with the Arab Socialist Union, arguing that

the Socialist Union has failed to prove itself a viable political organization that can rally behind it all national forces, and is today losing the freedom of independent action and thus the ability to become a focal point for the mobilization of the national forces. No doubt, it is going to be subjected to measures that aim at its liquidation or a further weakening, making it completely dependent on the ruling group, and ending by becoming the focal point for the reactionary forces. A situation of this sort will undoubtedly lead to changes in the positions, attitudes, and structures of the various national groups and blocs. It is not impossible, in such circumstances, to see the emergence of new elements, currents, and subsidiary organizations that will show firm opposition to the regime, even if they are few in number and [at present] have little influence.[66]

Finally, the report once again criticized the regime for its aggressive war against the Kurdish people.

After their success at the April and July meetings, the Baghdad section and other Party dissidents were now able to extract concessions from the Party leadership. They moved for the convening of a plenary session of the Central Committee and the advanced cadre. This group urged that all the Party's resources be devoted to implementing the principle of decisive action, and they again called for a condemnation of the August Line and the disciplining of those responsible

64 *Al-Akbar* (Beirut, 26 September 1965), pp. 3, 7; and *Ṭarîq al-Shaʿb* (Baghdad, end of August 1965).
65 *Al-Akbar* (Beirut, 26 September 1965), pp.3, 7.
66 Ibid.

for it, and for a specific date on which to hold a Second Congress that would evaluate both the Party and its activities during the previous decade. Twenty-five Central Committee members and advanced cadre attended this enlarged three-day Central Committee meeting in Baghdad, which began on 9 October and was dubbed in Party circles "the meeting of the twenty-five." Two main working papers, concerning how decisive action could be made operational, were presented. ʿÂmir ʿAbd-ul-lah adopted one view, which called for an immediate communist-led army coup since the ʿÂrif regime was now isolated and possessed little political support following the withdrawal of the Nasserites from government. In addition, the regime had its hands full dealing with the Kurdish rebellion in the north. ʿÂmir ʿAbd-ul-lah maintained that once the communists were in power as a result of the "decisive action," the other patriotic forces would rally to the Party's support. He stressed that the time was ripe for action, and if the Party did not seize this opportunity, others might.

The opposing view was represented by Bahâʾu-d-Dîn Nûrî, who argued that this was an adventurist policy that could unite all anti-communist forces against the Party, lead to a civil war, and end in the Party's demise. He called for collective action with other patriotic forces to carry out the coup, maintaining that the communists would have to share power with these other forces and might even have to play their role behind the scenes. In the final vote, ʿÂmir ʿAbd-ul-lah's position was chosen. Further, the old Central Committee was disbanded, and the new Central Committee that was elected included all the previous members of the Central Committee apart from one, Ḥusain al-Gumar (Walîd), and six new members. Al-Gumar had chaired the Central Organization Committee, antagonized the grass roots, and spearheaded the confrontation with the cadre group. Steps were taken to implement the "decisive action plan" with the creation of two new organizations. A military section was organized among Party members in the armed forces to recruit new members from their ranks, and an armed Party militia was also established to support the planned action.[67] The deliberations of the enlarged Central Committee meeting were communicated to the Central Committee and the secretary-general in Prague, who held a plenary session six weeks later on 18–19 November, to discuss this turn of events. In essence, the secretary-general had to deal with the immediacy of ʿÂmir ʿAbd-ul-lah's plan and the contrary conservatism of Bahâʾu-d-Dîn Nûrî. In addition, he had to accept the input of the grass roots on policy and organizational matters, a precedent that necessitated a change in both the Party's by-laws and its practice.

ʿAzîz al-Ḥâjj and Zakî Khairî led the opposition to ʿÂmir ʿAbd-ul-lah's plan. They considered it to be "irrational," arguing that the proposed coup was being

[67] Al-Ḥâjj, *Maʿa al-Aʿwâm*, pp. 229–236; al-Kharsân, *Ṣafaḥât min Târîkh al-Ḥarakah al-Shiyûʿiyyah fî al-ʿIrâq*, pp. 125–128; Hanna Batatu, *The Old Social Classes and Revolutionary Movements of Iraq* (Princeton University Press, 1978), pp. 1041–1045; Samîr ʿAbd-ul-Karîm, Iraqi Intelligence Service, *Aḍwâʾ ʿAlâ al-Ḥarakah al-Shiyûʿiyyah fî al-ʿIrâq*, vol. 4 (Beirut: Dar al-Mirṣâd, 1982), pp. 52–57.

forced on the grass roots who were not prepared for it. They both favoured a popular revolution that would include other popular forces. Zakî Khairî was very disturbed by what he perceived as violations of Party discipline, and he called the decisions of the enlarged meeting (such as disbanding the old Central Committee and electing a new one) a grass roots "coup" in organizational terms. He accused the trio in Baghdad of whipping the conference into a frenzy by promoting the principle of violence on the pretext that there was no other choice, and he claimed that this was a "cover-up" of the real crisis in the Party leadership. He considered the situation to be extremely serious, since the opposition to the Central Committee and the secretary-general

> is no longer confined to the Politburo, but has moved to the level of the cadre.... This situation is dangerous and threatens the leadership of the Party in its ability to direct the Party apparatus.... in my opinion, preparing a revolutionary military action requires a central leadership, skilled politically and militarily, and under the control of the secretary-general.[68]

While emphasizing the need for a Party conference, al-Ḥâjj also attacked ᶜÂmir ᶜAbd-ul-lah's report as being unrealistic, and described the trio as "unfit" to occupy the leadership position at home. He declared:

> In my opinion, the central efforts of the Party should, from now on, be directed to diligent and serious preparation for a Party congress.... all intellectual and political preparation for such a conference must take place in secrecy, but with a depth of analysis that requires exposing to the cadre all the documents, minutes, and basic theses related to the period, at least from 1963 on, including correspondence between the cadre and the [Central Committee in a discussion of the August Line].[69]

Both Khairî and al-Ḥâjj thought an important ingredient in the maturing of the path to revolution was to pay more attention to the Kurdish revolution and that this had been neglected by both reports, particularly that of ᶜÂmir ᶜAbd-ul-lah. Both also wanted to discuss the Party experience since 1963, though less publicly in Khairî's case.[70]

The secretary-general was cautious in his response to these developments, and he stated from the outset in various respects that the August Line did not seem to be an accurate analysis of the political situation within Iraq:

> Our position vis-à-vis other [national Iraqi] forces and the regime [is incorrect], and the influence of President Nasser on ᶜÂrif has been exaggerated... as proved by the issuing of the April pronouncement of the Central Committee.... those in charge of the Party [in Baghdad] have a complete right to express their views freely.... we attempt to give them specific directions to guide the rest of the cadre, and will provide them with objective facts.... My reservation centres around the fact that we might have different evaluations [of the situation], which may seem to incline towards a public exposure of our disagreements, and this is not very healthy. It does not mean that we do not say

[68] ᶜAbd-ul-Karîm, *Aḍwâʾ ᶜAlâ al-Ḥarakah al-Shiyûᶜiyyah fî al-ᶜIrâq*, pp. 64–70.
[69] Ibid., pp. 72–76.
[70] Ibid., pp. 61–81.

anything, and we can even pinpoint specific mistakes and, in the name of the Party, admit to making them. . . . however, in our present situation, it is incorrect to "compete" in exposing our faults. . . . We must confess that the August Line policy was incorrect in a number of ways, particularly vis-à-vis the regime, but [that] the future avenues of cooperation [with other regimes in the future] are correct. . . . We do not have to deal with past Party policies; we need to delineate the present direction. If we offer anything, we must formulate it fully.[71]

ᶜAzîz al-Ḥâjj, however, stated that, notwithstanding, a fear of admitting mistakes still seemed to exist, and he called for a more open discussion.

The result of the two-day mid-November meeting was a fifteen-page response, drafted on 18 December by the secretary-general with the help of his supporters on the Central Committee, excluding ᶜAzîz al-Ḥâjj and Zakî Khairî.[72] He directed his remarks to the home leadership, in a roundabout way criticizing the tone of the October enlarged Central Committee meeting and describing it as a hastily put together gathering:

Whereas the preparation for the meeting should have been discussed in the Central Committee first, and consultation with the other Central Committee members, outside [the country], should have taken place. All the suggestions advanced on the issue of leadership, which were connected to the concept of decisive action, have no justification. Rather they caused damage to the Party's position. All these suggestions and measures, I am sorry to say, appear to us irregular and irresponsible.

The enlarged meeting had no authority to elect either a temporary or permanent leadership, and what has taken place was in violation of the Party by-laws. In our opinion, this must be corrected.[73]

This response asked not that the decisions be reversed, but that the Party carry on as if they were formal and official until the Second National Congress – for which the rest of the Party leadership would gradually return – could take place in the safety of the Kurdish areas of northern Iraq. By then more than one view would be available for consideration.[74] However, in April 1966, the Central Committee plenum returned conditions almost entirely to what they had been previously by reseating the expelled members of the Central Committee and confirming those elected in the October meeting.[75]

On 13 April 1966 the Iraqi political scene dramatically changed when ᶜAbd-ul-Salâm ᶜÂrif's helicopter crashed and he was killed. Three days later, his brother, Major General ᶜAbd-ul-Raḥîm ᶜÂrif, the acting chief of staff, was chosen as his successors; al-Bazzâz continued in his role of prime minister. During the al-Bazzâz period, some oppressive measures against the communists were relaxed, and a certain stability emerged, brought about by the semblance of the rule of law. In an attempt to deal decisively with the Kurdish uprising,

71 Ibid., p. 64.
72 Al-Ḥâjj, *Ḥadatha Baina al-Nahrain*, p. 85.
73 ᶜAbd-ul-Karîm, *Aḍwâʾ ᶜAlâ al-Ḥarakah al-Shiyûᶜiyyah fî al-ᶜIrâq*, p. 84.
74 Ibid., p. 85.
75 Batatu, *Old Social Classes*, p. 1061.

ᶜAbd-ul-Raḥîm ᶜÂrif undertook a massive spring offensive, deploying sixty-five thousand troops in conjunction with heavy aerial bombardment of Kurdish strongholds. The offensive ended in a June ceasefire based on al-Bazzâz's twelve-point proposal. This proposal recognized Kurdish nationality from the perspective of fundamental law, accepted Kurdish as the official language in the Kurdish areas, and guaranteed the Kurds freedom of assembly, press, and association. In effect, it granted the Kurds political autonomy and proportional representation in the Iraqi parliament. Outraged army officers, who perceived the ceasefire to be a capitulation, were further offended when al-Bazzâz's finance minister complained that army expenditures had more than tripled in less than ten years.[76] The rebel officers managed to force al-Bazzâz's resignation on 6 August in favour of an ex-army officer, General Nâjî Ṭâlib, but by May 1967 ᶜÂrif had sacked Ṭâlib and had taken on the office himself, with the result that the Kurdish problem remained unresolved.

While the army was engaging with Kurdish opposition to the ᶜÂrif regime, Iraqi intelligence agencies were keeping close tabs on the activities of the Iraqi Communist Party. Having infiltrated every Party organization, including the Central Committee, they successfully monitored ICP activities.[77] Consequently, when preparations for the "decisive action" were being initiated in late 1965 and early 1966, the security forces began a crackdown on the Party. In less than ten months, six members of the Central Committee, including the official in charge of the military section of the Party, had been arrested: in fact, the massive number of arrests of ICP members across the country effectively defeated plans for the "decisive action." The Middle Euphrates section was completely crushed, and the clandestine Party press in Baghdad was confiscated and its staff imprisoned. To deal with the onslaught, the Central Committee went forward with their plans and started secretly moving back to Iraq; Zakî K͟hairî was the first to arrive in Baghdad, in the autumn of 1966. He had always been suspicious of the trio of Bahâʾu-d-Dîn Nûrî, ᶜÂmir ᶜAbd-ul-lah, and ᶜAbd-ul-Salâm al-Nâṣirî, and a year earlier had warned Secretary-General ᶜAzîz Muḥammad, "How could you leave Party affairs in the hands of these [vicious] bayonets [brutes], when you are outside the country?"[78] ᶜAzîz al-Ḥâjj arrived shortly after, followed by the secretary-general and the rest of the Central Committee. They were now forced to deal with the aftermath of both the enlarged meeting in October and the ensuing crackdown by government security forces.

If this were not enough, a more pressing problem, now spearheaded by the Baghdad section, began to surface, coalescing around what later became known as the Cadre Group. From 1964 to 1967, and specifically in reaction to the August Line, the Baghdad section had seethed with discontent. Their criticism

76 Ibid., p. 1065.

77 Interview by author with Colonel Ras͟hîd Muḥsin, director of military intelligence under President ᶜÂrif, Cairo (18 February 1973).

78 K͟hairî, *Ṣadâ al-Sinîn fî D͟hâkirat S͟hiyûᶜî ᶜIrâqî Muk͟hadram*, p. 263.

was focused on the leadership, which had not addressed the concerns of the cadre and had not implemented the resolutions of the enlarged meeting of October. To the Baghdad section members, holding the Second Party Congress was of the utmost importance so that the Party could deal with what they viewed as outstanding structural, political, and ideological issues. They regarded the leadership's inaction as an intentional delaying tactic, whose aim was to wear down the resolve of the grass roots and regain complete control of the Party. They therefore attempted to put into effect what they considered were the agreed to resolutions from the enlarged meeting by preparing a draft report in their own names. The report attempted to evaluate the Party's experiences and activities over the previous decade and point out what were seen as the causes and consequences of the contemporary situation. Although it hinted that the responsibility for the errors and failures fell on the Party leadership, the report did not identify particular individuals. The draft was offered for review to the member of the Central Committee who was at the time in charge of the Baghdad section, ʿAzîz al-Ḥâjj He saw nothing wrong in having the document circulated, not only to the Baghdad section but also to the entire Party cadre, for educational purposes. Encouraged by this response, the drafters of the report edited their copy, and although the nature of the report did not change, its tone became much harsher and its rhetoric more outspoken. They then distributed the edited reports. The Central Committee reacted by ordering immediate cessation of the distribution through formal Party channels, but hundreds of copies had already been sent out and the report's substance was circulating in discussions among the Party cadre.

It was in this atmosphere that the Central Committee and the secretary-general met in Baghdad for the first time since 1963. They agreed to take action on two fronts. First, they initiated a series of actions to disband what they considered to be the core group of agitators within the Baghdad section; the leaders of the Labour and East Karadah sub-sections were moved to other areas of the country or to Eastern Europe, or they were threatened with expulsion from the Party. The war of words between the Baghdad section and the Central Committee escalated in June 1966, when the Baghdad section issued a statement attacking the Central Committee for its inaction. It also challenged the Party leadership by calling for a popular, armed insurrection to overthrow the Iraqi military regime. In August the Central Committee responded in a statement rejecting this "adventurist approach," maintaining that "a military coup d'état is not a popular insurrection suitable to the special conditions of our country." Thus, the ideological lines between the two camps were clearly drawn. Their disagreement was no longer about approaches or personalities, but was now specifically ideological and philosophical.

The second outcome of the Baghdad meeting between the Central Committee and the secretary-general was a Central Committee plenary meeting that was held in February 1967 to plan the Party's response to the Baghdad agitation. During this meeting, the secretary-general notified the Central Committee that he intended accept a private invitation to go to Moscow and that Zakî <u>Kh</u>airî was to be in charge in his absence. He also replaced the Central Committee member in charge of Baghdad with ʿAzîz al-Ḥâjj, who had been promoted to the Politburo. Lastly, he charged al-Ḥâjj and Zakî Khairî, ʿÂmir ʿAbd-ul-lah, and Majîd ʿAbd-ul-Riḍâ with preparing for the Second Congress, which was scheduled to be held the following year. These moves saw ʿAzîz al-Ḥâjj now having to deal with issues he had once raised himself, and thus the Baghdad section now had a member of the Central Committee who was sympathetic to their concerns.[79]

The core group of the Baghdad section, however, refused to submit to threats or enticements and became more vocal, extending their activities across the entire Party. Viewing the actions of the Central Committee as an example of bad faith, the Party cadre and other sub-section leaders increased their support for the dissident Baghdad group, so that the conflict took on the form of a struggle between the Baghdad section, with the support of the majority of the rank and file in the countryside, and the newly reconstituted Central Committee. Again, the Baghdad section called for internal Party reform to be implemented through the holding of a Second Congress, charged the Central Committee with the responsibility for the August Line and its aftermath, and demanded that the Party leadership be held accountable for the Party's previous actions.

The battle then moved to the preparatory committee charged with organizing the Second Congress. Two working drafts of the proposed documents were prepared, each representing the view of one of the two competing factions. In support of those opposing the Party leadership, Zakî Khairî and ʿAzîz al-Ḥâjj resurrected their original 1965 report, though its language was toned down and no individuals were mentioned by name. As noted earlier, this report, "An Attempt to Appraise Our Party's Policies," was written in Prague in reaction to the August Line. It offered a critical evaluation of the Party's experience between 1956 and 1963, and blamed the leadership of the Party, namely the Central Committee and the Politburo, for the Party's missteps. The report maintained that the leadership had been responsible for all the setbacks suffered by the Party, particularly during the Qâsim era, when the ICP had become subservient to Qâsim whom the document identified as representing the interests of the bourgeoisie. It further claimed that towards the end of the Qâsim regime, when Qâsim's overthrow was clearly inevitable, the leaders had done virtually nothing to safeguard the Party from destruction. Indeed, they had actually strengthened the Party's association with Qâsim, who by then was becoming increasingly isolated from the masses. The report continued that the leadership had been impotent that it had reached its lowest point with the August Line, and that it had deepened the rift within the Party.

The second draft report, "A Contribution in the Appraisal of our Party's Policies," was written by ʿÂmir ʿAbd-ul-lah and Bahâʾu-d-Dîn Nûrî. They attempted to counter the views advanced by the al-Ḥâjj report, arguing that the

79 Ibid., p. 275; and al-Ḥâjj, *Maʿa al-Aʿwâm*, pp. 278, 279.

Party's policy during the Qâsim era (1958–1963) should not be simplified and treated as if it were a single unchanging approach. They pointed out that before succumbing to his dictatorial tendencies, Qâsim had been genuinely patriotic and could have been won over if the Party had exercised more tact in its dealings with him. Their report also cautiously rejected the Party's armed resistance to the February coup of 1963, led by the Baᶜth, admitting that this had been a tactical error and asserting that a strategy of "retreat to the countryside" should have been put into action instead. They argued that had the Party avoided resisting the coup by staunchly defending Qâsim, it could have mitigated the ICP's exposure to the horrors of the Baᶜthist backlash, and that instead of pursuing a direct armed confrontation with the new regime, the ICP should have marshalled its resources. Overall, the report was mild in its criticism of the Party leadership, and it completely ignored any discussion of the August Line.

The two reports were released soon after the February plenary session and were introduced to the cadre, along with an internal Party memorandum entitled "On Directing the Intellectual Activities," dated March 1967, in which the Central Committee admitted the confusion in the Party ranks. Even so, it did not take any responsibility for the divisions and instead attributed the Party's problems to international and organizational forces beyond its control, explaining:

> The triumph of the rightist deviation in 1964 took place in conditions and circumstances favourable to the growth of rightist ideas, which were helped by the pressure of petit bourgeois notions.... In addition, the confusion prevalent in the Arab and international communist movements... [and] also the huge gap in [the personnel of] the Party leadership structure, exacerbated the situation.... The August Line ignored the will of the cadre and Party organizations. A fundamental turning point in the Party's principles and policies, such as the 1964 about face, ought to have been preceded by an ongoing intellectual preparation which should have been contributed to, and accepted by, the majority of the Party.... The consequences of the August Line were the people's loss of confidence in the Party [leadership], and a wide-ranging internal confusion within the Party.... The reaction [of the cadre] to this deviation, and the methods used to superimpose it [on the membership], such as the violation of internal democracy, resulted in erroneous reactions [by the leadership] to the situation whose ramifications we are still dealing with now.... The April 1965 meeting corrected the Party's actual policy, but did not condemn the intellectually wrong rightist deviations.... the enlarged Central Committee meeting of October 1965, while condemning the August Line, did not solve the problem because the admission of the problem was not accompanied by a practical analysis or explanation to educate the cadre... and this confusion was transformed into a deep internal crisis.... This resulted in severe organizational implications in some of our most important and largest sections.

After winning Zakî Khairî to his side, the secretary-general appointed him acting secretary-general and despite the dissension within the Party ranks left Baghdad for Moscow in early April. However, the Party, though trying to sort out its most serious ideological and structural problems, continued to be so paralyzed by its internal dissension that it was quite unable to function, let alone be a dominant force on the Iraqi political scene.[80] In this environment, calls from the cadre for guidance mounted; when they were met with no response from the leadership, the cadre's demoralized state deepened. With the secretary-general gone and Party morale sagging, the ICP once again found itself unprepared as the region hovered on the brink of a confrontation between Israel and the Arab world. In Iraq itself, the regime of ᶜAbd-ul-Raḥîm ᶜÂrif was going through its own crisis of confidence, and in response, on 10 May 1967, President ᶜÂrif once again took over the premiership. On 17 May, three weeks before the outbreak of the Arab-Israeli war, the Party issued a vague statement denouncing Israeli threats. Under increasing pressure, Zakî Khairî called for an unscheduled meeting of the Central Committee. Though a quorum could not be achieved, it put out a rhetorical pronouncement calling for the mobilization of the masses.

Nevertheless, by the time of the June War, the Party and its leadership found they were still not prepared to play any sort of role in response to the widening crisis, and as far as the Iraqi political scene was concerned, they were completely irrelevant. When Zakî Khairî called for yet another meeting in early June, ᶜÂmir ᶜAbd-ul-lah and two of his close allies did not attend, assuming that a quorum again could not be achieved. Only on 5 June, with Israel launching attacks on Egypt, was the Central Committee able to achieve a hastily gathered quorum. Following the meeting, the final communiqué written by ᶜÂmir ᶜAbd-ul-lah, dealt once again only in vague generalities.[81]

Although the Party hierarchy proved ineffectual, the Party membership became part of the spontaneous public demonstrations against the Israeli attacks on Egypt, Syria, and Jordan. These efforts provided the ICP yet again with a chance to rejoin the national political scene, despite the schism between its grass roots and its leadership. In response to the grassroots mobilization, a rejuvenated Central Committee met continuously as the war raged,[82] and the secretary-general was asked to return from the USSR.

However, despite the increased Party activity on the organizational level, the conflict between the Central Committee and the Baghdad section continued. When in the July issue of *Munâḍil al-Ḥizb*, the Party's Central Organization Committee revealed that a crackdown on dissidents was imminent, the Baghdad section took the initiative and challenged the leadership by calling for an emergency meeting for the advanced cadre on 17 September. This meeting was

[80] Numerous interviews with participants in these events, most of whom left the Party; al-Ḥâjj, *Ḥadatha Baina al-Nahrain*, pp. 97–99; idem *Maᶜa al-Aᶜwâm*, pp. 232–278; Khairî, *Ṣadâ al-Sinîn fî Dhâkirat Shiyûᶜî ᶜIrâqî Mukhadram*, p. 269; ᶜAbd-ul-Karîm, *Aḍwâʾ ᶜAlâ al-Ḥarakah al-Shiyûᶜiyyah fî al-ᶜIrâq*, pp. 145–185; and al-Kharsân, *Ṣafaḥât min Târîkh al-Ḥarakah al-Shiyûᶜiyyah fî al-ᶜIrâq*, pp. 128–130.

[81] Khairî, *Ṣadâ al-Sinîn fî Dhâkirat Shiyûᶜî ᶜIrâqî Mukhadram*, pp. 277–281; al-Ḥâjj, *Maᶜa al-Aᶜwâm*, pp. 282– 283.

[82] Khairî, *Ṣadâ al-Sinîn fî Dhâkirat Shiyûᶜî ᶜIrâqî Mukhadram*, pp. 280–281; al-Ḥâjj, *Maᶜa al-Aᶜwâm*, pp. 293–301.

chaired by ᶜAzîz al-Ḥâjj, who gave a detailed report on the crisis within the Party. A long debate ensued, in which it was recognized that:

> the Party suffers from a deep structural, political and intellectual crisis which has stifled all its energy and hindered its activities.... The most important manifestation of this crisis, represented in a great intellectual confusion,... [has resulted in] organizational chaos, mistrust of the political leadership, the spread of liberalism and non-communist traditions, the exposure of the inner workings of the Party, the growth of cliques... and the increase in internal debilitating conflicts.... These have had a major negative impact in obstructing the Party's activities [as specially evidenced in the Baghdad district].... the crisis of the Party extends deeply, as it embraces all Party activities and reaches back in time to the July 1958 revolution, which had a far-reaching destructive effect on the Party and contributed to the forfeiture of the people's revolution. The crisis expressed itself fully with the imposition of the August Line of 1964 that created complete internal uncertainty, destroyed the trust of the grass roots in the leadership,... led to severe conflicts and splits, and exposed the Party to near ruin. The April meeting of 1965 did not resolve the issue but rather only brought about a temporary and partial relief.... It did not "cure" the rightist deviation, [or deal with] its ideological and strategic roots, [it] was not accompanied by a courageous self criticism, and no fitting structural measures, particularly in the composition of the leadership, were put in place. Soon after, the crisis rekindled and internal conflicts increased among the leadership and the cadre, particularly at the end of 1965 and the middle of 1966.... Our Party today does not only suffer from disarray and political backwardness, but is also confronted by the increasing reality of divisions.[83]

The 17 September meeting adopted the following decisions:

1. Those responsible for the Party between 1958 and 1964 would be expelled, and their final fates would be determined by the forthcoming Second Congress.
2. The August Line was to be condemned and annulled.
3. A temporary Central Leadership would be created whose main task would be to "cleanse" the Party of all those associated with the old leadership, along with bringing about a renewed commitment to the processes of democratic centralism, collective leadership, and criticism and self-criticism. The new temporary Central Leadership of the Party was also charged with holding local conferences and with providing drafts of Party programmes, internal by-laws, and evaluations of Party policies and internal affairs. In addition, the new leadership had the task of preparing for the next congress and of putting together an agenda of immediate Party concerns, including matters of national cooperation with progressive and democratic elements; economic policy, particularly related to the oil industry; and the development of an Arab policy.[84]

[83] "The Decisions of the Extraordinary Meeting of the ICP." Reproduced in al-Ḥâjj, *Ḥadatha Baina al-Nahrain*, pp. 165–172 [17 September 1967, pp. 1, 2].

[84] Ibid., pp. 3, 4, 5.

Finally, those at the meeting declared themselves to be a movement to "cleanse the Party."[85] Putting the slogan "to cleanse the Party" into effect, the new leadership temporarily detained Zakî Khairî and Bahâʾu-d-Dîn Nûrî, possibly through the use of physical force.[86] Although ʿAzîz al-Ḥâjj publicly condemned this action, he still wanted the leadership detained until things had settled down.[87]

In response, the embattled and isolated old Central Committee held an emergency meeting two days later and decided to expel ʿAzîz al-Ḥâjj and his accomplices. According to an internal Central Leadership circular distributed at the meeting, the Central Committee threatened to reveal the names of the Central Leadership faction to security agents. On 26 September, led by Bahâʾu-d-Dîn Nûrî and six others, the "emergency meeting" put into action a plan to forcibly detain a number of the leaders of the new Central Leadership, just as the Central Leadership had done to the Central Committee a week earlier.[88] From this point forward, the ICP was two separate parties: the ICP-Central Leadership (ICP-CL) and the ICP-Central Committee (ICP-CC), each one claiming to be the legitimate "ICP," and both publishing party newspapers (*Ṭarîq al-Shaʿb*) and internal party circulars (*Munâḍil al-Ḥizb*) with the same names. Each had its own ideological position, often attacking its counterpart, and expounded its own position as if it were the sole legitimate representative of the ICP. At this point, the ICP-CC again called for the secretary-general to return home, and convened a plenary session on 3 October 1967. There the ICP-CC attempted to regroup the Party's forces and to combat the new danger of the Central Leadership faction by preparing for the Third Conference, which, indeed, took place as soon as the secretary-general had returned in December 1967. Zakî Khairî, on behalf of the Central Committee faction, issued an internal circular in mid-October 1967 in which he declared: "It had been proved beyond a doubt" that the Baghdad section leadership was "determined to create a new party by splitting the Baghdad section [from the Party leadership]" and that one member of the rebel leadership "was demanding the holding of a conference for the Baghdad district, whether the Central Committee approved or not, and that this individual was calling for other sections to send representatives to choose a new leadership." Khairî continued to attack ʿAzîz al-Ḥâjj personally, saying:

> When he was in charge of the Party from 1948 [to] 1952, he was a rough bureaucrat and an oppressive whip on the comrades' backs. Then he changed to become an advocate of freedom, to the degree of becoming a liberal, and next switched to become an adventurist provocateur who imposed his viewpoint on others by force.

85 Al-Ḥâjj, *Ḥadatha Baina al-Nahrain*, p. 123.
86 Khairî, *Ṣadâ al-Sinîn fî Dhâkirat Shiyûʿî ʿIrâqî Mukhadram*, pp. 283, 284.
87 Ibid., pp. 284–285, and al-Ḥâjj, *Maʿa al-Aʿwâm*, p 237.
88 "Let Us Protect the Unity of Our Party from the Deviationist Troublemakers" (28 September 1967).

Khairî accused ʿAzîz al-Ḥâjj of arranging his (Khairî's) detention on 17 September, and he described the al-Ḥâjj group as "the worst clique in the history of the ICP," even going so far as to characterize al-Ḥâjj as a "Nasserite." In the rhetoric of the time, Marxists identified as having Nasserist tendencies would have been seen as revisionists, if not as Arab chauvinists.

As Khairî was launching his attack, the Politburo of the Central Committee was issuing directives to all cells and committees, alerting them to expel anyone associated with the Central Leadership. It continued its condemnation of the group through its "own" *Munâḍil al-Ḥizb*, asserting that one of the reasons for the split in the Party was the "exploitation [by the Central Leadership], and the non-principled tolerance of the [Central Committee] leadership, which feared an open split." According to the internal circular, the crisis within the Party, in the period 1958–1964, "struck such a hard political and organizational blow to the Party that it weakened its effectiveness ... reduced public confidence in the Party leadership ... and limited democracy in the planning of Party policies ... spreading liberalism and organizational fragmentation."[89]

The situation was complex and expressed itself in a delicate balance of power between the Central Committee and the grass roots, complicated by another precarious balance of power within the Central Committee itself, with Bahâʾu-d-Dîn Nûrî, Khairî, and Bâqir Ibrâhîm al-Mûsawî on one side, and the rest of the Central Committee either opposing them or accusing them of being opportunists who shifted from one side to another but would not take a stand. Thus, no group was strong enough to challenge the status quo, each group mistrusted the other, and each feared that a change in the balance of power would undermine its own position. Each group began to seek alliances with the various rebellious groups inside the Communist movement to strengthen its position while weakening that of the other. As a result, these rebellious groups, which had previously been isolated from the Party, achieved more influence than their actual size would otherwise warrant, and, in the process, gained increasing influence on the Central Committee.

In this unsettled situation, the small but articulate and well-organized Cadre Group emerged in a meeting on 30 June 1967. They disseminated a draft document for internal Party discussion only, which was delivered to both the Central Committee and the Central Leadership and eventually produced the 27 September memorandum. The genesis of this group's leadership went back to certain members in the Baghdad organization, especially in the Intelligentsia and the Student Committees that had been led at their inception by Najim Maḥmûd and other members of the ICP organization in Britain. Among these individuals was Khâlid Aḥmad Zakî, who, as a critic of Party policies (especially the August Line) had acquired followers of his own among Iraqis in London and other European cities, and who in 1966 had returned to Baghdad, where he successfully widened his circle of influence. Upon his return, he had been assigned the responsibility of the existing organization known as the "Ḥusain line," which

89 ICP-CC, *Munâḍil al-Ḥizb* (latter part of October 1967).

advocated calls for an "armed struggle" as Zakî had previously propagated. In his new role, he enlarged, invigorated, and intensified the group's activities, which added to the reputation he had established outside Iraq and further enhanced his credibility in the turbulent environment of Party politics.

This success enabled the Intelligentsia Committee members, who had no intention of splitting, and no desire to join the Central Leadership, to express their concerns openly. This group had reservations about the conduct of both the ICP-CC and the ICP-CL. On 26 September 1967 it issued an internal memorandum entitled "Let Us Transform the Crisis of the Party to a Principled Unity That Will Enable the Party to Lead the People's Revolution to Victory" and signed by "a group of the Party Cadre" (known thereafter as the Cadre Group) in which it condemned both the Central Leadership and the Central Committee:

For years our Party has suffered from a severe internal crisis which has caused it to forfeit any real unity, stifled all its energies, and nullified its role in the leadership of the people's revolutionary movement. Recently this has resulted in the Party being sickly, and eaten away by unprincipled and opportunist contradictions, engulfed by confusion [and by] doubt, and having no direction.

The crisis has been represented in the last few days by a foolish attempt taken by a group of people who played a major role in imposing and reinforcing the rightist, servile dismantling [of the Party] in [the August Line] of 1964. This was the fundamental reason why the Party's internal crisis intensified and became ossified, and thus, in our opinion, the latest attempt is a dangerous extension of this [earlier] crisis, and is [certainly] not an effective remedy for it. Because of the seriousness of the dangers the Party is facing, and the insistence of the Party leadership to continue with the same mentality, and [with] the same erroneous approach to deal with the crisis [for] and because the leadership refuses to acknowledge the very existence of the crisis of which they are pre-eminently responsible, [the crisis has] deepened to the point that the conflict has become non-principled. Moreover, those who led the latest attempt have claimed for themselves a revolutionary banner which they do not deserve. Thus we found it imperative to bring the truth to the attention of the grass roots of the Party. We are confident that it, and it alone, is able to deal with the Party crisis in the spirit of concern for the Party's health and principled unity without being affected by opportunist or personal considerations. In addition, our conviction is that any attempt to deal with the Party crisis must come from the grass roots and Party organizations, otherwise it will not succeed, and will only lead to a further damaging of the Party and a deepening of the crisis.... The majority of the Party membership and the popular masses realize that the Party leadership after the July [1958] revolution was unsound and, in fact, was a participant in the February [1963] reactionary coup, and responsible for the failure of the February [popular] revolution. The leadership of the Party bears great historic responsibility, because of its shortsightedness and inability to understand the nature of events in Iraq and prescribe the correct solutions [for] them, and for that reason it deserves condemnation as unworthy of the position it holds in the Party.... With the end of the Baᶜthist regime ... some Party leaders declared themselves to be the Party leadership without consulting Party grass roots or their organization.... They gave themselves the prerogative of amending Party basic principles and declared publicly the abandonment of the [principle] of the dictatorship of the proletariat and the vanguard role of the Iraqi working class to lead the national democratic revolution, and submitted themselves to march under the direction of the reactionary bourgeois leadership of ᶜAbd-ul-Salâm ᶜÂrif and his pathetic structure "the Arab Socialist Union," without authorization from a Party conference or the Party organizations. Rather, they went further and began implementing a sinister plan to dismantle our Party, "melting" it into the swamp of the reactionary bourgeois movement.

The memorandum went on to identify three "trends" or groupings within the Party. The first was that of the Party leadership. The Cadre Group considered them responsible for the August Line, for terrorizing those who disagreed with them, for applying without Party sanction to join the Arab Socialist Union of Iraq, and finally, for mobilizing the Party membership in support of the ᶜÂrif regime. The second grouping was identified as those who later became the Central Leadership. The document characterized them as similar to the first group, which "represented mercenaries of a sort who found themselves members of the communist Party, and who would criticize any Party or policy line, but reverse themselves and practice the opposite the next day, but for a price, such as [a] salary, leadership position or cheap privileges." According to the same memorandum, the "current conflict is, in essence, a struggle between two rightist trends, the ultra right of the Party leadership, and the rightists that want to take the leadership." The third trend identified by the Cadre Group represented the majority of the grass roots and the lower echelon of the cadre. This grouping went against both of the other trends and was seeking a way out of the Party's quagmire.

The document asserted that the "sole and correct resolution to the Party crisis is to achieve unity in all Party organizations from the leadership down." It proposed a number of criteria for evaluating the leadership: (1) their position vis-à-vis the August Line of 1964; (2) a principled commitment to Party tenets between 1958 and 1964; (3) their service as a role model in words and deeds; and (4) their free democratic election and their respect for Party organizations. It also emphasized the need for adherence to Party by-laws and for respect for Party principles. It proposed three basic solutions: (1) an immediate Party conference, in which all organizations would participate, to make the previous leadership accountable and to elect a new leadership using the criteria just outlined, (2) more grass roots participation in the running of the Party and in implementing its policies dealing with the crisis in the Party; and, (3) a second national congress to normalize as Party practice the leadership election principles and leadership accountability.

As there were no fundamental differences between the Cadre Group and the interim Central Leadership (CL) on ideological principles, ᶜAzîz al-Ḥâjj of the interim Central Leadership (CL) proposed a meeting with Najim Maḥmûd in mid-October to explain the CL position. A dialogue then ensued between the Cadre Group, led by Najim Maḥmûd and K͟hâlid Aḥmad Zakî (pseudonym Ẓâfir), and the CL, led by ᶜAzîz al-Ḥâjj. Al-Ḥâjj then proposed a merger with the CL to the enlarged cadre meeting of 2 January 1968. He argued that "the return of the cadre will strengthen the Party's struggle and will direct a blow at the right.... Among the cadres are elements with good ideas. They also have a strong membership. There is no difference between us ideologically."[90] This meeting also resulted in some changes in the composition of the leadership of the ICP-CL, based on an acceptance of the criteria set by the Cadre Group. Khâlid Aḥmad Zakî was made a member of the ICP-CL Politburo, and the majority of the Cadre Group joined the ICP-CL without any conditions. However, Najim Maḥmûd did not join or request a leadership position, symbolizing that his concern was not the pursuit of personal gain.[91]

ᶜAzîz al-Ḥâjj also pointed out that the Cadre Group desired to initiate armed struggle, but "the good thing is that some of them don't want to start without coordination with us, though the extremists are calling for an immediate start."[92] This desire to initiate an armed struggle proved alluring to many Party cadres, and autonomous groups took advantage of the Party's squabbles to break free and launch uprisings – especially in the south. One such group was a small faction that had sought cooperation with the Cadre Group (though it was not part of it). It initiated its own armed struggle, establishing the *Munaẓẓamat al-Kifâḥ al-Musllaḥ* (Organization of Armed Struggle) on 10 November 1967. This group, led by Amîn Ḥusain al-Khaiyyûn, advocated the continuation of the armed struggle as originally called for at the October 1965 Party conference (i.e., the armed forces would play the decisive role in overthrowing the ᶜÂrif regime). Al-Khaiyyûn proposed that the struggle should start in the south, particularly in the city of Basra. He argued that the Party position had given undue "weight" to the army and to Baghdad and he had neglected the rest of the country. He had been in charge of Basra's local Party committee, and had advocated the primacy of the south generally, and of Basra specifically, in the armed struggle. This position had been rejected by the ICP-CC at the time (1966–67), and as a consequence, al-Khaiyyûn had broken away from the Party leadership.

The Organization of Armed Struggle planned to launch its insurrection in the Chibaysh marshes in the province of Thiqar in December 1967. The initial operation was to be an ambush of the government paymaster in an effort to finance future operations. The operation was aborted when its details became known to the authorities, and Khaiyyûn was arrested on 24 February 1968. While he was in prison, a number of his followers denounced him for his dictatorial style. Shortly thereafter, the Organization of Armed Struggle faded away and the remaining active members of this group were either arrested or joined with the ICP-CL. Those who joined the ICP-CL became the nucleus of the "Brigade of Twelve," which initiated yet another armed struggle, this time

90 Minutes of the Central Leadership meeting, January 2, 1968, in al-Ḥâjj, *Ḥadatha Baina al-Nahrain*, p. 239.

91 ᶜAzîz al-Ḥâjj, *Shahâdah li al-Târîkh*: *Awrâq fî al-Sîrah al-Dhâtiyyah al-Siyâsiyyah* (London: al-Rafid Distribution and Publishing, 2002), p. 226.

92 Minutes of the Central Leadership meeting, 2 January 1968, in al-Ḥâjj, *Ḥadatha Baina al-Nahrain*, p. 235.

to implement the decisions reached at the first ICP-CL Party conference held in Baghdad in January 1968. The ICP-CL designated K̲h̲âlid Aḥmad Zakî to lead the brigade of the Front of the People's Armed Struggle (also known as the Brigade of Twelve) and provided him with funds acquired through a successful attack against a government paymaster in Sulaymaniyah at the end of May 1968.[93]

The genesis of the armed struggle was very closely associated with K̲h̲âlid Aḥmad Zakî, who believed that the marshes in Iraq were better suited to armed struggle than were the mountainous areas in the north.[94] When he began his activities, his aim was to announce the birth of the armed struggle, which would then, it was hoped, attract others to join in the assault. According to Najim Maḥmûd, Zakî insisted that the action would succeed, and that it should begin in the marshes and then expand to the Middle Euphrates before progressing to the countryside of Kut.[95] However, the ICP-CL leadership was not as committed as Ḍâfir was to the insurrection's material or moral support. The leader of the CL saw "the Front of the People's Armed Struggle as not the only alternative of [liberation], but rather as one of the very important struggle activities within a broad general strategy which had a role within a larger circle."[96] Maḥmûd received a communiqué from Zakî accusing the CL of not taking his ideas of armed struggle seriously and warning that "we should be vigilant." Within two weeks, Zakî launched his armed struggle, believing that if he hesitated any longer the "whole idea of armed struggle would die."[97] Thus, on the eve of the 28 May 1968, the Front initiated the "flame of the glorious partisan war in the marshes of the south," as reported in its first official military communiqué and published in the Front's news bulletin *Al-Lahîb*.[98]

The communiqué detailed the Front's first successful operation, which was against the police detachment of al-Ghumjah. Without any loss of life they managed to capture the police garrison and detain all the officers, whereupon the captured police, who were held in a single jail cell, were lectured on the political situation facing the country before they were released. A larger engagement took place two days later, on 30 May 1968, when an Iraqi military brigade of around seven hundred soldiers was dispatched to quell the rebellion. Arriving in helicopters, they surprised the Front members, eight of whom beat a hasty retreat into the marshes, where they were cut off from the outside world. Three Front members withdrew to safety elsewhere, but inclement weather forced the others to remain behind. The Front initiated a second attack after regrouping in the al-Ghumjah marshes around 20 kilometres from the city of Shatra. The

93 Al-Ḥâjj, *S̲h̲ahâdah li al-Târîk̲h̲*, pp. 243–246.
94 ʿAlî Karîm Saʿîd, *Al-ʿIrâq: Al-Biriyah al-Musallaḥah: Ḥarakat Ḥasan Sarîʿ wa Qiṭâr al-Mawt* (Beirut: al-Furât Publishing House, 2002), p. 214.
95 Interview by author with Najim Maḥmûd, Paris (5 June 1982).
96 Saʿîd, *Al-ʿIrâq*, pp. 219–219.
97 Interview by author with Najim Maḥmûd, Paris (5 June 1982).
98 Front of the People's Armed Struggle, "Communiqué No. 1," *Al-Lahîb* [News Bulletin], vol. 1, no. 1 (1 June 1968).

army, having overestimated the Front's numbers, did not press their advantage. Instead, they also regrouped and advanced cautiously before attacking deep in the marshes on the following day. Believing that a large rebel force was hiding in the marshes, they pushed on for three days, losing one army helicopter before the "high military command" of the Front was forced to surrender, having run out of ammunition. According to their final communiqué, dated 6 June 1968, of the eight members who had retreated into the marshes, three surrendered to the military, two were injured and subsequently captured, and on 3 June, three – including Khâlid Aḥmad Zakî – were killed after being surrounded by the army.[99]

In evaluating the impact of the Cadre Group and its contribution to the Central Leadership, ʿAzîz al-Ḥâjj, looking back a quarter of a century later, commented, "Whatever happened, one of the legacies of the Cadre Group [Brigade of Twelve] was that its continuous criticism of the Central Committee directly inspired [the CL] to initiate our armed formation in the marshes."[100] Despite the brigade's military defeat its legend continued to inspire leftists and progressives throughout the Arab world, as well as in expatriate communities in Europe and America. Indeed, the exploits of the brigade were immortalized by the Syrian novelist Ḥaidar Ḥaidar in his novel *A Feast for the Sea Weed: The Symphony of Death*.[101] The novel was reprinted several times, and in 2001, more than years later, the publication of a new edition created an uproar in Cairo for offending some religious groups. The controversy raised the profile of the novel sufficiently to propel it once more onto the best seller lists and to reintroduce the legend of the "Marsh Uprising" to a new generation. Yet despite their sacrifice at the time of their defeat by the government forces, the Brigade of Twelve was condemned by the ICP-CC for its partisan war, and ʿAzîz al-Ḥâjj and his group were written off as a "bourgeois, adventurist, individualist, intellectual clique."[102]

The Formation of the ICP-CL

While factions pursued the "armed struggle" with varied results, it is clear from the documentary record that the early stages of the Central Leadership were not an attempt to split the Party or to start a new political organization. Rather, the agitation can be seen as a questioning by the grass roots of a detached and remote Central Committee, cut off from Party members and living outside the country, predominantly in Eastern Europe. The Central Leadership was therefore created as a temporary caretaker "to cleanse the Party" from "revisionist control" until the Second Congress could be held. Refuting charges that it was "secessionist," the Central Leadership pointed to the Central Committee itself

99 Front of the People's Armed Struggle, "Communiqué No. 2: Partisans Fight Hundreds of Enemy Forces and Shoot Down One Helicopter," *Al-Lahîb* [News Bulletin], vol. 1, no. 1 (1 June 1968).
100 Al-Ḥâjj, *Shahâdah li al-Târîkh*, p. 226.
101 Ḥaidar Ḥaidar, *Walîmah li Aʿshâb al-Baḥr: Nashîd al-Mawt* (Beirut: Dâr Amwâj, 1988).
102 ICP-CC, *Munâḍil al-Ḥizb* (November 1968).

as a "breakaway" clique that ignored the will of the Party's grassroots majority. This antipathy gradually escalated until, by the end of 1967, each side's position had become entrenched; this made compromise extremely difficult, and the rift seemed irreparable. Both factions became firmly committed to going their own ways. To formalize its position, the temporary Central Leadership held its first plenary session on 7 and 8 November 1967, at which it formulated its ideological platform, namely, "to study the Arab political conditions, [and] internal affairs, and take a stand toward the provocative actions of the breakaway centre against our Party."[103] It attacked the Central Committee, which it considered to be in collusion with the ʿÂrif regime and declared that most of the country's Party sections supported the Central Leadership, particularly in Baghdad and most Kurdish areas, as well as in the sections of Diala, Hilla, ʿImarah, and Kut.[104]

The Central Leadership also addressed the political situation in the Arab world in the aftermath of the June 1967 Arab-Israeli War. It identified this event as the beginning of the UAR's retreat from its progressive anti-imperialist stand as a result of "imperial-reactionary pressure" that had strengthened the oppressive Iraqi dictatorship as well, even though Iraq had not participated in the June war.

> [The Iraqi dictatorship] played a very dirty role in enabling the policies of retreat to succeed.... [The Central Leadership called for the] overthrow of the dictatorial government [of ʿÂrif] and the establishment of a progressive, democratic coalition government which will open the door for Iraq to participate actively in the general Arab revolutionary struggle against imperialism and Zionism.[105]

The meeting also stressed "the necessity of invigorating and reactivating Party efforts to create and strengthen cooperation with all [other] progressive and democratic forces, in order to stand united against dictatorships, the challenges of Arab reaction, and Israel."[106]

With the split between the Central Committee and the Central Leadership being finally recognized as at an impasse, both sides intensified their internecine conflict in competition for support and membership, and with each committed to the demise of the other. The Central Leadership accused Bahâʾu-d-Dîn Nûrî and Zakî Khairî of being behind the campaign of intimidation against its members, claiming that

> the deposed breakaway leaders are hoping, from their organized and widespread campaign of terror, ... to conceal the principal and great issues which were the focal point of our conflict with them, deepen the split, make it permanent, expose our cadre and organization to danger, and distract our Party from its organizational, political, and public responsibilities.[107]

[103] A communiqué on the plenary session of the Temporary Central Leadership of the ICP, 8 November 1967.
[104] Ibid.
[105] Ibid.
[106] Ibid.
[107] Pronouncements of the Temporary Central Leadership, 2 November 1967.

According to the then leader of the Central Leadership, ʿAzîz al-Ḥâjj:

The Central Leadership was rapidly transformed into an exciting phenomenon, a focal point, and a symbol, not only among independent Marxists and communists but also among a wide circle of the revolutionary democratic left. We were supported by the majority of Baghdad's communist workers, especially those active in unions and all the communist student groups and their supporters.[108]

For the purpose of organizing their new Party structure and clearly delineating their ideological positions, a plenary session of the group cadre of the ICP-CL, attended by thirty-three active members, was held on 2 January 1968. A number of draft position papers discussing the most important strategic issues facing the Party, such as structural formalization and organizational issues, relations with the international communist movement, Arab unity and Palestine, and the Party's relationships with other political groupings on the Iraqi scene, were prepared for this meeting. As these were draft reports, circulated on a limited scale for security reasons, those participants who had not been able to obtain the drafts expressed some concern. A compromise solution was reached, however, in which only the most important documents were to be read at the conference. The group's plenum declared that on the organizational level the meeting

considers the condemned breakaway leadership as an element alien to the principles of Marxism-Leninism and the thoughts of the working class, and that the [ICP-CC] has transformed itself into a representative of the bourgeoisie. . . . The meeting calls upon all Party organizations to double their efforts to combat all intellectual appearances of deviation, whether this is in the working class [parties] or the general revolutionary movements.[109]

It went on to condemn the Soviet Union, which it considered "responsible for the deviation in the ICP leadership in its move to the right." It further accused the USSR of "encouraging imperialism . . . in its predatory dealings with other nations, and in instigating the policy of servitude in revolutionary movements."[110] Such condemnation signalled the ICP-CL's independence from the international communist movement, formerly led by Moscow. It was agreed also that Arab unity "is a necessity after the victory of the socialist revolution in more than one Arab country, and that real Arab unity will not be achieved without the leadership of the working class."[111] On the Palestine issue, it reiterated the idea of "establishing a unified, democratic Arab state in Palestine and the removal of the Zionist entity."[112]

A new leadership was elected. It considered itself to be the legitimately elected leadership, replacing the "cleansed" leadership of the ICP. From this point forward, Party organs carried the designation the Central Leadership of the

108 Al-Ḥâjj, *Ḥadatha Baina al-Nahrain*, p. 139.
109 "The Detailed Minutes of the Plenary Session," in al-Ḥâjj, ibid., p. 238.
110 Ibid., p. 222.
111 Ibid., pp. 227, 142.
112 Ibid., p. 142.

Iraqi Communist Party, with the label "temporary" removed. *Ṭarîq al-Shaᶜb* was now sub-titled "The central newspaper of the ICP Central Leadership," and also bore the slogan, "Communist Party – not Social Democracy." While the January plenary session of the cadre established the ideological foundation of the new Party,[113] the details of the Party's strategy and tactics were left to be developed at future meetings and through subsequent documents. The new *Ṭarîq al-Shaᶜb* continued to address immediate matters related to the day-to-day activities of the ICP-CL. In its first issue after the formalization of the structure of the new Party, an editorial commemorating the execution of Fahd in 1949 described his efforts to rebuild the fledgling ICP "on a sound revolutionary basis and waging a fierce war against the rightist, social democratic deviations under a slogan, 'Communist party, not Social Democracy.'" Thus, by following in the footsteps of the ICP's founder, and casting the Central Committee faction in the role of the rightist deviationists against which Fahd had fought, the ICP-CL portrayed themselves as the legitimate heirs of Fahd's Communist Party.[114] The Central Leadership then prepared an analysis of the problems facing Iraq, and proffered its own prescriptions for solving them, in *Ṭarîq al-Shaᶜb* declaring:

> Iraq, as our Party always maintained, is in desperate need [of] a revolutionary and drastic leap and fundamental, progressive reforms to eradicate its deep-seated problems... develop its national economy, solidify Arab-Kurdish brotherhood...and secure the participation of the country in a vanguard role in the struggle against Israel and imperialism.... The avenue to save the people and the country from their worsening conditions is a revolutionary armed struggle to overthrow the dictatorship and install a revolutionary democratic government representing the alliance of all classes and revolutionary forces united under the leadership of the working class which will move to deal with the most pressing issues. The foremost of these is granting popular freedoms, freeing all political prisoners, securing self-rule for Iraqi Kurdistan,... arming the people, following a policy of cooperation among all progressive Arab forces, creating the most solid form of military and political coordination with the liberated Arab states, rejecting any truce with Arab reactionary forces, nationalizing the shares of Britain, Holland, and the US in the oil industry,... solving the people's needs for daily survival (unemployment, inflation, housing, and taxes), and the implementation of serious agrarian reforms.
>
> The seriousness of any party or political movement in Iraq will be determined by its position vis-à-vis these burning fundamental issues... which determine the revolutionary transformation of the society in a popular democratic government led by the working class. The crisis of the country is, in essence, a crisis of governance and cannot be fundamentally dealt with by anyone except the working class and the rest of the popular masses.[115]

With a sounder internal base, the Central Leadership moved energetically to replace the inactive Central Committee on the Iraqi political scene by trying to win acceptance from the other major opposition groupings. To provide a safe haven for the activities of the Central Leadership, the ICP-CL began with

113 According to ᶜAzîz al-Ḥâjj, the session could be viewed as a founding convention and an equivalent to a Party conference.

114 *Ṭarîq al-Shaᶜb*, vol. 25, no. 1 (February 1968).

115 Ibid., no. 2 (April 1968).

the Kurdistan Democratic Party (KDP). The KDP was one of the most influential parties in the Kurdish national movement, which now controlled much of the north, and its leader, Mullah Muṣṭafâ Bârzânî, had previously had a close relationship with the secretary-general of the Central Committee. However, recognizing the split within the ICP, Bârzânî was careful to exploit both ICP groups, since he wanted to use them in his competition with other Kurdish rebel groups within the KDP, and within the broader opposition movement to the central government in Baghdad. The Central Leadership deftly avoided questions about Bârzânî's relations with Israel, the United States, and Britain, as well as about his tribal, corrupt, and "reactionary" leadership

> since the CL was more concerned with the position of his movement towards the central government. As long as the Kurdish movement opposes the central government, cooperation with this movement is possible and a necessity, as everything should be mobilized against the main enemy. In addition, communists who flee the country will be secure in the Kurdish areas under the control of Bârzânî.[116]

Furthermore, al-Ḥâjj was aware of the special relationship Bârzânî maintained with the Soviets as a result of his years spent in exile from Iraq (1946–1958). In spring 1968, ʿAzîz al-Ḥâjj went to Kurdistan to ask Bârzânî for support for the ICP-CL against the ICP-CC. Bârzânî advised al-Ḥâjj to return to the Party's fold and said that he would use his good offices to facilitate this. Shortly after the meeting, he declared, "I always support the side of ʿAzîz Muḥammad. You should always remember that."[117] He offered to use his influence with the Soviets, to mediate between the two communist factions.[118] To provide a place of refuge for the CL's membership, al-Ḥâjj avoided antagonizing Bârzânî and continued ICP-CL support for the Kurdish movement,[119] which the ICP-CL considered "an important wing of the Iraqi national movement."[120]

While sensitive to Kurdish sensibilities, the Central Leadership was even more attractive to other nationalist groupings because of its positions on Arab unity and Palestine. Its platform allowed the ICP-CL to appeal to both dissatisfied communists and a large number of dissatisfied Baʿthist and Arab nationalist opposition members, who were gradually moving to a class-based analysis and Marxist interpretation of Arab politics. Its position on the most pressing issues of the time – Arab unity and Palestine – also made the ICP-CL more appealing to a younger generation of Iraqis, who were frustrated following the defeat of the Arab governments in the June war, and were especially frustrated because of the Iraqi government's non-involvement. As a result, recruitment increased dramatically, as Zakî Khairî would recall twenty years later:

116 Al-Ḥâjj. *Shahâdah li al-Târîkh*, p. 228.
117 Masʿûd Al-Bârzânî, *Al-Bârzânî wa al-Ḥarakah al-Taḥarruriyyah al-Kurdiyyah*, vol. 3 (Arbil: Iraqi Kurdistan Ministry of Education Press, 2002), p. 88.
118 Al-Ḥâjj, *Shahâdah li al-Târîkh*, p. 228.
119 ʿAzîz al-Ḥâjj, interview on Baghdad television (3 April 1969).
120 Al-Ḥâjj, *Shahâdah li al-Târîkh*, p. 229.

In effect, they [the ICP-CL] tripled their size in a few months while we in the Central Committee kept losing more and more [members], to the degree that we could retain no more than ten per cent of what we had prior to the split, and these were mainly older cadre. This occurred not only because we literally stopped recruiting, but also because we devoted all the resources of the Party [ICP-CC] to fight[ing] the ᶜAzîz al-Ḥâjj group. Our obsession with ᶜAzîz al-Ḥâjj and the feeling of having been betrayed consumed all of us in the Central Committee.[121]

Another issue that made the Central Leadership popular was its call for "Independence [from the CPSU] among the communist parties [globally]... particularly in positions affecting the regional and local environment."[122] The ICP-CC, in contrast, attempted to reemphasize their solidarity with the CPSU and support of its leadership of the international communist movement.[123] On the basis of its newly acquired influence, the Central Leadership began offering its analysis of the Arab world, including Iraq, as the basis for a programme of action that could bring all active progressive and nationalist forces together. The Iraqi political scene after the fiasco of the June war, in which all Arab and Iraqi political forces had been demoralized and politically paralyzed, provided the Central Leadership with fertile ground. To the Central Leadership:

Confronting Israel, seriously and truly will be protracted and arduous, but it will have to start with: (a) The Arab masses taking charge of their destiny, arming themselves, imposing their [individual] freedoms on the liberated Arab countries, and increasing the struggle to overthrow the reactionary... regimes in the Arab countries, including Iraq; (b) The cooperation of all democratic and progressive forces in a unified and revolutionary front all over the Arab East, in general, and inside each Arab country, in particular; (c) Military union and political and economic coordination between the liberated Arab countries, in addition to cleansing their governmental and army structures of agents, reactionaries, and propagators of defeat and a truce [with Israel]...; (d) The support of all the liberated Arab governments, the masses of the Arab world, and its progressive forces, for Palestinian organizations through effective material and political aid, in order to help unify these [organizations] in one front so as to transform them into an able force that can engage in a protracted war of liberation; and (e) Increasing the struggle against the old and new imperialisms, [especially] their oil monopolies, propaganda, and designs.[124]

The Factions Face the Baᶜth

The ICP-Central Committee, now popularly known as the "Central Committee faction," had limited support among the cadre and was predominantly controlled by the older leadership living outside Iraq in the Soviet Union and Eastern Europe. In December 1967 this group proceeded to hold its own ten-day-long

121 Interview by author with Zakî Khairî, Damascus (15 March 1987).

122 "Pronouncements of the Enlarged Meeting of the Central Leadership," 5 January 1968 (internal party memo).

123 *Ṭarîq al-Shaᶜb*, Supplement, vol. 24, no. 5 (November 1967).

124 Ibid., vol. 25, no. 2 (April 1968).

Third Conference, in Iraqi Kurdistan, with fifty-five delegates in attendance. It was billed as the Third Party Conference, and not as the Second Congress as originally planned, because it was hoped that it would "give the dissidents, particularly among the cadre, the chance to return to their Party and participate in the conference." Two previously circulated reports, ʿAzîz al-Ḥâjj's "An Attempt to Appraise Our Party's Policies Between July 1958 and April 1965" and "A Contribution in the Appraisal of Our Party's Policies" by ʿÂmir ʿAbd-ul-lah were presented. However, the authorship of the first report was now credited to Zakî Khairî, with ʿAzîz al-Ḥâjj's name removed. ʿÂmir ʿAbd-ul-lah's report was rejected, and the meeting produced a mild, less radical Party programme. Its main aims were to combat the Central Leadership faction, which, nevertheless, continued to attract the younger and more dissatisfied cadre, as well as many of the Baghdad District members, who were the most active, the most organized, and the best financed in the Iraqi Communist Party.

The resolutions of the Third Conference also rejected the slogan promoting decisive action through a military coup in favour of "a popular armed uprising, in which the armed forces could play a role [along with the masses]." In addition, it reduced membership on the Central Committee to thirteen by removing those who had joined the Central Leadership. The ICP-CC further diluted its strategic aims by calling for a democratic coalition government as a transition to a "democratic revolutionary republic" under the leadership of the proletariat, which they believed had already taken place in the "People"s Democracies" of Eastern and Central Europe following the Second World War. To gain Soviet and international communist support for their faction, the ICP-CC accused the Central Leadership of being Maoist and attacked the Chinese communists, holding them responsible for the rift in the international communist movement.[125]

As the chapters that follow will show, the net effect of this entrenchment of the ICP-CC's position was to widen the gulf between the factions, such that reconcilation would be difficult. In effect, the conference advanced the polarization of the Party from a competition between rival factions of the same party to a division that demarcated two separate parties moving forward. The rupture was recognized as such at the time by the ICP-CL, which argued that the conference had "fixed the split."[126] With the Central Committee isolated from the cadres of the former ICP, who were clearly committed to more radical courses of action, its platform now offered more moderate policy formulations, and its leadership turned to searching for allies from amongst the other political forces in the country.

125 Khairî, *Ṣadâ al-Sinîn fî Dhâkirat Shiyûʿî ʿIrâqî Mukhadram*, pp. 286, 287; and al-Kharsân, *Ṣafaḥât min Târîkh al-Ḥarakah al-Shiyûʿiyyah fî al-ʿIrâq*, pp. 128–130.

126 "Reformist Opportunism: The Staunch Enemy of the Principled Unity of the Iraqi Communists" Central Leadership," *Munâḍil al-Ḥizb*, vol. 14, no. 3 (end of August 1968). See also *Ṭarîq al-Shaʿb*, vol. 25, no. 3 (end of September 1968).

According to Raḥîm ᶜAjînah, the conference produced "classic traditional Marxist rhetoric."[127] While it clearly forbade an ICP-CC alliance with the rightist faction of the Baᶜth Party, led by Michel ᶜAflaq and including the remainder of the Iraqi Baᶜth leadership, this changed after the coup of 1968. The ICP-CC's efforts to establish its own organizational presence within a front, with the aim of achieving power following a considerable period of absence from a leadership role in the country, soon appeared to bear fruit. In June 1968, Aḥmad Ḥasan al-Bakr, the secretary-general of the Baᶜth Regional Command of Iraq, requested a meeting with the ICP-CC leadership to discuss the current political situation in the country. The ICP-CC designated Mukarram al-Ṭâlabânî to act as liaison with al-Bakr, who told Ṭâlabânî that "we need peace and accommodation with the communists and we do not want to repeat the [confrontational] experience of 1963."[128] While the ICP-CC pursued negotiations to form a national front with the leftist anti-Bakr faction within the Baᶜth, the Arab socialist movement and the Kurdish parties, who were planning their own takeover, were careful not to break off contact with al-Bakr irrevocably.[129]

Sensing the weak position of the Party and the ICP-CC's indecisiveness and newfound ideological moderation, nationalist and Baᶜthist army officers who were planning a military takeover approached the Central Committee faction in April 1968 and asked if it would be interested in working with them to overthrow the ᶜÂrif regime.[130] According to Zakî Khairî, the ICP-CC "was very interested and seemed worried that the Central Leadership would exploit this direction and 'pull the rug [out] from under the ICP-CC.'" The ICP-CC asked for time before giving a final answer. In the end, however, the ICP-CC and Politburo refused to join in the takeover, but although the communists would not support the Baᶜthists, the ICP-CC was careful not to condemn the potential coup, leaving the door open for future dealings.[131] The Party conveyed [to the Baᶜth], "Be my guest; alone we will not stand in your way ... and we told them ... our position depends on the people's endorsement and your actions, which then will determine our reaction," thus giving a green light to the Baᶜth move.[132] Pragmatism prevailed, and the ICP-CC altered its stand, becoming willing to entertain such an offer in an effort to reappear on the Iraqi political scene and rejuvenate its presence after years of marginalization and internecine conflict. It was hoped that this would provide the ICP-CC leadership with legal status and, eventually, legitimacy. By this time, though, an increasing number of Arab-nationalist officers had become opposed to cooperation with the ICP

[127] Interview by author with Raḥîm ᶜAjînah, London (18 July 1975).

[128] ᶜAlî Karîm Saᶜîd, *Irâq 8 Shibât, 1963: Min Ḥiwâr al-Mafâhîm Ilâ Ḥiwâr al-Dam* (Beirut: Dar Al-Kunûz al-Adabiyyah, 1999), pp. 367–368.

[129] Ibid., p. 367.

[130] Zakî Khairî, *Ṣadâ al-Sinîn fî Dhâkirat Shiyûᶜî ᶜIrâqî Mukhadram*, pp. 292, 293, and interview with the author, Baghdad (17 March 1974).

[131] Ibid., pp. 299, 300.

[132] Ibid., p. 96.

as it now appeared weak and divided.[133] According to one prominent officer involved in the plot, those involved did not want to bail out the sinking ship of the ICP-CC.[134]

On 17 July 1968, a successful Baᶜth coup was launched. Communications between the Central Committee faction and the emergent Baᶜth regime became more formalized, despite the fact that state security agencies did not relent in persecuting the ICP-CC leadership. According to Raḥîm ᶜAjînah, who was active in these negotiations with the Baᶜth, some in the regime were interested in communicating with the ICP-CC but wanted to ensure that any arrangement with it would remain under their complete control. One Baᶜth leader made this clear during negotiations when he took a sheet of paper, drew a circle on it, and stated, "We will allow the ICP to be active only within this circle. If it ever tries to step outside of the boundaries, we will then push it back in."[135] At the same time, however, the ICP-CC was developing good relations with the Kurdish Democratic Party (KDP), which was also negotiating with the Baᶜth. The latter negotiations resulted in the Kurdish-Baᶜthist Agreement on self-rule on 11 March 1970. Summarizing the dilemma posed by negotiating with the Baᶜth while the ICP-CC was under assault, Raḥîm ᶜAjînah stated: "I used to feel, and I was not alone, the immense contradictions [in which] we were living.... As soon as you left the meeting(s) of the regional Baᶜth command you would receive reports of oppression, suppression, imprisonment and assassination of our cadre and ICP-CC leadership."[136]

Despite its precarious position, the ICP-CC continued sending out feelers to the Baᶜth about the possibility of being inclusion in a proposed national front, going so far as to produce a working proposal in September 1968. Entitled "Draft for a National Front," it attempted to curry favour with the new regime. The Baᶜth ignored the proposal but kept negotiations alive, even while the state security apparatus relentlessly continued its assault on the ICP-CC, as well as on the ICP-CL.

The ICP-CL maintained a much more antagonistic response than the ICP-CC to the Baᶜth coup. It rejected the regime's call for a front, considering the idea to be "unrealistic and impractical." On 30 September 1968 the ICP-CL declared:

> [With regard to] a front at the current stage, whether it was called a "Popular Front," or [a] "Progressive Revolutionary Front", or a "Democratic Front," its composition, content, aims, and means are the important things. It cannot be dealt with and analyzed realistically without analyzing the nature of this [historic] stage and the aims of the revolution.... When we speak of a political front, a progressive, true... front for the benefit of the majority of the people... in our opinion this must depend on the [input of the] people.... This front must adopt a comprehensive program, based on the realities of Iraq and its society.... What the country needs today is not partial reform, but a complete

[133] Interview by author with Zakî Khairî, Damascus (15 March 1987).
[134] Interview by author with General Ṣâliḥ Mahdî ᶜAmmâsh, Paris (27 October 1974).
[135] Raḥîm ᶜAjînah, *Al-Ikhtiyâr al-Mutajaddid* (Beirut: Dâr al-Kunûz al-Adabiyyah, 1998), p. 97.
[136] Ibid, p. 98.

turnaround and a revolutionary transformation of society, and since everything depends on the nature of the political authority, the state, then the achievement of the democratic, popular revolution is dependent on the transfer of power to the working class and [to] the political forces that represent them.... Any compromise government, even though it may be progressive to a degree... will be "hopping" between two camps: the masses and the right-wing reactionaries and imperialists.[137]

The ICP-CL went on to declare that all progressive forces, including the ICP-CC, should work together: (1) to give the masses a democratic voice while firmly silencing the reactionaries; (2) to find a solution to the Kurdish question on the basis of self-determination; (3) to reorganize the state entirely, placing it under popular control; (4) to arm the population throughout the country; (5) to reform the agrarian sector progressively and fundamentally; (6) to nationalize oil and create a national Iraqi oil sector; (7) to liberate the Iraqi economy from the domination of the oil sector; (8) to improve the conditions of the working classes; and, (9) to support all Palestinian organizations and achieve the participation of Iraq in the battle against imperialism and Israel.[138]

The intensification of the conflict between the Central Committee and the Central Leadership reached its height in a "war of words" that took an ideological turn, with each side trying to ridicule the other and challenge its Marxist-Leninist credentials. In response to the Third Conference, the Central Leadership blamed the Central Committee for splitting the Party:

As it did in 1964, the Central Committee accused any dissenting [voices] of being adventurist and leftist, even branding them as spies. In 1967, it used the same old methods and continued to push the erroneous idea that the true Communist Party was the Central Committee. [This might be true] if the Central Committee were following the Leninist strategies and the principles and revolutionary plans, but when it deviates from these, and persists in [its deviation], then it does not represent the Party's will.... The opportunists used to call for accountability and described opposition to their positions as "destructionist," "deviationist" and "against the unity of the Party." In their view, unity did not mean anything but their continuous control, as well as the continuation of rightist deviation that was prevailing in the Party. This Central Committee Third Conference fixed the split, and affirmed reformism, [along with] two different parties with two different internal by-laws.

According to the Central Leadership, the Central Committee differed from it in the following ways:

(a) The rightist program of the Central Committee rejected the social class nature of the Party. There was no reference, not even once, to improving the social [working-] class component of their membership, while our [Central Leadership] draft program emphasized this more than once.

137 The Central Leadership memorandum to all progressive democratic parties, groups, elements, and personalities in Iraq, in al-Ḥâjj, *Ḥadatha Baina al-Nahrain*, pp. 279–286.

138 Ibid.

(b) There was no reference, whatsoever, in their party program to the armed struggle and the commitment of the membership, particularly the leadership, to it, while our draft emphasized that emphatically.

(c) Their party program concentrated on centralism and the duties of the membership and the powers of the leadership, and dealt with the issue of party unity in isolation from the intellectual and strategic principles. It purposely ignored the responsibility of the Central Committee to safeguard the party against opportunist, rightist, leftist, and national bourgeois deviations. It only concentrated on its structural powers.... on the other hand, our draft party program (1) emphasized: the [Marxist-Leninist] principles as the foundation of our Party and its unity, (2) affirmed democratic centralism and the vigorous defence of Party unity based on [Marxist-Leninist] principles, (3) imbued the Party with the responsibility of the armed struggle, while the Central Committee Party programme, in its preface and contents, was more suitable to a peaceful, gradualist social evolution.... They borrowed heavily from the first Party programme, except when it related to strengthening the working-class component and its leadership, which the deviationists erased.[139]

The Party cadres held the Central Committee responsible for the split, endorsed the plenary session's decisions of 2 January, and reiterated that the split

> was between two [different] ideas, two directions and two policies and thus, between two parties, our Communist Party and the petit-bourgeois party of the Central Committee.... the guilty Central Committee is the one that broke away from the Party of the working class, and it alone is responsible for the splits between the communists and the fixing of this division constitutionally.[140]

When the Central Leadership held its meeting at the end of August 1968, it affirmed the decisions and resolutions taken by the plenary session of 2 January 1968. It also emphasized the rejection of a peaceful solution to the Arab-Israeli conflict and called on the Palestinian groups to unite in a common progressive programme against international imperialism, Arab reaction, and Israel:

> The existing split is between two parties: one communist and the other rightist and reformist. As every day passes, the guilty Central Committee party reveals its face to be more and more servile and against every revolutionary struggle. It shows the depths of its division in every area, to the degree of refusing even the simplest forms of cooperation or coordination between us.[141]

Despite the ICP-CL's calls, the ICP-CC equivocated. An ICP-CC pronouncement entitled "On the Most Pressing Issues of the Political Situation," issued in mid-October 1968, was more critical of the regime, accusing it of being "non-democratic... and in essence, based on the manipulation of power, it maintained its dance with the Baᶜthist regime and the various other nationalist parties for the next three years." When the Baᶜth eventually announced their

[139] "Reformist Opportunism," *Munâḍil al-Ḥizb*, vol. 14, no. 3 (end of August 1968).
[140] Ibid.
[141] *Ṭarîq al-Shaᶜb*, vol. 25, no. 3 (September 1968).

own framework for cooperation among the national forces, the ICP-CC hailed the 15 November 1971 the resulting National Action Pact as "a very positive step towards an anti-imperialist programme," one that "delineates a progressive programme for socio-economic transformation, clearly rejecting the path of capitalist development."[142] The ICP-CL, however, rejected the pact outright.

Following the visit of Iraqi Vice-President Saddam Hussein to Moscow in February 1972 and the visit of Soviet Premier Alexei Kosygin to Baghdad in April of that same year, a Treaty of Friendship and Cooperation was signed between the Soviet Union and Baᶜthist Iraq. This left the ICP-CC, already weakened following the split in the Party and decimated by the assaults of the security apparatus, now facing a Soviet-Baᶜthist alignment; it had little choice but to support the Baᶜth, and join the front as proposed. To have attempted to alter the conditions laid forth by the Baᶜth, and thereby to undermine its relationship with the CPSU, would have left the ICP-CC isolated from its long-time patron and subject to an unending Baᶜthist assault.[143] Neverthless, in September 1968, the ICP-CC produced what has come to be called the "Draft for a National Front," in an effort to carry further its flirtation with the new regime.

142 *The Politburo Circular* (27 November 1971).

143 *Al-Thawrah* (Baghdad, 6 July 1970; see also 13 May 1970).

4

Alliance with the Ba^cth

The autumn of 1967 found the Iraqi communist movement in disarray with schisms within the Party over the emergence of the Central Leadership and a decline in the Iraqi Communist Party-Central Committee (ICP-CC). Recognizing the communist movement's weakened condition, the Baʿth regime, which had assumed power in July 1968, expressed an interest in cooperating with the ICP-CC. Such a relationship would provide the Baʿth with an opportunity to consolidate its power domestically, through appearing tolerant to leftists generally and to communists in particular. Moreover, it raised hopes of a possible opening to a relationship with the Soviet Union.

In response to these overtures from the new regime in Baghdad, the ICP-CC invited representatives of the Baʿth Party into leadership positions within some International Front communist organizations, such as the *Majlis al-Silm al-Waṭanî* (Council of National Peace). To accommodate the Baʿth, and to distinguish the organization from its communist origins, which dated back to the 1950s, the council's name was altered to *Al-Majlis al-Waṭanî lil Silm wa al-Taḍâmun* (National Council for Peace and Solidarity). The Baʿthists responded favourably and accepted seats on the the National Council for Peace executive board. Their strategy was to reduce the influence the communists had acquired through their leadership of these mass organizations. In addition, the ICP-CC facilitated the Baʿth's move into the Afro-Asian Solidarity Council, which the communists had been involved with for almost two decades.[1] Through this marriage of convenience with the communists the Baʿth regime embarked upon a large-scale campaign to improve its image and simultaneously disassociate itself from its 1963 predecessor by moving towards more radical social and international policies. To signal this policy shift, and thereby garner popular support, the Baʿth needed to appear to move closer to the progressive and

[1] Raḥîm ʿAjînah, *Al-Ikhtiyâr al-Mutajaddid* (Beirut: Dâr al-Kunûz al-Adabiyyah, 1998), pp. 110–111.

leftist political forces. Weakened from the loss of the ICP-Central Leadership members, the ICP-CC proved willing to facilitate such Baᶜthist manoeuvres.

The outlook of the ICP-CC leadership was buoyant, as they expected the Party to expand, whereas the Baᶜth had sought their alliance to check any growth in the communist movement's popularity and, simultaneously, control the movement's activity. The period from 1970 to 1975, as described by Central Committee members,

> witnessed an expansion of the ICP-CC [as its] organization and activities increased, as well as its popularity both inside the country and on the Arab and international stage.... In addition, the Baᶜthists began ... to implement a plan to curb the popularity of the ICP and reduce the threat it posed [to Baᶜthist control].[2]

At the same time, the new Baᶜthist-controlled state apparatus intensified its campaign of terror against all factions of the ICP. While its popularity grew commensurate with its increased activity in opposition to the Baᶜthist regime, the ICP-CL came under increasing attack, with its members routinely facing arrest or worse. Even as the ICP-CL gradually weakened under the onslaught of the security services, its activities became more and more hostile to the policies of the Baᶜth. This allowed the ICP-CC to further develop its relationship with the Baᶜthist regime. By the time of its second national conference, in September 1970, in a village in the foothills of the Karokh mountains near Rawandoz, the ICP-CC was divided over which course to pursue. Despite the decline and the general disorder of the communist movement in Iraq, a carrot had been dangled, encouraging increased cooperation with the Baᶜth. The ICP-CC's resolutions reflected this vacillation: on the one hand, they condemned the Baᶜth for its oppression of national opposition parties and its human rights violations, while, on the other, they it expressed a willingness to support the Baᶜth in any anti-imperialist measures and progressive social reforms.

In October 1970, the regime asked the British-controlled Iraqi Petroleum Company for a credit of some twenty million pounds sterling, an amount that was forthcoming only after the Baᶜthists agreed to repay the money in two years.[3] The likely impossibility that the regime could actually meet this contractual requirement gave the ICP a massive amount of leverage over the Baᶜth government. The subsequent nationalization of the oil company appears to have had less to do with Baᶜth plans for economic independence than with the government's own poor management and planning, along with the fledgling government's constant need for cash. In August 1971, to raise the necessary funds to finance its proposed development projects, the regime also began negotiations with the Iraqi Petroleum Company on concessions and royalties. The support of the ICP-CC proved invaluable to the regime after 1 June 1972, when President Aḥmad al-Bakr announced the nationalization of

[2] Ibid., p. 136.
[3] *Le Monde* (9 January 1971), p. 5.

the Iraqi Petroleum Company.[4] Though the action was decisive, it was not part of a distinct nationalization plan put forward by the Baᶜth regime, since nationalization had been explored by every major Iraqi political actor since Qâsim had passed Public Law 80.

The nationalization suddenly and rapidly opened the door to closer Soviet relations and increased ties between Moscow and Baghdad. These developments made a stronger relationship with the ICP a requirement for the Baᶜth so that they could both control Soviet manipulation of the ICP and appear to their Soviet partners to be tolerant of the domestic communist movement. The secretary-general of the Iraqi Baᶜth Regional Command, ᶜAbd-ul-Khâliq al-Sâmarrâ'î, explained the position of the Baᶜth Party in a July 1971 interview:

> Most of us knew that the ICP-CC was weakened by the split from the Central Leadership and the ICP-Central Committee was looking for a way out of their predicament. In the meantime, they still had a reservoir of public sympathy and did have some credibility though the leadership was in need of some public exposure to appear politically viable vis-à-vis the ICP-CL. Most of us were genuinely interested in an accommodation with the Communist Party. However, there were two camps in our leadership whose reasons for this cooperation were different. One group wanted to cooperate with them [ICP-CC] to utilize their political and practical experience, their intellectual sophistication, and especially their theoretical grounding in social and international issues. Others, including Saddam Hussein and al-Bakr, felt we could not succeed as long as the communists were not under control, if not subdued, and within that group there were two factions: one, mainly conservative, the majority of whom were from the army and wanted the communists to be destroyed, and the others who wanted [the communists] to be neutralized and become an appendage to us.[5]

In 1972, on the eve of the regime's negotiations with the Iraqi Petroleum Company, the ICP-CC again proved itself valuable to the regime by mobilizing international support for the Baᶜthists through an August "Solidarity with Iraq" conference in Baghdad aimed at promoting the nationalization of the Iraqi oil industry. Soon after, in November, another international conference, with the theme "Oil as a Weapon," was convened, in which the ICP-CC again played an important role in rallying international support for the regime's nationalization efforts.

The declaration of the "Charter of National Action" by al-Bakr on 15 November 1971 indicated that the Baᶜth believed they were in a strong enough position to establish a working alliance with the weakened ICP-CC, an alliance in which the Baᶜth would have the dominant role. The ICP-CC considered the Charter both a positive step and a prelude to further debate, issuing a statement to that effect on 27 November. Its response affirmed the ICP-CC's willingness to enter talks on the language of a final version of the Charter as the basis for discussion of the establishment of a broad national front. This tentative

[4] Oles M. Smolansky, with Bettie M. Smolansky, *The USSR and Iraq: The Soviet Quest for Influence* (Durham, NC: Duke University Press, 1991), pp. 46–48.

[5] Interview by author with ᶜAbd-ul-Khâliq al-Sâmarrâ'î, Beirut (12 July 1971).

acceptance was almost certainly due in no small part to advice from the Soviet leadership, which argued that participation was at least symbolically necessary. On 14 May 1972, two cabinet portfolios were assigned to the ICP-CC leadership by the Revolutionary Command Council, with ʿÂmir ʿAbd-ul-lah as minister of state and Mukarram al-Ṭâlabânî as minister of irrigation. The following month, on 18 June 1972, a Kurdish-Arabic weekly journal, *Peri Noi: Al-Fikr al-Jadîd*, was published and was allowed to print political articles although it was licensed as a cultural organ. Moreover, the ICP-CC was licensed to publish its Party newspaper, *Ṭarîq al-Shaʿb* (The People's Path),[6] beginning 16 August 1972.

During al-Bakr's 1973 visit to Moscow, Leonid Brezhnev, the secretary-general of the Communist Party of the Soviet Union (CPSU), told al-Bakr "You are advancing on the right path" and expressed his support for the Baʿthist regime. In addition, the secretary-general of the ICP-CC, ʿAzîz Muḥammad, had a recommendation for his fellow communists on the CPSU:

> We must reach an understanding with the [Baʿthist] regime.... the Soviets felt an agreement was essential and that everything else amounted to mere details. Their impression was that the Baʿth would respond favourably to our overtures.... in response the Baʿthists produced a leaflet [entitled] "Discussion with the Communist Party" under the pseudonym of Salîm Sulṭan, in which they emphasized their intention to establish [improved] relations with other communist parties including the CPSU.... I believe the real reason behind this was to get closer to the Soviets and obtain arms from them.[7]

According to Raḥîm ʿAjînah, one of the most active negotiators for the ICP-CC, Soviet pressure on the Iraqi Party intensified with the signing of a fifteen-year "Treaty of Friendship and Cooperation" in April 1972 between the Iraqi Baʿthist regime and the Soviet Union.[8] The Baʿth regime became increasingly tolerant of the publication of communist ideas. At the same time, the Baʿth regime pursued negotiations with the Jalâl Ṭâlabânî–led splinter group of the Kurdistan Democratic Party (KDP), which would later become the Patriotic Union of Kurdistan. Their (unsuccessful) talks were aimed at creating a national front that would further cement Baʿthist control within Iraq. Ṭâlabânî's participation would have secured a split within the KDP, weakened the Kurdish position, and broken Bârzânî's monopoly in the north, while ICP-CC involvement would have legitimized the Baʿthist position, giving the party the appearance of addressing social problems with progressive policies. Under such an agreement, however, political power would remain firmly in Baʿthist hands.

Bâqir Ibrâhîm al-Mûsawî, a prominent member of the ICP-CC Politburo who was also instrumental in the final negotiations for the alliance when the national front was discussed, believed that to save itself the ICP-CC had no choice but to join the proposed front. Moreover, he argued that any attempt

6 According to Iraq's 1975 cultural statistics, it had an annual circulation of 6,712,140 issues compared to the Baʿthist *Al-Thawrah*'s 18,186,710.

7 "Interview with ʿÂmir ʿAbd-ul-lah," *Abwab*, Winter, no. 3 (London, 1995), p. 217.

8 Interview by author with Raḥîm ʿAjînah, London (16 July 1995).

to escape a formal alliance with the Baᶜth was unrealistic, if not impossible, in the ICP-CC's weakened state. As a result, between July 1968 and July 1973, the ICP-CC tried to walk "a *via media* between cooperation and opposition." However, this position repeatedly incurred the wrath of the Baᶜth regime. As Al-Mûsawî maintained:

> The known and declared position of leadership of the ruling party clearly stated that the freedom of the Party [ICP] to exist and work is conditioned on its acceptance to work within the alliance of the Front, and no other choice is left to the ICP except annihilation. And if the leadership of the Baᶜth did not specifically announce this, they, in effect, practised it for the five years preceding the signing of the [Front alliance]. . . . The justification of the ruling party for such a condition was that any activity outside the Front with its conditions and commitments meant [to the regime] the preparation by the [ICP] to strengthen itself with the aim of assuming power and was, in other words, conspiring [against the regime]. The main problem with the ruling party in Iraq stemmed from the fact that it was created and formulated on the foundation of the fixed belief that it alone possessed: the truth, commitment, ability, and power to lead the Arab nation and save it from its miseries. Because [the Baᶜth] saw itself as the solitary saving force, for the future of the [Arab] nation, this gave it pride, conceit, and the "right to destroy others," and annihilate those who would not accept these "truths." . . . I must mention that the Party [ICP], under the policy explained above, went through a period of decimation, and a dislodgement of its upper- and middle-level leadership from [its bases of operation] and their immigration to either Kurdistan or overseas, especially in the period from the end of 1970 through 1971. . . . Few people want to remember that the Party leadership of Baghdad was vacant for a long time with the exception of Zakî Khairî, myself (Bâqir Ibrâhîm), ᶜAdnân ᶜAbbâs, and Nazîhah al-Dulaimî, who were unable to move around. In this period, the Party's central organ, *Ṭarîq al-Shaᶜb*, and the rest of its clandestine publications were all halted.[9]

Raḥîm ᶜAjînah noted that that the secretary-general and the Politburo adopted the Moscow directive to join the national front: "and thus I was directed to proceed towards that end. I must admit though, that [at the time] I had questions but did not [wish to] pursue any disagreement with the [party] leadership."[10] Raḥîm ᶜAjînah believed that the ICP-CC was pushed by the CPSU to accept a subordinate position, supportive of and amenable to the Baᶜth. "Through the enactment of laws, as well as the use of oppression and terror, [the Baᶜth] maintained their stranglehold on state power."[11] The ICP-CC Politburo was divided, almost equally for and against, over joining the front. In the first Politburo vote, seven voted in favour, including the secretary-general, and eight were opposed. But the secretary-general insisted on a second vote, which saw a shift to a favourable response to the Baᶜth offer.[12] Writing more

9 Introduction to "Dirâsât fî al-Jabhah al-Waṭaniyyah," in *Al-Malaf al-ᶜIrâqî*, 104 (London, August 2000), p. 38.
10 Interview by author with Raḥîm ᶜAjînah, London (16 July 1995).
11 Ibid. Also, for more detail, see ᶜAjînah, *Al-Ikhtiyâr al-Mutajaddid*, pp. 114–118.
12 Bahâʾu-d-Dîn Nûrî, *Mudhakkarât Bahâʾu-d-Dîn Nûrî* (Sulaimaniyah, Kurdistan: n.p., 1992), pp. 302–303.

than a quarter of a century later, Bâqir Ibrâhîm al-Mûsawî, who sat on that ICP-CC Politburo, disagrees with those who criticized the Soviet involvement, maintaining that this was realistic advice that aimed

to take the most advantageous approach by cooperating and uniting in order to achieve the national and patriotic aims. How advantageous and useful if we had been able to do without Soviet advice! The fact that we sometimes need that advice is one of our problems. Our theoreticians and guides used sometimes to read the texts before they read the situation in our Iraqi and Arab life, and then ordered us to follow the text. Sometimes I found some of the Soviet thinkers more capable than our own leaders of directing our attention to our distinct Iraqi conditions, instead of clinging to the text.[13]

Continuing the apparent Baᶜthist tolerance of ICP-CC activities, *Al-Thaqâfah al-Jadîdah*, a monthly leftist journal identified as an ICP-CC publication, which had closed after the 1963 Baᶜthist coup, was allowed to resume publication in April 1969. ᶜÂmir ᶜAbd-ul-lah later claimed that the minister of justice position was also offered to the ICP-CC to secure its participation, but that the Party declined because of the position's function in meting out the death penalty, often to opposition figures. Furthermore, the ICP-CC did not wish to be complicit in the "reign of terror" that followed the appointment of the security chief, Nâẓim Gzâr, who would lead a failed take-over bid in July 1973.[14] The ICP-CC's statement, in an internal memo in late July 1973, on its participation was that

the leadership of the Baᶜth Arab Socialist Party presented, for discussion, the draft National Charter last November. Our Party favourably evaluated this draft project as it contained "a sound foundation for national cooperation." Our Party based its evaluation, which was contained in the Politburo's statement of 27 November 1971, on the fact that the proposed draft Charter was anti-imperialist, and underlined the importance of perseverance in bolstering cooperative relations with socialist states. Also, it declared total and unequivocal alignment with the camp of peoples fighting against imperialism. It formulated a progressive programme for socio-economic transformation, and rejected the capitalist approach to development as a matter of principle. It declared that the statement of 11 March 1970 provided a proper framework for safeguarding the Kurdish people's rights and ensuring the fulfilment of their national expectations, including autonomous rule. In addition, the draft Charter included a number of significant conclusions, which stressed the importance of joint action and alliance between the various groups of the revolutionary movement.

The leadership of the Baᶜth Arab Socialist Party asked our party to participate in the cabinet with two ministers until the final version of the Charter had been formulated so that a progressive national front could be established on its basis.

The ICP-CC noted, in one response to the Charter, that the failures of the revolutionary movement in the Arab world had been due to "an inclination to hold secondary contradictions between the detachments of the revolutionary movement above the main contradiction with imperialism, Zionism, and

[13] Bâqir Ibrâhîm [al-Mûsawî], *Mudhakkarât Bâqir Ibrâhîm* (Beirut: Dâr al-Ṭalîʾah, 2002), p. 37.
[14] Interview by author with Raḥîm ᶜAjînah, London (16 July 1995).

reaction."[15] A more direct invitation to cooperate with the Baᶜth is difficult to envisage. The communists would help the regime stay in power if the regime adopted a socialist and progressive agenda. The decisive meeting in the formation of the national front was held 15 July 1973 and

> was attended by Baᶜthists Saddam Hussein, Shiblî al-ᶜAisamî and ᶜAlî Ghannâm [of the Baᶜthist National Command]; Naᶜîm Ḥaddâd and Tariq ᶜAziz from the Baᶜthist Iraqi Regional Command; and from the ICP, ᶜAzîz Muḥammad, ᶜÂmir ᶜAbd-ul-lah, Mukarram al-Ṭâlabânî, Mahdî ᶜAbd-ul-Karîm, and Raḥîm ᶜAjînah.[16]

The debate on the Charter and the national front did not continue for long. Iraq's relations with the West were strained because of Iraq's decision to nationalize the Iraqi Petroleum Company. This move required domestic unity and stability to withstand the foreign pressure against it. Thus the need for solidarity between the ICP-CC and the Baᶜth was stressed in a statement that the ICP-CC released on 1 June 1972. On the subject of the negotiations with the Iraqi Petroleum Company, it stated:

> The nationalist government declared the nationalization of the Iraqi Petroleum Company thereby fulfilling the wish of our people in liberating its main national wealth, which had been the booty of the world oil monopoly for more than forty years.
>
> Since the monopolistic oil firms acquired their oppressive privileges, they did not confine themselves to robbing our oil wealth in accordance with the most inequitable terms, but they would deliberately humiliate our people and continue to subject them to destitution and misery. These oil firms violated our people's national pride, and gave their agents a free hand to sabotage the people's future so that they became the real masters of our nation.
>
> The Iraqi Communist Party calls upon the people to support the courageous step that has been undertaken by the patriotic government; namely, the nationalization of the Iraqi Petroleum Company. Our Party again declares its readiness to devote all [its] fighting energies in all domains to the battle against the monopolistic oil firms, and to support the historic decision that has been declared by the Revolutionary Command Council.
>
> The Iraqi Communist Party appeals at the same time to the national government, which has undertaken this liberating step, to make it possible for the parties and progressive forces to share the responsibility of government and play an honourable nationalistic role in mobilizing the people for this important battle against world imperialism and its monopolies, and to unleash the people's fighting energies which are capable of achieving miracles.[17]

In a ceremony held at the Republican Palace, the Nationalist Progressive Front Charter was signed on 17 July 1973, the fifth anniversary of the Baᶜth coup. The signatories were al-Bakr for the Baᶜth and ICP-CC secretary-general ᶜAzîz Muḥammad for the Iraqi Communist Party. The Baᶜthist daily *Al-Thawrah* (The Revolution) hailed the Charter as a great success for the

[15] *Baghdad Observer* (2 December 1971), p. 6.
[16] ᶜAjînah, *Al-Ikhtiyâr al-Mutajaddid*, p. 114.
[17] *Al-Thawrah* (Baghdad, 1 June 1972).

Baᶜthist goal of Arab unity, claiming that "The need is to unite the progressive national and democratic groups into a single front whose central task is to defeat the imperialist, Zionist, and reactionary aggression, and then proceed to establish the goals of the Arab revolution." The Baᶜthist analysis of the agreement continued in this geo-strategic vein, emphasizing the importance of the agreement for Arab unity and anti-imperialist goals, and stressing the durability of the alliance with the ICP-CC. As al-Bakr himself stated: "We want it to be a lasting and unshakeable front – a front with a strategic horizon and strategic long-range mission; and we want it to be a good model for all the progressive forces in the Arab homeland."[18]

Yet this sentiment would have the lie put to it in a matter of a few years. A Supreme Committee, consisting of the president of the Republic and the ICP secretary-general, was established and set the policies for the National Front. The Secretariat was composed of eight representatives from the Baᶜth and four from the ICP. Policies set by the Supreme Committee were operationalized using provincially based committees and bureaus made up of National Front representatives from both the ICP and the Baᶜth, who mobilized support for the Baᶜth regime.[19] Publicly, Kurdish and other parties were welcome to join the National Front, but the reality was that membership in the Front was designed to neuter potential opposition rather than to promote a plurality within the government. With the ICP-CC now temporarily removed from its long-standing role as the major opposition to the regime, the Baᶜth turned to neutralizing as many other sources of dissent as possible, starting with the Kurds. The remnant of the ICP-CL, as will be discussed in Chapter 5, totally rejected the agreement, claiming that it represented a convergence of Anglo-American interests (through the Baᶜth) and Soviet imperial interests (through the ICP-CC), allowing the two powers to act jointly against the Kurds and other nationalist opposition groups.

Nevertheless, its alliance with the Baᶜth, including its participation in the cabinet and other areas of governance, also freed the ICP-CC to act publicly. It acquired significant experience in administration and governance and continued to develop its own Party structure, despite Baᶜth and state security surveillance. The 1974 Report of the ICP-CC Politburo[20] had a positive tone.[21] In surveying the international scene its position was predictable. It included support for the new Soviet policy of "relaxing" of the tensions with the West, as evidenced at the Vladivostok summit; pride in the successes of leftist movements in Greece, France, and Portugal; and support for national liberation movements in Africa. It also trumpeted the cracks it claimed to identify in the foundations of the world capitalist system. Examples included the energy

[18] Ibid. (Baghdad, 2 August 1973), pp. 3–6.

[19] ᶜAjînah, *Al-Ikhtiyâr al-Mutajaddid*, pp. 119–120; see also *Al-Thawrah* (Baghdad, 26 August 1973), and *Al-Fikr al-Jadîd* (26 August 1973).

[20] *Ṭarîq al-Shaᶜb* (Baghdad, 2 March 1975), p. 1.

[21] Ibid., pp. 1–4.

crisis, labour unrest, and the success of the Organization of Petroleum Exporting Countries (OPEC) in using oil as a "weapon" against imperialism. The importance of worldwide communist unity was stressed, although the Chinese leadership vilified for portraying the USSR as a threat and for consorting with forces of rightism and reaction. Domestically, the report detailed the success of the Nationalist Progressive Front and the support of the Iraqi masses for its continued advancement, especially for the inclusion of new political parties. While stopping far short of criticism, the report did call for increased progress in joint political action within the Front and for a "consolidation of the concept of political alliance." Given Iraq's past history of political repression, it is ironic that the fact that much of this repression came at the hands of the Baʿth was not mentioned. Divisions in the Front and delays in politically mobilizing the masses were portrayed as "weapons handed to imperialism, Zionism, and reactionism" that would be used to divide the Iraqi revolution. The best tool for mobilizing the Iraqi masses, in the eyes of the ICP-CC Politburo, would be the union and professional movements in which the communists were traditionally strong. The Politburo also called for continuing and strengthening the purge of "parasitic elements" from government structures and bureaucracy. The report mentioned the restriction of democratic activities only briefly, doing so in a carefully calculated fashion that simply questioned the importance of tackling obstacles that wasted precious capabilities and time that ought to be devoted to the joint struggle.

The 1974 report also contained specific recommendations on economic and social management. It applauded growth, development, and increased production, as well as the rising level of employment in both the "productive and non-productive" sectors of Iraq's economy. Government management in the public sector was stressed as the best way to reject the capitalist model of development. The report's recommendations on management and planning included:

1. Quick growth in the economic and social development areas, and the realization of a relatively developed balancing among the branches of the national economy, necessitates a practical commitment to the central planning of the economy and society. It also necessitates a reconsideration of the structure and method of action of the planning machinery and its cadres at all levels. This further requires that the participation of the national parties and forces and of the professional and vocational organizations in the discussion of the development plan, before its final approval, should be taken into consideration. Moreover, practical use, without discrimination, should be made of the scientific capacities and cadres available in the country.
2. The task of expanding the public and cooperative sector in the branches of industry, agriculture, trade, transport, communications, and building will continue to receive the attention of the state and society in the next period. However, the improvement of the structure of the economic department and its methods of action, development of the democratic relations and the consolidation of their progressive notions in the various establishments, and the improvement

of the standard of production and services that these establishments extend to the masses will remain the essential and main task. This necessitates the expansion and improvement of the popular control practices by the apparatuses of the National Front, the vocational organizations, and the trade unions, and this control must be linked to the [state's] administrative and overall financial administration. Moreover, efficient administration requires improvement in the standard of response to the economic incentives, on the basis that this is an integrated system of economic indicators including productivity, costs, wages, rewards, prices, and profits.

3. For the state's policy of expansion in the construction of state and collective farms and of agricultural cooperatives to be sound, it is necessary to give more attention to the activities of these establishments, programme the agricultural production, improve and expand the services of agricultural machinery and equipment rental stations to cover the whole countryside, supply agriculture with modern means of production and guides, develop cooperative marketing and lending, and reactivate the role of the poor peasants and workers in leading and directing these establishments.
4. The use of international economic relations and trade exchange to expedite comprehensive development, strengthen the present structure of the national economy, and consolidate progressive trends makes it necessary to assert the importance of the programmed expansion of economic cooperation and coordination with the fraternal Arab countries and the socialist countries. These relations also necessitate the need to develop forms of coordination... benefit from the preferential treatment it offers, make use of all available possibilities for cooperation with it, and develop cooperation with the free developing countries. Economic cooperation with the capitalist countries is useful for obtaining the most up-to-date scientific, technical, and technological achievements suitable for the development of our economy and the implementation of projects. However, the experience of the developing states in this regard makes it imperative to stipulate strict controls that would contribute to the realization of the maximum possible benefits and insure that there will be no interference in the country's domestic affairs. Further, independence and national sovereignty must be respected, and the progressive tendencies of Iraq's liberation march must be safeguarded and developed.
5. It is necessary to increase interest in the expansion and development of primary services, particularly in the fields of technical and vocational education, transport, storage, construction of government and cooperative residential houses and buildings, communications, ports, and water supplies and drainage. These sectors have both a direct and an indirect effect on the process of the economic and social development, and on the standard of living of the population. The past two years' experience has proven that the push towards extensive development has clashed with the ability of the national economy to absorb [the changes] despite an improvement in this respect, and that the economy has stumbled attempting to implement these projects. There has also been a loss of balance between financial allocations and available financial, human, and technical capacities.

Support was also expressed under a sixth heading for a detailed system of employment-creation programmes, wage increases, price controls, and supply management. In addition, the 1974 report applauded the successes of the laws granting limited autonomy to Kurdistan in March of that year. Primary among these were the establishment of the official bodies of the autonomous government, and an improvement in the dire economic and infrastructure situation of the region since the passing of the autonomy laws. The autonomy laws were portrayed as a great blow against the foreign forces of rightism and reaction (primarily from Iran), which were influential among the Kurds. The report proposed the following steps to continue the revolutionary "struggle" in Kurdistan, advising the Baʿth to

1. Continue the measures pertaining to the application of autonomous rule and the activities of the resulting organizations, develop the powers of these organizations in managing the affairs of the area, and allow the programmes of these organizations the time and opportunity to solve the Kurdish people's political, economic, and social problems.
2. Achieve the cohesion of the national and progressive nationalist forces represented in the Front, within the framework of the social and vocational organizations of the Kurdish people, and rebuild these organizations on a democratic basis.
3. Permit the departments in the autonomous rule area to continue to play an important role in restoring the confidence of the masses in the regime, and in creating a state of stability and revival; this calls for strengthening the role of the loyal and efficient elements in these departments.
4. Avoid the adoption of any measures connected to the transfer of the Kurdish population, workers, officials, or citizens from their present places of residence.
5. Mobilize the vigilant and politically organized masses of the Kurdish people, and depend on them both to purge their areas of the forces of the rightist wing and to prevent their infiltration to carry out subversive activities.
6. Speed up the measures connected to the application of agrarian reform in the interests of the toiling peasants, adopt new measures on a larger scale to include Kurdistan in the development projects, employ manpower there, and provide essential consumer goods sufficient for the population in all the cities and villages within the autonomous rule area.
7. Adopt measures guaranteeing the safety of the citizens, and provide an atmosphere of reassurance and stability in the area.
8. Strive to develop and enrich the Kurdish national culture in the fields of publication, studies, radio and television, and other vital fields.
9. Aid and care for displaced persons in the area, through the Front's committees in the various provinces, and compensate those who have been harmed.
10. Expand the measures adopted to protect the national rights of the ethnic and religious minorities, and develop their language and national culture.

The ICP-CC staked its hopes on the continuation of its alliance with the Baʿth, expressed in its support for "unitary nationalism." However, despite the position it took in the 1974 report of the Politburo, the Party disbanded all of its professional organizations (students, youth, unions, etc.) and pledged not to operate in the army following its Third Congress, which took place in

Baghdad in May 1976. At this Congress, under the heading of "a consolidation of progressive forces," the ICP-CC in effect abandoned its role as a vanguard party by passing a resolution that endorsed the Baʿth party's leadership.

On the Kurdish issue, the ICP-CC had expressed implicit support for the government offensive in March 1974, which it justified in a statement on International Labour Day, 1 May 1974:

Let us devote our energies to the noble mission, the mission of consolidating Arab-Kurdish brotherhood and implementing self-rule.... The accomplishment of this mission requires the isolation of warmongers and provocative rightists, reactionaries, and imperialist agents who are today performing a dangerous role in the Kurdish nationalist movement. This would require the combating of their propaganda and falsehoods aimed at dragging the simpletons of the Kurdish people to an unwarranted military conflict that would only serve the schemes of imperialism and reactionary elements, as well as the interests of the exploitive and greedy elements in Kurdistan who are ready to sacrifice the real national interests of the Kurdish people for their selfish class interests.

The Third National Congress

Now that the ICP-CC was a committed member of the National Progressive Front with the Baʿth, the preparations for its Third Congress could be conducted publicly. For the first time in the ICP's history, a Party congress could be held openly. Preparations for the Congress began in late September 1975, when the two basic programme drafts, the "Programme of the Party" and the "Revision of the Internal By-Laws," were circulated to the cadres after they had been approved by the Central Committee in its session of 19–23 September 1975. The Party held its Third Congress in Baghdad between 4 and 6 May 1976, under the slogan, "For the Purpose of Strengthening and Deepening the Revolutionary March of Iraq in Its Path Towards Socialism." It was attended by prominent members of the national Baʿth leadership and by important political figures belonging to other Front groups. In addition to the congratulatory letters from the Baʿth leadership, there were greetings from many in the international communist movement, as well as from other Arab communist parties.

The congress began with the oldest member of the Politburo, Zakî Khairî, saluting the participants and calling for one minute of silence for the martyrs of the Party. Then Secretary-General ʿAzîz Muḥammad read the report of the Central Committee and announced:

The Third Congress of our Party [is being] held in the circumstances of establishing the National Patriotic and Progressive Front, the liberation of our oil wealth from the yoke of foreign monopolies, and the beginning of self-rule in Kurdistan. [There has been] a deepening of our country's progressive march in economic, social, and cultural areas. To this end, there must be a discussion on the direction of the country's development and the requirement to achieve more active participation from the Communist Party to deepen this march through cooperation with the Arab Baʿth Socialist Party, the Progressive National government, and all revolutionary forces of our people. For that reason, we are reconsidering our Party's programme so as to make it more compatible to the reality of our present situation.[22]

On the international level, the secretary-general saluted the international communist movement and re-affirmed the commitment of the Iraqi Communist Party to the resolutions of the 1969 meeting in Moscow of the International and Workers' Parties. The secretary-general also saluted the CPSU for helping the international revolutionary movement. He concluded by saying:

The international communist movement occupies the vanguard position in the international revolutionary movement, and represents the most powerful political force of our age.... Our Iraqi Communist Party formulates its policy on the basis of our country's special circumstances, guided by the principles of Marxism. The Party's independence in formulating its policies should not be an excuse to create an artificial conflict between national interests and international objectives. There should be no conflict between the principle of independence of every branch of the international communist movement and the mutual aims that unite them.... Marxism-Leninism emphasizes the interdependence between the general laws in building socialism, and the patriotic and national specifics that affect the conditions and forms of its construction.[23]

On the regional level, the report read by the secretary-general emphasized Soviet-Arab cooperation and offered its own analysis of the Arab liberation movement:

One of the symptoms and points of weakness in the Arab liberation movement is related to conflicts within this movement, particularly the conflict between the Arab progressive states and some segments of the Palestine resistance movement, in addition to the continuance of the phenomenon of the weakening, or non-existence, of democracy [in the Arab world], and a disrespect for the role of the people in planning and articulating a country's policies. No doubt the continuance of the denial of democratic freedoms and the disrespect of the people's will, will continue to be weak points in the Arab liberation movement in general, and in some of the progressive regimes in particular. Our Party sees that as a starting point to confront the imperialist Zionist plans, and to oppose the activities of the reactionaries and rightist forces, the differences and conflicts [among] the Arab liberated regimes must be settled, the masses must be mobilized, the national forces in alliances of fronts in every Arab country and on the international scale must be unified, and cooperation with the Soviet Union and other socialist countries must be strengthened.[24]

Ironically, this statement foreshadowed the direction of political discussion in the 1990s, as will be discussed in Chapter 6.

On the domestic level, the secretary-general of the ICP-CC applauded the progress that had taken place under the Baʿthists since they had assumed power in 1968. He emphasized the cooperation between the Baʿth and the Iraqi Communist Party Central Committee in the National Action Charter, particularly

[22] Iraqi Communist Party, Wathâ'iq al-Mû'tamar al-Waṭanî al-Thâlith Lil-Ḥizb al-Shiyûʿî al-ʿIrâqî," *Ṭarîq al-Shaʿb*, no. 8 (Baghdad, 1976), pp. 9–10.

[23] Ibid., pp. 21–24.

[24] Ibid., p. 37.

with regard to the structures within the National Front, such as the Supreme Committee and the Secretariat:

> No doubt the Arab Baʿth Socialist Party, because of its political authority in the country, occupies a specific and distinct point in the Front, possessing essential powers to transform the Front into a mass-mobilizing political agency that can actively participate in the transformation of the country and deepen the revolutionary march. This is also the duty of all allied forces of the Front, and our Party will devote its complete energies to achieve it.[25]

On the Kurdish issue, it implicitly supported the government's position, declaring:

> The Party always considered the Kurdish problem as part of the issue of democracy, and always called for its resolution [along] democratic and peaceful [lines] which would fulfil the just national aspirations of the Kurdish people through the establishment of national self-rule in Iraqi Kurdistan, within the framework of the Iraqi Republic, and through a strengthening of the fraternal ties between the two people in the unity of their struggle against imperialists and reactionaries, and for the sake of achieving progressive economic, social, and cultural transformations. The People's National Movement in Iraq must acquire a social content in addition to its struggle against oppression and racial discrimination. The refusal of the reactionary rightist leadership within the Kurdish national movement to recognize these facts, and their insistence on continuing the narrow national objectives based on their selfish class interests, and their regressive tribal conduct [have] led to dangerous tendencies which have resulted in grave damage to the Kurdish people, their national movement, and the revolutionary national movement in the country as a whole.[26]

The secretary-general criticized the Kurdish self-rule experience between 1970 and 1973, describing the actions of the Kurdistan Democratic Party as tribal, anti-revolutionary, and a rejection of progressive measures taken by the central government. In addition to the non-democratic practices against communists by the KDP and its support for reactionary tribal activities, the secretary-general accused the Kurdistan Democratic Party of responsibility for the Kurdish rebellion and its aftermath in 1973:

> The [1973] collapse of the Kurdish reactionary armed rebellion created the objective possibility to implement a peaceful democratic solution to the Kurdish issue, and ... the period that followed the collapse witnessed a number of actions in the development of the area, including increased health services and the development of its economy. Another important step was the enactment of Law 90 of 1971 to limit the size of agricultural ownership in the areas of self-rule. Its rapid implementation became an effective base to isolate the reactionary forces of the feudalists and strip them of their economic power. These events again proved that the just national issue of the Kurdish people cannot be solved in isolation from the democratic revolutionary transformations in Iraqi political and social life. A national Kurdish movement that marches in isolation

[25] Ibid., p. 45.
[26] Ibid., p. 51.

> from the march of the Iraqi people, and in isolation from the basic forces of the anti-imperialist international front, and in collaboration with the imperialist reactionary Zionist forces, cannot meet anything but the inevitable destiny the reactionary rebellion met in Kurdistan, and this is the most valuable lesson a Kurdish nationalist can learn.[27]

In the programme, the ICP-CC praised the Baʿth coup of 17–30 July 1968, and described it as a positive force that "established in Iraq a national progressive government." The Baʿth government's accomplishments were many, including

> legalization of oil as a weapon in the patriotic and national battle. It also supported all the Arab liberation movements, and Latin American, Asian, and African national revolutionary movements. It further strengthened local and economic cooperation with the countries of the Soviet bloc and developed, qualitatively, a relationship with the Soviet Union through the signing of the Treaty of Friendship and Cooperation [of 1972] between the two countries. In addition, it achieved a great revolutionary advance on the path of economic independence by nationalizing its oil wealth. . . . The government also implemented a plan which resulted in the expansion of the public sector into a number of areas where it occupied a leading position in the national economy. Agrarian reform was also expanded. The government, in addition, began implementing a number of programme laws for workers, government employees, and the popular masses.[28]

Thus, according to the ICP programme, these steps took Iraq along the path of non-capitalist development, and the duty of the ICP-CC was to work to complete the objectives of the democratic national revolution. The struggle to deepen this movement to socialism required the following: (1) ICP-CC support of the existing Baʿth government and an enlarging of its popular base; (2) strengthening and developing self-rule for the Kurdish people; (3) strong cooperation between the Soviet Union and the Iraqi government; (4) commitment to the public sector in the Iraqi economy; and (5) support for Arab liberation movements, including the Palestinian struggle.[29]

A tense atmosphere pervaded Third Congress. ʿAzîz Muḥammad controlled the deliberations and even orchestrated the agenda. He also controlled the minutiae of individual speeches, which were also cleared by ʿAbd-ul-Razzâq al-Ṣâfî, who managed matters on behalf of ʿAzîz Muḥammad. There were many people who insisted on speaking extemporaneously, but if they were expected to be critical of the Party alliance or of official Party policies, they were silenced and ignored. It seems that none of the leadership wanted anything but routine business conducted, and no transparency of any sort was allowed. As a matter of fact, the election for ICP-CC leadership was undertaken on a strictly pro forma basis and the results were entirely predictable. In one case, a nominee to the Central Committee, Fakhrî Karîm Zanganah, the protégé and trusted

[27] Ibid., pp. 51–54.
[28] Ibid., p. 102.
[29] Ibid., pp. 103–104.

friend of ʿAzîz Muḥammad, was not even on the nomination list, but he was declared elected anyway.[30]

The Baʿth Turn on the ICP-CC

The 1976 congress saw the ICP-CC at the apex of its public visibility and, in Baʿthist eyes, potentially in a position to accrue more influence within the Front. Although not in a position to directly challenge the Baʿth for power, the ICP-CC nonetheless represented the single largest source of opposition to the regime following the crushing of the Kurdish rebellion in 1975. In fact, Baʿthist leaders quickly realized that with the defeat of the Kurdish guerrillas, with Iraq's relationship with the Soviets now secure, and with alternative political parties either weakened or subservient to the Baʿth-led National Front, the regime no longer required ICP-CC support to achieve its goals.

In May 1976, soon after the conclusion of the Third Congress, a Baʿth-inspired campaign was initiated by the state security apparatus against communist activities throughout Iraq. No attempt was made to distinguish between ICP-CL and ICP-CC activities or activists, and the ICP-CC was increasingly frozen out of government decision making. Fewer meetings of the Supreme Committee of the National Front and of its Secretariat took place, and, as the new year began, open repression of ICP-CC activities became increasingly common.

When the ICP-CC met again in March 1977, a report that was highly critical of the Baʿth regime was presented to Party members. Though it was not published it was delivered to the Baʿthist leadership, thereby confirming the latter's fears of ICP-CC opposition to the regime. Alarmed by the ICP-CC's apparent betrayal, and reacting as well as to a failed April 1977 communist-led military coup in Afghanistan, the Baʿth took the initiative. A number of suspected communists and communist sympathizers in the military were arrested, and following short tribunals they were sentenced to death for treason. Despite appeals for clemency from Soviet leader Leonid Brezhnev, they were all summarily executed on 19 May 1977. The Baʿth identified the Brezhnev pleas as a communist gambit that represented an act of overt Soviet interference in Iraq's internal political affairs. When the Soviets repeated their calls for calm and an end to the crackdown, the Baʿth regime carried out a further round of executions of suspected communists ten days later.

On 4 December 1977 an ICP-CC statement published in *Ṭarîq al-Shaʿb* attempted to gloss over the attacks on the Party. It stated that the ICP-CC considered the National Progressive Front still to be a working arrangement, and stressed the Front's importance in "thwarting the plans of imperialism, Zionism and reaction" in the region. It was supportive of both the Iraqi regime's opposition to Egyptian president Anwar Sadat's "capitulationary step" at Camp

[30] Interview by author with Khâlid al-Salâm, Edmonton, Alberta (10 July 2002). Confirmed earlier by Thâbit al-ʿÂnî, Raḥîm ʿAjînah conversation with author, London (18 July 1995).

David and the Baʿthists efforts to create a united "progressive Arab front." The statement was pointedly anti-American, referring to the Soviet Union as the chief ally "of [efforts to] successfully thwart the imperialist-Zionist plot" and to ensure a comprehensive solution to the Palestinian question leading to a just peace in the region.

Despite such public concessions the Baʿth continued to move against the ICP-CC, which was becoming increasingly active in its own defence. Its resistance increased the ICP's popularity with a population that was increasingly disillusioned with the Baʿth regime. According to ʿÂmir ʿAbd-ul-lah, a Communist Party representative in the Baʿthist cabinet and a member of the Party Politburo, the growing popularity of the ICP angered Saddam Hussein, who told ʿÂmir ʿAbd-ul-lah "that the [Communist] Party newspaper circulated thirty thousand copies daily, and that the [creation of the] Front did not mean the gain of one side at the expense of the other," warning the communists not to overstep their bounds. According to ʿÂmir ʿAbd-ul-lah, arrests began to increase among the Party membership.[31]

The security agencies of the regime penetrated of the ICP-CC, making it vulnerable to being undermined and manipulated by the Baʿth. One such occasion occurred in late 1977, when the Kurdish section of the ICP-CC was attacked because of articles appearing in its internal monthly publication *Reikari Kurdistan* (The Kurdistan Path). In the articles the ICP-CC Kurdish section endorsed Kurdish national aspirations and criticized the regime for its denial of Kurds their rights and its oppression of Kurdish activists. The regime used the publication as evidence of the ICP-CC's betrayal of the policies it had agreed to support as part of its membership in the National Front. Forced to address the issue by public Baʿth pronouncements, the ICP-CC held a plenary meeting on 2 March 1978. Under the slogan "Oppression Against the Party and Its Supporters," it gave a detailed rebuttal of the regime's charges, which was eventually published as an ICP-CC report. It protested the crackdown against ICP-CC members and criticized the regime's denial of Kurdish self-determination, and it addressed methods by which the local autonomy arrangements granted to the Kurds could be improved.[32] In response, a paper put out by the government security agency denounced the report and accused the ICP-CC of violating the tenets of the Front. In fact, it initiated the formal process whereby the Front would be dissolved the following year.[33]

Increasingly, the ICP-CC was powerless to halt the Baʿth manoeuvres, for without a coercive force its own it was dependent on political machinations in the National Front, a forum in which its leverage had seemingly evaporated. As Raḥîm ʿAjînah explained, "When we protested [against the Baʿth actions] at the National Front Secretariat meeting on 1 June 1978 we were ignored. In fact,

31 "Interview with ʿÂmir ʿAbd-ul-lah," *Abwab*, Winter, no. 3 (London, 1995), p. 222.

32 *Ṭarîq al-Shaʿb* (4 March 1978).

33 A Progressive Writer, "A Critical Discussion of the Central Committee Report," *Al-Râṣid* (Baghdad, 7 March 1978), p. 1.

it was the final meeting of the Secretariat, and only one single meeting of the Supreme Committee of the National Front was held over the course of the entire year."[34] Perhaps what the Baʿthists found most alarming was the ICP-CC's infiltration of the army. Thus, the regime arrested a further thirty-one army officers on 21 November 1978 on charges of being part of a communist military conspiracy to overthrow the regime, in violation of the agreement between the Baʿth and the ICP-CC.[35] The officers were subsequently executed. This prompted the Iraqi Communist Party Central Committee leadership to issue a warning "encouraging anyone who could, to leave the country."[36] At the same time, other members of the Central Committee and Politburo called for an armed struggle, to begin in the northern Kurdish areas.[37]

The ICP-CC leadership had placed itself in an awkward position with its marriage to the Baʿth. Its relaxed vigilance enabled both security agents and Baʿthist agents to penetrate the Party. This infiltration allowed opponents of the ICP-CC to monitor the Party's activities and membership very closely, leaving it highly vulnerable. When the Third National Conference was held in May 1976, a member of the Central Committee, looking back on the situation within both the ICP-CC and the other non-Baʿthist members of the Front, described how the ICP-CC leadership

> consulted with [advisors] from the Soviet Union. [However,] we neglected the nature of the Baʿth Party and its complete rejection of, and subsequent antipathy towards, democracy, in addition to the Baʿth Party's monopoly of power through dictatorship and anti-communism. Although the documents of the Second Congress of 1970 emphasized these aspects of Baʿthist rule... an internal desire controlled us, and that was that the National Front must stay and be victorious [despite Baʿth actions].... we were subjected to an intellectual pressure on the thesis and concept of non-socialist transformation, which was not accepted by a number of the ICP-CC leadership and cadre. [It was initially] adopted as government policy after pressure from the Baʿth that Iraq was marching towards a non-capitalist development, which was referred to later on as a "socialist outlook." The Third Conference gave the ICP-CC more public exposure in both its activities and position. This exposure soon rang danger bells within the Baʿth Party. We should have expected that as in the Baʿth Party's calculation a special [position] had been delineated for the ICP-CC, within which the Party would be [severely] circumscribed in its manoeuvrability. Despite the fact that the National Front still existed, the ICP-CC [had] exceeded the limits imposed by the Baʿth.[38]

Following nearly three years of the crackdown, Baʿth attempts in February 1979 to begin talks on renegotiating the old pact and establishing a new National Front proved unsuccessful. The ICP-CC was no longer interested in working under Baʿth domination,[39] for it had resolved, in July 1978, to oppose

[34] ʿAjînah, *Al-Ikhtiyâr al-Mutajaddid*, pp. 134–135.
[35] "Editorial,"*Ṭarîq al-Shaʿb*, no. 3 (Baghdad, October 1979), p. 222.
[36] "Interview with ʿÂmir ʿAbd-ul-lah," *Abwab*, Winter, no. 3 (London, 1995), p. 222.
[37] Ibid.
[38] ʿAjînah, *Al-Ikhtiyâr al-Mutajaddid*, pp. 129–130.
[39] Ibid., p. 137.

the regime formally under the slogan "Ending Dictatorship." After the outbreak of the regime's campaign against the ICP-CC in 1977, a number of Party cadres fled north to the Kurdish areas, where they gradually established a partisan movement. By January 1979 they had established military units with bases in Irbil and headquarters in both Sulaimaniyah and Kirkuk. To further disperse its command and control structure to ensure that it was less vulnerable to the regime's attacks, the ICP-CC built additional bases in both Nineveh and Dohuk. Eventually, a unified Central Military Bureau was established to coordinate activities among the disparate forces and in 1980 a newspaper for the partisan movement began publication in Arabic (*Nahj al-Anṣâr*) and in Kurdish (*Ribazy Bashmarga*). In 1981 the partisan brigades could be found operating against government forces in all of the Kurdish provinces of Iraq, and by 1982 a decentralized military structure, based upon geographical location, had been adopted by the various units. This allowed them greater flexibility in harassing Iraqi government forces, although overall strategic planning remained under ICP-CC Party control with its first Central Military Council held in secret with partisan commanders, the ICP-CC Politburo, and the secretary-general himself in attendance.[40]

While this partisan apparatus was still in its infancy, however, the ICP-CC faced the full onslaught of the Baʿth Party, and with the Baʿth ensconced as the ruling regime, the full force of the state security apparatus as well. Relations between the Baʿth and the other parties in the National Front continued to deteriorate. Officially the alliance was maintained, the ICP-CC newspaper was still legally published, and joint communiqués continued to emanate from the regime. Attempts to mediate the dispute by both the Palestinians and the Soviets met with failure. ICP-CC cadres and supporters, afraid of a Baʿthist pogrom against the Party, began to flee Iraq to other countries or to Iraqi Kurdistan. Under this pressure, and despite the ICP-CC's July 1978 resolution to oppose the regime, the Party was issuing communiqués from Baghdad as late as August 1979 that made no overt mention of its recent misfortunes at the hands of the Baʿth. In a lengthy article printed in the Lebanese Communist Party's newspaper *Al-Nidâʾ* on 17 August 1979, the ICP-CC articulated its position on the Camp David accords as well as on other international issues but avoided any criticism of the Baʿth. It attacked Sadat's regime for making peace with Israel; for its opposition to Libya, the People's Democratic Republic of Yemen (PDRY), and the Palestine Liberation Organization (PLO); and for its support for reactionary regimes in Jordan, Sudan, Zaire, and elsewhere. It further accused Egypt of being the main perpetrator of imperialism in the Middle East and Africa.

The ICP-CC also proclaimed its own support for a list of Arab anti-imperialist groups, including the PDRY, various Palestinian factions, the Sudanese Communist Party, and the Egyptian Communist Party. The article praised the actions of the masses in Tunisia and Algeria and expressed approval of the Polisario Front in the Western Sahara. The Camp David accords were referred

40 Ibid., pp. 173–174.

to as the "mask of treason" that were intended to turn Egypt into a military client state and tool of the United States and Israel. Furthermore, the ICP-CC insisted on the special role of the USSR in the global struggle, asserting:

> The vital principle of dealing with the battle in a manner that would ensure its successful opposition, [ranging] from defining its international requirements to underscoring the utmost and urgent necessity for an alliance with the Soviet Union against imperialism and Zionism, has been ignored. In addition, efforts and schemes designed to minimize the role of the Soviet Union and to remove it from the Arab struggle for liberation have continued.

This paean to the Soviets continued with an examination of the socialist states' successes in developing their economies, in providing for their people, and in giving aid to the developing world. As usual, the ICP-CC toed the Soviet line by describing "the crisis in the capitalist countries," primarily in energy, inflation, unemployment, and widespread labour unrest. Perhaps in reference to the Arabs' own situation, the statement underlined the importance of national fronts and of democratic rule:

> A long time ago, the Arab peoples came to a sound and highly significant conclusion: a regime that restricts the freedom of an individual and paralyses the will of the masses cannot achieve victory in peace or in war; it does not have the ability to be steadfast or to confront its enemies.... revolutionary forces in Arab countries also have almost reached a consensus that the establishment of national fronts... and the achievement of political democracy for the masses, and for their revolutionary forces, constitute the road to a sound national unity, to pan-Arab solidarity in the struggle, and to a true and effective national struggle.

In outlining the ICP-CC's programme for the establishment of a true Arab national liberation movement, there was further implicit criticism of the Baᶜth. The previous line of argument was continued:

> First, the people are to be made effective partners in the political life of the country and in the decision-making process by repudiating autocratic modes of government, and [by] establishing broad national fronts to which all parties and national forces contribute, on the basis of a programme of struggle against imperialism, Zionism, and reactionaries. Second, the will of the masses is to be liberated by abolishing all restrictions, conditions, and organizations that suspend freedom. Freedom and democratic rights – political, union, and professional – of the popular masses, and of their parties, and [of] democratic national organizations are to be granted.

This articulation of the ICP-CC's position was unequivocal, yet it failed to address the increasingly dire oppression the Party faced at home.

The two ICP-CC ministers in the Baᶜth cabinet were dismissed in the spring 1979, and soon thereafter publication of *Ṭarîq al-Shaᶜb* ceased to be legal and was forced underground. Baᶜth-supported publications directed against on the ICP-CC, accusing it of having historical ties to the Zionist movement and of being the unwitting pawn of Moscow. A puppet pro-regime communist group, the Iraqi Communist Vanguard Organization, was established to erode the

ICP-CC's credibility by criticizing it and casting doubt on its legitimacy within the National Front. Despite this obvious public persecution of the ICP-CC, Baᶜthist propagandists accused the communists of "giving up the struggle" through their abandonment of the National Front.[41]

When the Baᶜth issued a statement in late 1979 ending its alliance with the ICP-CC, the communists' response was issued from Beirut, to which most of the Central Committee members had fled. There had been a tacit understanding that the ICP-CC leadership would be permitted to leave the country, and most though not all of them eventually avoided arrest by resettling in Eastern Europe, in what is now the former Soviet Union, in Syria, or in Lebanon.[42] Their departure from Iraq coincided with the outbreak of revolution in Iran and the return of the Ayatollah Ruhollah Khomeini to that country. The Iranian revolution posed a host of new challenges for the regime in Baghdad. Recent accommodations with the Shah's regime had left Baᶜth relations with the new Islamic revolutionary state virtually stillborn. However, the removal of the Shah and the evident anti-Americanism of the new Iranian regime also opened new foreign policy possibilities for the Baᶜth, and made Soviet goodwill less important to the Iraqi regime.

The first real attack on the Baᶜth regime by the ICP-CC following its dismissal from the government was in an article in the August 1979 issue of the now clandestine *Ṭarîq al-Shaᶜb*. Entitled "End the Dictatorship and Establish a Democratic Regime in Iraq," the article first accused the Baᶜth of launching a purge against progressive forces in Iraq, including the arrest of "thousands upon thousands of communists and democrats . . . whose fate is still unknown," and of using the regime's control of the media to discredit the communist movement, Marxism, and the Soviet Union. The attack on what the ICP-CC perceived to be the "Baᶜthification" of Iraqi society was severe, and deserves to be quoted at some length:

> These measures have been coupled with intensified Baᶜthisation of the state organs, the social organizations, the educational system, and cultural organizations throughout the country. A job ban has been imposed on the employment of non-Baᶜthists in the Ministries of Defence, the Interior, Foreign Affairs, Education, Higher Education, Culture and Information and their departments. Also the trade unions, peasant cooperative societies, women's, student and youth organizations, and vocational associations have been monopolized and transformed into instruments carrying out the policy of the regime. Laws have been enacted banning the formation of parallel organizations, and punishing those who exercise this right with life imprisonment. A terror campaign has been unleashed to force the people, especially the civil servants, into an affiliation with the ruling party and the organizations attached to it. The workers have been denied the right to strike, and thousands of them have become victims of arbitrary measures, persecution, and ill treatment by management. Apart from intimidation and threats, tempting privileges have been offered. Non-Baᶜthists have been denied any foreign scholarships.

41 Ibid.

42 Nûrî, *Mudhakkarât Bahâ'u-d-Dîn Nûrî*, pp. 340–341; and ᶜAjînah, *Al-Ikhtiyâr al-Mutajaddid*, pp. 136, 138.

In addition, non-Baʿthists have been denied admission to military colleges, as well as [to] arts and teachers' training colleges and institutes, and thousands of qualified students have been denied university and school education, or expelled from them. Tragic Baʿthisation has been enforced in the education system, where thousands of the finest teachers have been dismissed. This has caused a sharp decline in the standard of education, and resulted in the emigration from Iraq of a large number of teachers and specialists in various fields. A wider range of arbitrary terrorist laws which run counter to the [UN] Declaration of Human Rights have been passed. The number of death sentences based on political charges is unparalleled anywhere in the world.

The ICP-CC went on to criticize the economic management of Iraq under the Baʿth regime, accusing the government of spending the windfall from increased oil revenues since the 1973 war on "beefing up the organs of repression, intelligence, propaganda and conspiracies" and on bribes and payments to influence Western governments (including massive donations to keep socialists out of the French government and raise the fortunes of Jacques Chirac, the Israeli Zionists' friend). The ICP-CC pointed to Iraq's increasing inflation and to the slump in the value of the Iraqi dinar as evidence of the regime's poor management and the willingness of the Baʿth to sacrifice the Iraqi economy to gain foreign support and investment.

The article continued with an attack on the new class of "bureaucratic-parasitic bourgeoisie" that had developed because of its place within, or cooperation with, the dictatorial regime, a class that had positioned itself as part of the state's organs of administration and repression. It accused the Baʿth of taking the "reactionary" line in response to the Camp David accords by merely boycotting Egypt, thereby weakening Arab solidarity and making Iraq a major obstacle to the materialization of a unified stand that would match the gravity of the dangers facing the Arab nations. It also criticized the Baʿth's hostility towards the Iranian revolution and the "encouragement Iraq has received in this from 'the imperialist quarters.'" In addition to the steps it took to strengthen its political and economic relations with French imperialism, including selling substantial oil supplies to France at preferential prices,

the regime has further developed the areas of this cooperation by concluding huge arms deals with the French monopolies and other armament manufacturers in West Germany, Italy, Spain, and Brazil under the label of "diversification of the arms sources," the very label, it is to be recalled, which portended the degeneration of Sadat's policy and his plunge into anti-Sovietism.

Finally, the ICP-CC clarified its stand on its continued support for a truly national front' that was to be

democratic in form and content, a front essentially consisting of ideologically, politically, and organizationally independent parties, organizations, and forces, and whose decisions are taken unanimously; a front whose parties have the right of criticism and [the right] to solve any disagreement between them by democratic means; a front open to all anti-imperialists, anti-Zionists, and anti-reactionary forces which are struggling to achieve the tasks of the national-democratic revolution on an agreed programme.

To achieve this aim, the Party struggled for an end to dictatorship, an end to the state of emergency, a democratic solution to the Kurdish question, Arab solidarity, protection of peasants and workers, democratization, and an independent foreign policy. Throughout the events of the late 1970s, two strands important to the ICP-CC emerged. The first was the "official face" of the Party – the pronouncements, the interpretation of events, and the issues that it considered. However, the second was the internal fragmentation of the Party, which in practice rendered it largely ineffective.

The Public Dimension – Issues and Pronouncements

During the 1980s, the now-underground ICP-CC attempted to expand its links with other communist movements. In January 1980, ᶜAzîz Muḥammad visited the PDRY (Yemen), where he discussed the predictable topics of imperialism, pan-Arabism, and Palestine. The topics of the Iraqi regime and the ousting of the Party from the National Front appear to have been avoided except in reference to anti-communist sentiments being turned to the service of imperialism.[43] There was also a statement that "encroachment on the democratic rights of the Arab masses directly serves imperialism and reaction, and weakens the national and patriotic struggle of the Arab peoples."[44] The two sides also expressed their support for the Iranian revolution as "a struggle against US imperialism, national independence . . . and the 'anti-imperialist stand' of the Ethiopian revolution."[45]

The beginning of the 1980s saw continuing conflict between the ICP-CC and the Baᶜth regime. The ICP-CC denounced Saddam Hussein's oppression of democrats, communists, Kurds, and Shi'ites, while also accusing the Baᶜth of integrating the Iraqi economy into the capitalist system and undervaluing Iraqi oil to please Western oil firms.[46] Finally, the ICP-CC criticized the "reactionary characteristics" of the regime as manifested in the Baᶜth's rapprochement with Saudi Arabia, "the most reactionary regime in the world," and the regime's "capitulationism" in supporting the Camp David accords.

One of the ICP-CC's documents that casts serious doubt on its priority of "anti-imperialism" versus its relationship with the USSR was the article "We Greet You On Behalf of All Progressive Forces," published in January 1980 in *Ṭarîq al-Shaᶜb*. The article applauded the Soviet invasion of Afghanistan "in line with its principled policy of rendering support to people waging a struggle against imperialism, for the defence of their national independence, and their independent choice of the path to development." The language used to describe the Soviet action was excessively subservient even by the standards of the time ("the noble [Soviet] stand of resolute internationalism, [and] a creative

[43] *Ṭarîq al-Shaᶜb* (Baghdad, February 1980).
[44] Ibid.
[45] Ibid.
[46] *Lᶜ Humanite* (27 August 1980).

implementation of the Leninist policy of support for the people's struggle against imperialism and reaction"). In the article the ICP-CC also took the opportunity to attack the Baᶜth regime for its condemnation of the Soviet invasion:

Moreover, in its eagerness to slander the firm, principled policy of the Soviet Union, which is aimed at staunchly defending the people's right to freedom and independent development, this regime has gone even further than some of the most reactionary Arab regimes. This stance of the dictatorial Iraqi regime renders a direct service to US imperialism, facilitating the implementation of its vile intentions aimed not only against the revolution in Afghanistan and Iran, but against all our peoples and their just struggle against Zionist aggression.

Later, the ICP-CC's enmity towards the regime increased when the Baᶜth supported a Turkish attack on communist bases, as well as an attack by the Kurdish Patriotic Union of Kurdistan (PUK) on ICP-CC headquarters in northern Iraq.[47] For its part, the Baᶜth-controlled National Progressive Front (NPF) declared that it was expelling the ICP-CC on the grounds that the Party had undermined national unity by carrying out political activities in the army.[48]

Splits in the Party's ranks had appeared as early as 1977, when some ICP-CC members disagreed with concessions made to the Baᶜth in the name of "consolidation of progressive forces." Both cooperation with the regime in its war against the Kurds and the abandonment of communist influence in the armed forces and in mass organizations had been especially contentious. These members also accused the ICP-CC leadership of dependence on the USSR and of vacillating between cooperation and armed struggle as the means for establishing democracy. They further claimed that the ICP-CC leadership had neglected "political consciousness-raising" among the masses, had failed to engage in proper self-criticism, and had abandoned the Party's nationalist character.[49] For these dissidents, the Party had lost its nationalist and pan-Arab character. Moreover, its internationalist positions had become weakened, it could not keep pace with the current political situation, and it had become paralysed and incapable of affecting the course of social progress and development within Iraq. Finally, its slogans and decisions could not be practically applied to the real objective and subjective situation in Iraq.

A number of breakaway groups emerged out of the Party. One such group, the Iraqi Revolutionary Communists, though not large, articulated the basic reasons for the long-standing and general discontent with the Central Committee in its political newspaper *Al-Asâs*, which, the group declared in late 1978, was to be the voice of Iraqi communist revolutionaries. This group began raising questions even about the initial basis of the alliance with the Baᶜth and the process by which the Central Committee, in general, and the secretary-general, in particular, had conceived of and eventually joined the NPF. The group's questions focused as well on the dictatorial personality of the secretary-general

[47] *World Marxist Review* (February 1981), p. 74.

[48] *Al-Thawrah* (Baghdad, 12 September 1980), p. 4.

[49] *Al-Nashrah* (31 October 1983), pp. 9–11.

and on the irresponsibility of both an ineffective Central Committee and the Politburo, which it held responsible for the fiasco and its aftermath. The group regarded the ICP-CC's joining of the NPF as an ill-conceived expedient and a decision whose strategic impact had not been thoroughly examined by the leadership. It offered its own vision of a genuine revolutionary front, calling for

> the formation of a popular nationalist solid front now, which is not only ready to shoulder the responsibilities of the current political circumstances but is also able to create [and direct] the conditions for the future [political] stage. . . . This means, in communist terms, a search for the means of advancing towards the achievement of the socialist revolution . . . and the need to delineate this means to achieve the aim [of socialist transformation] within calculated political equations in a changing environment.

It also advocated the principle of self-criticism, "not in order to punish anybody but rather to learn from past mistakes." It began by identifying the existing political conditions, and locating the national forces that were genuinely revolutionary and committed to accepting Marxist-Leninist principles.

For its proposed front the Iraqi Revolutionary Communists advanced several conditions: the first was to be a general rejection of the oppressive Baᶜthist state and a commitment to struggle against the regime. To achieve this, a correct understanding of the class nature of the alliance was essential. In addition, the Baᶜthists had to be seen as the class enemy of the (general revolutionary) front, and therefore as the group that the front must struggle against. This was to be the principle that would bind groups together in such a revolutionary front:

> There must be not only our agreement regarding the oppressive and terrorist actions of the Baᶜthist dictatorial regime but also a clear understanding of the class nature of the regime, from its inception with a military coup, on 17 July 1968, up to the present. We must [further agree] to deal with the disagreement [that could arise] as to the means of the struggle against this regime. In other words, [we need to delineate] an analysis of the class nature of the regime and our position towards it, and our struggle against it, in order to force it to retreat from its non-democratic practices or to overthrow it, if need be, completely. . . . In our view [this] is the basis of [our] alliance. Next, the most important conditions to create this needed front by revolutionary means . . . are not only replacing those who are in power but changing the entire system. . . . any front would lose its raison d'être if it did not clearly determine its stand towards the regime as a whole, and this cannot occur unless the class nature of the regime is identified. This front must be progressive . . . in other words; we must delineate the enemy, the friendly and the allied camps. The third condition is the need for a revolutionary party, which is the most essential axis for the creation and success of any front.[50]

The Politburo and the secretary-general attempted to deal with this challenge by clandestinely issuing rebuttals through their newspaper *Ṭarîq al-Shaᶜb*, which was now underground. Beginning with the first issue, dated at the end

50 "Editorial on National Alliances and the Project of the Front," *Al-Asâs*, no. 8 (Baghdad, October 1979), pp. 1, 6–8.

of August 1979, they attempted to justify their previous partnership with the Baᶜth, and to salvage that partnership by asserting that they had tried to play the role of "balancer" within the National Progressive Front. However, by late 1979 it was evident that the Baᶜthists were interested only in the continuation of the dictatorial regime. The ICP-CC further claimed that throughout 1979 they had lobbied the regime to reduce its dictatorial tendencies. On 9 February 1979 they made a formal complaint to Saddam Hussein, protesting the regime's oppression against progressive forces, particularly communists. They accused the Baᶜthist regime of mounting a propaganda campaign, inside and outside the country, against communist and progressive forces as a prelude to the ICP-CC's expulsion from the NPF. The Baᶜthist campaign was given ideological overtones by claims that it was directed not just against the Iraqi Communist Party, but against all communists. Thus, in the 12 May 1979 issue of *Al-Thawrah*, the official Baᶜth Party newspaper, the Baᶜthists accused all the Arab communist parties of treason and of importing foreign ideologies. With this attack, the NPF had reached a point of no return.

The Central Committee also claimed to have called for increased democracy

> not for the ICP alone but for all the progressive, anti-imperialist forces and for a guarantee of the rights of political, labour, social, and professional organizations. The Baᶜthists monopolized all these activities and ensured that monopoly in a way not found anywhere in any country in the world, through severe punishments for any who violated the laws. . . . these laws [therefore] had to be abolished in order to create confidence among its citizens.[51]

The next editorial in *Ṭarîq al-Shaᶜb*, in November 1979, emphasized that the campaign against the opposition was basically a conspiracy involving the Iraqi regime, Saudi Arabia, and Arab reactionaries that was intended to

> destroy the liberation movements [and] revolutionary parties, strangle the Palestinian revolution and the Lebanese national movement, frustrate the activities of the national Arab regimes, conspire against the Democratic Republic of Yemen (PDRY), create difficulties for Syria, discourage Arab-Soviet cooperation, increase anti-communist animosity, suggest closer cooperation with Western Europe, and rehabilitate the reactionary traditional regimes such as Saudi Arabia, and the like under the slogan of national independence, by uniting the [Arab] nations in their fight against outside influence. . . . It is no coincidence that there were efforts by Iraq, Saudi Arabia, and Jordan to frustrate any effort in the Tunis Arab Summit to garner support for Iran in its battle with America, and to omit any condemnation of the US in the final communiqué.[52]

As a result of the NPF's collapse, calls for a Fourth Congress began to be heard, even amongst moderates in the complacent Central Committee, in order to assess: the impact of the failure of the alliance with the Baᶜth; the gradual compromises with the NPF to please the Baᶜth, the detrimental effect of those compromises on morale, recruitment, membership, and the popular image of

[51] Editorial, *Ṭarîq al-Shaᶜb*, no. 3 (Baghdad, October 1979), pp. 1–7.
[52] *Ṭarîq al-Shaᶜb*, no. 4 (Baghdad, November 1979), pp. 1, 3.

the Party; the subsequent decimation of the Party and to determine the accountability of those responsible. The agenda of the Central Committee's first meeting in June 1980 after the collapse of the NPF included "the holding of the Fourth Congress in order to discuss and evaluate the Party's previous policies, and articulate a revolutionary policy to respond to the new conditions as an opposition party ... and to elect the Party's new leadership."[53] In 1981, to channel these sentiments and energies, the leadership initiated an armed struggle against the Baʿthist government of Iraq, forming the *Anṣâr* partisans, a fighting force quartered in northern Iraq.

In a large Party meeting of the advanced cadre towards the end of 1981, chaired by the secretary-general, ʿAzîz Muḥammad made it clear that he had no intention of holding a congress in the near future, citing security conditions and personality clashes. Thus, in early November 1981, when the Central Committee met, it was evident that a strong group critical of the Party's submissiveness to the Baʿth and its overall ineffectiveness would be demanding radical changes, including the use of armed struggle in the Kurdish areas and its eventual extension to southern Iraq.

To build a genuine Marxist-Leninist Iraqi Communist Party, and to avoid what happened in 1965–1966 when a similar situation resulted in the formation of the Central Leadership faction, a compromise solution was reached at the November meeting. The Central Committee agreed not to adjourn the meeting, but to leave it open until it met again in Moscow, where Soviet theoreticians would be in attendance to mediate between the Iraqi factions. Thus, when the Central Committee met in Moscow at the end of November 1981, under the auspices of the CPSU, certain decisions were agreed upon to appease the rebellious groups, for example, that a Fourth Congress would be held in Iraq in a timely fashion and would prepare and discuss ideological, organizational, and theoretical documents among which would be a document evaluating the Party's experiences and future plans. The Central Committee also accepted the principle of armed struggle and even added members from the group critical of the Politburo, exactly as had happened to ʿAzîz al-Ḥâjj in 1966.

When the Central Committee announced the results of the meeting, it did not include the compromise solutions agreed to in Moscow. Nevertheless, the Central Committee began organizing itself and its supporters in preparation for the Fourth Congress, although without designating a date for its convening. It also tried to isolate those whom it considered troublemakers. Nine months later, the Central Committee defiantly declared "our party's policy is correct, its aims are very clear, its organizations are very healthy, its influence is very great, and its membership is very unified and possessed of iron discipline." This stance made it difficult for those who were calling for change. A splinter group was then formed by those who were dissatisfied,[54] and at the end of September

53 ʿAzîz Muḥammad, *Ḥadîth Shâmil bi Munâsabat al-Dhikrâ al ʾÛlâ li Inʿiqâd al-Mûʾtamar al-Waṭanî* (n.p.: Communist Party of Iraq, 1985), p. 10.

54 *Al-Niḍâl*, no. 1 (end September 1982).

1982, it published the first issue of *Al-Nidâ'*, calling for a challenge to the existing political leadership and appealing to the rest of the Party membership for support.[55]

In January 1983, a number of representatives of the Iraqi Communist Party cadre, among them members of the newly formed Revolutionary Current, a breakaway group, met to discuss the crisis that the Party was undergoing and the fragmentation that had begun. They evaluated all of the ICP's policies, and condemned the Party's organizational and ideological stagnation, particularly in relation to the leadership's submissiveness to the Baᶜth and abandonment of Marxist-Leninist principles. They also accused the leadership of fleeing the country and living pampered lives abroad. They described the policies of the Party leaders as "a rightist and opportunist current" and accused them of pushing the Party

> into non-nationalist positions, and towards sectarian exploitation . . . exemplified in their re-evaluation of the sectarian religious movements, . . . [and they asserted that] the historical experience in Iraq proved repeatedly that traditional methods within the Party showed it to be incapable of dealing with such a deep-rooted crisis. Even the promised Fourth Congress that many of the wishful-thinking cadre hoped [would deal with the crisis], as was rumoured by the condemned opportunist leadership, . . . even if it were held, it would not resolve the crisis within the Party. We can thus say that all avenues are closed in the face of the honest cadre in their desire to participate actively in resolving the Party crisis. The leadership has been able to remove a number of the cadre by non-principled means, and in flagrant violation of the Party by-laws, through expulsion or "freezing," . . . which has made it impossible to deal with the leadership in an honest [and] principled manner so as to redirect the Iraqi Communist Party onto the true path.[56]

Thus, they decided on the following:

1. To create a new communist organization under the name *Munaẓẓamat al-ᶜAmal al-Shiyûᶜî fî al-ᶜIrâq* (The Organization of Communist Action in Iraq). This would avoid having to use the name the Iraqi Communist Party, which was controlled by the current illegitimate leadership, and it would avoid inheriting the mistakes of this leadership, with its heavily loaded, deviationist past.
2. To work in a principled manner and with a strategic outlook. To encourage honest communists to join the new organization through such basic documents as its programme and by-laws, particularly those related to its general political line and current responsibilities.
3. To publish a central organ.[57]

55 *Ṭarîq al-Shaᶜb*, no. 8, vol. 46 (Baghdad, end July 1982); Editorial, *Al-Ghad* (On the Path of the People), nos. 18–19 (July 1985), pp. 156–158.

56 *Al-Ghad*, no. 18–19 (July 1985), p. 160.

57 "The Founding Declaration of the Iraqi Communist Action Group," *Ḥiwâr*, vol. 1, no. 1 (6 January 1983).

ICP opposition forces in Iraq increasingly found themselves under the tutelage of patrons whose own interests determined the level and effectiveness of the support they gave. During the 1980s, Syria was the most prominent of these supporters, and in late October 1980, it attempted to unify the major opposition groupings into *al-Jabhah al-Waṭaniyyah al-Taqaddumiyyah al-Dîmuqrâṭiyyah* (the Progressive National Democratic Front), which became known by its Arabic acronym, JWQD. Its nucleus was assembled in Damascus on 12 November 1982, bringing together the PUK (Patriotic Union of Kurdistan), HASAK (the Kurdish Socialist Party), and the ICP. The PUK insisted on excluding its main rival, the KDP (Kurdistan Democratic Party) and manoeuvred to keep it out of the JWQD. But two short weeks later, the ICP, HASAK, and the KDP formed *al-Jabhah al-Waṭaniyyah al-Dîmuqrâṭiyyah* (the National Democratic Front), which came to be known by its Arabic acronym, JWOD, thereby excluding the PUK. The ICP-CC had hoped to tie the two fronts together, forming an indirect alliance among all of the major Iraqi opposition groups, including the belligerent PUK and KDP. However, the PUK proved adamant and demanded the removal of HASAK and the ICP from the JWQD, which virtually destroyed any hope of a unified alliance against Baᶜthist tyranny.[58]

The separatist group, whose goals were primarily organizational and ideological, called itself the Communist Labour Organization of Iraq and claimed to be dedicated to the same ends as the ICP-CC, though through different means:

> We call for working with principled means, a strategic point of view, and a spirit of zeal, so that honourable Party [ICP-CC] members and communist cadres will attach themselves to the new organization. This requires that the cadres not exposed to the [corrupt] leadership work within the Party in order to influence the state of the Party [ICP-CC] and raise the consciousness of all Party cadres and members in a proper manner that should be followed by the communist movement in Iraq.
>
> Conflict and democratic-ideological intellectual dialogue must be used in the current stage as a basic tool for building the structure of the new organization. This can be done by preparing the necessary basic documents, especially the organization's programme and by-laws, and those documents having to do with its general political line, as well as the nature of the tasks currently facing the country.[59]

Further organizational difficulties surfaced throughout the 1980s. The ICP-CC alleged that Bahâᵓu-d-Dîn Nûrî (who would be ousted from the Central Committee in 1984) had been agitating for a split within the Party and was being supported by Jalâl Ṭâlabânî's Patriotic Union of Kurdistan (PUK). The PUK, in turn, held ᶜAzîz Muḥammad and the ICP-CC responsible for its own internal difficulties, while also joining other Kurdish groups in making moves

[58] Nûrî, *Mudhakkarât Bahâᵓu-d-Dîn Nûrî*, pp. 340–341; and ᶜAjînah, *Al-Ikhtiyâr al-Mutajaddid*, pp. 375–376; see also ᶜAjînah, *Al-Ikhtiyâr al-Mutajaddid*, pp. 194–196; and ICP Politburo bulletin, (Baghdad, 20 May 1982).

[59] Communist Labour Organization of Iraq, "Founding Document," *Al-Ghad*, no. 18–19 (London, July 1985), p. 160.

towards Iran and pressuring Bahâʾu-d-Dîn Nûrî, as a communist representative, to do so as well.[60]

Meanwhile, Bahâʾu-d-Dîn Nûrî, who had spent forty years on the advanced cadre of the Party, mainly on the Central Committee and Politburo, and who had been the secretary-general thirty years earlier, had settled in Qaradagh in the Kurdish area of northern Iraq and considered himself the inheritor and legitimate leader of the true Iraqi Communist Party. He declared the goals of his Party to be democracy for Iraq and autonomy for Kurdistan. Further, he issued a members-only publication called *Ḥayât al-Ḥizb* (The Party's Life), and resurrected the old Party mouthpiece *Al-Qâʿidah*, which the Party had published in 1943. Declaring it to be the main newspaper of the Iraqi Communist Party, Nûrî published issue Number 1 of Volume 41 in March of 1984. Starting in 1989, he also published *Ṣadâ al-Qâʿidah* for external consumption. But with the collapse of the Soviet Union in 1991, he ceased all his political activities.

Bahâʾu-d-Dîn Nûrî explained his position in "A Draft for Discussion to Evaluate the Policy of the Iraqi Communist Party for the Years 1968–1983." He noted that he had asked the Central Committee to circulate this document as a discussion paper five years earlier, citing precedents in 1965 and 1967 when the Party circulated documents that were later taken up by the Second Congress. He then recounted how, while on his way to meet the Central Committee in June 1984 to convey to them his views on the document, he had been kidnapped and detained for a month by the Central Committee.[61] This, he said, was why now, in early August 1984, he found himself forced to republish this document in which he identifies the problems with the Party. He maintained that the Party had been very cautious in 1968–1970 in dealing with the Baʿthist regime but later had taken "a wrong political direction [that abandoned the principles of central democracy]," and as such, the collective leadership and party organs were undermined.[62] In this situation, the secretary-general became the sole decision maker, and the Central Committee nothing more than a rubber stamp.

After 1973, according to Nûrî, the Party tied itself to a policy of cooperation with the ruling Baʿth̲ Party, first by agreeing to take a position in the cabinet in May 1972 and then by signing the National Patriotic Front's programme in July 1973. This meant

> accepting the leading role of the Baʿth̲ in this Front, completely conceding their role as the vanguard and leader of the working class, and retreating from the demand for a coalition government, contrary to the decision of the Central Committee.... [In fact,] the Secretary-General, on his own, offered another concession by withdrawing the Central Committee veto in Front discussions. By consenting to this, the Central Committee had also allied itself with a ruling party, and committed itself to the support of a regime, without that regime's conceding any power, and agreeing to the regime's monopolizing

60 Nûrî, *Mudhakkarât Bahâʾu-d-Dîn Nûrî*, pp. 424–438.

61 Bahâʾu-d-Dîn Nûrî, "A Draft for Discussion to Evaluate the Policy of the Iraqi Communist Party for the Years 1968–1983," *Al-Ghad*, no. 18–19 (July 1985), pp. 95–101.

62 Nûrî, *Mudhakkarât Bahâʾu-d-Dîn Nûrî*, pp. 424–438.

of activity among peasants, farmers, and students, any organization within the armed forces, and allowing it to completely monopolize all basic means of political communication.[63]

The secretary-general controlled everything after 1979, concentrating power in his own hands and in the hands of a few Politburo members. On top of this, the entire Central Committee was living abroad and unaware of the situation within Iraq, which resulted in internal Party dissension and crystallized the isolation of the Party leadership from the cadre.[64] In this environment, the Party entered a chaotic period, resulting in the crisis that eventually led to its disintegration.

Nevertheless, in the early 1980s the ICP began to call for the overthrow of Saddam Hussein, formally president since 1979, and the establishment of a democratic regime in Iraq.[65] ICP-CC member Nazîhah al-Dulaimî stated that this new regime would be a "national democratic coalition government that would achieve democracy for Iraq and real autonomy for the Kurdish people."[66] According to Party by-laws, the Fourth Congress of the ICP was supposed to be held no later than October 1984, to coincide with the fiftieth anniversary of the founding of the Iraqi Communist Party. Because Party conflicts might surface in such an event, challenging the hegemony of the leadership, the ICP sought the congress's delay. As a result, just prior to the congress, the ICP found itself plunged into further internal dissension within the Politburo and throughout the rest of the leadership.

The leadership of the Party was now old, increasingly detached from its cadre, and to some degree isolated from what was happening inside Iraq. Most of the leadership had been living outside Iraq since 1978, after the Party's failed experiment in cooperation with the Baʿthists and eventual expulsion from both the NPF and the country. With the leadership residing outside Iraq and enjoying a comfortable, even lavish, life under the protection of the Eastern bloc countries and the CPSU, the communist rank-and-file cadres inside Iraq were left to endure the ruthless fury of the Baʿthist intelligence services. A further split between the middle-ranking leadership of the cadre inside Iraq and those living outside it thus became inevitable.

During this period, the average age of Central Committee and Politburo members was over seventy years. By this time, the secretary-general himself had been in power for over a quarter of a century, and Zakî Khairî (who was incapacitated) and such other Central Committee leaders as Bahâʾu-d-Dîn Nûrî, Karîm Aḥmad, ʿÂmir ʿAbd-ul-lah, and Thâbit Ḥabîb al-ʿÂnî had also served the Party for over twenty-five years. The leaders were weak, old, subservient to the secretary-general's wishes, and totally dependent on their Party salaries, which were controlled by the secretary-general. As soon as its members were located in Eastern Europe, the Central Committee sought to

63 *Al-Ghad*, no. 18–19 (London, November 1987), p. 71.
64 Ibid., no. 18–19 (London, July 1985), pp. 64–103.
65 *Merip Report* (21 June 1981), p. 74.
66 *Al-Hurriyah* (27 February 1983).

mobilize support from other enemies of the Baᶜthist regime in Iraq; it moved closer to the Syrian Baᶜthists and joined alliances dedicated to bringing down the Iraqi Baᶜthists. It also began to cooperate with the People's Democratic Republic of Yemen. The secretary-general, along with Politburo members and a number of the Central Committee members, established liaison offices in Damascus and Aden. Furthermore, when the war broke out between Iraq and Iran, the leaders condemned the Iraqi aggression against Iran, considering it to be a continuation of the deterioration of political conditions in the Arab and international spheres. Indeed, they re-emphasized this viewpoint at every meeting of the Central Committee, particularly the meetings of November 1981 and September 1982.[67]

As a way for the non-aligned community to condemn the Baᶜth regime and its policies, the leadership also considered the postponement and relocation of the non-aligned nations' conference scheduled to be held in Baghdad in 1982. Indeed, they considered the proposal to hold the conference in Baghdad to be a ploy by Saddam Hussein to

> hi-jack the non-aligned movement from its revolutionary, anti-imperialist content, whereby the movement helped oppressed nations achieve freedom and independence . . . and serve American imperialism, whose basic aim was to demolish the movement from inside and cause it to deviate from its original aims and slogans of independence and freedom from the influence of both superpowers.[68]

In its meeting at the end of September 1982, the Party gloated over the repulsion of Baᶜathist agression by Iranian forces. It also "took note of the military and political defeats, and the increase in Iraq's isolation, inside and outside the country."[69]

During the 1980s the Iran-Iraq war widened the serious division between the Baᶜth and the ICP-CC. According to the communists, the Baᶜth "represents the interests of the bureaucratic, parasitic, and anti-people bourgeoisie,"[70] and the war reflected the reactionary nature of the regime. As noted by Secretary-General ᶜAzîz Muḥammad of the ICP-CC: "The unleashing of this armed conflict was the continuation and outcome of the domestic policy pursued by the reactionary dictatorial regime in Iraq, as reflected in its foreign policy."[71]

According to the ICP-CC, the war with Iran only increased the Iraqi regime's oppressive policies. In October 1987 a message from the ICP-CC to the UN secretary-general and Security Council pointed out:

> The war has been used as a pretext to commit even more blatant violations of human rights in our country, up to and including crimes against humanity, for which the guilty are to be prosecuted by the international community and tried in national or international courts in accordance with legal instruments adopted more than forty years ago.[72]

67 Voice of the Iraqi People broadcast, 11 October 1982.
68 *Ṭarîq al-Shaᶜb*, vol. 47, no. 1 (Baghdad, August 1982).
69 Statement by the Central Committee, dated end of September 1982, p. 1.
70 *Information Bulletin* (November 1984), p. 9.
71 *World Marxist Review* (September 1987), p. 110.
72 *Information Bulletin* (October 1987), p. 15.

These crimes included the disappearance of political prisoners, the execution of children, and the use of chemical weapons against Kurdish civilians. The war was perceived not only as intensifying the ruling regime's repressive domestic policies but also as destabilizing the entire region. The ICP-CC claimed that the war

> plays into the hands of US imperialism, by providing it with a pretext for the unprecedented escalation of its military presence in the Persian Gulf area. The war also benefits the Zionist rulers of Israel, because it has assured them of the most favourable conditions for brazenly trampling the Palestinian people's legitimate rights, for their devastating invasion of Lebanon, and subsequently for the imposition of a capitulationist agreement on the victim of the aggression.[73]

In a September 1987 article, ᶜAzîz Muḥammad argued further that

> the US deftly used its knowledge of the Iraqi regime, of its expansionistic and chauvinistic ambitions. In our region the US wants to restore the influence it lost when the Shah's regime was overthrown, make Iraq more heavily dependent on US imperialism and reaction, and paralyse Iraq's potential for participating in the confrontation with Israel.[74]

The communists called for an end to the war almost as soon as it began. The Party secretary-general summed up the ICP-CC's position at the Fourth Party Congress in November 1985:

> The Congress urged an immediate cessation of the hostilities and a peaceful settlement of outstanding disputes. The Party condemned the war and the occupation of Iranian territory by Iraqi troops, called for their earliest [possible] withdrawal and, at the same time, categorically rejected Iran's attempts to invade Iraq, occupy Iraqi territory and expand the scope of hostilities. True to our principles, we reject Iran's intention to export, by way of war, the "Islamic Revolution" to Iraq and impose the "Iranian Model" on our people.[75]

The ICP-CC believed that the end of the war and the downfall of the ruling regime were closely related issues. As Zakî Khairî argued. "It is impossible to carry through a democratic peace when one of the sides is an aggressive, belligerent dictatorship.... both governments ... will hardly be able to get out of it on their own since a defeat is likely to mean the defeat of either government."[76]

The post-ceasefire stand of the ICP-CC is worthy of examination as it was a continuation of its position during the war. One of the issues the ICP-CC sought to address was its desire to see a reduction in the American military presence in the region. According to an ICP-CC statement:

> It is necessary to force the imperialist countries, the United States in the first place, to remove their aggressive naval forces, which were sent into the Gulf on the pretext of the war, so as to turn it into an arena of aggressive US and NATO action, in order to

73 *World Marxist Review* (February 1981), p. 75.
74 Ibid. (September 1987), pp. 111–112.
75 Ibid. (November 1986), p. 34.
76 *Land of Folk* (East Berlin, 25 August 1983).

establish their imperialist domination, to threaten the sovereignty of the countries in the region, and to plunder their national wealth.[77]

The ICP-CC issued a list of measures that it believed were necessary to move beyond a ceasefire into something more lasting.[78] The first demand was that the international community refrain from making further arms sales to both Iran and Iraq, coupled with a call for stricter worldwide controls on the manufacture and use of chemical weapons. The second important point was a call for a moratorium on international aid to both Iran and Iraq until the two states began to negotiate in good faith. It also issued its own programme outlining how it believed negotiations should be conducted. The first stage, in the ICP-CC's view, would consist of a POW exchange and amnesty for Iraqis who had fled to Iran to escape Baᶜthist persecution. The Party also called for the deployment of a UN force to monitor the ceasefire, supervise troop withdrawal, and clear and patrol the Shaṭ al-ᶜArab waterway. The second stage would address a review of the 1975 agreement between Iran and Iraq, with particular attention to the status of the Shaṭ al-ᶜArab; it would also identify "those who started the war and those who insisted on its continuation," an action clearly directed at the regime of Saddam Hussein.

The ICP-CC was attempting to make the maximum political capital from the end of the war – by addressing internal oppression by Saddam's regime in its first round of hypothetical negotiations, and in the second, by attempting to force global acknowledgement of Saddam Hussein's culpability, which, it hoped, would lessen his international support and thus the strength of the regime. The two main tasks facing the ICP-CC were to end the war and overthrow the Baᶜth regime:

The beginning of the end of the war ... brings to the fore the problem of uniting the forces in the fight to overthrow the dictatorship and set up a coalition government to ensure democracy in the country and Kurdistan's genuine autonomy. Attention must be focused on the problem of democracy and human rights in Iraq.[79]

The ICP-CC pressed for progress on human rights in both Iran and Iraq, as one of the strongest guarantees of peace, calling on the world community, notably the UN General Assembly and the UN Human Rights Commission to act towards this end.[80] The post-war focus on democracy and human rights was also manifested in the writer Bilâl al-Sâmir's article "Human Rights and Global Security," in which he stated:

Everything indicates that a new stage, characterized by a relaxation of tension, is beginning in world development. The Cold War clouds are gradually dissipating.... However, the favourable international situation is incompatible with the existence of

77 *Information Bulletin* (December 1988), p. 6.
78 *World Marxist Review* (June 1989), p. 72.
79 *Information Bulletin* (December 1988), p. 6.
80 *World Marxist Review* (June 1989), pp. 72–73.

a dictatorship, which defies the times and principles of the Universal Declaration of Human Rights.[81]

This article dismissed the recent statements about "a general amnesty" and "pluralism" that had been made by Saddam Hussein, viewing them "as an attempt to blunt the protest abroad" and as "proof of the dictatorship's inability to prolong its days by force" in the current international environment. The article further argued that

international cooperation for the defence and advancement of the values of freedom, democracy, and individual and national rights will be expressed in vigorous actions to uproot racism, chauvinism, and all forms of discrimination, and in joint solutions to the problems of ethnic minorities, refugees, and immigrant workers.

Undoubtedly, the ICP-CC viewed the post–Cold War environment as conducive to its struggle against Saddam Hussein's regime.

Another very important issue on the ICP-CC's agenda in the 1980s was Kurdish autonomy. The ICP-CC had supported the Baʿthist war against the Kurds in 1974–1975, but as the regime turned on the ICP-CC, the ICP-CC reversed its stance and sought an alliance with some Kurdish groups. According to Zakî Khairî, "The second most important issue in the Middle East (besides the Palestinian issue) is the Kurdish issue. The Kurdish national movement is an element that contributes to creating the basis for revolution in the area."[82] The Fourth Party Congress of November 1985 adopted the attainment of Kurdish autonomy as one of its main tasks for the 1980s. ʿAzîz Muḥammad identified the other tasks as ending the war, overthrowing the dictatorship, and implementing a democratic alternative.[83] The importance of the Kurdish national movement to the ICP-CC grew with time, and in October 1988, ʿAzîz Muḥammad even referred to the Kurdish liberation movement as part of the Iraqi democratic movement.[84] Also in 1988, the ICP-CC and five Kurdish parties formed the Front of Iraqi Kurdistan. According to the ICP-CC:

The National Front targets its activity at the solution of the common tasks in today's difficult conditions resulting from the tragic Iran-Iraq war ... the fascist terror being conducted against the people, and the national oppression of the Kurds.[85]

The alliance with the Kurds was seen as an integral part of the ICP-CC's "common front" policy at this time, and the ICP-CC viewed the overthrow of the ruling regime as "a joint struggle of the entire Iraqi people."[86] Thus,

the ICP-CC has exerted colossal efforts to unite the struggle of Iraq's national patriotic opposition forces through a broad nation-wide front open to all the patriotic and

[81] Ibid. (July 1989), p. 44.
[82] *Land of Folk* (East Berlin, 25 August 1983).
[83] *World Marxist Review* (November 1986), p. 35.
[84] *Information Bulletin* (October 1988), p. 21.
[85] Ibid., p. 20.
[86] Ibid., p. 21.

democratic forces without exception. Those include the ICP-CC, the Arab national movement, the Kurdish national movement, the religious movement, and the national minorities. [The ICP-CC considers its union with the five Kurdish parties as the] first positive step in this direction.[87]

In response to the Baᶜth regime's oppression and slaughter, the ICP-CC went underground in the late 1970s, and the armed struggle became a basic strategy of the Party. According to Zakî Khairî, "We found no other option for fighting the dictatorship ... than taking up arms."[88] Until that point, the ICP-CC had renounced violence in favour of "peaceful and democratic struggle." This had been a fundamental point that had led to its split with the ICP-CL. The renunciation of a non-violent approach was in large part philosophical, but also pragmatic. While it often had considerable public support, the ICP generally had little influence in the routinely purged armed forces and none whatsoever in the security services. The Baᶜthists had been organized to utilize force and had proved to be committed to using violence to achieve their ends. The ICP-CC's inability to compete in this area was not in doubt, as the ICP-CC had committed itself to peaceful change, though Soviet influence probably played a role as well. Violent communist agitation could have destabilized Iraq, making the exercise of Soviet influence in the country more difficult. Khairî attached importance to the role of the armed forces in future revolutionary success. "Our revolution will only be a success if it is supported by the overwhelming majority of the Iraqi people and if it is supported by the army." He seemed optimistic about the possibility of military support, noting that "the Iraqi people [were] armed"[89] for the first time in Iraq's history, because of the war with Iran.

The ICP-CC was increasingly interested in establishing its own armed forces and conducting a guerrilla struggle against the Baᶜthist dictatorship. However, a serious problem with dissent, and charges of conspiracy, surfaced in the Party in 1983. During its armed struggle against the Baghdad government, the Central Committee mustered and stationed its *Anṣâr* fighting force in the north and began cooperating with the Patriotic Union of Kurdistan (PUK). Two weeks after its alliance with this group, the Party rather clumsily switched its alliance to the PUK's rival, the Kurdistan Democratic Party (KDP), and in doing so directly involved the Iraqi Communist Party Central Command in the conflict between the two competing Kurdish political groups. Its abandonment of the PUK, coupled with the fact that the PUK had successfully negotiated a new relationship with the Baghdad government, resulted in a massacre by the PUK of 150 cadre and Central Committee members in May 1983, when the Central Committee stationed its forces in a disputed area (called Pasht Ashan) that both Kurdish groups wished to control. The ICP-CC's headquarters were subsequently looted, its radio station was destroyed, its ammunition and food supplies were stolen, and a number of Central Committee and Politburo

87 Ibid.

88 *Land of Folk* (East Berlin, 25 August 1983).

89 Ibid.

members were captured. According to Bahâʾu-d-Dîn Nûrî, this was as disastrous a setback as the one that occured in 1978–1979, when the Baʿth had turned on the ICP-CC.[90] Sources in the ICP's Central Leadership claimed that this massacre had been deliberately brought about by the Central Committee leadership to get rid of those members who opposed the Central Committee's policies, and who had been outspoken in calling for the Fourth Congress.[91] The ICP-CC eventually settled its differences with the PUK, but for all practical purposes the now decimated Anṣâr guerrillas ceased to be an effective fighting force.

In this environment, the surviving members of the partisan movement of the ICP-CC (*al-Anṣâr*) found themselves confined in the Kurdish environment, since their area of operations from 1983 to 1985 was restricted to the northern Kurdish regions. Under the protections offered by the northern frontier and by the central government's distraction during the war with Iran, *al-Anṣâr* was able to grow in both stature and effectiveness – as long as the partisans could keep their actions within the prevailing Kurdish balance of power. This made their operations extremely difficult, as no Kurdish group actually trusted the communists.

Moreover, the complexity of the Kurdish military and political make-up was surpassed only by the antagonistic relationships among the groups in the region, which were further complicated by the shifting alliances when one of them would periodically negotiate with the central Baʿthist government. The KDP, as well as the PUK, negotiated with the Baʿthist central government in an effort to gain an advantage over other Kurdish groups and to legitimize themselves as full-fledged partners with the central government. This constant flux among Kurdish groups unsettled the ICP-CC, and as it could never again negotiate with the Baʿthist government itself, it was always left on shakey ground. Ultimately, the use of chemical weapons by Saddam Hussein against the civilian population of northern Iraq from March to August of 1988 ended the possibility of any further complicitous relationship between an opposition group and the Baʿth – until after the Gulf War of 1991.

Always paying the steepest price for the shifting Kurdish alliances, and always the outsider, the ICP-CC needed to bring a coalition of oppositional forces to bear on the Baʿth, or be constantly attempting to stay ahead of these shifting alliances in Iraqi-Kurdistan. The Enlarged Plenary Meeting of the ICP-CC in 1985

> considered the activity of the communist guerrilla movement and its successes, and discussed ways of raising its level, and enhancing its role in the people's heroic struggle for the overthrow of the dictatorship, in alliance with the guerrilla forces of the parties united in the Democratic National Front, and also those not forming a part of it.[92]

[90] Nûrî, *Mudhakkarât Bahâʾu-d-Dîn Nûrî*, pp. 400–405.

[91] *Al-Ghad*, no. 21 (London, November 1987), p. 22.

[92] *Information Bulletin* (January 1986), p. 28.

Moreover, the Fourth Congress of the ICP-CC also

stressed anew that among the various and interrelated methods of struggle, the armed struggle was now the chief one, and underscored the need to strengthen guerrilla units qualitatively and quantitatively, making them more active, and enhancing their role in the struggle.[93]

[93] Ibid. (April 1986), p. 19.

5

The Rebirth of the Central Leadership in the 1970s

In 1969 the ICP-CL faced an organizational deadlock as a result of the brutal treatment it had experienced at the hands of the Ba'thist regime. The ICP's split into factions left the CL temporarily rudderless, with the defection of the secretary-general and the submission of the rest of the leadership to the Baᶜthists in the National Front. This was further compounded by the ICP-CL's refusal to be reconciled with the ICP-CC. There seemed to be no option left for its cadre except to face annihilation at the hands of the Baᶜth security and police apparatus (as had already happened to their leadership) or to abandon political activism altogether. However, a new generation of committed cadre emerged, who concentrated their efforts on rejecting all cooperation, let alone the formation of an official alliance, with the Baᶜth, and who aimed for a very tightly knit, secretive organizational structure and more defined ideology. Of course, such an organization took time to develop and when Party activists met for a plenary session in Qaradagh, a mountainous area in the vicinity of Sulaimaniyah in Iraqi Kurdistan, the regime had detailed knowledge of both the timing and place of the meeting. It dispatched three MIG fighters and a Badger bomber to fly low-level runs over the location from 2:00 PM to 8:00 PM to signal the regime's ability to destroy the CL if it so desired.

> The meeting was held in the area's main mosque. The planes attacked but the local population was sympathetic and warned the delegates by shouting. The safety devices on the bombs had not been removed and the pilots dropped them in a valley nearby, giving the families of the delegates who happened to be in the school a chance to escape into the nearby cemetery. The fact that no one was killed or even injured indicated that the pilots themselves did not want a slaughter to occur and were perhaps sympathetic to the cause, since the sites could have easily been destroyed.[1]

This attack forced the cancellation and relocation of the ICP-CL meetings. The Party moved them to a mountainous area where Najim Maḥmûd was

[1] Interview by author with Najim Maḥmûd, Beirut (20 July 1976).

unanimously elected to be the new leader of the ICP-CL.[2] As Maḥmûd later recounted, this period was very sensitive for the CL and for their relationship with Muṣṭafâ Bârzânî, their host in Kurdistan, "as we were completely dependent on Bârzânî's good-will." Maḥmûd related:

> We heard rumours that Andrei Primakov, a close personal friend of Saddam Hussein and a high-ranking Soviet official and Middle East specialist, had been mediating between Muṣṭafâ Bârzânî and the Baᶜthist government. Rumours in traditional areas like the Kurdish north usually have a base in reality, more than in other places, as the leaders talk freely in their social interactions and this information gradually filters down to the rest of the population. In addition, we saw government delegates visiting Bârzânî and we also had soldiers and officers, sympathetic to us, who alerted us to what was happening. As a result, we formulated our policies and carefully monitored the negotiations.[3]

Despite the virtual annihilation of the ICP-CL on the structural level, remnants of the young, committed, ideologically oriented leadership headed by Najim Maḥmûd issued a manifesto in the form of several articles in successive issues of *Al-Hurriyah*, the Beirut-based Arab nationalist newspaper. It had become the voice of the Palestinian Marxist-Leninist Popular Front for the Liberation of Palestine (PFLP), and in order to revitalize the ICP-CL and to distinguish its ideological tenets from those of the ICP-CC, Maḥmûd had the articles published in that paper. The ICP-CL's manifesto was entitled "A Look at the Political and Social Situation in Iraq."[4] It laid out the ideological foundations of the Central Leadership and accused the Central Committee both of becoming a movement dedicated to the interests of the bourgeoisie and of being sensitive to "corrupting influences prevalent in the international sphere at the expense of the masses, the army, and of any real revolutionary progress." It accused the ICP-CC of abandoning the class struggle, replacing real socialist economic development with bourgeois domination, and ignoring the workers and peasants.

At the root of past communist failures, according to the ICP-CL, was Iraq's "old, deep-seated, and chronic" political crisis, which led to the pursuit of short-term goals through the cynical building and abandonment of coalitions, rather than by revolutionary progress. This process had led to the "military dictatorial regime which, to the ICP-CL, was neither progressive nor socialist." The ICP-CL argued that the Baᶜth represented no change from the ᶜÂrif regime (especially as it included many of the same key figures) and that it served the interests of the only bourgeoisie and international imperialism. This tradition of complicity would be abandoned by the ICP-CL in favour of a long-term struggle against the Iraqi regime that would necessitate a Party presence in the army and within the Kurdish nationalist groupings. The ICP-CL identified strongly with

2 Interview by author with a number of activists, in London, Paris, Frankfurt, Berlin, and Vienna, between September 1979 and October 1989.

3 Interview by author with Najim Maḥmûd, Beirut (20 July 1976).

4 *Al-Hurriyah* (Beirut, 14 July 1969), pp. 13–15; (21 July 1969), pp. 14–15; (28 July 1969), pp. 12–14.

the Kurdish masses (though not with Kurdish tribal leaders, who were seen as "bourgeois pawns") as they were often the first targets of Baghdad's oppression by the army and its "toiling base" of soldiers. Indeed, the ICP-CL laid almost personal claim to the revolutionary movement in general. In the ICP-CL's view, the Central Committee members were nothing more than collaborators eager to share in power without benefit to the Iraqi people, and were referred to as "toys in the hands of the bourgeoisie." The ICP-CC was further accused of derailing professional and student unions from a true revolutionary course through rigged elections.

The document criticized the theoretical foundation of the "progressivism" underlying the regime, asserted that the rapprochement between the Baʿth and the ICP-CC was not genuine, and claimed that the real aim of the "reformists" (the ICP-CC) was to cooperate in the subjugation of the Iraqi people in the service of foreign imperialism. It also criticized the (then) current conception of democracy in Iraq, arguing that it was designed only to "legitimize the regime" and to prevent the development of true popular democracy. The provisional Constitution of 1970 was dismissed as merely giving the regime "a free hand to deal despotically, and in a fascist and reactionary way, with all the progressive and nationalist forces in general, and workers and farmers in particular." In the ICP-CL's portrayal, the regime was "completely infiltrated by agents of foreign imperialist and Zionist spy networks, who operate to divide the masses along sectarian, racist, provincial, and tribal lines," and the ICP-CL was of the opinion that these networks, which were seen as primarily sponsored by Britain, were not only tolerated but were also "supported by high officials of the regime." Internal division – between Kurds and Arabs, workers and peasants – was encouraged by these foreign agents and Iraqi collaborators and was the primary obstacle to revolutionary progress in Iraq.

The ICP-CL also saw negotiations, such as those that culminated in the 11 March 1970 agreement to end the Kurdish uprising, or that saw the ICP-CC secure the "National Front" proposal with the Baʿth, as betrayals of the Kurdish and Arab peoples. In this charged political environment, and with detailed information in hand, a pronouncement in late December 1969 by the Central Leadership described these moves as

> an attempt to strengthen the dilapidated Baʿth regime ... in order to allow them to catch their breath so that they could prepare another bloody round against national and progressive forces, and prepare for another massacre of the Kurdish people, taking advantage of the new deceptive circumstances [and] exploiting the alliance with the opportunist right-wing ICP internally and with the Soviet deviationists internationally.

Prior to the official announcement of the 11 March agreement, a secret delegation of government envoys from Baghdad visited the KDP to negotiate, and when the discussions ended, they were safely escorted by KDP members through Kurdish-controlled territory back to the demarcation line between themselves and territory controlled by the government of Iraq. After dispatching their interlocutors, the KDP group then visited the CL encampment. However, the

CL members had already heard via the BBC Arabic news service that an agreement had been reached between the Ba'thist government and the KDP, though it had not yet been made public. Therefore, the CL responded, in early March 1970, by issuing a Party circular warning the Kurdish leadership against the pending agreement. This antagonized Bârzânî, who dispatched his son Idrîs to see Maḥmûd and to protest about the CL's position, which was described as "premature and inaccurate."[5]

One of the first tasks faced by the new leadership was to clarify the ideological tenets of the ICP-CL. Thus, at the end of August 1969, in a bold move made during an enlarged meeting for the advanced cadre, the leadership was instructed "to study the conditions of the international communist movement, analyze the dangers of the rightist revisionist [impacts] on the global revolutionary movement, and pinpoint its international centre" and issue a report on its findings.[6]

The Basic Ideology of the ICP-CL

During the the ICP-CL's formative years in Iraqi Kurdistan, from 1969 to 1974, its positions became crystallized. Its political stances were organized into a clear and coherent intellectual framework by Najim Maḥmûd while he was "in a more peaceful setting after leaving the battlefield of Iraqi Kurdistan."[7] The series was initiated with a draft of "The Iraqi Communist Party and Contemporary International Revision: Positions and Experiences" for discussion by the cadre. This work, with its analysis of the crises since the mid-1950s (the essence of these being attributed to a "revisionist" tendency in the CPSU), can be considered the cornerstone document of the Party's theoretical foundations.[8] It noted that "the roots of revisionism in Iraq spring from international sources, and cannot be limited simply to a criticism of the rightist leadership of the Party [ICP-CC] . . . since it is an extension of an international trend of revisionism."[9] The draft accused the Soviet Union of "exploiting its position in the international communist movement to impose its opportunist rightist strategy on the rest of the international communist movement."[10]

In a way, the CPSU coerced and diverted a number of communist parties from the "revolutionary Marxist-Leninist principles,"[11] and in abandoning the international class struggle in favour of peaceful economic competition and coexistence, betrayed these principles. This revisionism had assumed that peaceful

[5] Interview by author with Najim Maḥmûd, Beirut (20 July 1976), reaffirmed in Paris (18 September 1982), and clarified further in February 2006.

[6] ICP-CL, "Al-Ḥizb al-Shiyûʿî al-ʿIrâqî wa al-Taḥrîfiyyah al-ʿÂlamiyyah al-Muʿâṣirah: Mawâqif wa Tajârub," *Silsilat Dirâsât Thawriyyah*, no. 1 (1969), p. 1.

[7] Interview by author with Najim Maḥmûd, Paris (18 September 1982).

[8] ICP-CL, "Al-Ḥizb al-Shiyûʿî al-ʿIrâqî wa al-Taḥrîfiyyah al-ʿÂlamiyyah al-Muʿâṣirah," p. 4.

[9] Ibid., pp. 4–8.

[10] Ibid., p. 13.

[11] Ibid., p. 23.

competition between the socialist and capitalist systems would result in the success of socialism, which then would be emulated by the rest of the world. According to the report, this entailed "a sacrifice of the interests of the countries of Asia, Africa and Latin America, and all people oppressed by imperialism, on the altar of claimed economic competition."[12] The document then accused the Soviet Union of "intentionally separating the national and social liberation movements from the international socialist movement on the pretext that, as the majority of their documents show, [national liberation] is not a fundamental movement."[13] As such, national liberation movements were of secondary importance in the CPSU's revisionist vision,[14] a position that, by itself was described as a betrayal of the basic tenets of Leninism.[15] Accordingly,

> the contemporary international revisionist movement strives to change the struggle for socialism in the tri-continent countries that cannot be led by anything but the working class and its Marxist-Leninist party, and calls for them to march after the petite bourgeoisie on the basis that they are a substitute for real socialism. Rather, it considers the petite bourgeoisie regimes "socialist" or able to build socialism . . . and as such, it is a substitute for the working-class parties that have to dissolve themselves and merge with these bourgeois regimes to build socialism.[16]

It went on to condemn the Soviet Union's attempt to "falsify" Marxism-Leninism to justify its own revisionism and foreign policy objectives, since it "manipulated the facts, misrepresented the text, and confused reactionaries and [imperialist] puppets with what is genuinely revolutionary."[17] Thus, according to the ICP-CL analysis, the revisionists introduced the concept of the "non-capitalist path to socialism" and "social progress" as being socialist, although in essence it was nothing less than state capitalism. However,

> to describe progressive reforms, or the appearance of progressive reforms, as socialism, and state capitalism as another form of socialism, and to refer to the possibility of moving to socialism under the banner of the leadership of the petite bourgeoisie [is to make] erroneous claims whose basic purpose is to divert people from socialism, the revolutionary path, and successful national struggle.[18]

All these were described as false claims made by the revisionists and a betrayal of Leninism, since Marxist principles gave primacy to the role of the proletariat in building socialism, and the aim of the contemporary revisionists was "to distort" this major point.[19]

[12] Ibid., p. 38.
[13] Ibid., p. 41.
[14] Ibid., p. 43.
[15] Ibid., p. 51.
[16] Ibid., p. 58.
[17] Ibid., p. 61.
[18] Ibid., p. 71.
[19] Ibid., p. 81.

Moreover, according to this analysis, military regimes in the Third World were erroneously portrayed by the new revisionists as

> the true vanguard of social progress, and as such, the most suitable substitute for the revolutionary Marxist-Leninist parties.... [They] began to depend on them ... and worked to dissolve the communist parties or keep them from assuming power, as a vanguard for the people's revolutionary movement.[20]

The document maintained that the military regimes contributed to the end of colonialism and the old regimes, but that the regimes also had their reactionary side, and that as soon as they assumed power, their primary class interests prevailed against those of workers and peasants:

> [This] would block the path to complete the democratic revolution and initiate the socialist revolution ... and would do anything possible to stop the working class from achieving its historic goal of leading the revolution. The attempts of the new ruling elites to frustrate revolutionary development take different forms, e.g., one is the imposition of a "fictional" one-party system which they use as a pretext to destroy the working-class party, utilizing the local revisionist [communist] tendencies, as happened in the case of Algeria, Egypt, and the attempt [in 1966] in Iraq.[21]

The analysis went on to assert that as Marxist communists, the ICP-CL considered the army, as an institution, to be "the most important oppressive tool at the disposal of the ruling regimes."[22] However, within the army it excluded individuals and groups whose destiny was tied to the "revolutionary movement," since "the most important base of the military is soldiers and non-commissioned officers who commonly come from the working classes, the peasantry, and other toiling groups whose views are very influenced by the general political conditions in the country, and whose views reflect those of the peasants and other workers outside."[23] The document cites the Rashid Uprising of 3 July 1963 as an example of this idea, although, in the case of Iraq, the revisionists wanted to keep the Party out of the military. The systematic refusal to organize in the army may be the reason why the uprising failed, since those participating in the uprising, both military men and civilians, could not rely on the organizational capacities and strengths of the ICP. The Party generally insisted that the army, as an institution, be dissolved on assuming power. Thus, the emergence of a popular uprising by rank-and-file soldiers, as opposed to a coup by career high-ranking officers, was outside Party thinking, if not a surprise. It went against the grain of the gradual arming of the populace (Shaᶜb Musallaḥ) envisioned by the Party hierarchy.[24]

[20] Ibid., p. 82.
[21] Ibid., p. 87.
[22] Ibid., p. 88.
[23] Ibid.
[24] Ibid., p. 89.

The document then stated that, in the special conditions of Third World countries, the major enemy was imperialism, and the reactionary forces of the bourgeoisie who cooperate with it. "Although there is a segment of the bourgeoisie that is anti-imperialist, this sometimes also clashes with the working class and may end up hurting the interests of the proletariat, and stopping it from completing its historic mission." Consequently, the document insists that in the Third World, for the hoped-for revolution against imperialism and foreign exploitation to succeed, the workers and peasants must be the main forces "for a new class alliance" in which a "revolutionary" front would be formed "to carry the banner of the armed struggle," influenced primarily by the local conditions of each region or country and operating independently.[25]

However, the revisionists, led by the Soviet Union, advocated

> the necessity for total dependence by the Third World countries on revisionist socialist support to attain socialism.... this revisionist policy is still the official view of the CPSU elite, the socialist countries, and all communist movements marching to the tune of the International revisionists.... What is left for Third World countries except an armed struggle in facing the aggression and terror of the imperialists and the reactionaries.[26]

With regard to Iraq and the Soviet Union's special relationship with the Iraqi Communist Party, the oppression by a series of regimes against the Party had resulted in a complete dependence on, and affinity with, the CPSU

> in times when the CPSU policies, in general, were still Marxist-Leninist. However, this support for the Soviet Union took the form of an excessive adulation, and a subjective outlook, based on a narrow and blind understanding of proletarian internationalism that restricted the international socialist revolution to the confines [and objectives] of the foreign policy aims of the Soviet Union. As long as the general trend of the Soviet Union remained internationalist, revolutionary, and socialist, it was difficult to perceive the harm in this outlook.... However, when the Soviet policy revisionists deviated towards the rightist, opportunist interest of American imperialism, and stood against revolutionary movements, and created obstacles for the proletarian struggle in the Third World, it should have been patently obvious that the illusions regarding the Soviet Union would disappear.... However, some of the revisionist leaderships were divided into two groups: The top controlling echelon, who consciously understood the nature of the opportunist role it was playing, along with a limited, politically blind number of this group, became tools in the hands of international revisionism ... while the second group, which did not have any influence in the policy formation of the rightist opportunist party, also became a tool to be manipulated by the first group.[27]

In addition to this tradition of subservience to the CPSU, the document described the culture of the ICP as practising "the worst intellectual backwardness" as a result of being forced to go underground.[28] Thus their main means of survival became support from the Soviet Union, and accordingly,

[25] Ibid., pp. 102–103.
[26] Ibid., p. 105.
[27] Ibid., pp. 114–115.
[28] Ibid., p. 117.

the ICP had to adopt whatever the CPSU dictated. When the 1958 revolution took place and the possibility of the Party's taking over the reins of the state from Qâsim in 1958 emerged, the ruling military bourgeoisie fought to stay in power and strengthen its control. For its part, the Soviet Union supported the Qâsim regime and used its influence in the Party to reinforce this support. A rift began to open between Salâm ᶜÂdil, the secretary-general, who supported Jamâl al-Ḥaidarî from the Politburo, and the rest of the Politburo and the Central Committee, who accepted the dictates of the Soviet Union. This ended with both ᶜÂdil's and al-Ḥaidarî's being frozen out of the ICP leadership, and both being accused of leftist extremism. This condition, the document maintained, ultimately initiated "a situation that resulted in the bloody 1963 decimation of the Party after the first ᶜÂrif-Baᶜthist coup. The fleeing rightist opportunist groups landed in Moscow after the coup and became even more dependent on, and subservient to, the Soviet Union.[29]

In 1964 the Soviet "deviationists" arranged for an Arab Communist Party meeting in Moscow, in which the ICP "presented the [Soviet] deviationist line to the rest of the Arab communist parties."[30] Thus, when the new Arab government in Iraq declared its socialist measures on 14 July 1964, the ICP "blessed" these moves, and declared them to be steps towards the path of non-capitalist development. The same scenario was repeated when the Baᶜth came back to power in 1968. As a result,

> the Soviet "deviationists" did not stop with this political support but interfered directly in the internal affairs of the country, on behalf of the Baᶜthist agents to the new imperialism, ... and participated in the deceit of the Baᶜthist, racist, fascist government. [In passing,] the Kurds were given autonomous rule in Kurdistan to allow the Baᶜthists more time to get out of their [initial] crisis, and as a means to eliminate the revolutionary and progressive parties in Iraq.[31]

As noted earlier, the document accused the Soviet Union of "falsifying" Marxism-Leninism and of exploiting the international communist movement, making the movement

> an intellectual police force that served the narrow interests of a major power [the Soviet Union].... revisionism denies the right of every people to choose the path to socialism, in accordance with its own [cultural] conditions and its own special local environment, and it tries to impose a specific elastic interpretation, in the name of the non-capitalist path, on all Third World non-socialist countries.[32]

The analysis concluded that "the international struggle today is against contemporary international revisionism, and is the beginning of the decisive global battle against imperialism and reactionism."[33]

[29] Ibid., pp. 118–134.
[30] Ibid., p. 127.
[31] Ibid., p. 135.
[32] Ibid., p. 141.
[33] Ibid., p. 143.

Soon after, another study appeared in the series of articles entitled "On the Strategy of Popular Armed Struggle in Iraq." For the first time, there was an attempt to comment on the Marsh Uprising, limited though it was, demonstrating a decisive demarcation between the ICP-CC and the ICP-CL. In the introduction to the study, the reasons for the January 1968 adoption of the strategy of armed struggle were attributed without any solid theoretical basis. The study identified the contradictory signals coming from the leadership of the Party following the CPSU's Twentieth Congress in 1956, and the leadership's notions of evolutionary development and international coexistence. This confusion of ideas and actions led to the condensed and disastrous marsh operation, and to the devastating effects it had on the Party, caused by the ICP leadership's servile following of the Soviet line on the nature and methods of a struggle. The Soviet view of coexistence and the non-capitalist path of development, which resulted in the August Line of 1964, was reversed by the 1965 grassroots rebellion against it. The ICP simultaneously adopted an ill-defined notion of armed struggle, which really meant either a popular urban uprising or a military revolutionary coup. But no attention was given to the rural dimensions of the struggle until after the Party split. With the formation of the ICP-CL, the rural dimension of armed struggle was highlighted, contrary to, or in opposition to, the international deviationist position outlined in the earlier study entitled "On the Strategy of Popular Armed Struggle in Iraq." This strategy emphasized the role of peasants, and the secondary, if not actually hindering, role of urban dwellers, in the revolution.

In an article he wrote under the pseudonym "Nazâr ᶜAbbûd," Najim Maḥmûd offered a critical discussion of this study, in which he asks, "What does the emphasis on the secondary role of towns mean? Because the study concludes that this would be a hindrance to the Iraqi revolutionary movement, now and in the future, yet ignores the presence of workers who are concentrated in the towns." In doing so, he concluded, the study denied the proletarian role in the revolutionary armed struggle.[34]

Maḥmûd's Grounding of ICP-CL Thought

While he was in Paris in 1980, Najim Maḥmûd, the secretary-general of the Central Leadership, published his celebrated work on the ICP-CL's ideological tenets. Outlining the basic framework in *Al-Ṣirâᶜ fî al-Ḥizb al-Shiyûᶜî al-ᶜIrâqî wa Qaḍâyâ al-Khilâf fî al-Ḥarakah al-Shiyûᶜiyyah al-ᶜÂlamiyyah* (The Conflict in the Communist Party, and the Issues of Disagreement with the International Communist Movement), he traced the development of the ICP-CL from its inception within the ICP in the 1950s through its evolution into a force that questioned the ICP's actions, ideological tenets, structure, and relationship with the CPSU.

34 Nazâr ᶜAbbûd, "Contribution to the Discussion on the Strategy of Popular Armed Struggle," *Al-Hurriyah*, s46, vol. 11 (Beirut, 21 December 1970), pp. 6–7.

The intellectual and political struggle that led to the establishment of the Central Leadership had been complicated through the use – by both sides in the Party split – of poorly defined concepts such as "revisionism" and by reliance upon the textual validity of Marx's works and their interpretation. The internal struggle can be traced back to the post-1956 period, which witnessed the end of the Iraqi monarchy. As ICP-CL literature pointed out, "The struggle in the ICP was often a continuation of the tendencies that prevailed within the global communist movement. The phenomenon of 'contemporary revisionism' was a universal phenomenon as it was not confined to a single socialist state or a particular party."[35] This "revisionist tendency," traced back by Maḥmûd to the rise of Khrushchev in the mid-1950s,[36] was asserted to be the opposite of the "revolutionary tendency" that underlined the Marxist-Leninist spirit and presented state power as the major issue in all political struggles. According to Maḥmûd, the developments in the People's Republic of China (PRC) that paralleled the Bolshevik Revolution led the two revolutions to deviate from each other until socialism ended and a hybrid bureaucratic capitalism emerged in both the USSR and China. From this point of view, revisionism was characterized by bargaining with "reactionary regimes," by giving precedence to economic modernization over revolutionary transformation in politics, culture, and society (which, for Maḥmûd, led to gaps between urban and rural populations and class groups), and, finally, by attempting to downplay the accomplishments and magnify the errors of socialism in an effort to justify capitalist tendencies (such as extension of privilege to bureaucrats) and bar the masses from revolutionary transformation.

With the fall of the monarchy and the establishment of the Republic in July 1958, Maḥmûd saw the ICP, having turned itself over to the service of the new order, reflecting on its harsh treatment at the hands of the Hashemite security organs. Still, he noted, during Qâsim's regime the Party was the only member of the United National Front not allowed to participate in the initial post-revolution cabinet. The ICP referred to this in the Party plenum of September 1958 as "a defect in the power-sharing formula" of the new regime. As Maḥmûd pointed out, despite the Party's flexibility and support for the interests of the Qâsim regime, the regime did not respond to its demands. For example, on 29 April 1959, an ICP appeal published in *Ittiḥâd al-S̲ha*ᶜ*b* demanded communist participation in the government, including the important Ministry of the Interior and three other cabinet posts. Qâsim ignored this appeal and, furthermore, took steps to remove communist influence from the army.[37] "Between September 1958 and July 1959," the first Party secretary of the ICP-CL,

[35] Najim Maḥmûd, *Al-Ṣirâ*ᶜ *fî al-Ḥizb al-S̲hiyû*ᶜ*î al-*ᶜ*Irâqî wa Qaḍâyâ al-K̲hilâf fî al-Ḥarakah al-S̲hiyû*ᶜ*iyyah al-*ᶜ*Âlamiyyah* (n.p.: Publications of the Iraqi Communist Party [Central Leadership], 1980), p. 5.

[36] Ibid.

[37] Ṣalâḥ al-K̲harsân, *Ṣafaḥât min Târîk̲h al-Ḥarakah al-S̲hiyû*ᶜ*iyyah fî al-*ᶜ*Irâq*, (Beirut: Dâr al-Furât, 1993), p. 120; and ᶜAzîz al-Ḥâjj, *Ḥadat̲ha Baina al-Nahrain* (Paris: n.p., 1997), p. 91.

ʿAzîz al-Ḥâjj, asserted, "it was the Politburo that was formulating the Party's policy and determining its basic positions regarding the most serious and [most] minor issues.... The Central Committee, as an organization, was isolated from the disputes, contradictions, and conflicts that erupted in July 1959."[38] The ideological seeds of the ICP-CL were planted during the 1959–1961 period as a result of the disenchantment of various factions within the ICP. Although opposition voices were not always strong enough to alter the ICP's course, dissent continued to fester, exacerbated by the crack in the Party's ideological make-up. In both the July 1959 Plenary Session of the Central Committee of the Party and the 1960 Moscow meeting celebrating the Twentieth Congress of the CPSU, the ICP would see this fissure widen until a true split in the Party appeared.

The Plenary Session of the Central Committee (July 1959)

The crystallization of Soviet policy following the CPSU's Twentieth Congress resulted in the ICP-CL's perception that Soviet officials saw the Iraqi revolution merely as an opportunity to bolster the USSR's own position in its dealings with the United States. It was logical for Khrushchev to consolidate Soviet relations with the revolutionary regime under Qâsim and to refrain from any actions that would threaten this relationship. The ICP-CL literature argued that the USSR was militarily and economically weaker than the United States, leading Soviet policy to concentrate on friendly overtures to American imperialism at the expense of "revolution" in the satellite states. Criticizing the impoverished intellectual orientation of the ICP's leadership, Maḥmûd asserted that the Soviets did not find much difficulty in directing ICP policy even when political conditions and the interests of the Iraqi revolution should have dictated a different line. Thus, according to Maḥmûd, the ICP blindly accepted the Soviet appraisal of Qâsim's regime and of the role that communists should have in it. Rather than take advantage of the popular support in Iraq for revolutionary change by combining sound tactics and the support it enjoyed among the masses, the ICP adopted a complacent attitude towards the Qâsim regime, based on the false hope that such a regime would gradually turn into a democratic Iraqi state.[39]

This contradiction erupted in the July 1959 Plenary Session of the Central Committee, which concentrated on the Party's strained relations with the Qâsim regime. Instead of reassessing the situation created by the growing opposition, especially in the lower ranks of the Party, to the regime and by Qâsim's measures to suppress it, the Party leadership became deeply divided, falling into

38 ʿAzîz al-Ḥâjj, *Maʿa al-Aʿwâm: Ṣafaḥat min Târîkh al-Ḥarakah al-Shiyûʿiyyah fî al-ʿIrâq Baina, 1958–1969* (Beirut: Al-Muʾassasah al-ʿArabiyyah lil Dirâsât wa al-Nashr, 1981), p. 63.

39 Maḥmûd, *Al-Ṣirâʾ fî al-Ḥizb al-Shiyûʿî al-ʿIrâqî wa Qaḍâyâ al-Khilâf fî al-Ḥarakah al-Shiyûʿiyyah al-ʿÂlamiyyah*, p. 26.

the regime's trap to split and further weaken the ICP. Meanwhile, the Qâsim government adopted a balance-of-power approach in its relations with the ICP, playing progressives and nationalists off against each another in the following ways:

1. Speaking on the occasion of the 31st May celebration, Qâsim attacked partisanship in general and the communists in particular, signalling a shift in his relations with the left.
2. Concluding an agreement with the National Democratic Party's leadership to suspend partisan activities, followed by the dissolution of the NDP in May 1959, on the grounds that the "necessities associated with the interim stage dictated this step," and forcing the ICP to take a similar step or diverge from the nationalist ranks.
3. Dismissing officers with communist ties from sensitive posts.
4. Using the security apparatus to detain communists on questionable legal grounds, such as their connections to the 1959 Mosul demonstrations.
5. Assassinating communists, a strategy that claimed several hundred lives between 1959 and 1962; the assassinations were planned and carried out either by government agents or with the regime's complicity.
6. Attacking on the headquarters of professional organizations and unions that were closely tied to the communists.
7. Mounting an anti-communist media campaign.

But the Party leadership did not respond to these provocations. The resolutions of the plenary session attempted to contain internal opposition to the Party's position vis-à-vis the Qâsim regime; they overlooked the regime's attacks against the Party and its cadres, and adopted a severe degree of self-criticism, as manifested in the following text from the 23 August 1959 issue of *Ittiḥâd al-Sha*ᶜ*b*:

The Party organization became preoccupied with the conflicts [centred on] conspiratorial activities, so that they did not have much opportunity for indoctrination. The Party organizations' qualitative development thus fell behind development of its numerical strength. There were other factors that militated against the Party's resolution of the problem of keeping its organizations clandestine, however public its political activity was. It was this which made it difficult to ensure the leadership's thorough monitoring of the Party's bases. This led to the committing of mistakes and abuses. The Party failed to firmly stand against such conduct. The Party made mistakes as a result of the euphoria of victory and conceit resulting from its major triumphs. It thus made political miscalculations by overestimating its power and underestimating the role of the other nationalist forces, which caused it to commit leftist political mistakes that affected its organizational plan. The Party violated the Leninist principle of collective leadership and encroached upon the rights of the Central Committee. To the extent that collective leadership was compromised and monolithic leadership prevailed, bureaucratic tendencies emerged and the level of criticism and self-criticism declined especially among some Party cadres who thus discredited the Party.

The ICP emerged from the July 1959 plenary session ready to subordinate every other consideration to "the Republic's independence," to "democratic rule," and especially to "the restoration of solidarity with Qâsim" – in other words

> [persisting] in the rightist approach to clientism in the monolithic military government and its pressures and policies, which were against the interests of the mass movement. The possibility of abandoning Qâsim and seeking out other allies among other nationalist forces to rally and defend the masses was ignored. Rather than criticizing Qâsim's authoritarian actions, the resolutions of the plenary session contained justifications for more and more humiliating concessions to the regime. The leadership failed to realize that fighting against the progressive, democratic forces that the July 1958 revolution had thrust to the fore could not preserve the young republic.[40]

Still, no number of concessions from the ICP brought it official recognition or tolerance from the government.[41] The Party's official newspaper, *Ittiḥâd al-Shaᶜb*, was closed in September 1960, and the communist-supported Iraqi Union of Democratic Youth was banned in April of the following year. The union's secretary, Nûrî ᶜAbd-ul-Razzâq Ḥusain, was arrested and detained at the same time. These incidents contributed to the deepening of the intellectual conflict in the ICP in its early stages, well before the official split in 1967. Two ideas were at the root of this conflict.[42] One was the idea of "armed struggle," either as an uprising in the towns or as a military coup, and the other was the "peaceful reformist tendency," which came from the CPSU's Twentieth Congress in 1956 and was reflected in the report of the ICP's Second Conference in the same year, which stated that it was possible to achieve a "peaceful transformation" under Nûrî al-Saᶜîd and the royal regime.

The gains in popular support made by the ICP and the upsurge of mass popular activity terrified the Qâsim regime and its bourgeois supporters. According to the ICP-CL literature, the masses were capable of thwarting the bourgeoisie's attempts to assume control of the entire country, owing to the wide influence of the ICP and other revolutionary forces among the masses, in particular, among the peasants and the rank and file of the army. However, the leadership of the ICP at the time was deeply influenced by the worldwide "revisionist movement." Instead of taking the initiative to rally the masses against the ruling class's retreat from the revolution and reaction against the democratic gains it had brought, the ICP asked the masses to surrender submissively and stand behind the regime. In this, the ICP was following the new Soviet line, a course made possible only by the temporary removal in 1959 of Party Secretary-General Salâm ᶜÂdil, as well as of the head of the Party's Kurdish branch, Jamâl al-Ḥaidarî, to "study" in the USSR: "The Party, at this point,

40 Al-Ḥâjj, *Maᶜa al-Aᶜwâm*, pp. 68–69.

41 Al-Kharsân, *Ṣafaḥât min Târîkh al-Ḥarakah al-Shiyûᶜiyyah fî al-ᶜIrâq*, p. 120; and al-Ḥâjj, *Ḥadatha Baina al-Nahrain*, p. 96.

42 "Ḥawla Istirâtîjiyyat al-Kifâḥ al-Shaᶜbî al-Musallaḥ fî al-ᶜIrâq," *Silsilat Dirâsât Thawriyyah*, no. 3, Publications of the Iraqi Communist Party (Central Leadership) (1970), p. 5.

began to fall under the sway of a clique of opportunistic leaders who had no connection to the ICP's revolutionary bases and cadres."[43]

The Moscow Meeting (November 1960)

According to the early literature of what would become the ICP-CL, the pressure on the Party from its lower ranks to act more boldly was increasingly irresistible. A demonstration was staged by the ICP on 1 May 1959, demanding a role for the ICP in the Qâsim government. When this was ignored by the regime, the ICP considered a hastily drawn plan for a July coup, which would capitalize on the support of communist elements in the army. However, according to the ICP-CL, the plan could not be put together in time, and the revisionist elements in the ICP's leadership managed to stifle enthusiasm for such an uprising.[44] Foremost among these revisionist elements was the so-called Clique of Four, who were violently opposed to ᶜÂdil and al-Ḥaidarî, whom they accused of fanaticism. The dispute between the Clique of Four and the ICP leadership began at the July 1959 plenary session. The major issue was the Party's stance vis-à-vis the Qâsim regime. ᶜÂdil's and al-Ḥaidarî's deep reservations about the regime identified the causes of the crisis with Qâsim, but they were dismissed by the majority of those Central Committee members attending the meeting. ᶜÂdil's and al-Ḥaidarî's colleagues in the Politburo (namely, the Clique of Four,[45] led by Bahâʾu-d-Dîn Nûrî) tried to place the reason for the tension with Qâsim on the secretary-general's "leftist extremism" and on the leadership's demands for a communist voice in government. The plenary session endorsed this line, but failed to serve the purposes of the four by refusing to dismiss ᶜÂdil despite Bahâʾu-d-Dîn Nûrî's savage criticism of his "monolithic" leadership.

By the spring of 1959 resistance to the Qâsim regime (evidenced in the Mosul uprisings of the previous September) was intensifying. The Berlin crisis was also under way, and

> preparations were being made for Khrushchev's visit to the United States, where the superpowers would parcel out spheres of influence worldwide. At this time, the Soviets took the initiative to reassure the West regarding their intentions in Iraq, sending George Tallû, a member of the ICP Politburo, to Baghdad to suggest to the ICP leadership that the campaign against Qâsim should be stopped, and the officials responsible for it be dismissed.[46]

The betrayal of the Iraqi (Qâsim) revolution, and the preservation of "Western imperialism's interests" in the region was, to the Soviets, an acceptable price

43 Maḥmûd, *Al-Ṣirâᶜ fî al-Ḥizb al-Shiyûᶜî al-ᶜIrâqî wa Qaḍâyâ al-Khilâf fî al-Ḥarakah al-Shiyûᶜiyyah al-ᶜÂlamiyyah*, pp. 38–40.

44 Ibid., p. 36.

45 Ibid., pp. 38–41; see also ᶜal-Ḥâjj, *Maᶜa al-Aᶜwâm*, p. 64.

46 Maḥmûd, *Al-Ṣirâᶜ fî Ḥizb al-Shiyûᶜî al-ᶜIrâqî wa Qaḍâyâ al-Khilâf fî al-Ḥarakah al-Shiyûᶜiyyah al-ᶜÂlamiyyah*, p. 68.

to pay for successful talks with the Americans.[47] Soviet intervention in early July 1959 signalled the beginning of the dominance of the "revisionist" faction within the ICP leadership, when the balance of power tipped in favour of the anti-ᶜÂdil/anti-Ḥaidarî Clique of Four. The two leaders were sent to Moscow under the pretext of finishing their studies, and the Party Secretariat was re-formed around the Clique of Four, which assumed leadership while the first secretary of the Central Committee (Salâm ᶜÂdil) was in the USSR.[48]

The Soviet leadership was able to intervene directly in the affairs of the ICP because at this time the Iraqis lacked vision, experience, and a sound analysis of the revolutionary situation, and as such were "open to suggestion." The Soviets had no interest in the ICP except as a bargaining chip with the West, as Allen Dulles, the director of the American Central Intelligence Agency (CIA) had been quite apprehensive about the evolution of the Iraqi revolution and the possibility of a communist takeover of Iraq.[49] The ICP leadership was too naïve to realize that it was being used by the Soviets in this fashion, and they failed to stand up to the Soviets as Comrade Fahd had done when he rejected the partition of Palestine despite Soviet support for it in the United Nations. Nor were the ICP leaders sufficiently resolute to deal with Qâsim's divergence from the path of the revolution and with his unleashing of reactionary forces.[50]

According to the ICP-CL literature, the bias of the new Soviet leadership in favour of their own interests was not confined to compromising on Iraqi national interests, but extended to exploiting the respect the ICP enjoyed in the world communist movement. This respect was due to the Party's influence with the Iraqi masses and other Iraqi forces following the July 1958 revolution. At the World Communist Parties Conference held in Moscow in November 1960, both the CPSU and the Chinese Communist Party (CCP) attempted to win over the ICP. This rivalry for its favour enabled the ICP to take a leading role in a number of international democratic organizations and leftist unions, such as the International Student Union and World Democratic Youth.[51] The Clique of Four, however, which assumed leadership in July 1959, lacked a clear position on many issues, including on the general conflict in the world communist movement as the CPSU and the CCP competed for the support of communists internationally.[52] Internally divided, the Clique of Four, agreed only on their mutual opposition to the Party's previous position endorsing a coup to overthrow the Qâsim regime. Not unnaturally, the Soviet leadership at the World Communist Parties Conference was apprehensive about the new leadership of the ICP for several reasons. First was the recent reprinting in *Ittiḥâd al-S̲h̲aᶜb* of a critique by the CCP of Krushchev's policies, entitled "Long

[47] Ibid., pp. 36–37.
[48] Ibid., p. 39.
[49] Ibid., p. 38.
[50] Ibid., pp. 40–44.
[51] Ibid., p. 47.
[52] Ibid., p. 46.

Live Leninism." Second was Bahâʾu-d-Dîn Nûrî's speech at the conference, which, although it praised the CPSU's role in the world communist movement, failed to criticize either the Chinese or Albanian parties.[53]

The Soviets successfully exerted pressure on the Iraqi delegation to the Moscow conference, and on 24 November the rehabilitated Jamâl al-Ḥaidarî was allowed to return to prominence so that he could oppose the ICP leadership, which was perceived as being friendly to the Chinese. To make their point, the Soviets blocked the nomination by the Chinese of an ICP delegate to the committee assigned to write the conference's closing statement and replaced him with Khâlid Bakdâsh of the Syrian Communist Party, who was a Soviet loyalist.[54] To further undermine the Clique of Four, the Soviets invited Salâm ᶜÂdil to attend the Twenty-second Congress of the CPSU, where he delivered a speech on behalf of the ICP, attacking the Chinese and Albanians, and expressing the support of "the whole of the Iraqi people" for the CPSU's programme.[55] The ICP-CL's literature portrayed the Moscow meeting as an attempt to impose "revisionism" on the world communist movement and to isolate those who did not agree.[56] The final documents of the conference were vague and focused on topics such as peaceful coexistence and the non-revolutionary transition to socialism. The most important resolution passed by the conference dealt with the revolutions in Asia, Africa, and Latin America. "The question of the labour class's leadership in such revolutions became an urgent matter, and became a subject of bargaining between world revisionism and the United States."[57] Khrushchev's CPSU leadership succeeded in getting the rightist line endorsed in the ICP, which called for the acceptance of nationalist bourgeois leadership of the revolution and renunciation of the leadership of the working class – as expressed in the slogan "the non-capitalist path to development and democratic nationalism."[58]

The Failures of the National Democratic Movement

The ICP's subsequent relationship with the Qâsim regime on the one hand, and the USSR on the other, led to an unprecedented indecisiveness and fragmentation with ICP ranks. The ICP-CL claimed that the fundamental error of the ICP following the 14 July 1958 revolution was its failure to grasp the essence of governance and the state. Because there was no purge of the state organs (army, police, and security forces), the reactionary forces opposed to the revolution remained in place. The Party then became involved in the struggle between two military cliques – that of Qâsim and that of ᶜAbd-ul-Salâm ᶜÂrif – and

[53] Ibid., pp. 47–50.
[54] Ibid., pp. 48–49.
[55] Ibid., p. 57.
[56] Ibid., p. 50.
[57] Ibid.
[58] Ibid.

supported the Qâsim faction without reservation. Subsequently, the politically susceptible National Union Front collapsed.

According to its literature, the ICP had had two possible courses of action following the revolution. The first was to preserve the National Union Front and avoid the Qâsim-ᶜÂrif conflict. The second was to point out the dangers of the Qâsim-ᶜÂrif a confrontation and call for Arab unity and for a legitimate, representative, democratic government in Iraq. After the opportunity to take the latter course passed, and Qâsim became a virtual dictator, the ICP needed to cooperate with the Kurdish Democratic Party to establish a democratic government. The ICP interpreted Qâsim's rule as the "bourgeois democratic stage" and thus marched behind him, rallying the masses to support his regime – which they did, believing that the grassroots ICP supported him. Nevertheless, after it became clear that cooperation with other progressive and democratic parties would be difficult and that Qâsim desired to demolish all other political groups, it still would have been possible to remove him and his military supporters in a coup and replace them with a communist regime. The ICP leadership refused to seize the opportunity, however, and banned any attempts by the progressive military elements loyal to the ICP to do so. The ICP-CL analysis of the Qâsim–ICP relationship pointed out that although the regime eliminated all communist participation in the government and continued to persecute the communist movement by detaining and killing thousands of cadres, the ICP leadership remained out of touch, providing no direction for the cadre or for other progressive Iraqis. The leadership continued to hold onto false hope, waiting for the "return of the genuine leader [Qâsim] to the sound nationalist path." The ICP-CL also attacked the ICP's decision to support the Qâsim regime against the Kurdish revolt of September 1960, which the ICP claimed had the potential to spark a national revolution. Instead in its blind and unswerving support of Qâsim, the ICP sacrificed any possibility of future Kurdish cooperation.

The division of the ICP into two camps served the Baᶜth well. Unable to destroy the entire communist movement in one fell swoop, the Baᶜth found themselves able to conquer what was already divided. Iraq's new rulers first turned their attention towards the ICP-CL. The ICP-CL's more radical views attracted more public attention than the views of the ICP-CC, and its lack of an international sponsor (such as the ICP-CC's link to the Soviet Union) cut it off from potential foreign support. The development of a Baᶜthist-ICP-CC–nationalist alliance, as examined in Chapter 4, allowed the regime to have a much broader power base and laid the foundation for its actions against both the ICP-CC and the ICP-CL.

Nevertheless, the ICP-CL was able to endure the severe blows delivered against it by the Baᶜth regime. These included the February 1969 detention of the Party's secretary and main ideologue, ᶜAzîz al-Ḥâjj, as well as a persecution of other members of the Central Committee. Along with the arrest of the entire Party leadership, the disclosure of the names and whereabouts of Party members, details of Party organization and financing, and the schedule for Party activities led to the execution of some of al-Ḥâjj's compatriots, while other, less influential, Party members simply faded from the political milieu, fearing for their lives. Although it is not clear what motivated al-Ḥajj, one explanation may be that he feared the complete annihilation of the communist movement in Iraq. As he had devoted over thirty years of his life to the ICP, and needed a means to ensure its survival, his actions may be seen as a way to alleviate the Baᶜthist wrath that was decimating the ICP-CL. To this end, he appeared on Iraqi television, calling on his followers to renounce violence. He justified this action on the basis of a re-evaluation of the political situation and, most importantly, on the basis of his finding common ground with several progressive Baᶜthist notions (such as the Baᶜth positions on Palestine, Arab unity, and social transformation). The Baᶜth assault on the CL faction resulted in the virtual elimination or the surrender of the leadership and of the known advanced cadre.

However, some small cells that were unknown to security agencies and untouched by the crackdown continued to function and strove to reorganize the Party in the CL vision. Those who had not been in formal leadership positions were now elevated and assured of prominent roles in the Party's rebuilding, particularly in the Baghdad section. Among these new leaders was Najim Maḥmûd, who had been detained earlier but had escaped execution because he was relatively unknown. Though he had acquired some degree of influence among students, intellectuals, journalists, and other professionals in the Baghdad section while he had been in charge of these groups eighteen months earlier, he was removed for questioning and for challenging the Party leadership prior to the split.

On his release, the remaining cells, along with previously disaffected cadres, gathered around Maḥmûd and he began slowly rebuilding the Party. One of the first steps in this process was taken at a meeting convened at the end of August 1969 to deal with the Party's situation. At "The Plenum to the Advanced Cadre," a number of resolutions to "explain the Party's strategy and tactics and its general political evolution were passed."[59] Most important, it considered the strategy of "popular armed struggle" to be the "essence of its struggle."[60] It emphasized the relationship between "our people and brotherly nations, as well as other revolutionary movements throughout the world," and continued that the rebuilding of the Party structure "should reflect the strategy of popular armed struggle in combating anarchy and liberalism in the Party's [daily life], as well as respecting grassroots views, strengthening centralism, and rejecting old dilapidated styles of work and organization."[61]

Maḥmûd argued that the liberation of Iraq and the hopes of the people of the Middle East were clearly undermined by the now divided communist movement. In his opinion, the ICP-CC was unable to lead an effective "'popular

[59] "Ḥawla Istirâtîjiyyat al-Kifâḥ al-Shaᶜbî al-Musallaḥ fî al-ᶜIrâq, pp. 1–2.
[60] Ibid.
[61] Ibid. p. 4.

armed struggle" or implement a policy to remove the imperialist presence in the region. After the August 1969 meeting, "popular armed struggle" was seen as the only way to alter the social and political conditions within Iraq:

> Violence is the only path for class and national struggle in Iraq. All classes and ruling regimes, most especially [the] reactionary and treasonous regimes, which have ruled Iraq, have always resorted to violence, terrorizing the masses and thereby retaining their control over the country. There is no other way to face this reactionary violence, except with a revolutionary violence, combating arms with arms. Popular armed struggle in its highest forms becomes "popular war," and has been the path followed in a number of victorious revolutions. The history of the people's struggle in Iraq extends deeply into our national revolutionary history.
>
> Necessity requires all progressive and revolutionary forces that aspire to create a new socialist Iraq to unify themselves into a broad revolutionary alliance. These forces will include all revolutionary classes in society, whether they are workers, peasants, revolutionary intellectuals, or the revolutionary wing of the petit bourgeoisie. This alliance must also include the entire Iraqi population in all its different Arab and Kurdish nationalities, in addition to all other national minorities. While the alliance between peasants and workers is the solid foundation of this revolutionary "front," for it to be created in reality and move from simply talk into practice, there must be certain prerequisites.[62]

The plenary session resulted in an ICP-CL policy, which included the following six major points:

1. "The popular armed struggle," which did not begin until 1967, was an unsuccessful path for the party because it was not adopted sooner; it was not properly pursued once it was adopted, and it was impossible to pursue it after 1967. With the weakness and division of the party, it had a purely rhetorical nature.
2. As the ICP-CL was the Marxist-Leninist party of the proletariat and the vanguard of the "popular armed struggle," it ought to be led by the Iraqi people's interest and not by foreign interests.
3. The enemies facing the Iraqi people were international oil imperialists, who were "following an approach of neo-imperialism in eradicating the revolutionary movement." As the agents of the "new" imperialists – Baʿthist fascism and reactionary governments – united under a single banner, this necessitated the creation of a "united national revolutionary front" to combat the interests of international oil in an effort to create a socialist Iraq.
4. The conditions of the imperialist imposition would require that this "front" be trans-national and encompass all of the Arab revolutionary movements, which would adhere to the central tenets of such a front: (a) belief in the national liberation of Arab states from imperialist and Zionist capitalist forces; (b) popular democracy; (c) socialism; and (d) achievement of revolutionary Arab socialist unity.

[62] Ibid., pp. 1–2.

5. The Iraqi revolution was part of the international socialist revolution in general and an integral part of the tri-continental revolutionary movement. The tri-continental movement signified the experience of Asia, Africa, and Latin America in suffering the dual oppression of foreign imperialism and local reactionary governments, highlighting the need for movements from these regions to work together to combat imperialism and oppression.
6. Finally, the central task facing the Iraqi party would be the creation of the "Iraqi People's Army," without which it would be impossible to combat the forces of the new imperialism and establish the people's rule and popular democracy under the leadership of the working class.[63]

The ICP-CL's position regarding Palestine centred on the legitimacy of the Jewish state, which it viewed mainly as an instrument of imperialist and capitalist forces wishing to establish a base in the region. As outlined in a November 1968 Party study, the Palestinian cause was seen as an Arab cause with the Palestinian people either scattered by or held down under the strong occupation tactics of the Israelis, and with Israel posing an "expansionist threat" to the entire region. Further, the issue of Israel's legitimate existence was presented as an international issue, since it represented a threat to socialist and progressive regimes throughout the world. The following principles outline the ICP-CL's position:

1. It is impossible to separate Zionism from imperialism, as Zionism is the tool invented by imperialists to contain the people of the region.
2. Israel must be surrounded by all the progressive force of the world masses in order to secure and protect liberation movements in the region.
3. Zionism is racist, expansionist, and fascist, and must be distinguished from the Jewish religion and Jewish masses that have been misled by Zionist propaganda.
4. The reactionary Arab governments must be opposed in order to end their tacit support of imperialist aims and Zionist occupation of Palestine.
5. The 1948 basis for the state of Israel should be contested, not its 1967 aggression and expansion, as Israel represents a threat to progressive regimes and forces, no matter what its form.
6. Finally, the ICP-CL rejects any form of "political" settlement, instead regarding an unconditional victory by progressive forces to be the only resolution to the threat posed by Zionism and imperialism.

Thus the ICP-CL proposed strategies to eradicate the Zionist influence in the region based primarily on changes within Arab society (aimed principally at reactionary governments) and the adoption of a popularly based progressive and socialist cadre to lead the struggle against Israel.[64]

[63] "Ḥawla Istirâtîjiyyat al-Kifâḥ al-Shaᶜbî al-Musallaḥ fî al-ᶜIrâq," pp. 105–112.
[64] Ibid.

Many of al-Ḥâjj's inexperienced comrades in the ICP-CL leadership were not as lucky at the hands of the security police as he was, and many, including the Politburo members Mattî Hindî Hindû and Aḥmad Maḥmûd al-Ḥallâq, died as a result of torture during interrogation.[65] Al-Ḥâjj himself was the last of the ICP-CL communists to leave prison in 1969. The Baghdad section of the Party was particularly hard hit; the south and Kurdistan were less affected. According to Central Leadership literature from 1970, reconstruction of the decimated Party was well underway, although the documents reveal great losses owing to the imprisonment of al-Ḥâjj. With the stewardship of the ICP-CL clearly in the hands of Najim Maḥmûd, the revitalization of the Party accelerated. After a lapse of one full year the ICP-CL's official newspaper, *Ṭarîq al-Shaᶜb*, resumed publication with clear ideological positions, particularly with regard to the Soviet Union. In its editorials, the ICP-CL openly accused the USSR of collusion with the regime, condemning it as the main supporter of the "opportunist fascist state" and for "goading" the ICP-CC into aiding the Baᶜthist regime. *Ṭarîq al-Shaᶜb* asserted:

The ruling Baᶜth regime is conducting a manoeuvre, beginning with the political and demagogic position vis-à-vis the Kurdish issue, and ending up with some [minor] cabinet posts being "charitably" assigned to the so-called coalition government [made up of] those forces that are willing to traffic with it, so that it can claim to be ruling the country with a "Progressive front," in order to request military and economic aid from the "revisionist" states, in the process of preparing for new campaigns against the country's revolutionary forces, and so as to attack the Kurdish people from a position of strength and power.... No political force can escape facing the following truth: whoever cooperates with the Baᶜth, in any fashion, will have to bear responsibility for all the crimes committed against the Iraqi people: Arabs, Kurds, and other national minorities.[66]

The editorial went on to analyze the Soviet Union's negative impact on the international communist movement, and on the Iraqi situation in particular, declaring:

We must assert here that the new revisionism has progressed from an internal opportunist trend in the contemporary international communist movement [USSR]... [and] as in 1958, the new revisionism played a role in confusing and undermining the policy of the Iraqi Communist Party, and was one of the most crucial factors in forfeiting the chance of the Iraqi toiling masses to resolve the crisis of the Qâsim regime in their favour. It was one of the factors that prepared the ground for the apostatization of February 1963 [the first Baᶜth-ᶜÂrif coup]. After the coup of 18 October 1963, the Soviet revisionists rejected the Party's position of 19 October that considered the coup nothing more than an extension of the "apostasy of February 1963."

The revisionist [Soviet] newspapers presented the regime of October as a nationalist one, and in July 1964, the policies of the revisionist leadership of the ICP were nothing more than an echo to the revisionist propaganda claims of the [Soviet] press, under shiny

[65] Hanna Batatu, *The Old Social Classes and Revolutionary Movements of Iraq* (Princeton, NJ: Princeton University Press, 1978), p. 415.

[66] Editorial, *Ṭarîq al-Shaᶜb*, vol. 27, no. 1 (January 1970), pp. 1, 3.

slogans such as "Iraq on Its Way to a Socialist Transformation." Today, the revisionists were among the first to call for a trafficking with the fascist oppressors, and intervened directly between the Baʿthist regime and other political forces. . . . It is a mistake to believe that the revisionism and the policies adopted by the rightist, opportunist, revisionist Central Committee is an Iraqi phenomenon reached independently.[67]

At the same time, the Baʿth continued its attempts to establish its "National Progressive Front" with the weaker ICP-CC. By co-opting it into the regime, the regime's ongoing attempts to bolster Baʿth influence and power were advanced, bringing to the fore the need to achieve the pacification of the Kurdish region. Yet at the same time, the Baʿth concentrated the efforts of all their security agencies and party organizations in a ruthless attack on the remnants of the ICP-CL, which now grew more active, visible, and bold, especially among the young college-aged activists who bore the brunt of the brutal oppression. This led to hundreds of arrests and to "improvements" in the interrogation dungeons of the secret police, especially in the notorious Qasir al-Nihiyah (a palace turned into a prison).

Portrait of a Torture Victim from the ICP-CL

Born into a wealthy Kurdish family in Iraq in 1950, Haifâʾ Zanganah graduated with a degree in pharmacy from the University of Baghdad in 1974; she now lives in London. Zanganah is both a talented artist, who has exhibited her work in the United Kingdom and the United States, and a writer who has contributed to many publications. When she was twenty, she was arrested under suspicion of membership in the ICP-CL and taken to the detention centre at Qasir al Nihiyah. The head of the "Palace" (*qasir*), as it was called, was Nâẓim Gzâr, a technical institute student who held the post of general director of security. (Four years later, he was himself arrested, tortured, and executed by the government.) When he questioned her, Gzâr talked quietly to Zanganah, as if she were an old friend, while she stood naked before him. On her way to the toilet, the guards forced her to face the wall, as other prisoners, dripping blood, filed past her in the hallway. During her first interrogation, a series of bloodied people, some unable to stand on their own, came in to identify her. "Many more were brought into the room. All alike had been tortured and disfigured to the extent that I only recognized them by their voices. . . . One of the men came nearer and began beating me and kicking me in the groin. My underwear was wet with blood and urine and I took a further kick in the head."

The Palace where Zanganah was held had originally been built for Crown Prince el-Qasir and was opened to the public after the Qâsim revolution. It had beautiful gardens, and in the front were stables that were later turned into cells. After her arrest, the authorities brought in her friends, one by one: "All had tortured bodies and a strange emptiness in their eyes." Taken to a cell,

[67] Ibid., p. 2.

she found the floor stained thick with blood and the walls covered with the names of earlier prisoners. On her third night in the prison, "I heard the kind of screams I had never heard before.... It was a mixture of a human voice denying knowledge of anything and a continual animal howling interrupted by sudden screams and pleading for mercy." Later, blindfolded and expecting to be executed, she was taken by car to another, "better" prison. She would be released six months later.

Zanganah was rearrested and sent again to the Qasir. "Do you know that the three people arrested before you have been executed?" asked a guard. Later, her door opened and a fat interrogator with bulging eyes said, "It has come to our attention that while you were in prison you were still in touch with certain bastards and that you, bitch, sent them information about what was happening to you.... Do you think a few whores and bastards can jeopardize our regime?" She was forced to sign a statement:

> I, the undersigned ... joined the Communist Party on ... and was arrested on.... In my room were found hand grenades, explosives and pamphlets against the revolutionary regime and the National Front. I state of my own free will that I did not join the Party for political reasons but to meet men and have sex with as many of them as I could. My relationships were all immoral. I admit I had sex with ... and I affirm that I was not a virgin when I entered Qasir al Nihiyah. I have been well treated by the security forces.

She was then forced to tape record what she had written. She remained in prison this time for a year.

Haifâ᾽ has said that she writes to "ward off forgiveness" and to prevent her from even thinking of returning "to a country where they still practice their repulsive rituals."[68]

The Third Party Conference (January 1974)

The signing by Muṣṭafâ Bârzânî of the 11 March 1970 declaration with the new Baᶜthist regime saw the KDP cease hostilities with the Baᶜth. In so doing, the safe houses in the north were removed, and the ICP-CL in Kurdistan was left vulnerable. The ICP-CL and especially Najim Maḥmûd had warned Bârzânî against this move, which the communists considered to be detrimental to the interests of the Kurdish people and of the rest of the country as well. Such an agreement would provide the regime with a breathing space in which to strengthen its grip on Iraq. As a result of the ceasefire, the KDP limited the ICP-CL's freedom of movement, particularly that of its *Anṣâr* militia.

Yet the ICP-CL persevered in this trying situation, due mainly to Maḥmûd's personality, skills, and connections. The Party continued to mature, becoming an important actor on the Iraqi political scene, acquiring credibility and

[68] Haifâ᾽ Zanganah, *Through the Vast Halls of Memory*, translated from Arabic by Paul Hammond and Haifâ᾽ Zanganah (Paris/London: Hourglass, 1991).

acceptance within the Kurdish and Iraqi national opposition forces and with progressive forces in the Arab world, as well as with China and others in the international communist movement. At the same time, the ICP-CC was losing its international prominence, except with the USSR, and its influence within Iraq was diminishing as it grew increasingly dependent on the goodwill of the Baʿth regime. The ICP-CL, however, grew more confident under its new leadership and refused to become an appendage to the controlling Kurdish forces that dominated the area in which the ICP-CL was operating. Tension between the ICP-CL and Bârzânî intensified, however, and finally reached its height at the end of 1973; ultimately, their differences proved irresolvable. For his part, Bârzânî perceived all progressive elements as communist and all communists as his enemies. Thus even when the ICP-CL was under his protection, and despite his positive personal relationship with Najim, the ICP-CL was watched carefully by KDP forces. As long as the ICP-CL was seen as a thorn in the side of the Baghdad regime, Bârzânî was prepared to countenance its presence in Kurdistan, but if it deviated from the role he envisioned for it, the Party was informed that he would not tolerate its dissent. Despite these limitations and before the return of Kurdistan to the Baʿthist fold, the Party was strong enough to hold its Third Conference, in which it reflected on the previous three years. This was the last official Party conference before the ICP-CL was forced into exile, and it proved to be a watershed in both ideological and organizational terms. Indeed, it could be described as the zenith of the Party's power – articulating a clear ideological formulation that provided the intellectual underpinnings of the ICP-CL for the next two decades, and was testimony to Najim's adroit leadership and ideological vision.

When the Third Conference of the ICP-CL took place in Iraqi Kurdistan in early January 1974, it was attended by a large representation from all over Iraq, especially the Kurdish region, as well as by representatives from outside the country, particularly from Europe, Syria, and Lebanon. The secretary-general gave a detailed report in which he identified the Baʿth regime as the product of an Anglo-American "détente" that had resolved the tension between

> British interests [that had] controlled the Iraqi economy, and American interests [that had] aspired to extend their influence to the entire Gulf region and replace the British.... However, this "détente" vanished when the British-supported group took over power in July 1968 ... From the beginning, this new fascist regime practised a dual policy of bloody oppression and political deception.... While it announced an amnesty for political prisoners, the reinstatement of fired government employees, and closure of the desert prison Nuqrat al-Salman, it reopened the slaughter house of al-Nihiyah in Baghdad. It also organized secret units to assassinate and torture citizens. The agencies of the regime brutally attacked all the national forces without exception, so much so that the oppression was extended even to loyal fascist forces such as the revisionist [ICP-CC] party that had supported the new fascist regime from the beginning. Our Party [ICP-CL] experienced the most vicious of the bloody acts of the campaign.... At the same time the regime resumed its aggression against the Kurdish people ... with the failed military campaign against the Kurdish National Liberation Movement.

With the persuasion of British diplomacy, the regime took a second step of political deceit to gain time [for themselves] since, with the end of 1971, the British withdrawal from the Gulf was approaching and there was an impasse in British–American negotiations on sharing influence in the Gulf after the withdrawal. British interests advised the regime to stop fighting in Kurdistan, and assigned the role of mediator to the Soviets and their local supporters in order to achieve a new armistice between the Kurds and the regime, and to reinforce the regime's hold on power and save it from certain collapse.... British diplomacy was aiming, after the cessation of fighting in Kurdistan, to use the Iraqi regime to bargain with American imperialists who had pushed the Shah's regime in Iran to occupy a certain parts of the Shatt al-ʿArab [waterway] and threaten Iraqi sovereignty and its national waterways. As a result, the regime stopped the fighting in Kurdistan after prolonged negotiations, and on 11 March 1970, announced the March Declaration.... [This] promised that autonomous rule would be achieved in four years, and the regime exploited this condition [of peace] to strengthen its hold over the country.... During this time it rearmed its military forces with Soviet weaponry, and continued to prepare for another chauvinist war to be waged, at the right time, against the Kurdish people.... At the beginning of 1972, a crisis emerged between the regime and its British imperial friends as a result of the deal between the Iranian reactionary regime and Britain over Iran's occupation of the Gulf islands. This eventually resulted in a break in diplomatic relations between the two [Iraq and Britain], and an accusation [by Iraq] against Britain of masterminding a coup against the regime. At the same time, the British pressed the regime to annul [the Qâsim] Law 80 [on oil exploration] and abandoned the agreement on North Rumailah, which was about to be concluded. Thus, the [British-controlled] Iraq Petroleum Company reduced its production from the Kirkuk oilfields in order to exert new pressures on the regime and to persuade [it] not to nationalize the more productive Basra oilfields.[69]

This idea was developed more fully some two decades later in Najim's *Al-Muqâydah: Berlin–Baghdad*.

According to the secretary-general's report, the isolation of the regime had given it no alternative but to nationalize the Iraqi Oil Company in June 1972 after promising not to do so in relation to the Basra field. However, because of the nature of the regime, Najim argued that the nationalization was nothing more than a bargaining ploy with the British:

The Iraqi Oil Company was given compensation, many times more than its real asset value. In the meantime, it allowed the non-nationalized Basra Oil Company to raise its production to 80 million barrels, which, in effect, annulled the impact of the nationalization by transferring the profits of the foreign companies from the nationalized Kirkuk field to the larger field of Basra.... Thus, the nationalization process and the bargaining that followed were simply a transfer of profits of foreign monopolies from "one pocket to another." During this period, the regime moved to strengthen its crumbling rule, turned towards Soviet imperialists and concluded an unequal treaty on 9 April 1972 with the Soviet Union, violating Iraq's national sovereignty and giving Soviet fleets easy access to Iraqi ports. Saddam Hussein declared his intention of creating "a strategic alliance," between the regime and the Soviet Union. However, despite this new "strategic

[69] Iraqi Communist Party – Central Leadership, *Al-Taqrîr al-Siyâsî lil Qiyâdah al-Markaziyyah al-Muqaddam Ilâ al-Kûnfrans al-T͟hâlit͟h lil Ḥizb al-S͟hiyûʿî al-ʿIrâqî* (Kurdistan, 1974), pp. 4–8.

alliance," British influence did not disappear from Iraq. In fact, increased Soviet interest in Iraq allowed the regime to "skip on more than one imperial rope," especially when Soviet imperialists were ready to offer "the appropriate support," because of their desire to seek a foothold in the Arab Gulf, and because of the decline of Soviet influence in Egypt.

All these manoeuvres failed to save the regime either from its endemic crisis or its alienation from the popular masses. In fact, the crisis deepened, rather than being resolved, and this was reflected in the internal struggle within the regime.... The regime became clearly tribal, and power became concentrated in the hands of the President as he amended the constitution for that purpose, and the existing political system was transformed into a one-man dictatorship.... Because of the deepening of the crisis and the diminution in [the numbers of the] ruling inner clique, the regime resorted to political manoeuvres and minor retreats, whose basic aims were to garner support for its weakened foundations, and widen its narrow [popular] base. For these reasons, it announced the creation of the "Progressive Nationalist and Patriotic Front" with the deviationist Iraqi party [ICP-CC] and, after the Party had appointed two of its [ICP-CC] leaders to cabinet positions, permitted it to publish a daily organ and to open headquarters in major cities, completely transforming the deviationist party to a subservient follower of the regime whose basic aim was to decorate its "black" history and work to strengthen Soviet influence in Iraq.... All these measures reflected the [weakened] situation of the regime and revealed its attempt to forge ties with more than one imperial state while pretending independence.[70]

The report went on to challenge the notion of the non-capitalist path of development that the Soviets bestowed on the Iraqi regime, and it asserted that the class nature of the Baʿth regime was

nothing more than one more segment of the bureaucratic bourgeoisie which has alternated control over the state of Iraq ever since the coup of 8 February 1963. This class is composed of the military and tribal cliques who depend, in essence, on the thin layer of the military bureaucracy, which permeates the state infrastructure.

The existing regime is represented by the Baʿth Party, which suppressed the national democratic and communist movements, and is known historically for its foreign imperial connections. After the bloody internecine struggle among the ruling elite... the regime moved to an open semi-dictatorship, despite the fact that it kept the façade of party rule. This bureaucratic bourgeois class derives its position from being in control of the state agencies. If it was out of power it would represent only a small number of certain classes, mainly from the high-ranking military, the sons of the feudalists, and the scum of the proletariat (killers, thieves,... employees of the race track, etc.) whose ambition is to regain control of the state, which would then afford them privileges, income and "respectable" positions. Social background does not mean much for this class, for its main aim is to control the state, its military apparatus, [and its] bureaucracy, and to have access to the tremendous assets of the state. This class is against the interests of the majority of the population, and one can see this fact in the contradiction between the bureaucratic bourgeoisie and the national and petite bourgeoisie, [on the one hand], and the other popular classes, the workers and peasants.

70 Ibid., pp. 8–11.

However, a great number of the petite bourgeoisie's interests are very closely tied to the state bureaucracy which [in essence] ties the class to the ruling bureaucracy.... In a way, the bureaucratic bourgeoisie, through political terrorism, inflation, detention and dismissal [from government employment], makes survival difficult for a great number of students, intellectuals, minor state employees, and those with a limited income who, as a result, are opposed to this bureaucratic bourgeoisie. Consequently, they make up the main forces of the anti-fascist, anti-imperialist, and anti-reactionary national progressive front.

The national bourgeoisie and the bureaucratic bourgeoisie are, in essence, antithetical to each other, since the latter, in 1963, replaced the Qâsim regime which, to a large degree, represented the interests of the national bourgeoisie, and in 1964 brought about the nationalization that dealt a crippling blow to the interests of the national bourgeoisie and directed [the economy] towards the bureaucratic bourgeoisie of the ᶜÂrif regime, with these measures transferring the capital of the national bourgeoisie to the state bureaucratic sector.

The Baᶜth rule after 17 July 1968 adopted more aggressive policies directed against the national bourgeoisie, exercising terror, banning all means of popular expression, and closing all avenues of political organization, as it had done with other national classes.... The national bourgeoisie became immobilized with the demise of its political and economic power, and the loss of its prominent political leaders, yet there remained a section of this group that was able to engage in national action, and could be included in the anti-fascist and anti-bureaucratic front.... The ruling regime also tried to create a rural social base through the enlargement of the state's capital investment in agriculture, in order to form a rural bourgeoisie closely connected to the bureaucratic bourgeoisie. To achieve this, it allowed the sons of urban bureaucrats to control [state farmland] rental by reviving the old feudal [relationships], and the recruitment of thieves to combat revolutionary peasants and terrorize poor farmers.... Half of the Iraqi peasants are still landless, while non-cultivated and feudal lands make up half of the possible arable land.[71]

The report then explained that the existing regime had to be challenged through the creation of a genuine progressive national front that would work to end the "fascist-tribal" system and create a national democratic coalition government that would deal with the immediate issues facing Iraq, chiefly the issue of Kurdish self-rule, and lead the way towards "the creation of the democratic people's republic under the leadership of the working class."[72]

The Kurdish issue being the most important at the time was given prominence, and the report suggested that

solving the Kurdish issue on the basis of national self-determination included the right to separate ... which was compatible with the realities of the national issue in Iraq, and could be extended to other minorities such as Turkomans, Assyrians, and Armenians because their common enemy is imperialism and reactionism.[73]

[71] Ibid., pp. 12–17.
[72] Ibid., pp. 21.
[73] Ibid., pp. 25–27.

The report also affirmed that the ICP, since its inception in 1935, had rejected the call for the "imposed integration" of all national minorities and had for that reason rejected the "chauvinist" military campaigns against the Kurdish national liberation movement. At the same time, the report condemned what it termed ethnic "isolationism," as this was detrimental to both Kurds and Arabs and would result in the overall weakening of the national struggle, as well as permit imperialism and reactionism to eradicate the national movement in Iraq generally, and in Kurdistan in particular. It also condemned the ICP-CC for its support of the regime with regard to its Kurdish policies.[74]

Nevertheless, despite the 1970 ceasefire in Kurdistan, tension began to build once again between the KDP and the regime in Baghdad. On 11 March 1974, the Baᶜth, having failed to negotiate a mutually acceptable agreement with the KDP, unilaterally declared the law of regional autonomy. The KDP considered this action a violation of the ceasefire agreement, and in April 1974 full-scale conflict erupted once more. These events seemed to mirror the forecast contained in the secretary-general's report. Three months earlier, the report had suggested that these manoeuvres would lead the Baᶜth to superimpose their policies in an effort to gain time to strengthen the regime's hold on the country and to rebuild Iraq's armed forces, which would once again be used against the Kurds; all of this was to happen with the help of the Soviet Union and the ICP-CC.

The report explained that the country's economic situation was nothing more than a symptom of the crisis caused by the existing bureaucratic bourgeoisie, an inevitable result of the state bureaucratic capitalism practised in the country and of its parasitic consuming nature, since in Iraq the state controlled all means of production.[75] From the founding of the state in 1932, 85 per cent of foreign trade was always under state control. During the time that Britain had control of Iraq, British policy impeded the development of national industry. The royal regime that followed did nothing to change this situation, since the British merely transferred what had been under their control, for example, electricity, the ports, and the railways, to the new Iraqi state. When the 1964 nationalization of industry took place, even more capital was transferred to the state. By the time the nationalization of oil occurred, state revenues had increased exponentially, whereas private industry had declined, making the state Iraq's major economic enterprise, with huge resources at its disposal. Thus control of the state and of its resources became the main and true aim of all the military coups.[76] The report also explained how Iraqi bureaucratic capitalism was "backward," since it was nothing more than an extension of the semi-colonial economy and was dependent on one natural resource: oil.

Further, the bourgeoisie who managed the state were, according to the secretary-general, "greedy," inexperienced, and from "tribal and feudal" backgrounds. Many of them were unable to manage the country along "modern"

[74] Ibid., pp. 27–28.
[75] Ibid., pp. 29–30.
[76] Ibid., p. 30.

capitalist lines, as "the bureaucratic state capitalism in Iraq is, in essence, a parasitic, consuming system whose basic aim is not to achieve profits, but rather to provide high salaries . . . for this parasitic bureaucracy."[77] The rampant growth in the bureaucracy and spendthrift governmental policies resulted in massive failures of mega-projects and losses in revenue. Indeed, the state's policies on agriculture resulted in "the destruction of agricultural output, and the impoverishment of the peasantry," emptying the countryside of productive labourers and filling the cities with these unemployed peasants, and thus strengthening even further the hold the feudal class had over agriculture and exacerbating the sorry conditions of the working class in the cities. As a result, the rich became richer, and the poor became even more impoverished.[78] The report advanced a programme to overthrow the bureaucratic bourgeoisie who were the ruling regime and to institute a popular national democratic revolutionary government that would "save the people" from dependency, fascism, hunger, and destruction.[79]

In its examination of international affairs, the report concluded that because of the regime's narrow social base and limited popular appeal, its primary concern was to maintain its hold over the state, and that to achieve this it had to seek external imperialist support from both the United States and the Soviet Union. Indeed, given the international situation and the imperialist rivalry between the two major powers, the regime was able to deal with both because "the imperial powers compete to achieve more influence for themselves, though at the same time they are both united against the people's struggle for national liberation and social progress."[80] The report also criticized the two superpowers for supporting Israel, eradicating the Palestine national movement, and gradually dividing the Arab national liberation struggle, in this way weakening the Arab front. Further, it predicted a new status for the Arab bourgeoisie as servants of American and Soviet interests.[81]

Commenting on the crisis that occurred in the Party five years earlier, and the surrender of the Party leadership in 1969 to the Baʿth Party, the report concluded:

> Contemporary revisionism is the main danger to the Party and [to the entire] international communist movement, and it [the ICP-CL] took an important decision in identifying the international source, the "apostate" Soviet leadership. Thus, our Party engaged in a continual intellectual struggle against contemporary revisionism and imperialist socialism, and struggled to educate the grass roots and Party cadre on its danger in their march to the revolution, and [on] its responsibility in the series of setbacks that have afflicted the Party since 1959. . . . We will work to improve our Party, and prepare it to enable it to achieve the revolutionary goals. For that reason, we must struggle

77 Ibid., p. 31.
78 Ibid., pp. 33–38.
79 Ibid., p. 40.
80 Ibid., p. 49.
81 Ibid., pp. 49–52.

to combat the ignorance of Marxism-Leninism, political adventurism, isolationism in popular activities, and bureaucratic liberalism in organization. We must adhere to [the concept of] the international proletariat, and fight chauvinist mega-nations and national parochialism.

Our Party must operate from the principles of internationalism [but must adhere to] independence and self-reliance. Our basic aim is to prepare our Party so as to become able to mobilize and organize, and lead the masses in their struggle to achieve national liberation, democracy, and to end the fascist regime [which will lead to] the creation of a national democratic coalition that will [achieve] self-rule in Iraqi Kurdistan, and pave the way to the creation of the people's democratic republic under the leadership of the working class.[82]

With their continued presence in Kurdistan untenable and the report of the Third Conference complete, the Central Leadership dispersed across Europe, with London and Paris becoming the primary centres of their activities. When the Baᶜth reneged on their commitment to Bârzânî, and the Kurdish rebellion flared up again, remnants of the Kurdish section of the ICP-CL declared in their official paper, *Ṭarîq al-Shaᶜb*, that

the interest of the Iraqi masses requires us to stand together united to face the attacks of this immoral, unprincipled bunch. All national forces, Kurds in particular, and the Iraqi national forces in general, should watch carefully and responsibly to guard the interests of the Iraqi people . . . should not be swayed by some temporary gains, and should abandon their narrow paradigms in their political analysis. . . . the experience of the last few years of Iraqi history should be a lesson to lead us towards the necessity of a [real] nationalist front. . . . if the Iraqi nationalist forces had unified their ranks from the time the fascists [Baᶜthists] came to power, our people would not have suffered these black days.[83]

With the resumption in April 1974 of fighting between the Baᶜth regime and the Kurds, *Munâḍil al-Ḥizb*, the internal Party newspaper, issued a detailed analysis of the Kurdish question at the end of December 1974 outlining the ICP-CL's position on self-determination. It reiterated the basic thesis of the secretary-general's Third Conference report, which considered the Baᶜthist actions to be "chauvinist, unjust, and waged by a bureaucratic, reactionary bourgeoisie against a people who were [simply] seeking their national rights and democracy. What distinguishes this from past wars is the fact that it took place in unique international and local conditions."[84]

On the subject of local conditions, the analysis argued that the Baᶜth had decided to apply the "final solution" to the Kurdish issue, and because the Baᶜth regime was weak when it had taken power in 1968 and was unable to implement this policy, it attempted to gain time to solidify its control, as the ICP-CL had consistently maintained. However, when conditions became favourable in the spring of 1974, the regime turned once again to military alternatives. The regime

82 Ibid., pp. 58–60.
83 *Ṭarîq al-Shaᶜb*, branch of Kurdistan, vol. 29, no. 1 (August 1974), p. 2.
84 Republished in *Al-Mushtarak*, vol. 45, no. 2 (July 1988), p. 6.

successfully cultivated Iraqi public opinion antagonistic towards the Kurdish national movement by portraying the movement as tribal, reactionary, and separatist, while at the same time presenting itself as a "moderate, progressive" regime.[85]

On the class nature of the Kurdish national movement, and on its political leadership as represented by the KDP, the report described the leadership as "duplicitous" because

> on one hand, it supports the Kurdish people's struggle for legitimate national rights... and as such represents a democratic progressive force, while on the other hand, and because of its own special conditions, only looks after its immediate and short-range interests, without considering the long-term ramifications of some of its positions and relations for the Kurdish liberation movement, or even [for] the leadership's own class interests.
>
> Despite the new fascist Iraqi regime of 1968, and the Kurdish experience in 1963 at the hands of the Baᶜth, the KDP leadership went along with the new regime. Nevertheless, a few months later, in 1969, the regime resumed its war against the Kurds.... [Once again] a truce followed, between March 1970 and March 1974, with the Baᶜth and a number of the KDP members of the Baᶜthist cabinet, and others assuming official positions in the Kurdish areas, giving the fascist regime an extended period to gather its forces and prepare once more for a vicious war against the Kurds. At the same time, the regime directed strong blows against other progressive [Iraqi] forces. In doing so, the fascist regime limited the discussion of the Kurdish issue to itself and the KDP, to the exclusion of other forces, and thus created the illusion of dividing power between the two allied parties. The KDP accepted this in the hope of gaining more concessions for itself, and did not consider that devastating blows were being directed against either national force.[86]

The report went on to delineate the international circumstances that had fostered the renewal of fighting against the Kurds. It argued that because of the oil crisis and the relationship between the two superpowers, Iraq had become

> the main arena for the confrontation between the two superpowers and other imperial states, as it [Iraq] represented the main gateway to the oil-rich reserves of the Arab Gulf, and the land bridge connecting the Gulf areas and the Indian Ocean to the countries of the Mediterranean. Thus, with the signing of the Unequal Treaty [of 1972], Soviet interests, which were in decline in Sadat's Egypt, coincided with those of the Iraqi Baᶜthist rulers who had initially been brought to power by Anglo-American subversion.[87]

The report also analyzed the rise of Russian interests in Iraq, which coincided with those of Britain, and the reaction of the United States to this situation. It argued that the United States countered Soviet influence by supporting the Shah's regime in Iran, which, in turn, supported the Kurds in their war with the Baᶜthists. Such machinations fostered American hopes of overthrowing the regime in Baghdad and thereby reviving US influence in Iraq. It went on to

85 Ibid., pp. 7–9.
86 Ibid., p. 10.
87 Ibid., p. 11.

conclude that Soviet long-term interests were not served by the continuation of the war, although the Soviets acquired further concessions from Iraq through the increasing sale of arms to the country. It further concluded that the only outcome of the impasse would be either the "overthrow" of the Baᶜthist regime or a peaceful solution to the Kurdish war, and that the United States held the key to this dilemma by virtue of its relationship with Iran.

The report suggested, therefore, that the Soviets were also interested in a peaceful solution in order to preserve their own influence with the Baᶜthists. Indeed, all signals pointed to the fact that

> the Iraqi Baᶜthist regime is moving to strengthen its ties with American imperialism and with Western states in the hope of soliciting their support in solving the regime's [Kurdish] crisis. However, American imperialism is not in a hurry, and aspires to greater concessions. Its final aim is to exchange the leadership of the regime with other agents who will be obedient to its [US] dictates.[88]

By the time the Treaty of Algiers was signed between Iraq and Iran in March 1975, the Kurdish rebellion had collapsed and Bârzânî had landed as a political refugee in the United States. This temporarily ended the domination of the Bârzânî clan over the KDP and led to the splintering of the Kurdish party and, ultimately, in the late 1970s, to the emergence of the Patriotic Union of Kurdistan (PUK) as a rival for leadership of the Kurdish nationalist cause.

The few remaining cadres of the ICP-CL in Iraq were forced to flee the conflict. Najim Maḥmûd, the ICP-CL secretary-general, was compelled to leave Iraq against the wishes of a handful of cadres who wanted to remain and continue fighting for the liberation of the country. However, the majority followed Najim Maḥmûd and withdrew to Syria, eventually moving on to Paris and London. As a result of their flight, an opposition group within the ICP-CL began to crystallize, calling for a Party congress to evaluate the experiences of the Central Leadership and to look for new directions for the Party. About this time, the Baᶜth contacted "Fârûq" (an alias for an ex-Politburo member who had severed his Party connections but continued his friendship with and admiration for Maḥmûd). More than three decades later, Fârûq told the author:

> Ghânim ᶜAbd-ul-Jalîl, who was then a member of the Baᶜth Regional Command and in charge of Saddam Hussein's office, asked me why the CL could not enter into a national front and consequently become partners in the Baᶜth government. Although I emphasized that I was no longer connected to the Party and had no intention of betraying my ex-comrades among the Iraqi people, I [indicated] would be willing to carry the message, with no guarantee of even connecting with the ICP leadership outside.... ᶜAffân Chilmîrân and I were given passports and allowed to leave. ᶜAffân did not return though I did, but Maḥmûd emphatically refused even to consider opening the topic.... All this took place in the General Security Office of the Baᶜth, and was completely recorded.[89]

[88] Ibid., p. 12.

[89] Telephone interview by author with Fârûq Mullah Rasûl from Iraqi Kurdistan to London (15 March 2003).

Wiḥdat al-Qâᶜidah and the Splintering of the ICP-CL

The proposed meeting between the ICP-CL and the government exacerbated tensions within the ICP-CL and led to a split in the Party. In the absence of a Party congress, one group, led by ᶜÂdil Mahdî, a Central Committee member, put out a publication entitled *Wiḥdat al-Qâᶜidah* (Unity of the Cadre) to discuss issues relevant to the membership. Najim Maḥmûd rejected the meeting's demands, considering this move a challenge to Party solidarity and discipline in a time of crisis, and expelled the splinter group's leadership. He also formally warned the cadre about the danger of this move. *Wiḥdat al-Qâᶜidah*, however, continued on as a minor splinter group, declaring itself to be the legitimate representative of the Iraqi Communist Party (ICP-CL) and expelling the secretary-general. As the group had initially had no intention of breaking away, and wished only to address organizational concerns, not to fuel ideological and intellectual disagreements, ᶜÂdil Mahdî and his supporters had not expected such a dramatic reaction from Maḥmûd. Their expulsion forced the group to make the split public, taking a large number of cadres with them and recruiting new supporters in both Britain and France.

> Past experience – all of it – taught our Party valuable lessons . . . to rebuild itself and unify all Marxist-Leninists in a healthy [party] capable of leading the working class and the masses in order to achieve our objectives. From this time, our Party has started to cleanse itself from policies of regression and confusion, and from non–Marxist-Leninist analysis in thought and organization, and has marched bravely forward to achieve the rebuilding of the party of Fahd, the party of the Iraqi working class. For that reason this party journal, *Wiḥdat al-Qâᶜidah*, was issued to stand up against the policies of retreat, treason and opportunism, utilizing the Marxist approach in analyzing the concrete reality.[90]

Both groups claimed to be the legitimate ICP-CL, and both continued to produce *Ṭarîq al-Shaᶜb*. In September 1976, *Wiḥdat al-Qâᶜidah*, acting as if it were a preparatory committee for a Party congress, held a meeting under the slogan "Toward Rebuilding Our Party: Toward the Unity of All Marxist-Leninists in One Iraqi Communist Party." The meeting was attended by the majority of the noteworthy Party members, both foreign and domestic, as well as by other Iraqi Marxists. Following the procedures of a proper Party congress, beginning with a report by the *Wiḥdat al-Qâᶜidah* editorial board, similar to that of past secretary-generals' reports, the group began to lay out its vision for the communist movement in Iraq. The meeting discussed two reports, the first entitled "An Assessment of Our Party's Shortcomings Between February 1969 and March 1975," and a second, more relevant, report entitled "Our Positions and Current Objectives." An interim leadership called the "Board of Central Organization" was elected, which was entrusted with leading the Party through this period, guided by the decisions of the September meeting. The meeting declared the Maḥmûd leadership to be null, void, and illegitimate and recommended the creation of a number of publications to rebuild the Party intellectually and

90 *Wiḥdat al-Qâᶜidah*, no. 16 (April 1977), p. 1.

explain its ideological basis. *Wiḥdat al-Qâʿidah* was to continue as the public organ, and plans were made for the establishment of a Kurdish publication along the same lines. The group also published an internal Party newspaper entitled *Al-Kâdir al-Shiyûʿî* (The Communist Cadre),[91] which outlined its basic ideological tenets as follows:

1. On the nature of the regime and the ruling class,

> the regime is basically a backward compradorean state capitalism, which is an appendage to the international capitalist system in the age of imperialism and monopolies – and the ruling elite is a bureaucracy of bourgeois-fascists whose recent roots are in the semi-feudal and semi-imperial system.[92]

2. On the conditions of the working class and the Iraqi Communist Party, the group considered the Central Committee faction as a reformist, rightist group responsible for the rise of the Baʿthist regime at a time "when the Marxist-Leninist current [of the old Central Committee group] was unable to stand intellectually or organizationally, and which . . . allowed the opportunist leadership to control the Party."[93] For that reason,

> we consider the principal danger inside the communist and workers' movement is that of deviationism, and the main task then is to rebuild a party on Marxist-Leninist foundations and strengthen its relationship with the working class and the masses. . . . bourgeois influence is the main source of internal deviation and surrender under the pressures of imperialism is the external source.[94]

3. On the conditions of the revolution, the group called for the creation of a popular national democratic front at a stage when many objectives of the socialist revolution would be intertwined with the national democratic revolution. Thus, an alliance between the working class, peasantry, petit bourgeois, and national bourgeois would be an essential condition for a successful revolution.[95]

4. On the national issue, it called for solving the Kurdish issue based on Marxist-Leninist principles,

> on the basis of total recognition of the Kurdish people, their self-determination and their acquisition of complete national rights, including their right to secede, and the creation of their national state. . . . the Kurdish issue is an integral part of this democratic struggle for the entire Iraqi nation. At the same time, while we support the right of the Kurdish people in its national unity, we see that [the existing] conditions of the present working-class struggle require the unity of the Arabs and Kurdish nations, and other national minorities in Iraq, in a common struggle against exploitation, oppression, reactionism, imperialism and Zionism.[96]

It also called for preparation for a progressive popular armed struggle in Iraqi Kurdistan under the leadership of the Marxist-Leninist Communist Party, since

[91] *Al-Kâdir al-Shiyûʿî* (September 1976), p. 1.
[92] Ibid., p. 3.
[93] Ibid., p. 4.
[94] Ibid., p. 5.
[95] Ibid. p. 6.
[96] Ibid., p. 7.

the tribal and bourgeois leadership of the Kurdish uprising had been responsible for its failure.[97]

5. On the issue of Arab nationalism, the faction condemned the mistakes of communists

> in considering Arab nationalism as [merely] a reservoir for the reactionary forces and imperialism, and realizing the democratic, progressive, anti-imperialist aspects of Arab nationalism.... [It called for] complete liberation, the achievement of Arab unity, and the maturity of the Palestinian and Arab struggle to face Israel.[98]

6. On the Arab regional and international situation, it called for the support of the Arab masses in the revolution against reactionary bourgeois Arab governments and imperialism. In the international sphere, it condemned both super powers as their détente

> will have an effect of increasing the internal contradiction, providing an opportunity to suppress revolutions and of interfering in the internal affairs of [Arab] nations.... for that reason we are committed to complete independence and rejection of all coercive means, influence and control. We are committed to stand up against imperialism, deviationism, and foreign influence, and to support the struggle of the proletariat and oppressed nations.[99]

It also condemned the Soviet Union and its satellites, considering them responsible for the schisms in the communist movement.[100] It concluded by emphasizing that "Our slogans, planning our programme, and our working agenda [are] based on the foundation of initiating and executing the revolution in Iraq, and in this we do the greatest service to the international revolution."[101]

Gradually this faction grew, drawing substantial support from Iraqis abroad, mainly in France and Great Britain. Although they were not able to hold a congress, they were able to call for an enlarged meeting for their cadre, and the Board of Central Organization continued to play the role of a Central Committee until 1979. Further, they expanded their contacts with other activist groups internationally, thereby gaining in popularity and recognition at both the Arab and the international levels. By the end of 1978 and into early 1979, some members of the board had begun propagating Chinese Marxist interpretations, including the theory of the "Three Worlds" (first world, capitalist; second world, communist; third world, non-aligned).

At this point, the Baghdad regime, facing the possibility of dissolving its formal alliance with the ICP-CC and expelling it from the Progressive National Front, approached the Unity of the Cadre to replace the ICP-CC. Promising to implement democracy and allow a more liberal political environment in Iraq, the Baᶜth, triggered a split among the leaders of this group as well. One faction continued to propagate the Three World Theory, while the other took

[97] Ibid., p. 8.
[98] Ibid.
[99] Ibid., p. 9.
[100] Ibid.
[101] Ibid.

an independent line. Thus both factions continued to publish separate editions of *Wiḥdat al-Qâᶜidah* in 1979, with different contents and with each describing the other faction as illegitimate.

By the early 1980s, both groups had gradually disappeared, with their leadership going in divergent directions. Some adopted Islamic ideas and joined the Iranian-based opposition groupings. ᶜÂdil Mahdî and his followers continued to flirt with the Iranian revolution, initially by espousing the ideas of Abul Hasan Bani Sadr, the first post-revolutionary president of Iran, and then by issuing any number of pronouncements on the relationship between the Iranian people's struggle and the Iraqi struggle against the Baᶜthist regime. Eventually, they adopted Iranian Islamic ideas, and when Ayatollah Khomeni eradicated the communists and other liberal opposition groups in Iran, ᶜÂdil Mahdî merged with the Islamists. He continued his association with Iran and gradually amalgamated his group with the Iranians, rejecting his Marxist past and devoting all his group's time to propagating Khomeni's ideas and organizing the Muslim communities in France on behalf of the Iranian revolution. He eventually was made a member of the Supreme Council of the Islamic Revolution in Iraq (SCIRI). In the meantime, the Baᶜthist alliance with the Central Committee came to an end, and the *Wiḥdat al-Qâᶜidah* group disappeared.

Najim Maḥmûd and his group were able to revitalize themselves, and they began issuing *Ṭarîq al-S̲haᶜb* on a more routine basis. In addition, their theoretical-intellectual newspaper *Al-Ghad* now appeared more regularly, evolving into an intellectual "umbrella" for all left-wing progressive groupings. Their most serious contribution came in 1983, however, with the publication of *Al-Mus̲htarak*, which remained their theoretical foundation for the rest of the century.

Soon after leaving Iraq, Najim settled in Paris, where, in May 1981, he earned a doctorate in Islamic history at the Sorbonne, studying under Jacques Berque, an internationally distinguished historian of Islam. While studying, Najim continued his organizational activities, conferring with exiled Iraqi leaders from a number of different groups, among whom was the well-known former communist, Colonel Salîm al-Fak̲hrî. Fak̲hrî had been a close Qâsim associate, as well as Qâsim's radio and television director, and the prime minister–designate of the leaders of the July 1963 Rashid putsch. Najim, al-Fak̲hrî, and others established an umbrella organization called "The Democratic 14 July Movement," which published a manifesto in November 1979. Entitled "A Project for a National Pact," the manifesto's basic aims were described as "the overthrow of the Baᶜt̲h and the achievement of democracy." It called upon all political forces

> to join in a wide national front that will renew the vitality of the [1957] National Front, and mobilize the energies of all the people, Arabs, Kurds, and other national minorities, in one struggle to overthrow the rule of the Baᶜt̲h and achieve the aims of the people in national liberation, democracy, and a better life.[102]

[102] The Supreme National Committee, *Ḥarakat 14 Tammûz al-Dîmuqrâṭiyyah* (Baghdad, November 1979), p. 3.

Its objective was the return of the 14 July 1958 revolution, which it perceived as the "embodiment of the aims of the Iraqi national movement" that had been "diverted" from its true path by Qâsim and his military associates, allowing the Baʿth to come to power in 1963 with the help of "foreign imperial forces."[103] The movement's programme included: (1) full participation of Kurds in the Iraqi government, and their right to self-determination through a referendum; (2) democratization of the army, which was seen to be semi-feudal and dehumanizing; (3) rationalization of Iraq's economic development and energy policy; (4) more towards the adoption of the non-aligned movement's cause of introducing democratic freedoms in every member state, parallel to the aim of preserving world peace; and (5) economic integration of Arab countries to guarantee freedom of movement, work, and the flow of information among them as steps towards a democratic Arab federation.[104]

Najim concentrated on propagating these ideas and mobilizing the opinion-making leadership by preparing it intellectually through the publication of *Al-Ghad*, with himself at its head. Its first issue (May-June 1978) *Al-Ghad* described itself as a national and democratic journal whose aim was to "participate in the awakening of a new patriotic democratic movement in Iraq and the Arab world" by becoming:

1. *An open forum for liberal thought* in a time when the simplest form of freedom of expression is denied, especially the freedom of the press, all over the Arab world, and when there is an organized programme of misinformation, and a total obfuscation of the truth from the public, and when only controlled and oppressive official body of information is provided.
2. *An open forum for the interchange of ideas* in the democratic national camp related to the problems of the country. The editorial board of the journal declared its willingness to publish even ideas that were contrary of the journal's positions, as long as they were part of the debate within the general national movement, thus putting into practice the principle of freedom of expression and participating the affirmation of democratic traditions.
3. *A wide-ranging forum* where discussions on economics and politics meet issues of culture and education in an environment that encourages historic and scientific research, and debate on the most important events and struggles of the Iraqi people.

Disagreements emerged almost immediately, however, with Salîm al-Fakhrî considering himself to be the spokesperson for the group and the true inheritor of the 1958 revolution. In July 1980, al-Fakhrî negotiated independently with Jalâl Ṭâlabânî, leader of the PUK, and offered "to form a national front" with

[103] Ibid., p. 4.
[104] Bashir Mehdi, *Memorandum: Middle East Currents* (n.p. April 1980), pp. 2–3.

Ṭâlabânî, claiming to have authorization from Iraqi democrats inside and outside Iraq.[105] This assertion was immediately disputed by the other participants, since no such discussions had taken place and a unilateral move of this sort was considered to be a violation of the principle of "collective leadership." Soon after, at the beginning of 1981, the movement collapsed, although *Al-Ghad* continued to be published by Najim for more than a decade.

With the progressive opposition now aging and scattered internationally, the lack of a viable organizational structure left a vacuum for those wishing to challenge the regime to fill. Two significant works – *Al-Mushtarak* and *Al-Muqâydah* – emerged to anchor the secular opposition intellectually.

The Theory of *al-Mushtarak*

In 1983, following a series of Iranian military victories during the Iraq-Iran war, the ICP-CL issued a highly detailed and articulate theoretical treatise entitled *Al-Mushtarak: Niẓâm al-Ishtirâkiyyah al-Dîmuqrâṭiyyah fî Ḍawʾ Târîkh al-Mujtamaʿ al-Islâmî wa khibrat al-Thawrât al-Ishtirâkiyyah al-Ḥadîthah*, in which it proposed an indigenous interpretation of Marxist thought within the Islamic and Arab social milieu. An equivalent English translation would read *Al-Mushtarak: A Democratic Socialist System from Islamic History and Modern Socialist Revolutions*. The treatise consists of 193 pages divided into a preface; a derivation of terms and their socio-linguistic justification; an introduction; chapters on the concept of *al-mushtarak* in Islamic history, the Soviet Union (even predicting its demise), and the prospect for communism's replacing the Baʿth regime in Iraq; and a conclusion.

The treatise demonstrates the relevance of two terms germane to the prospective application of this new theory of communism in Iraq. The first term is "*al-mushtarak*" itself, the Arabic word that the theory asserts is equivalent to ideas behind the 1871 French "*commune*"; it refers to a democratic-socialist revolutionary system whereby a community in a certain locale would have equal access to economic resources and would constitute an armed political and administrative unit that was autonomous within a hierarchy of similar units.[106] The second term, "*al-dîmuqrâṭiyyah al-ishtirâkiyyah*," is roughly equivalent to "democratic socialism" and refers to proletarian democracy, which the ICP-CL viewed as "true socialism."[107] Five years later, the term "democratic socialism" was clarified to mean a socialist system based on democratic principles.[108]

Further, the book uses the word "Islam" in a narrow and specialized sense, referring to the social formations that corresponded to the modes of Islamic

[105] Letters dated 27 and 28 July 1980, exchanged between Salîm al-Fakhrî and Jalâl Ṭâlabânî, p. 1 (in the possession of the author).

[106] ICP-CL, *Al-Mushtarak: Niẓâm al-Ishtirâkiyyah al-Dîmuqraṭiyyah fî Ḍawʾ Târîkh al-Mujtamaʿ al-Islâmî wa khibrat al-Thawrât al-Ishtirâkiyyah al-Ḥadîkhth* (London: Communist Party of Iraq, 1983), pp. 12–13, 114, 117–118.

[107] Ibid., pp. 14–15.

[108] *Al-Mushtarak*, vol. 45, no. 7 (July 1988), p. 3.

governance.[109] As Islam spread to the lands of other ancient civilizations (e.g., Iraq and Persia), it faced uncompromising resistance from pagan belief systems, particularly those that derived from Gnosticism. Therefore the use of the term "Islam" becomes fraught with the risk of historical selectivity, which the authors believed we should be wary of. The theory is an outline of hypotheses for the establishment of a democratic-socialist system, based on the election of its leadership by secret ballot by all citizens, which would be spearheaded by a revolutionary proletariat that was self-confident and politically aware. In the theory, this model society would transform Iraq into a classless and a stateless society in which citizens could enjoy an extensive range of human freedoms without fear or discrimination. For that objective, an armed citizenry would be required to take the place of the regular army, and the politico-administrative structure would be based upon the experience of the 1871 "Commune de Paris," while the economic system would likewise be transformed. Thus, the people would enjoy equal rights and unfettered access to the sources of power, as encapsulated in the spirit of *al-mushtarak*.[110]

In the introduction, the treatise sets out the socio-political topography of Iraq, emphasizing the monstrous bureaucratic machine of the state and its control and ownership of 90 per cent of the economic resources. The political and socio-economic formations, with the exception of the "new" Iraqi Communist Party-Central Leadership, would be powerless to effect a revolutionary democratic change as they either would become agents for the state or would be incorporated into the state agencies that engulfed civil society and exercised tyranny over it. The treatise attempts to infer, from Arabic historical chronicles, the prior existence of *al-mushtarak* and its correlated structure of power. However, the quotation footnotes are not complete and are given in such a manner that it is practically impossible to trace the quoted sources for confirmation.[111] The theory traces selective versions of *al-mushtarak* in pre-Islamic Arabia to the exclusion of other structures, arguing that Islam's adoption of *al-mushtarak* gave the religion its dynamism and vitality in its early stages of development and expansion.[112]

Based on such thinking, the ICP-CL asserted that when Muslim rulers deviated from the political norms of consultation and election, and departed from the communal ownership of economic resources, a despotic institution – the Islamic state – was born.[113] The new Islamic state took ownership of the principal economic resources within its jurisdiction, enacting exorbitant taxes for the purse of its rulers, and used a standing army to suppress any voices of protest

[109] CPI-CL, *Al-Mushtarak*, p. 16.

[110] Ibid., pp. 118, 120, 124, 162–176.

[111] For example, the book quotes "al-Râzî" but which "Râzî"? Fakhr al-Dîn, Muḥammad Ibn Zakariyyah, or Abû Ḥâtim? See ibid., pp. 72–74.

[112] CPI-CL, *Al-Mushtarak*, pp. 45, 47–49.

[113] Ibid., pp. 53–57.

or calls for human freedom.[114] The theory attributes the loss of human freedom to the hereditary nature of the Umayyad and ʿAbbasid regimes, although no such interpretation of the Islamic political system can be found in any recognized secondary sources. According to the theory, there were a number of political movements, social revolutions, and uprisings, as well as intellectual protests, against Umayyad and ʿAbbasid state despotism. This ICP-CL theory selectively maintains that, among the political movements, both that of Bâbik al-Kharramî in the ninth century,[115] and that of al-Qaramita (Carmathians) in the tenth century,[116] called for a return to the life of *al-mushtarak*. But the theory fails to identify the roots of these movements in Gnosticism, which predated Islam and enjoined communal ownership of property. Indeed, the practices of *al-mushtarak* were earlier condemned by the major schools of Islamic jurisprudence, such as those of Imam Abû Ḥanîfa (699–767) and al-Jâḥiẓ (776/7–868/9).

The treatise also refers to the al-Zanj uprising in Basra (869–879),[117] and it briefly examines the emergence of syncratic philosophers such as al-Fârâbî (870–950), al-Râẓî (865–925), and al-Maʿarrî (973–1057),[118] who attempted to recast a communal lifestyle – or *al-mushtarak* – as an attack on the newly founded Islamic state. The significance of this analysis is in its attempt to suggest that Islamic thought and history provided an indigenous tradition of an egalitarian communal structure without oppression or class privileges. In a word, the treatise was a call to resurrect *al-mushtarak*,[119] though it did neglect to mention the "Ikhwân al-Ṣafâ" movement, which had been active during the late Abbasid period.[120] This movement had called for human equality and proposed a communal lifestyle based on egalitarian work, but it also went further by proposing a political programme and an administration system on which to build a society on a basis similar to that of *al-mushtarak*.[121]

114 Ibid., pp. 53–59.

115 Ibid., pp. 65–66. Bâbik al-Kharramî, one of the most profound social movements in Islamic history, developed in the ninth century in southern Iraq among poor, dispossessed blacks and many other marginalized socio-economic groups. Calling for social justice, it advocated progressive taxation, communalism, guaranteed employment or all members of society, and the abolition of private property. Until Bâbik al-Kharramî was crushed by the state, it tied Islamic principles to secular and materialist development.

116 Ibid., pp.68–70.

117 Ibid., pp. 67–68. See also Philip K. Hitti, *History of the Arabs*, 8th ed. (London: Macmillan, 1964), pp. 467–468. The Zanj rebellion, one of the bloodiest and most destructive witnessed in West Asia, saw African slaves rebel throughout the marshlands south of Baghdad, repeatedly defeating punitive forces sent by the Caliph to subdue them. Led by ʿAlî Ibn-Muḥammad, a self-proclaimed messiah, the slaves managed to maintain their domain for fourteen years (869–879) with large numbers of casualties in near constant bloodletting, until the brother of the Caliph personally led the mission that captured the rebel stronghold of al-Mukhtarah and killed ʿAlî Ibn-Muḥammad.

118 CPI-CL, *Al-Mushtarak*, pp. 72–78, 90–96.

119 Ibid., pp. 98–99.

120 Ibid., pp. 82–89.

121 Ibid., p. 88.

The treatise pursues a methodical and sophisticated survey and analysis of the emergence of the European state system within its historical context as seen from a Marxist perspective. Quoting from the works of Marx and Engels, Maḥmûd's *Al-Mushtarak* concludes that a political revolution is the first prerequisite for the establishment of a socialist society.[122] Such a political revolution would replace the state with a model derived from the "Commune de Paris" of 1871, which demonstrated direct political participation by all the citizenry.[123] This theory, which follows Lenin's line of thought in *The State and Revolution* (1917), contends that in this historical model, armed citizenry replaced the standing army, and all citizens became equal from a perspective of power.[124] Further, to explain the inadequacies of the socialist regimes in the USSR, China, and Eastern Europe during the period of its writing, *Al-Mushtarak* emphasized the fact that Marxism did not fully elaborate the role of the state in the socialist revolution. More important, it failed to establish the "scientific" relationship between the role of the army and that of the state. Additionally, there had been external interference in the post-Bolshevik Russian Revolution. In citing the historical context of Marxism, the theory indirectly excuses the founders of Marxism for the inappropriate treatment of the issue of the state and the standing army as found in their texts.[125] The treatise outlines traditional Marxism, drawing four conclusions: first, the state is the instrument of the dominant class to maintain the status quo to the detriment of the rest of the people. Second, the state is a privileged social institution that cannot voluntarily extinguish itself. Third, the state, whether in a socialist or a capitalist system, is a self-perpetuating institution; and fourth, a revolutionary proletarian leadership is not sufficient to counterbalance the power of organized bureaucracy. The revolution needed to build popular democratic institutions that had sufficient power to counteract that of the bureaucracy.[126]

The treatise then proposes an agenda for a "new" Iraqi Communist Party in which an Arab and Islamic heritage and the scientific analysis of Marxist historical evolution would be combined. Thus the ICP-CL's proposed political programme would be based on direct democracy, with its vision of *al-mushtarak* deriving from the historical precedent of the short-lived revolutionary experience of the Paris Commune.[127] To counterbalance the power of the hierarchy of communalism, which is freely elected, a supreme national body of notables, with the power to review the acts of the executive should there be complaints, would be formed. The role of the "new" Iraqi Communist Party would be pivotal in leading and consummating the socialist revolution, but its membership

122 Ibid., pp. 110–111.
123 Ibid., p. 118.
124 Ibid., pp. 119, 124.
125 Ibid., pp. 132–136, 138–141, 145–150.
126 Ibid., pp. 156–158.
127 Ibid., pp. 162–163. The Paris Commune occurred from 18 March to 28 May 1871.

and actions would be subject to independent investigation and supervision, with no privileges attached to Party membership.[128] From the experience of the Paris Commune, the Party would establish an armed citizenry in place of a standing army, support the national bourgeoisie, realize the full extent of democratic freedoms, and solve the Kurdish problem in keeping with the historical rights of the Kurds, all within the framework of *al-mushtarak*.[129]

It is curious that the ICP-CL programme did not elaborate on the fate of contemporary state-owned economic resources, which was estimated to include some 90 per cent of the economy in modern Iraq.[130] The treatise concludes with a rhetorical vision of some six tasks to be immediately undertaken that would lead to the overthrow of the Baʿth regime.[131] It appears that such a vision could have been intended to serve as a transitional phase until the establishment of *al-mushtarak*, but the treatise neither sets a timetable for transition nor delineates the form and content of the political process during that transition.

A vehement response to the use of Islamic history in the communist interpretation expressed in *Al-Mushtarak* came from a Shîʿî religious ideologue, al-Najdi, in a series of articles entitled "Islam: From a Contemporary Marxist Perspective" in the journal *Al-Tawḥîd* (published in Tehran). Ridiculing the Marxist interpretation of Islam, al-Najdi's article went so far as to deny to the "godless" the right to venture into religious doctrine, stating, "Islam doesn't need to be studied by the Marxists." Al-Najdi contended that *al-mushtarak* was an Islamic ideal and needed no justification or promotion from secular political groupings:

> Some people may see in *al-mushtarak* a new, positive initiative to study Islam in a scientific spirit.... however, since we do not wish to disappoint them [the Marxists] we will say... we are not optimistic with this first attempt, which does not represent anything but disagreements in approach between two Iraqi Marxist groups: Islam does not need in any way to be studied through the prism of communist theory, Islam does not need to be vouched for by any secular organization. Other [political groups] need the legitimization only Islam can bring, as it is the only comprehensive international scientific theory that provides conscious cultural solutions for the future of all humanity.[132]

Al-Ghad responded to this criticism over two consecutive issues,[133] with a detailed critique of the ideas expressed in *Al-Tawḥîd*, as well as with its own sophisticated interpretation of the role that Islam had played in regional history.

[128] Ibid., pp. 164–165.
[129] Ibid., pp. 166–178.
[130] Ibid., pp. 174–176.
[131] Ibid., pp. 192–193.
[132] Al Najdi, "Islam; From a Contemporary Marxist Perspective," *Al-Tawḥîd* (Tehran) no. 22–24 (May–September 1986), pp. 144–145, as quoted in *Al-Ghad*, no. 21 (October 1987), pp. 56–57.
[133] *Al-Ghad*, no. 21 (October 1987), pp. 55–67, and *Al-Ghad*, no. 22–23 (February 1992), pp. 79–102.

While maintaining its adherence to Marxist dialectical materialism, *Al-Ghad* concluded that the author of the *Al-Tawḥîd* piece

[had] built his arguments on arrogance and fanaticism, rather than on logic.... instead of bringing forward a counter argument to repudiate to the idea of *al-mus̲h̲tarak* ... we were hoping that *Al-Tawḥîd* would treat the subject objectively, with the spirit of academic dialogue and open the doors to serious discussion of Islamic culture, rather than an irresponsible and rigid [response] of fanaticism and incrimination.[134]

Five years later, this theory became the ideological foundation of the ICP-CL, and an official organ, under the same title of *Al-Mus̲h̲tarak* (but subtitled "Towards Democratic Socialism and Towards the Republic of al-Mushtarak"), was now billed as the central publication of the Party. With the change of name from *Ṭarîq al-S̲h̲aᶜb* to *Al-Mus̲h̲tarak*, the paper considered itself to be a direct continuation of *Ṭarîq al-S̲h̲aᶜb*, and *Al-Mus̲h̲tarak*'s first issue of March 1988 was therefore published as number 1 of volume 45. In its editorial, it explained that the new name was necessitated by

the changed political circumstances ... and the conditions of Iraq after the ruling fascists had become entrenched. This required a new political direction that would deal with the new issues, and that would take into consideration the new generation that has grown up during the fascist [Baᶜthist] rule and the war [with Iran], in addition to the deviation of the international socialist movement that has taken place.... It became imperative for the central Party organ to reflect this new direction in its political stance ... and for us to distinguish between the banner of the People's revolution and that of the opportunists [ICP-CC].

As already discussed, the term "*al-mus̲h̲tarak*" refers to democratic socialism, which, according to the editorial, now reflected the Party's concept of scientific socialism. At the same time, it also referred to a special concept for "the international proletariat, and differentiates *al-mus̲h̲tarak* from the obsequious concept that prevailed in the international communist movement from the time of the Second World War, and deepened after the Twentieth Congress of the CPSU in 1956." The treatise continued to explain that, according to Marxism-Leninism, the idea of the international proletariat was based on solidarity among the communist parties around the world founded on "equality and independence, and not a blind servile following." It asserted that, on this basis, while the interests of the international working-class movements were similar, their specific conditions often differed. Thus, "independence and an innovative understanding of their objective circumstances are two quintessential prerequisites for the advancement and victory of communist parties." *Al-Mus̲h̲tarak* promised to devote its pages "to the concerns of the popular masses, and [to] struggle to achieve the pressing national objectives which could be summarized [as] the overthrow of the fascist Baᶜthist regime, the cessation of the war with Iran, and the achieving of democracy which includes self-rule in Kurdistan."

[134] *Al-Ghad*, no. 22–23 (February 1992), p. 102.

At the same time, the theoretical journal *Al-Ghad* continued to espouse discussions of the concept. Both the *Al-Ghad* and *Al-Mushtarak* newspapers ceased publication in Iraq in the early 1990s, although *Al-Ghad* continued to publish in London until the mid-1990s, carrying on as the primary intellectual forum for leftist and critical thought in the circles the of democratic opposition forces. It was dedicated to the promulgation of a critical analysis of both Iraqi politics and the CC faction of the ICP, going so far as to publish interviews, excerpts, and manifestos of those who chose to break away from the ICP-CC ranks.

The Interpretations of *al-Muqâydah*

Another milestone in the thinking of the Central Leadership (ICP-CL) was the concept of *al-muqâydah* (barter),[135] which described the faction's position vis-à-vis both ideological poles of the Cold War. The secretary-general, Najim Maḥmûd, introduced the thesis, which was founded on the historical premises that because of Iraq's rich resources it was of immense importance to the great powers. As such, the ICP took it upon itself to mobilize against the Western powers and to chart a new path for the country. This was particularly necessary as the established parties were beholder to regional and/or international powers and thus were compromised.

The Iraqi Communist Party Central Committee, which was the focus of *Al-Muqâydah*, continued to be subservient to Soviet influence, especially during the Khrushchev era (1958–1964). "The policy of General Qâsim, the leader of the Revolution, was not a sweeping popular change for the benefit of the masses; [instead, he] played off one party against the other, for the ultimate goal of complete power for himself." But Qâsim did not attempt to achieve a strong radical stand against Western interests in Iraqi oil, something that the Iraqi Communist Party had initially called for. The international political arena was polarized by the Cold War, and regional powers like Egypt and Iran were tied to one or the other of the ideological blocs.

Al-Muqâydah argued that none of the Iraqi political parties was aware that the Western powers, led by the United States, had their tactical differences over Western capitalist goals in the Middle East; instead, the Iraqis saw the Western alliance as a monolithic bloc. Divisions, when identified and exploited, allowed some room for the Soviets to manoeuvre but did not prevent them from attempting to barter away their influence over the Iraqi revolution to achieve their more important policy objective of demilitarizing Germany. The political parameters of Western strategy during the Cold War were always centred on the containment of the "Red scare," and on securing the flow of cheap oil from the Middle East.

[135] Najim Maḥmûd, *Al-Muqâyḍah: Berlin – Baghdad, al-Thawrah al-ʿIrâqiyyah, 14th Tammûz fî al-Siyâsah al-Dawliyyah* (London: al-Ghad Society, 1991).

In Europe, Britain opposed the Common Market proposed by France – an arrangement in which Germany would again play a leading role in European affairs. The Soviets were aware of this British stance and attempted to use it to bring Britain closer to the views of the USSR. The Soviets proposed exchanging support for the ICP and, by extension, influence over the Iraqi revolution and the country's oil reserves, in return for a neutral and demilitarized Germany. This left the ICP isolated and clearly left Iraq within the West's sphere of influence. The administration in the United States was, in the main, opposed to such an understanding between the Soviets and the British. First, Washington had assumed an uncompromising stance against the USSR. Second, the United States believed at the time that the revolution in Iraq could be favourably compromised through Western regional agents such as the United Arab Republic and through actions such as the 1959 Mosul uprising, which had been instigated by the Arab nationalists. Third, at the time responsibility for the American decision-making process was spread almost equally among the president, the National Security Council, the CIA, the State Department, and Congress. As no one could accurately predict the outcome of the interaction of such factors in the policy process, wide contradictions in US policy began to appear.

Al-Muqâydah provided a historical overview of the strategic and economic importance of Iraq in Britain's political calculations. Throughout the nineteenth century and up to the First World War, Iraq had been a strategic garrison post, protecting British interests in both India and the Middle East.[136] Between the two world wars, Britain sought to control Iraq without developing the country's rich natural resources; instead, in an effort to quell popular resistance, it introduced a policy of economic stagnation. Iraq became a military base for Britain, and its oil a strategic reserve. In the 1950s, Iraq cemented its alliance with the West through the Baghdad Pact. However, at this time Britain began a political and military retreat from the entire Middle East, after facing increasing popular resistance in countries like Egypt and Iran that were concerned with indigenous calls for the nationalization of oil. With the British retreat, the United States, under the Eisenhower doctrine, stepped forward to fill the vacuum. Demonstrating that they were not to be seen as benign, the Americans used military force to influence events after the outbreak of the Iraqi revolution on 14 July 1958, with the landing of US Marines in Lebanon.[137]

Al-Muqâydah saw the Anglo-American actions in the Middle East, particularly after the Iraqi revolution, as no less than a deliberate redrawing of the political map. Regional agents of change were to be utilized to attack Arab governments. Israel would invade Egypt and Syria and annex the West Bank of Jordan,[138] and Turkey would invade Iraq from the north under American air cover.[139] Britain would occupy Iraq and Jordan in the aftermath. London,

[136] Ibid., pp. 21–22.
[137] Ibid., pp. 23, 30–32, 35.
[138] Ibid., p. 53.
[139] Ibid., p. 52.

however, was worried about the Turkish role (an American plan) for fear of Soviet intervention. Another reason for Britain's abandonment of military intervention was that the Iraqi revolution had summoned remarkable popular support, and that all the members of the royal family had been killed immediately after the 14 July 1958 revolution.[140] A final reason for cancelling military intervention was that Qâsim had pledged to respect the existing international agreements that regulated oil production in Iraq; nationalization of the oil industry was not on his political agenda.[141] The US strategy to take over the Middle East from Britain resulted in the demotion of Britain to the level of a junior strategic partner, broadening the rift in Anglo-American relations and forcing Britain to seek the influence of a countervailing power, namely, the USSR, while exploiting the phobias and conflicts among the Arab rulers.[142]

Maḥmûd then offered a cogent analysis of the history of Anglo-Russian interests in blocking German influence in the Middle East before the Second World War. *Al-Muqâydah* concluded that US policy with regard to the Iraqi revolution was to isolate the regime, both internally and externally, by exacerbating the poor relations between Egypt and Iraq (Egypt feared communist influence), and then by dislodging Soviet influence in Iraq and containing whatever weight the Iraqi Communist Party wielded in the country's internal politics. Conducting such a policy was easier after Qâsim made it clear that his goals for Iraq would focus on economic development and the welfare of the Iraqi people.[143] The United States was confident that, because of its policy of isolating the regime it would be easy to arrange for an internal coup in the future by one of the many competing political forces that would better serve American interests. Moreover, Soviet strategy after the Second World War was premised on creating discord among the Western allies who were pursuing from their self-interested policies.[144] During the same period, West Germany was admitted into NATO. Furthermore, the world began to see an accelerating rate of de-colonization and the emergence of many new states, making up what came to be known as the Third World. These Third World countries gave the USSR a new political card to play against its Western foes during the Cold War.[145] Meanwhile, Britain attempted to play the German card with the Soviets in order to make gains in the Middle East generally and in Iraq in particular and to reduce the increasing American hegemony over its international affairs.[146]According to Maḥmûd, Britain's tactical objective was to establish a convenient Anglo-Russian axis to balance the Franco-German axis in Europe, as well as balancing American power throughout the Middle East region.[147]

[140] Ibid., p. 37.
[141] Ibid., p. 54.
[142] Ibid., pp. 56–57.
[143] Ibid., pp. 64–65.
[144] Ibid., pp. 78–79.
[145] Ibid., pp. 82–83.
[146] Ibid., pp. 85, 89.
[147] Ibid., p. 99.

The Soviets were so concerned about the emergence of the Iraqi Communist Party in 1934, with its popularity and its independence from Moscow, that they constantly tried to weaken it internally so they could control it and use it as a pawn in achieving their own policy interests.[148] The emergence of the People's Republic of China in 1949, and its immediate recognition of the Iraqi revolution on 16 July 1958, was greeted enthusiastically by both the Iraqi people and the Iraqi Communist Party. Their appreciation intensified on 17 July 1958 when China announced that it had made thousands of volunteers available to defend Iraq against potential Anglo-American intervention.[149] Concerning the Soviets' fear of a strong, united Germany and their political gambits in the Middle East, Maḥmûd highlighted Soviet readiness to exchange its influence in Iraq and in its huge oil deposits for a divided and powerless Germany by manipulating Britain's position in Europe and British relations with the United States.[150]

Maḥmûd focused on the factors that shaped the political positions of Britain and the USSR and that would bring the two powers to a closer "understanding" of the potential advantages of a Soviet desertion of Iraq, thereby leaving Iraq in the British sphere of interest while Britain gave up Germany to Soviet designs. The solution of the German question now lay solely in the hands of the Americans – over whom the Soviets had no leverage. Britain, like the USSR, was concerned about the prospect of a strong and unified Germany, but Britain was more concerned about protecting its principal Middle Eastern interests in the Persian Gulf and Iraq, interests that were more important to it than those it held in Europe at this time. The Iraqi revolution was a threat to these British interests, and the Soviets, who now had a strong foothold in Iraq, used their influence with the ICP as a strong negotiating lever with Britain. Britain constituted the weakest link in the Western front, but it was the only member of that bloc with which the Soviets could negotiate.[151]

The Soviet foothold in Iraq consisted predominantly of its influence over the Iraqi Communist Party, which was likely to prove instrumental in mobilizing the masses behind the nationalization of the oil industry and lend political support to Qâsim's regime. Another item of Soviet influence came from the generous economic agreement the USSR reached with Qâsim on 16 March 1959, valued at £49 million.[152] However, a later Iraqi request for Soviet arms alarmed Britain. Maḥmûd stressed that the failure of Colonel ʿAbd-ul-Wahhâb al-Shawwâf's coup on 8 March 1959 had far-reaching repercussions. In Iraq the ICP, enjoying wide popular revolutionary support, demanded that Qâsim provide support for the Algerian revolt against the French, withdraw from the Baghdad Pact, and close two British air bases that still remained in Iraq. However, Iraq had become regionally isolated owing to the severe propaganda campaign launched

148 Ibid., pp. 105–106, 110.
149 Ibid., pp. 113–122.
150 Ibid., pp. 124–125.
151 Ibid., pp. 130–131.
152 Ibid., p. 151.

against Qâsim by the United Arab Republic, which accused the Iraqi leader of being a puppet of the communists. On 23 March 1959, Qâsim declared in a press conference that he would consider nationalizing the French shares in the Iraqi Oil Company as a measure of solidarity with the Algerian revolt. Maḥmûd identified that declaration as a domestic gambit by Qâsim to give himself more leeway to manoeuvre, since he was actually seeking an increase in oil revenues.[153]

On 9 April 1959, the Qâsim regime formally requested that foreign oil companies increase the Iraqi share of profits, increase oil production, invest in raising oil-pumping capacity, and forfeit their contractual rights to the unexplored areas. The request was preceded by the Qâsim regime's denial of any intention to nationalize oil.[154] However, fearing that the Iraqi Communist Party would force Qâsim to nationalize the oil industry, the British responded by adopting a two-pronged policy that would both maintain the status quo of in Iraq, and thereby contain the communist force internally, and also allow the USSR to rein in the ICP.[155]

The oil industry developed comparatively late in Iraq, principally during the 1930s, "because it was the goal of British imperialism to keep Iraqi oil as a reserve, and consequently, there were no capable indigenous technical cadres available to run the industry. Kuwaiti oil was the top priority for the British."[156] Throughout the 1950s the Iraqi Communist Party championed the popular demand for the nationalization of oil, supported in this by other parties even though that neither the National Unity Front nor any other party had formally demanded that the Iraqi revolution undertake nationalization.[157] The only demand with regard to oil made formally by the ICP was that the revolution impose "strict control on the foreign oil companies."[158] Maḥmûd, however, identified "strict control" as nationalization.[159]

In April 1959, the ICP re-drew its policy to compromise with the regime and, according to Zakî Khairî, declared that "strict control meant no more than the existence of Iraqi representatives in the foreign oil companies, to ensure fair operation." Going back to the international stage, Maḥmûd believed that the USSR might have been behind this volte-face,[160] and that Qâsim's retreat from nationalizing the French oil shares, and the shift in ICP policy (under Soviet pressure) regarding the nationalization of oil, might have led the French to look more favourably at the Anglo-Soviet position with regard to a European summit to examine the German question.[161]

[153] Ibid., pp. 153, 158, 164.
[154] Ibid., p. 165.
[155] Ibid., p. 172.
[156] Ibid., pp. 163, 190.
[157] Ibid., pp. 190–191.
[158] Ibid., p. 174.
[159] Ibid., p. 192.
[160] Ibid., pp. 179–181.
[161] Ibid., pp. 199–202.

Maḥmûd also attempted to explain the intricate dialectics between the regional powers – Iraq and Egypt – and the international powers – Britain, the United States, and the USSR. Maḥmûd maintained that Egypt feared the influence of communism domestically, as well as in Iraq, since this might undermine its ambitious plan for regional leadership. To topple Qâsim and introduce their agents through the failed al-Shawwâf coup satisfied both the Egyptian and the US policy designs in the region. The United States hoped that a new regime would be friendlier to American interests than to those of either Britain or the USSR.[162] The Iraqi regime itself also feared the Iraqi Communist Party and was ready to seek political support, even from Egypt's Nasser, to contain the Party's influence – a position that served Anglo-American interests well. Thus, to help the Iraqi leader control the ICP, the United States exploited its good relations with Nasser to get him to ease up on his attack on Qâsim.[163]

Faced with the American efforts in the region, Britain was forced to steer a middle course; this indirectly supported the American-Egyptian attempts to remove Qâsim and control the communists and would also, the British hoped, enlist American support for a European summit with the Soviets to study the German question. Such a strategy would have left Iraq out of the Soviet sphere.[164] Maḥmûd maintained that the Soviets used Iraq as a pawn with which to threaten Anglo-American interests in the Middle East, alluding to the foothold the USSR had obtained through its financial loans and economic assistance to the Iraqi government after the 1958 revolution, as well as to the influence it had over the Iraqi Communist Party. For the West, particularly the United States, which feared that Iran would be in great danger if Iraq fell completely to the Iraqi Communist Party and, consequently, to Soviet influence, the Middle East took precedence over Europe. Iran was seen to be the weakest link in the Baghdad Pact, and the Baghdad Pact represented both the *cordon sanitaire* around the southern Soviet Union and security for the largest petroleum reserves in the world. Believing that the communists could easily penetrate Iran from Iraq, the United States agreed to a European summit, "with Iraq the sacrifice on the altar of international politics."[165]

Maḥmûd outlined an exchange of messages between the Soviet Union and Nasser, which he believed was evidence that the Soviets would exaggerate their propaganda attack on Nasser to further win over the British and restrain the ICP in Iraq.[166] Furthermore, he asserted that an unwritten agreement between the USSR and Egypt outlined their respective spheres of interest in the Arab world, thus, Nasser "agreed" to abandon Iraq to the Soviet sphere of influence and accept Qâsim's regime in return for a Soviet promise to prevent the ICP from achieving power in Iraq. In addition, the Soviets would recognize Nasser

[162] Ibid., pp. 210–214.
[163] Ibid., pp. 217–218.
[164] Ibid., pp. 217, 224–225.
[165] Ibid., pp. 227–228.
[166] Ibid., p. 241.

as the leader of Arab nationalism – excluding Iraq.[167] With Iraq now isolated, and the ICP abandoned by its patrons in Moscow, Maḥmûd continued his exposé by outlining the failure of Soviet policy under Khrushchev to attain its German objective, leading ultimately to Khrushchev's removal from the Soviet Presidium.

Maḥmûd argued that to secure Germany, Khrushchev had made concerted efforts to involve Egypt, Britain, and Cuba, in addition to Iraq.[168] However, the American administration was well aware of the Soviet coordination with Egypt, and it made certain that Khrushchev's pending visit to the United States in 1959 would not be annouced until after the Soviet leadership stopped the Iraqi Communist Party from taking over the Iraqis government. The Soviets demanded that the ICP withdraw its call for cabinet seats in the Qâsim government, and the ICP obliged. At the same time, Qâsim began mending fences with Nasser and took to releasing nationalist and right-wing prisoners.[169] On 15 April 1959, Khrushchev arrived in Washington, withdrew his ultimatum about Germany, withdrew his consent to help China manufacture nuclear weapons, and obtained the approval of the American president for a summit conference in Paris to discuss the German question. Thus, as Maḥmûd argued, "The price for the Soviets was the loss of China and Iraq, and the strategic psychological repercussions of the ultimatum without gaining any concrete advantage."[170]

In 1962 the Soviet Union sent military units to Cuba, where they installed nuclear warheads, an act that resulted in the Cuban missile crisis. At the same time, ICP members who were in Moscow returned to Iraq with instructions to be ready for a takeover when they "received the green light." Maḥmûd interpreted such actions as political *démarches* on the Soviet part, in a continued effort to force American concessions on Germany, by defusing the Cuban crisis, while still playing the Iraqi card and the communist scare, which, in Maḥmûd's estimation, were more important than Cuba to the West.[171] Inexperienced in international machinations, the Iraqi Communist Party easily fell prey to the Soviet's ruthless political games.[172]

Al-Muqâydah then provided the historical background for the tensions between Iraq and Kuwait, which had arisen as a result of British strategic interests in Kuwait and in the trade routes to India. From the eighteenth century until the outbreak of the First World War in 1914, Kuwait had been part of Basra province, [173] and indeed, the Anglo-Ottoman Treaty of 1913, which was not ratified owing to the outbreak of the war and the ensuing British occupation of both Iraq and Kuwait, had recognized that Kuwait was a part of Basra.[174]

167 Ibid., p. 236.
168 Ibid., p. 249.
169 Ibid., pp. 249–251.
170 Ibid., pp. 251–252, 257.
171 Ibid., pp. 262–264.
172 Ibid., p. 266.
173 Ibid., p. 490.
174 Ibid., p. 498, Appendix 7.

Britain chose not to transform Iraq into a British colony and, after the popular revolt of 1920, formed an independent royal government to rule in Baghdad. From that point, Britain pursued a policy of containment towards Iraq in an effort to control it both economically and militarily. In the process, Kuwait was unilaterally severed from Basra by Britain in 1923 and declared a British protectorate. This act undermined the emerging Iraqi state economically, since it blocked Iraq's only sea route to the Persian Gulf. As a result, Kuwait became a constant political issue in Iraqi politics, reaching a crisis point under King Ghazi in 1932, under the government of Nûrî al-Saᶜîd in 1957–1958, in June 1961 in Qâsim's time,[175] and in 1991 with Saddam Hussein's invasion of the country.

After the Iraqi revolution in 1958, Britain reached an understanding with the United States Kuwait should remain in British hands at all costs because it was Britain's primary source of fuel, producing an annual 70 million tonnes of oil, more than twice what was produced by Iraq.[176] For his part, Qâsim proposed the recovery of Kuwait in return for lenient terms for the companies,[177] Having analyzed various sources, Maḥmûd concluded that to drive a wedge between Qâsim and the Iraqi Communist Party, and to ensure that no nationalization of Iraqi oil would take place, Britain may have indicated its consent to the formation of some kind of union between Iraq, Kuwait, and Jordan.

At the same time, Britain entered into secret negotiations with Kuwait to grant it sovereignty and independence as soon as British plans for preventing Qâsim's nationalization project succeeded. The declaration of the independence for the State of Kuwait in June 1961 came as a complete surprise to Qâsim and was among the reasons for his downfall.[178] Maḥmûd noted that the Iraqi Communist Party had been unclear as to the position it should assume towards Qâsim's plans in Kuwait.[179] However, he argued, it was clear that Kuwait had assumed paramount importance in Western policy designs in the Middle East.[180] In an attempt to unravel the tangled web of causes behind the ICP's demand in May 1959 to take part in Qâsim's government, Maḥmûd examined the March failed coup of al-Shawwâf. Arguing that the communists played a prominent role in foiling this attempt to topple Qâsim, Maḥmûd contended that two main issues remained: oil, and the nature of the ruling power that now resided solely in the person of Qâsim.[181] In early May 1959 the Iraqi Communist Party announced that there was a need for cooperation among all political parties and that the National Unity Front should be revived. Such a front constituted a threat Qâsim's the political power, since the popular appeal of such an alliance might force him into a confrontation with the foreign oil

[175] Ibid., pp. 286–289.
[176] Ibid., pp. 290–291.
[177] Ibid., pp. 292–295.
[178] Ibid., pp. 295–296.
[179] Ibid., pp. 297–298.
[180] Ibid., p. 299.
[181] Ibid., pp. 304–305.

companies, after he had pledged to Western powers that he would abandon the nationalization of Iraq's oil resources.[182] Maḥmûd maintained in *Al-Muqâydah* that Qâsim had lured the ICP away from its political mobilization efforts by insinuating in *Al-Thawrah*, the government newspaper, that the ICP must take seats in the cabinet to properly represent the popular forces.[183]

Although the ICP, under Soviet influence, suspended its drive for the nationalization of oil, its participation in the government was so gratifying that it drew the Party "away from its national projects and left it isolated in the political arena for Qâsim to squash."[184] Shortly afterwards, in April 1959 the communist newspaper *Ittiḥâd al-Shaᶜb* requested representation of the ICP in the cabinet,[185] believing in Qâsim's promise that he would legitimize political parties and give access to political activity, following a short transitional period that would end in early 1960. When the time came, however, Qâsim denied approval for the ICP and instead, created a substitute communist party, which was subordinate to the regime.[186] Abandoned by its Soviet patrons, and now outmanoeuvred by Qâsim, the ICP had not foreseen its own destruction. After nationalizing the oil industry and provoking the ire of the international community, Qâsim, despite having ousted the ICP was himself overthrown in a bloody coup by the Baᶜth Party on 8 February 1963.

Maḥmûd incorporated into his analysis the Party's activities up to the Iraqi invasion of Kuwait in 1990. He stated that

> the "new" international environment – an environment that started with the "bartering of Baghdad for Berlin" by the CPSU and the uprooting of the 14 July 1958 coup – was crowned by the 1991 Gulf War, which resulted in the final destruction of Iraqi society. The ICP-CL has maintained, as its Party platform, the hope of a new age of freedom and progress based on the end of the "one-man-rule system" to achieve democracy in order that the Iraqi people may determine their own future.[187]

Maḥmûd concluded *Al-Muqâydah* by examining the 1991 Gulf War in the light of the devastation of Iraq at the hands of the Western powers. He linked the two wars in the Gulf region and the destruction of the ICP as evidence of a plan to control Iraqi oil reserves, as seen in 1991 when Iraq faced an American-led military coalition in the Second Gulf War. Maḥmûd must be credited with a great deal of perceptiveness, since his predictions appear quite accurate even though his book was published in 1991, before the results of the war were clear.

Maḥmûd began his analysis by examining the global political environment at the time of the war's outbreak. He pointed out the deteriorating American financial system, which was suffering under an internal debt of $10 trillion, a federal deficit of $3 trillion, and an annual interest of $150 billion in

[182] Ibid., pp. 309–312.
[183] Ibid., pp. 315–316.
[184] Ibid., pp. 312, 315–319.
[185] Ibid., p. 305.
[186] Ibid., pp. 324–325.
[187] Ibid., p. 416.

1990. Increasingly, American oil imports, 15 per cent of which came from the Gulf region, were being consumed by exporting states themselves.[188] Furthermore, Maḥmûd maintained, the emergence of Japan and the South Asian "little tigers," appeared to be an increasing economic threat to the diminishing American economy, while a unified Europe, led by the German economy, posed yet another danger to American global dominance. Therefore, the United States began to dismantle its military installations in Europe for financial reasons as much as for strategic concerns; it needed to re-deploy its forces closer to the oil reserves of the Middle East, not only to control the oil physically but also to influence the oil-hungry economies of Japan and Germany.[189] Such a manoeuvre proved difficult, because the pro-Western and pro-American regimes of the Arab Gulf were concerned that there would be a domestic backlash if American forces were stationed on their soil.

Maḥmûd portrayed the American "rescue" of Kuwait as a ruse to secure a base for American forces in the strategic heartland of Middle Eastern oil. He placed the Gulf War within the broader context of the conflicts that American forces had engaged in during the Cold War (China, Korea, and Vietnam), pointing out how its lack of victory in each one had left socio-psychological scars on American society and promoted American's isolationist tendencies. But the Iranian revolution and the 444 days of detention endured by the American hostages in Tehran, the fiasco of the American rescue operation, and the failure in the regional balance of power all generated an urge to revive and reinvigorate "the invincible American spirit." The *International Herald Tribune* reported that the parade celebrating victory in the Gulf War, down the "canyon of heroes" in New York,[190] was more a celebration of "defeating the ghost of Vietnam" than a celebration of military victory over Iraq.[191] Furthermore, Maḥmûd argued:

> The American instigation and support of the Iraq-Iran war was [undertaken in an effort] to exhaust both countries, and woo over the Iranian regime through indirect military assistance (under the Reagan administration) . . . [This] was simply a reversion to the old game of regional balance of power, which had failed when Iran moved closer to Moscow, and Iraq succeeded in building [what was] numerically the largest army in the region. It was at that moment that the Western powers ended the war, and that [the] US began considering direct intervention as a policy, especially when Israel was so distracted by the Intifada that it could not fully act as a balancing military regional power and as the custodian of American interests.[192]

Although Iraq had built the largest army in the region, it was also the largest debtor state, having incurred an estimated debt of US$120 billion as a result of its war with Iran. The United States pursued a policy of secretly enticing Kuwait and the United Arab Emirates to lower oil prices through over-production,

[188] Ibid., pp. 354–355.
[189] Ibid., pp. 357–358.
[190] *International Herald Tribune*, issue 10 (June 1991).
[191] Maḥmûd, *Al-Muqâyḍah*, pp. 367–370.
[192] Ibid., pp. 358–360.

while lending public support to Iraq's call for higher oil prices (to $25 per barrel), which Iraq required in order to free itself from its staggering economic crisis. The purpose of the American policy was to keep the Iraqi regime to its assigned regional role and firmly under US domination, beneath the umbrella of an American "new world order."[193]

Maḥmûd outlined the course of American policy on Iraq. First, America sought to "insinuate to Iraq that the US had neither a defence treaty with nor any interests in Kuwait,"[194] Second, although Kuwait, unlike Saudi Arabia, lacked historical, cultural, or religious significance in the region, its strategic geographical position and its proximity to the oilfields in Iran, Iraq, and Saudi Arabia made it an excellent base of operations to serve American interests in the "new world order."[195] Third, the American administration anticipated that, given Saddam Hussein's personality and the prevailing political circumstances, Saddam would react to the American policy by taking over the oil-rich neutral zone and the two small islands of Rubiah and Bubian, to allow Iraq access to a deep-water port in the Persian Gulf.[196] Fourth, in the face of overwhelming American power, Saddam would not dare to challenge the interests of the United States directly with any bold military adventure.[197] Fifth, according to the American scenario, after Saddam's foray the United States would land its forces in Kuwait under the pretext of safeguarding oil and would establish a permanent military presence there that would bring all the region, including Iran and Iraq, under US control.[198]

Saddam appeared to have experienced enough American duplicity to be able to determine at least a portion of the American strategy, because, as he told King Hussein of Jordan, "I have to take all of Kuwait and then negotiate with the US in order to end up with the two islands and the oil field."[199] In other words, Saddam felt forced to attack so that he could in order to begin "negotiations with the maximum, before settling for the optimum." However, the United States did not accept the fact that Saddam could go beyond his scripted role in the American plan for the new world order.

Maḥmûd argued that the administration of President George Bush saw an extra advantage to the United States in the Iraqi occupation of Kuwait through which to realize its plans for the region, namely the crippling of the Iraqi military and the establishment of American military bases throughout the Gulf. For that goal, the Americans insisted on having their ground forces stationed in Saudi Arabia before the war, despite the fact that Kuwait could have been liberated by intensive air strikes.[200] Maḥmûd concluded that "crippling the Iraqi army and leaving the regime intact sustains the perception of the existence of a military

[193] Ibid., p. 363.
[194] Ibid., p. 363.
[195] Ibid., p. 360.
[196] Ibid., p. 365.
[197] Ibid., p. 364.
[198] Ibid., p. 365.
[199] Ibid., pp. 366, 372.
[200] Ibid., pp. 272–273.

threat to the region, and justifies permanent American military bases in Kuwait, Qatar and Saudi Arabia." The war against Iraq, and the destruction of the country was all undertaken for the control of its oil, as has been the case since the 1958 Iraqi revolution.[201]

The Iraqi Progressive Opposition After the First Gulf War

Soon after the 1991 Gulf War, some Iraqis living in exile, including several Iraqi communists, many of whom disagreed with the Party's political leadership and had ceased to have any contact with it, rallied together to examine the impact on Iraq of the bombings and economic sanctions. In attempting to deal with the basic issue of what was to be done, they came together, as Iraqis, at a time when the nation was under considerable threat. One of the earliest responses came from a group of Iraqi ex-communists living in Algeria. Calling themselves the Leninist Group in the Iraqi Communist Movement (*al-Farîq al-Lînînî fî al-Ḥarakah al-Shiyûʿiyyah al-ʿIrâqiyyah*), they were followers of two professors at the University of Algeria, Khâlid ʿAbd-ul-lah al-Salâm and Khalîl al-Jazâʾirî, who had long been critics of the Party leadership and who had gathered around themselves a number of former communists, independent democrats, and other leftists. From the late 1980s, the group had taken it upon itself to challenge the ICP leadership, regularly publishing a broadsheet, *Al-Nashrah*, with a circulation limited to opinion leaders and activists. While its main purpose was to report on pressing Iraqi national issues, including the crisis within the country and Baʿthist oppression, it did not shy away from pinpointing the responsibility of the ICP leadership for the crisis within the Party and for its role in the national crisis. The invasion of Kuwait, and the war that followed, brought this group more actively into the Iraqi political scene since, as Iraqis whose nation was in danger, they belived that political forces of all persuasions now had an obligation to rally in support of Iraq in the aftermath of the "imperial" aggression. Communication among these disparate groups intensified, and a call to all nationalist, leftist, and progressive forces outside the country appeared to win the approval of the desperate regime in Baghdad. The official Baʿthist newspaper *Al-Thawrah* published an editorial statement from a large number of democratic and leftist exiles, including the *Nashrah* group, on 9 December 1991. Appearing in the "free opinion" section, the article was attributed to Mâjid ʿAbd-ul-Riḍâ, had been a member of the Central Committee and Politburo for three decades before quitting the Party. The statement declared that

> the aggressive war against our country brought entirely new conditions that affected all national, Arab, and international realms and requires analysis and the derivation of necessary conclusions... in a broadly based democratic dialogue.... We see it necessary to concentrate [our efforts] on the pressing issues since the aggressive war has...

[201] Ibid., p. 391.

endangered the country's independence, threatened its unity with the aim of interfering in its internal affairs, and placed the country in the miserable condition of dependency... [under conditions] of encirclement and starvation. We condemn any cooperation or coordination with the enemy, whatever its excuse.... On the contrary, we think we see our national duty as requiring us to struggle for the sake of safeguarding Iraq's unity, both its land and people, to strive to strengthen its internal solidarity, united against its enemy, and to work to remove economic sanctions. We call on all nationalists and the sons of the nation to rebuild their devastated country.

Taking advantage of the pardon for all exiles, al-Salâm and al-Jazâʾirî, representing the Algerian Arab Committee for the Support of Iraq and Palestine, participated in a conference of the popular forces in Baghdad in the autumn of 1991. Behind the scenes, negotiations took place between themselves and the regime that resulted in the two being invited again to Baghdad on 25 December 1991, where they were joined by Mâjid ʿAbd-ul-Riḍâ. The three held informal negotiations with the government representative to discover whether there was the possibility of "forming a political movement on a legal democratic, transparent and peaceful basis."[202] They agreed to continue discussions in which the regime and the Party representatives could formalize future relations.

Mâjid ʿAbd-ul-Riḍâ was the most active in these discussions as he had been the first to return to Iraq following the war. The idea of the group was to form a political grouping "which would not carry the name of the Communist Party." In January 1992, Tariq ʿAziz, then Iraqi's minister of information, met the group three times on behalf of the government; the group agreed not to form a political party and promised not to organize in the army, since they were meeting him "as individuals," not as representatives of any party, and would not attempt to act in any way against the regime. They requested only a newspaper that would allow them to express their views. Tariq ʿAziz informed them that the government leadership did not want to license a paper unless a political party was formed that required such a voice. Khâlid ʿAbd-ul-lah al-Salâm felt that a party was premature and more than they wanted. "The idea was to establish a paper and develop a clear position after which we could claim [to have a base] to form a party."[203] Others, led by Mâjid ʿAbd-ul-Riḍâ and Khalîl al-Jazâʾirî, were more optimistic and were willing to discuss the regime's proposal.

After their return to Aligers from Baghdad on 3 May 1992, ʿAbd-ul-Riḍâ and al-Jazâʾirî summarized their ideas in a letter to Bâqir Ibrâhîm al-Mûsawî, who had been a member of the Central Committee from July 1959 and member of the Politburo from 1962 until his resignation from the Party in 1984. They noted that

there is a huge vacuum in the country of democrats, including the Iraqi Communist Party, which requires our presence in the country in order to humbly and practically

[202] "Notes on the Visit to Baghdad," Khâlid ʿAbd-ul-Salâm and Khalîl al-Jazâʾirî, *Al-Nashrah*, no. 27 (2 March 1992).

[203] Letter from Khâlid ʿAbd-ul-Salâm to author, dated 3 September 2002.

participate . . . to find solutions to the country's problems. . . . We call upon all to return to the country, though our call is particularly directed to those who were expelled from the Party for any reason, and who are still active.[204]

They explained the reasons for a return to Iraq as a need to generate a discussion among the people based on

national, democratic, and general socialist aims reflecting the current international situation, including the communist movement, derived from our experience in the Party. . . . We want to emphasize that this open grouping is not directed against the Communist Party or any other group, and is not a substitute for these.[205]

Their vision of the independence of the group from the regime, and its democratic orientation and openness, was clear, though "open for discussion." Under the present conditions, they hoped that the regime would also be open to their ideas. Al-Salâm and al-Jazâʾirî completed the academic year and resigned their posts; in July, al-Jazâʾirî accepted a university position in Iraq, while al-Salâm returned in December 1992.[206] However, by the time both were back in Iraq, the regime was more firmly in control, and their relations with the Baʿthists soured, although there was no apparent conflict. A week after he returned, Khâlid al-Salâm's car was involved in an accident in which it mysteriously exploded and his entire family was killed. He was badly burned and remained hospitalzed until the end of June, when he received permission to travel to Paris. A few days later, al-Jazâʾirî was found chopped to pieces in his apartment in Baghdad, and thus their experiment with patriotic support for the regime came to a bloody end.[207] Khâlid al-Salâm continued to work with other groups and engage in democratic activities, but them outside Iraq.

Between 9 and 10 December 1995, a group of independent Iraqi political activists met in Paris with academics from Britain and France to discuss conditions in Iraq. They issued a declaration condemning

the disastrous effects of the continued, oppressive sanctions, whose basic goal is the destruction of Iraq and the future of its generations by imposing foreign designs on our people and the region. The dictatorial and oppressive regime is one of the main factors that led to the morass of the Kuwaiti invasion and the regime's inability to deal with its consequences. The exploitation of economic sanctions as a tool to achieve political gains by some states, particularly the US, is a condemned and unacceptable action, nationally, humanely, and morally. A serious action to lift the sanctions would require a credible [Iraqi] governmental policy in its dealing with the UN Security Council resolutions, and a democratic relaxation [by the regime] towards the people and their national forces . . . Effective popular participation means free representative institutions which require democratic practices that will allow the supremacy of the law, respect

[204] *Al-Malaf al-ʿIrâqî*, no. 50 (February 1996), p. 35.
[205] Ibid.
[206] Interview by author with Khâlid ʿAbd-ul-Salâm, Edmonton, Alberta (20 July 2002).
[207] *Al-Masaʾ* (Algiers, 5 February 1996), and *Ṭarîq al-Shaʿb*, no. 13 (end of September 1993).

for human rights, and a peaceful transfer of power. For that reason, there must be a government of national unity. These democratic institutions are our only path to a strong national solidarity, in order to stand against the racial and sectarian designs currently circulating.

The partnership of Kurds and Arabs in one "homeland," and securing the national rights of the Kurds, is one condition for the steadfastness of Iraq and its democratic progress.[208]

The ICP-CL Responds to the American Empire (1990–Present)

The ICP-CL had continued issuing statements in the 1980s and into 1990 on crucial issues facing the Party and on the Iraqi political landscape. In early August 1990 it circulated a number of pronouncements in which it discussed the Iraqi occupation of Kuwait;

The Kuwaiti crisis has given an excuse for the forces of the United States to occupy Saudi Arabia in an attempt to resurrect the old Baghdad Pact, now with direct US military control . . . the Kuwaiti crisis comes in to inaugurate the post–Cold War era . . . the age of American imperial control over the ugly Soviet capitalism . . . Soviet capitalism showed its dependency on American imperialism when it supported the American incursion against Iraq . . . and in this subservient policy they [the USSR] dropped the last of the "progressive veils of their ugly face."[209]

The pronouncements called upon all Arab people to overthrow the Arab regimes participating in the American imperial aggression and put an end to the "fascist conditions and the means of oppression and terrorism . . . that shackle the Arab people's energy to resist aggression and the impediments to democracy, in order to stand up to the imperialist-Zionist challenges." As the air war raged over Iraq, with American and allied forces destroying Iraqi infrastructure and showing no hesitancy in targeting civilians, the ICP-CL published another announcement, stating:

These acts of hatred against Iraq, before all else its popular masses, regardless of their class . . . even before the regime of Saddam Hussein . . . was created by American designs and maintained by American armaments, and has continued its mistreatment to terrorize the Iraqi people . . . with the help of American aid . . . as well as the regime's aggressive war against Iran – brought about by the US, its allies, and international agents . . . it is no longer a secret that the American ambassador to Baghdad is the one who encouraged Saddam to invade Kuwait . . . to be used as an excuse for the United States occupation of the Gulf region, to destroy Iraq and enslave its people . . . the US invasion does not target Iraq alone but all Arab nations, and all of the nations of the region.[210]

208 *Al-Quds al-ʿArabi* (London, 14 December 1995).

209 ICP-CL, Pronouncement, "The Kuwaiti Crisis" (early August 1990).

210 ICP-CL, Pronouncement, "Our People Should Stand Up to Defeat American – Zionist Invasion and Save the Nation: Arab People Must Awaken in Order to Overthrow the Governments of Treason and Shame" (18 January 1991).

The ICP-CL again called on the Arab people to rise up against their oppressors, both the capitalist West and the regional "reactionaries," while clearly placing the Iraqi experience within that of the larger international political experience.

Our country is now exposed to a new imperial aggression whose basic aim is to fragment Iraq and break up its political structure . . . in order to secure permanent American control over the region's oil wealth, and abort any progressive national efforts towards scientific and civil progress in Iraq, the Arab and Islamic countries. The American aerial campaign in Kurdistan and the encouragement of reactionary elements [throughout the region] will open the door to the destruction of Iraq and the creation of a number of small and feudal states who would be constantly embroiled in conflict with one another, all under the control of Washington and Tel Aviv, just as happened in Lebanon and Yugoslavia.[211]

It further argued that

what distinguished this latest aggression from the chain of wars was its implementation of international economic sanctions, starvation, and the complete devastation of Iraqi society in an effort to break up the very unity of the country by instigating sectarian violence, and the employment of mercenaries and thieves from the old regime, who engaged and promoted Shiᶜi and Sunnî sectarianism, and who live on the misery of the Kurdish people . . . why the forces of imperialism and their agents in the Arabian Peninsula and the Gulf lit the fire of sectarianism is unclear . . . they all know who will be the first to be burned by its flames . . . namely the sheikhs of Saudi Arabia and the Gulf . . . who practice the worst forms of sectarian oppression on their own populations, particularly the Shi'a minorities in the world today.[212]

From this point forward, the activities of the ICP-CL, particularly those of Najim Maḥmûd, were concentrated on the formation of *Tajammuᶜ al-ᶜIrâqiyyîn ḍid al-Ḥarb wa al-Ḥiṣâr* (the Iraqi Coalition Against War and Sanctions), a broad progressive front of leftist and democratic opposition, to deal with the terrible conditions that existed in Iraq in the aftermath of the 1991 Gulf War. Following the American invasion and occupation of Iraq in 2003, this front was transformed into *al-Dîmuqrâṭiyyûn al-'Irâqiyyûn ḍid al-Iḥtilâl* (the Iraqi Democrats Against Occupation; IDAO). The IDAO continued publication of *Al-Ghad* as the "voice of the Iraqi left" and initiated publication of an electronic journal. The aims of IDAO included

supporting and facilitating the struggle of the Iraqi people . . . to rescue Iraq from Anglo-American colonialism . . . to establish democratic freedoms in all facets of public life . . . to eradicate the despised occupation, and oppose the attempts and pressure of occupying forces to create artificial political parties connected to it . . . to eradicate the remaining vestiges of Saddam's bloody regime, ensure that the new structures of oppression do not succeed . . . and to build the [national] infrastructure with Iraqi hands to guarantee the future needs of development [for Iraqis], not foreign corporations.[213]

211 ICP-CL, Pronouncement, "The American Conspiracy to Balkanise Iraq" (late August 1992).
212 Ibid.
213 www.idao.org/2004/10/blog-post.html, accessed 2 February 2005.

Soon after the occupation, on 26 July 2003, the IDAO presented a discussion paper to a seminar in London dealing with national unity and issues confronting the Iraqi people and progressive political forces. It called for an end to the occupation and for the establishment of an elected government in a free, democratic, and united Iraq. It called for free elections to be held as soon as possible: (a) to choose a government that represented the will of the Iraqi people and established constitutional guarantees to protect the national and religious rights of all the people within a united and unified Iraq; (b) in a transitional period, to choose representatives, independent of the occupation forces, in order to draft a new secular constitution and prepare for a free general election; (c) to call for appropriate compensation from the United States and Britain for the death and destruction as a result of their barbaric bombardment of 1991. It also called for an independent body to investigate the organized pillaging of the Iraqi state after the occupation and called for the Iraqi people to deal with the aftermath of the Saddam Hussein regime to guarantee human rights in an attitude of reconciliation.

In an October *Al-Ghad* editorial entitled "Federalism in Southern Iraq," the journal also rejected the notion of federalism in the south. The editorial argued that such federalism was an American scheme to "partition the country in order to dismantle Iraq," which was similar to the British scheme in the 1920s that had intended "to separate Basrah, Amarrah and Nasiriyah from [Iraq]." In March 2004, the ICP-CL issued a further statement on the continued occupation, reaffirming its desire for a unified Iraq and its rejection of American plans. The strong nationalist position of the ICP-CL continues to this day, though its effectiveness has diminished in a disintegrating environment of rising sectarian tensions.

Al-Ghad called for a united front for a free democratic election in January 2005 "supervised by international bodies and [with] a timetable for the withdrawal of occupation forces."[214] *Al-Ghad* also warned that the election, as organized and controlled by the United States, could lead to "civil war manufactured with Iraqi hands directed by the occupation authorities."[215]

[214] *Al-Ghad*, vol. 26, no. 23 (29 September 2004).
[215] Ibid., No. 26 (22 November, 2004).

6

Crisis

Disintegration or Renewal?

When the Central Committee held its Fourth Party Congress in Ziwiah Ka on the Iraq-Iran border from 10 to 15 November 1985, it found itself divided once more over the direction and objectives of the Party. The split in the Central Committee into two distinct groups along ethnic lines had become evident by the plenum of June-July 1984, and crystallized at the 1985 Congress. The Kurds congregated around Secretary-General ᶜAzîz Muḥammad, while the Arab groups gathered under the leadership of Bâqir Ibrâhîm al-Mûsawî, a member of the Politburo; ᶜÂmir ᶜAbd-ul-lah; Mahdî al-Ḥâfiẓ, Mahdî ᶜAbd-ul-Karîm; Nûrî ᶜAbd-ul-Razzâq; Mâjid ᶜAbd-ul-Riḍâ; ᶜAdnân ᶜAbbâs; Muḥammad Ḥasan Mubârakj and ᶜAbd-ul-Wahâb Ṭâhir. In addition to personal animosities between the two cliques, there was also a clear split between the leadership inside Iraq and that from outside that exacerbated their political differences.

The two objectives dividing the Party were whether its immediate priority should be the overthrow of the Baᶜth or the defence of the country in the ongoing war with Iran. Zâkî Khairî led the faction calling for a concentration of Party activities against the possibility of an Iranian occupation of Iraq.[1] The dispute resulted in the expulsion of many in the Arab faction and in a reduction in the size of the Central Committee from forty-four members, which had been elected by the Third Congress, to only twenty-four, as it was announced that twenty members of the Third Congress Central Committee would not be running for re-election. Bahâʾu-d-Dîn Nûrî, Nûrî ᶜAbd-ul-Razzâq Ḥusain, Mahdî al-Hâfiẓ, Muḥammad Nâyib ᶜAbd-ul-lah, Mâjid ᶜAbd-ul-Riḍâ, and Thâbit Ḥabîb al-ᶜÂnî, all long-time members of the Central Committee, were expelled, either because they were accused of being agents of the Iraqi government or because they were described as rightist deviationists. Only sixteen loyal members of the old Central Committee were re-elected. Ibrâhîm al-Mûsawî did not re-nominate himself for the Central Committee, and others were expelled for supposedly

[1] Raḥîm ᶜAjînah, *Al-Ikhtiyâr al-Mutajaddid* (Beirut: Dâr al-Kunûz al-Adabiyyah, 1998), p. 191; and interview by author with Raḥîm ᶜAjînah, London (18 April 1995).

not possessing leadership qualities. The secretary-general was authorized "to choose ten new additional members to the Central Committee at will, with the sole condition that if they were from the south or central regions of the country they had to be of Arab descent, or willing to relocate to these regions."[2]

Raḥîm ᶜAjînah was selected to be on the Central Committee again and eventually became one of the seven Politburo members. Within the deep ethnic split in the Party, he was seen as a moderate. Looking back on this period, he noted:

In hindsight, I was a token Arab who had a good relationship with many of the Kurdish groups, and was always willing to find an accommodation between the disparate factions of both movements. I was easy-going, but sometimes feel it difficult to understand that some in the Party leadership can be so motivated by personal gain. However, I had my own doubts regarding the intellectual bankruptcy of many in the leadership, not least of which [ᶜAzîz Muḥammad] who, as Party leader, was never to be found in the country.[3]

The result of the Fourth Party Congress was disarray within the ICP-CC. The rebel Politburo, Central Committee, and other expelled members took their case directly to the cadre, bringing to their attention the non-democratic practices of the secretary-general. They even went so far as to accuse him of "treason" and "deceit" and of violating a number of Party by-laws, as well as of manipulating and falsifying the results of the Fourth Party Congress, which was a charade of a congress. As evidence, they cited the fact that those who were expelled were known to have been important figures in the ICP-CC leadership for years.

My past experience with some members of the Politburo is not free of real suffering. This, in essence, stems from the bureaucratization and jingoism prevalent within the Party. This destroyed free speech within the Party, and led to an overall lack of criticism in dealing with [corrupt] practices . . . on the basis that dealing with such issues might negatively affect the Party and its activities. These activities were not unknown to either the secretary-general or members of the Politburo.[4]

One of the early responses to the ouster came from Mâjid ᶜAbd-ul-Riḍâ in circulars to the ICP-CC cadre beginning in early October 1985. Many media outlets, both those outside Iraq and clandestine Party publications within the country, published the circulars, giving them great exposure. This exposure also reinforced Riḍâ's special stature, achieved through his personality and the leadership positions he had held in the Party for over half of its life. Riḍâ followed this up in November 1986, when he stated:

During the last few years, a gulf between myself and other Party leaders had arisen and the reason was basically differences of opinion on a number of important issues . . . some facets of general Party policy, mainly the means of struggle and public activity, and some . . . conclusions on the Party program all, of which related to the approach to Party internal life. This gulf increased after the Fourth Congress . . . because of the preconceived intentions to orchestrate its composition . . . and in a private Central Committee circular

[2] ᶜAjînah, *Al-Ikhtiyâr al-Mutajaddid*, pp. 192–193.
[3] Interview by author with Raḥîm ᶜAjînah, London (18 April 1995).
[4] ᶜAjînah, *Al-Ikhtiyâr al-Mutajaddid*, p. 194.

dated the 26 December 1984, a proposal was clearly stated including the names of those involved in a clique inside the Central Committee indicating the means of containing and eradicating this group... and subsequently, on 9 October 1986, I was expelled and my study fellowship was revoked.... As a member of the Central Committee for 21 years and a member of the party for 31.... I do not regret this. I participated in preparations for the Second and Third Congresses... have never been involved in the actions of any breakaway group, and on the contrary, have always defended the unity of the Party.[5]

He gave a more detailed response in December 1987 in the form of an open letter to the cadre. He spoke of the deterioration of the Party after it came under the control of the secretary-general and the Politburo, saying it was "in the hands of a limited number of the Party's Central Committee members," and he delineated the "grave mistakes" of the Party leadership in several areas. In the political sphere, he emphasized that the Party leadership, for personal gain and not for principle, had used "revolutionary phrases" instead of realistic analysis, such as when the ICP became involved in the premature armed struggle involving inter-Kurdish rivalries rather than anti-regime actions that resulted in the loss of a quarter of the Party's *Anṣâr* forces. He also emphasized the Party's contradictory position on the Iran-Iraq war, which saw it prioritize opposition to the regime over the national cause – despite the fact that it had condemned the Iranian violation of Iraqi territory and rejected Iran's declared expansionist intentions in regard to Iraq. But this position did not crystallize into a clear policy that worked to immediately end the conflict, nor did it frankly condemn Iran, whose basic aim was "to confiscate the right of our people to choose the political system they desired and impose an Islamic government by force, or condemn Iranian aggression, in support of the defence of Iraqi independence, its national sovereignty and its right to protect the country from Iranian occupation."[6]

On the organizational level, he emphasized

the phenomenon of bureaucratization, the development of the personality cult, and a control never experienced in the entire history of our Party. The small clique of the leadership substituted orders [and] arbitrary decisions from the top in disregard of the principle of collective leadership.... All this was very often subject to personal whim, nepotism and the encouragement of servile behavior.... Accompanying this was a taking of revenge against those who did not accept these conditions by expulsion, firing and freezing from the Party.[7]

He also condemned the chauvinist (anti-Arab) approach of the secretary-general and the Kurdish groups and their control over the Central Committee,[8] citing the example of their punishing Party members they did not like by sending them to the *Anṣâr* forces.[9]

5 Mâjid ʿAbd-ul-Riḍâ, "Open Letter Towards a Comprehensive Solution of the Party Crisis: Safeguarding Its Unity, and Strengthening It on the Foundation of Legitimacy, Principles and the Primacy of Its Internal Life," unpublished MS (December 1987), p. 11.

6 Ibid.

7 Ibid., p. 13.

8 Ibid., p. 14.

9 Ibid.

ᶜAbd-ul-Riḍâ also pointed out that the leadership completely orchestrated the Fourth Congress and even kept the Central Committee in the dark about its arrangements, under the guise of "security measures." He advanced the idea that the Fourth Party Congress was not legitimate because the attendees had not been elected "and Party organizations had not been consulted, or even told [of the congress] in some cases."[10] According to Riḍâ, seven members of the Central Committee, which amounted to a quarter of its membership, were not even invited to the congress, and a unilateral decision made on the eve of the event by those in control of the Central Committee reduced the number of members on the Central Committee to fifteen.[11] Furthermore, half of the Central Committee were expelled from the new Central Committee – the half that happened to be Arab – and the secretary-general was given extraordinary powers to add the votes needed to select ten more members for the new committee.[12] In addition, no serious discussion of the basic Party documents was permitted,[13] and the results of the election were not even announced at the congress. Thus, ᶜAbd-ul-Riḍâ branded the Fourth Party Congress illegitimate and called for its annulment.[14]

As a result of this confusion, splinter groups proliferated. The young cadre, disillusioned with the political leadership of the Party and under threat from the Baᶜthist regime, began to form splinter organizations in the absence of a credible leadership. One such group described itself as *Munaẓẓamat Fahd al-Thawriyyah* (Fahd's Revolutionary Organization). This group emerged in the middle of 1985, publishing a newspaper called *Al-Munâḍil al-Shiyûᶜî* (The Communist Combatant). Describing itself as an internal circular, the paper called for a rejection of the old leadership that had been unable to fulfil the aspirations of Iraqi communists committed to a more democratic practise within the Party; in fact, it called for a new Marxist-Leninist party altogether. "We must work hand in hand, must work seriously and hard to create the necessary conditions for a new Iraqi experiment, represented in the building of a contemporary party for the working class by emulating Lenin and the revolutionary spirit of Fahd."[15]

Another such group dedicated itself to the challenge of the Party leadership. It issued a circular at about the same time, along the same lines, entitled *Al-Thawrî* (The Revolutionary), which claimed to be directed at Iraqi communists and called for the rebuilding of an Iraqi Communist Party that was now

> suffering from a crisis which had reached a terminal point, and which was a direct result of the rightist opportunism which now permeated all the spheres of political action, in intellectual, organizational and popular spheres ... which is why we call for the rebuilding of the Iraqi working-class party.

[10] Ibid., p. 18.
[11] Ibid., p. 20.
[12] Ibid., p. 21.
[13] Ibid., p. 22.
[14] Ibid., pp. 23–30.
[15] *Al-Munâḍil al-Shiyûᶜî*, vol. 2, no. 11 (July 1986), p. 11.

According to the *Thawrî* group, the Party was now in a fight between two cliques. One was "those who prepared, and succeeded in manipulating their [legitimacy], and all its privileges, which would guarantee them [the right to] any responsibility and the winning of followers." The other group was blamed by the first group for all the negative outcomes and rightist mistakes, having "[falsely] resorted to 'wearing the cloak of revolutionaries' to win more supporters."[16] The *Thawrî* group rejected both quarrelling factions as being equally at fault for the Party's disarray.

Though the Party experienced a number of splits, the faction under the leadership of ᶜAzîz Muḥammad continued to be the group recognized by the USSR. Schisms and confusion became the norm, and the Party was effectively paralyzed. To add to this confusion, the Twenty-seventh Congress of the CPSU was held in Moscow in February 1986, at which the new policy of Perestroika (Economic Restructuring) was introduced. The Iraqi Communist Party saw this policy as nothing more than standard Soviet rhetoric. Thus, because of its traditional loyalty to the Soviet Union, ᶜAzîz Muḥammad, in the report of the Central Committee to the Fourth Congress, addressed Perestroika as if it were related only to internal Soviet affairs and not to the Iraqi situation.[17]

The Iraqi Communist Party and Kurdistan

The five major forces historically represented in the Kurdish region of northern Iraq were the Kurdistan Democratic Party (KDP), the Patriotic Union of Kurdistan (PUK), the People's Kurdish Democratic Party (HASAK), the Socialist Kurdish Party (BASOK), and the Iraqi Communist Party (ICP). Each of these groups controlled certain areas of Iraqi Kurdistan; the KDP in Bahdenan, the PUK in Sulamaniyah, and the KDP and ICP in Arbil. Generally, the ICP maintained a fair if uneasy relationship with the other groups, though it had a special relationship with the KDP because of their similar progressive ideological orientations with regard to Kurdish issues. Attempts were made to bring together all of the Kurdish active groupings into some sort of "Kurdish Front" organization after the mid-1980s. This effort intensified after the PUK was unsuccessful in establishing its own relationship with the Baᶜthist central government in 1985. Consequently, the truce between the PUK and Baghdad collapsed, and fighting quickly escalated, bringing the PUK firmly back within the opposition fold.

The ICP attempted to broker some form of accommodation between the PUK and HASAK, hoping, in turn, to gradually improve PUK-KDP relations as well. Even while the PUK continued to flirt with the Baᶜthist regime, the ICP believed that the PUK's "shifting and temporary" views could not in the end support the chauvinist regime in Baghdad. "[Rather, the PUK would be forced] to return to the JOQD [Patriotic National Democratic Front] opposition, as eventually the negotiations with the regime would reach an impasse forcing the

[16] *Al-Thawrî*, no. 3 (1986), p. 2.
[17] *Al-Thaqâfah al-Jadîdah*, vol. 33, no. 4 (January 1986), p. 76.

PUK to reassert its opposition to the regime."[18] Indeed, by the end of 1984, the PUK had turned against the Iraqi government, prompting the ICP to bring it back into the JOQD fold.

Soon thereafter, the PUK began negotiations with the ICP, allowing Kurds to be brought together under the banner of the "Kurdish Front" with the ICP invited to join. The conciliatory role played by the ICP in its formation allowed seven Kurdish parties (HASAK, PUK, KDP, HASHDIK – the People's Democratic Party of Kurdistan, PASOK – the Kurdistani Socialist Party, and two minor parties) to establish the Kurdish Front on 12 May 1988. In addition to its conciliatory role, it was hoped that the ICP would become a coordinating force, acting as a contact between Arab Iraqi political groupings and the Iraqi Kurds, a role the ICP had played in the 1957 front.[19] To facilitate both its unique role and its non-Kurdish membership, the ICP was exempt from the Front's agreement binding members from joining any other alliances.[20]

The Iraqi Communist Party and Perestroika

Despite the attempts of the Iraqi Communist Party-Central Committee to appear to accommodate the restructuring contained in Soviet leader Mikhail Gorbachev's Perestroika, it did not actually go through with a complete reorientation of its decision-making process. Rather, it introduced some cosmetic changes by apparently opening up discussion, for the first time allowing the entire cadre, as well as the public, access to the main documents of the Party program and to its proposed by-laws. Thus the ICP-CC's response to Perestroika floundered on the two organizational flaws of the style and the approach of its leadership, which was all the while clinging to the old oligarchic style of decision making. According to the testimony of Raḥîm ᶜAjînah, a long-time member of the Central Committee and Politburo,

> When Gorbachev was selected to be the Secretary-General of the CPSU, reports began to arrive in Iraq . . . from the leadership abroad on how the ICP would react to the new directives from Moscow . . . and as a Party organ responsible for Party organization, we arranged indoctrination meetings for the membership, including the international communist movement as one of the subjects of indoctrination. We held discussion groups to identify international transformations through the march of the communist movement(s) . . . discussing the changes in different parties, as well as the "new" issues and questions raised within the movement, in addition to the latest positions on the intellectual and organizational principles [of the movement]. . . . Then we began receiving, from our CPSU contacts, the positions as they were being dealt with in the *World Marxist Review* and at their conferences. We began receiving *al-Nahj* and *al-Thaqâfah al-Jadîdah* as well as other journals that were full of discussions centered on Perestroika. . . . Soon after, members of the Party leadership who had been outside [Iraq] began to arrive and arrange lectures and seminars on the changes in communism and new ideas [emanating

[18] ᶜAjînah, *Al-Ikhtiyâr al-Mutajaddid*, p. 196.

[19] Ibid., p. 201.

[20] Ibid., p. 204.

from Moscow]....The pressure was very strong for almost everybody because of our blind parroting that we always suffered from. I had reservations regarding the developments arising from Gorbachev's ideas but did not express them publicly. However, I say now in all truth, my views were not hidden from the [Party] leadership or our cadres....In my last Central Committee meeting (May 1988)...I offered a detailed intervention on conditions in the socialist countries, and my own view of it concluded by saying... "I confess to you that what Gorbachev and other Soviet leaders are doing is something that I do not understand, [and is] beyond my mental capabilities to comprehend, and I reject it wholeheartedly."[21]

By the late 1980s, the ICP-CC had seemingly been reduced to an appendage of the Kurdish Front, and in practice the Party had come under the sway of its Kurdish wing. This change was due to the combination of CPSU pressure,[22] the Party's isolation in the northern regions of Iraq, and the Party's obsequious position in the Kurdish political milieu. By early 1988, the *Anṣâr* movement had been transformed "into an activity [solely] under the Kurdish wing of the Party, truncating it and eventually leading to its abolition."[23] After May 1988, the Central Committee formally made *Anṣâr* part of the Kurdish section of the Party and dismantled its independent Central Military Bureau.[24]

By the outbreak of the 1991 Gulf War, the Party had been considerably weakened within the Iraqi political environment. Confined as it was – for the most part – to acting only within the Kurdish areas, it was further marginalized by its subservience to the Kurdish political agenda. With its secretary-general and many of its Central Committee and Politburo members residing abroad, principally in Prague and Moscow, internal divisions, "Kurdification," and charges of rampant corruption besieged the Party. *Lajnat Tanẓîm al-Khârij* (the Committee for Outside Organization), which was now led by Raḥîm ʿAjînah, and the Central Committee met in Prague in the summer of 1989 and called for a conference in November of 1989 to discuss the Party's deteriorating status, decline in morale, and apparent organizational chaos that had all intensified following the Fourth Party Congress. Draft reports were prepared for discussion at the conference, including a "Political Report" by Raḥîm ʿAjînah, as well as reports on "Democratic Reform" within the Party and "Improving Structures within the Party Organization," and, to combat rampant corruption, a thorough report on "Financial Reorganization," which were all written by ʿAjînah's wife, Bushra Parto. As ʿAjînah noted in his report,

the last setback of the Party and the Kurdish opposition groupings, after the Iran-Iraq war ended, and the intellectual and propaganda campaign against the Party intensified from the Baʿthist dictatorship – in addition to the destructive [elements] from both right and left – resulted in the intellectual [malaise] of the Party.... depending heavily on the vigor of the members' intellectual behavior, Party organization, as well as the

[21] Ibid., pp. 205–206.
[22] Ibid., p. 180.
[23] Ibid., p. 261.
[24] Ibid., p. 181.

organizational structure of the Party, could not stem the onslaught and internal disintegration. The unity of the Party, as well as its strategic and tactical policies, in addition to its future, became of concern for all comrades and all levels of the Party organization. Discussions and intellectual conflicts, both within and outside of the Party, between both Party members and non-members . . . [allow for] the scientific analysis [which] delineates the failures and problems [of the Party]. . . . the bitterness of our comrades should not push us to become single-minded. Defeatism and disappointment became very common among our younger cadre, which is clearly evident in emigration – such as the large number seeking political refuge in Sweden – resignation from the Party, and an overall reluctance to attend Party functions. . . . they [the young cadre] wanted a quick way to overcome the [Baᶜthist] dictatorship, and therefore, [they have] put all of their hope upon the *Anṣâr* movement and by inference, the Kurdish movement. . . . in these conditions, the Party cannot achieve any form of political victory. . . . What we hope to achieve is a clarity of thought, intellectual unity and a solid Party organization . . . which will require us to redouble our hard work.[25]

Members of the Politburo allowed the conference to proceed despite their increasing uneasiness about the content of the reports. Especially disquieting for them was ᶜAjînah's "Political Report," which was interpreted as an indirect attack on the Party leadership by discussing the chauvinistic orientation among the membership of the Kurdish wing.[26] Furthermore ᶜAjînah identified four cliques from both within and outside the Party membership: (1) a right-wing faction within; (2) a right-wing faction outside of the Party apparatus; (3) an adventurist – albeit comfortable – executive; and finally, (4) a Marxist-Leninist faction that still existed within the Party.[27] Party members from the United States, Britain, France, West and East Germany, Sweden, Czechoslovakia, Bulgaria, Italy, Greece, and Australia attended the conference. Even the Party secretary-general, ᶜAzîz Muḥammad, as well as much of the Central Committee and Politburo, attended. Although the conference and the reports allowed for a critical public evaluation of the Party and its activities, the Politburo considered any discussion of issues and policies within its jurisdiction as outside the purview of the conference to amend or alter, nor would it permit the Party leadership to be accused of wrongdoing. Soon after, the tenor of the conference was established – condemning the performance of the Party executive. Nevertheless, the Politburo hijacked the proceedings, as well as the circulation of the conference's findings and its final communiqué, which the Politburo then sanitized before its dissemination to the ICP-CC membership. A new Party newspaper was established, and a new committee, *Lajnat al-Tanzîm al-Markazî* (the Committee for Central Organization), was put in charge of all political activities. Comprising members of the Central Committee who were close to the secretary-general, the committee was put under the direct control of the Politburo.[28]

[25] Ibid., pp. 334–335.
[26] Ibid., pp. 338–339.
[27] Ibid., p. 340.
[28] Ibid,. p. 258.

Internal dissension became evident during the conference when Fakhrî Karîm physically threatened other members of the Politburo during discussions. Karîm, however, faced no sanction, owing to his friendship with the secretary-general and his personal power base in the Kurdish region. Karîm's financial dealings were criticized at the conference, especially those involving a Party-financed journal, *Al-Nahj*, that was supposed to be the newspaper for Arab communist parties. Instead, it had become a private profit-making venture for Karîm, while its funding, staff, and [initial] circulation base continued to be provided by the ICP.[29] Eventually, Karîm expanded his operations to include the Al-Mada International Arab Publishing House.

The outside cadre considered the conference to be a disappointment and a failure, as it had not addressed what many of them considered the most pressing issues facing the Party.[30] The Party newspapers and other information channels, which were now controlled by the secretary-general, the Politburo, and the Central Committee, gave the conference minimal coverage, thereby making it a non-issue and a non-event. In its first meeting following the conference, the Central Committee – meeting in Damascus – again criticized the activities of the "outside cadre." Yet despite his criticism, the Central Committee promoted one of its most active members, Raḥîm ʿAjînah, to the Politburo.

Preparations for the Fifth Congress

The eight years between the ICP-CC's Fourth Congress and its Fifth (12–25 October 1993) were a bitter and difficult period, during which tangled and bloody events cast their shadows, not only over the Party but also over Iraq and its people as a whole. The same period also witnessed tumultuous developments and dramatic changes on the international political scene. The Iran-Iraq war ended without the establishment of a deeply rooted peace, and while Iraq recovered from this terrible conflict, Saddam Hussein embarked on the ill-fated invasion of Kuwait in August 1990. This conflict brought even greater ruin to Iraq, both from Western weapons and from comprehensive United Nations economic sanctions. Finally, the period witnessed the uprisings in March 1991 that followed the ravages of the Gulf War and ended in ruthless massacres and the displacement of tens of thousands of inhabitants of central and southern Iraq. Parallel to this uprising was another, more successful one, in Kurdistan, in the summer and autumn of 1991, resulting in the elimination of Baghdad's authority in the region and its replacement with the de facto rule of the Kurdish Front.

Internationally, these eight years of turbulence saw first the retreat of the USSR and its allies, then the collapse of the global socialist bloc, and finally the demise of the Soviet Union itself. These developments meant disequilibrium in the accepted power relationships and constituted a challenge to the legitimacy

[29] Ibid., pp. 287–290.
[30] Ibid., pp. 254–258.

of existing socialist and communist parties and polities. The Iraqi regime's wars, along with the disintegration of the USSR, opened the door for the United States and the West to consolidate their presence in the Gulf region, a factor of tremendous prominence in regional politics. Examining the draft documents of the Fifth Congress allows us to observe the intellectual, political, and organizational background of the Party in the light of which the ICP's tasks were later determined.

The "Political and Organizational Report" began with a recounting of the events that followed the Fourth Congress and then moved on to analyse Iraq's political and economic situation, arguing that

> the rulers (the leadership of the ruling Baᶜth Party and the senior state officials) turned into a large bureaucratic parasitic bourgeoisie that established a fascist dictatorship under Saddam Hussein. The latter rules through the security organs and intelligence, which is presided over by his family and a clique of civilians and military officials of the Baᶜth Party and state leadership.[31]

After presenting this gloomy picture of the situation in Iraq, the report concluded that Saddam Hussein's regime survived its political isolation and the deterioration of economic and living conditions because of the factors underlined by the Fourth Congress: Iraq's large oil revenues; the regime's control of the print and electronic media, and its "buying" of overseas media to mislead domestic and international public opinion; the regime's monopoly on partisan, syndicalist, and mass activity; the violent suppression of all forms of opposition; the great support the regime received from the socialist bloc and the West in the past; imperialist zeal in maintaining Saddam Hussein's regime as a means of blackmailing the region's peoples; the fragmentation of the opposition; and finally, the fact that most opposition activity was now forced to take place abroad.

The report also affirmed the soundness of the Party's position towards the Iran-Iraq war. It then examined the invasion of Kuwait and stressed the Party's position at that time, which encompassed both a denunciation of the aggression as an outrage that subjected the region to further American intervention and a call for the withdrawal of foreign fleets, and the Iraqi army, from Kuwait, out of respect for Kuwait's sovereignty. The report then looked at the human, material, and environmental balance sheet resulting from the war. Regarding the uprising of March 1991, the report mentions four factors responsible for its failure to topple Saddam's rule in southern Iraq – namely, the haphazard nature of the uprising, the failure of opposition leaders to perform a political role and be present in the field, the lack of unity of the opposition groups, and the lack of support by the United States and the Gulf states. About the international resolutions that followed the invasion of Kuwait, the report affirmed the Party's acceptance of most of them, though with certain reservations. The Party also

[31] Iraqi Communist Party, *Wathâʾiq al-Muʾtamar al-Waṭanî al-Khâmis* (Baghdad: Tarîq al-Shaᶜb, 1994), p. 32.

pointed out, however, that the United Nations' sanctions had become a crushing burden for the Iraqi people. The Party therefore

1. Called for the lifting of UN sanctions, and for securing food and medicine for those who needed them through the direct provision of the United Nations; and
2. Appealed to the international community to tighten the noose around the Baᶜth dictatorship and to try Saddam Hussein and his senior officials for their crimes before an international tribunal.

The Party also expressed its reservations about the international demarcation of the border between Iraq and Kuwait, as the people of neither state had been given the opportunity to freely endorse it.

Rejuvenation of the Party was another concern of the report, and it endorsed a number of older Party slogans, such as "the necessity of rejuvenation" for the apparatus and leadership. The report recorded the efforts already made in this direction, such as the general distribution of the Politburo's bulletin (September 1989) that called on all organs and members of the Party to take part in the selection of Party leadership and in the formulation of Party programme documents. The Central Committee meeting of September 1991 resulted in

> our Party's examination of theoretical generalizations and concepts, driven by a revulsion against blind imitation of another country's experiences. It is inspired by the Marxist approach, and hence, the objective examination of reality and its possible development, our people's struggle and their problems, traditions, and revolutionary heritage, as well as [the intention to] benefit from global experience.[32]

On the organizational level, the report mentioned that the Party had adopted the formula of democratic centralism on the basis of proper theory, which is different from the faulty application of bureaucratic centralism evident in the world communist movement. It also encouraged intellectual exchange within the Party and discussed, in favorable terms, the activities and role of the Party's guerrilla units since the adoption of the armed struggle in 1980–1981.

As for national alliances, the document pointed out that the ICP-CC decision to participate in the founding of the Unified Nationalist Iraqi Congress was central to the dislodging of the Baᶜth, the modest role assigned to the ICP-CC in the convention's central organs notwithstanding. The decision to join the convention was based on the view that being a part of this institution, which included the majority of the active opposition forces, was better than remaining outside of it. It also drew attention to the Party's criticism of the convention, centered on its own weak representation and the degree of foreign influence. Regarding the Kurdish issue, the report hailed the cessation of conflict between the Kurdish parties and the eventual formation of the Unified Kurdish Front. Though the end of the Iran-Iraq war allowed Saddam Hussein to deploy his full military forces against the Kurds, the Gulf War, the 1991 uprisings, Western

[32] Ibid., p. 58.

"no-fly zones," and Western support for the Kurds had forced Saddam to withdraw from the northern regions. As a consequence, regional autonomy was inaugurated; a Kurdish cabinet was installed, in which the communists held one ministerial position; and several communists were elected to the National Kurdistan Legislative Council. In addition, the Central Committee endorsed a call for the establishment of a separate Kurdish Communist Party parallel to the ICP-CC. The report summed up the Party's tasks as being (1) to rally the masses, (2) to establish and consolidate the national alliance among opposition forces, (3) to preservate and expand democracy in Kurdistan, (4) to consolidate Party organization, and (5) to establish intellectual traditions for the study of the Iraqi context.

In the report, the ICP-CC also attempted to sum up the causes of division and fragmentation in the Arab political context. On religious groupings, the Party believed that it was now necessary to distinguish between the groups on the basis of their aims. Yet the Party would continue to criticize their backward ideological propositions. Finally, regarding the international situation, the report outlined the factors that led to the collapse of the international socialist experiment: a lack of democracy; the prevalence of bureaucracy; technological backwardness in the Soviet state; the burdening of society with a costly arms race; rigid dogmatism; the alienation of workers from public ownership; and the subversive role played by domestic and foreign forces hostile to socialism.

The report, therefore, did not consider the collapse of the socialist bloc to be a defeat, but rather an opportunity for further education regarding the proper application of theory under real conditions. The Fifth Congress was the first that followed the tumult of Perestroika and, thus, was a watershed regarding the various tendencies manifested in the general debate. Indeed, at the congress, many of these tendencies were endorsed as the future direction of the Party, either intellectually or organizationally. However, the "Political and Organizational Report" did not break away from the substance and form of the old discourse. In fact, the programme, the second document endorsed by the Fifth Congress, was only slightly and insubstantially modified. The most important of these modifications regarded the structure of the document, the delineation of the interim, the Party's long-term objectives, and a coalition government's functions – namely, the establishment of democracy following dictatorship. The most striking feature of the programme is that it does not outline the Party's ideological character. Such small changes may have been acceptable before the 1990s, as it was possible to determine the intellectual orientation of Arab communist parties supporting the Soviets as soon as they declared their commitment to Marxism-Leninism. However, in the early to mid 1990s, such an omission required attention, especially with regard to parties that had declared their rejection of what they termed the bureaucratic (or distorted) model.

Nevertheless, the Party continued to support the slogan calling for "rejuvenation," though it did not outline its goals or any methods of securing them. The document is strikingly truncated and general, although the latter characteristic may have been intentional, to avoid disputes and preserve unity. ʿAzîz

Muḥammad, the secretary-general, declared on Kurdish television on the eve of the Congress: "It is difficult to overburden the Congress.... Our Congress' task is therefore to deal with the 'ripe issues,' the essential features, of which the comrades are informed, so that they will reach a common appraisal of these issues and leave the other controversial issues to the future." Supporting these comments is the fact that, in general, the document did not contain anything new and the leadership's discussion of rejuvenation did not appear to have been translated into anything concrete. It is probably fair to say that the document represented an interim programme that could be presented by any social democratic party, with certain additions as follows: the checking of parasitical activity, the assignment of some role in the economy to the public sector; and the implementation of certain social reforms.

Under the title "The Tasks for Whose Fulfillment the Party Is Striving," the document outlined the functions of the interim government that would replace the dictatorial regime, which included:

1. Eradication of the consequences of the dictatorial regime's war.
2. Reconstruction and revitalization of the national economy.
3. Defence of the rights of the labouring class through legislation, safeguarding of union freedoms, and implementation of a social security system.
4. Development of productive forces in the countryside.
5. Protection for consumers against the excesses of parasitical activity.
6. Repair of the environmental damage caused by Saddam's wars.
7. Provision of free healthcare.
8. Reappraisal of the educational system.
9. Rebuilding of the armed forces on a democratic basis and rejection of militarism, as well as establishing freedom of political action for members of the military.
10. Affirmation of the Kurdish people's right to self-determination.
11. Continuation of the struggle to emancipate women.
12. Assigning to youths and students a more concrete role within the Party and affirming of their right to establish their own organizations.
13. Reduction of the negative impact of Saddam's dictatorship on Arab relations.
14. Support for efforts to resolve the Arab-Israeli conflict on the basis of international legitimacy and the liberation of all occupied Arab territories.
15. Establishment of security and a just peace as well as neighborly relations, in the region.
16. Establishment of a just world order and world peace, as well as the writing off of Third World debt.

Among the controversial points in the document was number 9, which would not only make the politicization of the army possible but would also potentially involve the military in conflicts among the various political forces in Iraq, this in a country where the military is the most effective institution with regard to organization and capacity for action. The document stipulated that the Party adopt Marxism, though with a conspicuous absence of Leninism. Apart from this modification, there is little to indicate what model the Party intended to follow, especially given the public questioning of the Soviet system.

The "document of the by-laws" followed the same pattern and reiterated the goal of rejuvenation, also without giving any concrete direction. On the contrary, old discourse was recycled for a new application. The by-laws also emphasized democratic centralism, a doctrine that had already been abandoned by many communist and leftist parties. Outside of top Party groups, the document aroused suspicion among many communists for two reasons: first, democratic centralism would continue the power of the bureaucracy, and second, democratic centralism had proven in practice to be a stumbling block on the way to democracy. The "Political and Organizational Report" stated that "The democratic centralism we are striving to preserve, however, is not the centralized bureaucracy and misapplication which the international communist movement has supported for a substantial part of the Communist Party of the Soviet Union's existence." Yet the features of democratic centralism outlined by the by-laws presented nothing novel to suggest a break with the past.

Regarding the rights of minorities and of the lower Party organs, the report also presented nothing new. These rights could easily be withdrawn at any moment, a fact that had been confirmed in the experience of many communist parties, especially the ICP-CC. The by-laws also referred to the lower groups' monitoring of the upper ones, without explaining either the nature of the regulatory mechanism or how such regulation could be made mandatory, a clear starting point for corrective action. It was also assumed that under such centralized democracy, the references in the document to elections and secret balloting were purely cosmetic. Further, the ICP-CC's by-laws provided for such a democratic right to be revoked when the Party's hierarchical powers, such as the Central Committee, determined the election rules and proportions of representation at the National Congress. Article 14 of the by-laws stipulated that those who would attend the Congress be "those concerned prominent Party personalities whom the Central Committee names as members of the congress, subject to the endorsement of the congress and provided that they do not exceed 10% of the total number of delegates." Also, according to Article 18, the secretary-general's function was "to represent the Central Committee and the Politburo in all Party organizations and in public. He holds primary responsibility for the implementation of its resolutions, in addition to his supervision of the preparation of reports of Central Committee meetings." ... Thus, the by-laws invested the secretary-general with broad and unchallenged authority. It was in this Stalinist tendency that the ICP-CC's dilemma lay, expressed in the context of highly complex, circumstances.

The Central Committee did, however, realize the need to provide at least some method for Party cadres to have input on the draft documents under consideration for the Fifth Congress. This was clearly expressed in the directive that came from the meeting of the Central Committee to the cadre in the middle of September 1991:

> The meeting reviewed the great changes that have taken place in the international situation and the collapse of the socialist camp in the countries of Eastern Europe and the Soviet Union that have resulted in a setback to international communism . . . and reached a number of preliminary conclusions regarding them. . . . The Central Committee continued its work through an exhaustive discussion [on the topic resulting in] the appropriate decision to hold the Fifth National Congress of the Party in order to approve the drafts of the two documents of the new Party program and its by-laws in the light of the felt need to renew itself intellectually, politically, and organizationally, and to distribute [the documents] to all Party organizations to study and provide feedback.[33]

The discussion initiated by Central Committee and the subsequent responses that were published in its journal, *Al-Thaqâfah al-Jadîdah*, evidenced the confusion within the cadre(s). Some of the comments were profound in their call for complete change, including the need for "new realistic discourses free of the [personality] cults and the old sterile moulds, and suggested ways to steer away from two dangerous tendencies: first, the conservative outlook which refuses change and the integration of [new] phenomena in life, and second, the radical view which rejects all the past along with its positive aspects."[34] A question that was raised by Sâmî Khâlid (a journal participant) was the degree to which the programme documents were synchronized with the current developments in the local, Arab, and international spheres, and whether they accommodated these developments.[35] The journal allowed non-Iraqis, non-communists, and even some known anti-communists to participate in the Party's soul searching. One warned that in the renewal taking place in the Iraqi communist movement, two considerations must be taken into account, namely, the peculiarities of the Iraqi situation, and "the need to learn from the pioneering experiments that others were engaged in without completely imitating them."[36] The discussion in *Al-Thaqâfah al-Jadîdah* continued for over two years prior to the opening of the Fifth Congress, and the responses varied from a rejection of Perestroika to a rejection of the entire Marxist-Leninist past. The majority of the discussion centred on three themes: the international situation, the Arab front, and the local level.

33 "Pronouncements on the Meeting of the Iraqi Communists," *Al-Thaqâfah al-Jadîdah*, vol. 38, no. 12 (November 1991), p. 5. The Party programme and the proposed by-laws were disseminated in many forms, but for our documentation we are using "The Draft of the Iraqi Communist Party Programme Document," *Ṭarîq al-Shaʿb*, vol. 57, no. 7 (mid-October 1991), pp. 6–7, and the "Draft of the Proposed By-Laws," *Al-Thaqâfah al-Jadîdah*, vol. 39, no. 1 (November 1991), p. 13.

34 Sâmî Khâlid, "A Contribution to the Discussion of the Draft of the Party Programme." *Al-Thaqâfah al-Jadîdah*, vol. 39, no. 4 (February 1992), p. 15.

35 Ibid., p. 17.

36 ʿAlî Ibrâhîm, "On the Draft of the Internal By-laws and the Political Programme and Other Thoughts," *Al-Thaqâfah al-Jadîdah*, vol. 39, no. 4 (February 1992), p. 17.

The International Situation

Most of the contributors to the discussion in *Al-Thaqâfah al-Jadîdah* accepted both the premise that democracy was the essential component of the current international environment and the liberal interpretation of democracy. For example,

> It ["democracy"] is not any longer an abstract term but a specific political structure expressed in a supremacy of the law, a multi-party system, parliamentary life and organization, press and party freedoms, and that these concepts now have new specific meanings based on the right of human beings to live freely and with dignity.[37]

The Central Committee's document did not truly explain the reason for the failure of the Soviet experiment. Rather, it skirted the issue, dealing with democracy only in traditional communist discourse, as a capitalist bourgeois phenomenon, in the same way it would have been discussed prior to Perestroika. Democracy, human rights, and social justice as described in the feedback in the Party's journal were interpreted as positive features of the technological and scientific revolutions that are still taking place. However, according to Suᶜâd Khairî, an old hand in the Party but by this time outside the Central Committee, the negative aspects of this revolution were ignored, and

> the structural crisis which has engulfed the entire world [economy] is the cause of the backwardness of the relations of production in socialist and Third World countries in comparison to highly developed capitalist countries, because of the [success] of the technological revolution.... a number of factors have played a role in the explosion of the crisis in the socialist countries. Foremost among them is the sensitivity of the more conscious society [the socialist camp] to the negative ramifications of espousing the technological and scientific revolution and its principles, and that this brings about a great distortion to relations of production in socialism.[38]

In other words, the technological revolution tilted the international balance in favour of capitalism and created the crisis in the communist movement. Khairî proposed taking the following three steps to deal with the crisis in the social and economic spheres: (1) work seriously to understand the ramifications of the technological revolution, (2) work to spread this understanding, and (3) create internationally committed local and public organizations that would coordinate their activities to readjust the international balance and impose new international relations based on "the respect for human rights everywhere in today's world, and progress to the world of prosperity, freedom and brotherhood," and in this way stop the exploitation inherent in capitalism.

[37] Ibid.; see also Khâlid, "Contribution to the Discussion," p. 17.

[38] Suᶜâd Khairî, "The Responsibilities of the Communists Today," *Al-Thaqâfah al-Jadîdah*, vol. 39, no. 5 (March 1992), p. 33.

The Arab Front

The Party draft document was less contentious when addressing issues regarding the region. The majority of those who wrote responses in the Party journal more or less supported the Party's draft programme, accepting it as a guide for the future. There were no disagreements on the general notion of Article 13 of the draft programme, which emphasized the Arab nationalist component of the Party's future direction. What was innovative in the document was that

1. The platform of the Party, for the first time, emphasized nationalist orientations in that it declared that one of its responsibilities would be "to participate actively in all mutual [Arab] struggles against imperialism, Zionism and Israeli expansionist policies in the defence of the Arab people." This was quite a departure from the traditional Marxist and the Arab communist views in which Arab reactionaries were placed among the enemies that the communities were united to fight against. In the proposed draft this orientation was completely dropped.
2. The Party insisted on "mobilizing the mutual cooperation among the party's political, cultural and popular organizations in the Arab world for the cause of democracy and the respect of human rights."[39] The main activity of the Iraqi Communist Party was now political and no longer predominantly economic, the direction that had been the essence of all previous Party stands. Furthermore, this struggle was open to all other parties and did not give the communists a special leadership role.

Some of the responses did not see this programme to be a switch or to be opportunism, but rather looked upon it as being a realistic understanding of the political environment of the Arab world. There was a "need to acquire support and legitimacy from the Arab brethren because it [was] a time when the Arab states are in their 'golden age' [of control] through severe oppression, the effectiveness of suppressive state organs and [in] their neglect of human rights." According to the same response, "democracy should be the most important component of the Party ... which is not only a political issue but a humanitarian one. When we call loudly for democracy we must call for it with the same level of enthusiasm for everyone.... It is this that distinguishes us from others."[40] This also, according to the same author,

> did not mean the truce with reactionaries in the Arab world was to continue indefinitely. When the time comes, the pragmatic position of the Iraqi Communist Party today will give the Iraqi democratic movement the position of being an active Arab force for the creation of a democratic Arab solidarity which will restore self-confidence to the Arab citizen ... and which will increase the demand for democratic rule and peace, based on the rejection of military aggression, respect of neighbors, and destruction of military

39 Saʿd Ṣâliḥ, "The New Draft Programme Document Between Discourses and Questions of the New Reality," *Al-Thaqâfah al-Jadîdah*, vol. 39, no. 5 (March 1992), p. 20.

40 Luṭfî Ḥâtim, "Yes for a National Comprehensive and Transitional Government," *Al-Thaqâfah al-Jadîdah*, vol. 39, no. 5 (March 1992), p. 74.

bases. These aims will form realistic steps towards Arab cooperation of different forms which will promote the work to achieve collective unity between all the different trends and Arab political groupings.[41]

Thus Arab nationalism was given a democratic content through the building of a civil society and the protection of human rights. A number of responses to the Party programme and by-laws emphasized this: "The national issue, until now, has been a patriotic question with a social content and thus it is a democratic issue and cannot succeed without a democratic framework."[42] Accordingly, the building of a civil society, in addition to a dialogue among the political and social groups in different Arab countries, became an imperative in order to initiate the process of interaction and discourse that would advance solutions to common Arab issues.[43]

The Local Level

Another notion that emerged on the local level was no different than that expressed by other Iraqi opposition groups. The Party delineated as its most basic task the support of a transitional democratic coalition government after the overthrow of the Baʿth dictatorship (see Article 1), learning from the experience of other socialist countries. An examination of the reactions to the draft programme reflected the following three themes:

1. A new role envisaged for capital in Arab, and regional economic development in the new democratic Iraq through the encouragement of investment in the private sector.
2. A new role for the military establishment as envisaged in Article 9 of the Party programme draft, and a reduction in the military's size and influence, with civilian control in a new civil society.
3. A new perspective on the issue of Kurdish self-determination that world translate into real self-rule in Iraqi Kurdistan and the establishment of a federal democratic republic in Iraq. What the term "self-determination" implied was the right to separate (see Article 10).

The draft of the Party's platform was purported to have been formulated by the Central Committee to fulfil the objective of toppling the existing dictatorship and establishing a democracy in Iraq. That objective required a broad political alliance of all social forces, which would be the most effective means of forming a transitional, democratic coalition government. This inclusive approach reflects three aspects of ICP-CC theorizing: first, pragmatic understanding of the balance of power; second, abandonment of concepts such as the leading role of the working class and its party; and third, a commitment to joint action in the broadest possible alliance. Most studies of the Party's programme

41 Ibid.

42 Ibid.; see also Khâlid, "Contribution to the Discussion," p. 18.

43 Khâlid, "Contribution to the Discussion," p. 19.

point out the significance of the objective assessment of local conditions, as well as the need to assimilate the experience of previous socialist experiments. These analyses lead to the realization that an urgent and massive task exists, namely:

> the building of a new modern party that would adopt a theory based on universal socialist thought in harmony with Iraqi reality. The Party's current objective is the establishment of a democratic society in which social justice would prevail. Socialism is the long-term objective of the post-capitalist stage. It is more developed than capitalism in all respects. Development in the direction of socialism should occur naturally and gradually, and hence the rejection of the concept of so-called "revolutions" or coups, the jumping of stages, and the theory of non-capitalist development and other concepts which aim at the realization of what may otherwise have been a gradualist natural development, through coercion, thus creating a stagnant, malformed society.[44]

One commentator queried how the Party's programme could be articulated to establish harmony among the alternatives (ranging from nationalism to Islamism). The document, however, does not suggest absolute limits or irrevocable formations, and references are made to coalition government and a pluralist democracy and to direct universal suffrage. Nor does the document merely name the post-dictatorship period; it "outlines the tasks that must be accomplished during what is appropriately called the stage of 'democratic tasks,' as this is its major objective based on the close link between political democracy and social development."[45] The communists' responses found in *Al-Thaqâfah al-Jadîdah* were not unified as to the significance of national alliances.[46] Some supported an alliance only of the "Left," whereas others wished to unify only the "major" forces and to disregard the more marginal. Still others rejected alliances with Islamic groups because the foundation of those groups' ideological tenets was identification of communism as the enemy and because of the belief that Islamists would form the primary opposition to democratic forces in the future. These divisions helped keep the Iraqi opposition movement as a whole, not just the communists, from moving against Saddam Hussein's regime. Many respondents argued, however, that it was necessary to avoid vetoing cooperation with any opposition force at this stage, so long as the group supported the overthrow of the Ba'thist regime and agreed to a temporary national coalition government and to national elections at the soonest possible juncture.[47]

The communists' publications identified several topics, theses, and concepts in the new programme of the Party that can be considered wholly "new". First, there was a new conception of the role of capital in development that acknowledged the benefits of an expansion of the local private sector and consolidation of its production of goods and services. It also recognized the internationalization of the production process, accepting a role for Arab and international

[44] Ibrâhîm, "On the Draft," p. 25.
[45] Khâlid, "Contribution to the Discussion," p. 25.
[46] Amîn Dâûd, "Outline on Critical Subjects," *Al-Thaqâfah al-Jadîdah* (January 1992), p. 37.
[47] Ṣâliḥ, "New Draft Programme Document," p. 19.

capital in future development. The question at the intellectual level was distinguishing between productive and non-productive capital. Second, the programme presented a new, more limited role for the military establishment, determined as the defence of the nation's independence and sovereignty, and cast aside the old conception of the military's "nationalist role." The military would be subjected to civilian auditing and disclosure. This could be established only by rebuilding the military in a democratic manner, to prevent it from rising above civilian society, as it frequently had. Care had to be taken to avoid the infiltration into the military of hegemonic forces, which could encourage the emergence of another dictator to lead Iraq to "victory." Third, a new two-level strategic approach to the Kurdish question was presented. The first of these was the ICP's recognition of the need to establish a Kurdish homeland. The second was the view that Kurdish autonomy and self-determination should be a step towards the establishment of a democratic federal republic, a completely new concept for the Party. However, it is unclear what the line between self-determination and outright secession was. Further, there is a sense in the document that the emphasis on self-determination did not negate the need for a rapprochement between the democratic forces of the two peoples or for realistic solutions to inter-communal tensions. These new elements in the Party's programme cannot be fully understood without examining the Party's new by-laws and their relation to the programme. In addition, until they were actually put into practice, the new elements suggested in the programme could not really be tested.

An Examination of the By-laws and Their Relationship to the Party Programme

Most comments published in *Al-Thaqâfah al-Jadîdah* were based on the assumption that, as one commentator asserted, "It is necessary to abandon passive listening to the main Party organs. To be alert intellectually and politically can shake us up."[48] Most of the responses also stressed that the writers did not aim at breaking with Marxist theory only for the purpose of destruction, but sought to contribute to a constructive critique leading to a progressive reconstruction of the Party. The objective was to sharpen the Party's insight and streamline the Party organization. Saᶜd Ṣâlih stated that a cessation of the "veneration" of Party documents would help rid the Party of dogmatism and needless self-flagellation, and create a suitable atmosphere for a useful dialogue that would strip the veneer of "sacredness" from the documents and allow room for insight, opinion, and sagacity. This would also reduce the tendency to stop at generalities, to cover theoretical and intellectual weakness with the rhetoric of class struggle, or to use clichés propagated by the "Big Brothers" in Moscow.

[48] Saᶜd Ṣâliḥ, "The New Draft of the Party Programme and By-laws Between the Clash of the Old Discourses and the Burning New Issues," *Al-Thaqâfah al-Jadîdah*, vol. 39, no. 3 (January 1992), p. 6.

The responses pointed out the frequent contradictions between the programme (the Party's objectives) and the by-laws (the Party's structure),[49] which generally centred on the orientation towards democracy on the one hand, and adherence to old concepts, such as centralized democracy, on the other. The programme focused on renovation, whereas the by-laws went to great lengths to preserve the old procedures and concepts. Further, the documents did not have the linkages and coherence required to prevent a plurality of opinions and interpretations regarding the Party's structure and objectives. Their positions can be traced as follows:

1. Position vis-à-vis the government. The draft programme emphasized "getting rid of, ending, overthrowing, and eliminating"[50] the dictatorial regime. In contrast, the preamble to the by-laws asserted that the party should fight not only against economic and social exploitation, and political and nationalistic persecution, but also for national liberation, the establishment of a democratic socialist society, and the realization of social progress. The question then arises as to the Party's priorities, which the by-laws confirm as being both economic and political. However, the by-laws do not identify the class enemy or the nature of the authority that the struggle is directed against.[51]
2. Guidance by the Marxist approach and the Leninist heritage. This "guidance" is confirmed within both documents: Marxism no longer belongs to a certain party; it has joined the most important theories of human thought in the last century and a half. No one is entitled to exclusive reference to the theory, nor is the communist movement its exclusive guardian. The ICP, however, asserts an entitlement to distinction on account of its being guided by the scientific approach of dialectical materialism in its policy, organization, struggle, and perception of every natural, political, and intellectual phenomena. Adherence to a single venerated theory, one ICP commentator has argued, caused the Party to commit tactical errors in the course of its struggle, by attempting to mould current reality into a theory that was formulated under a different set of circumstances. Therefore, an objective, critical stance must be adopted regarding theory in response to the tremendous developments in the fields of science and technology and in light of society's new spiritual and material needs. Adherence to the scientific, Marxist, dialectical approach will contribute to a progressive conception of the Party's inspiration from around the globe and, especially, from Iraqi civilization.[52]

49 ᶜAbd-ul-Laṭîf al-Saᶜdî, "Theory . . . Programme . . . Organization . . . Objectives," *Al-Thaqâfah al-Jadîdah* (February 1992), p. 30.

50 Abû-Inâs, "A Look at the Programme Draft and the Proposed By-laws," *Al-Thaqâfah al-Jadîdah*, vol. 39, no. 4 (February 1992), p. 30.

51 Ibid.

52 Ibid.

Unfortunately, there existed irresolvable contradictions in this theoretical analysis. A remarkable example is Article 8, which stipulates that "the Iraqi Communist Party is a voluntary association of those who struggle and share the same ideology and devote their lives to the cause of the working class and the masses." Considering that the preamble specifically states that the Party adopts only the Marxist approach, and not the Leninist heritage, this vagueness and its departure from Leninism would seem to leave the ICP without a clear theory to unite its ranks. Article 8 also contradicts the introduction, wherein the Party is described as the "party of the working class, the peasants, intelligentsia and the rest of the masses" and which says nothing about a strict working-class struggle, being rather more inclusive.

This contradiction can be attributed to intellectual and political factors within the ICP, such as "the weakness of the intellectual cognitive aspect in some formulations" and the "use of vague phraseology to avoid provoking future controversy and splits in the Party."[53] There are phrases in the Party documents that were carried over from the old mould, to avoid a massive abandonment of Marxist communist concepts and terminology. Despite attempts to infuse them with a new spirit, they show a tentativeness and fear of future dissent that leads to vagueness and contradiction. The experience of the Party's own discussion regarding these documents proved the necessity of democratic discourse. From 1993 on, the Party has been genuinely open to the democratic approach to resolving political and intellectual issues. One commentator insisted, "If this is truly to be the case, however, the democratic approach must also extend to the response of the main organs to the criticism, and suggestions expressed by the contributions of members and others."[54]

The Concept of Democratic Centralism

The concept of democratic centralism, which became the cause of major differences, not only in the ICP but also in the Arab and world communist movements, is still divisive. This is especially true after the implementation of Perestroika and the collapse of the Soviet system along lines that questioned the value of centralism. The prominence of democratic centralism is due to its historic position as an essential aspect of the ICP's leadership process. It is considered by most analysts to be an obstacle to change and the reform that has not yet been achieved by the new draft by-laws. The principle of democratic centralism

> had an adverse effect on the course of the Party, which was not experienced by other parties that did not practice democratic centralism. In contrast, we note that the democratic parties whose constitutions and by-laws do not embody the concept of centralized

53 Saᶜd Ṣâliḥ, "New Draft of the Party Programme and By-laws," p. 12.

54 Kâmil ᶜAlî, "Observations on the Drafts of the Programme and By-laws of the Iraqi Communist Party," *Al-Thaqâfah al-Jadîdah*, vol. 39, no. 5 (March 1992), p. 7.

democracy have achieved greater unity by their inner democracy with the passage of time.[55]

Subsequent developments confirm this viewpoint. The maintenance of centralized democracy in the draft by-laws was perceived as useful only to limit democratic debate and lead to decision making without consultation. Under Lenin, democratic centralism was dependent on certain historical and social conditions. Its continuation, especially under Stalin, turned it into a check on any process of change, renewal, or response to initiatives from below and ensured the tight grip on power of a clique that blindly supported the decisions of an increasingly isolated inner circle; it became mere centralization rather than democratic centralism.[56]

The Fifth National Congress

Under these circumstances, within both the Party and the country, the Fifth Congress took place in Shaqlawah in the district of Arbil in Iraqi Kurdistan on 12–25 October 1993. It convened under the slogan, "For the purpose of mobilizing our people, lifting the economic sanctions, overthrowing the dictatorship, the establishment of a unified federal democratic Iraq and the defense of the toilers interests." The two basic documents discussed at the congress were the "Party Programme" and the "Internal By-laws," in addition to the political, financial, and organizational reports. Under the tutelage of the Kurdish authorities, the communists received congratulations from the two main Kurdish parties, the Kurdistan Democratic Party (KDP) and the Patriotic Union of Kurdistan (PUK). In addition, the communists received a message of support and congratulations from the majority of the opposition groupings, including the conservative and religious ones, as well as from the regional Tudah of Iran; the Turkish Communist Party; the communist parties of Syria, Lebanon, Jordan, and Sudan; and the Syrian Baᶜth and its Iraqi affiliates, in addition to the French, British, American, Cypriot, German, and Korean communist parties.[57] Over the course of two weeks, the Fifth Congress devoted its entire time to the slogan "Democracy and Renewal" and asked, "What is to be done to translate this slogan into a left-wing reality in the internal life of the Party in all spheres of its activities?"[58] According to the Party newspaper, the peculiarities of the situation in Kurdistan required that the congress give more attention to the role that the Kurdish communists should play in that area, and the congress approved all the decisions taken by the Kurdish region's organization and the documents it prepared. The congress also endorsed the

55 Muḥsin Ḍâbit al-Jailâwî, "Violating the Established Limit for Discussions," *Al-Thaqâfah al-Jadîdah* (March 1992), pp. 44–45.

56 Zuhdî al-Dâûdî, "Notes on the Draft Programme and By-laws," *Al-Thaqâfah al-Jadîdah*, vol. 39, no. 5 (March 1992), p. 56.

57 *Ṭarîq al-Shaᶜb* (November 1993), pp. 1–5.

58 Pronouncements of the Iraqi Communist Party on the Fifth Congress, 26 November 1993.

"creation of the Iraqi Kurdish Communist Party – which accepts the [complete] independence of this Party in dealing with all Kurdish affairs based on the general programme principles of the ICP."[59]

The Fifth Congress showed its concern about the growth of the "Black" (religious) fundamentalists as a result of the Arab governments' failure to deal with the problems of the masses, and their denial of people's democratic rights. Regarding Iraq, the congress gave

> exceptional attention to the issue of economic sanctions imposed on the country since 1990. These have taken our people to unbearable limits and ignore all the evidence that the existing ruling clique is the cause of all the disasters that have afflicted our people and nation. [The sanctions] are used as a cover for [the government's] responsibilities [for] these disasters."[60]

The congress called for the removal of the sanctions, and it also condemned UN Security Council Resolution 773, which established the borders between Iraq and Kuwait, considering this resolution to be a decision made under duress. The ICP considered itself to be "the Party of the working class, peasants and all toilers," and it identified the toilers as those who work "with their hands and those who work with their brains for the defence of the popular masses and their rights and struggle for the creation of a unified, federal Iraq." Although it declared its adherence to Marxism in thought and as a guide for achieving its socialist choice, it did not commit itself to Leninism. Rather, it avoided the traditional emphasis on Marxism-Leninism and even avoided going into an explanation for the failure of the socialist experiment. Indeed, "it rejected the claim that the collapse [in the socialist countries] is a defeat [for] socialist thought."[61]

Shortly following the Fifth Congress, in a public meeting in November in Arbil attended by two thousand the new secretary-general of the Party, Ḥamîd Majîd Mûsâ, attempted to outline the innovative changes agreed to by the congress participants:

> We have agreed, as delineated by the Party by-laws, that Marxism will be a guide to lead the Party in its struggle, efforts, and activities to understand the realities of Iraqi society in its specific traits, and this will become the intellectual identity. And we mean by "Marxism" the thoughts of the founders, Marx, Engels, and Lenin, and all the developments that took place after Lenin's death by Marxist theorists and the international communist movement. As communism did not disappear with the collapse of the Soviet Union we must work to develop and enrich Marxism with the new realities.... Marxism is a basic direction and a guide, which will always be enriched by innovation....
>
> The Fifth Congress examined the principle of democratic centralism.... while we disagree with those who believe that democratic centralism is the reason for the collapse of the Soviet Union... democratic centralism, known to us in theory, was derogated

59 *Ṭarîq al-Shaʿb* (November 1993), p. 8.
60 Ibid.
61 Ibid.

during the years of the "personality cults" and ideological rigidity which dominated the CPSU.... This was not only limited to the CPSU, but extended to the communist parties of Eastern Europe and was carried to the underground parties, among them, ourselves. It is important that we develop this principle [of democratic centralism] from these distortions, which transformed the principle to an authoritarian, administrative bureaucracy.... The Fifth Congress forbade the transformation of democratic centralism to one of a central bureaucracy....

Iraqi communists are serious about strengthening dialogue, understanding, and a respect [for] other views.... For that reason we are moving away from copying, imitating, and a mechanical reproduction.[62]

In reality, the Fifth Congress covertly transformed the Party from a Marxist-Leninist party into a mild, social democratic one. Also in evidence was the absence of such traditional communist slogans as "the proletariat," "the vanguard party," "class struggle," "state economy," and "the mobilization of the masses" in preparation for a socialist state. Although the "Pronouncement of the Central Committee" emphasized the creation of a unified, federal and democratic Iraq, the internal by-laws still stressed democratic centralism, as in the past.[63] Furthermore, despite the fact that Party pronouncements after the congress claimed that more than half of the Central Committee members were new, in reality there were not many new names on the Central Committee or Politburo; although some members may not have held a post in the previous Central Committee, an examination of the names of the newly elected members showed that most of them were from the old groups.

Ḥamîd Majîd Mûsâ was a devoted ally, if not a disciple, of ᶜAzîz Muḥammad, and after the close of the congress, the old secretary-general, accompanied by his replacement, visited all the Kurdish parties and affirmed their commitment to Kurdish unity and national aspirations. On 11 November 1993, they met with Masᶜûd Bârzânî, the head of the KDP, and on 15 November 1993, Jalâl Ṭâlabânî, the head of the rival PUK, received them. On 14 November 1993, a delegation from the ICP visited the Conservative Party of Kurdistan in Arbil, where they affirmed the Party's commitment to cooperation and support for the aspirations of the Kurdish people and the overthrow of Saddam Hussein. On 16 November 1993, ᶜAbd-ul-Razzâq al-Ṣâfî, a member of the Politburo, met with the rest of the Iraqi opposition groupings in Damascus, briefing all of them, including the Baᶜth leadership in Syria, on the congress's activities, after which he received their blessings. And on 17 November 1993, the Party of the Toilers of Kurdistan paid a call on the ICP at its headquarters in Arbil, Kurdistan. Among the first to visit the ICP-CC at its Arbil headquarters was the conservative, pro-American, Dr. Aḥmad al-Chalabi, head of the Iraqi National Congress (INC), who congratulated the new leadership of the ICP.[64] On 28 November 1993, the secretary-general was invited to speak before the Organization of Islamic

[62] Ibid., vol. 59, no. 4 (late November 1993).
[63] Ibid., p. 2.
[64] Ibid. (November 1993), p. 1.

Action, Iraq, where he conveyed his Party's commitment to be open to all opposition groupings and to avoid ideological conflicts.[65]

As decided at the Fifth Congress, the by-laws moved the Party from a traditional Marxist-Leninist discourse into the contemporary framework of liberal democratic parties. They described the ICP as

> democratic in its essence, aims, structure, organization, and activities, and in its relationship with other political and social forces. It rejects all forms of totalitarian, oppressive rule, and the violation of human rights. The party struggles to create a democratic political system that ensures social justice. Thus, the ICP is an independent national party that places the primary interests of the people and the nation above any other interests. It defends the welfare of the working class, the peasants, and the rest of the toilers, and seeks [to protect] the aspirations and national interests of the Iraqi people, as well as taking pride in the achievements and revolutionary traditions of the Iraqi people, and derives from these its determination and commitment to strengthen Iraqi independence and national sovereignty.[66]

The "Party Programme" document delineated the ICP's Iraqi-centered orientation:

> The Party derives, in its programme, everything that's progressive [in] the civilization of the nations of Mesopotamia and the human civilization, in addition to the accumulated experiences of struggle for the Iraqi nation.... It assembles its programme document based upon the study of the class, national, and religious realities of contemporary Iraqi society, guided by Marxism, taking advantage of all socialist and human heritage.[67]

To achieve these aims and challenge the oppressive dictatorial regime of Saddam Hussein, the ICP pledged to work in an alliance with all social and political groups, in hopes of forging a unified front to overthrow the regime.[68]

The Kurdish Connection

ʿAzîz Muḥammad's long association with the Kurdish region, stemming from his own Kurdish heritage and from his personal relationship with Muṣṭafâ Bârzânî (and, after Bârzânî's death, with Bârzânî's sons, who inherited his leadership position), in addition to his role as head of the Kurdish section of the ICP-CC since the 1960s, gave the Kurdish issue a special meaning for him personally and, by extension, for the ICP-CC. This focus reached its peak after 1979, when ʿAzîz Muḥammad's control of the entire Party also reached its zenith. With the demise of Party influence in the Arab region of Iraq, and with the increased in influence of the Kurdish national parties, the main theatre of ICP-CC operations became the northern Kurdish region. These activities reached a climax in the 1990s, in the aftermath of the 1991 Gulf War that saw

[65] *Ṭarîq al-Shaʿb* (late November 1993), p. 1.

[66] Iraqi Communist Party, *Wathâʾiq al-Muʾtamar al-Waṭanî al-Khâmis*, p. 114.

[67] Ibid., p. 100.

[68] Ibid., p. 101.

the retreat of Saddam Hussein from the region on the heels of the disintegration of the ICP-CL leadership. The ICP-CL had also been very active in the northern region between 1973 and 1978, while the ICP-CC and the Baᶜth National Front were allies.

The Party became increasingly active only in Kurdistan, through its Kurdish section, and was an involved partner in the political life of the northern region, so much so in fact, that at the Plenary Session of the Central Committee in September 1991, it was decided that the Party's Kurdish section should be semi-autonomous. For this reason the Party decided to hold its much-delayed Fifth Congress in Kurdistan. The secretary-general maintained that preparations for the Congress had taken place in a very democratic environment and that the election of delegates, and later their participation in the congress, had been completely unrestricted, although ᶜAzîz Muḥammad lamented the non-participation of the other sections of the country still under the control of Saddam Hussein.[69] This condition undoubtedly strengthened the tendency of the cadre to develop in a totally divergent direction and establish itself as a faction suspicious of the Central Committee. Thus, in 1993, the Fifth Congress formally sanctioned the de facto status of the Kurdish section. By then the Party was openly identified with the Kurdish region and recognized by the Kurdish leadership and government. As such, it was able to participate publicly in the political life of Kurdistan and in its parliament and government, though Kurdish suspicions towards the communists did not disappear. The Party's press operated legally, and its leadership was now able to call for and hold mass public meetings. This allowed Secretary-General ᶜAzîz Muḥammad to tour the main cities of the region and to hold mass meetings with ICP-CC members. At one such meeting, in Kifri, he was only a few meters from the territories still controlled by the regime of Saddam Hussein.[70]

Nevertheless, basically because of the complicated nature of the Kurdish groupings, the ICP, operated on the periphery of Kurdish politics, concentrating on attacking the common enemy, the Baghdad regime, in every possible way. It avoided becoming directly involved in the internal conflicts among the Kurdish national groupings, especially after its disastrous experience in 1983, in the Pasht Ashan region, when its involvement in intra-Kurdish conflicts led to the capture and massacre of the *Anṣâr*. Instead, in the 1990s, the ICP played the role of a pressure group and peacemaker in a number of incidents among the conflicting Kurdish groupings; for example, in August 1994 it organized public demonstrations and marched on the Kurdish parliament to condemn the fighting that had broken out between the Patriotic Union of Kurdistan and the Kurdistan Democratic Party two weeks earlier and to call for a reconciliation between the two groups.[71] It remained careful not to offend any Kurdish party on any matter. For example, the Kurdish election of 1992 was criticized by the

69 *Ṭarîq al-Shaᶜb* (June–July 1993), p. 9.
70 Ibid. (mid-May 1992), p. 1.
71 Ibid., vol. 60, no. 2 (September 1994), p. 1.

secretary-general because of irregularities and violations, but he did not place the blame on any particular party.[72] On the ideological front, however, the Party continued playing it safe, emphasizing the slogans of Kurdish self-rule it had been advancing since the 1950s. In the early 1990s, such policies included a call for the self-determination of Kurdish people, with an emphasis on self-rule for Kurdistan within the Iraqi Republic.

ᶜAbd-ul-Razzâq al-Ṣâfî, a member of the Politburo, stated that the federalism slogan would be considered "when it becomes possible to unify all parts of Kurdistan, as we believe that all separated areas have the complete right of self-determination." However, he was careful to indicate that the possibility of this would be determined by "local, regional and international circumstances."[73] His calls were not echoed by the new secretary-general, Ḥamîd Majîd Mûsâ, however, they would personally have received his blessing.

The 1993 Fifth Congress of the ICP also accepted the Central Committee's draft recommendation in Article 1, re-emphasizing "the Kurdish nation's right to self-determination in all of its land, its right to national unity . . . and [the need] to increase the mutual struggle and Arab-Kurdish brotherhood, in order to agree on constitutional and [legal] arrangements for the Kurdish region." The ICP delineated its vision of a democratic, federal, multiparty government after the removal of the Saddam Hussein dictatorship. At the congress, ᶜAzîz Muḥammad outlined the Party's plan for Iraqi Kurdistan, which had emerged from the ICP Kurdish section's Second Congress in mid-1993. It called for:

1. The unity of all Kurdish Iraqi forces and their full participation in all legislative institutions.
2. The participation of the Kurdish masses in government.
3. The winning of Arab regional support and the elimination of Arab regional concerns.
4. The strengthening of relations among all democratic and nationalistic Iraqi forces.[74]

The Party continued its attempt to work with all other opposition groupings to gain both legitimacy and acceptance, and slowly reduced its rhetoric to generalities, while reiterating its commitment to Kurdish issues. At the Plenary Session of the Central Committee, which took place between 19 and 24 March 1994, the IPC-CC emphasized the rhetoric of its previous congress, calling for closer cooperation among all opposition groupings.

The Sixth Congress

The Party continued its formal activities preparing for the Sixth Congress, which was supposed to be held at the end of 1996. However, according to the

[72] Ibid., vol. 57, no. 18 (June 1992), p. 1.
[73] Ibid., vol. 57, no. 7 (mid-March 1992), p. 3.
[74] Ibid. (June–July 1993), p. 1.

secretary-general, because of "legitimate circumstances related to the complicated and dangerous security conditions that emerged after the dictatorial forces [of the Baghdad government] occupied Arbil city [the capital of Iraqi Kurdistan] on 31 August 1997,"[75] the Party held its Congress nine months late, on 26–29 July 1997. Preparation for the congress had begun when the Central Committee produced a draft document entitled "Fundamental Topics for Discussion on the Party's Policies and Positions" at the end of April 1996, circulating the document among friends, Party members, and all who were interested in a "democratic" alternative. In the document, the Party described the nature and practice of power by the regime as

> large, bourgeois, bureaucratic, and parasitic, and which gave birth to a dictatorship of a comprehensive fascist pattern headed by Saddam Hussein, who rules the country through security and intelligence agencies headed by his family members and a limited clique that controls the leadership of the state and the [Baᶜth] party.... the social base thus became narrower and the limited few exploited most of the social wealth, and political and economic life [of the country] ... after it had destroyed most of the middle class.... The last three years [ending in 1997] also witnessed a conflict within the ruling clique itself extending to the core of Saddam Hussein's family which was, in effect, the leadership of the regime, over and above state organizations and the ruling party itself.... In addition, the regime strengthened its grip on the special security agencies with the formation last year [1995] of new paramilitary formations to the army, the security forces, and the party. He also created the social strata known as "the friends of Saddam" ... as a distinct class, not based upon huge salaries and benefits, but on great privileges, which allowed this group to become prosperous through access to power and state funds. This stratum served the purpose of creating a new social and economic base for the regime after its grassroots support had withered away over the past few years. The regime also tried to widen its social base to win the support of tribal groups by creating new chiefs and sheikhs through gifts and bribes.[76]

The document identified the dilemma in the political system as a "social, moral, political and economic crisis, which intensifies daily."[77] On the situation in Kurdistan, the document asserted "our Party, particularly its Kurdish section, has tried to stop the conflict between the Kurdish groupings since May 1994, and supports the concept of forming a coalition government from among the various groupings in Kurdistan to bring peace to the region."[78] Additionally, the internationalization of the Iraqi issue as a result of the Kuwaiti venture, and the US/UN control of Iraq through economic sanctions, resulted in a process of demoralization and a dependence on foreign forces to bring about change in Iraq. The ICP-CC called for a new policy, which would strive "to create open political alliances on the principles of intellectual, political and organizational

[75] *Al-Thaqâfah al-Jadîdah*, no. 280 (January–February 1998), p. 82.
[76] Ibid., no. 270 (June–July 1996), pp. 7, 8.
[77] Ibid., p. 9.
[78] Ibid., p. 20.

independence for every group . . . for all political forces that are willing to work for the overthrow of the dictatorship."[79]

On the internal front, the Central Committee complained: "Establishing democracy is a complicated and arduous process. As a result of distorted theoretical notions, the experiences, traditions and practises of the past, this has been made difficult to attain in such a short time."[80] The document went as far as admitting the existence of three competing ideological trends within the Party that could hinder democracy, the first being "a conservative trend rooted in the past and not willing to entertain any change, the second being a radical liberal one which wanted to divorce itself from the past, and the third being a moderate trend that sought to adapt realistically to the conditions of the Party and the country."[81]

The document determined the immediate Party aims to be "the overthrow of the ruling dictatorship and the creation of the democratic alternative as an imperative necessity, needed to lead the country out of its crisis and save the Iraqi people from their predicament, and the removal of the comprehensive international sanctions against Iraq."[82] It suggested the following means to achieve these aims: (1) the formation of a democratic coalition government representing all political groupings, which would, with neutral international supervision, oversee elections to elect a constituent assembly that will enact a constitution for a democratic system; (2) the removal of economic sanctions against Iraq and the return of Iraq to the international community as a sovereign state; (3) the recognition of the legitimate rights of the Kurdish people through a federal system and a guarantee of the national administrative and cultural rights of all minorities; (4) the rejection of violence among political forces and a peaceful democratic transition of power; (5) the eradication of the oppressive infrastructure of the Saddam Hussein regime, including the abolition of arbitrary laws and of the police security agencies; (6) the improvement of the conditions of workers, poor peasants, and government officials, and the restoration of national development plans, along with a rebuilding of the national economy; and (7) the development of positive relations with neighboring countries based on mutual interest and non-interference in one another's internal affairs.[83]

This draft programme was circulated and widely discussed for a year and a half in the Party's theoretical journal *Al-Thaqâfah al-Jadîdah*. Some contributors argued for it and some against, but when the Sixth Congress did finally take place, the basic ideas of the document became the Party's political report. Further, the congress discussed a report on relations between the Party and its

[79] Ibid., p. 25.
[80] Ibid., pp. 29, 30.
[81] Ibid., p. 30.
[82] Ibid., p. 32.
[83] Ibid., pp. 33, 34.

Kurdish section, and one that evaluated the experiment of the military arm of the Party, the *Anṣâr* or partisan, movement, in the decade 1979–1988.[84] In the document on the *Anṣâr* movement, the Central Committee admitted that cooperation with the Baᶜth in the National Front alliance of 1973 had been a fatal error. According to this account, documents captured during the 1991 uprisings showed that the Baᶜth had indeed maintained a strategy for annihilating the ICP. As the Baᶜthists began implementing their plan, the Party developed no strategies for defending itself.[85] The document argued that by April 1979, when the *Anṣâr* partisan movement emerged, the political and military leadership of both groups – the partisans and the Politburo – were not compatible.[86] In November 1981, when the Party decided to officially adopt the armed struggle into its praxis, the Politburo took control of the *Anṣâr* movement and unilaterally established a military bureau for the purpose of directing the partisans. According to the Sixth Congress report, this led to confusion and ill-conceived decisions that ultimately resulted in the death of over 150 partisans in June 1987, decimating the movement and effectively bringing it to a halt a year later. The Central Committee, in its meeting of June–July 1987, officially returned control of the *Anṣâr* movement back to the Kurdish section of the Party, condemning it years later at the Sixth Congress as "the wrong application of the armed struggle as the main avenue of liberation"[87] The document argued that this praxis

> pushed the *Anṣâr* movement into unjustified large battles that could otherwise have been avoided, reducing the great casualties suffered by the Party. This sometimes happens because of the miscalculations of the Party leadership, as it happened clearly when the Party became a participant in the conflict between the various Kurdish forces, resulting in the setback of Pasht Ashan in 1983. The difference of opinion amongst the leadership on the necessity of the *Anṣâr* had a negative impact on the movement altogether. Two faulty trends emerged regarding this. One faction underplayed the significance of the movement, while the second exaggerated its importance.... Furthermore, the partisan movement failed to transform itself into a mass movement for both city and countryside.... In addition to the non-principled friction between the [Party] leadership and the partisan cadre... the negative impact of the conflict between Kurdish forces resulted in demoralization and despair amongst the masses, aided by the Party entering into the conflict in favour of one side over the other.... The contradictions and conflicts between the civilian and military wing created difficulties for *Anṣâr* activities and the rebuilding of the Party organization, resulting in the martyrdom of some cadre members who had been designated to help rebuild the Party. Thus, the *Anṣâr* movement was set back in 1988.[88]

84 *Ṭarîq al-Shaᶜb*, vol. 63, no. 1 (August 1997), p. 10.

85 Iraqi Communist Party, *Wathâᵓiq al-Muᵓtamar al-Waṭanî al-Sâdis* (Baghdad: Tarîq al-Shᶜb, 1998), pp. 81–83.

86 Ibid., pp. 84–89.

87 Ibid., p. 99.

88 Ibid., pp. 99–101.

A Central Committee and Politburo were finally elected and Ḥamîd Majîd Mûsâ was reaffirmed as Party secretary-general. In reality, however, the Kurdish section of the ICP-CC was now the true center of power, and the rest of the ICP-CC was merely an arm of the Kurdish section. If any serious activity, including the holding of a congress, was to take place in Iraq, it was forced to be in Kurdish territory and under the tutelage of the Kurdish section. The ICP-CC now confined its activities to the more than two million expatriate Iraqis in Europe, where the secretary-general toured for two months in early 1998, explaining the Party platform and justifying the latest developments.[89] Further, the Party published a monthly news journal called *Risâlat al-ᶜIrâq* (The Iraqi Message), and *Al-T͟haqâfah al-Jadîdah*, which, following the Sixth Congress, transformed itself into an independent leftist journal, no longer solely Marxist. *Al-T͟haqâfah al-Jadîdah* declared in its editorial in February 1998 that

> while it had emerged in 1953 as a vehicle of Marxist and leftist intellectuals whose main mission was to propagate scientific thought and progressive culture, today, while it is still leftist in orientation, within the Marxist orientation, it is now open to whatever is enlightened and democratic in all other intellectual and political currents, on the basis of a respect for other views and a rejection of rigidity and personal political polemics.... while the journal has a special relationship with the ICP-CC... and it publishes some of the central documents of the Party, it welcomes insightful discussion in order to implement democracy, renewal, and dialogue which are the true embodiment of the thoughts and actions of the Party itself.[90]

With the Party journal now transformed, a new editorial board reflecting this change in orientation was put in place, though it was still headed by a member of the Central Committee, Ḥamdân Yûsuf. However, the intellectual confusion within the ICP and its publications was clearly illustrated when the editor of *Al-T͟haqâfah al-Jadîdah*, in explaining the Sixth Congress's policy of free elections in Iraq under the supervision of the UN – as published in *Risâlat al-ᶜIrâq*, the official monthly communist publication – interpreted this idea as a personal view rather than as Party policy, incensing its author, Ḥamdân Yûsuf.[91] Given the radical changes in the Party, this confusion was to be expected. Since the Fifth Congress, the ICP-CC had been transformed into a social democratic party, abandoning many of its Marxist-Leninist revolutionary and proletarian positions, and it was now willing to work with non-revolutionary and non-socialist groupings, including right-wing, religious, and staunchly pro-capitalist parties, to achieve a democratic alternative for Iraq. The Sixth Congress clearly mandated this position when it formulated its vision of a "national democratic project" for the other democratic political forces in Iraq, which would "initiate the building of a democratic multiparty Iraq on the ruins of the dictatorship and

[89] *Risâlat al-ᶜIrâq*, no. 39 (March 1998), p. 6.
[90] *Al-T͟haqâfah al-Jadîdah*, no. 280, (January–February 1998), pp. 5, 6.
[91] *Risâlat al-ᶜIrâq*, vol. 4, no. 40 (April 1998), p. 16.

its agencies and institutions."[92] The secretary-general of the Party found a bond between the national democratic parties, in general, and the Iraqi Communist Party, especially on basic issues such as democracy, human rights, and the rejection of dictatorship. He pledged "dialogue and continuous communications" to influence the "right wing" of the national democratic parties to be more understanding of Third World problems.[93] In the meantime, past–Secretary-General ʿAzîz Muḥammad achieved a large measure of personal acceptance within both camps in the Kurdish dispute, so much so that in mid-1988 he was entrusted with initiating a dialogue between the two major opposing parties in Iraqi Kurdistan.[94]

The Iraqi Communist Party held its first annual conference for expatriate Iraqi communist organizations in Europe, 15–16 May 1998, under the slogan "Supporting the Party's Struggle Within Iraq: The Removal of Economic Sanctions, the Eradication of the Dictatorship, and the Establishment of a Unified Federal and Democratic Iraq." The secretary-general, a number of Central Committee members, and members of both Iraqi and Kurdish sections of the Iraqi Communist Party were in attendance. In accordance with the policies and decisions of the Sixth Congress, the election of the political leadership of these expatriate organizations took place.[95] In the meantime, it was reported that the dissident group headed by Mâjid ʿAbd-ul-Riḍâ had applied for a licence to publish a newspaper for the Communist Party in Baghdad,[96] perhaps, a continuation of ʿAbd-ul-Riḍâ's efforts of 1992.

The march of the Party towards becoming a liberal-democratic left-wing party was tolerated, but when the secretary-general met some American government officials during his visit to Washington, DC, in late November 1999, grassroots criticism of this direction began to be expressed.[97] This discontent would later manifest itself in 2003 with the re-emergence of the ICP cadre as an alternative pseudo-communist force in Iraq within the context of the US occupation.

The ICP and the US Occupation

The Anglo-American–led war on Iraq and Iraq's subsequent occupation led to a further transformation of the ICP from a Party with ideological ties to Marxist, Leninist, and neo-Marxist transformation theories, to an intellectually uprooted and largely pragmatic parliamentary contestant. Originally maintaining a stance somewhat hostile to the United States, seeing the American government as the champion of capitalism and imperialism, the ICP then diluted

[92] *Ṭarîq al-Shaʿb*, vol. 63, no. 1 (August 1997), p. 10.
[93] Interview with the secretary-general, *Risâlat al-ʿIrâq*, no. 39 (March 1998), p. 6.
[94] *Al-Qabas* (Kuwait, 31 May 1998). See interview with Ṭâlabânî.
[95] *Risâlat al-ʿIrâq*, no. 42 (June 1998), p. 9.
[96] Morning news bulletin Monte Carlo Radio, Arabic Broadcasting (12 November 1999).
[97] *Al-Wasat*, no. 389 (7 December 1999), p. 18.

its anti-capitalist rhetoric almost overnight. The outcome of this transformation was obvious: a seat on the Governing Council of Iraq and official political recognition for the Party's leadership by the occupation authorities. However, the cost for the Party was astronomical and involved its being cut off from the movement against the occupation forces, as many of the individuals engaging in active resistance came to see the members of the Governing Council, including the ICP, as "collaborators." In its attempt to hasten the end of the occupation by working in the political structure established under theUS-dominated authorities, the ICP managed to secure for itself a place in the interim Iraqi government, but it divorced itself from its communist roots and the sectors of the population it claimed to represent.

The ICP Before Occupation

Prior to the Anglo-American invasion in 2003, the ICP Central Committee, operating largely in exile, maintained that the only solution to the Iraqi question was unite the efforts of the Iraqi "patriotic forces" to overthrow the hated Saddam Hussein regime and lift the economic sanctions that were strangling the Iraqi people. The Seventh Party Congress, held between 25 and 28 August 2001, followed a meeting of various "patriotic forces" in Paris, to which the ICP had sent a delegation seeking common ground from which to overthrow the Saddam Hussein regime. The Party Congress reiterated the commitments made at the Fifth and Sixth Congresses, emphasizing that the basic aims of the Party were the lifting of sanctions, the overthrow of the dictatorial regime, and the creation of a federal, democratic Iraq.[98] In the secretary-general's political report, he noted that

> the majority of our people are not under the illusion that the US has the intention of overthrowing the dictatorial regime and creating a democratic system, which is sought after by our people. The American administration, whether Democrat or Republican, looks only for a change of leadership and to halt the emergence of a mature popular movement that aims to overthrow the existing dictatorship. Its primary strategy is to protect and guarantee its vital interests in the region, including control over Iraqi oil as well as the economy of the country today and into the future. And this is contrary to the interests of our people and their rights, as well as the country's independence and national sovereignty.[99]

In a plenary meeting held 18 December 2001, following in the wake of the 11 September attack on the World Trade Center in the United States, the Party reiterated its commitment to an internally inspired, popular overthrow of the Baᶜth government and a rejection of the UN-imposed sanctions. However, the dangerous potential of the American "war on terrorism" and its implications for Iraq were already beginning to emerge, forcing the Central Committee to

[98] Iraqi Communist Party, "Wathâʾiq al-Muʾtamar al-Waṭanî al-Sâbiᶜ," *Ṭarîq al-Shaᶜb* (November 2001), p. 87.

[99] Ibid., pp. 62–63.

address this issue. While the ICP joined the public chorus denouncing the attacks on the World Trade Center and the use of terrorism, it also highlighted the danger of leaving too much ambiguity in the definition of "terrorism" and it stressed

> the need to adopt, under the auspices of the United Nations, a clear and precise definition of terror, distinguishing it from peoples' legitimate right to struggle against occupation, for self-determination and [for] free choice of their social-political systems, and to struggle against dictatorial and fascist regimes.[100]

The Party asserted that the United States had used the tragedy as a pretext for advancing a predetermined agenda of "imperialist hegemony."[101] Furthermore, the Party continued to criticize the United States for its unabashed support for "the terror policy of [Israeli Prime Minister] Sharon's extreme right-wing government," as well as for US President Bush's abolition of the norms established in treaties with the USSR on ballistic missiles.[102]

Mild criticism of the US government and US hegemony continued well into 2002. At the International Meeting of Communist and Workers' Parties, in Athens, Greece, on 21–23 June 2002, the ICP Central Committee's head of the International Department, Dr. Ṣubḥî al-Jumailî, presented a paper in which he asserted that some fundamental questions had not been answered about the events of 11 September 2001. The most important of these was "Why did it happen?"[103] He laid the responsibility for the factors that contribute to international terrorism, and specifically anti-American terrorism, primarily on US foreign policy, the US government's hegemonic designs, and the mounting inequality in the world that terror organizations can feed off.[104] The ICP-CC also officially rejected what it referred to as "the war option" and "foreign military intervention." This stance would remain consistent until the US-led invasion began.

The Central Committee continued to push for a "patriotic" solution in which the Iraqi opposition parties would seize the mantle of Iraqi power and institute a democratic and federal government. Included in the ICP-CC's position at the Athens conference was a complete rejection of any participation in the American effort.[105] The history of the duplicity of the US government, especially from the communist perspective, with regard to Afghanistan and Vietnam, indicated to the Party that efforts at "liberation" were typically sought to further the

100 "Communiqué Issued by the Meeting of the Central Committee of the Iraqi Communist Party" (20 December 2001). http://www.iraqcp.org/framse1/00112CC%20-%20Communique%20(20-12-2001)1.htm
101 Ibid.
102 Ibid.
103 Ṣubḥî al-Jumailî, "The New World Situation After the 11th September and Its Impact on the Situation in Iraq" (paper delivered at the Athens International Meeting of Communist and Workers' Parties, discussing "The New World Situation After the 11th September," 21–23 June 2002). http://www.iraqcp.org/framse1/002622ICP%20-%20Athens%20Meeting%20(21-6-2002).htm
104 Ibid.
105 Ibid.

ends of the US elites and rarely served to improve the conditions of the people being "liberated." As war became more inevitable and the US government began to discuss methods of administrating a "post-Saddam Iraq," the ICP-CC continued to protest against the "war option" and insisted that the people of Iraq would unconditionally reject any occupation or foreign military rule, stating, "The declared intention to get rid of Saddam Hussein and his hated regime does not give anyone the right to occupy the country and impose military rule on the people!"[106]

Throughout 2002, the ICP-CC continued to reject any cooperation with the United States and even criticized America for "a return to McCarthyism" and "an evident desire to exercise direct control of the future development of [Iraq], pushing it in a direction suitable with American views and plans, so as to reshape the situation in the area in accordance with strategic interests of the United States."[107] Further, the Party refused to participate in the US-sponsored Iraqi "Opposition Conference" because of the apparent US intentions in the region. The Party's secretary, Ḥamîd Majîd Mûsâ, emphasized that the Central Committee was not interested in taking part in any event that subverted the interests of the Iraqi people to the objectives of the American government. He declared that

> salvation from the dictatorial regime is our cause and the cause of the Iraqi people, and it does not make sense to ignore this and to pin hopes on American war, American invasion and American "liberation". No! This is what the Iraqi opposition should take care not to fall into.[108]

In March 2003, on the eve of war, the ICP-CC, having protested vehemently against "the war option" and US unilateralism, remained visibly undeterred in its stance on separating the liberation of Iraq from the American war movement. In fact, it went even further in tying itself to a potential anti-occupation movement by calling on the Iraqi people,

> caught between the US hammer and the regime's anvil, to remain steadfast and patient, ready to defend their life and their rights, to persist in their endeavour to determine their own destiny themselves, and to establish the unified democratic federal Iraq we all aspire to.[109]

106 "Our Iraqi People Reject Occupation and Foreign Military Rule," *Iraq News: A News Bulletin Issued by the Iraqi Communist Party Information Bureau Abroad* (16 October 2002). http://www.iraqcp.org/framse1/0021017Iraq%20News%20-%20Our%20People%20Reject%20Occupation-%20(16-10-2002).htm

107 "Communiqué Issued by the Meeting of the Central Committee of the Iraqi Communist Party" (15 August 2002). http://www.iraqcp.org/framse1/002823ICP-1%20(22-8-2002).htm

108 "Iraqi Communist Party Leader Explains Reasons for Refusal to Participate in 'Opposition Conference,'" *Iraq News: A News Bulletin Issued by the Iraqi Communist Party Information Bureau Abroad* (24 November 2002).

109 "While the Catastrophe of War Is Looming the Regime Terrorizes the Iraqi People," Iraqi Communist Party Radio, Voice of the Iraqi People, based in Iraqi Kurdistan (18 March 2003). http://www.iraqcp.org/framse1/0030322ICPstatement(18-3-2003).htm

It should be noted, however, that even at this point, the condemnations of the United States and of a potential occupation of Iraq were relatively mild; they did not go beyond the level of analysis provided by the liberal factions of the international anti-war movement and, as later would become clear, were likely to have been merely posturing and empty rhetoric rather than stem from deep convictions or a firm commitment to Marxist principles. Nonetheless, the Central Committee still maintained its public posture of opposition to US invasion and occupation as a means to liberate the Iraqi people.

The position of the ICP-CC shifted in the aftermath of the war. By the end of June 2003, the Party had already reduced most of its rhetoric condemning the United States and the intentions of the Bush administration. Additionally, it opened an office in Iraq in which it entertained visits by US and British representatives,[110] exposing an inconsistency in the Party's proclamations of "Refusing to take part in the American effort."[111] In an interview with Ḥamîd Majîd Mûsâ in *Al-Sharq Al-Awsat*, criticism of the Anglo-American occupation now focused on the Americans' inability to control the occupation scenario, rather than reject the occupation as altogether illegitimate.[112] The ICP reduced its programme for Iraq largely to the forging of a federal system, abandoning its principles in favor of the ends. This stood in contrast to the position declared by the Party at the beginning of the month, when Mûsâ committed the Party to resistance to the occupation, declaring its desire to construct a federal government regardless of the American intentions. In an interview with the Italian daily *il Manifesto*, on 6 June 2003, he said: "They [the Americans] did not come for the sake of Iraqis, but on the basis of a strategy which is in line with their objective and desire to impose their control over the world."[113] He added, "We know very well that the Americans want a government which is in line with their interests."[114] But Mûsâ was careful not to indicate whether the ICP was willing to join in any non-political resistance to the occupation, only warning the Americans of the very real threat of resistance by the Iraqi public if the occupation were to continue.[115] By the end of the month, however, the Party began to drop elements of its earlier program that were consistent with its long-held

110 Visits by representatives of the United States and Britain are confirmed in an interview with Mûsâ by Naṣîr al-Nahr of *Al-Sharq Al-Awsat*, the London-based Arabic daily. "We Could Not Prevent the War... Others Could Not Prevent the Occupation and We Are Dealing Realistically with the Situation" (23 June 2003). http://www.iraqcp.org/framse1/0030705icpLeadershariq.htm

111 Al-Jumailî, "New World Situation."

112 Ḥamîd Majîd Mûsâ interviewed by Naṣîr al-Nahr for *Al-Sharq Al-Awsat*. "We Could Not Prevent the War... Others Could Not Prevent the Occupation and We Are Dealing Realistically with the Situation" (23 June 2003). http://www.iraqcp.org/framse1/0030705icpLeadershariq.htm

113 Ḥamîd Majîd Mûsâ interviewed by *il Manifesto* (6 June 2003). http://www.iraqcp.org/framse1/0030705icpLeader.htm

114 Ibid.

115 Ibid.

ideology, analysis, critique, platform, and demands. Coinciding with this came their active participation in the Governing Council.

The Governing Council

After the Anglo-American–led invasion and the passage of UN Security Council Resolution (UNSCR) 1483, "which in effect gave legitimacy to the occupation authority in Iraq,"[116] the Party emerged with a platform to reclaim a post-Baᶜth Iraq from the "problems which burden the lives of the broad masses" and have "even gotten worse."[117] Mûsâ laid out the basic tenets of the ICP's platform in his *il Manifesto* interview:

> I am talking about what the Iraqis want: A broad government that is born out of a national conference representing all the spectrum of Iraqi society and Iraqi political parties which fought against dictatorship and tyranny. We are now working for establishing a front of political forces, which have a common position with regard to setting up the government. The agreement with regard to this provisional government would deal with: eliminating remnants of the dictatorial regime; striving to rebuild Iraqi institutions and the whole country after the destruction caused by the war; working to formulate new laws and preparing for free elections under the auspices of the UN; preparing a draft constitution and putting it to a national referendum; and then conducting negotiations about the presence of foreign forces and their departure from the country. In this way, the country can return to real life.[118]

He further asserted that the issues at hand would be resolved only by an Iraqi government with "real powers," and not the one referred to in UNSCR 1483.[119] He questioned the US government, arguing that if it was serious about establishing stability in Iraq it should adopt the ICP's solution, which constituted a different plan than the Bush administration's meager "consultative role" for the Iraqi opposition forces.[120] The ICP's platform up until this point had demanded instead that the "patriotic" opposition groups convene a "broadly based National Conference to elect a transitional coalition patriotic government which enjoys full authority" and prepare for free elections "under UN supervision."[121] However, the Party eventually revised its earlier position – that the process must be done properly, and with the broad participation of

116 "Statement Issued by the Meeting of the Central Committee of the Iraqi Communist Party" (24–25 July 2003). http://www.iraqcp.org/framse1/0030805statementissuedbythemeeting.htm

117 "Big Issues Are the Business of Iraqi Governments," *Ṭarîq al-Shaᶜb – Central Organ of the Iraqi Communist Party*, no. 20, Year 68 (6–12 July 2003). http://www.iraqcp.org/framse1/0030706Tareeq20.htm

118 Ḥamîd Majîd Mûsâ interviewed by *il Manifesto* (6 June 2003). http://www.iraqcp.org/framse1/0030705icpLeader.htm

119 Ibid.

120 Ibid.

121 Salâm ᶜAlî interviewed by *Left Greek Weekly EPOHI* (6 July 2003). http://www.iraqcp.org/framse1/0030709InterviewwitIraqiCP.htm

the Iraqi public[122] – and agreed to the establishment of the Governing Council. Not only that, they agreed to participate on it. According to Paul Bremer, the US administrator for occupied Iraq,

> as we worked to broaden the Governing Council the first week of July [2003], the British came up with the idea of including someone from the Iraqi Communist Party . . . [and] asked me if I had any principled objection to the idea. I said I had none, provided we could find someone who had cast off communism's misbegotten ideas about how to run an economy.[123]

Bremer interviewed both ʿAzîz Muḥammad, the ICP's former long-standing secretary-general, and Ḥamîd Majîd Mûsâ, the presiding secretary-general. Affirming his suitability for Bremer, Mûsâ was appointed.[124]

According to the ICP, the Governing Council emerged as "a compromise between the general desire of Iraqis for establishing an Iraqi provisional patriotic coalition government" and the governing system endorsed by the UN Security Council in its Resolution 1483.[125] While stating its awareness of the need to be suspicious of the US government, the ICP joined the Governing Council of Iraq, thereby making the Party a de facto partner in the occupation and reconstruction of the country under the auspices of the Americans. The Party justified this move in two ways: first, it claimed that the Governing Council was a transformable body, even under the US occupation; and second, it claimed that large sections of the Iraqi public wished to see the ICP participate.[126] The ICP now called upon the people of Iraq to support the work of the council, encouraging critics to offer constructive criticism. One can only assume that by encouraging only constructive criticism, the Governing Council meant to deflect any rejection of the its legitimacy, knowing full well that a substantial portion (very likely the majority) of the Iraqi public viewed the Governing Council as "collaborators" or as "puppets" of the US-led occupation forces.

Once it fully engaged with the Governing Council, the ICP ceased any systemic critique of the occupation that might be considered anti-imperialist and saved its public condemnations primarily for internal security affairs. Although these events were obviously tragic in their own right, the Central Committee failed to condemn the occupation as perhaps the root cause of Iraqi frustration. While the ICP had been capable of arguing compellingly that the United States had been targeted for terrorism on 11 September 2001 because of its foreign

[122] "Communiqué Issued by the Meeting of the Central Committee of the Iraqi Communist Party" (15 August 2002). http://www.iraqcp.org/framse1/002823ICP-1%20(22-8-2002).htm

[123] L. Paul Bremer III, *My Year in Iraq: The Struggle to Build a Future of Hope* (New York: Simon & Schuster, 2006), p. 95.

[124] Ibid.

[125] "About the Formation of the 'Governing Council,'" *Ṭarîq al-S͟haʿb – Central Organ of the Iraqi Communist Party*, no. 21, Year 68 (13–19 July 2003). http://www.iraqcp.org/framse1/0030714IRAQNEWS.htm

[126] "The Iraqi Communist Party and the 'Governing Council,'" *Ṭarîq al-S͟haʿb – Central Organ of the Iraqi Communist Party*, no. 22, Year 68 (20–26 July 2003).

policy, it seems that the Party now had difficulty elucidating the Iraqis' overwhelming distaste for the "Coalition" occupation and how US and other troops stationed in Iraq were possibly responsible for the proliferation of hostilities. It appears that by joining the council and becoming engaged in pragmatic political manoeuvres the ICP had severely weakened what was left of its ability to offer a credible critique of the occupation.

Whither Socialism?

At this time, the Party also abandoned a large portion of what remained of not only its Marxist but also its socialist platform. The issue of privatization of the oil economy came to be expressed primarily in terms of intellectual positions, rather than in programmes consistent with communist praxis. This was evident when the Greek leftist weekly *EPOHI* questioned Central Committee member Salâm ʿAlî in July 2003 on the US privatization of the Iraqi oil industry. In all logic, this issue would be considered a major concern for the ICP, given its own analysis of why the United States had invaded Iraq in the first place – global hegemony. However, although ʿAlî's reaction indicated that the control of oil was crucial to the Iraqi people and that securing Iraqi control of the oil was necessary for the establishment of a democratic Iraq, he failed to state explicitly whether the ICP would be willing to forge a federal government that would deal with this issue, even in defiance of US designs.[127]

One month earlier, the Party had reacted to the increasing reports of contracts being handed out by the US administrators of the occupation with a strong statement in favour of Iraqi self-determination over the country's resources.[128] Yet even this statement was subdued, in that it failed to name the parties responsible other than as the "Coalition Authority." Indeed, the Party never fully tackled this issue and seemed to dismiss it as a matter of concern for future Iraqi governments, despite the fact that a national oil industry was a historical demand of Iraqi Marxist and socialist organizations, since the degree of privatization or nationalization of the oil industry has a direct impact on the political economy of the country, especially on the conditions of the working classes.

Additionally, the ICP never managed to adequately explain how a federal government, established under the supervision of and in a space provided by the US-led occupational authority, would be bold enough to re-nationalize the country's wealth. This is especially pertinent considering that it was not capable of even a minor murmur of distaste, let alone have the tenacity to stop the process or even to demand an end to the privatization of Iraq's wealth. Instead, when questioned on this issue by Richard Bagley on 20 April 2004, Salâm ʿAlî

127 Salâm ʿAlî interviewed by *Left Greek Weekly EPOHI* (6 July 2003). http://www.iraqcp.org/framse1/0030709InterviewwitIraqiCP.htm

128 "Big Issues Are the Business of Iraqi Governments," *Ṭarîq al-S͟haʿb – Central Organ of the Iraqi Communist Party*, no. 20, Year 68 (6–12 July 2003). http://www.iraqcp.org/framse1/0030706Tareeq20.htm

indicated that the strategy of the ICP-CC was to place as much sovereignty as possible in the hands of the Governing Council, where a consensus had been established to retain "the oil industry as an Iraqi state asset."[129] He admitted that the ICP-CC had "no illusions that the power handed over [from the Coalition Authority to the Governing Council[130]] on 30 June [2004] will be total or complete."[131] He argued that even the US-led Coalition Provisional Authority (CPA) had "decided to shelve any large-scale privatizations for the simple reason that they know it would aggravate not only the economic situation but the social and political situation." However, ᶜAlî's position did not take into account the external pressures that mount upon even "sovereign" states to adhere to privatization programmes demanded by global investment organizations such as the World Bank or the International Monetary Fund, a position well understood in most anti-colonial and socialist circles. Nor did his position address the already problematic level of privatization that had occurred in Iraq up to that point. Furthermore, it did not consider the effect of the resistance movement in delaying and discouraging private investment, or as a possible driving force in the decision to delay privatization programs. If extended the benefit of the doubt, it is possible that the ICP-CC dropped its strong commitment to a class-based analysis in order to overcome a national crisis – an approach not unique to the ICP – but given the Party's later behavior, it would indicate that this approach either may not have been well-crafted or may have been a compromise intended to lead to political inclusion.

The Iraqi Communist Party Cadre

A more plausible explanation than the one provided by the ICP-CC may be found presented by the ICP Cadre (*al-Ḥizb al-S̲h̲iyûᶜî al-ᶜIrâqî – al-Kâdir*) in their assessment of the Central Committee's role in the invasion and occupation. The Cadre, led by Nûrî al-Murâdî, split from the ICP in 1985 as a result of the consolidation of authority in the hands of Fak̲h̲rî Karîm, whom they saw to be a petty dictator undermining the Party's principle of "democratic centralism."[132] They claimed that the reversal of communist policy by the Central Committee was a result of "two full decades of retreats and backtracking led by the former Secretary, ᶜAzîz Muḥammad, accompanied by the financial and propaganda officer of the Party at that time, Fak̲h̲rî Karîm."[133] Even after being reprimanded by a Party tribunal for relations with the Baᶜt̲h̲ regime, Fak̲h̲rî Karîm still managed to return to the Party on the orders of ᶜAzîz Muḥammad

[129] Richard Bagley, "We Need Support Not a Lecture," *The Morning Star* (20 April 2004). Hosted on the ICP-CC website: http://www.iraqcp.org/framse1/0040421salam.htm

[130] As agreed on in the Law of State Administration in the Transitional Period, which came into effect on 8 March 2004. http://www.cpa-iraq.org/government/TAL.html

[131] Bagley, "We Need Support."

[132] Iraqi Communist Party (Cadre), "Appeal to Fraternal and Friendly Communist Parties," trans. Muḥammad Abû-Naṣr (20 July 2003). http://www.neravt.com/left/war/cadre1.html

[133] Ibid.

and continued to be highly influential in Party affairs. He cemented his position by subverting the democratic principles of the Party in the 1984 Party Congress.[134] This was considered the point of departure for the Party by the Cadre:

The Party's top concern then became the finding of an ally that would fight on its behalf. The ideological undermining of the Party resulted in its becoming a mouthpiece for the chauvinist tendency within the Kurdish movement, while organizationally the undermined Party became an army of informers serving Fakhrî, who spied on his comrades, searching out ways to bring them down should they try to expose him.[135]

The Cadre asserted that under Fakhrî Karîm the Party found its way into cooperation with the US government as a means of ridding Iraq of Saddam Hussein. However, according to the Cadre, this alignment would not serve the interests of the communist movement, nor would it bring "liberation" to the beleaguered Iraqi people, and indeed its only result would be to secure a position for an ideologically compromised communist Party on the near-powerless Governing Council. They pointed out that the ICP, having resisted the powerful Soviet Union in order to remain faithful to the integrity of its programme, was now in collaboration with the other superpower – the United States. The Cadre asserted that the integration of the ICP-CC's agenda and the US government's agenda resulted in a scenario in which the editors of Fakhrî's paper "began directly to work for the Central Intelligence Agency" by 1993.[136]

The Cadre claimed that the current leader of the Central Committee, Ḥamîd Majîd Mûsâ, having ascended to the position of secretary-general, plunged the Party headlong into open activity with the US government. Mûsâ had supported the division of the ICP over national identity and had agreed to the partition of the ICP in 1993 and the founding of the Kurdistan Communist Party – Iraq (*Hizbi Komunisti Kurdistan / al-Ḥizb al-Shiyûʿî al-Kurdistânî*). The ICP Cadre argued that the 1993 Congress was the Kurdish Section's point of departure from the communist movement and solidified a turn towards the highly chauvinistic tendencies of the Kurdish movement.[137] In fact, the Cadre compared the divisive nature of the Governing Council to the 1993 split of the ICP:

The Party has become nothing but an additional spokesman for the most chauvinist part of the Kurdish movement and a propagandist for the partition of Iraq on a federal basis. It was the renegade Ḥamîd Majîd Mûsâ himself who was the first to prepare the way for the partition of Iraq when he partitioned the Communist Party into one Iraqi and one Kurdistani party, despite the fact that all federal states, for example Russia, Germany, India, and Canada, and others, without exception have in them only one Communist Party. Furthermore, since 1990 the Party lost its own identity, as it cast about for those whom they could fight for, leaving themselves nothing to do but issue assessments and

134 Ibid.
135 Ibid.
136 Ibid.
137 Ibid.

declarations of principle that could never go beyond saying "we are against" or "we are for." All its alliances were with forces tied to regional states and world imperialism, such as the Islamic Council and the two Kurdish parties.[138]

Further, according to the Cadre, when Ḥamîd Majîd Mûsâ joined the Governing Council, he did so on a number of conditions put forth by the administrators of the occupation forces. These conditions included the following: he was not to represent the Communist Party, but rather the Shiᶜite confessional community; the ICP must reformulate its programme to eliminate any references to "colonialism," "imperialism," "national independence," "defence of the homeland," and any other such references; the ICP must cooperate with the occupational forces against "saboteurs" and other agents of discord; the ICP must be disarmed; the ICP will focus their celebrations only on American-approved holidays; and, the Party will help to reduce extremism among Shiᶜite Muslims.[139] Indeed, the actions of the Central Committee in post-Baᶜth Iraq appear to corroborate this argument. Since Ḥamîd Majîd Mûsâ acquired a position on the Governing Council these conditions have been met in full; moreover, the party appears to have accepted the sectarian "logic" of contemporary Iraq, putting its support behind a federalism scheme that formalizes Iraq's social divisions.

First, the Governing Council gave tacit support to the elimination of the celebration of the July 1958 revolution, replacing it with a holiday celebrating the US "liberation" of Baghdad. There were no protestations emerging from the Central Committee despite the fact that "communists took great pride in the revolution of July 1958" and "communists [had] therefore acculturated themselves in the firm principles and successes of that revolution for the last forty years."[140] Second, press releases by the ICP focused its condemnations on events such as the bombing of the UN office in Baghdad[141] and the assassination of Ayatollah Saiyyid Muḥammad Bâqir al-Ḥakîm,[142] and paid no negative attention to the occupying forces, with the single exception of the Abu Ghraib torture scandal,[143] which would have been virtually impossible for any Iraqi organization to ignore, and which was discussed even by pro-occupation American media outlets. The ICP even went so far to suggest that the "sabotage" of pipelines and other such actions of resistance were all activities of the

[138] Iraqi Communist Party (Cadre), "Appeal from the Iraqi Communist Party (Cadre)," trans. Muḥammad Abû-Naṣr (8 August 2003). http://www.neravt.com/left/war/cadre2.html

[139] Iraqi Communist Party (Cadre), (20 July 2003).

[140] Ibid. (8 August 2003).

[141] Political Bureau – The Iraqi Communist Party, "Iraqi Communist Party Condemns Terrorist Attack on UN Office in Baghdad" (20 August 2003). http://www.iraqcp.org/framse1/0030823icp.htm

[142] Political Bureau – The Iraqi Communist Party, "The Iraqi Communist Party Denounces the Criminal Assassination of Ayatollah Saiyyid Muḥammad Bâqir al-Ḥakîm" (29 August 2003). http://www.iraqcp.org/framse1/0030902icp.htm

[143] Center for Human Rights – Iraqi Communist Party, "Iraqi Communist Party Calls for Effective UN Supervision of Human Rights during the Transitional Period," (4 May 2004).

"crumbling remnants of [the Hussein] regime."[144] While there is plenty of room to draw analogous arguments for the violence occurring under the occupation in Iraq and the case already put forth regarding the impetus for the attacks in the United States on 11 September, the ICP failed to connect these issues. In fact, once Ḥamîd Majîd Mûsâ joined the Governing Council, the Central Committee ceased to make any statements that would indicate support for any groups engaging in acts of sabotage or violence against the occupying armies, or even for the resistance movement in general. Instead, they treated the resistance as though it were solely a by-product of the remnants of Saddam's regime and random criminal elements in society.

The ICP-CC, adopting a position similar to that of the US government, refused to acknowledge any legitimate resistance emerging even in areas where it was overwhelmingly popular, as it was in Fallujah in April 2004. Rahul Mahajan, reporting from Fallujah on 12 April 2004, was emphatic that the resistance in that city was not simply the work of a few extremists, but was supported by the vast majority of the population:

> Among the more laughable assertions of the Bush administration is that the mujaheddin are a small group of isolated "extremists" repudiated by the majority of Fallujah's population. Nothing could be further from the truth. Of course, the mujaheddin don't include women, very young children (though we saw an 11-year-old boy with a Kalashnikov), or old men, and are not necessarily even a majority of fighting-age men. But they are of the community and fully supported by it. Many of the wounded were brought in by the muj[aheddin] and they stood around openly conversing with doctors and others. They conferred together about logistical questions; not once did I see the muj[aheddin] threatening people with the ubiquitous Kalashnikovs.[145]

However, Salâm ʿAlî, in speaking to Richard Bagley, claimed that the rebellion of Muqtaḍâ al-Ṣadr in Najaf and the muj(aheddin) of Fallujah did not indicate a growing trend of resistance. He asserted that "they don't command much support, but the way that the Americans have been dealing with them has been giving them more weight than they deserve."[146] ʿAlî dismissed the existence of a growing national resistance movement, suggesting that the insurgencies were really directed by opportunists and old elites, and that the nascent resistance was directionless and had no concrete programme:

> What alternative are they putting forward for Iraq and the region as a whole apart from violence and destabilization and turning Iraq into a battlefield to fight their own wars against America? ... Anybody can go to Baghdad and they can detect straight away that the people simply are not part of it.[147]

144 Political Bureau – The Iraqi Communist Party (20 August 2003).

145 Rahul Mahajan, "Report From Fallujah – Destroying a Town in Order to 'Save' It," *Empire Notes* (12 April 2004) http://www.empirenotes.org/fallujah.html

146 Bagley, "We Need Support."

147 Ibid.

The ICP-CC refused to acknowledge any trend towards the emergence of a nationalist anti-colonial movement with broad support, despite the increasing public hatred of the occupying forces and the increasing xenophobia that is typical of rising nationalism. These sentiments were dramatically amplified following the Muqtaḍâ al-Ṣadr and Fallujah uprisings and the release of the photographs of abuse and humiliation of Iraqi detainees in the Abu Ghraib prison. In fact, the ICP-CC maintained a discourse similar to that of the occupation forces, where there was an attempt to distinguish between the "terrorists" and civilians, despite reports that the muj(aheddin) in many cases, especially in Fallujah, intermingled freely with civilians and were increasingly drawn from the ranks of the public.[148] By July 2004, even US intelligence had admitted that there was a significantly popular resistance movement, estimating that direct participation in the insurgency, including part-timers, may have included as many as twenty thousand people.[149] An analyst for the Center for Strategic and International Studies claimed that the previous estimate of five thousand participants in the insurgency "was never more than a wag and is now clearly ridiculous,"[150] an observation that corroborated claims that the United States was seriously underplaying the significance of the resistance. Even after the "transfer of sovereignty" to the Iraqi Interim Government on 28 June 2004, the insurgency failed to show any signs of weakening, as a suicide bomber detonated a car bomb outside of the headquarters of the Interim Government and the British embassy as early as 14 July 2004.[151] The continuing daily attacks suggested that the insurgents, quite possibly in accordance with the analysis provided by much of the international left, viewed the new government primarily as a "puppet" of the occupation forces, granted limited control of the country only in order to "draw the heat" off of the disintegrating Coalition Forces who no longer wished to deal with the disastrous occupation.

Furthermore, the appointment of John Negroponte as US ambassador to Iraq (later relieved) failed to stimulate any response from the ICP-CC despite the fact that while he was the US ambassador to Honduras under the Reagan administration, he oversaw much of the campaign against the Sandinistas in Nicaragua.[152] Negroponte was closely connected to the training of the Nicaraguan Contra (counter-revolutionary) forces, indicating that he was experienced in combating anti-colonial and socialist movements, and under his watch human rights violations in Honduras peaked, reaching a death toll in excess of ten thousand in the 1980s.[153] Indeed, the fact that he was appointed to the US embassy in Iraq, "the largest embassy in the world," even prompted

[148] See Dahr Jamail, "Fallujans Declare Victory!" *Iraq Dispatches* (11 May 2004).

[149] "Iraq Insurgency Larger Than Thought," Associated Press (9 July 2004).

[150] Ibid.

[151] "Baghdad Car Bombing Kills 10, Injures 40," Associated Press (14 July 2004).

[152] Peter Watt, "Negroponte, Honduras and Iraq" Znet (9 July 2004). http://www.zmag.org/content/showarticle.cfm?SectionID=15&ItemID=5852

[153] Ibid.

comparison with the British "colonial office."[154] Given the ICP-CC's repeated references to "human rights" and its concern over the sovereignty of a federal Iraq, it seems highly suspect that the appointment of Negroponte as ambassador, a well-established "enemy" of the "old" left, would fail to illicit any response from the ICP-CC. Rather, while the majority of the "international left" was condemning the transfer of sovereignty to the interim government as a charade, the ICP-CC praised it, stating, "The transfer of power represents a principal milestone along the path of completing... the political process and achieving its objective: completing the transitional process[,] building elected constitutional and democratic institutions, and regaining and consolidating full sovereignty."[155] Meanwhile, the ICP-CC continued to condemn the acts of the insurgents with rhetoric analogous to that of the Bush administration, declaring that the sufficient arming of Iraqi police and armed forces would allow them to "defeat the forces of darkness, evil[,] sabotage and terrorism, and foil their heinous schemes and attempts to destabilize the situation and obstruct the timetable of the political [process]."[156]

On 11 October 2006, the Iraqi parliament narrowly passed a controversial federalism scheme, which allows Iraq's provinces to form autonomous regions with the power of self-rule. Seeing in the scheme an attempt to formalize Iraq's social divisions, and hurry the implosion of the Iraqi nation, it was summarily rejected by the Sunni Accord Front as well as by the Shiᶜi, though nationalist, Sadr movement and Fadhilla Party.[157] The ICP, however, now having acceded to the sectarian (il)logic of contemporary Iraq, put its backing behind the divisive bill. Rejected by the Party's own Nationalist List coalition, and repudiated by much of Iraqi society, Mûsâ feebly defended himself, characterizing the action as consistent with the country's constitution.[158] As a "concession" to Sunni and nationalist opposition, the ICP agreed to delay the scheme's implementation for eighteen months. The ICP, having once presented itself as a progressive national movement, thus appears to have abandoned the project of Iraq, instead adopting an increasingly sectarian identity and throwing its lot in with the American-backed United Iraqi Alliance.

The inability of the ICP-CC to provide any analysis of the rapidly changing psychology of the Iraqi public, especially with regard to the emergence of a possible nationalist revolt, attests to the overall weakness of the Party. Indeed, the ICP Cadre's claim that the Central Committee had ultimately compromised and sacrificed its entire communist legacy for a position of (negligible) authority bears considerable weight. They argued that this compromise served to make the ICP-CC irrelevant not only to the Iraqi working class, but even to the

154 Ibid.

155 "Transfer of Power Is a Landmark Towards Regaining and Consolidating Full Sovereignty," *Ṭarîq al-Shaᶜb – Central Organ of the Iraqi Communist Party*, no. 49, Year 69 (30 July 2004). http://www.iraqcp.org/framse1/0040705icp.htm

156 Ibid.

157 Qassim Abdul-Zahra, "Baghdad Passes Federalism Law," Associated Press (12 October 2006).

158 *Al-Hayat* (16 October 2006).

occupational authority.[159] The Cadre considered Mûsâ's actions to be treasonous and even alluded to him in a number of statements as Abû Rughâl – famous as the Muslim traitor who led an Ethiopian army to conquer Mecca and destroy the Kaaba. Seeing themselves as the true representatives of the communist legacy and the Communist Party in Iraq, and having assumed a different trajectory from the one chosen by the Central Committee, they declared that

> the renegade, Hamîd Majîd, by collaborating with the American Administration prior to the occupation and by joining one of its institutions after the occupation, has committed the crime of high treason against the nation. In his activities, he does not represent the Iraqi Communist Party or Iraqi patriots.[160]

[159] Iraqi Communist Party (Cadre), (8 August 2003).
[160] Iraqi Communist Party (Cadre), (20 July 2003).

7

Conclusion

From Vanguard Activism to Rearguard Opportunism

Vanguard activism and rearguard opportunism represent signposts in the ICP's journey through Iraq's political development from a backwater outpost of the Ottoman Empire in the early twentieth century to what is effectively a US mandate in the twenty-first century. The purpose of this chapter is to retrace the main pathways of this journey as it unfolded in the previous chapters.

Vanguard Activism

The story of the ICP's journey began in the inner recesses of Iraq's semi-feudal class structure. The last decades of the nineteenth century witnessed the growth of a land-owning aristocracy composed mainly of tribal chiefs, wealthy city merchants, upper-level bureaucrats, and religious leaders. Semi-feudal relations prevailed, but with the introduction of modern communications and transport, internal markets opened up to private financial institutions that were closely connected to the international capitalist markets. This process became more prominent following the opening of the Suez Canal in 1869. European goods began to flood Iraqi markets, almost wiping out indigenous production and transforming the traditional agricultural barter system into a market economy. The British occupation of Iraq in 1917 accelerated this process, as railways, electrical companies, and waterways were opened, and the port of Basra was expanded to serve the economic demands of the British Empire. However, perhaps the most important development in this change was the introduction and development of the oil industry, which tied Iraq inextricably to the international oil monopolies.

A second significant change was the wholesale expansion of semi-feudal relations. In 1929 an expert from the Egyptian Service of the British colonial administration, Sir Ernest Dowson, was invited to study and report comprehensively on Iraqi land settlement. His 1932 report led to the establishment of a Settlement Department and the passage of a law recognizing the right of *lazma*, a complex term essentially implying inheritable tenancy over government land (*miri*).[1] As a result, the majority of state and tribal lands were handed over to a few tribal chiefs, thereby turning them into feudal lords and in effect feudalizing the tribal system. This subsequently led to massive emigration of landless peasants to the cities, prompting fundamental changes in the country's socio-economic structure. The rapid growth of an unskilled surplus labour force provided very cheap workers for nascent industries such as construction, transportation, and oil.

The end of the 1920s witnessed the formation of Marxist circles in major urban centres (Baghdad, Basra, Nassiriyah), paving the way for the formal emergence of the Iraqi Communist Party (ICP) in 1934. At this point, the formation of a modern working class was just beginning, especially in the railway and the emerging oil sector. Though the Marxist groups were relatively insignificant in number, they were credited with influencing the first major labour strike of the railway workers in 1927, when workers in the main depot in Baghdad collectively demanded better working conditions and the drafting of labour laws. When their demands were not met, a strike ensued. It was so successful that two years later, in 1929, they formed the first labour union in Iraq, and in 1936 a national Labour Law was promulgated.

Although the Party aspired to be the vanguard of the proletariat, the leaders and members of the newly constituted ICP were recruited mainly from the salaried sections of the middle class and were predominantly civil servants, teachers, clerks in commercial firms, writers, and journalists. These groups not only were excluded from political power, but often found themselves in a very precarious and unstable economic situation as well. Not surprisingly, when the Party was formed there were very few workers among its members, and according to its first secretary-general, ᶜÂṣim Flayyiḥ, his selection for the post was based almost entirely on the fact that he was an artisan, "the closest of the group to being a worker."[2]

The Party became active in Iraqi affairs almost immediately upon its formation. It was heavily involved in the peasant uprisings in the Euphrates region in the mid-1930s, in the infant working-class movement of the time, and in supporting the Bakr Ṣidqî coup d'état in 1936. One of its leading intellectuals at the time, Yûsuf Ismâᶜîl al-Bustânî, even wrote a pamphlet in support of the military coup entitled "Al-Ṭaiyyârah."[3] At the same time, Saiyyid Muḥsin Abû Ṭabîkh, a prominent tribal landowner who opposed the coup, wrote a book, *Al-Mabâdi' wa al-Rijâl*, which depicted the leaders as conspirators without principles. However, it also attributed a far more significant role in the coup to the

[1] Stephen H. Longrigg, *Iraq, 1900 to 1950* (London: Oxford University Press, 1953), p. 214; Albertine Jwaideh, "Aspect of Land Tenure in Lower Iraq," in Tarif Khalidi (ed.), *Land Tenure and Social Transformation in the Middle East* (Beirut: American University, 1954), pp. 335–338.

[2] Interview by author with ᶜÂṣim Flayyiḥ, Baghdad (18 February 1959).

[3] Unfortunately, the author was unable locate the pamphlet, although its existence was confirmed by more than a dozen people. The content of the pamphlet was conveyed to me by the author himself in an interview: Tareq Y. Ismael, Baghdad (18 December 1959).

Communist Party than was suggested by others at the time. In his memoirs, Abû Ṭabîkh reiterated that he had opposed Ṣidqî because of his communist tendencies, "as these values were contrary to our religious, social, moral, and political heritage."[4]

After the Second World War, the numbers of the working class began to increase significantly as a result of the development of indigenous modern industries, such as textiles and cement. Additionally, state capitalism was strengthened with the increase in oil revenues, and the state-controlled sector of the economy grew rapidly as a result of the state monopoly over electricity, railroads, public transportation, refineries, large factories, and banking. In conjunction with the development of state industries, the compradorial and bureaucratic classes increased, dominating the import and export sector, as well as investing in major industries. In this changing economic environment, the social base of society was controlled through the legal and political strengthening of the semi-feudal system, whose foundation had been laid in the 1930s. There was a merging of the major urban bourgeoisie with the semi-feudal class of urban landowners and the burgeoning civil (state) bourgeoisie. This amalgamation was achieved through laws enabling the urban bourgeoisie and the upper echelon of the state bureaucracy to own agricultural land that had previously been *miri*, or state land. Thus, the new city landowners became partners with the feudal tribal chiefs (*shaikhs*), increasing the gulf between the propertied classes and the poor (dispossessed and proletarianized peasantry). A feudal bourgeoisie of a very unusual nature emerged in Iraq, in which the urban bourgeoisie owned land and feudalists were partners with them in industry. The urban bourgeoisie and wealthy rural feudalists had similar life styles and were both involved in the international capital markets. In this way the classical Marxist distinctions and antagonisms between the two groups were significantly blurred, and the interests of both often coincided.

During the creation of the modern Iraqi state, the complex course of national awakening was followed by the process of nation building. In political terms, the country changed over the next half century from its semi-colonial status under the British mandate and traditional monarchy to a totalitarian nationalist dictatorship, with only brief periods of a working parliamentary regime and liberal institutions. While relatively modern socio-economic institutions were imposed to integrate the country into the global capitalist market, the important role of tribal institutions and feudal relations did not disappear but were in fact integrated into the modern institutional framework. To mediate the relationship between the global market and feudalized tribal institutions, the state apparatus was given preponderant influence in the socio-economic life of the country. In the context of Iraqi social and political realities, the new and old structures remained very much interwoven.

4 *Mudhakkarât al-Saiyyid Muḥsin Abû Ṭabîkh: 1910–1960* (Amman: Dâr al-Fâris, 2001), pp. 342–343. Also see Zakî Khairî and Suʿâd Khairî, *Dirâsât fî Târîkh al-Ḥizb al- Shiyûʿî al-ʿIrâqî*, vol. 1 (n.p., 1984), pp. 23–47.

In this context, the influence of the ICP among the intelligentsia, civil servants, workers, and slum dwellers grew rapidly in the pre–World War II era. The Party's success in mobilizing popular support behind the issues it championed – women's rights, minority rights, workers' rights, better working conditions – and its central role in mobilizing public support for national liberation and non-sectarian principles of political change, especially in times of national crisis such as the 1948 national uprising (*al-wat̲h̲bah*), were indicative of the vanguard role played by the Party in Iraq's political development. However, with the onset of the Cold War following World War II and the suppression of the ICP, the ICP turned to the Communist Party of the Soviet Union (CPSU) for support. This resulted in its greater dependence on the Soviet Union and a commensurate loss of its identity as an Iraqi party. In other words, the influence of Soviet interests – both ideological and political – became evident in Party policy and practise.

While the ICP looked to the CPSU for guidance and solidarity, there were Iraqi voices of dissent over Soviet dictates, and even a rejection of aspects of CPSU theoretical interpretation and Soviet foreign policy, particularly as these related to Iraqi national and Arab issues. Though these disagreements were sometimes manifested as a form of personality conflict, which led to splits and schisms, this internal dissent became a feature that, from its inception, strongly characterized the ICP. Festering for the most part in the background, this dissension did nevertheless surface when the local political situation was relaxed or when a serious national crisis developed. An example of this pattern was the grassroots opposition to Soviet dictates to the Iraqi Communist Party after the ᶜÂrif-Baᶜt̲h̲ military coup in 1963. Grassroots opposition to the Party's leadership for its kowtowing to Moscow ultimately resulted in the emergence of two clearly competing ideological wings of the Party, each claiming to be the true representative of Marxism-Communism in Iraq. In 1968 this division finally culminated in a major schism, represented in the formation of a major splinter, the ICP-Central Leadership (CL).

The ICP-CL maintained a distinct ideological orientation centred on asserting its independence from Soviet control and making Iraqi-Arab national questions its priority issues. Meanwhile, the remnants of the ICP, now known as the ICP-Central Committee (CC), consisted primarily of the "old guard" and their allies. However, this turmoil did not reduce the ICP-CC's subservience to Moscow – rather, it increased it. Furthermore, those who had challenged the Party leadership in the early stages of the split were looked on as renegades, and these factions became isolated, even within the international communist movement, which was now divided into two major camps: Russian and Chinese. The ICP-CC, for its part, clung even more closely to the USSR and the CPSU as its sponsors, especially in the period between 1960 and 1991. The ICP-CL adopted a more independent anti-Soviet position and assumed increasingly cordial relations with China.

The ICP-CL continued to develop outside the sphere of Soviet influence and began to define a distinctive ideological framework for itself. Over time, this group developed its own interpretations of Marxism and socialism, combining these with its particular emphasis on domestic and regionally specific concerns. ICP-CL's first secretary-general, ʿAzîz al-Ḥâjj, commented that "the experience of the Central leadership [from] 1967–1969 . . . with all its faults, was a pioneering step [for the communist movement] in the Arab world," noting how "its rejection of unconditional acceptance of Soviet dictates, and grassroots rejection of the Party's hierarchical bureaucratic control"[5] enabled the rejuvenation of progressive secular alternatives in Iraqi politics. This combination of Marxist internationalism and an Arab regional discourse was blended into historic Islamic interpretations, producing an elaborate and sophisticated discourse, a creative amalgam that had the potential to serve as a vehicle for the revitalization of Marxism in Iraq by making it more relevant to the country, the region, and Iraq's cultural heritage.

However, the ICP-CL faced overwhelming internal suppression from the Baʿthist government as well as the ICP-CC. By 1974 its members had been annihilated or driven into Iraqi Kurdistan or exile. ʿAzîz al-Ḥâjj exclaimed, "This experiment failed, not only because of its own mistakes but also because its opponents successfully united against it." Thereafter, the ICP-CC was the only operational representative of the ICP in Iraq. In addition to unending theoretical and political debates, the ICP's frequent splits reflected the fissured nature of Iraqi society – particularly along ethnic Arab-Kurdish lines. Progressive Kurds often utilized, and were attracted to, the Iraqi communist movement as a means of protecting and advancing their own ethno-cultural interests in the face of the Arab majority and the oppressive regimes in Baghdad. Indeed, in the 1990s, the Kurdish section of the Iraqi Communist Party's Central Committee became the only genuinely functioning communist group, with the ICP in the remainder of the country becoming subservient to the Kurdish section. The negative reaction by the Arab masses, including the Arab members in the ICP hierarchy, to chauvinist demonstrations of Kurdish nationalism by those in Iraqi Kurdistan, could not be avoided. The heightening of the ethnic, confessional, and tribal divisions of Iraqi society by the Baʿthist regime also contributed to the ICP's fragility and lack of internal cohesion.

The Iraqi nation-building process and the capitalist development of the country remained incomplete and distorted, largely owing to the meddling of foreign forces in Iraqi affairs. Throughout the history of the ICP, the Party found itself, in one way or another, under the tutelage of an external ideological mentor, although there were short periods in its history when attempts were made to assert an independent ideological course. Regional and local events almost inevitably compelled the Party to return to dependence on an outside centre. A case in point was Secretary-General Fahd's attempt in the early 1940s to move the Party away from blind subservience to the Soviet Union and to assert a more independent course. With his arrest and eventual execution, the drive for an independent voice coincided with the Party's revival in the late 1950s

5 ʿAzîz al-Ḥâjj, *S̲hijûn ʿIrâqiyyah* (Paris, 1998).

and Salâm ᶜÂdil's efforts to forge an independent Iraqi-centred course in the early 1960s. Such a path was again aborted with ᶜÂdil's arrest and execution following the 1963 ᶜÂrif-Baᶜth coup. The Party again turned to the safety of Soviet patronage, and this control resulted in the splitting of the Party into two camps – the ICP-CC and ICP-CL – in 1968, and continued to hang over the ICP-CC until the demise of the Soviet Union in 1991.

Thus, the ICP-CC failed to develop an independent political culture on either an ideological or organizational level. Furthermore, its cadre became accustomed to receiving diplomatic, moral, and financial support from a leadership completely subservient to the Soviet apparatus. There was only minimal input from the grass roots, and power was concentrated in the hands of the secretary-general and his Politburo. Consequently, with this hierarchical model of decision making, policies flowed in one direction, from the top to the bottom. This outcome resulted in frustrations that subsequently led to numerous challenges and ultimately to schisms, which appeared to be the only avenue available for any questioning of ideology and praxis in this inflexible environment.

The long-lasting and sometimes overwhelming Soviet influence in the ICP had many negative outcomes. Starting from the importation of a rigid ideology that was inconsistent with Iraqi realities and the level of development in the country, Soviet leaders frequently neglected the real interests of their Iraqi comrades, sacrificing them on the altar of their own global political agendas. Numerous examples of the deleterious impact of Soviet misdirection are provided by Soviet relations with various Iraqi regimes after July 1958, and by recurring Soviet pressures on the Iraqi communists to submit to the demands of these regimes in spite of their harsh repression of the communists. Beginning in the 1960s, Soviet interference and Moscow's alliance with the oppressive ᶜÂrif regime generated growing discontent among Iraqi communists, many of whom doubted whether the reforms that had been introduced by the ruling Baᶜthist regime (which was then, according to the Soviets, "socialist oriented") had resulted in any fundamental changes in the mode of production, while simultaneously remarking on the fact that the executions and persecutions of leftists and communists that had taken place under the ᶜÂrif regime in a single year exceeded those of the entire monarchical period. As a result, the regime could not be described as progressive, let alone socialist.

Rearguard Opportunism

The culture of dependency fostered by the ICP Central Committee's reliance on Soviet tutelage, along with the pyramid-like structure of leadership, became the norm for the ICP following the suppression of the ICP-CL challenge. To support their activities as an underground party and maintain their cadre, the ICP relied on the Soviet Union for stable financial support, and for a safe haven for the Party's exiled leaders whenever they were in exile. The Soviet Union provided significant diplomatic and financial support, including the acquisition of a printing press for the Party to publish its newspapers and literature and to ensure its voice in the Iraqi political milieu. Reflecting the Party's dependence on Soviet support, the printing press had to be smuggled in with bribes. In addition, the Party needed a secret location, supplies, and underground personnel to operate it. Moreover, the families of Party members in jail and of those in hiding required financial means to survive, as did the leadership, both inside and outside the country. The Soviets and their allies supplied all of this, in addition to the diplomatic protection of the Soviet state, any necessary mediation with other states, and the often invaluable travel documents.

The price for this support was that the ICP became an extension and agent of the Soviet state apparatus, making the CPSU the sponsor of the ICP to the Soviet state and, by extension, its ideological mentor. Thus, any freedom of independent action or thought by the ICP was viewed by the Soviets as either disloyalty or ideological betrayal. Meanwhile, the cadre, relying as it did on the leadership to survive, came to expect this wide-ranging support, and did not challenge any leadership decision. This ultimately allowed the secretary-general and the Politburo to attain absolute and virtually unquestioned power. In this framework, power was concentrated in the hands of the secretary-general, criticism within the cadre was silenced, and a "cult of personality" was fostered. This scenario reduced the Party to little more than the fiefdom of the secretary-general, whose primary aim was to please the CPSU and to preserve the flow of support. Thus, the Party remained in the firm control of the "old guard" and lost touch with, and relevance to, the Iraqi milieu. Pro forma conferences and congresses were the norm, and by the late 1980s, when the Soviet Union gradually withdrew its support for the ICP, the confusion within the leadership that resulted from the cessation of both material and diplomatic backing immediately eliminated the secretary-general's source and means of Party control. ᶜAzîz Muḥammad, who had been in control of the ICP for thirty years, was forced to relinquish the helm of the Party in the storm of criticism and mass resignations that followed the Fifth National Congress in October 1993, soon after the collapse of the Soviet Union.

In 1993, a new secretary-general, Ḥamîd Majîd Mûsâ, was selected and the Party attempted to regroup around his leadership. Not surprisingly, the Party structure fell apart, and the secretary-general was then able to reshape it as he saw fit. Utilizing the aura of the office of the secretary-general and its established power, Majîd Mûsâ transformed the Party into today's ICP, although it bears little resemblance to Fahd's original Party in form, substance, and even ideology. The established practice of accommodation, developed with the Soviet Union, found a striking new expression with the end of the Cold War and the advance of US power in the region. Bâqir Ibrâhîm al-Mûsawî, commenting in *Al-Quds Al-Arabi*, pointed this out, observing

> the sharp transformation in the Iraqi Communist Party from its clear rejection of international imperialism as the number one enemy of our people, to direct ally with it and – a

partner – in its designs for Iraq [under the US occupation]. It surprised a great number of people, and others might have considered it a sudden transformation; however those that closely followed developments of the Party positions, particularly the last fourteen years, will discover that this public transformation is old in its history, deep and imbedded in its contents, in addition to its immediate and long-term aims. I speak here as one of those who followed the transformation and was a member of that organization that was transformed.[6]

Indeed, the ICP eventually joined the US-sponsored anti-Baᶜthist coalition that included Kurds, Islamists, nationalists, and pro-American groups. By the time the American occupation of Iraq began in April 2003, the Party leadership found no difficulty in endorsing it, or even in being appointed by the US occupation administration to the newly installed Governing Council, with a member of its Politburo serving in its cabinet as minister of culture.

Journey's End?

Reflection on the ICP's journey in Iraq from vanguard activism to rearguard opportunism provides some insight into the dynamics of Iraqi political development over the course of the twentieth century. First and foremost, it is important to note that, from its very inception, the ICP mapped out the pathway of vanguard activism and provided the modern Iraqi state with a model for a modern political party. It articulated ideological positions, raising relevant socio-economic and political issues and solutions. The ICP possessed quasi-administrative organizational units to identify and articulate public concerns, and it suggested solutions that incorporated these into the political process via public mobilization. Clandestine party literature became a cardinal feature of the process of raising public consciousness. Being an illegal, radical, and revolutionary party, the underground cell system became its essential means of survival and the trademark of its organizational structure – a model emulated by other radical political movements. The ICP contributed significantly to the increase in public awareness of political, social, and economic issues and encouraged public participation in the country's political life, activities that had previously been the exclusive domain of the upper classes.

This part of the ICP's journey was based on the Party's responsiveness to the grass roots of Iraqi society. Throughout the monarchical era (1921–1958), the Party's connection to the expanding ranks of the urban poor – dispossessed peasant migrants into the cities – was more symbolic than substantive in the sense that the Party was more successful in raising the political consciousness of the urban masses than in recruiting them into the party. Nevertheless, the road of vanguard activism was mapped out on this grassroots base. The base, however, was singularly urban, and the ICP was completely out of touch with

[6] Bâqir Ibrâhîm al-Mûsawî. "The Transformation of the Iraqi Communist Party: Is it a Complete Turnaround or a Passing Mistake?" *Al-Quds Al-Arabi* (6 January 2005).

the rural realities that occupied the majority of Iraq's population. The rural reality came to the fore in Iraqi politics in 1963 with the emergence of the Baʿth in alliance with reactionary forces entrenched in the tribal structures and religious fatalism of Iraq's impoverished villages. Perhaps because of its brief flirtation with political empowerment under the Qâsim regime (1958–1963), or because the new wave of rural immigrants into the urban core were already intoxicated with nationalist dreams and anti-communist phobias, or perhaps because of the Pol Pot–style slaughter of the urban intelligentsia unleashed by the Baʿthists in their short-lived reign of terror in 1963 – or some combination of these factors – the ICP lost touch with the grass roots in the 1960s. Successive splits within the Party, culminating with the emergence of the ICP-CL as a major fracture, reflect efforts within Party ranks to realign party praxis with the grass roots. With the collapse of the CL's efforts to displace the CC's control over the Party's apparatus, many communists abandoned communism altogether and returned to their national (Arab or Kurdish) and Islamic roots.

For all practical purposes, the Party never recovered from the Baʿathist blow after 1963. And within a few months, the Party was reduced to a shell, with no political organization at home and only a symbolic structure outside. Fully dependent on the Soviet State, the secretary-general was selected by a limited number of cadre outside the country. He received direct financial subsidies from the Soviet party, which he utilized to reinforce his control over the Party apparatus and to implement Soviet dictates.

Disconnected from Iraq's popular classes, by 1967 the ICP had lost the confidence of Baghdad's intelligentsia and working classes, and found itself essentially confined to the Kurdish areas, under the tutelage of Kurdish leaders. The grassroots revolt against the Soviet-sponsored August Line in 1964 catalyzed the formation of the CL by party activists and the younger cadre, leaving only the old guard in the formal party. Thus, when the Party accepted Paul Bremer's offer to join the Governing Council in 2003, it had no ideological difficulty in integrating with the occupation forces and participating in the programme of occupation.

Disaffected from communism, the young activists initiated alternative sociopolitical analyses of the region along other paths of development. With their wealth of experience in vanguard activism, their ideological sophistication, and their skill in public mobilization, these former communists "pollinated" the landscape of politics throughout the Middle East with political activism, revitalizing political movements throughout the region with skills and expertise acquired in the communist movement. In light of the fact that Iraqi communists have included, and still include, some of the most prolific intellectuals in the country,[7] and that their political discourse has traditionally been more sophisticated than that of most other political movements, their potential influence on the future of the country should not be underestimated.

[7] Ibid.

The ICP-CC's success over the ICP-CL for control over the Party apparatus marks its turning down the road of rearguard opportunism. In effect, the Party sold out to the Soviet Union, and the voice it maintained in Iraqi politics reflected Soviet interests, not the interests of the Iraqi people. The Party was effectively out of touch with the needs and problems confronting ordinary Iraqis, and this was reflected in its policies and programmes and vacuous ideological discourse, clearly manifested after the withdrawal and subsequent collapse of the Soviet Union. The Party's relatively easy accommodation with the US occupation was and is entirely consistent with the comprador role it had been playing in Iraqi politics under Soviet tutelage. Still on the road of rearguard opportunism, the Party merely followed a new foreign master. As an old veteran of the ICP lamented when reflecting on the Party's cooperation with the occupiers, "The struggle to defend the nation against attempts to occupy it or oppress the people is the noble aim that could return the communist party to the vanguard."[8]

Clearly, the party faithful never achieved the hopes and aspirations for ordinary Iraqis that motivated the best of them and for which so many, like those hanged in Baghdad in February 1949, paid with their lives. But in the end, history's judgement on their role will go beyond the childlike simplicities of action versus thought, of success versus failure. Language and concepts do shape outcomes, even if indirectly, and there are intermediate spaces for partial, though still meaningful, realizations between success and failure. Almost certainly, the Party's most lasting and valuable contribution has been its politicization of the social issues of poverty and injustice that had previously been beyond the scope of public political discourse. In Iraq, mainly because of the communist input in the public debate, the class-determined socio-economic issues highlighted by communist analysis have had to be addressed, and differing positions justified, in response to the Party's demands for social justice. Thus, through the intellectual and ideological discourse of the communist movement, grounded in Marxist terminology and concepts, Iraqi political thought and literature have been enriched. The concerns raised have also become woven into the programmes of most of the other political groupings. At a time when the future of Iraq is once again being decided, the intrinsic linkage between socio-economic and national-political issues that the Party brought to the forefront will certainly become more manifest. The legacy of the Iraqi communist movement may be its remarkable ability to affect the Iraqi polity in these critical ways even as it continues, organizationally, to recede from the contemporary political scene.

However, the journey of the ICP does not end on the road of rearguard opportunism. Despite the ICP-CL's failure to displace the ICP-CC, remnants of it survived and restructured to emerge as an umbrella organization encompassing a number of progressive nationalist groupings, both within Iraq and

[8] Jamâl Muḥammad Taqî, "The Orphaned Left of Iraq," *Al-Quds Al-Arabi* (London, 22 April 2006).

in the diaspora, during the 1980s and 1990s. This experience allowed the ICP-CL to play a powerful role in the formation of Iraqi Democrats Against Occupation following the US invasion of March 2003,[9] thus forging a new pathway through the minefield of Iraqi politics.

[9] The development of the ICP-CL is very interesting indeed, and is worthy of its own volume. Unfortunately, a more detailed analysis of its history and impact is outside of the scope of this book.

Index

^{c}Abbâs, ^{c}Adnân, 170, 264
Abbassid period (eighth century), 7, 243
^{c}Abbûd. *See* Auerbach, Haim
^{c}Abbûd, Nâṣir, 44, 53, 63, 117
^{c}Abd-ul-Ḥamîd, Ṣamad, 101
^{c}Abd-ul-Ḥamîd II, 3
^{c}Abd-ul-ilah, Regent and Crown Prince, 34–35, 36, 40, 42
^{c}Abd-ul-Jalîl, Ghânim, 235
^{c}Abd-ul-Karîm, Mahdî, 48, 172, 264
^{c}Abd-ul-lah, ^{c}Âmir, 63, 75–76, 79, 81–98, 101, 104–106, 119, 121, 130, 134, 139–146, 160, 169–172, 182, 196, 264
^{c}Abd-ul-lah, Muḥammad Nâyib, 264
^{c}Abd-ul-Qâdir, ^{c}Adnân, 112
^{c}Abd-ul-Qâdir, Yûsuf, 23
^{c}Abd-ul-Razzâq, ^{c}Ârif, 116, 128, 129
^{c}Abd-ul-Razzâq, Nûrî, 264
^{c}Abd-ul-Riḍâ, Majîd, 144, 258, 259, 264–267, 296
Abu Ghraib, 308
Abû Ja^{c}far. *See* Salmân Khiḍr
Abû Salâm. *See* Ḥabîb, Muḥammad
Abû Ṭabîkh, Saiyyid Muḥsin, 312–313
Abû-lailah, Sulimân Aghâ, 1
Abû-l-^{c}Îss, Muḥammad Ḥusain, 92, 94, 96, 104, 105
Abu-l-Timmân, Ja^{c}far, 11
Action (publication). *See Al-^{c}Amal*
^{c}Âdil, Salâm (^{c}Âdil Ḥusain Aḥmad al-Râḍî), 46–62, 64, 66–67, 75, 76, 80–83, 86–98, 101, 104–108, 110, 211, 216–219, 316
Advanced Cadre Abroad. *See al-Kâdir al-Mutaqaddim fî al-Khârij*
Afghanistan, 181, 188
^{c}Aflaq, Michel, 161
Afro-Asian Solidarity Council, 166
aghas, 13
agrarian reform, 32, 122
agricultural production in Iraq, 8, 14
Ahâlî (group), 19, 22, 24–25
Aḥmad, Karîm, 44, 53, 196
Aḥmad, Munîr. *See* Nûrî, Bahâʾu-d-Dîn
Aiyyûb, Thûnûn (Qâdir), 27
^{c}Ajînah, ^{c}Abd-ul-Raḥîm, 49, 117, 118, 161, 162, 169, 170, 172, 265, 269–272
^{c}Ajînah, Anîs, 50
al-^{c}Ablî, Muḥammad Ṣâliḥ, 63, 105, 108, 112, 114
al-Ahâlî (group), 21–25, 90
Al-Ahâlî (newspaper), 21–22, 90
al-^{c}Ahd (Allegiance Party), 12
al-^{c}Ahd (secret society), 4, 6
Al-Ahram, 59
al-Aḥrâr (Liberal Party), 35
al-^{c}Aisamî, Shiblî, 172
al-Aiyyûbî, ^{c}Alî Jawdat, 73
Al-^{c}Amal (Action, publication), 29
al-^{c}Ânî, Thâbit Ḥabîb, 104, 117, 119, 196, 264
al-^{c}Ârif, Ismâ^{c}îl, 96–97
Al-Asâs (The Foundation, newspaper), 40, 189
al-A^{c}ẓamî, Hâdî Hâshim, 96, 97, 105, 108
al-Bakr, Aḥmad Ḥasan, 112, 161, 167, 169, 172–173
al-Bayâtî, ^{c}Abd-ul-Khâliq, 49
al-Bazzâz, ^{c}Abd-ul-Raḥmân, 129, 130, 142
Al-Bilâd (The Country, newspaper), 23
al-Bustânî, ^{c}Abd-ul-Qâdir Ismâ^{c}îl, 20, 21, 22, 23, 86, 88, 97

al-Bustânî, Yûsuf Ismâʿîl, 20, 22, 23, 312
al-Châdirchî, Kâmil, 22, 35, 67, 71, 77, 86
al-Chalabi, Aḥmad, 288
al-Chalabî, Sâlim, 44, 53
al-Darrajî, ʿAbd-ul-laṭîf, 77–78
"al-dîmuqrâṭiyyah al-ishtirâkiyyah (defined), 241
al-Dîmuqrâṭiyyûn al-ʿIrâqiyyûn ḍid al-Iḥtilâl (Iraqi Democrats Against Occupation, IDAO), 262
al-Dîn Maḥmûd, Nûrî, 42
al-Dulaimî, Nazîhah, 127, 128, 170, 196
al-Fakhrî, Salîm, 131–132, 239, 240
al-Falâḥî, Ṣâdiq, 44
al-Fârâbî, 243
al-Farîq al-Lînînî fî al-Ḥarakah al-Shiyûʿiyyah al-ʿIrâqiyyah (Leninist Group in the Iraqi Communist Movement), 258
al-Fikr al-Jadîd (weekly), 169
al-Gailânî, Rashîd ʿAlî, 12, 26–27
Algeria 1954 revolt in, 43
Algerian Arab Committee for the Support of Iraq and Palestine, 259
Al-Ghad (newspaper), 118, 125, 239, 240, 241, 245–247, 262–263
al-Gumar, Ḥusain (Walîd), 133, 139
al-Ḥâfiẓ, Mahdî, 264
al-Ḥaidarî, Jamâl, 31, 44, 45, 63, 81, 92–93, 96–97, 101, 104, 105, 108, 114, 211, 216, 217, 219
al-Ḥaidarî, Ṣalâḥ, 31
al-Ḥâjj, ʿAzîz, 64, 81, 92, 117, 118, 119, 125–129, 132, 139–144, 147–149, 151–152, 154, 156, 158–160, 192, 214, 220–221, 224, 315
al-Ḥakîm, Ayatollah Saiyyid Muḥammad Bâqir, 306
al-Ḥallâq, Aḥmad Maḥmûd, 224
al-Ḥaqiqah (The Truth), 40
al-Hâshimî, Yâsîn, 12
al-Hayy, 67
al-Hilâl (journal), 4
al-Ḥilw, Farajallah, 76
al-Ḥizb al-Ḥurr al-ʿIrâqî (Liberal Party of Iraq), 11
al-Ḥizb al-Shiyûʿî al-ʿIrâqî – al-Kâdir (ICP Cadre), 304
al-Ḥizb al-Waṭanî (National Party), 11, 17
al-Ḥurriyyah (newspaper), 205
ʿAlî, Ibrâhîm Muḥammad, 110
ʿAlî, Muḥammad, 2
ʿAlî, Musṭafâ, 18, 20
ʿAlî, Salâm, 303–304, 307
al-Ikhaʾ al-Waṭanî, 12
al-ʿIṣâmî, Shiblî, 172
al-Istiqlâl (Independence Party), 35, 41, 51, 52, 54–55, 65, 67, 71, 75, 78, 85, 87, 91
al-Ittiḥâd (The Union), 40
al-Ittiḥâd al-Waṭanî (National Unity Party), 35, 37, 38, 39
al-Izzarjâwî, ʿAṭshân Khaiyyûn, 63
al-Jabhah al-Shaʿbiyyah al-Muttaḥidah (Popular Unified Front Party), 41, 42
al-Jabhah al-Waṭaniyyah al-Dîmuqrâṭiyyah (National Democratic Front, JWOD), 194
al-Jabhah al-Waṭaniyyah al-Muttaḥidah: Ṭarîqunâ wa Wâjibuna al-Târîkhî (The United National Front Is Our Path and National Duty, pamphlet), 37
al-Jabhah al-Waṭaniyyah al-Taqaddumiyyah al-Dîmuqrâṭiyyah (Progressive National Democratic Front, JWQD), 194
al-Jâḥiẓ, 243
al-Jawâhirî, Muḥammad Mahdî, 100
al-Jazâʾirî, Khalîl, 258–260
al-Jumailî, Ṣubḥî, 298
al-Kâdir al-Mutaqaddim fî al-Khârij (Advanced Cadre Abroad), 119
al-Kâdir al-Shiyûʿî (The Communist Cadre, newspaper), 237
al-Khaiyyûn, Amîn Ḥusain, 152
al-Kharramî, Bâbik, 243
Al-Lahîb (news bulletin), 153
al-Lajnah al-Qiyâdiyyah al-ʿUlyâ li al-Ḥizb al-Shiyûʿî al-ʿIrâqî (Supreme Leadership Committee for the Iraqi Communist Party), 131
al-Lajnah al-Thawriyyah (Revolutionary Committee), 110, 131
Allegiance Party. *See al-ʿAhd*
al-Maʿarrî, 243
al-Mabâdiʾ wa al-Rijâl (book), 312
Al-Mabdaʾ (The Principle, newspaper), 98, 99, 101
al-Mada International Arab Publishing House, 272
al-Madfaʿî, Jamîl, 25
Al-Majlis al-Waṭanî lil Silm wa al-Taḍâmun (National Council for Peace and Solidarity), 166
al-Mukhtarah, 243
al-Munâḍil al-Shiyûʿî (The Communist Combatant, newspaper), 267
al-Muqaṭṭam (journal), 4
al-muqâydah (barter), 247

Al-Muqâydah: Berlin-Baghdad, 228, 241, 247–255
al-Muqtaṭaf (journal), 4
al-Murâdî, Nûrî, 304
al-Mûsawî, Bâqir Ibrâhîm, 112, 113, 114, 121, 149, 169–171, 259, 264, 317–318
Al-Mushtarak (newspaper), 246–247
al-mushtarak defined, 241–243, 245, 246
Al-Mushtarak: Niẓâm al-Ishtirâkiyyah al-Dîmuqrâṭiyyah fî Ḍawʾ Târîkh al-Mujtamaʿ al-Islâmî wa khibrat al-Thawrât al-Ishtirâkiyyah al-Ḥadîthah (Al-Mushtarak: A Democratic Socialist System from Islamic History and Modern Socialist Revolutions, treatise), 239–244
al-Nâbulsî, Sulaimân, 42
al-Nahâr (newspaper), 127
al-Nahj (journal), 269, 272
al-Najdi, 245
al-Najmah (The Star), 40
al-Naqîb, Maḥmûd, 11
Al-Nashrah (broadsheet), 258
al-Nâṣirî, ʿAbd-ul-Salâm (Anwar Muṣṭafâ), 44, 105, 117, 118–121, 126, 130, 142
al-Nasiriyah Marxist circle, 20
Al-Nidâʾ (newspaper), 184, 193
Al-Niḍâl (The Struggle, newspaper), 46
Al-Qâʿidah (The Base, newspaper), 28, 44, 45, 46, 52–53, 55–57, 60, 195
al-Qâʿidah (the Grassroots), 40
al-Qaramita (Carmathians), 243
al-Qazzâz, Muḥammad Ṣâliḥ, 15, 20
Al-Quds Al-Arabi, 317
al-Raḥḥâl, Ḥusâin, 1, 5–6, 17–20
al-Raḥḥâl, Rashîd, 17
al-Rashid Putsch, 109–113, 209, 239
al-Râzî, 243
al-Ṣadr, Muḥammad, 11, 40
al-Ṣadr, Muqtaḍâ, 307–308
al-Ṣâfî, ʿAbd-ul-Razzâq, 44, 180, 288, 291
Al-Ṣaḥîfah (The Journal), 18, 19
al-Saʿîd, Nûrî, 12, 25–26, 35–38, 41, 42, 53–55, 59, 69, 71, 72, 74, 77, 254
al-Saiyyid, Maḥmûd Aḥmad, 18–19, 20
al-Salâm, Khâlid ʿAbd-ul-lah, 258–260
al-Sâmarrâʾî, ʿAbd-ul-Khâliq, 168
al-Sâmir, Bilâl, 199
al-Ṣawâb (The Right), 40
al-Shaʿb (People's Party), 35–37, 38, 39, 45
al-Shabîbî, Ḥusain Muḥammad (Ṣârim), 28, 37, 38
al-Shaʿbiyyah (populism), 22–24, 39
al-Shaghîlah, Râyat, 60

al-Shaikh, ʿAzîz Aḥmad, 63, 101
al-Shaikh, Sharîf, 40
al-Shaikhlî, ʿAbd-ul-Karîm, 108
Al-Shams (journal), 20
Al-Sharârah (The Spark, journal), 27–30
Al-Sharq Al-Awsat, 300
al-Shawwâf, ʿAbd-ul-Wahhâb, 87, 250, 252, 254
al-Shishaklî, Adîb, 42
Al-Ṣirâʿ fî al-Ḥizb al-Shiyûʿî al-ʿIrâqî wa Qaḍâyâ al-Khilâf fî al-Ḥarakah al-Shiyûʿiyyah al-ʿÂlamiyyah (The Conflict in the Communist Party, and the Issues of Disagreement with the International Communist Movement), 212
al-Siyâsah (journal), 4
al-Suwaidî, Tawfîq, 35, 36, 38
Al-Ṭaiyyârah, 66, 312
al-Ṭâlabânî, Mukarram, 161, 169, 172
Al-Tawḥîd (journal), 245–246
al-Thaqâfah al-Jadîdah (journal), 171, 269, 278–279, 282, 283, 293, 295
Al-Thawrah (The Revolution, newspaper), 172, 191, 255, 258
al-Thawrî (The Revolutionary, circular), 267
al-ʿUmarî, Arshad, 35–37
al-ʿUmarî, Muṣṭafâ, 42
al-ʿUṣbah al-Ḥamrâʾ (Ottoman Decentralization Party), 4
ʿAlwash, ʿAmmâr, 108
Al-Waṭan (The Homeland, newspaper), 37, 45
al-Waṭanî al-Dîmuqrâṭî (National Democratic Party), 35, 37, 38, 39, 41, 51, 52, 54, 65, 67, 71, 75, 77, 78, 80, 85, 90, 95
al-Wathbah (the Leap, 1948), 16, 39, 314
al-Zanj uprising (866–879), 243
Al-Zawrâʾ (newspaper), 3
al-Zigam, ʿArrâk, 85
ʿAmara province, 13
Amarrah, 263
American hostages in Tehran, 256
Anglo-American actions in Iraq, after the 1958 revolution, 248
Anglo-German Agreement (15 July 1914), 9
Anglo-Iraqi Treaty
  (1922), 11
  (1926), 11
  (1930), 12, 16, 37, 56, 80
Anglo-Ottoman Treaty (1913), 253
Anglo-Persian Oil Company, 9
Anglo-Russian interests in Iraq, 249
Anglo-Turkish Agreement (29 July 1913), 9

Anṣâr (Partisan Movement, 1979–1988), 192, 201, 202, 226, 266, 270, 271, 290, 294
Anwar Muṣṭafâ. *See* al-Nâṣirî, ᶜAbd-ul-Salâm
April plenary session, report of, 137
Arab Baᶜth Socialist Party. *See* Baᶜth
Arab Central Committee, 66
Arab Front, 280–281
Arab-Israeli conflict (1948), rise of Soviet popularity after, 51
Arab-Israeli War (June 1967), 155
Arab League, 103
Arab Mutual Security Pact, 59
Arab Nationalist Movement (ANM), 41–42
Arab Revolt of 1916 (against the Ottomans), 11
"Arab socialism," 21, 126
Arab Socialist Alliance, 124
Arab Socialist Union, 116, 124, 136, 138, 151
"Arab Unity: The Greatest Hope of the Arabs" (declaration, 14 November 1957), 73
Arbil, occupation of (31 August 1997), 292
ᶜÂrif, ᶜAbd-ul-Raḥîm, 141, 142, 146
ᶜÂrif, ᶜAbd-ul-Salâm, 77–78, 80, 82, 85–86, 107, 109, 112, 115–134, 137–141, 146, 161, 219–220
ᶜÂrif-Yaḥya, 135
Artisans' Association. *See Jamᶜiyyat Aṣḥâb al-Ṣanâʾiᶜ*
Association of the People's Reform. *See Jamᶜiyyat al-Iṣlâḥ al-Shaᶜbî*
"Attempt to Appraise Our Party's Policies Between July 1958 and April 1965, An," 144, 160
Auerbach, Haim (ᶜAbbûd), 20
August Line (1964), 121–123, 125–147, 150–151, 212, 319
Azadi (Freedom, newspaper), 63
ᶜAziz, Tariq, 172, 259

Baghdad, 67
  Arab nationalist societies in, 4
  British occupation of 1917, 9
  first communist cells in (1935), 25
  Industrial Conference (11 February 1965), 128
  Marxism in, 1
  Pact, 41, 42, 51, 52, 58, 59, 62, 66, 68, 69, 72, 73, 75, 76, 80–81, 83, 248, 250, 252, 261
  population growth in, before 1831, 2
  Section Conference (August 1958), 82
  as a semi-autonomous state, 1
  "Worker's Committee," 110
Baghdad-Basra railway, 9
Bagley, Richard, 303, 307
Bahrain, 9
Bakdâsh, Khâlid, 60, 75–76, 82, 219
Bandung Conference (April 1955), 43, 59
Bani Sadr, Abul Hasan, 239
Bârzânî, Idrîs, 207, 235
Bârzânî, Masᶜûd, 103, 288
Bârzânî, Muṣṭafâ, 103, 114, 115, 158, 205, 207, 226–227, 235, 289
Base, The (newspaper). *See Al-Qâᶜidah*
"Basic Foundations of the Concept of National Unity," 99
Basîm. *See* Nûrî, Bahâʾu-d-Dîn
Basîm, Zakî Muḥammad (Ḥâzim), 28, 39
BASOK. *See* Socialist Kurdish Party
Basra, 67, 263
  Arab nationalist societies in, 4
  British occupation of, 9, 253
  declared a British protectorate (1923), 254
Basra Oil Company, 228
Batatu, Hanna, 6, 15, 16, 40
Baᶜth, 41, 65, 67, 71, 77, 78, 85, 87, 91, 107–112, 119, 123, 161, 165, 171, 186–187
  ᶜÂrif coup (February 1963), 107, 114, 224, 314, 316
  cooperation with the ICP-CC, 166
  coup (17–30 July 1968), 162, 180
  government accomplishments of, 180
  Military Bureau, 108
  National Guard, 107
  oppression of the Kurds, 134
  purge of, 109
  tension with Nasser, 109
  see also National Progressive Front
Baᶜth Arab Socialist Party, *see* Baᶜth
begs or *aghas*, 7
Berque, Jacques, 239
Bertrand Russell Peace Foundation, 127
Board of Central Organization, 236, 238
Bolshevik Revolution in the People's Republic of China, 213
Bolshevik Ṣâliḥ, 5–6
Bolshevism Iraqi interest in, following the October 1917 revolution, 5
Bosnia, 4
Bremer, Paul, 302, 319
Brezhnev, Leonid, 131, 169, 181
Brigade of Twelve. *See* Cadre Group
British Committee for the Defence of Human Rights in Iraq, 127

British East India Company, 2, 7
British Imperial market system (mid-nineteenth century), 7
Bubian, 257
Bulgaria, 4
Bureau of Central Organization, 114
bureaucratic bourgeoisie, 13, 229, 233
bureaucratic state, centralized, 12
Bush, George H. W., 298

Cadre Group [Brigade of Twelve], 142, 149–154
Cairo conference (March 1921), 10
Camp David Accords, 181–182, 184–185, 187, 188
capital, role of, in development, 282
Castro, Fidel, 92
CCP. *See* Chinese Communist Party
Center for Strategic and International Studies, 308
Central Committee, 27, 60, 62, 79, 82–84, 119, 121, 144–146, 205, 214, 218, 237, 264, 290, 314–321
  ʿÂdil appointed secretary-general by, 58
  and the Baʿth, 166–202
  commitment to nationalist causes under ʿÂdil, 59
  distinct from Central Leadership, 147–165
  first, 21
  memorandum of (1955), 55
  in 1970–1975, 167
  plenary session of the
    1956, 83
    1958, 83, 85, 213
    1959, 93, 97, 214
    1962, 104, 114
    1964, 121
    1967, 148, 156–157
    1978, 182
    1985, 202
    1991, 290
  Pronouncement of, 288
  and the Qâsim coup, 75
  radical action programme of the, 56
  reconstructed by Nûrî, 44
  and the removal of ʿUthmân as secretary-general, 58
  reorganized under ʿUthmân, 53
  response to Perestroika, 269
  see also National Progressive Front
Central Intelligence Agency (CIA), 107, 218, 305
Central Leadership, 97, 114, 147–165, 166, 204–214, 224, 233, 314–321
Central Military Bureau, 184, 270
Central Military Council, 184
Central Treaty Organization (CENTO), 42
chalabis (rich merchants), 6
Chamoun, Camille, 77
Charter of National Action, 168
Chilmîrân, ʿAffân, 235
China, People's Republic of (1949), 43, 76, 250
Chirac, Jacques, 187
Churchill, Winston, 10
Cilician plain, in Asia Minor, 9
Clique of Four, 92–94, 96, 97, 101, 102, 105, 106, 217–219
Coalition Authority, 63
Coalition Provisional Authority (CPA), 304
Cohen, Yaʿqûb (Fâḍil), 27
Cold War, 109, 247, 256
collective leadership, 44, 93, 95, 96, 123, 147, 195, 215, 241, 266
Cominform, dissolution of the (17 April 1956), 60
Comintern, 23, 28
Committee for a Marxist Understanding. *See* *Lajnat al-Waʿi al-Mârkisî*
Committee for Central Organization. *See* *Lajnat al-Tanẓîm al-Markazî*
Committee for Combating Imperialism and Exploitation. *See Lajnat Mukâfaḥat al-Istiʿmâr wa al-Istithmâr*
Committee for National Cooperation. *See* *Lajnat al-Taʿâwun al-Waṭanî*
Committee for the Defence of Democratic Freedoms and Rights in Iraq, 102
Committee for the Organization of Members Abroad. *See Lajnat Tanẓîm al-Khârij*
Committee for the Preservation of the Republic, 87
Committee for the Protection of the Revolution, 85
Committee of Democratic Activities, 58
Committee of the Workers' Organization, 57
Communist Cadre, The (newspaper). *See* *al-Kâdir al-Shiyûʿî*
Communist Combatant, The (newspaper). *See* *al-Munâḍil al-Shiyûʿî*
Communist Labour Organization of Iraq, 194
Communist Party
  of Britain, publications of, 4
  of China (CCP), 218
  of East Germany (DDR), 76
  of Egypt, 124, 184

Communist Party (*cont.*)
of Iraq. *See* Iraq: Communist Party of
of Kurdistan. *See Hizbi Komunisti Kurdistan / al-Ḥizb al-Shiyûʿî al-Kurdistânî*
of Lebanon, 76
of Sudan, 76, 184
of Syria, 60, 219
of Syria and Lebanon, 31, 50, 75
of the Soviet Union (CPSU), 75–76, 90, 92, 115, 131, 169, 207–212, 214, 218–219, 314–317, 320. *See also* Cominform; Comintern; Soviet Union
"Communist Party – not Social Democracy," 157
Communist University of the Toilers of the East (KUTV), 20, 125
Conference of Communist and Workers' Parties (November 1957), 76
conscripts, 32
Conservative Party of Kurdistan, 288
constitution of Iraq, 3, 4, 11, 32, 206
Constitutional Monarchy in Iraq (1921), 12
Constitutional Union (party), 53
Contra forces, 308
"Contribution in the Appraisal of Our Party's Policies, A," 144–145, 160
Council of Ministers, 81
Council of National Peace. *See Majlis al-Silm al-Waṭanî*
Country, The (newspaper). *See Al-Bilâd*
CPA. *See* Coalition Provisional Authority
Crete, 4
crop production in Iraq (1867–1913), 8
"Cry of May, The," 56–57
Cuban missile crisis (1962), 253

Ḍaiyyûl, ʿAtshân, 53
Dâûd, Karîm Aḥmad, 47
Dâûd Pasha, contributions of, 2
"Death Train," 112
Debate on the General Direction of the International Communist Movement, A (publication), 131
"Declaration on the Anniversary of the Aggression against Egypt, A" (29 October 1957), 72
Declaration 13 (8 February 1963), 107
Decree 16 (22 August 1954), 53–54
Decree 19 (22 September 1954), 54, 55
Decree 24 (10 October 1954), 54
Decrees 17 and 18 (22 August 1954), 53–54
Defence Organization and Mutual Arab Cooperative (March 1955), 58
democracy, 279–281
liberal interpretation of, 279
"Democracy and Renewal" (slogan), 286
Democratic Arab Federation, 240
democratic centralism, 64, 277, 285–288, 304
Democratic 14 July Movement, 239
democratic freedoms, 136
Democratic National Front, 202
Democratic Reform (report), 270
Democratic Republic of Yemen (PDRY), 191
democratic rights, 125
democratic socialism, 241
demonstrations, public (1927–1928), 17
"Documents of the Plenary Session of the ICP," 134–135
"Down with the Pakistan-Turkey Treaty," 51
Dowson, Sir Ernest, 311
"Draft for a National Front" (September 1968), 162, 165
"Draft for Discussion to Evaluate the Policy of the Iraqi Communist Party for the Years 1968–1983, A," 195
due process, 99
Duglah, Ṣâliḥ Mahdî, 63, 115
Dulles, Allen, 218
duties, import, imposed on the British, 2

economic classes in Iraq, prior to World War I, 6
Economic Organization for Banks, 116
education, 32
Egypt, 32, 58–59, 68, 184
Israeli-French-British attack on (29 October 1055), 59
July 1952 revolution in, 42
Tripartite aggression against (1956), 67, 71, 74
Egyptian Free Officers, 75
Eisenhower doctrine, 73, 75, 248
election
17 January 1953, 42
9 June 1954, 53, 55
12 September 1954, 55
11 March 1970 Declaration, 226, 228
11 September 2001, causes for, 298
el-Qasir, Crown Prince, 225
"End the Dictatorship and Establish a Democratic Regime in Iraq," 186
"Ending Dictatorship," 184
Enlai, Zhou, 75–76
Enlarged Central Committee, 139, 145

Enlarged Plenary Meeting of the ICP-CC (1985), 202
EPOHI (weekly), 303
Euphrates River, 8
European imports into Iraq, through Basra, 1868–1909, 8

Fâḍil. *See* Cohen, Yaᶜqûb
Fadhilla Party, 309
Fahd (Yûsuf Salmân Yûsuf), 5, 20–31, 34, 38–39, 44, 63, 157, 218, 315, 317
Faiṣal, Amir, 11
Faiṣal I. *See* Faiṣal, Amir
Falah, Kakah, 44
fallâḥ (peasants), 19
Fallujah, 307
"Fârûq," 235
Fattâḥ, Muḥammad Sâlim, 18, 20
Feast for the Sea Weed: The Symphony of Death, A (novel), 154
February Plenary Session, 145
"Federalism in Southern Iraq, 263
federalism scheme (11 October 2006), 309
Fî al-Maizân: Ḥawla Risâlat al-Ahâlî; Muṭâlaᶜât fî al-Shaᶜbiyyah (pamphlet), 23
Field Committee, 71
Fifth National Congress (12–25 October 1993), 272–279, 283–291, 295, 317
Financial Reorganization (report), 270
First Conference of International Communist Parties (October 1956), 76
First Congress of the Communist Party of Syria and Labanon (31 December 1943–2 January 1944), 31
First Party Conference. *See* National Charter Conference
First Party ("Organization") Congress (19 April 1945), 33, 44
Flayyiḥ, ᶜÂṣim, 17, 20, 21, 23, 312
"For Strengthening National Independence, for Genuine Democratic Government, and Toward an End to the Dictatorship and the Abnormal Situation in the Country," 119
"For the purpose of mobilizing our people, lifting the economic sanctions, overthrowing the dictatorship, the establishment of a unified federal democratic Iraq and the defense of the toilers interests" (slogan), 286
"For the Purpose of Strengthening and Deepening the Revolutionary March of Iraq in Its Path Towards Socialism," 177
Foundation, The (newspaper). *See Al-Asâs*
14 July 1958 Iraqi revolution, 248
Fourth Party Congress (10–15 November 1985), 191, 192, 196, 198, 200, 202–203, 264–268, 270
Forward (journal). *See Ila al-Amâm*
France, 9
Frankûl, Yûnân, 21, 23
free elections, 125
"Free Homeland and a Happy People, A" (slogan), 33
Free Officers' Movement, 77, 79; *see also* Supreme Officers' Committee
Freedom (newspaper). *See Azadi*
"Freedom for the Patriots in Iraq," 126
Friends of the Peasant associations, 85
Front of Iraqi Kurdistan, 200
Front of the People's Armed Struggle (Brigade of Twelve), 153
"Fundamental Topics for Discussion on the Party's Policies and Positions" (April 1996), 292–295

Gailânî revolt (April–May 1941), 27
"Gather around *Al-ᶜAmal* to form a unified and strong Iraqi communist party," 6
General Union of Iraqi Students, 41, 73, 85
General Union of Labour, 88, 91
Germany, 9, 247
Ghannâm, ᶜAlî, 172
Ghâzî I, King, 25, 254
Gnosticism, 242, 243
Gorbachev, Mikhail, 269
Governing Council of Iraq, 302
grain production in Iraq (1860s–1920s), 8
Grassroots. *See Qâᶜidah*
"Grave Responsibilities" (editorial), 54
Great Britain, 7–17, 26, 39–41, 51, 250–254, 258, 263, 311
Gulf War (1991), 255–258
Gzâr, Nâẓim, 171, 225

Ḥabîb, Muḥammad (Abu Salâm), 110–112
Ḥabîb, Mûsâ, 21, 23
Ḥaddâd, Naᶜîm, 172
Ḥaddâd, Nicola, 18
Ḥadîd, Muḥammad, 22, 24, 78
Ḥaidar, Ḥaidar, 154
handloom industry, domestic, in Iraq, 8
Ḥanîfa, Imam Abû, 243
Ḥarîm, 19
HASAK. *See* Kurdish Socialist Party / People's Kurdish Democratic Party

Ḥasan, Muḥammad Salmân, 2
Ḥasan, Qâsim, 23
Hashemite Union, 76–77, 80, 213
Hâshim, Hâdî, 53
Hâshim, Mahdî, 21, 24
HASHDIK. *See* People's Democratic Party of Kurdistan
Ḥayât al-Ḥizb (The Party's Life, publication), 195
Ḥâzim. *See* Basîm, Zakî Muḥammad
Ḥijâb (veil), 19
Hindû, Mattî Hindî, 224
Ḥizb al-Muʾtamar al-Waṭanî (National Congress Party), 65
Ḥizb al-Nahḍah al-ʿIrâqiyyah (Iraqi Renaissance Party), 11, 17
Ḥizb al-Shaʿb. See al-Shaʿb
Ḥizb al-Taḥarrur al-Waṭanî (Party of National Liberation), 37
Hizbi Komunisti Kurdistan / al-Ḥizb al-Shiyûʿî al-Kurdistânî (Kurdistan Communist Party – Iraq), 305
Homeland, The (newspaper). *See al-Waṭan*
"Human Rights and Global Security," 199
Ḥurriyyat al-Waṭan (The Liberation of the Motherland, newspaper), 57
Ḥusain, Jamîl, 17
Ḥusain, Nûrî ʿAbd-ul-Razzâq, 117, 118, 216, 264
Ḥusain, Sharîf, 11
"Ḥusain line," 149
Hussein, King, of Jordan, 168, 172, 188, 191, 196, 197, 257
Hussein, Saddam, 165, 168, 172, 182, 191, 196–202, 228, 254, 257, 261, 272–275, 282, 290–293, 297, 305

Ibn-Muḥammad, ʿAlî, 243
Ibrâhîm, ʿAbd-ul-Fattâḥ, 22, 35
ICP. *See* Iraq: Communist Party of
"ICP Calls the Iraqi People to a General Strike in Solidarity with the Arab People in Support of Egypt," 66
IDAO. *See al-Dîmuqrâṭiyyûn al-ʿIrâqiyyûn ḍid al-Iḥtilâl*
Ikhwân al-Ṣafâ, 243
il Manifesto (newspaper), 300, 301
Ila al-Amâm (Forward, journal), 27, 28, 30
imperialism, 17, 61, 119, 122, 136, 155, 171, 185, 188, 280
"Imperialism and Its Allies, An Account of the ʿUmarî Cabinet Actions and the Events That Have Occurred Under It," 36
Improving Structures Within the Party Organization (report), 270
"In Whose Interests Are Events Occurring?" 36
INC. *See* Iraqi National Congress
independence of Iraq (1932), 12
industrial working class in Iraq, prior to the 1920s, 7
industrialization, 12
Intelligentsia Committee, 150
"Interests of the People Above All Other Interests" (editorial), 22
International and Worker's Parties meeting (1969), 178
International Herald Tribune, 256
International Labour Office, 14
International Meeting of Communist and Workers' Parties (21–23 June 2002), 298
International Student Union and World Democratic Youth, 218
International Youth Festival (1955), 45
Iran, 252
Iran-Iraq war, 197, 272, 273
Iraq
  before World War I, 1–4, 6
  British influence in, 7–17, 39–41, 51
  Communist Party (ICP) of, 1, 268
    activities in the 1940s, 25–40
    activities in the 1950s, 40–58
    development of (1930s–1940s), 34
    Kurdish Branch Committee, 105
    Kurdish branch of, 63, 66, 114, 216, 290
    ideological trends within the, 293
    influence of 1930s–40s, 26
    influence of, in 1948, 40
    military involvement with (1930s), 25
    origins, 20
    separate women's party section of, 58
    see also Central Committee; Central Leadership; Communist Party
  as cornerstone of the British Indian Empire (1830–1880), 7
  as a dependent market for Great Britian, 8
  early communist organization in, 20–24
  effects of World War II on Iraqi society, 15
  first experiment in autonomy, 2
  foreign influences on, 4–7
  importance of, to British, 248
  interim government of, 308
  Iraqi-British agreement (4 April 1955), 52
  Iraqi-British Treaty (1930), 34
  Iraqi Coalition Against War and Sanctions. *See Tajammuʿ al-ʿIrâqiyyîn ḍid al-Ḥarb wa al-Ḥiṣâr*

Iraqi Communist Vanguard Organization, 185
Iraqi Democrats Against Occupation. *See al-Dîmuqrâṭiyyûn al-ᶜIrâqiyyûn ḍid al-Iḥtilâl*
Iraqi Interim Government, 308
Iraqi Kurdish Communist Party, 287
Iraqi Message, The (journal). *See Risâlat al-ᶜIrâq*
Iraqi National Congress (INC), 288
Iraqi Petroleum Company, 41, 167, 168, 172, 228, 251
Iraqi Press Syndicate, 100
Iraqi Renaissance Party. *See Ḥizb al-Nahḍah al-ᶜIrâqiyyah*
Iraqi Revolutionary Communists, 189–190
Iraqi Students' Society (UK), 50
Iraqi-Turkish-Pakistani Pact, 56
Iraqi Union of Democratic Youth, 79, 216
labour movement purges, 100
Mamluk suzerainty in, 1–2
Napoleonic interest in, 7
oil in, 12, 122, 231, 247, 250, 251, 254–257, 303–304
Ottoman influence on, 1–4
"Iraq on Its Way to a Socialist Transformation" (slogan), 225
"Iraqi Communist Party and Contemporary International Revision: Positions and Experiences, The," 207
Irbil, 21, 67
Islam, 241–242
"Islam: From a Contemporary Marxist Perspective," 245
Islamic-German and Bolshevik alliance, 6
Israel, 159
Istanbul, Council of State in, 3
Ittiḥâd al-Shaᶜb (newspaper), 61, 67, 73, 75, 86–92, 94, 97–100, 213, 215, 216, 218, 255
Ittiḥâd al-ᶜUmmâl (The Unity of Workers, newspaper), 57

Jabr, Ṣâliḥ, 39–40
Jaddûᶜ, ᶜAbd-ul-lah, 18, 20, 23
Jalâl Ṭâlabânî, 169
Jamîl, Ḥusain, 17, 20, 22
Jamᶜiyyat al-Aḥrâr al-lâ-Dîniyyah (Secular Liberal Society), 20
Jamᶜiyyat al-Iṣlâḥ al-Shaᶜbî (Association of the People's Reform), 24, 25
Jamᶜiyyat Aṣḥâb al-Ṣanâʾiᶜ (Artisans' Association), 15
Jandal. *See* Khairî, Zakî
Joint Presidential Council between Egypt and Iraq (1964), 116
Jordan, 76–77, 184, 254
Jordanian Communist Party, 76
Journal, The. See Al-Ṣaḥîfah
July 1958 Revolution, 16, 218, 306
June 1957 uprising (Diwaniyah district), 74
June War, 146
JWOD. *See al-Jabhah al-Waṭaniyyah al-Dîmuqrâṭiyyah*
JWQD. *See al-Jabhah al-Waṭaniyyah al-Taqaddumiyyah al-Dîmuqrâṭiyyah*

Kafih, 23
Karîm, Fakhrî, 272, 304–305
KDP. *See* Kurdistan Democratic Party
Kerr, Miss, 5
Khairî, ᶜAmr, 94, 149, 155, 158, 160, 161, 170, 177, 196, 198, 200, 201
Khairî, Suᶜâd, 64–65, 279
Khairî, Zakî, 17, 20, 21, 24, 25, 44, 64, 79, 86, 88, 89, 92, 94, 99, 101, 104, 105, 106, 126, 128, 132, 134, 139–149, 155, 158–161, 170, 177, 196, 198, 200–201, 251, 264
Khajadûr, Ara, 117, 118
Khâlid, Sâmî, 278
khans (inns), 2
Khomeini, Ayatollah Ruhollah, 186, 239
Khrushchev, Nikita, 76, 116, 213, 214, 218, 219, 253
Kifâḥ al-Shaᶜb (The Struggle of the People, newspaper), 23, 131
Kirkuk, 25, 91
Kojaman, Hesqal, 63–64, 78, 79
Komer, Robert, 107
Kosygin, Alexei, 165
Kubbah, Ibrâhîm, 72, 78
Kubbah, Muḥammad Mahdî, 35
Kurdish-Baᶜthist Agreement on self-rule (11 March 1970), 162
Kurdish Democratic Party (KDP), 30, 39, 66, 71, 91, 103, 104, 158, 162, 169, 179, 194, 201, 220, 226, 231, 235, 268–269, 275, 286, 288, 290, 295
Kurdish Freedom Party. *See* Rizgari Kurd Party
Kurdish Front, 268–269, 272

Kurdish issue, 33, 62, 83–84, 103–104, 106, 116–117, 134–138, 141–142, 158, 163, 177, 179–180, 182, 200, 205–206, 224, 230, 234–235, 237, 245, 261, 274–276, 283, 291
Kurdish National Liberation Movement, 227
Kurdish political autonomy, 142
Kurdish Socialist Party (HASAK), 194
Kurdistan, 6, 157, 170, 176, 177, 179, 180, 211, 226–228, 262, 281, 290–291, 292, 295
Kurdistan Communist Party – Iraq, 305
Kurdistan Path, The (monthly). *See Reikari Kurdistan*
Kurdistan uprising (1991), 272
Kurdistani Socialist Party (PASOK), 269
Kut province, 13
Kuwait, 9, 77, 102–103, 105, 253–255, 273, 274, 292
  crisis in, 261
  importance of, to British interests, 254
  independence of (June 1961), 254
  invasion of (August 1990), 272

labour and peasant organizations after the Revolution, 84
labour conditions in Iraq in the, 1920s, 12
Labour Day rally (1 May 1960), 100
Labour Law No. 72 of (1936), 32, 312
Labour Monthly, The, 128
labour unions, 16
Laftah, Ḥâfiẓ, 110
Lajnat al-Taᶜâwun al-Waṭanî (Committee for National Cooperation), 39
Lajnat al-Tanẓîm al-Markazî (Committee for Central Organization), 130, 271
Lajnat al-Waᶜi al-Mârkisî (Committee for a Marxist Understanding), 45
Lajnat Mukâfahat al-Istiᶜmâr wa al-Istith̲mâr (Committee for Combating Imperialism and Exploitation), 20, 21
Lajnat Tanẓîm al-Kh̲ârij (Committee for the Organization of Members Abroad / Outside Organization), 117–119, 270
land ownership, 13, 136
Law 80, 228
Law of Association (1 January 1960), 99
Lâwî family, 15
lazma (inheritable tenancy over government land), 312
Lazmah Law (land tenure law), 13
League for the Defence of Iraqi Women's Rights, 73, 79, 91
League for the Defence of the Unity of the National Forces, 78
League of Iraqi Women, 79, 85
League of Women's Rights, 41
Leap, The. *See al-Wath̲bah*
Lebanon, 8, 32, 77, 262
Lenin, 244
Leninist Group in the Iraqi Communist Movement. *See al-Farîq al-Lînînî fî al-Ḥarakah al-Sh̲iyûᶜiyyah al-ᶜIrâqiyyah*
"Let Us Transform the Crisis of the Party to a Principled Unity That Will Enable the Party to Lead the People's Revolution to Victory," 150
L'Humanité (newspaper), 5
Liberal Party. *See al-Aḥrâr*
Liberal Party of Iraq, *See al-Ḥizb al-Ḥurr al-ᶜIrâqî*
Liberation of the Motherland, The (newspaper). *See Ḥurriyyat al-Waṭan*
Libya, 184
London Conference (16 August 1956), 65
"Long Live Leninism," 218–219
"Look at the Political and Social Situation in Iraq, A," 205

Mahajan, Rahul, 307
Mahdî, ᶜÂdil, 236, 239
Maḥjûb, ᶜAbd-ul-Kh̲âliq, 76
Maḥmûd, ᶜAbd-ul-Wahâb, 21
Maḥmûd, Najim, 133, 149, 151, 153, 204–205, 207, 212–214, 221, 224, 226–228, 235, 236, 239–241, 244, 247–258, 262
Majîd, Ḥamîd (from Nasiriyah), 20, 21
Majlis al-Silm al-Waṭanî (Council of National Peace), 166
Mao Tse Tung, 76
March 1991 uprising, failure of, 273
Marsh Uprising, 152–154, 212
Marxism, 287
Mattî, Yûsuf, 21, 23
May 1983 massacre, 201
McKenzie, Donald M., 5
meeting of the twenty-five, the, 139
Mesopotamia, 8, 9
middle class in Iraq, after the 1920s, 13
Middle East
  spheres of influence in, after World War I, 10
  Western capitalistic goals in the, 247–249
Midḥat Pasha, 3, 4
military, Iraqi, 57
military coup, first Arab (29 October 1936), 24
minorities, 6, 32, 277

miri (state land), 31, 312, 313
Mond, Sir Alfred, 17
Morocco, 43
Mosul, 4, 9, 67, 217, 248
Movement for the Defence of the Iraqi People, 118, 125
Mubârak, Muḥammad Ḥasan, 264
Mubârak, Ṣabîḥ, 112
Muḥammad (prophet), 11
Muḥammad, ᶜAzîz (Nâẓim ᶜAlî), 44, 105, 113, 121, 125, 142, 158, 169, 172, 177, 180, 188, 192, 194, 197–198, 200, 264, 265, 268, 271, 276, 288–291, 296, 302, 304, 317
Muḥammad, Faḍîl, 20
Muḥyî-d-Dîn, ᶜAbd-ul-lah ᶜUmar, 53
mujaheddin, 307
Munâḍil al-Ḥizb (newspaper), 146, 148, 149, 233
Munaẓẓamat al-ᶜAmal al-Shiyûᶜî fî al-ᶜIrâq (Organization of Communist Action in Iraq), 193
Munaẓẓamat al-Kifâḥ al-Musllaḥ (Organization of Armed Struggle), 152
Munaẓẓamat Fahd al-Thawriyyah (Fahd's revolutionary organization), 267
Mûsâ, Ḥamîd Majîd, 287–288, 291, 295, 299, 301, 302, 305–310, 317
Muṣṭafâ ᶜAlî, 18
Muṭâlaᶜât fî al-Shaᶜbiyyah (Studies in Popularism, leaflet), 22
Muṭlaq, Rashîd, 20, 75

Nâdî al-Taḍâmun (Solidarity Club), 17
Nâdir, Sâmî, 20, 21
Nahj al-Anṣâr (newspaper), 184
Najaf, 67, 307
Nashrah group, 258
Nâṣir, Buṭrus Abu, 20
Nasiriyah, 263
Naṣṣar, Fû'âd, 76, 82
Nasser, Gamal Abdel, 58–59, 68, 70, 75, 76, 80, 86, 109, 116, 126, 252–253
Nasserist Pan-Arabism, 43
National Action Charter, 178
National Action Pact (15 November 1971), 165
national bourgeoisie, 230
National Charter (1944), 32–33
National Charter Conference (February 1944), 28, 31
National Committee for the Union of Officers and Soldiers, 57
National Congress of Peasant Societies, 91
National Congress Party. *See Ḥizb al-Mu'tamar al-Waṭanî*
National Council for Peace, 166
National Council for Peace and Solidarity. *See Al-Majlis al-Waṭanî lil Silm wa al-Taḍâmun*
National Council of the Revolutionary Command, 130
National Defence Council, 130
National Democratic Front. *See al-Jabhah al-Waṭaniyyah al-Dîmuqrâṭiyyah*
National Democratic Party. *See al-Waṭanî al-Dîmuqrâṭî*
national front, 34, 37, 51, 55, 59, 61, 62, 67, 69, 70, 136, 161
National Front, 41, 52, 53, 55, 56, 72, 73, 74
National Front Against Imperialism and War, 10
National Front of Iraqi Kurdistan, 295
"National Front Struggle Against War and Imperialism," 47–48, 50
National Kurdistan Legislative Council, 275
National Liberation Party, 38
National Oil Company Law, 122
National Party. *See al-Ḥizb al-Waṭanî*
National Progressive Front (NPF), 172–186, 189–191, 195, 225, 238
National Progressive Front Charter (17 July 1973), 172
National Union Front, 220, 251, 254
National Unity Party. *See al-Ittiḥâd al-Waṭanî*
nationalism, 4, 102
Nationalist List coalition, 309
nationalist movement after the Revolution, 85
Nazâr ᶜAbbûd. *See* Maḥmûd, Najim, 212
NDP. *See al-Waṭanî al-Dîmuqrâṭî* (National Democratic Party)
Negroponte, John, 308–309
newspapers and journals, 36
  Arab, in Iraq, 1894–1914, 4
  Egyptian, in Iraq, 4
Nicaraguan Contra, 308
Nieuwenhuis, Tom, 2, 3
Nihâd. *See* Nûrî, Bahâ'u-d-Dîn
Nineteenth Infantry Brigade, 77
nonalignment, five principles of, 43
"non-capitalist path to development and democratic nationalism, The," 41
Northern Tier defence system, 42
November 1936 demonstrations, public, demands of, 24
NPF. *See* National Progressive Front

Nuqrat al-Salmân (prison), 46, 112
Nûrî, Bahâ'u-d-Dîn (Bâsim), 43–45, 47, 81, 86–97, 97, 101, 104, 105, 106, 119, 121, 123–125, 130, 132–134, 139, 142, 144, 148, 149, 155, 194–196, 202, 217, 219, 264

"Observations on Neo-Imperialism and How It Should Be Combated," 129
"Observations on the Chinese-Soviet Dispute," 131
October Enlarged Central Committee, 141
October 1917 revolution,
interaction between Iraqis and Russians following the, 5
officers, military, role of Arab, in quest for independence, 4
"Oil as a Weapon," 168
"On Directing the Intellectual Activities," 145
"On the Most Pressing Issues of the Political Situation," 164
"On the Strategy of Popular Armed Struggle in Iraq," 212
OPEC. *See* Organization of Petroleum Exporting Countries
"Opposition Conference," 299
"Oppression Against the Party and Its Supporters," 182
Organization of Armed Struggle. *See Munaẓẓamat al-Kifâḥ al-Musllaḥ*
Organization of Communist Action in Iraq. *See Munaẓẓamat al-ᶜAmal al-Shiyûᶜî fî al-ᶜIrâq*
Organization of Islamic Action, Iraq, 289
Organization of Petroleum Exporting Countries (OPEC), 174
Ottoman Decentralization Party. *See al-ᶜUṣbah al-Ḥamrâ'*
Ottoman Empire, 9
Ottoman influence in Iraq, 5
Ottoman Land Code (1858), 10
Our Political Plan, 63
"Our Political Plan for Our National and Patriotic Liberation," 61
"Our Positions and Current Objectives," 236

Palestine, 32, 137, 156, 178, 188, 223
Palestine Liberation Organization (PLO), 184
Pan-Arabist party, 126
Paris Commune, 241, 242, 244, 245
Parliament of Iraq dissolved (1922), 11
Partisan Movement. *See Anṣâr*
Parto, Bushra, 270
Party Conference (1952), 44
Party Congress (1984), 305
Party of National Liberation. *See Ḥizb al-Taḥarrur al-Waṭanî*
Party of the Toilers of Kurdistan, 288
Party of the Unity of Communists in Iraq. *See Waḥdat al-Shiyûᶜî fî al-ᶜIrâq*
Party Programme, 286, 289
Party's Life, The (publication). *See Ḥayât al-Ḥizb*
Pasht Ashan, 201, 294
PASOK. *See* Kurdistani Socialist Party
Patriotic National Democratic Front (JOQD), 268
Patriotic Union of Kurdistan (PUK), 169, 189, 194, 201, 235, 240, 268–269, 286, 288, 290, 295
PDRY. *See* People's Democratic Republic of Yemen
Peace Partisans, 41, 42, 75, 85, 87
Peasants' Bureau, 105
Peasants' Association of the Party, 74
Penal Code if Iraq, 25, 38, 53
People's Democratic Party of Kurdistan (HASHDIK), 269
People's Democratic Republic of Yemen (PDRY), 184, 197
"People's Imperative, The," 36
People's Kurdish Democratic Party (HASAK), 268–269
People's National Movement in Iraq, 179
People's Party. *See al-Shaᶜb*
People's Path, The (newspaper). *See Ṭarîq al-Shaᶜb*
"People's Primary Demands and the New Cabinet, The" (editorial), 36
Perestroika, 268, 269–272, 275, 278, 285
Peri Noi: Al-Fikr al-Jadîd (journal), 169
Persian Gulf, 9, 257
"personality cults," 288
Plenum to the Advanced Cadre, 221–223
PLO. *See* Palestine Liberation Organization
Polisario Front, 184
Politburo, 62, 64, 80–81, 83–84, 89–93, 121, 149, 173–176, 192, 214, 271, 316
Political and Organizational Report, 273–278
political parties, official, in Iraq after 1946, 35
political parties banned by British High Commission (1922), 11
Political Report, 270, 271
popular armed struggle, 237
Popular Committees for the Defence of the Republic, 79

Popular Forces conference (1991), 259
Popular Front for the Liberation of Palestine, 205
Popular Front Party, 54
Popular Resistance Forces, 87
Popular Resistance Militia, 79
Popular Unified Front Party. *See Al-Jabhah al-Shaʿbiyyah al-Muttaḥidah*
popular uprising, 27, 61, 209
"popular war," 222
population of Iraq
  Arab, pre–World War I, 6
  Armenian, pre–World War I, 6
  of cultivators, pre–Word War I, 10
  demographics, pre–World War I, 6
  growth (1930–1947), 12
  Kurdish, pre–World War I, 6
  middle class (1920s–1950s), 14
  Muslim, pre–World War I, 6
  nomadic, pre–World War I, 9
  Persian, pre–World War I, 6
  prior to World War I, 6
  priviledged, pre–World War I, 7
  religious makeup, pre–World War I, 6
  sedentarization of, in Iraq pre–World War I, 9
  Turkoman, pre–World War I, 6
  urban/rural/Bedouin, 6, 9–10, 12, 14, 15
  urban middle class, pre–World War I, 7
Portsmouth Treaty with Britain (15 January 1948), 16, 39, 40
postal services, role of foreign in bypassing Ottoman censorship, 4
Prague Plenary Session, 121
Pravda, 121, 127
Primakov, Andrei, 205
Principle, The (newspaper). *See Al-Mabdaʾ*
private property in Iraq, prior to World War I, 6
"Problem of the National Liberation Movement of the Arab People," 126
professional organizations after the Revolution, 85
Progressive National Democratic Front. *See al-Jabhah al-Waṭaniyyah al-Taqaddumiyyah al-Dîmuqrâṭiyyah*
Progressive Nationalist Patriotic Front, 181
"Project for a National Pact, A," 239
proletariat exploitation, causes of (Faud), 31
Pronouncement of the Central Committee, 288
property tax, shaikh and agha immunity from, until 1927, 13
public lands (*miri*), 32
Public Law 80, 168
PUK. *See* Patriotic Union of Kurdistan

Qâdir. *See* Aiyyûb, Thûnûn
Qâsim, ʿAbd-ul-Karîm, 41, 74–82, 85–107, 211, 213–216, 218–220, 247, 249–255, 262, 319
Qasir al Nihiyah, 225
Qatar, 258
Qazanchî, Kâmil, 39
Qurainî, ʿAbd-ul-lah Masʿûd (Riyâḍ), 28

Râbiṭat *al-Shiyûʿiyyîn al-ʿIrâqiyyîn* (League of Iraqi Communists), 29
Râḍî Shubbar, Muḥammed, 44
railway workers trade union (7 September 1944), 33
Râyat al-Shaghîlah (The Worker's Banner), 45, 60, 81
Razzâq, ʿÂrif ʿAbd-ul-, 116
Reikari Kurdistan (The Kurdistan Path, monthly), 182
rejuvenation, 277
Report of the ICP-CC Politburo (1974), 173, 174, 176
republic, Iraq as a (1958), 77
Response to Bourgeois Chauvinist Dismantlers, A, 66
revisionism, 207–211
Revolution (newspaper). *See Shursh*
Revolution, The (newspaper). *See Al-Thawrah*
Revolutionary, The. See al-Thawrî
Revolutionary Command Council, 169, 172
Revolutionary Committee. *See al-Lajnah al-Thawriyyah*
Revolutionary Current, 193
Revolutionary Popular Council, 132
revolutionary transformation, 61
Ribazy Bashmarga (newspaper), 184
Rich, C. J., 2
Rifʿat, Kamâl, 76
Riley, 5
Risâlat al-ʿIrâq (The Iraqi Message, journal), 295
Rizgari Kurd Party (Kurdish Freedom Party), 30
Rubiah, 257
Rufâʾîl, Nûrî, 21
Rughâl, Abû, 310

Ṣadâ al-Qâʿidah (publication), 195
sadah (descent from the Prophet), 6

Sadat, Anwar, 181, 184
Sadr movement, 309
Saif, Mâlik, 40, 63
Salâm ʿÂdil, 61
Ṣâliḥ, Dhâfir, from Basra, 20, 21
Ṣâliḥ, Saʿd, 35, 283
Salmân, Khiḍr (Abu Jaʿfar), 133
San Remo conference (April 1920), 10
Sandinistas, 308
Sarîʿ, Ḥasan, 110, 111
Ṣarîfa, 15
Ṣarîfas (shanty towns), 14
Saudi Arabia, 59, 258
Ṣâyegh, Dâûd, 28, 29, 98, 99, 101
SCIRI. *See* Supreme Council of the Islamic Revolution in Iraq
Second Congress (IPC Kurdish, 1993), 291
Second London Conference of the Communist Parties within the Sphere of British Imperialism, 49
Second National Congress (1993), 79, 141, 143, 183, 291
Second Party Conference (1956), 61, 65, 70, 216
Second Party Congress (1970), 143–144, 183
secret societies, 4
secretary general, 43, 316, 317
Secular Liberal Society. *See Jamʿiyyat al-Aḥrâr al-lâ-Dîniyyah*
self-determination, 281
semi-feudalism in rural areas of Iraq, 13
separatist movements,
non-Turkish, 4
September 1956 uprisings, 67, 68
Settlement Department, 311
Settlement of Land Rights Law (1932), 13
Seventh Party Congress (25–28 August 2001), 297
Shaʿb Musallaḥ, 209
Shaikh al-mashâyikh (chief of tribal confederations), 7
shaikhs (feudal tribal chiefs), 10, 13, 313
Sharîf, ʿAbd-ul-Raḥîm, 60, 63
Sharîf, ʿAzîz, 17, 35, 37, 45–46, 85
Sharon, Ariel, 298
Shaṭ al-ʿArab, 9, 199, 228
Shâʾûl, Ibrâhîm, 64
Shâwî, Nicola, 82
Shiʿi Ulama, 6
Shiʿism, 6
Shukr, ʿAlî, 33, 85
Shumaiyyil, Ibrâhîm Nâjî, 39
Shumaiyyil, Shiblî, 18
Shursh (Revolution, newspaper), 30
Shursh group, 30
Sibâhî, ʿAzîz, 34
Ṣidqî, ʿAwnî Bakr, 18, 20, 23
Ṣidqî, Bakr, 24–25, 312–313
Sînamâ al-Ḥayât (Theatre of Life, journal), 19
Sixth National Congress (26–29 July 1997) 291–296
Socialist Bloc, 272
Socialist Kurdish Party (BASOK), 268
socio-economic transformation of Iraq (1930s–1940s), 14
Solidarity Club. *See Nâdî al-Taḍâmun*
"Solidarity with Iraq," 168
Sovereignty Council, 78, 81
Soviet Union, 27, 55, 68, 115–118, 156, 180, 188–189, 201, 224–225, 232, 234–235, 238, 248–253. *See also* Communist Party: of the Soviet Union
Spark, The (journal). *See Al-Sharârah*
Spartacist, uprising (1918), 1
Stalinism, 34
standard of living in Iraq (1920s–1950s), 14
Star, The. *See al-Najmah*
State and Revolution, The (1917), 244
State Security Agency, 102
status, hierarchial, in Iraq at the turn of the century, 6
stratification, internal social, in Iraq at the turn of the century, 6
"Strengthen Your Party Structure and Strengthen the National Movement's Organization" (slogan), 33
strikes, 102, 107, 312
Struggle, The (newspaper). *See Al-Niḍâl*
Struggle of the People, The (newspaper). *See Kifâḥ al-Shaʿb*
Student Federation, 100
Studies in Popularism (leaflet). *Muṭâlaʿât fî al-Shaʿbiyyah*
Sublime Porte, 2
Sudan, 43, 184
Suez Canal, 8, 59, 311
Ṣûfî, 6
Sulaimân, Ḥikmat, 12, 24
Sulaimaniyah, 67
Sulṭân, Ḥusain, 117
Summit Conference, Paris, 253
Sunni Accord Front, 309
"Supporting the Party's Struggle Within Iraq: The Removal of Economic Sanctions, the Eradication of the Dictatorship, and the

Establishment of a Unified Federal and Democratic Iraq," 296
Supreme Committee of the Front, 173, 179, 181, 183
Supreme Committee of the Movement for the Defence of the Iraqi People, 127
Supreme Council of the Islamic Revolution in Iraq (SCIRI), 239
Supreme Executive Committee, 73, 74
Supreme National Committee, 73
Supreme Officers' Committee, 74–75, 82
Supreme Student Committee, 71
suqs (markets), 2
Sykes-Picot agreement (1915), 10
Syria, 4, 8, 32, 58–59

Ṭabrah, Khâlid, 108
Ṭâhir, ᶜAbd-ul-Wahâb, 264
Ṭâhir, Waṣfî, 79
Tajammuᶜ al-ᶜIrâqiyyîn ḍid al-Ḥarb wa al-Ḥiṣâr (Iraqi Coalition Against War and Sanctions), 262
Ṭâlabânî, Jalâl, 169, 194, 240–241, 288
Ṭâlib, Nâjî, 142
Tallû, George, 105, 217
Ṭalyah, Wadîᶜ, 21
Tanzimat, Age of, 3
tapu sanads (title deeds), 10
Ṭarîq al-Shaᶜb (The People's Path, newspaper), 94, 104, 106, 133, 148, 157, 169, 170, 181, 185, 186, 188, 190, 191, 224, 233, 236, 239, 246
"Tasks for Whose Fulfillment the Party Is Striving, The," 276–277
tax farming, 10
terrorism, defined, 298
Thâmir. *See* Abû-l-ᶜÎss, Muḥammad Ḥusain
Theatre of Life (journal). *See Sînamâ al-Ḥayât*
Third Conference (January 1974), 177–181
Third Congress (May 1976), 176–181, 183
Third Party Conference (December 1967), 160, 163, 183, 227, 235
31 March 1934 communist meeting, 21
Three World Theory, 238
Tigris River, 7, 8
title deeds (*tapu sanads*), 10
"To the New Government," 36
"Toward Rebuilding Our Party: Toward the Unity of All Marxist-Leninists in One Iraqi Communist Party," 236
trade unionism in Iraq (1928–1940s), 26
Treaty of Algiers (between Iraq and Iran, March 1975), 235
Treaty of Friendship and Cooperation (between the Soviet Union and Iraq, April 1972), 165, 169
"Treaty Is Null and We Must Declare Its Abrogation, The," 39
Tribal Criminal and Civil Disputes Regulation (1916), 13
Tripartite Pact of Unity (between Iraq, Egypt, and the Baᶜthist regime in Syria), 109
Ṭuᶜmâ, Farḥân, 63
Tuᶜmâ, Farmân, 53
Tûmâ, Jamîl, 17
Tunisia, 43
Turkey-Pakistan Treaty, 52
Turkification, 4
Turkish Communist Party, 286
Turkish-Iraqi Mutual Cooperation Pact (24 February 1955), 52
Turkish-Pakistani Pact for Friendship and Co-operation for Security, 55, 56
Truth, The. *See al-Ḥaqiqah*
Twentieth Congress (of the CPSU, 1956), 43, 60, 212, 214, 216, 246
Twentieth Infantry Brigade, 77
Twenty-second Congress (of the CPSU), 219
Twenty-seventh Congress (of the CPSU, February 1986), 268
23 August 1922 demonstrations, 11

UAR. *See* United Arab Republic
ulama, 6
ul-Karîm, Mahdî ᶜAbd-, 48
Umayyad regime, 243
Understanding of Military Assistance (21 April 1954), 51
unemployment, 136
Unequal Treaty (1972), 234
Unified Kurdish Front, 274
Unified Nationalist Iraqi Congress, 274
Unified Political Command, 116
Union, The. *See al-Ittiḥâd*
Union of Democratic Youth, 41, 73, 79, 85, 91, 100, 216
Union of Peasant Associations, 85
United Arab Republic (UAR), 76, 80, 84, 155, 251
United Iraqi Alliance, 309
United National Front, 71–73, 74–75, 77, 78, 80, 85, 89, 91, 118, 120
United Nations sanctions against Iraq, 274
United Nations Security Council Resolutions
  UNSCR 773, 287, 301
  UNSCR 1483, 301

United States, 232, 234, 247–249, 252–258, 261, 263, 297–303, 318
Unity of the Cadre. *See Wiḥdat al-Qâᶜidah*
Unity of the Communists in Iraq, 60
Unity of the Struggle. *See Waḥdat-al-Niḍâl*
Unity of Workers, The (newspaper). *Ittiḥâd al-ᶜUmmâl*
Universal Declaration of Human Rights, 200
Uprising of 1956, 70
"Uprising of 1956 and Our Responsibilities in the Current Conditions, The," 67–70
"Urgent Demands," 36
ᶜUthmân, Ḥamîd, 31, 47, 53, 56–58
ᶜU<u>th</u>mân, Mullah <u>Sh</u>arîf, 21, 63

vilayets, 9
Vladivostok summit, 173
Voice of the Iraqi People (radio station), 118, 119

Wahbî, ᶜAbd-ul-Jabbâr, 108, 114
Waḥdat-al-Niḍâl (Unity of the Struggle), 30
Waḥdat al-<u>Sh</u>iyûᶜî fî al-ᶜIrâq (Party of the Unity of Communists in Iraq), 45, 46
Wâlî, 1, 3
Wâlîd. *See* al-Gumar, Ḥusain
war of liberation against Great Britian, 1920, 10
water, British control of, pre–World War I, 9
Wa<u>th</u>bah (uprising), 39
"We Greet You on Behalf of All Progressive Forces," 188
Wiḥdat al-Qâᶜidah (Unity of the Cadre), 236–239
women's rights, 19, 32
"Workers and Peasants of the Arab World Unite," 21
Workers' Central Committee, 110
"Workers of the World Unite," 6
workers' union movements (in Iraq, 1930s), 15
World Communist Parties Conference (November 1960), 218
World Marxist Review, 76, 102, 121, 123, 125, 126, 128, 269

Yazbak, Yûsuf Ibrâhîm, 18
Yemen, 58
Young Turks, revolution of (1908), 4
Yugoslavia, 262
Yûnus, Nafiᶜ, 31
Yûsuf, Ḥamdân, 295
Yûsuf, Peter, 133
Yûsuf. Salmân Yûsuf. *See* Fahd

Ẓâfir. *See* Zakî, <u>Kh</u>âlid Aḥmad
Zaire, 184
Zakî, <u>Kh</u>âlid Aḥmad (Ẓâfir), 127, 133, 149–154
Zanganah, Haifâʾ, 225–226
Zanj Rebellion, 243
Zanjanah, Fa<u>kh</u>rî Karîm, 180
Zionism, 17, 33, 42, 61, 155, 171, 174, 181, 185, 221, 223, 280